QUINN'S PRINCIPLES AND PRACTICE OF NURSE EDUCATION

SUZANNE J. HUGHES
FRANCIS M. QUINN

SIXTH EDITION

CENGAGE

Australia • Brazil • Japan • K...   ...United Kingdom • United States

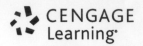

Quinn's Principles and Practice of Nurse Education, 6th Edition
Suzanne J. Hughes and Francis M. Quinn

Publishing Director: Linden Harris

Commissioning Editor: Annabel Ainscow

Production Editor: Alison Cooke

Production Controller: Eyvett Davis

Marketing Manager: Lauren Mottram

Typesetter: Integra Software Services Pvt. Ltd. India

Cover design: Adam Renvoize

While the publisher has taken all reasonable care in the preparation of this book, the publisher makes no representation, express or implied, with regard to the accuracy of the information contained in this book and cannot accept any legal responsibility or liability for any errors or omissions from the book or the consequences thereof.

Products and services that are referred to in this book may be either trademarks and/or registered trademarks of their respective owners. The publishers and author/s make no claim to these trademarks. The publisher does not endorse, and accepts no responsibility or liability for, incorrect or defamatory content contained in hyperlinked material.

For product information and technology assistance, contact **emea.info@cengage.com**.

For permission to use material from this text or product, and for permission queries, email **emea.permissions@cengage.com**.

British Library Cataloguing-in-Publication Data
A catalogue record for this book is available from the British Library.

ISBN: 978-1-4080-7282-0

Cengage Learning EMEA
Cheriton House, North Way, Andover, Hampshire, SP10 5BE
United Kingdom

Cengage Learning products are represented in Canada by Nelson Education Ltd.

For your lifelong learning solutions, visit **www.cengage.co.uk**

Purchase your next print book, e-book or e-chapter at **www.cengagebrain.com**

Printed in United Kingdom by CPI Antony Rowe
Print Year: 2016   Print Number: 03

BRIEF CONTENTS

DETAILED CONTENTS

6   Teaching strategies 189

7   Assessment of learning 242

8 Student feedback 291

9 Information literacy and study skills 307

10 Quality and evaluation 327

PART THREE

SPECIFIC TEACHING CONTEXTS 355

11 Placement learning 356

12 Interprofessional education 409

13 Teaching patients, clients and their families 429

FOREWORD

I am delighted to welcome readers to the sixth edition of *Quinn's Principles and Practice of Nurse Education*. This book has been an indispensable text for teachers of nurses and other health professionals for nearly four decades, serving an international and multi-disciplinary readership.

The sixth edition has been extensively updated to take account of recent developments and we have introduced new chapters on "Student Feedback, Quality and Evaluation, and Interprofessional Education." The balance between theoretical issues and practical application , which is so important to the practising teacher, has been maintained; all of which will ensure the book remains at the cutting edge of nurse education.

I would like to express my sincere gratitude to my co-author Suzanne Hughes, who has taken on the role of Lead Author for this new edition. My thanks also go to Annabel Ainscow and Carol Usher at Cengage Learning EMEA Limited for their help and patience in bringing the project to fruition.

Lastly, I must offer thanks to my wife Carole and my children Hamnet and Tara for their support throughout the years since the first edition was published.

Francis M. Quinn
Ventnor, Isle of Wight, UK

ABOUT THE AUTHORS

SUZANNE J. HUGHES

Suzanne has been a lecturer in adult nursing studies at Cardiff School of Nursing and Midwifery Studies, Cardiff University since 2002. She has clinical experience in practice education within an operating theatre department and clinical experience in anaesthetic, surgery and post-anaesthetic care nursing.

FRANCIS M. QUINN

Was the sole author of *Quinn's Principles and Practice of Nurse Education*, first published in 1980, until 2000. He was formerly director of education in the school of post compulsory education and training at the University of Greenwich, London.

PREFACE TO THE SIXTH EDITION

It is a pleasure to introduce the sixth edition of *Quinn's Principles and Practice of Nurse Education*. Learning and teaching is a subject that involves all qualified nurses and midwives; they work in a constantly learning profession where the teaching and supervision of students feature greatly in their daily lives. To be able to develop and implement a range of teaching and learning strategies that are effective across a variety of educational settings, and to be able to create and develop opportunities for students to identify and undertake experiences to meet their learning needs, are objectives that many seek to achieve to meet the requirements of qualified teacher status. These are in line with the current vision and strategy of Jane Cummings, Chief Nursing Officer for England, that Nurses, Midwives and Care-Givers should have the following 'Six Cs' values to unite their professions: care; compassion; competence; communication; courage and commitment.

The book is primarily aimed at lecturers who are new to nursing and midwifery education, practice educators and students undertaking a postgraduate certificate in education, and teaching and assessing and mentorship programmes.

The overall structure of the book remains relatively unchanged, although a few new chapters have been introduced. These include 'Student Feedback', 'Quality and Evaluation' and 'Interprofessional Education'. A number of pedagogical features accompany the sixth edition including chapter aims, teaching suggestions, chapter summaries of significant points and a glossary of key terms. An online resource centre via the Cengage Learning website provides further information and guidance for readers.

The sixth edition is divided into four parts. Part One focuses on adult learning theory and perspectives on teaching and learning; Part Two focuses on learning, teaching and assessment; Part Three addresses specific teaching contexts, and Part Four explores the spectrum of professional development within the university and clinical practice environment.

Suzanne J. Hughes

ACKNOWLEDGEMENTS

I would like to express my gratitude to the people who have helped and supported me during the last year.

It remains an honour to co-author the sixth edition with Francis Quinn and I thank him enormously for his continued encouragement and support.

I would like to acknowledge the support and commitment given by Annabel Ainscow, acting commissioning editor at Cengage Learning; and a big thank you to Carol Usher, development editor, whose inspiring enthusiasm and encouragement has been invaluable.

I would also like to express my appreciation to the excellent reviewers for their constructive feedback and suggestions during the planning and development of this book; your willingness to give your time so generously is much appreciated.

Finally, my special thanks are extended to my husband Charlie, my son Oliver, Mitzi and my mum and dad for their unequivocal support and patience.

Suzanne J. Hughes

The publishers would like to thank Stephen McGhee, Ian Murray, Mike Parkinson, Louisa Sheward and Ben Stanfield Davies for their insightful review comments on the manuscript. Stephen McGhee and Ian Murray, both Nursing lecturers at the University of Stirling are also to be thanked for all their excellent work on the digital support resources which accompany the new edition.

DEDICATION

To Oliver
'One more story'
Love, Mummy x

WALK-THROUGH TOUR

CHAPTER AIMS Listed at the beginning of each chapter, these emphasise the key topics that are covered in that chapter.

TEACHING TIP This feature provides tips to help develop your teaching practice.

REVIEW QUESTIONS At the end of each chapter, these give you the opportunity to review your understanding of the key issues raised.

SUMMARY The summary summarizes the key points included in the chapter.

FURTHER READING References are provided, which will provide further information about points raised in the chapter.

DIGITAL RESOURCES

Dedicated Instructor Resources

To discover the dedicated instructor online support resources accompanying this textbook, instructors should register here for access:

http://login.cengage.com
Resources include:

- Answers to Review Questions in the book
- Teaching Tips
- PowerPoint slides

Online Student Resources

Instructor access

Instructors can access the online student resources by registering at **http://login.cengage.com** or by speaking to their local Cengage Learning EMEA representative.

Instructor resources

Instructors can use the integrated Engagement Tracker to track students' preparation and engagement. The tracking tool can be used to monitor progress of the class as a whole, or for individual students.

Student access

Students can access the online platform using the unique personal access card included in the front of the book.

Student resources

A range of interactive learning tools tailored to *Quinn's Principles and Practice of Nurse Education sixth edition* are available on the online platform, including:

- Quizzes and self-test practice questions
- Critical Thinking Questions
- Discussion Questions
- Case Studies
- Interactive eBook

CHAPTER 1
INTRODUCTION: NURSE EDUCATION

THE AIMS OF THIS CHAPTER ARE:

- To outline key regulatory developments within the nursing profession

- To provide a brief overview of health and social care legislation

- To summarize the main standards that underpin learning and teaching in higher education

KEY TERMS

NMC standards   PREP
Competency framework   Developmental framework
NMC

The focus of this book is education within nursing, midwifery and specialist community public health nursing, and this introductory chapter identifies some key developments relevant to these professions.

Variety is one of the hallmarks of nurse education, consisting as it does of a variety of disciplines, engaging in a variety of activities, carried out by a variety of staff, in a variety of settings. The disciplines involved are nursing, midwifery and specialist community public health nursing, but within these main groups there are numerous sub-groupings such as community midwives, intensive care nurses, liaison specialist community public health nurses and so forth.

The activities of nurse education range from the formal, academic type of teaching through to the impromptu teaching that occurs spontaneously in day-to-day work. The former includes a range of academic awards including diploma of higher education, bachelors' degrees, postgraduate diplomas, masters' degrees and research degrees at master's and doctoral levels.

This teaching is delivered by nursing personnel such as university lecturers, lecturer/practitioners, mentors, clinical and community practitioners, students themselves and also by a range of non-nursing personnel including medical practitioners and members of the professions allied to medicine.

The settings in which nurse education takes place include university departments of nursing, hospitals in both public and private sectors, clinics, GP surgeries, prisons, nursing homes and patients'/clients' own homes.

THE INSTRUMENTAL IDEOLOGY OF NURSING CURRICULA

Nurse education comes under the overall umbrella of post-compulsory education and training, i.e. education that takes place after completion of compulsory schooling at age 16. The principles of nurse education are based upon the theory and practice of adult learning, and as such differ significantly from the education of children in school. One of the main differences between curricula in nursing and the national curriculum for children is that nurse education curricula are instrumental; i.e. their purpose is the production of a nursing workforce that is equipped to deal with the demands of the role, and vocational relevance is therefore a key principle. This is not to say that nursing curricula omit the wider aspects of education such as the needs, aspirations and personal growth of the individual, but these considerations are secondary to the main purpose. Nurse education takes place within two major contexts, the National Health Service (NHS) and the university sector within the UK, and each of these is subject to continuing development and change. There are also important developments in professional nursing that have a major impact on the design and delivery of nurse education. The following sections will highlight some of these current developments, and reference will be made to the appropriate chapters of this book in which further discussion of some of these issues can be found.

DEVELOPMENTS IN THE NURSING PROFESSION

The Nursing Midwifery Council

The Nursing Midwifery Council (NMC) was set up by Parliament to protect the public by ensuring that high standards of care are provided by nurses and midwives. The NMC was established by the Nursing Midwifery Order 2001 and came into effect on 1 April 2002. The Nursing Midwifery Order 2001 provided legislative powers for the NMC to approve and monitor the standards of educational programmes that lead to entry on to the register and the educational institutions delivering these programmes. The main objective of the NMC in exercising its functions is to:

> *'Safeguard the health and well-being of persons using or needing the services of registrants.'*

The principle function of the NMC is to:

> '*Establish from time to time standards of education, training, conduct and performance for nurses and midwives and to ensure the maintenance of these standards.*'

There are three parts to the NMC register for nurses, midwives and specialist community public health nurses, with five recordable post-registration qualifications: Lecturer/Practice Educator; Teacher, Specialist practitioner; Nurse independent/supplementary prescriber and Community practitioner nurse prescriber. A number of important developments relating to the NMC are also included here.

Standards for pre-registration nursing education *(NMC 2010)*

New NMC standards for pre-registration nursing education were introduced in 2010 to ensure that nurses of the future are fit for practice, reflecting changes in healthcare delivery and are able to meet the needs of patients and the public safely and effectively with compassion. The new standards came into effect at the beginning of the academic year 2011/12 and after this time, approved education institutions could request approval of new programmes. From the start of the academic year 2013/14 students are only able to commence a programme that meets the new standards.

To support the introduction of a new curriculum, the NMC made the following statement:

> '*Nursing education across the UK is responding to changing needs, developments, priorities and expectations in health and healthcare. Nurses who acquire the knowledge, skills and behaviours that meet our standards will be equipped to meet these present and future challenges, improve health and wellbeing and drive up standards and quality, working in a range of roles including practitioner, educator, leader and researcher*'
>
> NMC (2010)

The aim of the standards is to enable nurses to provide and support high quality care in rapidly changing healthcare environments by reflecting how future services might be delivered, acknowledging public health priorities and addressing the challenges of long-term conditions, and providing more care outside hospitals. The NMC subsequently decided that degree-level registration was required to make new nurses fit for purpose. In 2009 the government reported that all nurse pre-registration education programmes would become degree-level by September 2013. The NMC (2010) stipulate that nurses must be equipped to lead, delegate, supervise and challenge other nurses and healthcare professionals and must be able to develop practice, and promote and sustain change.

As nursing graduates they must be able to think analytically, use problem-solving approaches and evidence in decision-making, keep up with technical advances and meet future expectations.

A competency framework identifies the standards for competence and associated competencies that all nursing students must achieve prior to registration. The framework details four domains of competence for each of the four fields of adult, child, mental health and learning disability nursing including:

■ Professional values
■ Communication and interpersonal skills
■ Nursing practice and decision making
■ Leadership, management and team working

Once students have met all requirements of the preregistration nursing programme, the NMC (2010, p. 5) maintain that the public can be confident that all new nurses will:

■ Deliver high quality essential care to all
■ Deliver complex care to service users in their field of practice
■ Act to safeguard the public, and be responsible and accountable for safe, person-centred, evidence-based nursing practice
■ Act with professionalism and integrity, and work within agreed professional, ethical and legal frameworks and processes to maintain and improve standards
■ Practise in a compassionate, respectful way, maintaining dignity and wellbeing and communicating effectively
■ Act on their understanding of how people's lifestyles, environments and the location of care delivery influence their health and wellbeing
■ Seek out every opportunity to promote health and prevent illness
■ Work in partnership with other health and social care professionals and agencies, service users, carers and families ensuring that decisions about care are shared
■ Use leadership skills to supervise and manage others and contribute to planning, designing, delivering and improving future services

All approved education institutions and their partner practice learning providers are required to fully comply with these standards and requirements in all UK pre-registration nursing programmes.

Standards for pre-registration midwifery education (NMC 2009)

New standards for pre-registration midwifery education were introduced in 2009 to prepare midwifery students to practise safely and effectively so that, on registration, they can assume full responsibility and accountability for their practice as midwives. The guiding principles relate to professional competence and fitness for practice, and the promotion and facilitation of the normal physiological process of childbirth, which includes competence in identifying any complications that may arise, accessing appropriate assistance and implementing correct emergency measures.

A competency framework identifies the standards for competence and essential skills clusters that all midwifery students must achieve prior to registration within four domains of competence:

- Effective midwifery practice
- Professional and ethical practice
- Developing the individual midwife and others
- Achieving quality care through evaluation and research

The NMC (2009, p. 4) standards outline that midwifery students must demonstrate competence in:

- Sound, evidence-based knowledge of facilitating the physiology of childbirth and the newborn, and be competent in applying this in practice
- A knowledge of psychological, social, emotional and spiritual factors that may positively or adversely influence normal physiology, and be competent in applying this in practice
- Appropriate interpersonal skills to support women and their families
- Skills in managing obstetric and neonatal emergencies, underpinned by appropriate knowledge
- Being autonomous practitioners and lead carers to women experiencing normal childbirth and being able to support women throughout their pregnancy, labour, birth and postnatal period, in all settings including midwife-led units, birthing centres and the home
- Being able to undertake critical decision-making to support appropriate referral of either the woman or baby to other health professionals or agencies when there is recognition of normal processes being adversely affected and compromised

The post-registration education and practice (PREP) standards (NMC 2011a)

The NMC issued the new PREP standards in 2011, identifying two standards that affect a practitioner's registration. These are:

The PREP (practice) standard: The practice standard requires nurses, midwives and specialist community public health nurses to have completed a minimum of 450 hours of practice during the three years prior to renewal of registration.

The PREP (continuing professional development) standard: The continuing professional development (CPD) standard requires a commitment from registrants to undertake CPD and undertake at least five days or 35 hours of learning relevant to practice during the three years prior to renewal of registration, and maintain a personal professional profile of learning activity

Registrants must also comply with any request for auditing of the practitioner's personal professional profile by the NMC. PREP is discussed in Chapter 17.

Standards to support learning and assessment in practice (NMC 2008)

The NMC have devised a developmental framework to support learning and assessment in clinical practice, which outlines the knowledge and skills that nurses and midwives must apply in practice when supporting and assessing students undertaking NMC approved programmes that lead to registration or a recordable qualification. The framework identifies prescriptive outcomes for mentors, practice teachers and teachers to ensure clear accountability for making decisions that lead to entry to the register and which can be applied within the context of inter-professional education. There are eight domains in the framework with identified outcomes at the four developmental stages. These include:

1. Establishing effective working relationships
2. Facilitation of learning
3. Assessment and accountability
4. Evaluation of learning
5. Creating an environment for learning
6. Context of practice
7. Evidence-based practice
8. Leadership

The framework is underpinned by five principles for supporting learning and assessment in practice for any student undertaking an NMC approved programme leading to registration or a qualification that is recordable on the register are that nurses and midwives who make judgements about whether a student has achieved the required standards of proficiency for safe and effective practice must:

- be on the same part or sub-part of the register as that which the student is intending to enter
- have developed their own knowledge, skills and competency beyond that of registration through CPD by holding professional qualifications at an appropriate level to support and assess the students they mentor/teach
- have been prepared for their role to support and assess learning and met NMC defined outcomes
- Nurses and midwives who have completed an NMC approved teacher preparation programme may record their qualification on the NMC register.

TEACHING TIP

Other teaching qualifications may be assessed against the NMC teacher outcomes through the NMC accreditation route.

DEVELOPMENTS IN THE NHS SECTOR

Health and Social Care Act [2012]

The Health and Social Care Act, which received royal assent in 2012 puts clinicians at the centre of commissioning, frees up providers to innovate, empowers patients and gives a new focus to public health. Modernization of the NHS is essential due to rising demand and treatment costs, the need for improvement and the state of public finances. The key policy areas of this Act are identified below:

- *Clinically led commissioning*: This will empower NHS professionals to improve health services for patients and communities. It will remove political interference and micromanagement in decisions about people's care.

- *Provider regulation to support innovative and efficient services*: This enables patients to access a range of providers who can offer services which are tailored to their particular needs.

- *Enhanced patient voice*: A key part of patient empowerment is to offer increased choice about their care. The views and experiences of patients, carers and the public will influence the commissioning process and improve the quality of health and social care services.

- *New focus for public health*: In order to improve the nation's health, there will be a drive towards health improvement by pulling together the work done by the NHS, social care, housing, environmental health, leisure and transport services.

- *Greater accountability at national and local level*: This strengthens and clarifies accountability for and within the NHS nationally and improves and introduces new mechanisms for local accountability within the health system.

- *Streamlined public organizations*: The Act contains provisions to restructure the health and care public bodies sector to create better organizations with greater freedoms, clear duties and transparency in their responsibilities to patients; and to increase the proportion of money going to frontline services.

- *Regulation of support workers*: The Act reveals that high standards for support workers can be assured without imposing statutory regulation and have created a system of external quality assurance for voluntary registers, which aims to be operational from 2013. Skills for Health and Skills for Care have been commissioned to accelerate production of a code of conduct and minimum standards for training in order to identify appropriately skilled and qualified support workers.

DEVELOPMENTS IN HIGHER EDUCATION

The UK Quality Code for Higher Education *(QAA 2012)*

The UK Quality Code for Higher Education is used to assure the standards and quality of higher education in the United Kingdom. It is developed and maintained by the Quality Assurance Agency for Higher Education (QAA) through consultation with the higher education sector and is used by individual higher education providers to ensure students have the high-quality educational experience they are entitled to expect (p. 2). The Code gives individual higher education providers a shared starting point for setting and maintaining the academic standards of their higher education programmes and awards, and assuring the quality of the learning opportunities they provide for students.

The purpose of the Quality Code is to:

- Safeguard the academic standards of UK higher education
- Assure the quality of the learning opportunities that UK higher education offers to students
- Promote continuous and systematic improvement in UK higher education
- Ensure that information about UK higher education is publicly available

It consists of a series of separate chapters grouped in three parts:

Part A: Setting and maintaining threshold academic standards: **focuses on issues** relevant to the setting and maintaining of academic standards including:

- The national level
- The subject and qualification level
- The programme level
- Approval and review
- Externality
- Assessment of achievement of learning outcomes

Part B: Assuring and enhancing academic quality: refers to issues relevant to ensuring that the quality of learning opportunities meets expectations and is continually being enhanced:

- Programme design and approval
- Admissions
- Learning and teaching
- Student support, learning resources and careers education, information, advice and guidance
- Student engagement
- Assessment of students and accreditation of prior learning
- External examining
- Programme monitoring and review
- Complaints and appeals
- Management of collaborative arrangements
- Research degrees

Part C: Information about higher education provision

This part addresses how providers make available information that is fit for purpose, accessible and trustworthy.

The UK Professional Standards Framework for teaching and supporting learning in higher education *(HEA 2011)*

The professional standards framework was borne out of the White Paper *The Future of Higher Education* in 2003. In response to the white paper, Universities UK (UUK), Standing Conference of Principals (SCOP) and the UK HE funding bodies invited the Higher Education Academy to consult with the sector to develop a National Professional Standards Framework for institutions to apply to their professional development programmes and activities in order to demonstrate that professional standards for teaching and supporting learning are being met.

Underpinning this framework is acknowledgement of the distinctive nature of teaching in higher education, respect for the autonomy of higher education institutions, and recognition of quality enhancement for improving student learning (HEA 2011, p. 2). The framework recognizes that the scholarly nature of subject inquiry and knowledge creation, and a scholarly approach to pedagogy, combine to represent a unique feature of support for student learning in higher education institutions.

The aims of the UK Professional Standards Framework are to:

- Support the initial and continuing professional development of staff engaged in teaching and supporting learning
- Foster dynamic approaches to teaching and learning through creativity, innovation and continuous development in diverse academic and/or professional settings
- Demonstrate to students and other stakeholders the professionalism that staff and institutions bring to teaching and support for student learning
- Acknowledge the variety and quality of teaching, learning and assessment practices that support and underpin student learning
- Facilitate individuals and institutions in gaining formal recognition for quality enhanced approaches to teaching and supporting learning, often as part of wider responsibilities that may include research and/or management activities

The framework is a descriptor based approach whereby higher education institutions determine their own criteria in the application of the standards framework. Six areas of activity, core knowledge and professional values are applied to learning outcomes and assessment activities within the institution's professional development programmes so that application of the standards can be demonstrated.

Review questions

1. Make a timeline of the key developments in nursing education from 2000 to the present day.
2. The NMC standards consist of a framework of competencies and skills for pre-registration student nurses, post-registration nurses and nurse educators. Summarize these in a diagram.
3. What do you consider are the three most important developments in the NHS sector? Explain your answer.
4. How do the developments in the NHS affect developments in nursing education?

SUMMARY

- The activities of nurse education range from the formal, academic type of teaching through to the impromptu teaching that occurs spontaneously in day-to-day work.
- Teaching is delivered by nursing personnel such as university lecturers, lecturer/practitioners, mentors, clinical and community practitioners.
- Nurse education comes under the overall umbrella of post-compulsory education and training.
- The role of the Nursing Midwifery Council is to protect the public by ensuring that high standards of care are provided by nurses and midwives.
- There are three parts to the NMC register for nurses, midwives and specialist community public health nurses, with five recordable post-registration qualifications.
- Standards for pre-registration nursing education ensure that nurses of the future are fit for practice and are able to meet the needs of patients effectively with compassion.
- Standards for pre-registration midwifery education prepare midwifery students to practise safely and effectively so that, on registration, they can assume full responsibility and accountability for their practice as midwives.

(continued)

- The PREP standards identify two standards that affect a practitioner's registration, namely the PREP (practice) standard and the PREP (continuing professional development) standard.

- Standards to support learning and assessment in practice outline the knowledge and skills that nurses and midwives must apply in practice when supporting and assessing students.

- The Health and Social Care Act puts clinicians at the centre of commissioning, frees up providers to innovate, empowers patients and gives a new focus to public health.

- The Quality Code for Higher Education is used to assure the standards and quality of higher education in the UK.

- The UK Professional Standards Framework for teaching and supporting learning in higher education ensures that professional development programmes demonstrate that standards for teaching and supporting learning are being met.

References

Health and Social Care Act [2012] http://www.legislation.gov.uk/ukpga/2012/7/notes/contents

HEA (2011) *The UK Professional Standards Framework for Teaching and Supporting Learning in Higher Education*. York: Higher Education Academy

NMC (2008) *Standards to Support Learning and Assessment in Practice: NMC Standards for Mentors, Practice Teachers and Teachers*. London: Nursing Midwifery Council

NMC (2009) *Standards for Pre-registration Midwifery Education.* London: Nursing Midwifery Council

NMC (2010) *Standards for Pre-registration Nursing Education.* London: Nursing Midwifery Council

NMC (2011a) *The PREP Handbook.* London: Nursing Midwifery Council

NMC (2011b) *Guidance on Professional Conduct for Nursing and Midwifery Students.* London: Nursing Midwifery Council

QAA (2012) *The UK Quality Code for Higher Education: A Brief Guide.* Gloucester: Quality Assurance Agency

Further Reading

Council of Deans of Health (2012) *Clinical Academic Careers for Nursing, Midwifery and the Allied Health Professions: Position Statement.* London: CoDH

DELNI (2011) *Graduating to Success: A Higher Education Strategy for Northern Ireland.* Belfast: Department for Employment and Learning

DH (2012) *Developing the Healthcare Workforce: from Design to Delivery.* London: The Stationary Office

DH (2012) *Developing the Role of the Clinical Academic Researcher in the Nursing, Midwifery and Allied Health Professions.* London: The Stationary Office

NHS Future Forum (2012) *Education and training: Next Stage - A Report from the NHS Future Forum,* http://www.dh.gov.uk/prod_consum_dh/groups/dh_digitalassets/documents/digitalasset/dh_132025.p

Scottish Government (2011) *Putting Learners at the Centre: Delivering Our Ambitions for Post-16 Education.* Edinburgh: Scottish Government

Welsh Government (2009) *Post Registration Career Framework for Nurses in Wales.* Cardiff: WG

PART ONE
THE PSYCHOLOGICAL BASIS OF LEARNING AND TEACHING

CHAPTER 2
ADULT LEARNING THEORY

THE AIMS OF THIS CHAPTER ARE:

■ To explore the underpinning principles of adult learning

■ To consider different learning styles utilized in nursing education

■ To outline approaches to learning

KEY TERMS

Andragogy	Cognitive	Pedagogy	Congruent
Experiential learning	Self-actualization	Ethology	
Schemas	Autonomy	Improvidence	

Similar to all members of the human race, adult learners in nursing, midwifery and specialist community public health nursing differ widely from one another in their personal characteristics. These individual differences encompass physical characteristics, such as age and gender, and psychological characteristics, including motivation, personality, intelligence, learning styles and expectations. The literature of adult education points out that adult learners do, however, have one thing in common; they are all voluntary participants. Whilst this is true at face value, it ignores the pressures that employers and the professional nursing bodies exert upon individuals to undertake continuing education.

This chapter begins with a review of human development across the lifespan, and then focuses on the main theoretical underpinnings of adult learning, namely humanistic approaches exemplified by Abraham Maslow and Carl Rogers, the work of Malcolm Knowles on andragogy, and the experiential learning approach exemplified by David Kolb, and, finally, Peter Jarvis's typology of learning.

A useful list of seven general characteristics of adult learners is identified in Table 2.1 (Rogers and Horrocks, 2010).

TABLE 2.1 General characteristics of adult learners
1. They are adult by definition
2. Their process of growth is continuing, rather than starting
3. They come to the learning situation with a set of experiences, knowledge and values
4. They come to the learning situation with aspirations and intentions
5. They come to the learning situation with expectations of the learning process
6. They have competing interests
7. They have established patterns of learning

HUMAN DEVELOPMENT ACROSS THE LIFESPAN

Given that an individual's physical development seems to stop once adulthood is attained, one might be forgiven for thinking that human development is therefore complete. On the contrary, it is a continuous process throughout the lifespan of an individual, and it is possible to identify a series of broad stages of development, commencing with infancy and progressing through childhood, adolescence, adulthood and finally, old age. The term 'development' is normally taken to mean some form of physical, intellectual or social improvement as an individual progresses through the developmental process, but in the case of ageing the changes may be degenerative. This section focuses on three aspects of human development: the first is concerned with intellectual development, the second with adult development, and the third with ageing.

Piaget's theory of cognitive development

Piaget's work focuses on the intellectual development of individuals and their adaptation to the environment (Piaget and Inhelder, 1969). For adaptation to occur, there must be some form of organization within the individual, and these two processes work interdependently and in parallel.

Schemas

The internal organization of an individual consists of schemas, which are ways of giving meaning to, and dealing with, aspects of the environment that are encountered. They can be likened to mini-theories that develop as a result of the infant's interactions with the environment. In early infancy, schemas equate to reflexes but as development progresses these schemas become more complex, and this occurs through two processes: assimilation and accommodation. When children encounter a new situation, they try to assimilate it into their existing familiar schemas but if the latter are inadequate then their schemas have to be modified to accommodate the new situation. For example, a child's schema for 'dog' may include all smallish, four-legged animals such as cats and foxes, but as accommodation progresses these become schemas in their own right. Hence, the child's knowledge of the world is modified and extended by the processes of assimilation and accommodation, and these processes are in balance with one another; Piaget calls this balancing process *equilibration* – a dynamic process that prepares the child for new learning. In Piagetian theory, motivation is intrinsic and arises from the application of schemas to the environment.

Stages of cognitive development

Cognitive development is seen by Piaget as consisting of four stages:

1. sensorimotor (birth–2 years)
2. pre-operational (2–7 years)
3. concrete operational (7–11 years)
4. formal operational (12 years and up)

Sensorimotor stage (birth–2 years)   At birth, the infant is equipped only with basic reflexes and these serve as the first schemas, hence thinking equates with doing. Gradually 'self' becomes differentiated from objects, and intentional behaviour begins at eight months or so. The infant begins to understand that objects exist even when they cannot be seen; this object permanence is an important characteristic at this stage because it demonstrates that a mental representation of the object must be present. It also indicates the beginnings of a move away from the egocentric focus of early infancy.

Pre-operational stage (2–7 years)   This stage is called pre-operational because children are unable to use mental rules or operations for transforming information. They are still egocentric, focusing on general aspects instead of on the individual aspects of a situation. This is strikingly demonstrated in the child's lack of conservation; for example, if presented with two balls of clay of equal size, the child will indicate that the balls are the same size. If one ball is then rolled into a cylindrical shape, the child will say that that ball has more clay. Lack of conservation also applies to numbers: if two rows of coins are evenly spaced out, and then in one row the coins are moved closer together, the child will indicate that the original row contains more coins. Thus, the child lacks reversibility, i.e. the ability to understand that if an operation is reversed matter reverts back to its original state.

Concrete operational stage (7–11 years)   During this stage, the child develops conservation and the ability to undertake mental operations. However, these operations are limited to the here-and-now; in other words, the child cannot reason hypothetically.

Formal operational stage (12 years and up)   This final stage is characterized by the ability of children to reason hypothetically, i.e. they can focus on the form of a problem without being limited to the concrete aspects as in the previous stage.

Implications for teaching and learning

Piaget's work does not consider individuals beyond the age of adolescence, but Tennant (2006) suggests that Piaget's work is relevant to adult learning because:

- it emphasizes qualitative rather than quantitative development;
- it emphasizes the active role of individuals in constructing their own knowledge;
- the concept of formal operations is seen as representing adult thinking.

It is possible to extrapolate from Piaget's approach some implications for the teaching of adults; for example, the active involvement of adult students in their own learning might assist them in their own knowledge construction. When teaching difficult abstract concepts to adult students, the teacher could initially try to frame explanations at Piaget's concrete operational level and, once these have been understood, could then adopt a more abstract approach.

Piaget's work has been subject to criticism on a number of grounds, including criticism of his experimental methodology. Some researchers reject his claim that the stage of formal operations marks the end of any further structural change; another criticism is that his approach fails to consider affective or emotional aspects of development.

Levinson's adult development model

Levinson (1986) has developed a model of adult development that identifies four major periods or eras.

The eras are relatively stable periods, but the periods of transition between stages are characterized by turmoil. The era of early-adulthood marks the adolescent's entry to the adult world. It is a time for exploring possibilities and for the beginnings of stability in life. The age 30 transition is a period of settling down, of taking a more serious approach to life and work. The transition stage into middle adulthood or midlife has become synonymous with the term 'midlife crisis'. For some 80 per cent of Levinson's sample this transition period was extremely stressful and characterized by self-doubt and a realization that their career progression had probably reached its limit. In the midlife era, there are added pressures such as worry about elderly parents, children becoming independent young adults, and the beginnings of physical decline exemplified by the need to wear spectacles. However, there is a positive side to midlife, such as being financially more secure, and enjoying life as a couple again after children have left home.

Implications for teaching and learning

Levinson's model may help teachers to gain greater insight into the developmental stage of their adult students and an appreciation of the factors that might help or hinder such students in their studies. For example, the mid-life crisis may provide a useful explanation for some of the difficulties that adult students may experience whilst undertaking studies in middle age. Although Levinson's methodology was sound, the model has yet to gain universal acceptance.

The ageing process and the adult learner

Technically speaking, ageing begins at birth but the accompanying decline in human performance does not significantly manifest itself until the onset of old age between approximately 60 and 65 years of age. A number of sub-categories of old age can be found in the literature: the term 'young elderly' applies to those aged between 65 and 75, and the 'old elderly' to those over 75. Another classification is that of the 'third age' and the 'fourth age', the former referring to those elderly individuals who are independent and active and the latter to those who are dependent upon others for activities of living.

General effects of ageing

There are many theories that attempt to explain why the human body ages but the general effects of the process are well documented, the usual classification being physiological and psychological ageing.

Physiological ageing   The ageing process involves a decline in the effectiveness of many bodily functions, including breathing, circulation, digestion and elimination but the most obvious deterioration is in eyesight and hearing. The main eyesight problem in the elderly is concerned with the ability to focus correctly, leading to long-sightedness or, more seriously, loss of acuity or sharpness of vision. Hearing loss of varying degrees is common in the elderly and can be attributed to a range of factors, such as wax blocking the auditory canal, degeneration of the small bones that conduct sound in the middle ear, and degeneration of the nerves of the inner ear. Perception of high-frequency sounds sustains greater loss than that for low-frequency sounds, and the ability to discriminate pitch may be affected (Stuart-Hamilton, 1996).

Psychological ageing   In considering the effects of ageing upon psychological functioning, it is useful to distinguish between two types of intelligence: crystallized intelligence, which indicates the knowledge acquired by an individual throughout the lifespan, and fluid intelligence, which is concerned with information-processing and problem-solving, and which is much less dependent upon acquired knowledge. Crystallized intelligence is often equated with wisdom, i.e. the accumulated knowledge gained over a lifetime, whereas fluid intelligence equates with wit, i.e. the ability to deal with novel or abstract problems. Research studies indicate that there is a decline in fluid intelligence in old age, but that crystallized intelligence is largely unaffected. Many elderly people feel that their memory has declined as they have grown older, and research findings support the fact that memory does indeed decline with ageing.

Implications for teaching and learning

From the foregoing outline of ageing, it is apparent that no significant deterioration in intellectual abilities is likely to be present in those adult learners in nursing, midwifery and specialist community public health nursing who are below the age of 60–65 years. However, the teacher may be able to assist the adult learner to compensate for the gradual decline in some aspects of functioning that occurs progressively during adulthood. With regard to eyesight problems, the teacher can ensure that adequate lighting is provided by simply switching on the classroom lights at the commencement of the lesson. It may also be helpful to ensure that PowerPoint presentations and accompanying lecture notes are available for students in hard copy format or to download from a virtual learning environment prior to the teaching session. The teacher can help students with hearing problems by suggesting that such students sit at the front of the class, and by ensuring that the volume of his or her voice is sufficiently audible and the speed of delivery is not too fast. Also, particular attention needs to be given to the volume and tone settings of audiotape and video presentations.

Given the comments about the decline in fluid intelligence with ageing, the teacher may, when setting problem-solving activities in the classroom, need to allocate extra time for older students to complete the activities. Similarly, in the light of the decline in memory with ageing, the teacher should, when asking questions, allow older students a little longer to structure their reply, as they may be slower to recall the information that they require to answer.

In addition to these specific aspects of ageing, older students may lack confidence in their academic and study ability, especially if they have not been engaged in formal study for some considerable time. If older students are in the minority within a group, they may feel marginalized or isolated from the younger students. It is not always easy to bridge the 'generation gap' and mix freely with a younger group, so teachers may need to offer additional support to older students if they become isolated. On the other hand, the younger students may benefit enormously from the experience and stability of the older students.

THE HUMANISTIC BASIS OF ADULT LEARNING THEORY

Adult learning theory has been strongly influenced by humanistic psychology, although there is no single theory that represents the humanistic approach. However, all theories share a common view that this approach involves the study of people as human beings, with thoughts, feelings and experiences. This is in direct contrast to the stimulus–response theorists, who study people from the point of view of their overt behaviour, disregarding inner feelings and experiences. Humanistic differs from cognitive theory also, in that the latter is concerned with the thinking aspects of behaviour, with little emphasis on the affective components.

Exponents of humanistic theory claim that the other two theories omit some of the most significant aspects of human existence, namely feelings, attitudes and values. Humanistic theory is closely related to the philosophical approach called phenomenology, which asserts that reality lies in a person's perception of an event and not in the event itself. The humanistic viewpoint has never been better crystallized than in this definition:

> 'It is a psychological stance that focuses not so much on a person's biological drives, but on their goals; not so much on stimuli impinging on them, but on their desires to be or to do something; not so much on their past experiences, but on their current circumstances; not so much on life conditions per se, but on the subjective qualities of human experience, the personal meaning of an experience to persons, rather than on their objective, observable responses.'
>
> Hamachek (1978)

Humanistic theory, then, is concerned with human growth, individual fulfilment and self-actualization and it is claimed that this approach is 'intuitively right', as it agrees with the ideas that most people have about what is uniquely human. However, the behaviourist approach is not considered to be wrong; rather, humanistic theory prefers to emphasize the affective aspects of humans as being of equal importance to the cognitive and psychomotor elements. There are two main principles that apply to the humanistic approach to learning and teaching, namely teacher–student relationships and the classroom climate. The former stresses the importance of the interpersonal relationship between learner and teacher as a major variable affecting learning and this in turn affects the climate of the classroom. The presence or absence of conflict and tension will depend largely on the quality of relationships within the classroom setting. Mastering information and facts is not the central purpose of the humanistic model of learning. Instead, fostering curiosity, enthusiasm, initiative and responsibility is much more important and enduring and should be the primary goal of any educator (Braungart and Braungart, 2008).

Self-direction, empowerment and autonomy

Humanism's emphasis on the importance of the Self is reflected in three of its key tenets, i.e. self-direction, empowerment, and learner autonomy. The term 'self-direction' is used in three different senses within the literature of adult learning (Tennant, 2006):

■ the ability of adult students to plan and manage their own learning;

■ a personal characteristic of adult learners associated with personal autonomy;

■ a way of organizing teaching that allows greater student control over the learning process.

The basic underlying concept in each of these is the belief that adults are naturally self-directing and autonomous with regard to learning, if given the opportunity to be so. Autonomy is one of the basic values of Western society; its literal meaning is 'self-governing', which implies independence and a sense of control over external forces. Hence, learner autonomy is really about the re-distribution of power; self-directed learning aims to shift the power base away from the educational organization (teachers, curriculum, etc.) and towards the adult learners themselves. Autonomy is not an all-or-nothing phenomenon, but a continuum from lesser to greater autonomy; it is also a characteristic that can be developed (McNair, 1996). Mailloux (2006) emphasizes the importance of empowerment in developing autonomy in the following statement:

> 'Educational systems that facilitate the empowerment of students seek to increase the students' readiness to assume more control throughout their educational experiences thus providing a means of acquiring greater perceptions of autonomy'
>
> Mailloux (2006)

Humanistic psychology: Maslow's approach

Abraham H. Maslow (1908–1970) was a major exponent of the humanistic approach to psychology and has also made a significant contribution to motivation theory with his theory of a hierarchy of needs. He coined the term 'third force' psychology because he considered the first force to be Freudian psychotherapy and the second to be the stimulus–response school. The latter school, he felt, had little relevance to the human personality: 'these extensive books on the psychology of learning are of no consequence, at least to the human centre, to the human soul, to the human essence' (Maslow, 1971).

One of the key concepts that Maslow defined was 'self-actualization', and he studied the behaviour of people whom he classified as self-actualizers. Maslow stated eight ways in which an individual self-actualizes; these include 'experiencing fully, vividly, selflessly, with full concentration and total absorption' (Maslow, 1971, p. 44). He mentions the 'peak experience', which is an ecstatic moment that can be brought on by such experiences as classical music and religious experiences. For the humanist, the goal of education is to assist the individual to achieve self-actualization, or, as Maslow puts it, 'to help the person to become the best that he is able to become' (Maslow, 1971, p. 163). This intrinsic approach is in contrast to the extrinsic educational ethic, in which the transmission of factual knowledge is seen to be more important than the development of an individual. The ideal college, according to Maslow, would be one in which the main objectives would be the discovery of one's identity and the destiny or vocation for each person.

Humanistic psychology: Rogers' approach

Carl R. Rogers made his reputation as a psychotherapist, developing a new approach that he called client-centred therapy (Rogers, 1951). This involves the therapist in a non-directive role in which the client is encouraged to develop a deeper understanding of his or her 'self'. The role of the therapist is to provide a non-critical atmosphere, in which there is no attempt to interpret for the client, but simply a reflecting back of the statements made in order to assist the client in developing self-awareness. This concept of client-centred therapy led Rogers to formulate his student-centred approach to learning, which is contained in his most important work on the subject (Rogers, 1969; Rogers and Freiberg, 1994). In this work, he stated ten principles of learning.

These principles illustrate Rogers' approach to learning and his emphasis on relevance, student participation and involvement, self-evaluation and the absence of threat in the classroom. Rogers saw the teacher as a facilitator of learning, a provider of resources for learning, and someone who shares feelings as well as knowledge with the students.

Rogers further articulated his approach to education in his book *Freedom to Learn for the 80s* (Rogers, 1983). He saw learning as being a continuum, with much meaningless material at one end and significant or experiential learning at the other. The former could describe many curricula, which are seen as virtually meaningless by the students for whom they are intended.

Experiential learning, on the other hand, has a number of qualities such as personal involvement, self-initiation, persuasiveness, self-evaluation and meaningfulness. Rogers contrasts the kind of learning that is concerned solely with cognitive functioning with that involving the whole person.

Teaching, according to Rogers, is a highly overrated activity, in contrast to the notion of facilitation. Teaching by giving knowledge does not meet the requirements of today's changing world; what is required is the facilitation of learning and change, which calls for a different set of qualities in the facilitator.

Qualities required in a facilitator

The most important factor is the relationship that exists between facilitator and learner, and Rogers suggests a number of qualities that are required for this: genuineness, trust and acceptance, and empathetic understanding.

Genuineness   The facilitator should come across as a real person rather than as some kind of ideal model. Hence, it is important that facilitators show 'normal' reactions to their students.

Trust and acceptance   The facilitator should demonstrate acceptance of the student as a person in his or her own right as a person worthy of respect and care.

Empathic understanding   Facilitators need to put themselves in the students' shoes in order to see and understand things from their students' perspective.

Rogers suggests that it is possible for the teacher to build into a programme the freedom to learn, which students require. This can be done by using students' own experiences and problems, so that relevance is obvious, and by providing resources for the students in the form of both material and human resources. The goal of education is that the student should become a fully functioning person.

Implications for teaching and learning

Rogers' ten principles of learning can be used as a basis for planning the educational experiences of adult learners. Their natural potential for learning can be exploited by strategies that arouse curiosity and present problems or challenges. The importance of relevance cannot be over-emphasized; theoretical concepts should be framed in the context of the real world of adult students, for example applied to the workplace, or to wider society. Rogers sees the psychological environment of the classroom as being of paramount importance to learning; by their very nature, classrooms can be perceived by students as places where their ignorance or lack of ability may be exposed to ridicule by both teachers and peers. The first step in creating a psychologically safe atmosphere in the classroom is for the teacher to state clearly from the outset the ground rules of the teaching and learning interaction. These will include the expectation that students will actively participate in the learning process, that learning is a partnership between teacher and students, that students' contributions will be accepted with respect by other students and the teacher, and that challenge and debate will be part of the agenda.

TEACHING TIP

Think about ways in which you might positively encourage students from the outset to actively contribute in classroom discussions, and recognize the value of challenging discussions and debates.

A facilitative learning environment can take some time to come to fruition, given that its development depends on the establishment of trust and respect between all parties in the teaching and learning situation. It should be an environment where psychological safety exists and where the students feel at ease. Some of the barriers between teacher and learner may be lessened by the rearrangement of the seating and the use of small-group techniques. These also facilitate the discussion of feelings and values, an aspect that is considered crucial in the humanistic approach. The humanistic approach to education centres on the relationships between teachers and students, each learner being considered as an individual. The use of forenames between teacher and learner can increase the feeling of identity for the learner and help to reduce barriers to communication.

Involvement in decision-making is one step further in helping the students develop a sense of personal value and worth. While it is impossible to involve each learner in major planning decisions, it is useful to have student representatives on course and pathway committees to contribute ideas and suggestions from their peer group or cohort. Most teachers are aware of the individual differences between students prior to commencing an educational programme, but they also need to be sensitive to the fact that they will still have differences at the end of the course. It is important to remain aware that the students are individuals, even though they have been exposed to a common educational programme, and to encourage them to maintain their unique attitudes and values, rather than aiming for a conformist, homogeneous end product.

According to the humanistic approach, the role of the teacher is that of helper and facilitator, rather than conveyor of information. In other words, the teacher becomes another learning resource for the learner. In order to perform their role satisfactorily, teachers must fully understand themselves and be flexible in their approach to teaching. Rogers' approach encourages active involvement by the student in learning, and this can be achieved by the inclusion of strategies such as project work, practicals and field-based studies. It is also important that students be encouraged to follow up topics or issues that have particular interest for them, although it is often difficult in practice to make provision for this in a prescribed curriculum. Adult students should be encouraged to engage in self-evaluation of their learning, so that they do not become reliant on external feedback from the teacher. Lastly, Rogers emphasizes the importance of students' knowing how to learn, so study skills advice should be made available, usually in the form of study skills workshops or learning packages.

One of the specific applications of humanistic psychology is in the use of learning contracts, which give the students the opportunity to take responsibility for their own learning. Learning contracts are discussed below in the section on andragogy.

Critique of the humanistic approach

One of the most serious criticisms of the humanistic approach is that it is lacking in empirical evidence to support its claims, relying upon observations and assumptions of human behaviour. The humanistic approach has also been criticized for promoting self-centred learners who 'cannot take criticism or compromise their deeply felt positions'; charged with being more of a philosophy or a cult, than a science, the tactile approach of humanists can make some students and lecturers feel uncomfortable (Braungart and Braungart, 2008). The humanist educational theory in nurse education has raised the issue of which interests are served by humanist ideology; Purdy (1997) has previously suggested that the need to produce safe practitioners compromises the humanist model. He also warns of the dangers it poses in nurse education and makes the following statement:

'Far from seeking genuinely to empower the learner, the humanist perspective's goals are essentially conservative. Rather than confronting and challenging 'conditions' that may lead to the individual becoming alienated, disempowered, devalued and passive, the humanists offer only a means for individuals to accommodate themselves to the demands of the 'system'. In short, the perspective enables the individual to adapt to the system, but not to change it.'

Purdy (1997)

Humanistic psychology's emphasis on the *self* and on *feelings* may be seen as devaluing intellectual aspects of learning; the acquisition of knowledge and facts is a quite legitimate educational aim. It could also be argued that the emphasis on personal growth and self-exploration in humanistic theories makes them less useful for some types of vocational education and training. In recent years however, Braungart and Braungart (2008) have emphasized how humanistic learning theory has modified the approach to education and changing behaviour by focusing more on the individual needs and feelings of the student and by redefining the role of the educator. They believe that humanistic principles have been a cornerstone of self-help groups, wellness programmes and palliative care; it has also been found to be suitable when working with children and young people undergoing separation anxiety due to illness, surgery and recovery (Weidner *et al.*, 2011) and for working in the areas of mental health and palliative care (Spandler and Stickley, Barnard *et al.*, 2006).

The writings of Carl Rogers are about the education of children in schools, and the application of his ideas to the teaching of adult professionals, whilst attractive, may have little or no validity. Sigman (1995), in a telling critique, points out that humanistic psychology originated in the US, a different culture from the UK, and suggests that the principles may not easily translate to the UK culture. He argues that it began as a psychological therapy for illness, but has now become a general approach for the pursuit of self-fulfilment through change. According to Sigman, contentment has been replaced by the need for personal growth and fulfilment, and to illustrate this he contrasts the sayings of a generation ago, such as 'count your blessings', with society's current motto, 'go for it'. He claims that the constant emphasis on self-improvement may lead to self-disapproval and rejection of one's own identity, which may be made worse by failure to achieve the desired changes.

ANDRAGOGY: THE TEACHING AND TRAINING OF ADULTS

In recent years, 'andragogy' has become the preferred term in the literature for describing the teaching and training of adults. (It is used as a contrast to pedagogy: a pedagogue is literally a leader of children.) One of the foremost contributors to this area is the American educationalist Malcolm S. Knowles, whose approach is based upon the differences that he perceives between the teaching of adults and children (Knowles, 1990). He maintains that educational systems, including those for adult students, are based on a pedagogical model. Noting that all the great teachers in history, such as Socrates and Confucius, were teachers of adults, Knowles uses the term andragogy, i.e. a leader of man (adults), to describe his approach. He points out that the term 'adult' has a number of meanings:

- biological adulthood is the ability to reproduce;
- legal adulthood is defined by the law;
- social adulthood is the stage at which adult roles are performed; and
- psychological adulthood is when self-direction is assumed.

The two models, pedagogy and andragogy, are based on different assumptions about the learner on six dimensions:

- the learner's need to know;
- the learner's self-concept;

- the role of the learner's experience;
- the learner's readiness to learn;
- the learner's orientation to learning; and
- the learner's motivation.

The different assumption for pedagogy and andragogy are outlined in Table 2.2.

TABLE 2.2 The different assumptions of pedagogy and andragogy		
Assumptions	**Pedagogy**	**Andragogy**
Learner's need to know	Students must learn what they are taught in order to pass their tests	Adults need to know why they must learn something
Learner's self-concept	Dependency: decisions about learning are controlled by teacher	Self-direction: adults take responsibility for their own learning
Role of learner's experience	It is the teacher's experience that is seen as important. The learner's experience is seen as of little use as a learning resource	Adults have greater, and much more varied experience which serves as a rich resource for learning
Learner's readiness to learn	Learner's readiness is dependent upon what the teacher wants the learner to learn	Adult's readiness relates to the things he or she needs to know and do in real life
Student's orientation to learning	Learning equates with the subject-matter content of the curriculum	Adults have a life-centred orientation to learning involving problem-solving and task-centred approaches
Student's motivation	Student's motivation is from external sources such as teacher approval, grades and parental pressures	Adult's motivation is largely internal such as self-esteem, quality of life and job satisfaction

Knowles argues that traditional education conditions the learner to react to teacher stimuli, and this reactive learning does not equip the learner with the skills for lifelong learning. Andragogy encourages a proactive approach to learning in which enquiry and autonomy feature predominantly. However, pedagogy and andragogy should be seen as parallel rather than as opposing models, and Knowles acknowledges that both may be appropriate for children and adults depending upon the given circumstances. For example, it might be that a pedagogical or dependent approach involving didactic teaching would be more appropriate when the learner first encounters new or unusual learning situations, provided that an andragogical approach is used overall. Similarly, Knowles believes that andragogy can be appropriate for children, with its emphasis on a classroom climate conducive to learning and the concept of increasing self-direction and autonomy.

Two aspects of Knowles's work have had a particularly strong influence on nurse education curricula: his process model for human resources development, and the use of learning contracts.

Process model for human resources development

Knowles uses the term 'human resources development' to cover the whole range of continuing education and training in a wide variety of contexts, and the implementation of the andragogical model involves a 'process model' as opposed to the pedagogical one of a 'content model'. There are seven elements to the process model.

1. *Establishing a climate conducive to learning* This involves both the physical, and the human and interpersonal environment; the former takes account of the seating arrangements, decor, ventilation and lighting, and the latter such things as the organizational climate, mutual respect, collaboration, mutual trust and supportiveness, openness and authenticity and a climate of pleasure and humanness.

2. *Creating a mechanism for mutual planning* This is one of the cardinal principles of andragogy; all those concerned with the educational enterprise should be involved in its planning.

3. *Diagnosing the needs for learning* According to Knowles, a learning need is a gap between the specified learning outcomes of a programme and the existing state of the learner in relation to these. Andragogy emphasizes the importance of the learner's own perception of this gap, but there may be tension between the needs of participants and the needs of the organization, and this conflict must be negotiated with care.

4. *Formulating programme objectives* Knowles acknowledges the widely differing viewpoints on the nature of objectives and suggests cautiously that behavioural objectives might be more appropriate for training and for more process-orientated outcomes for education.

5. *Designing a pattern of learning experiences* Self-directed learning is central to andragogical design models and involves a choice of learning methods that are appropriate to the learner's objectives.

6. *Operating the programme* This involves the administration of the learning programme, and the quality of learning resources is a crucial factor.

7. *Evaluating the programme* Knowles favours a five-step approach to evaluation:
   a) reaction evaluation is ongoing evaluation during the programme;
   b) learning evaluation is the gathering of data about the learning outcomes achieved;
   c) behaviour evaluation takes a wider view of the changes in behaviour, culled from supervisors' reports, etc.;
   d) results evaluation is organizational data such as costs, efficiency, absence, etc.;
   e) re-diagnosis of learning needs is really a repeat of Step 3 above, and involves helping students to re-evaluate where they are in relation to programme objectives.

Learning contracts

As Knowles points out, individuals have a need to be self-directing in their learning, yet traditional curricula were largely controlled by the educational institution. Learning contracts are a means of reconciling the learning needs of the student and those of other interested parties such as educators and employers. The focus of nurse education is the promotion and maintenance of professional competence; what constitutes such competence is decided not only by the individual nurse but also by employers and professional bodies. The needs of each of these key players may well conflict on occasions, and learning contracts provide a useful way of negotiating an acceptable compromise. Knowles offers a step-by-step approach for developing a learning contract (Figure 2.1).

FIGURE 2.1 Stepped approach to learning contracts (Knowles 1990)

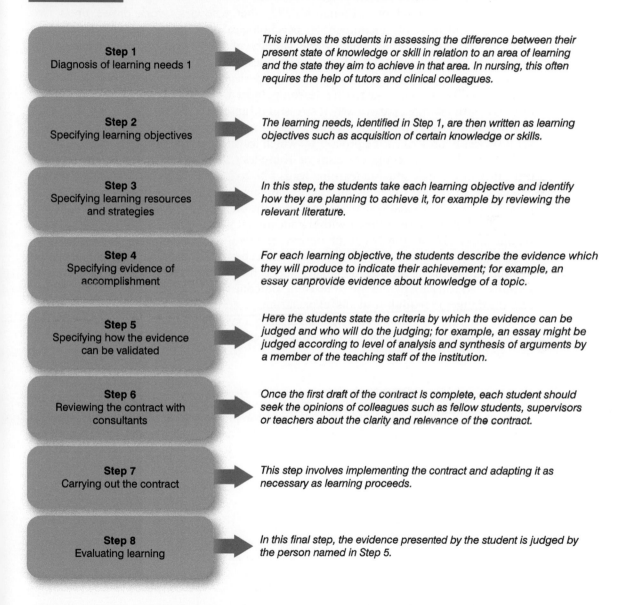

Step 1
Diagnosis of learning needs 1

This involves the students in assessing the difference between their present state of knowledge or skill in relation to an area of learning and the state they aim to achieve in that area. In nursing, this often requires the help of tutors and clinical colleagues.

Step 2
Specifying learning objectives

The learning needs, identified in Step 1, are then written as learning objectives such as acquisition of certain knowledge or skills.

Step 3
Specifying learning resources and strategies

In this step, the students take each learning objective and identify how they are planning to achieve it, for example by reviewing the relevant literature.

Step 4
Specifying evidence of accomplishment

For each learning objective, the students describe the evidence which they will produce to indicate their achievement; for example, an essay can provide evidence about knowledge of a topic.

Step 5
Specifying how the evidence can be validated

Here the students state the criteria by which the evidence can be judged and who will do the judging; for example, an essay might be judged according to level of analysis and synthesis of arguments by a member of the teaching staff of the institution.

Step 6
Reviewing the contract with consultants

Once the first draft of the contract is complete, each student should seek the opinions of colleagues such as fellow students, supervisors or teachers about the clarity and relevance of the contract.

Step 7
Carrying out the contract

This step involves implementing the contract and adapting it as necessary as learning proceeds.

Step 8
Evaluating learning

In this final step, the evidence presented by the student is judged by the person named in Step 5.

Although used extensively as a model in nurse education curricula, Knowles's approach has been criticized on a number of grounds. Given the humanistic value basis of andragogy, the assumptions of andragogy should apply as equally to children as to adults, for example the importance of self-direction and autonomy. The self-directing characteristic of adults is a cornerstone of Knowles's theory, yet experiences with open learning programmes indicate that many adult students find it difficult to unlearn their dependence on tutors and take considerable time to develop self-direction in their learning. This voluntary relinquishing of self-direction is particularly noticeable when students have to learn something new; it does not mean that they are adopting a child-like approach to their learning.

It has been pointed out (Tennant, 1997) that Knowles' work draws upon two opposing (and mutually incompatible) psychological theories, humanistic psychology and behaviourism, thus weakening the validity of his approach. The superiority of experience in adult learning has also been questioned. Although adults, by virtue of having lived longer than children, have more experience, they do not automatically bring a better quality of experience to their learning. Indeed, previous experiences may serve to interfere with learning, particularly if stressful or upsetting. There is inconsistency in the fact that Knowles is opposed to teachers prescribing the content of what is to be learned, yet he actually prescribed the process by which learning should occur.

Perhaps the most telling criticism of Knowles's approach is that his focus on the centrality of the individual in learning leads him to ignore the power of social forces in education. In reality, the individual has relatively little power in comparison with the power of the educational system to determine the organization of learning. For example, although choice may be offered within educational programmes, it is almost invariably within a prescribed framework of options imposed by the award regulations. Many commentators on andragogy highlight the conflict between the interests of the educational institution and those of the individual student, for example the restriction placed upon self-directed learning by the use of learning outcomes and award requirements. There is also the danger that adult students' expectations of adult education will be raised unduly by the rhetoric of self-directed learning. They may enter adult education expecting something completely different from what they experienced at school, an expectation all too commonly disappointed.

Tennant's reconstructed charter for andragogy

Tennant (1997) offers a useful generic guide for practising teachers in the form of a 'reconstructed charter for andragogy'. He identifies eight characteristics of critical adult education practice that can be considered generic to all forms of teaching; these are outlined below.

1. *Valuing the experiences of learners* Learners' life-worlds should be included in all aspects of the teaching and learning enterprise; it is not sufficient merely to have a positive attitude towards them.

2. *Engaging in reflection on experiences* This involves both the students' existing experiences and the new experiences introduced as part of the teaching. The latter encourages students to progress beyond their own experiences, which in turn helps them to generalize their experiential learning.

3. *Establishing collaborative learning relationships* Tennant points out the necessity for collaborative group learning, where students' experiences and learning can be shared and enriched from multiple perspectives.

4. *Addressing issues of identity and power relationships between teachers and learners* This will depend to some extent on the context of learning, but it is important that these issues are addressed.

5. *Promoting judgements about learning that are developmental and which allow scope for success for all learners* All judgements about students' learning should encourage further development, and should not be framed with reference to other students' success or failure.

6. *Negotiating conflicts over claims to knowledge and pedagogical processes* It is important that students should feel able to express differences of opinion with regard to educational knowledge, and that this is accepted as an important aspect of the teaching process.

7. *Identifying the historical and cultural locatedness of experiences* Students should be aware of the social and cultural context of their experiences and be encouraged to question the assumptions arising from this.

8. *Transforming actions and practices* This relates to 7 above, and refers to new actions and practices adopted by students as a result of their recognition of the social and cultural context of their experiences.

Neary's approach to learning contracts

We have come to understand how the use of learning contracts requires handing over the control of learning to the student. Neary (2000a) warns us how this might challenge the assumption underlying the traditional approach to health education, so some antagonism and resistance to this idea should be expected. The rate of helping students move towards independence is likely to be quite slow initially, but, as confidence, experience and autonomy increase, independence will accelerate.

The purpose of learning contracts is clearly explained by Neary (2000a, p. 77) who offers a concise eight-point set of criteria outlined below.

Learning contracts provide the following:

1. The safety for students to make decisions about their learning within the boundaries set by the curriculum framework and objectives.

2. The opportunity for teachers and students to utilize the individual's internal motivation to learn and/or change.

3. A framework for supporting students who may fail to do well because of their unstructured approach to learning.

4. A vehicle by which the external needs of the organization and the internal needs of the individual can be met.

5. A means for identifying the individual's preferred learning styles.

6. A means whereby the pace of learning can be adjusted to the needs of the individual.

7. A vehicle for integrating theory and practice, which is extremely important for practice-based professions.

8. The basic unit for auditing the learning programme and the identification of performance indicators:

   ● students;
   ● teachers; and
   ● programme.

THE EXPERIENTIAL LEARNING APPROACH TO ADULT LEARNING

Within the past 25 years, experiential learning has become firmly established in nursing, midwifery and specialist community public health nursing curricula. At its simplest, experiential learning is learning that results from experience, but, since almost everything in life constitutes experience, this becomes an impossibly global notion. Essentially, experiential learning is learning by doing, rather than by listening to other people or reading about it. This active involvement of the student is one of the key characteristics of this form of learning, together with student-centredness, a degree of interaction, some measure of autonomy and flexibility and a high degree of relevance.

Kolb: the theory of experiential learning

David Kolb is a major exponent of experiential learning theory.

> 'Experiential learning theory offers a fundamentally different view of the learning process from that of the behavioural theories of learning based on an empirical epistemology or the more implicit theories of learning that underlie traditional educational methods, methods that for the most part are based on a rational idealist epistemology. This perspective on learning is called 'experiential' for two reasons. The first is to tie it clearly to its intellectual origins in the work of Dewey, Lewin and Piaget. The second reason is to emphasize the central role that experience plays in the learning process …'
>
> Kolb, 1984, p. 20

Kolb sees learning as a core process of human development and makes a distinction between development and simple readjustment to change. Development results from learning that is gained through experience, and this is the basis of the 'experiential learning model' (or 'experiential learning cycle'). The cycle has become known as 'Kolb's Cycle', but it is interesting to note that Kolb himself refers to it as the 'Lewinian Experiential Learning Model'.

The cycle, as shown in Figure 2.2, begins with some kind of concrete experience, professional or personal, that the student considers interesting or problematic. Observations and information are gathered about the experience and then the student reflects upon it, replaying it over again and analyzing it until certain insights begin to emerge in the shape of a 'theory' about the experience. The implications arising from this conceptualization can then be utilized to modify existing nursing or midwifery practice or to generate new approaches to it.

FIGURE 2.2 Experiential learning model (Kolb, 1984)

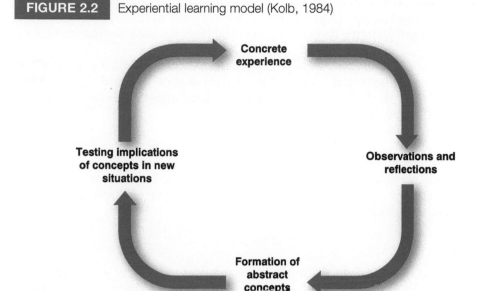

Generic adaptive abilities

There are four generic adaptive abilities required for effective learning:

1. *Concrete experience (CE)* The students must immerse themselves fully and openly in new experiences.
2. *Reflective observation (RO)* The students must observe and reflect on concrete experiences from a variety of perspectives.
3. *Abstract conceptualization (AC)* The students must create concepts that integrate their observations into logical theories.
4. *Active experimentation* The students must apply these theories in decision-making and problem-solving.

Primary dimensions of learning process

These four generic adaptive abilities consist of two pairs of opposites, forming two primary dimensions of learning:

- concrete experience – abstract conceptualization; and
- active experimentation – reflective observation.

During a learning situation, the student moves from action to observation to a varying extent according to the nature of the situation, both dimensions being important aspects of the learning process. This approach is compatible with other theories of cognitive development such as those of Piaget and Bruner.

Implications for teaching and learning

Kolb's work has provided a theoretical basis for the implementation of experiential learning in adult education; experiential learning is discussed in Chapter 6 in the context of small-group teaching and also forms a very useful theoretical basis for the Accreditation of Prior Experiential Learning (APEL), discussed in Chapter 7. Experiential learning theory can be applied to individual differences; for example, Kolb (1976) identified four learning styles based upon the theory of experiential learning; these are outlined later in the chapter.

The experiential learning cycle has been influential in curricula for nursing and midwifery, However, the model does not have a great deal of empirical support, and it is unlikely that every single learning situation will demand an integrated approach using the four general adaptive abilities.

Jarvis' typology of learning

Peter Jarvis has proposed a typology of learning based upon three forms of learning response to experience: non-learning, non-reflective learning and reflective learning (Jarvis and Gibson, 1997).

Non-learning

Jarvis points out that individuals do not necessarily learn from any given experience, and he identifies three types of non-learning. The first is presumption, i.e. the tendency for individuals to rely uncritically on their past experiences as a basis for their behaviour. The second is an individual's failure to respond to a potential learning situation, which Jarvis terms 'non-consideration'. The third type is rejection, where the individual rejects the possibility of learning from the experience; bigots would come under this category.

Non-reflective learning

As the name implies, this is learning that does not involve a reflective process; it includes memorization, skills learning and preconscious learning. The latter is also called incidental learning, i.e. the learning that occurs without the individual being aware of it.

Reflective learning

In contrast to the two previous forms of learning, this involves a process of reflection. Jarvis's research identified different types within this category: contemplation, reflective skills learning, and experimental learning.

Implications for teaching and learning

Jarvis's typology is useful in that it expands our view of what constitutes learning; it also emphasizes the importance of the reflective process in learning.

REFLECTION AND ADULT LEARNING

Although reflection as a concept had been established in education since the turn of the century, it was the work of Donald Schön (Schön, 1983, 1987) in the mid-1980s that put it well and truly on the agenda of professional practice in both the teaching and the nursing professions. The significance of reflection in nursing lies in its close relationship to learning in professional practice settings, and the concepts of reflective practice in nursing are discussed in detail in Chapter 15.

HUMAN MOTIVATION

Theories of motivation attempt to explain the processes by which human actions are directed; there is an implicit assumption here that human actions are purposeful as opposed to random, and are therefore directed towards some goal or another. Motivation is considered an important factor in the learning process, and one of the key aims of teaching is to increase students' motivation to learn.

Explanations of human motivation inevitably reflect the standpoints of the different schools of psychology. For example, the behaviourist approach sees motivation as being due to factors in the environment, rather than arising within an individual. In this approach, a person's current actions are determined by the success or otherwise of past actions, i.e. whether or not these were reinforced by past environmental events. In this approach, an individual's motivation to attend a concert is determined by the fact that previous visits to concerts were pleasurable, and concert-going behaviour was therefore reinforced.

The mediationist approach adopts the opposite stance to behaviourism; i.e. whilst not ignoring the role of the environment in motivation, it emphasizes the importance of an individual's perceptions, attitudes and beliefs in mediating their behaviour (Mook, 1996). The following sections highlight some of the most influential theories of human motivation.

Motivation as instinct

Instincts are aspects of animal behaviour that are innate and untaught, and which govern much of their total repertoire of behaviour.

Ethology

Ethology is a branch of psychology concerned with the study of animals in their natural settings rather than in the artificial surroundings of the laboratory. One of the founders of this school was Konrad Lorenz; he demonstrated that animals possess instinctive behaviours called fixed-action patterns (FAPs), which can be triggered off by innate releasing mechanisms (IRMs). Nikko Tinbergen (1951) has described these in relation to the male stickleback; fixed-action patterns of attack or courtship are released by the red underside of another male, or the swollen abdomen of the female respectively. Another example of a fixed-action pattern, according to Lorenz, is imprinting (Lorenz, 1958). This occurs in young animals within two days of birth or hatching and consists of the animal following the first moving object that it encounters. This is normally the parent, and the process has survival value to the species, in that the young animal follows and remains close to the parent. Lorenz showed that imprinting will occur on the first moving object, even if this is a human being or an inanimate object, but that it is difficult or impossible after two days, when fear of strange objects has developed.

Some psychologists believe that certain aspects of human behaviour are instinctual; Eibl-Eibesfeldt has summarized the innate releasing mechanisms in man, citing examples such as the cues in an infant's appearance, which trigger off caring behaviour in adults (Eibl-Eibesfeldt, 1971). Bowlby (1970) considered that the attachment behaviour of the newborn infant towards a preferred figure is a form of imprinting.

Freudian psychoanalytic theory

Another theory that utilizes the concept of instinct is that of Sigmund Freud. His psychoanalytic theory sees humans as being motivated by two basic instincts or drives, Eros and Thanatos. The former are life drives and are divided into ego drives, which are concerned with self-preservation, and libido, which is concerned with sexual drive and preservation of the species. Thanatos is composed of self-destructive drives and aggressive drives, and constraints imposed on these by self or society result in their repression below the level of consciousness. According to Freud, such repressed drives function as powerful unconscious motivators of behaviour (Freud, 1923).

Motivation as needs and drives

Drives are internal states of arousal of an organism that occur as a consequence of some form of need, either biological or non-biological. Biological needs are homeostatic needs such as hunger, thirst and body temperature control, which work on the principle of negative feedback. A negative feedback loop operates as follows: when a given level of production output is detected by sensors within the organism, mechanisms come into play that 'switch off' further production, allowing the output level to fall. When the output falls below a given level, the negative feedback loop is inhibited, allowing output production to resume.

To clarify the process of negative feedback, let us take the example of maintenance of body temperature. The hypothalamus controls the sympathetic and parasympathetic nerves supplying the smooth muscle of blood vessels, and hence controls vasoconstriction and vasodilatation; it also contains a 'thermostat' i.e. a collection of cells that detect body temperature. When the thermostat detects a rise in body temperature, the negative feedback loop operates to 'switch off' vasoconstriction and thereby allowing vasodilatation to increase the blood flow to the skin, where heat loss occurs by sweating and evaporation. One interesting example of a homeostatic approach to the acquisition of motives is the opponent–process theory, which is outlined below.

The opponent–process theory

The opponent–process theory (Solomon and Corbit, 1974; Solomon, 1980) focuses on emotional states and their role in motivating individuals' behaviour. The basis of the theory is similar to the concept of homeostasis, i.e. the tendency of an organism to counter any changes from the normal state by producing a counter-effect to that change, as in the example of temperature regulation However, the theory focuses on emotional states such as pain and pleasure, rather than on physiological ones.

The basic principle is as follows: when some circumstance or other generates an emotional reaction within an individual, this will in turn generate the opposite emotional state; for example, a visit to the theatre may generate a feeling of happiness, but this in turn generates the opposite emotion, i.e. unhappiness. Similarly, an unpleasant experience will generate displeasure, and this will trigger off the opponent emotion, i.e. pleasure. In other words, the processes are pulling in opposite directions, resulting in modification of the initial emotional state and a consequent reduction in the level of intensity.

One of the most important characteristics of the opponent–process is that, whilst the initial emotional reaction (Process A) does not change when experienced frequently, the opponent–process (Process B) increases in intensity each time. An imbalance therefore develops between them, with the original emotional reaction (Process A) getting smaller and the opponent–process (Process B) getting stronger and stronger. The theory has been used to explain the development of drug tolerance in addictive behaviour: with each dose of the drug, the unpleasant opponent–process emotions (Process B) become more powerful at the expense of the initial pleasurable emotions (Process A), so that bigger and bigger doses of the drug are required to produce the pleasurable emotional reaction.

When the drug is withdrawn completely, there is no longer any Process A emotional state, so the Process B opponent emotions (withdrawal symptoms) are left free to wreak their havoc.

The theory has been criticized for being overly general, in that it can be applied to a very wide range of situations. For example, it is quite usual for a student teacher to experience a degree of anxiety when he or she delivers the first few lectures. This unpleasant emotional state (Process A) triggers off the opposite or opponent process, i.e. a relaxed emotional state (Process B). As student teachers' exposure to lecturing increases, this relaxed state grows progressively bigger at the expense of the anxious emotional state, until this relaxed state becomes the normal reaction to lecturing. Apart from homeostatic needs, human beings have other forms of need, including cognitive, emotional and social needs. Abraham Maslow's influential theory of human motivation incorporates this wide range of human needs, and is outlined below.

Maslow's theory of human motivation: the hierarchy of needs

Abraham Maslow was one of seven children and a rather shy and nervous child. His father was a colourful character who liked to drink and fight. Maslow began by studying the law but then changed to study psychology, eventually becoming a trained therapist. He published his 'theory of human motivation', in which there are five classes of need arranged in hierarchical order, from the most basic up to the highest level (Maslow, 1971). Each class of need is stronger than the one above it in the hierarchy, in that it motivates the individual more powerfully when both needs are lacking. Gratification of needs is a key concept in this theory; when a need is gratified at one particular level, the next higher need emerges. The needs are arranged in a hierarchy as shown in Figure 2.3.

Physiological needs are the most basic and include hunger, thirst, sleep, maternal needs, etc. Individuals dominated by these needs see everything else as being of secondary importance, and this can occur to such an extent that they no longer see anything beyond the gratification of those needs. The next class is the safety needs, which include security, stability, protection, the need for order and structure, etc., and above this come the belongingness and love needs, including affection, friendship and sexual needs, although the latter can also be classified with physiological needs.

Esteem needs are concerned with strength, achievement, mastery and competence and also include reputation, prestige and dignity. Self-actualization is the highest class of needs and is concerned with the fulfilment of one's potential. This will vary greatly from person to person, according to how the individual perceives that potential. There are two further classes of need that Maslow originally included in the hierarchy – the need to know and understand and the aesthetic needs. These are now seen to be interrelated with the basic needs, rather than as separate classes. The order of these remains fixed for most people, but there are exceptions. For example, some people prefer assertive self-esteem to love. There are examples in life where lack of basic needs seems to be subjugated to the attainment of self-actualization, as with monks who fast for lengthy periods.

FIGURE 2.3   Maslow's hierarchy of needs

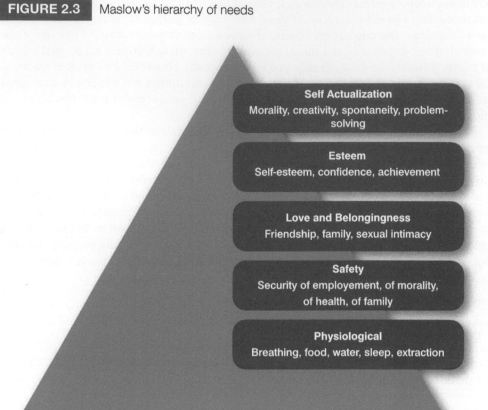

Characteristics of self-actualizing individuals

Maslow examined the lives of well-known public figures and came up with a list of shared characteristics, which are hallmarks of self-actualizing individuals:

- more efficient perception of reality;
- acceptance of 'self' and others;
- spontaneity, simplicity and naturalness;
- problem-centring;
- quality of detachment, a need for privacy;
- autonomy, independence of culture and environment;
- continued freshness of appreciation;
- peak experiences;
- deeper, more profound interpersonal relations;
- democratic character;
- philosophical, non-hostile sense of humour;
- creativeness;
- transcendence of any culture.

Maslow's theory is open to criticism on a number of counts. The imperative to satisfy basic needs before becoming motivated at the next level does not accord with the facts. There are many documented incidents of individuals becoming highly creative despite a lack of basic needs; for example, in concentration camps during the Second World War. Martyrdom is another example which conflicts with the theory; some individuals embrace the prospect of certain death as the ultimate fulfilment of their purpose on earth. There is no convincing evidence for the hierarchy of needs, but despite this the theory has influenced many curricula in nurse education.

One of the major problems with conceptualizing motivation as needs and drives is that it does not explain why animals or people try to achieve things that are not associated with biological deficits, such as watching television and reading books. It is likely that most real-life situations are characterized by multiple motivations, where the individual is motivated by a number of different motives. These may be in harmony, thereby increasing the strength of motivation or they may be in conflict, with some producing a positive incentive and others a negative incentive. This has been described as 'approach–avoidance conflict' and there are three types (Bourne and Ekstrand, 1985):

- approach–approach conflict, i.e. conflict between two equally desirable courses of action;
- avoidance–avoidance conflict, i.e. the choice is between two negative motivators, neither of which is desirable;
- approach–avoidance conflict, i.e. incentives have both positive and negative components, such as eating and weight gain.

LEARNING STYLES (COGNITIVE STYLES)

We have already seen that there are differences in motivation and personality between individuals, but there are also differences in their preferred ways of learning or processing information. In other words, individuals differ in their learning styles (also termed cognitive styles). In practice, andragogy might be understood to mean that adult learners need to focus on the learning process as opposed to content, in order to promote independence and a self-directed approach to learning. Reece and Walker (2007) suggest a move from behaviouristic principles towards a more humanistic approach, which they see as more appropriate for adult learners. This implies that a good teacher develops a feeling for the students' emotional needs, social background and cognitive development (Fontana, 1972) and that an interest in the welfare of students promotes learning (Wragg, 1984). This is particularly pertinent in health care settings, where students regardless of who they are will come from a variety of backgrounds, cultures and age groups, therefore nurse educators must be adaptable to meet such diverse needs.

Reflective and impulsive styles

These styles refer to an individual's tendency either to produce an answer to a problem very quickly or to spend some time in reflection before giving an answer. The kind of test used in this situation is called the 'matching familiar figures test' (Kagan, 1965) and consists of a number of pictures of familiar objects that the individual has to match with another picture. There are two styles of answering the problem: some people answer very quickly, whereas others take time to answer. Kagan considers the former to be impulsive and the latter reflective, taking only the speed variable into account. Thus, whether or not a person is accurate is not relevant to the test. Students can be taught to become more reflective by the use of self-instruction and scanning strategies.

Kolb's learning style inventory

Another approach to cognitive style is Kolb's learning style inventory (LSI, Kolb, 1976). Kolb's experiential learning theory is discussed earlier in the chapter, and the learning styles inventory utilizes concepts from the theory. There are two dimensions measured by this approach, concrete to abstract, and action to reflection, and four types of learning styles are identified.

- *Converger* Convergers are so called because they tend to do best in situations requiring a single correct answer or solution. Convergers excel in the application of ideas to practical situations, and their dominant learning abilities are abstract conceptualization (AC) and active experimentation (AE). Persons with this style tend to prefer things to people and often work in engineering and other physical sciences.

- *Diverger* Divergers, as the name implies, are the opposite of convergers. They tend to do best in situations requiring generation of ideas, and they tend to excel in the use of imagination and the organization of concrete situations into meaningful wholes. Their dominant learning abilities are concrete experience (CE) and reflective observation (RO). Kolb suggest that this style is characteristic of people with humanities and liberal arts backgrounds, and also of counsellors and personnel managers.

- *Assimilator* Assimilators tend to do best at creating theoretical models and inductive reasoning; they are less interested in practical applications. Their dominant learning abilities are abstract conceptualization (AC) and reflective observation (RO). People with this style tend to be found in basic maths and science, and in research and planning departments.

- *Accommodator* Accommodators tend to do best at carrying out plans and experiments. They tend more than the other styles to be risk-takers, and they excel in situations where they need to accommodate and adapt to the specific circumstances. Their dominant learning abilities are concrete experience (CE) and active experimentation (AE). People with this style tend to be found in action-oriented positions such as marketing or sales.

D'Amore *et al.* (2012) examined the learning styles of 285 nursing and midwifery students within their first year of the undergraduate programme using the Kolb and Kolb (2005) learning style inventory. The results found that the majority of students were of the diverging style, which are introverted with valuing or thinking skills, and feeling or intuition personality types. This was closely followed by the assimilating style, the accommodating style and finally the converging style. The authors propose the need for 'educators and students to be made aware of existing student learning styles, to encourage the development of a balanced learning style as espoused in Kolb's experiential learning theory'.

Serialist and holist strategies

In a series of experiments on learning strategies, Pask and his co-workers realized that subjects could be classified into two categories: serialist and holist (Pask and Scott, 1972; Pask, 1975, 1976). A system of classification for imaginary Martian animals was used as the learning task, and it was found that participants approached the problem in very different ways. Those who adopted a serialist strategy tended to proceed in a step-by-step manner, whereas the holists took a more global approach to what was to be learned. Pask suggests that these strategies reflect basic learning styles: holist strategies reflect a comprehension learning style and serialist strategies an operation learning style. Some students are able to employ both serialist and holist strategies as appropriate, and this learning style is referred to as versatile. Pask has related specific learning pathologies to the two strategies. The holist is prone to the pathology called 'globe-trotting', which involves a tendency to over-generalize from insufficient evidence and to use inappropriate analogy. Serialists, on the other hand, are prone to improvidence, which means that they may not build up an overview of how the subcomponents of the topic interrelate, nor utilize important analogies. In an experiment that matched and mismatched holist and serialist students with holist and serialist teaching styles, there was a clear superiority of outcome for students whose learning style matched the teaching style; however, the sample size was small.

Deep approach and surface approach

Marton and his co-workers at Gothenburg focused on how students read academic articles (Marton and Saljo, 1976). Students were given an academic article to read and were then interviewed afterwards to ascertain their approach to the article. These interviews were recorded and the audiotapes transcribed and analyzed in terms of level of understanding and approach to learning. The latter showed a clear-cut distinction between deep approaches and surface approaches. Those adopting a deep approach commenced with the intention of understanding the article, relating it to their own experience and evaluating the author's evidence. Those adopting a surface approach concentrated on memorizing the important points and were guided by the type of questions they anticipated being subsequently asked. The researchers suggest that these approaches are indicators of the students' normal approach to study.

Sutherland (1999) undertook a study of nurse tutors taking a professional qualification using a semi-structured interview. He reported a general rejection of the surface approach in favour of the deep approach as participants' dominant approach to learning.

Lancaster inventory of study strategies

Entwistle and his colleagues at Lancaster also studied how students read academic articles (Entwistle *et al.*, 1979; Entwistle, 1981), and this culminated in the development of the Lancaster Inventory of Study Strategies. The inventory contained the following scales:

1. *Achieving* relates to competitiveness and organized methods.
2. *Reproducing* relates to surface approach and the syllabus-bound concept.
3. *Meaning* relates to deep approaches and intrinsic motivation.
4. *Comprehension* reflects a holist strategy.
5. *Operation* reflects a serialist strategy.
6. *Versatile* indicates a versatile approach to learning.
7. *Pathological* indicates pathological symptoms in learning.
8. *Overall academic success* is prediction for success.

Shorter versions of the inventory have subsequently been developed (Entwistle, 2001).

Honey and Mumford's learning styles

Honey and Mumford (2000a) developed a scheme of learning styles involving a questionnaire of 80 items and scoring methodology. They believe that a pre-requisite to becoming an 'all-round' learner (an individual with a strong preference for several learning styles) is an awareness of a preferred learning style (Honey and Mumford, 2000b). Within the cycle of learning, they identify four dependent stages although a preference for one stage over another may be developed. The learning styles associated with each cycle of learning (Table 2.3) are classified under four headings – activists, reflectors, theorists and pragmatists – and the questionnaire data reveal the participant's scores on each of these variables. The authors emphasize the importance of acknowledging that identifying a learner with a string preference for a particular learning style does not necessarily mean that the style is used to its full effect.

Recent studies have revealed the preferred learning styles of students. Rassool and Rawaf (2007) investigated the learning styles preferences of undergraduate nursing students from three educational institutions using the Honey and Mumford (2000a) learning style questionnaire and an additional questionnaire to retrieve demographic data. Reviewing the questionnaire of 110 participants with a range of diverse backgrounds, the reflector group was found to be the highest category, followed by the activist category, theorist and pragmatist category. Flemming *et al.* (2011) examined changes in preregistration student

TABLE 2.3 Cycle of learning and learning styles

Cycle of learning	Learning style	Learning style characteristics
Experiencing	Activist	*Activists* are characterized by openness to new experiences and challenges with a sociable nature, albeit rather egocentric and impulsive. They prefer involvement with others, assimilation and role-play. They enjoy problem solving, and small group discussions.
Reviewing	Reflector	*Reflectors*, on the other hand, tend to be cautious people who like to explore things carefully before coming to a decision. They are observers rather than participants. They prefer to learn from activities that allow them to watch, think, and review events. They like to use journals and brainstorming and find lectures are helpful if they provide expert explanations and analysis.
Concluding	Theorist	*Theorists* are logical, rational people who like theories and systems; they are unhappy about subjective impressions and ambiguity. They enjoy lectures, analogies, systems, case studies, models, and readings and prefer to think problems through in a step-by-step manner. Talking with experts is normally not helpful to them.
Planning	Pragmatist	*Pragmatists* like very much to apply things in practice and to experiment with ideas; they tend to be impatient and like to get going with new ideas. They enjoy laboratories, field work, and observations; also feedback, coaching, and obvious links between the task-on-hand and a problem.

HONEY AND MUMFORD 2000A, HONEY AND MUMFORD 2000B

nurses' learning styles in their first and final year of the undergraduate programme, using Honey and Mumford's (2000a) 80-item questionnaire and scoring methodology. The results found that the preferred learning style of the students was that of 'Reflector' in the first and final year of study, and this was following by 'Activist' (first year) and 'Pragmatist' (final year).

Syllabus-bound and syllabus-free students

Malcolm Parlett (1970) classifies students into two types: syllabus-bound (sylbs) and syllabus-free (sylfs). The terms are largely self-explanatory. Sylbs tend to accept the system and are very much examination orientated and like to know exactly what is required of them in assignments. Sylfs, on the other hand, find the confines of the syllabus very limiting and wish to explore much more widely than that. They are happy to find things out for themselves and take responsibility for learning.

VARK approach to learning

VARK was developed by Neil Fleming in 1987 and first published in 1992 (Fleming and Mills, 1992). The VARK uses four sensory receivers to reflect the learning experiences of students: visual, auditory, read/write, and kinaesthetic (Kitchie, 2008). It is sometimes known as VAKT (visual, auditory, kinaesthetic and tactile) and is based on modalities, which are channels by which human expression can take place and comprises of a combination of perception and memory. Kitchie (2008) outlines the work of Fleming and Mills (1992), stating that a person learns most comfortably and effectively by one of the ways identified in Figure 2.4.

FIGURE 2.4 VARK learning approaches *(adapted from Fleming and Mills, 1992; Kitchie, 2008)*

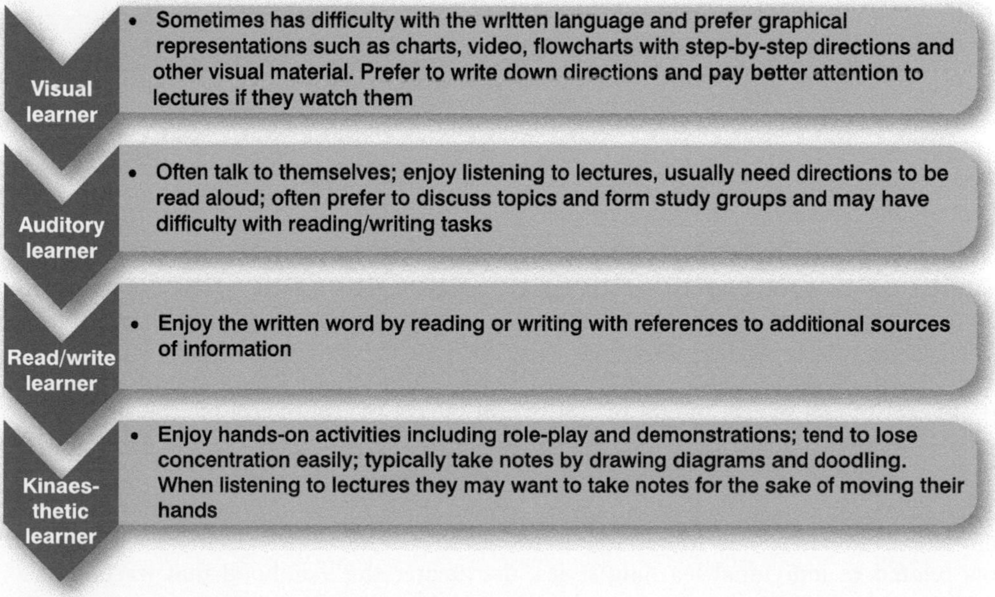

Visual learner
- Sometimes has difficulty with the written language and prefer graphical representations such as charts, video, flowcharts with step-by-step directions and other visual material. Prefer to write down directions and pay better attention to lectures if they watch them

Auditory learner
- Often talk to themselves; enjoy listening to lectures, usually need directions to be read aloud; often prefer to discuss topics and form study groups and may have difficulty with reading/writing tasks

Read/write learner
- Enjoy the written word by reading or writing with references to additional sources of information

Kinaesthetic learner
- Enjoy hands-on activities including role-play and demonstrations; tend to lose concentration easily; typically take notes by drawing diagrams and doodling. When listening to lectures they may want to take notes for the sake of moving their hands

Within the VARK learning preference, recent studies have revealed that kinaesthetic learning has been the mode preferred by students of nursing and midwifery programmes. This demonstrates a requirement for learning and teaching activities to be more interactive with the use of case studies, demonstrations, simulations and clinical laboratory experience (James *et al.*, 2011; Meehan-Andrews, 2011). While the research has shown a connection with modalities and learning styles, it has so far been unable to prove that using one learning style provides the best means for learning a task or subject. This is probably because VARK is not a fully-fledged learning style as it focuses on only one dimension of the complex amalgam of preferences that make up a person's learning style (Leite *et al.*, 2010); therefore it could be perceived more of a preference, rather than a style.

Problems with the concept of learning styles

The validity of attempting to match teaching styles with learning styles is criticized by Tennant (1988) on the grounds that it would produce harmonious viewpoints between teacher and student, but that educational growth is more likely to occur when students have to move outside the confines of their own learning style. In other words, a degree of challenge or conflict may well result in more creative learning. Tennant goes on to suggest that teachers should use the theories of learning styles to assist students to understand how they may approach learning, to facilitate expansion of their learning styles, and to provide a learning climate in which diversity is encouraged.

However, Rogers (2007) emphasizes that the first challenge is to know yourself and identify which style you are naturally drawn to. She asks us to remember that different subjects and circumstances will have their own imperative and quotes a very relevant example that many of us are able to relate to:

> 'If you are teaching people how to drive a car, there is probably no great place for theory – to drive a car successfully does not depend on knowing how the internal combustion engine works, though to pass the driving test you do need to know the Highway Code, a reflective activity; but mostly, learning to drive needs an activist approach. It cannot be learnt through reading books.'
>
> Rogers (2007)

A succinct summary of such learning styles is recognized by Petty (2009) and DeYoung (2007) who observe that student learning styles can be categorized in a number of ways. They claim that it is now thought that all students can learn in all these learning styles and that the more learning styles each learner experiences, the better. Recognizing that people have different approaches to learning can assist lecturers to understand the differences in educational interests, and needs of diverse populations. Kitchie (2008) clearly emphasizes that no learning style is either better or worse than another and that provided with the same content, the majority of learners can assimilate information with equal success, but how they go about mastering the content is usually determined by their individual style. The more flexible the lecturer is in using teaching methods and tools related to individual learning styles, the greater the likelihood that learning will occur (Kitchie, 2008).

APPROACHES TO LEARNING

All qualified nurses are involved in teaching and learning. They live in a constantly learning profession, in which the teaching and facilitation of students features greatly in their day-to-day life. Whilst exploring the theoretical underpinnings to teaching and learning, Dix and Hughes (2004) demonstrate how they can be applied to teaching and learning situations by discussing the strategies and approaches that can be adopted by nurse teachers and nurses working in the clinical setting to support students effectively. They presented four biographical vignettes of adult learners and described some of the strategies and approaches that might assist these students to learn more effectively. An example of those vignettes can be seen in Box 2.1.

BOX 2.1 | Four biographical vignettes

Katie

Katie is a 45-year-old nursing student with three grown-up children. She left school at the age of 15 without any formal qualifications. She has 25 years' experience as a health care assistant on an acute surgical ward. In order to acquire the necessary academic qualifications for nurse training, she has, for the past five years attended evening classes at her local FE College and achieved five GCSEs and passed an access to nursing course. Katie is now in her second year of the three-year programme, which leads to the award of Bachelor of Nursing. Although she was apprehensive about returning to full-time education, as she would probably be older than most of her colleagues and some of the lecturers, she is a popular student, who willingly contributes openly to class discussion and is keen to share her life experiences. She also possesses excellent interpersonal skills, which enable her to motivate other students and, overall, improve group dynamics. The quality of Katie's clinical work is exemplary, and her enthusiasm and motivation are demonstrated and documented well within her clinical placement reports. However, Katie is dyslexic and is particularly anxious about the continual theoretical assessments and examinations. Although Katie has passed all of her college-based assignments to date, she still feels that she is unable to demonstrate and apply her analytical thoughts and reflective skills adequately in a theoretical context. Her objectives during the second year are to improve on her assessment grades and achieve good passes instead of borderline passes. Factors that inhibit learning can be described as internal or external in nature. The most common barriers have been identified by numerous authors, and can include pressure of time and workload, lack of support from work organization and family, underachievement at school with a fear of further learning, social and family commitments, cultural and age (Ashcroft and Foreman-Peck, 1994; Huddleston and Unwin, 1997; Reece and Walker 2007). Factors likely to inhibit Katie's learning are lack of self-belief, age, exam anxiety and dyslexia.

Peter

Peter is a 28-year-old first year nursing student aiming for the award of Diploma (HE) Nursing. He lives at home with his parents and has a son of 18 months, who lives with his girlfriend. Peter takes his parental responsibilities seriously and hopes to be able to support his family when he qualifies. His parents are very supportive of his career and encourage Peter to study in the evenings to prevent him socializing with his friends. They think his friends are a bad influence on his social behaviour and blame this for his persisting truancy when he was at school. Peter reflects negatively on his school years and states that his lack of educational qualifications is due to his boredom and disinterest in class, and subconsciously highlights some of the consequences associated with the hidden curriculum (Vallance, 1974). For the past ten years

(continued)

BOX 2.1   Four biographical vignettes (*continued*)

Peter was employed as an operating theatre assistant but felt restricted in his role. This led to him applying for nurse training but he was advised to provide evidence of further education to support his application in order to satisfy the entrance requirements. He enrolled on a part-time course based at his local college and achieved a Diploma in Anatomy and Physiology, which led to his success in gaining a nurse-training place. Initially, Peter's enthusiasm was faultless; however, within the first four months, he has accumulated six episodes of sickness and presented mostly unbelievable reasons for his absence. On one occasion he was absent from lectures because he claimed that his best friend had died the previous night, but a request for a compassionate leave day for the funeral was never made.

Peter is a pleasant student with a vibrant personality and is eager to please his mentors on clinical placements. He also has many enduring qualities that have not gone unnoticed when caring for patients. However, he has had recent difficulties meeting deadlines for assignment submission and his personal tutor has noticed several inconsistencies in his style of writing, which is beginning to raise concerns amongst academic staff. Although he appears to be achieving clinical competence, oral questioning and written assessments confirm that knowledge is not evident. Peter is failing to progress and achieve the required assessment standard. In line with the equal opportunities of the college, Peter's personal tutor has offered him assistance in terms of help and support with academic writing skills in an attempt to overcome his learning difficulties but this has been declined. Peter maintains that he is as motivated as ever to achieve professional registration. Factors likely to inhibit Peter's learning are social and family commitments, underachievement at school and surface learning.

Melissa
Melissa is 32 years old and is a first-year nursing student. She is a recently separated parent with two young children, one of whom has profound learning disabilities. Melissa has extremely supportive parents who care for both children whilst she is at university but she is beginning to feel guilty for leaving them and burdening her parents for up to nine hours per day on most weeks. Prior to commencing the three-year nurse education programme, Melissa worked as a health care assistant and undertook a nursing access course in the hope of realizing her childhood dream. Although Melissa is enjoying the clinical aspect of the course, she is finding it increasingly difficult to juggle her shifts and home life. Her academic assignments are also proving difficult and she is just managing to achieve a borderline pass each time. The concept of adult learning is becoming difficult to grasp and she is losing confidence in her academic ability. During recent weeks, Melissa has contemplated the idea of leaving the course and becoming a full-time mum. Her drive and determination to succeed in qualifying as a Registered Nurse are slowly diminishing.

Nathan
Nathan is also a first year student nurse, nine-weeks into training; with a plethora of GCSEs and A levels, he is, as a result, following the degree pathway. Nathan is an only child and spent his secondary education at an all-boys school. He is finding the transition from further education to higher education quite difficult, and his quiet disposition and lack of self-confidence are inhibiting his ability to form solid friendships. As nursing is a predominately female profession, Nathan is also finding it difficult to adjust to this new culture of being surrounded by women, and feels embarrassed during lectures when animated slides often depict the nurse in a feminine form. As the only boy in his seminar group, Nathan is reluctant to participate in classroom discussion and has missed several seminar presentations because of this. A general surgical ward is to be Nathan's first clinical placement and, although he is excited, he is also anxious about the forthcoming six-week placement. Nathan is aware that he has a number of clinical competencies to achieve during this time and is concerned as to whether these can be accomplished.

ADAPTED FROM DIX AND HUGHES (2004)

Factors that inhibit learning

Factors that inhibit learning can be described as internal or external in nature. The most common barriers have been identified by numerous authors and can include pressure of time and workload, lack of support from work organization and family, underachievement at school with a fear of further learning, social and family commitments, culture and age (Armitage *et al.*, 2012; Reece and Walker, 2007).

Factors likely to inhibit each student's learning are demonstrated in Table 2.4.

TEACHING TIP

Recognizing the factors likely to inhibit the learner's learning and helping them to overcome these factors with confidence building techniques is a key element to effective teaching of nurse education. Think about the potentially inhibiting factors suggested in Table 2.4 above, in relation to your students, and try to identify a list of key factors you should be aware of.

TABLE 2.4 Potentially inhibiting factors	
Factors that are likely to inhibit the learner's learning	
Katie	**Melissa**
Lack of self-belief	Lack of self-belief
Age	Family commitments
Exam anxiety and dyslexia	Surface learning
Peter	**Nathan**
Social and family commitments	Lack of self-belief
Underachievement at school	Group participation
Surface learning	Gender issues

ADAPTED FROM DIX AND HUGHES (2004)

Strategies and approaches that offer effective support for learners

Adult learners in nursing differ widely in their personal characteristics, and these individual differences encompass physical characteristics that might include age and gender, and psychological characteristics such as motivation, personality, intelligence and learning styles. The students identified within the vignettes have found the transition from further education to higher education quite difficult to deal with, and this, the common factor that they all share, is potentially inhibiting their learning. Many students' previous educational experiences, before entering higher education have accustomed them to a fairly passive pedagogical approach to learning (Knowles, 1990). This model of learning is very much teacher centred, and students must learn what they are being taught. Students do not always find it easy to adapt to a learning situation in which they must take responsibility for what happens during their time together with the teacher (Ewan and White, 2000).

Learning contracts

These students would perhaps benefit from individual learning plans or learning contracts to assist them through this transitional phase, by setting out their intrinsic goals (Wallace, 2005; Walkin, 2000), in addition to the extrinsic goal of successfully completing their nurse education. Although andragogy relies on the learner engaging in self-directed learning (Neary, 2000a) it is evident that the learners are not responding to this strategy and a more structured and combined andragogical/pedagogical approach could be adopted to meet their learning needs. A learning contract can be designed by the teacher and student to specify what the student will learn, how it will be achieved, the time-span and the criteria for measuring its success (Bailey and Tuohy, 2009; DeYoung, 2007; Neary, 2002a). Learning contracts with identified objectives can bridge the practice–theory gap and demonstrate the transfer of knowledge to clinical practice (Rolfe, 1996).

As described in Box 2.1, Katie's dyslexia sometimes interferes with her academic work and causes her anxiety, which can affect her learning process. Although some of the best performances are undertaken in anxiety-provoking situations, if this becomes intolerable, Katie will be unable to learn. This supports Knowles's theory that adults learn best when not under threat. To ensure equal opportunities, a learning contract can ensure that the students are able to access a support network that can include one-to-one study skills tuition, IT training and assistance with exam technique (Reece and Walker, 2007).

The success of individualized learning often depends on the student being an active, rather than passive, responsible participant (Allen and Prater, 2011; Bradshaw, 2011). In the cases of Katie, Melissa and Peter, the submission of academic work could possibly be negotiated within a learning plan, thereby recognizing students as individuals, with other commitments of value outside of academic life. Nathan on the other hand could be encouraged to join one of the many college societies and begin to develop a circle of friends with the same interests as him. Regular feedback sessions should be arranged to review students' progress, concentrating on the positive aspects of learning and developing action plans for any identified problems. Neary (2000a) identifies ten key points for giving constructive feedback, which could be adapted to this situation.

Whilst on placement, students are allocated a mentor, to facilitate the learning experience during a six-week clinical practice. Many authors describe a good mentoring relationship as a dialogue between two people committed to improvement (Gopee, 2010; Quinn and Hughes, 2007; Neary, 1994). A mentor guides and formalizes clinical learning by use of a learning contract. In order to comply with nursing and midwifery standards, adequate support must be available to students to meet their professional development needs (NMC, 2010; NMC, 2009; NMC, 2008).

Gender issues

Nathan could be reluctant to participate in classroom discussion for a number of reasons, although Rogers and Horrocks (2010) believe that the causes of reticence are rarely clear. They also suggests trying to persuade the student to talk outside of the group session, to find out some opinions that they hold, some skill or experience that they possess and then try to guide the work of the group into these fields so that eventually the student can fittingly (but never easily) make some contribution. One possible reason for Nathan's apparent shyness could be that he is surrounded by female classmates and, as previously mentioned, is finding it difficult to adjust to this predominantly female profession. The fact that most of the animated visual aids used in teaching depict the nurse as female is not helping; this is indicative of the hidden curriculum as described by Jarvis (2010) who explains that some students may learn values that may be unrecognized and unintended by those who formulate them. Updating these teaching aids and depicting men as well as women in the role of nurse could possibly help the situation, not just for Nathan but for future male nurses.

Deep learning

Melissa is slowly losing her intrinsic motivation to continue with her nurse training, which in turn could be affecting her approach to learning. There are deep learners and surface learners, and an important role of the teacher is to help students become aware of different approaches to learning. The idea that a surface approach to learning is a less effective approach is not necessarily true, as not all learning tasks (e.g. learning keyboard skills) require a deep approach (Armitage et al., 2012; Jarvis, 2010; DeYoung, 2009; Petty, 2009; Reece and Walker, 2007). Melissa's lack of motivation could be affecting her deeper approach to learning, which could be the reason why she is finding her academic work increasingly difficult. Obviously, this motivational factor could be rooted in her social circumstances, and in such a situation referral to a counselling service could possibly be of some help. Regular positive reinforcement, providing encouragement and praise could help to increase Melissa's self-motivation; however, motivation depends as much on the attitudes of the teacher as on the attitudes of the students (Rogers and Horrocks, 2010). Peter has also been demonstrating characteristics of surface learning, so he might need encouragement to engage in applying his learning to problem-based situations and in structuring his reflective skills.

Learning through reflective practice

Reflection is an important human activity in which people re-capture their experiences, analyze them and evaluate them (Boud et al., 1985), in order to progress from a novice to expert practitioner as characterized by Benner (1984). To facilitate the learning process and to make learning as active and participative as possible, using a model of reflection the learners can be encouraged to demonstrate their understanding of concepts, knowledge, skills and attitudes within educational and clinical practice (Burns and Schutz, 2008; Jarvis, 2010; Neary, 2000a). A portfolio offers a dynamic, positive means of showing that a person is developing knowledge and competence, and of encouraging the learner to engage in lifelong learning; a portfolio is an ideal vehicle for reflection whilst providing evidence of achievement (Priest and Roberts, 1998). All the learners identified in the vignettes would benefit from the concept of reflective practice, to enable them to understand and learn through lived experiences and as a consequence take congruent action towards developing increasing effectiveness, within the context of what is understood as desirable practice (Johns, 1995). Nursing students are expected to reflect on experiences and situations whilst on clinical placements, and Neary (2000b) explains that students need help and guidance to reflect on their experience and to record that experience, with advice often given to the student by their mentors in clinical practice.

Drawing on experiences and valuing strengths

Katie expresses ageist views against herself and, although she is clinically and academically competent, requires a great deal of positive feedback. Like Katie, older students may lack confidence in their academic ability. Both Kate and Melissa need to be encouraged to reflect on and use their life experiences to help them contextualize and conceptualize new information. Maslow's hierarchy of basic human needs (1970) demonstrates progressive steps from physical needs to self-actualization where students aspire to be motivated and positive regarding their future. Reece and Walker (2007) believe that students are more likely to learn effectively if they possess a feel-good factor about themselves.

Time management

Owing to family and social commitments and his continual absence, Peter is struggling to meet assignment deadlines. Melissa is also struggling with juggling family and university life. Armitage *et al.* (2012) encourage the use of an empathetic approach, to communicate an understanding of students' situations, and the use of probing to help students to clarify and focus on issues of concern. A strategy to support and improve students' time management, using learning resources to develop appropriate study skills, could enable them to assume responsibility for their own learning; however, taking responsibility for their own learning may make students feel threatened and insecure.

Review questions

1. Consider how schemas need to be reconstructed to reflect a student moving into higher education.

2. Give five examples of problems a mature student might encounter with learning and give strategies a teacher could adopt to help with each one.

3. Construct a spider diagram or similar to show how the learning theories relate to each other.

4. Consider how the different schools of learning styles are similar and differ.

SUMMARY

■ Adult learning theory has been strongly influenced by humanistic psychology.

■ Humanistic theory is concerned with human growth, individual fulfilment and self-actualization.

■ According to the humanistic approach, the role of the teacher is that of helper and facilitator.

■ One of the most serious criticisms of the humanistic approach is that it is lacking in empirical evidence to support its claims, relying upon observations and assumptions of human behaviour.

■ In practice, andragogy might be understood to mean that adult learners need to focus on the learning process as opposed to content to promote independence and a self-directed approach to learning.

■ The rate of helping students move towards independence is likely to be quite slow initially, but as confidence, experience and autonomy increase, independence will accelerate.

■ Motivation is considered an important factor in the learning process, and one of the key aims of teaching is to increase students' motivation to learn.

■ All qualified nurses are involved in teaching and learning. They live in a constantly learning profession, in which the teaching and facilitation of students features greatly in their day-to-day life.

References

Allen, S.S. and Prater, L.S. (2011) Chapter 26 - Crafting the clinical experience: a toolbox for healthcare professionals. In. Bradshaw MJ, Lowenstein AJ, *Innovative Teaching Strategies in Nursing and Related Health Professions* (5th Edn). London: Jones and Bartlett Publishers International

Armitage, A., Evershed, J., Hayes, D., Hudson, A., Kent, J., Lawes, S., Poma, S. and Renwick, M, (2012) *Teaching and Training in Lifelong Learning* (4th Edn). Maidenhead: Open University Press

Ashcroft, K., Foreman-Peck, L. (1994) *Managing Teaching and Learning in Further and Higher Education*. London: Routledge Falmer

Bailey, M.E. and Tuohy, D. (2009) Student nurses' experiences of using a learning contract as a method of assessment. *Nurse Education Today* 29(7) 758–762

Barnard, A., Hollingum, C. and Hartfiel, B. (2006) Going on a journey: understanding palliative care nursing. *International Journal of Palliative Nursing* 12 (1): 6–12

Benner, P. (1984) *From Novice to Expert: Excellence and Power in Clinical Nursing Practice*. Addison-Wesley, California

Bradshaw, M.J. (2011) Chapter 1 – Effective learning: what teachers need to know. In: Bradshaw, M.J.and Lowenstein, A.J. *Innovative Teaching Strategies in Nursing and Related Health Professions* (5th Edn). London: Jones and Bartlett Publishers International

Braungart, M.M. and Braungart, R.G. (2008) Applying learning theories to healthcare practice. In: Bastable SB (Ed) *Nurse as Educator: Principles of Teaching and Learning for Nursing Practice* (3rd Edn). Boston: Jones and Bartlett

Boud, D., Keogh, R. and Walker, D. (eds) (1985) *Reflection: Turning Experience into Learning.* Kogan Page, London.

Bourne, L. and Ekstrand, B. (1985) *Psychology: Its Principles and Meanings*. Holt, Rinehart & Winston, New York

Bowlby, J. (1970) *Attachment*. Penguin, Harmondsworth

Bulman, C. and Schutz, S. (2008) *Reflective Practice in Nursing* (4th Edn). Oxford: Wiley-Blackwell

Cuthbert, P.F. (2005) The student learning process: Learning Styles or Learning Approaches? *Teaching in Higher Education* 10(2) 235–249

D'Amore, A., James, S. and Mitchell, E.K.L. (2012) Learning styles of first-year undergraduate nursing and midwifery students: A cross-sectional survey utilizing the Kolb Learning Style Inventory. Nurse Education Today 32(5) 506–515

DeYoung, S. (2007) *Teaching Strategies for Nurse Educators* (2nd Edn). New Jersey: Prentice Hall

Dix, G. and Hughes, S.J. (2004) Strategies to help Students Learn Effectively. *Nursing Standard*, 18(32), 39–42.

Eibl-Eibesfeldt, I. (1971) *Love and Hate*. Methuen, London.

Entwistle, N. J. (2001) Styles of learning and approaches to studying in higher education. *Kybernetes* 30(5/6) 593–602

Entwistle, N. (1981) *Styles of Learning and Teaching*. Wiley, Chichester.

Entwistle, N., Hanley, M. and Hounsell, D. (1979) Identifying distinctive approaches to studying. *Higher Education*, **8**, 365–380.

Ewan C. and White, R. (2000) *Teaching Nursing: A Self-instructional Handbook*, (2nd revised edn). London: Nelson Thornes

Fleming, N.D. and Mills, C. (1992) Not another inventory, rather a catalyst for reflection. *To Improve the Academy* 11: 137

Fleming, S., Mckee, G. and Huntley-Moore, S. (2011) Undergraduate nursing students' learning styles: A longitudinal study. *Nurse Education Today* 31(5) 444–449

Fontana, D. (1972) What do we mean by a good teacher? In D. Chanan (ed.) *Research Forum on Teacher Education*. National Foundation for Educational Research, Windsor.

Freud, S. (1923) *The Ego and the Id*. Translated by J. Riviere (1962), Norton, New York.

Gopee, N. (2010) *Practice Teaching in Healthcare*. London: Sage

Hamachek, D. (1978) Humanistic psychology: theoretical–philosophical framework and implications for teaching. In: D. Treffinger, J. Kent Davis and R. Ripple (eds) *Handbook on Teaching Educational Psychology*. Academic Press, New York.

Honey P., and Mumford, A. (2000a) *The Learning Styles Questionnaire 80-item Version*. Berkshire: Peter Honey Publications Limited

Honey P. and Mumford, A. (2000b) *The Learning Styles Helper's Guide*. Berkshire: Peter Honey Publications Limited

Huddleston P., Unwin, L. (1997) *Teaching and Learning in Further Education: Diversity and Change*. London: Routledge Falmer

James, J., D'Amore, A. and Thomas, T. (2011) Learning preferences of first year nursing and midwifery students: Utilizing VARK. *Nurse Education Today* 31(4) 417–423

Jarvis, P. (2010) *Adult Education and Lifelong Learning: Theory and Practice* (4th Edn). London: Routledge

Jarvis, P. and Gibson, S. (1997) *The Teacher Practitioner and Mentor in Nursing, Midwifery, Health Visiting and The Social Services*. Stanley Thornes, Cheltenham.

Johns, C. (1995) Framing learning through reflection with Carper's fundamental ways of knowing. *Journal of Advanced Nursing*, 22(2), 226–234.

Kagan, J. (1965) Reflection-impulsivity and reading ability in primary grade children. *Child Development*, 36(3), 188–190.

Kitchie, S. (2008) Determinants of learning. In: Bastable SB (Ed) *Nurse as Educator: Principles of Teaching and Learning for Nursing Practice* (3rd Edn). Boston: Jones and Bartlett

Knowles, M. (1990) *The Adult Learner: A Neglected Species*, 4th edn. Gulf Publishing, Houston.

Kolb, D.A. (1976) *The Learning Style Inventory: Technical Manual*. McBer and Co., Boston.

Kolb, D.A. (1984) *Experiential Learning: Experience as the Source of Learning and Development*. Prentice Hall, Englewood Cliffs, NJ.

Kolb, AY. and Kolb, D.A. (2005) The Kolb Learning Style Inventory. Boston: Hay Group Holdings

Leite, W.L., Svinicki, M. and Shi, Y. (2010) Attempted Validation of the Scores of the VARK: Learning Styles Inventory With Multitrait-Multimethod Confirmatory Factor Analysis Models. *Educational and Psychological Measurement*. 70: 323–339

Levinson, D. (1986) *A conception of Adult Development. American Psychologist*, 41(3), 13.

Lorenz, K.Z. (1958) The evolution of behaviour. *Scientific American*, 199(6), 67–78.

Mailloux, C.G. (2006) The extent to which students' perceptions of faculties' teaching strategies, students' context, and perceptions of learner empowerment predict perceptions of autonomy in BSN students. *Nurse Education Today* 26(7) 578–585

Maslow, A. (1971) *The Farther Reaches of Human Nature*. Penguin, Harmondsworth.

McNair, S. (1996) Learner autonomy in a changing world. In R. Edwards, S. Hanson, and P. Raggatt (eds) *Boundaries of Adult Learning*. Routledge, London.

Meehan-Andrews, T.A. (2009) Teaching mode efficiency and learning preferences of first year nursing students. *Nurse Education Today* 29(1) 24–32

Mook, D.G. (1996) *Motivation: The Organization of Action*. Norton & Co., London.

Neary, M. (1994) Teaching Practical Skills in Colleges. *Nursing Standard*, 27, 35–38.

Neary, M. (2000a) *Teaching, Assessing and Evaluation for Clinical Competence: A Practical Guide for Practitioners and Teachers*. Nelson Thornes, Cheltenham.

Neary, M. (2000b) Responsive assessment of clinical competence: part 2. *Nursing Standard*, 15(10), 35–40.

NMC (2010) *Standards for Preregistration Nursing Education*. London: Nursing and Midwifery Council

NMC (2009) *Standards for Preregistration Midwifery Education*. London: Nursing and Midwifery Council

NMC (2008) *Standards to Support Learning and Assessment in Practice: NMC Standards for Mentors, Practice Teachers and Teachers*. London: Nursing and Midwifery Council

Parlett, M. (1970) The syllabus-bound student. In L. Hudson (ed) *The Ecology of Human Intelligence*. Penguin, Harmondsworth.

Pask, G. (1975) *The Cybernetics of Human Learning and Performance*. Hutchinson, London.

Pask, G. (1976) Styles and strategies of learning. *British Journal of Educational Psychology*, **46**, 128–148.

Pask, G. and Scott, B. (1972) Learning strategies and individual competence. *International Journal of Man-Machine Studies*, 4, 217–253.

Petty, G. (2009) *Teaching Today: A Practical Guide* (4th Edn). Cheltenham: Nelson Thornes

Piaget, J. and Inhelder, B. (1969) *The Psychology of the Child*. Basic Books, New York.

Priest, H. and Roberts, P. (1998) Assessing students' clinical performance. *Nursing Standard*, 12(48) 37–41.

Purdy, M. (1997) Humanist ideology and nurse education: limitations of humanist educational theory in nurse education. *Nurse Education Today* 17(3) 196–202

Rassool, G.H. and Rawaf, S. (2007) Learning style preferences of undergraduate nursing students. *Nursing Standard*. 21(32) 35–41

Reece I., and Walker, S. (2007) *Teaching Training and Learning: A Practical Guide* (6th Edn). Sunderland: Business Education Publishers Ltd

Rogers, A. and Horrocks, N. (2010) *Teaching Adults*, 4th Edn. Maidenhead: Open University Press

Rogers, C. (1951) *Client Centred Therapy*. Houghton Mifflin, Boston.

Rogers, C. (1969) *Freedom to Learn*. Merrill, Ohio.

Rogers, C. (1983) *Freedom to Learn for the 80s*. Merrill, Ohio.

Rogers, C. and Freiberg, H.J. (1994) *Freedom to Learn*, 3rd edn. Macmillan, New York.

Rogers, J. (2007) *Adults Learning*, 5th edn. Open University Press, Buckingham.

Rolfe, G. (1996) *Closing the Theory–Practice Gap*. Butterworth Heinemann, Oxford.

Schön, D. (1983) *The Reflective Practitioner: How Professionals Think in Action*. Basic Books, New York.

Schön, D. (1987) *Educating the Reflective Practitioner: Towards a New Design for Teaching and Learning in the Professions*. Jossey Bass, San Francisco.

Sigman, A. (1995) *New, Improved? Exposing the Misuse of Popular Psychology*. Simon & Schuster, London.

Solomon, R.L. (1980) The opponent process theory of acquired motivation: the costs of pleasure and the benefits of pain. *American Psychologist*, 35, 691–712.

Solomon, R.L. and Corbit, J.D. (1974) An opponent process theory of acquired motivation. *American Psychologist*, 35, 119–141.

Spandler, H. and Stickley, T. (2011) No hope without compassion: the importance of compassion in recovery-focused mental health services. Journal of Mental Health 20(6) 555–566

Stevenson, A. (2010) (Editor) Oxford Dictionary of English. Oxford: Oxford University Press

Stuart-Hamilton, I. (1996) *The Psychology of Ageing*, 2nd edn. Jessica Kingsley, London.

Sutherland, P. (1999) A study of the learning of mature adult students on a professional course. *Journal of Further and Higher Education*, 23(3), 381–389.

Tennant, M. (1997) *Psychology and Adult Learning*, 2nd Edn. Routledge, London.

Tennant, M. (2006) *Psychology and Adult Learning*, 3rd Edn. Routledge, London.

Tinbergen, N. (1951) *The Study of Instinct*. Oxford University Press, Oxford.

Walkin, L. (2000) *Teaching and Learning in Further and Adult Education*. Stanley Thornes, Cheltenham.

Wallace, S. (2005) *Teaching and Supporting Learning in Further Education* (2nd Edn). London: Learning Matters

Weidner, N.J., Cameron, M., Lee, R.C., McBride, J., Mathias, E.J. and Byczkowski, T.L. (2011) End-of-life care for the dying child: what matters most to parents. Journal of Palliative Care 27(4) 279–286

Wragg, E.C .(1984) *Classroom Teaching Skills*. London: Croom helm

Further Reading

Illeris, K. (Ed) (2009) *Contemporary Theories of Learning: Learning Theorists ...* In Their Own Words. Oxford: Routledge

Jarvis, P. (2010) *Adult Education and Lifelong Learning: Theory and Practice* (4th Edn). London: Routledge

Knowles, M.S., Holton, E.F. and Swanson, R.A. (2011) *The Adult Learner: The Definitive Classic in Adult Education and Human Resource Development* (7th Edn). London: Butterworth-Heinemann Title

Kolb, A.Y. and Kolb, D.A. (2009) The learning way: meta-cognitive aspects of experiential learning. *Simulation and Gaming* 40(3) 297–327

Kolb, D.A. (2005a) *The Cycle of Learning* (Version 3.1). Boston: Hay Group Holdings

Kolb, D.A .(2005b) *Learning-Style Type Grid* (Version 3.1). Boston: Hay Group Holdings

Morrall, P.A. (2005) Quality assurance in nurse education – The social context of learning. *Nurse Education Today* 25: 620–624

Rassool, G.H. and Rawaf, S. (2008) Educational intervention of undergraduate nursing students' confidence skills with alcohol and drug misusers. *Nurse Education Today* 8(5) 284–292

Tennant, M. (2012) *The Learning Self: Understanding the Potential for Transformation*: San Francisco: John Wiley & Sons

VARK: A guide to learning styles. Available from: http://www.vark-learn.com/english/index.asp

CHAPTER 3
PERSPECTIVES ON LEARNING AND TEACHING

THE AIMS OF THIS CHAPTER ARE:

- To explore the three domains of learning

- To analyze cognitive theories of learning and instruction

KEY TERMS

Episodic knowledge	Retroactive interference	Incubation
Semantic knowledge	Proactive interference	Satisficing
Declarative knowledge	Sensation	Proprioceptive
Procedural knowledge	Perception	Obliterative subsumption
Psychomotor	Predicate	Augmented feedback
Propositions	Premise	Systematic desensitization

The term 'cognition' refers to the internal mental processes of human beings, and encompasses the domains of memory, perception and thinking. These are of fundamental importance to education, given that learning involves all three domains. The first part of this chapter deals with these three domains of cognition, and the remainder is devoted to the specific cognitive perspectives on teaching and learning of David Ausubel, Jerome Bruner and Robert Gagné.

MEMORY

Memory is the process that allows human beings to store experiences from the past, and to use these in the present. There are three basic aspects of memory function: encoding, storage and retrieval, and three stages of memory: sensory, short-term and long-term.

Encoding, storage and retrieval

The first of these basic aspects is encoding, i.e. putting information into the memory in some form of code such as acoustic or visual coding. Storage is also known as the memory trace; the trace is kept until it needs to be remembered. Retrieval is the bringing to mind of stored, coded information when required. For example, on first being introduced to a stranger, we encode the person's name into our memory in the form of an acoustic (sound) code, where it is then stored. When we meet that person again we try to remember (retrieve) that individual's name.

The three types of memory

One of the most influential models of memory is that of Atkinson and Shiffrin (1971). The three types of memory, sensory, short-term and long-term, may indeed be separate systems within the brain or merely different kinds of storage within the same system. Nonetheless, each of the three memory systems has distinctive characteristics, outlined below.

Sensory memory

The sensory memory is fleeting and registers incoming stimuli for a very brief period. It is a high-capacity system that registers all sensory inputs in their original form – visual stimuli as images or icons, and auditory stimuli as echoes of the sounds. Visual stimuli last for about one second and auditory stimuli for about four seconds, and we are unaware of these stimuli. However, when a stimulus is registered in sensory memory, contact is made with long-term memory to check whether there is an existing pattern for that stimulus. The role of sensory memory is to prolong stimuli just long enough to allow for selective attention to important ones. This aspect of memory also features in the section on perception later in this chapter.

Short-term memory (working memory)

This is also called working memory, primary memory and short-term store, and its main purpose is summed up nicely by Logie (1999):

> 'In its broadest sense, working memory can be thought of as the desktop of the brain. It is a cognitive function that helps us keep track of what we are doing or where we are moment to moment, that holds information long enough to make a decision, dial a telephone number, or repeat a strange foreign word that we have just heard.'
>
> Logie (1999)

DeYoung (2007) points out that short-term memory 'consists of whatever we are thinking about or that impinges on us from an external stimulus at any given time' (p.17). This particularly memory can last up to 20 seconds unless the item is repeated mentally or verbally. Short-term memory is characterized by a limited capacity for storage, of about seven chunks of information. The term 'chunks' is deliberately vague and applies to any unit that is familiar to an individual (Miller, 1956). Hence a chunk may be a single word or a single letter, and it is possible to increase the amount of data in short-term memory at any one time by incorporating more information into each chunk. In addition to this storage function of short-term memory, there are control processes such as rehearsal, which can be divided into maintenance rehearsal and elaborative rehearsal (Craik and Lockhart, 1972). Maintenance rehearsal consists of going over and over the material in short-term memory in order to keep it there; it does not affect the long-term recall of the material. Elaborative rehearsal, on the other hand, processes the material much more deeply by relating it to existing material in long-term memory. Short-term memory is also involved in the processes of both thinking and language by providing the working area for these, hence the alternative name, working memory. It is likely that information is coded in the form of both acoustic and articulatory codes in working memory; the former involves the sound of a word and the latter involves the way that it is pronounced. Baddeley and Hitch (1974) and Baddeley and Leiberman (1980) describe working memory as having a 'central executive' and two slave systems, the 'phonological (or articulatory) loop' and the 'visuo-spatial sketch pad'. The central executive has an overall co-ordinating and control function; the phonological loop is concerned with speech-based information, and the visuo-spatial sketch pad with spatial information.

Long-term memory

There appears to be no limit to the capacity of long-term memory, and information stored here has been subjected to considerable processing. Craik and Lockhart (1972) have suggested a levels-of-processing approach, which states that information is processed at a variety of levels, from the physical characteristics of the stimulus through to the identification of the stimulus's meaning. Deeper-level processing results in better remembering of information, because it allows more elaboration of the stimulus, i.e. more links are made with relevant information already existing in long-term memory. This means that the information has been subjected to considerable top-down processing and is therefore more susceptible to distortion and bias. It seems likely that there are two kinds of information stored in long-term memory – episodic knowledge and semantic knowledge. Episodic knowledge is associated with particular events in time and space, such as the memory of an encounter with a particular student, whereas semantic knowledge consists of general concepts unrelated to specific events or episodes (Tulving, 1972). Autobiographical memory differs from other knowledge structures in the degree of self-reference and the sensory/perceptual nature of the knowledge stored (Conway, 1991).

Representation of knowledge in long-term memory

It is useful to distinguish between declarative knowledge and procedural knowledge; the former is about 'knowing that' and the latter is about 'knowing how'. Declarative knowledge consists of knowledge of factual information and can be transmitted verbally to others. Procedural knowledge, on the other hand, is concerned with knowing how to do something, such as administering an injection, and is often more difficult to explain. Indeed, the most effective way of explaining procedural knowledge to someone is by demonstrating the procedure to them, and this is the basic way of teaching a psychomotor skill.

Research suggests two main theories about the way in which knowledge is represented in long-term memory, the 'propositional code theory' and the 'dual-code theory'.

Propositional code theory　Anderson and Bower (1973) and Pylyshyn (1973) state that information is coded in the form of propositions, i.e. the smallest unit that can be judged true or false. Propositions contain a central relationship called the predicate and a number of arguments, and are thus units of knowledge that can stand as separate assertions. All sentences are composed of propositions, and computers can store information in this form also. According to this theory, information in long-term memory is stored in terms of the meanings of propositions rather than their exact words, hence the term 'semantic' memory. Information is thus organized into a network of propositions that is hierarchically arranged via nodes and connections.

Figure 3.1 shows how a simple two-dimensional network hierarchy for 'tissues' in semantic memory might appear. The spatial orientation of the nodes is irrelevant, in that it is the connections that matter not the location. (Propositions can also be represented in three dimensions.) It is claimed that these networks can represent both perceptual and linguistic information in long-term memory and that this single-code explanation is more parsimonious than the dual-code theory.

FIGURE 3.1　Simple two-dimensional network hierarchy in semantic memory

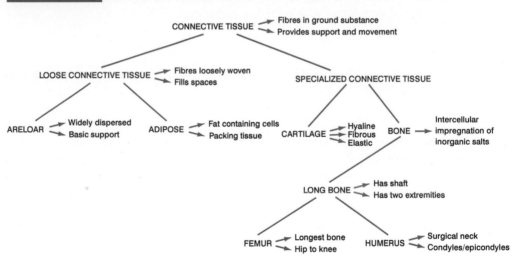

Network systems have been utilized in several computer models. The earliest is Collins and Quillian's Teachable Language Comprehender (TLC), which assumes that knowledge is represented in the form of propositional networks. The TLC was tested by giving participants sentences (such as the following) to verify and then measuring their reaction times.

- A canary is a canary.
- A canary is a bird.
- A canary is an animal.

According to the theory, participants should take longer to verify the third sentence because more nodes have to be traversed than in the first or second sentences, and this indeed was the finding. However, later work has shown that this is not always the case; for some concepts, the search is faster for sentences with more nodes to traverse. The sentence 'A dog is a mammal' should be verified faster than 'A dog is an animal', but participants found the latter more quickly, suggesting that familiarity plays a part in the speed with which propositions are searched (Collins and Quillian, 1969).

Dual-code theory   The dual-code theory (Paivio, 1969) states that there are two different kinds of knowledge representations in long-term memory: verbal and imagery. If information is encoded in both modes, there is a much better chance of remembering it; some words are easier than others to encode with imagery, such as words that describe concrete concepts like 'forceps'.

The information-processing approach

The information-processing approach is important in cognitive psychology and was developed out of psychologists' interest in the way that computers process information. It is claimed that computer programs can provide an analogy for the workings of the human mind, and the interest of cognitive psychologists is more on the 'software' or 'programs' that underlie an individual's thinking, than on the 'hardware' (the physiology of the brain). One branch of psychology, artificial intelligence (AI), involves devising programmes that will make computers simulate intelligent behaviours such as reading or translating.

The information-processing model is commonly used to explain a number of human psychological processes, including memory and perception. Information-processing consists of a flow of information through a system, with this flow taking a finite amount of time. Some parts of the system have a limited capacity for processing information and there are overall control processes that govern the flow.

The flow of information begins in the sensory receptors, which detect stimulus inputs from the environment and transfer them to the sensory memory; the latter records all stimuli encountered in a form similar to the actual stimulus: visual stimuli in iconic form, and auditory stimuli in echoic form, i.e. as an auditory echo. As the sensory memory registers stimuli for approximately one second only, we are not aware of this process. It does, however, allow time for further processing if the particular stimuli are given attention. When stimuli are attended to, the next stage in information flow is to the short-term memory, which has both storage and control functions but is very limited in capacity. Information can be transferred to long-term memory by further processing, particularly rehearsal. Information required for outputs must first be retrieved from long-term memory and put back into the short-term memory, from whence it can be used to generate outputs via effector organs. There is one other pathway in the flow of information that connects the sensory registers with long-term memory. This is not a direct pathway for storage of stimuli, but it is hypothesized that whenever a stimulus enters the sensory registers, contact is made with long-term memory to see if the stimulus has been encountered and stored before. This process is called pattern recognition.

So far we have examined the flow of information from the external environment through the system, but information can also arise from within an individual, i.e. from his or her own memory. Thus, people often sit and think about things and their thoughts may trigger off a course of action, with a flow of information through the system. This kind of processing is termed 'knowledge-driven' or 'top-down' processing; the processing of stimuli from the environment is termed 'data-driven' or 'bottom-up' processing.

Remembering

An early pioneer of memory study was Ebbinghaus (1885) who used himself as the subject of experiments in which he used nonsense syllables to eliminate any interference from previous knowledge of the words to be remembered. One group of very effective techniques is called mnemonics. These make the subject think about the item to be remembered by using some kind of scheme. The following offers a selection of these techniques.

Method of loci

In this method, the student first imagines a familiar place such as home or work and chooses a sequence of rooms to remember. The student then pictures an item to be remembered in each room until the whole list of items has been used. When the student wishes to recall the list, he or she simply does a mental walkabout through the house or workplace to find the items in their locations.

Natural language mediation

This mnemonic is useful for learning unfamiliar words, such as many of those encountered in nursing; it consists of turning the strange word into one that the student already knows and which relates to the new word. For example, students trying to learn the name of the drug streptomycin might think of 'strapped the mice in', which implies containment of the spread of the pest.

Key word method

This can be helpful when learning the vocabulary of a foreign language; the student first chooses a French word such as 'pain' (bread) and then makes a visual image of a loaf of French bread 'crying out in pain'.

Acronyms

These are lists of letters arranged vertically to form a word, with each letter itself forming the first letter of a horizontal word. For example, the curriculum components might be remembered thus:

A – (Aims)
C – (Content)
M – (Methods)
E – (Evaluation).

Forgetting

It was pointed out earlier in this section that there are three stages of memory: encoding, storage and retrieval. Encoding involves putting representations into the memory system, storage is maintaining these in memory, and retrieval is the recovery of memories from the memory system. There are a number of explanations for forgetting, but all of them involve either the original memory trace not being available, or being available but not accessible. The latter is termed the 'tip of the tongue' (TOT) phenomenon and is a familiar experience for most people.

Decay theory

Forgetting was originally ascribed to a simple process of fading or decay over a period of time. However, this explanation is insufficient to explain forgetting, as it takes no account of the influence of an individual's experience of forgetting.

Interference

This states that forgetting is due to interference from other memories. Retroactive interference (retroactive inhibition) occurs when new learning material interferes with that previously learned. Student nurses may attend two or three lectures during an afternoon, and the first one may be forgotten due to retroactive interference from the ones that followed it. Proactive interference (proactive inhibition) means the opposite; the second lecture of the afternoon is largely forgotten due to interference from the first.

Encoding specificity theory

The key point of this approach is that all forgetting occurs because the cues that were present when the memory was encoded are not present when it is retrieved. It is claimed that the best cues for remembering something are the cues that were present when the memory was encoded. It is well established that, when someone visits a place where he or she lived as a child, the context cues the recall of memories long thought to have been forgotten.

Consolidation theory

In this theory, the idea is that every experience sets up a trace in the brain and this trace needs to be consolidated if the information is to be remembered. Hence, the trace can be destroyed before it has had time to be consolidated, as in electro-convulsive therapy and retrograde amnesia following head injury.

PERCEPTION

In order to discuss the processes involved in perception, we need to refer again to the diagram of the information-processing system in Figure 3.1 It can be seen that sensory inputs from the environment are first registered in the sensory receptors such as the cells of the retina in the eye. These receptor cells transform the physical stimulus into electrical impulses and transfer it to the brain. Sensation is the term given to the initial processes of reception of the stimulus by the sense organ, whereas perception is used for the processes that occur centrally in the information-processing model. Perception can be defined as an organized process in which the individual selects cues from the environment and draws inferences from these in order to make sense of his or her experience.

Organization

When a particular stimulus such as the letter 'T' impinges on the cells of the retina, the information is transmitted to the cells of the visual cortex and it is here that the process of perception begins. These cortical neurones are designed to respond to particular types of stimuli or patterns, with some responding to vertical lines, some to horizontal, others to acute angles and so on.

Perception in practice-based learning

There are a great many implications for nurse education in both teaching and practice-based learning. In practice settings, students need to be taught about the factors that affect their perception of things, particularly the influence of 'top-down' processing, which might make them miss cues that patients might emit. Nurses need to recognize that a patient's perception may be altered by illness and must make the necessary allowance for this by giving more frequent explanations and reassurance, in case the patient may not have perceived the message. Selective attention will operate in clinical areas where patients may be kept awake by jangling drug keys or the sound of a trolley. Some patients may become disoriented and so experience perceptual distortion; the nurse's role in this case is to reduce stimulation by maintaining a quiet, dark environment. In teaching, it is important to use methods that hold the attention of the students with, for example, bright visual aids and changes of activity at frequent intervals. The teacher should maintain a central position as 'figure' separate from the 'ground' of background noise and distractions. The teaching should be for 'insight' rather than just giving factual information, so that students experience 'penny-dropping' when learning concepts.

THINKING

Thinking is a cognitive process consisting of internal mental representations of the world, and it includes a wide range of activities including problem-solving, reflecting and decision-making. Some mental representations are in the form of pictures in the mind, while others are in the form of propositions.

Propositional thought

Propositions are assertions or claims that relate a subject and a predicate, and they may or may not be true. For example, the proposition 'nursing is a caring profession' relates the subject (nursing) to the predicate (is a caring profession). Propositional thinking is made up of symbolic building blocks called concepts.

Concepts

Concepts can be defined as 'objects, events, situations or properties that possess common criterial attributes and are designated by some sign or symbol' (DeYoung, 2007; Ausubel *et al.*, 1978). A concept is thus a category or class of objects, rather than an individual example, each member of that class sharing one or more common characteristics.

- The word 'cell' represents a concept, in that it stands for a class of things that possess a number of common qualities or attributes, such as a cell membrane, cytoplasm, and nucleus and so on.
- The words 'Florence Nightingale' do not represent a concept, since there is only one example of this individual.

The common characteristics that members of a concept share can be either structural or functional attributes or both; for example, the concept 'bandage' contains a wide variety of shapes and sizes, but the functions are largely identified as support, pressure and securing of dressings.

In order to qualify as a member of a particular concept group, an individual example must possess certain key characteristics called critical attributes. Without these, the individual example cannot be classified as one of the concept in question; for example, the concept 'myocardial infarction' is a class of events that includes chest pain, vomiting, pain in the arms, breathlessness and myocardial necrosis.

Individual examples (i.e. patients), exhibit much variation in these features making it difficult to decide the critical attributes of this concept; it is possible to suffer from a myocardial infarction without experiencing pain, vomiting or breathlessness, so it seems that the only critical attribute of the concept is myocardial necrosis. The concept 'angina pectoris' may share the attributes of chest pain and breathlessness, but lacks the critical attribute of myocardial necrosis and hence does not belong to the class of concepts called 'myocardial infarction'.

Concrete and abstract concepts

Concepts that can be observed are termed 'concrete' whereas those that are not observable are termed 'defined' or 'abstract'. 'Liver' is an example of a concrete observable concept, whereas 'intelligence' is an abstract one. Abstract concepts tend to be more difficult to learn than concrete concepts. Concepts form hierarchies, with the most inclusive ones at the top and the more specific ones below and they also cluster together with other related concepts.

CRITICAL THINKING

Within higher education, the aims of undergraduate programmes tend to be of two kinds: the specific aims of the pathway in relation to its subject area, for example nursing or midwifery, and the more general educational aims that apply to all undergraduate programmes, for example development of skills in communication, problem-solving, evaluation and critical thinking. At post-graduate or post-registration level, typical learning outcomes require the students to reflect upon and critically evaluate their own professional practice.

'Critical' is a very common term in education, but it has a very different connotation from the lay use of the word. In society, the term is equated with 'criticism', which carries negative overtones from childhood and schooldays. In this context, it usually meant hostile or unkind comments about aspects of an individual's behaviour, and this notion may carry through to adult life. Critical thinking is very different from criticism, in that it is basically a positive activity. To question established assumptions may be interpreted as undermining them, but in reality such critical appraisal of situations is a positive and necessary process for growth and development to occur within a society or an organization.

Critical thinking is not confined solely to learning in higher education, but permeates all the activities of adult life including interpersonal relationships and work. The process of critical thinking involves purposeful thinking and reflective reasoning where practitioners examine ideas, assumptions, principles, conclusions, beliefs and actions in the context of nursing practice (Brunt, 2005).

Critical thinking is a cognitive activity and Cottrell (2011) points out that by using mental processes such as attention, categorisation, selection and judgement enables a person to learn to think in critically, analytical and evaluative ways. Price and Harrington (2010) outline their contemporary definition of critical thinking:

'A process, where different information is gathered, sifted, synthesized and evaluated, in order to understand a subject or issue. Critical thinking engages our intellect (the ability to discriminate, challenge and argue), but it might engage our emotions too. To think critically, we need to take account of values, beliefs and attitudes that shape our perceptions. Critical thinking then is that which enables the nurse to function as a knowledgeable doer – someone who selects, combines, judges and uses information in order to proceed in a professional manner'

Price and Harrington (2010, p. 8)

The nature of critical thinking

Within the literature there is considerable variation in what is considered to be critical thinking, but it is commonly interpreted as a core concept consisting of a number of abilities such as those identified in Figure 3.2.

FIGURE 3.2   Critical thinking stages

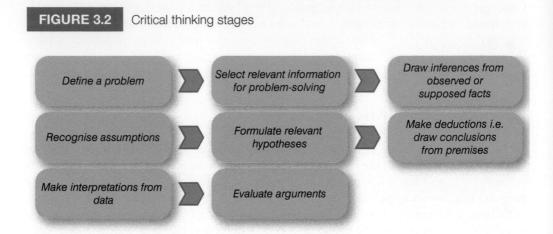

However, interpretations like these that equate critical thinking to a set of generic cognitive skills or procedures have been criticized as unhelpful (Bailin *et al.*, 1999a). They point out that these are simply lists of what people must be able to do (e.g. make deductions), and that they shed no light on the psychological processes involved in critical thinking. They also question the view that critical thinking is a generic skill that can be applied to any situation, because this ignores the importance of context. For example, the ability to evaluate arguments is included in the above list of critical-thinking abilities, but in order to do this one needs to have specific knowledge of the context in which it takes place. Nurses may be able to evaluate arguments within the field of their nursing specialism, but this would not generalize to the ability to evaluate arguments on the merits or otherwise of a Samuel Beckett play.

Bailin *et al.* (1999a, p. 287) suggest that there are three features of critical thinking:

- It is done for the purpose of making up one's mind about what to believe or do.
- The person engaging in the thinking is trying to fulfil standards of adequacy and accuracy appropriate to the thinking.
- The thinking fulfils the relevant standards to some threshold level.

Given their antithesis towards lists of abilities, Bailin *et al.* tackle the problem of identifying the characteristics of critical thinkers by suggesting the intellectual resources necessary for critical thinking:

- *Background knowledge* The depth of a person's background knowledge in a specific context determines the degree to which they can think critically about that context.
- *Operational knowledge of the standards of good thinking* This is acquired by analysis of current critical-thinking practices, but judgement must be used in their application to specific contexts.
- *Knowledge of key critical concepts* Critical concepts are those that enable the critical thinker to differentiate kinds of intellectual products such as arguments or statements. Examples of critical concepts are **premise** and conclusion.

- *Heuristics (strategies, procedures, etc.)* Critical thinkers require a repertoire of heuristic devices, such as double-checking something before accepting it as fact.
- *Habits of mind* This can be summarized as having a 'critical spirit' and refers to attitudes and values to which the critical thinker is committed, for example respect for truth, open-mindedness, etc.

An alternative approach by Brookfield (1987) identifies four characteristics of critical thinkers:

- *Identifying and challenging assumptions* Critical thinkers ask awkward questions in order to identify and challenge the assumptions that underlie issues and problems.
- *Challenging the importance of context* Critical thinkers are aware that beliefs, actions, and established practice reflect the context in which they are set, both cultural and professional. For example, opinions about the standard of appearance for nurses and midwives may be based upon the norms of a generation or more ago, such as a particular view of what constitutes an acceptable hairstyle. Modern hairstyles that are entirely appropriate in a social context may be perceived as being 'unprofessional' in a nursing or midwifery context. The same may be said about so-called 'designer stubble' in male nursing or medical staff.
- *Imagining and exploring alternatives* Critical thinkers have the ability to imagine and explore alternatives to established ways of thinking or behaving, because they are aware of the assumptions and the context of issues or problems.
- *Reflective scepticism* Reflective thinkers take a sceptical view of established dogma and practices, carefully scrutinizing them and questioning their current validity. For example, this approach is encouraged in initial programmes of nurse education, but it may be perceived as threatening by qualified nurses whose own professional education did not foster such an approach. Hence, their reflective scepticism needs to be handled with some sensitivity by students if they are to avoid conflict with qualified colleagues.

According to Popil (2011) and Brunt (2005) critical thinking skills are necessary in the nursing profession to provide safe and comprehensive care. She further substantiates this in the following statement:

> 'As providers of health services, nurses should be self-directive, creative, critical thinkers who strive for personal and professional growth, regardless of their level of practice. Nurses use critical thinking skills to problem solve and to make appropriate clinical decisions on an everyday basis.'
>
> Popil (2011, p. 204)

Teaching students how to obtain, organize and use information to solve complex problems is an empowering activity for both the learner and the teacher (Brunt, 2005). A number of authors believe that both lecturers and students should view learning as a shared responsibility; and if the lecturer empowers the student to think critically, they are more likely to take responsibility for the process of problem-solving (Cook, 2011; Sobocan and Groarke, 2010; DeYoung, 2007). Figure 3.3 outlines an example of strategies that can enhance the critical thinking skills of students.

FIGURE 3.3   Strategies to enhance critical thinking skills

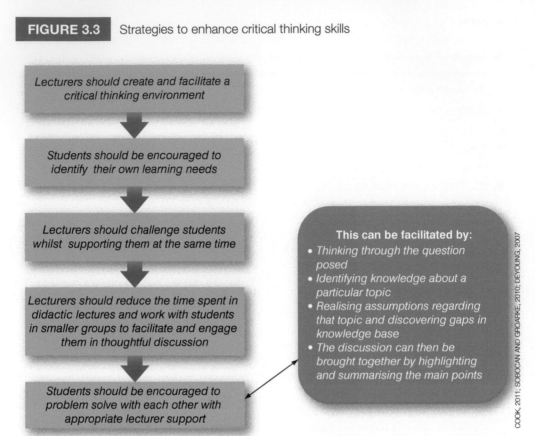

Assessing critical thinking

Assessing the critical thinking skills of students is an important element of nursing education (Cook, 2011) and higher education institutions should be encouraged to develop tools that aid and assess the critical thinking skills that reflects the philosophy of individual programmes. Critical thinking can be advanced through student-centred learning and teaching strategies such as discussion forums, small group teaching and also via concept mapping and clinical placement opportunities (Cook, 2011; DeYoung, 2007). Such skill development is evident within the NMC (2010) Standards for pre-registration nursing education, which states that higher education institutions must ensure that students develop their critical thinking skills in order to assist with clinical observations, assessment and effective decision making.

There are a number of tests of critical thinking in common use and, although these tests contain different sorts of items, there is considerable overlap within them. A classic example is the Watson–Glaser critical thinking appraisal (Watson and Glaser, 1961). This tests the person's ability on five aspects of critical thinking: inference; assumptions; deduction; interpretation; and evaluation of arguments.

Inference

This is a conclusion based upon facts or observations. For example, from looking at a post-operative patient's facial expression and body posture, a nurse may infer that the person is in pain. However, there may be other, equally plausible, explanations, such as anxiety about whether the person will still have a job when he or she is well enough to leave hospital.

Assumptions

An assumption is something assumed or taken for granted. For example, a nurse may assume that a post-operative patient will wish to be given analgesia as soon as pain is experienced. However, the patient may have a negative attitude to taking any form of drug, and so reject the offer of analgesia.

Deduction

This consists of drawing conclusions from stated premises. Either the conclusion follows from the statements, or it does not. For example, consider the two statements:

■ Some nurses look untidy.
■ Being untidy is unprofessional.

It is possible to deduce the conclusion that 'some nurses are unprofessional'. However, the conclusion that 'unprofessional nurses look untidy' does not follow from the two statements given, since unprofessional nurses may well look tidy, and yet have other shortcomings that contribute to their being considered unprofessional.

Interpretation

This involves judging whether or not a conclusion follows, beyond a reasonable doubt, from the facts given. Let us take a purely hypothetical example: suppose a survey of professional misconduct within the Barsetshire Region found that female nurses were involved in 34 cases of complaints from patients, but male nurses were involved in only 22 cases of complaint. The following conclusions might be drawn:

■ A There were more complaints by patients against female nurses than male nurses in Barsetshire.
■ B Patients are generally more satisfied with male nurses than female nurses.

Conclusion A follows beyond a reasonable doubt, since it is a factual statement supported by the evidence of the numbers involved. However, conclusion B does not follow beyond a reasonable doubt, as it makes unwarranted generalizations from the given data; for example, it takes no account of the number of male: female nurses – 34 may represent 1 per cent of female nurses, while 22 may represent 5 per cent of male nurses.

Evaluation of arguments

When attempting to make important decisions about an issue or problem, it is necessary to be able to distinguish between strong and weak arguments. Watson and Glaser use two criteria for a strong argument: it must be important, and it must be directly related to the issue or problem. If one of these is absent, then the argument is considered to be weak.

Teaching critical thinking

If critical thinking is considered an important aspect of professional practice in nursing, midwifery and specialist community public health nursing, then nurse teachers need to be able to facilitate its development.

> 'Teaching critical thinking is best conceptualized not as a matter of teaching isolated abilities and dispositions, but rather as furthering the initiation of students into complex critical practices that embody value-commitments and require the sensitive use of a variety of intellectual resources in the exercise of good judgement.'
>
> Bailin *et al.* (1999b, p. 298)

The authors go on to suggest that teaching critical thinking involves three components:

- engaging students in dealing with tasks that call for reasoned judgement or assessment;
- helping them to develop intellectual resources for dealing with these tasks;
- providing an environment in which critical thinking is valued and students are encouraged and supported in their attempts to think critically and engage in critical discussion.

TEACHING TIP

Critical thinking is a challenging skill for students to develop. Remember the ten-point critical thinking checklist in Table 3.1 above when teaching it, and encouraging students to hone their skills.

According to Cook (2011), academic written assessments relating to clinical practice is key to developing the critical thinking skills of students. Wiggs (2011) furthers this by referring to collaborative testing 'as a means to foster critical thinking by allowing students to solve complex patient problems within an examination environment' and explains that:

> 'Collaborative testing affords the nurse educator a unique opportunity to actively influence the development of critical thinking skills directly influencing the nursing student's ability to solve complex patient problems.' (p. 279)

TABLE 3.1   Ten point checklist for teaching critical thinking

1	*Affirm critical thinkers' self-worth*	It is important when teaching critical thinking to maintain an atmosphere of psychological safety, whereby students' thinking can be challenged, but they are not made to feel threatened or insulted
2	*Listen attentively to critical thinkers*	During training the teacher must attend carefully to students' verbal and non-verbal signals, so that interventions are both appropriate and sensitive to the situation
3	*Show that you support critical thinkers' efforts*	Students do not become critical thinkers overnight; their initial efforts need support and encouragement if they are to progress, and there is a delicate balance between this and the necessary degree of challenge and upset that is important for critical thinking skills' development
4	*Reflect and mirror critical thinkers' ideas and actions*	Trainers can foster the development of critical thinking by using reflection techniques that let the students see how their behaviours and attitudes are perceived by others.
5	*Motivate people to think critically*	There is a delicate balance between motivating students to think critically and helping them to estimate the risks involved in criticizing and destabilizing established practices. It would be naive to think that by simply criticizing the status quo, change will automatically follow. In reality, established organizational practices and systems tend to be relatively entrenched, and critical thinking may result not in change but only in the loss of the critical thinker's job
6	*Regularly evaluate progress*	One of the important roles of the trainer is to encourage students to engage regularly in reflective evaluation of their critical-thinking skills, so that behaviour patterns are identified and insights gained
7	*Help critical thinkers to create networks*	Networking is a common educational strategy, and is akin to self-help groups. Students should be encouraged to network with other students who are developing critical-thinking skills, so that experiences and insights can be shared and analyzed
8	*Be a critical teacher*	Teachers themselves can adopt a critical-thinking approach to their teaching by questioning assumptions, promoting inquiry, and experimenting with new ideas during their teaching
9	*Make people aware of how they learn critical thinking*	This focuses on helping students to understand their own learning styles in relation to critical thinking, such as how they sustain their motivation, how they integrate new ideas and experience, and how they approach new areas of knowledge
10	*Model critical thinking*	Observing a good role model can help students to become critical thinkers, so teachers should model these skills during their everyday teaching

BROOKFIELD (1987)

INTUITION

Intuition is an interesting cognitive phenomenon that has been largely neglected in psychology this century (Claxton, 1998). In lay terms, intuition is thought of as some sort of extra-sensory perception or 'sixth sense', and was at one time thought to be a particularly female characteristic, 'women's intuition'. The essence of intuition is a sense of knowing something almost unconsciously; it occurs without deliberation and there appears to be no articulated reason for this feeling of certainty.

However, intuitive learning, or learning intuitively, may actually be superior in some cases to rational problem-solving; as an example of this, Claxton cites children's ability to solve the Rubik's cube puzzle. The cube is notoriously difficult for adults to solve, yet children seem to be able to solve it more readily, and the explanation may well lie in the different approaches used by each. Adults tend to use a logical, problem-solving approach, which is inappropriate for the complexity of the Rubik's cube, whereas children rely on intuitive learning rather than on thinking about it.

PROBLEM-SOLVING AND DECISION-MAKING

Problem-solving is a good example of the inter-relationship of all the components of an information-processing system of cognition. Active learning can assist students to makes links between theory and practice where they are encouraged to focus on problem solving, critical thinking, and teamwork as illustrated by Yuan *et al.* (2011).

This first section addresses two approaches to problem-solving: insightful learning and an information-processing approach.

Problem-solving and insightful learning

The Gestalt school of psychology identified a type of learning called learning by insight (or insightful learning), in which the student's perception of a situation or problem undergoes a restructuring, and he or she sees the aspects of the situation in a new relationship to one another. This new relationship forms a unified whole, or gestalt, which is meaningful to the student, who is then said to have insight into the problem or situation.

Köhler (1925) demonstrated insight learning in the chimpanzee during a series of classic experiments in Tenerife during the First World War. In one experiment, the chimpanzee was placed in a cage which had a banana suspended out of reach and several boxes scattered around. It was impossible to reach the banana by standing on only one of the boxes and the animal would manifest trial-and-error behaviour, including great restlessness. Suddenly, it would pile the boxes one on top of the other and climb up to the banana. Köhler noticed that this sudden activity often followed a period when the animal had been sitting quietly, not attempting to reach the fruit. He interpreted the behaviour of the chimpanzee as that of gaining insight into the problem, by seeing the banana and the boxes in a new relationship that was meaningful and thus perceiving the solution to the problem.

The Gestalt laws of proximity and closure can be said to be at work in the insightful learning of the chimpanzee, the former being shown by the fact that all the aspects of the problem, namely the banana and the boxes, must be in the animal's visual field at the same time for insight to occur. Closure is suggested by the sudden awareness of the relationship between the boxes as a means of climbing to the banana, bringing the previously unrelated boxes into a complete, closed gestalt.

This sudden insight into the problem or situation applies to human learning also and has been termed the 'aha' phenomenon. Most people have had, at some time, the experience of suddenly grasping or understanding a problem that has previously perplexed them and have uttered the expression, 'Aha, now I understand!' According to the Gestalt psychologists, the cognitive restructuring that occurs in insightful learning occurs also in rats running in a maze. The rats achieve insight into the correct path to the food by a series of partial insights, gained by discovering that certain patterns of movement are non-productive, whilst others lead to food.

Problem-solving and information-processing

The other main approach to problem-solving research is information-processing, which seeks to explain the sequence of operations that people use in solving problems. The problem situation is termed the 'problem space' and is composed of an 'initial state' in which the individual is currently in, a 'goal state', which is the desired end state, and one or more 'operators', which are a set of operations that transform the initial state into the goal state (Smythe *et al.*, 1987).

Stages of problem-solving

Howard (1983) gives the following stages:

1. Encode the problem in the working memory.
2. Search the long-term memory for a plan or production system.
3. Execute the production system.
4. Evaluate the results.

This sequence may or may not be successful, depending upon the problem.

When individuals carry out problem-solving tasks, they tend to exhibit similar types of phenomena, such as rigidity, incubation and insight, and 'satisficing'. Rigidity implies that people tend to become entrenched in one particular way of seeing a problem, which prevents them from finding a solution. They are also influenced by perceptual set, which makes them respond to the problem as they have done in the past, even if this is not appropriate to the current problem. Incubation and insight refer to the lapse in time between tackling the problem initially and going back to it later, if unsuccessful. There is an increased chance of arriving at a solution after incubation; indeed, it very often results in a 'penny-dropping' insight into the problem. 'Satisficing' is a word meaning that people tend to settle for good choices rather than seeking better ones.

Conditions of learning for problem-solving

Gagné (1985) suggests that there are both intrinsic and extrinsic conditions for problem-solving. The conditions within the student that must be met are:

- recall of relevant rules that have been learned previously;
- possession of verbal information organized in appropriate ways, i.e. schemata; and
- cognitive strategies learned previously.

The extrinsic conditions in the learning situation are the verbal instructions issued by the teacher to stimulate recall of rules.

Problem-based learning

Gagné (1985) suggests that the most effective problems for student learning are those that are novel to the students and within their capabilities. Barrows and Tamblyn (1980) recommend problem-based learning as a strategy in teaching health studies and define it as learning that results from the process of working towards the understanding or resolution of a problem. Problem-based learning is different from other problem-solving teaching strategies, because the problem is given to the student prior to any form of input; usually, traditional methods involve the giving of information followed by the application of that information to clinical problems. Problem-based learning starts with the problem, and students have to find out what they need to know in order to solve it. This approach is very much a discovery-type approach and can be very motivating (Allen and Murrell, 1978).

TEACHING TIP

As a teaching technique, problem-based learning is excellent for encouraging a discovery-type approach to problem-solving and can be very motivational.

Problem-based learning lends itself well to computer-assisted learning, with the use of simulation and case method. Students are given basic data about a patient and are then asked to produce a suitable care plan. Having selected a series of interventions, the nurse can check to see whether, in the real case, the ones chosen were actually selected for the patient. This is explored further in Chapter 5.

Decision-making

Professional practitioners in nursing, midwifery and specialist community public health nursing spend a significant part of their professional lives making decisions: many are routine and predictable, and others are life-or-death decisions.

Decision theory offers an explanation for how people decide to take one kind of action rather than another. The theory assumes that people choose the action that they think will have the most value or utility for them. However, given that decisions are made before the outcomes are known, the choice of action is based upon the probability that the outcome will have the expected utility.

When faced with a range of possible actions, the decision about which one to take is made by multiplying the utility by the probability, which gives the expected utility of that action (Mook, 1996). However, in real life this calculation takes the form of deciding how well we like the outcome of each alternative action and how likely it is that the outcome will follow that action. Let us take an example relating to student assessments: it is common practice in higher education for tutors to offer formative feedback on drafts of students' assessment assignments. Institutions normally have a policy about what constitutes a draft, and it is considered inappropriate for tutors to comment on almost-final drafts, as this would constitute pre-marking of the assignment. However, the issue is not straightforward, since it is often difficult to specify what is acceptable as a draft; this can range from a simple outline of the structure of the assignment, through to several pages of text. Hence, the teacher's dilemma is how to decide which drafts are appropriate for feedback, and which are virtually the finished article.

MOTOR SKILLS

Earlier in this chapter the difference between declarative knowledge and procedural knowledge was identified: the latter being knowledge about how to do things. This procedural knowledge is an essential part of motor skills, hence the preferred term 'psychomotor skills'. Motor skills are an extremely important aspect of the practice of nursing, since nursing science is largely a practical endeavour, but the notion of skill pervades the whole of society; indeed, the concept of social class is very much influenced by the degree of skill of the occupations in each category of the Registrar General's classification. Motor skills are concerned with movements and a skilled person exhibits certain characteristics over a novice.

Human motor skills can be divided into three broad categories (Oxendine, 1984):

- *maturation-dependent* skills, such as crawling, walking and speaking;
- *educational-related* skills, such as writing, reading and observation; and
- *intrinsic-value* skills, such as recreational and vocational skills.

It might be useful, at this point, to look at some definitions of motor skill:

- a persistent change in movement-behaviour potentiality as a result of practice or experience (Oxendine, 1984);
- a learned ability to bring about a predetermined result with maximum certainty and minimum time and effort (Fitts and Posner, 1967).

Obviously, not all motor performances need to be learned from scratch, as many of the component skills will already have been mastered. Take the example of a nurse learning how to do a drug round; although she will not have done the motor performances before, such as taking a medicine pot to the patient, she will, since childhood, have acquired the skill of picking up and carrying a small container of fluid without spilling. Hence, the nurse teacher needs to consider the entry behaviours that students bring to the motor-skill learning situation. Three dimensions of motor skills are commonly identified in the literature: fine/gross, continuous/discrete, closed/open looped.

Dimensions of motor skills

Fine versus gross

Gross performance involves the whole body, or large muscles, such as in lifting a patient. Fine performance involves fingers and wrists, as in removing sutures.

Continuous versus discrete

The former involves continuous adjustment and corrections to stimuli, such as the continuous movements of external cardiac massage, while the latter is a movement made in response to an external stimulus, such as switching off a patient's nurse-call button.

Closed-looped versus open-looped

Closed-looped performance relies entirely on proprioceptive feedback, so could be performed with eyes closed, whereas open-looped is affected by external stimuli. For example, the painless removal of sutures requires some reaction from the patient, which indicates comfort or otherwise.

Learning motor skills

Unlike other forms of learning, acquiring motor skills requires practice, and practice consists of repetition of a procedure under specific conditions. These conditions are that the students must intend to learn the skill and they must obtain feedback about their performance. The reason why motor skills require practice is because of the importance of kinaesthetic feedback from the students' own body; it takes time to produce skilled, efficient movements. It is useful to distinguish between physical and mental practice; the former means the actual physical repetition of the procedure, whereas the latter involves thinking about the skill in between practice sessions. Mental practice or imagery is not a substitute for physical practice, but evidence suggests that it is a very useful way of encouraging skills learning when used in conjunction with physical practice. Reminiscence is the term used to describe improvements in performance occurring without physical practice and may be due to mental practice.

The acquisition of a motor skill normally follows a smooth curve when plotted against the time and the number of trials. The occurrence of plateaux, in which the student seems to stay at the same level of performance, is fairly rare. There are also no obvious stages, but Fitts and Posner (1967) suggest that three processes occur (Figure 3.4).

FIGURE 3.4   Acquisition of a motor skill (*Fitts and Posner, 1967*)

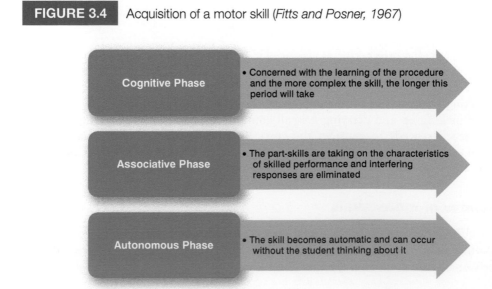

The frequency and distribution of practice can affect learning of motor skills; distribution can be divided into massed practice and distributed practice, the former having little or no rest from beginning to end of practice, and the latter having practice sessions separated by rest periods or by longer intervals of time. Distributed practice is generally more effective for learning motor skills, possibly because of the avoidance of boredom, fatigue or loss of attention. Simple tasks, however, are better learned in one session, and short practice periods are preferable to long ones. Of course, student motivational level will influence the amount of practice that the student can accommodate.

As pointed out earlier, one of the key features of practice is that, in order to help them improve, students must be receive feedback about their performance. Thorndike (1931), in a classic experiment asked participants to draw four-inch lines whilst blindfolded, and they were not told how close to four inches their efforts were. There was much variability in the lengths of the lines drawn, but no trend towards improvement over the trials. Feedback can be classified as intrinsic or extrinsic. Intrinsic feedback is feedback arising within the performer and is further subdivided into reactive and operational feedback: reactive feedback consists of the kinaesthetic feedback from the performer's body muscles and joints; and operational feedback is the observation of the effect of the action by the performer, also termed knowledge of results (KOR). Extrinsic feedback is external to the performer and is also termed augmented feedback; it can be given by teachers, peers or coaches and may be given concurrently during the performance, or terminally when it is finished.

When student nurses learn a new skill, it is likely that there will be some element of transfer from previously learned skills; transfer means that a previously learned skill has a positive or negative influence on the new one, and this is termed proactive transfer. It is also possible for the new skill to influence the old one, a phenomenon called retroactive transfer. Transfer of skill may be specific or non-specific; specific aspects that are transferred in nursing are such things as lifting patients without injuring oneself, whereas general transfer occurs less obviously, in areas such as problem-solving ability.

Positive transfer of skills is enhanced by similarity between them and also if well-learned responses can be used in the new skill. On the other hand, well-learned habits may interfere with new responses, as in driving a car with different controls. There is evidence to suggest that an understanding of the underlying principles will enhance transfer to a different activity.

COGNITIVE THEORIES OF LEARNING AND INSTRUCTION

A number of influential learning theorists have taken a cognitive approach in an attempt to explain how people learn, and from their theories have derived principles for instruction or teaching.

Ausubel: assimilation theory of meaningful learning

The psychologist David P. Ausubel is somewhat unusual amongst educational psychologists in that he focuses very much on presentational methods of teaching and also on the acquisition of subject matter in the curriculum. He draws a distinction between psychology and educational psychology, the former being concerned with problems of learning whilst the latter is an applied science, the function of which is to study those aspects of learning that can be related to ways of effectively bringing about assimilation of organized bodies of knowledge.

Ausubel *et al.* (1978) distinguish between types of learning by using a model consisting of two orthogonal dimensions of learning: one on the continuum from rote to meaningful learning; and the other on the continuum from reception to discovery learning. These dimensions are unrelated and consist of four quadrants:

- meaningful reception learning;
- rote reception learning;
- meaningful discovery learning;
- rote discovery learning.

Ausubel maintains that most classroom learning is of the reception type, in which information is presented in its final form to the student. Discovery learning, on the other hand, consists of allowing students to discover for themselves the principles of content. Discovery learning may fall at any point on the continuum, and it is more usual to find a form of guided discovery learning in use in the classroom. Whilst acknowledging the place of discovery learning, Ausubel claims that it is simply not feasible for transmitting large quantities of knowledge, since discovery learning requires greater time and resources. The second, unrelated, dimension is rote/meaningful: rote learning is defined as any learning that does not meet the criteria for meaningfulness.

Types of meaningful learning

There are three types of meaningful learning.

- *Representational or vocabulary learning* All other types of learning depend upon this basic form, which consists of the learning of single words or what is represented by them.
- *Concept learning* Ausubel defines concepts as 'objects, events, situations or properties that possess common criterial attributes and are designated by some sign or symbol'. He identifies two kinds of concept acquisition: the first occurring in young children, called concept formation; and the second occurring in school children and adults, called concept assimilation.
- *Propositional learning* In this form of learning, it is not simply the meaning of single words that is learned, but the meaning of sentences that contain composite ideas. Syntax and grammatical rules must also be understood.

Ausubel takes pains to point out that there is a difference between meaningful learning and the learning of meaningful material. In order for material to be learned meaningfully, it is necessary to meet three criteria:

1. The student must adopt an appropriate learning 'set', which is a disposition to approach a learning task in a particular way. In the case of meaningful learning, the student must adopt a set to learn the task in a meaningful, as opposed to rote fashion.
2. The learning task itself must have logical meaning, in that it can be related to the student's own cognitive structure in a sensible way. This cognitive structure is said to provide anchorage for the new information, with both components being modified in the process of assimilation.
3. The student's own cognitive structures must contain specifically relevant ideas with which the new material can interact.

Rote learning, on the other hand, can be considered as any learning in which these conditions are not present. For example, the student may adopt a set to learn the material in a word-for-word fashion, in which case the new material would be linked to the existing structure in a simple, arbitrary way without any real interaction. Such linkage prohibits the direct use of existing knowledge and, in addition, the word-for-word nature of learning will place limits on the amount of material that can be learned and retained. Ausubel considers that pure rote learning plays little part in everyday classroom learning beyond elementary school level.

These conditions form an integral part of Ausubel's assimilation theory, which states that most meaningful cognitive learning occurs as a result of interaction between new information that the individual acquires and the specifically relevant cognitive structures that he or she already possesses. This interaction results in the assimilation or incorporation of both the new and the existing information to form a more detailed cognitive structure. The pivotal nature of this idea to Ausubel's theory can be seen in the statement:

> 'If I had to reduce all educational psychology to just one principle it would be this: The most important single factor influencing learning is what the student already knows. Ascertain this and teach him accordingly.'
>
> Ausubel *et al.* (1978, p. 163)

Assimilation theory forms the basis of Ausubel's ideas on the organization of instruction; the main variables affecting learning are outlined below.

- Cognitive variables:
  - the student's previous knowledge of related ideas – seen to be important to the learning of new material and forms the basis of the notion 'transfer of learning';
  - developmental readiness, which is the stage of cognitive development the student has reached;
  - intellectual ability of the student;
  - practice;
  - arrangement of instructional materials in order to facilitate learning.
- Affective/social variables:
  - motivation and attitudes;
  - personality;
  - group and social factors;
  - teacher characteristics.

One of the key strategies for learning advocated by Ausubel is the concept of 'advance organizer', a strategy introduced in advance of any new material in order to provide an anchoring structure for it. This strategy is based on assimilation theory, which, as we have seen, states that new information is subsumed or incorporated into an anchoring structure already present in the student. Typically, an advance organizer consists of ideas that are similar to the material that is to be learned, but are stated at a higher level of generality and inclusiveness, so that the new material may then assume a subordinate relationship to the advance organizer. The concept is similar to an overview (or summary), except that the latter is presented at the same level of generality or inclusiveness. Advance organizers form the link between the student's previous knowledge and what is needed to be known, before any meaningful learning can take place. A further advantage is that it provides a highly specific anchoring structure because the content is virtually identical to the material that follows, although, to be effective, it must obviously be potentially meaningful and capable of being understood.

The process of forgetting meaningfully learned material is also explained by Ausubel in terms of assimilation theory. Learning, as we have seen, consists of the interaction between new information and knowledge already present in the cognitive structure of an individual. During the process of assimilation, this new information gradually loses its discrete identity as it becomes part of the modified anchoring structure; this process is termed obliterative subsumption. This gradual loss of separate identity ends with the meaning being forgotten when the idea falls below the threshold of availability. This threshold forms a level below which an idea cannot be retrieved, but the level is subject to variation, for example due to anxiety.

Implications for teaching and learning

How effective are advance organizers in practice? Barnes and Clawson (1975) reviewed 32 studies involving the use of advance organizers and found that 12 reported significant effects and 20 reported non-significant. They analyzed the studies according to selected variables, finding that length of treatment was not critical and that the ability levels of students had no differential effects on learning. Similarly, no clear pattern emerged in relation to the grade level of the students or to the types of organizer. They concluded that the efficacy of advance organizers had not been established. Ausubel, however, states that Barnes and Clawson failed to take into account the fact that most studies did not analyze the students' relevant subsumers or the conceptual material to be learned (Ausubel *et al.*, 1978). Meena (1980) reports a study in which advance organizers were used prior to information presented in an instructional film; results showed that learning and retention were significantly superior for the organizer groups. Nicholl (1978) studied the effects of advance organizers on a cognitive social-learning group, but the results were not significant.

The most obvious application of assimilation theory is that of advance organizers for lectures. As was pointed out earlier, an advance organizer is a form of introductory material, introduced and taught to the students in advance of the main body of the lecture, and its purpose is to provide the necessary specific anchoring structures for the information presented in the main body of the lecture. In order to do this, the advance organizer must fulfil certain criteria.

1. It must form a bridge between what the student already knows and the new information to be encountered in the lecture.
2. The advance organizer must be more general and inclusive than the material that follows it in the main body of the lecture; it must abstract out from that knowledge the key essence of the lecture.
3. It must be taught and learned just like any other information, either immediately prior to the lecture, or some time in advance of it.

One of the difficulties of grasping the concept of an advance organizer is that Ausubel only ever gave one example, because the organizer must relate intimately to the teacher's subject matter and thus cannot be written by anyone else. In order to see how the organizer is structured, it is always necessary to have the subject matter of the lecture available as well. Figure 3.5 shows an example of an advance organizer for a lesson on the circulatory system, including the lesson plan for the main lecture.

FIGURE 3.5   Example of a lesson plan with advance organizer for 'the circulatory system'

Introduction
Good morning and welcome to this lecture on the circulatory system. Before we begin I would like
to include some introductory material to help you understand the lecture.

Advance organizer
You are all very familiar with the notion of transport systems in society; for example, road, rail, air and
sea transport. Any transport system has a number of basic components as follows:

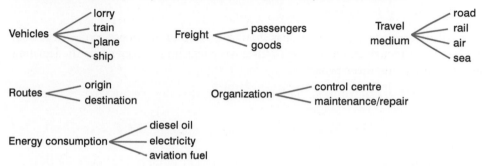

The circulatory system in the body is another example of a transport system with the same basic
components. We can usefully examine the system using these components as follows:

Vehicles: In the bloodstream, certain cells act as vehicles for transporting substances, as does the liquid
part of the blood, called plasma.

Freight: Many 'goods' are transported in the blood, including foodstuffs, oxygen, chemical messengers
and waste products.

Travel medium: the liquid part of the blood is the transport medium.

Routes: There are many routes involved in the circulation. For example, oxygen originates at the
lungs (the supplier) and its destination is the tissue cells (the consumer).

Organization: There is a complex organization of circulation, both from central control in the brain to
local control in the tissues.

Energy consumption: Like all other body systems, the circulation burns up glucose to make energy.

Main body of the lecture
1. Composition of the blood

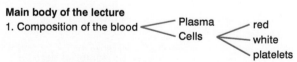

2. Greater and lesser circulation
3. Functions of blood
4. Control of circulation

The advance organizer is taught at the beginning of the lecture and is then followed
by the main body of information. The advance organizer contains all the elements of
the lecture that follows it, but at a much more abstract level. For example, it talks about
'certain cells' rather than giving specific names; the names are introduced later in the
lecture. The advance organizer also contains information that the student already knows,
i.e. the transport systems of society and so forms a bridge between this prior knowledge
and the new information about the circulation.

The principle of meaningful learning can be applied at all levels of nurse education, and it is particularly important to ascertain students' prior knowledge when working in the clinical setting. A few minutes spent clarifying what the student understands about the nursing care of a patient will be rewarded by providing a framework upon which further explanation can be hung. Nurse teachers should try to discourage students from learning material in a rote fashion and, instead, encourage them to learn it meaningfully, by ask them to try to explain the material to a fellow student.

Bruner: discovery learning

The work of Jerome Bruner (1960) has had a profound influence on educational thinking; he is particularly associated with 'discovery learning'. Bruner sees the learning of a subject as involving three processes.

1. *The acquisition of new information* This usually builds on something that is already known, albeit tentative or vague.
2. *Transformation of information* New information is analyzed and processed so that it can be used in new situations.
3. *Evaluation* All aspects of the processing of information are evaluated to check if they are correct.

Subject matter is usually broken down into a series of units or learning episodes and each episode involves the three processes above.

Structure of a subject

According to Bruner, the purpose of learning is that it should be useful to us in the future, and this is accomplished by the process of transfer. Transfer of learning can occur in two main ways – transfer of specific skills or transfer of general principles. The latter type of transfer is fundamental to the educational process and is dependent upon a thorough understanding of the structure of subject matter. The concept of structure is explained as follows:

> 'Grasping the structure of a subject is understanding it in a way which permits many other things to be related to it meaningfully. To learn structure, in short, is to learn how things are related.'
>
> Bruner (1960, p. 7)

Structure, then, involves the basic patterns and ideas of the subject but not the details or specific facts. If students understand the structure, they should be able to work out for themselves much of the fine detail. The structure is made up of concepts or categories, and Bruner sees learning as a process of categorization of objects. Classes of objects are seen to be characterized by common properties, and it is these properties that are used as a basis for identifying new objects that are encountered. The new object is compared with the properties of a category, to see if it belongs there. If the object fits a particular category, then we infer that it possesses the characteristics of that category. A category has certain distinguishing properties that differentiate it from other categories and it also has a certain order in which the characteristics are combined. For example, the category 'bed' has the following components: frame, legs, headboard, footboard, mattress, pillows, blankets and counterpane. These characteristics are assembled in a certain order, such as the legs underneath, the mattress on the frame, the pillows and blankets on top, etc. There are also limits of acceptance for objects to fall within a category. For instance, a bed would still be a bed if there were no headboard, but it would not constitute a bed if there were no frame.

When categorizing an object, an individual tends to follow a sequence of four stages. The first involves isolating the object from its background, a process called primitive categorization. A search for cues then follows, which may be conscious or unconscious, and the individual attempts to categorize the object using the cues available. He or she may employ a conscious cue search by saying, 'I wonder what this can be?' Having made a cue search, the individual makes a tentative categorization and this then narrows down the search to those cues that will confirm the tentative categorization. This is termed confirmation check. The fourth stage involves ceasing the search for cues; additional cues are more or less ignored. This stage is called confirmation completion and the object is identified and categorized.

Coding systems for information

The learning of more complex information is explained by Bruner in terms of coding systems. A coding system is a set of general categories that an individual uses to classify and to group information about the world. These systems are hierarchically arranged, with the more specific information in the lowest categories. As one rises in the hierarchy, each category is more general and less specific than the one below; to recall a specific item, it is necessary to recall the coding system of which it is a member. Thus, the general principles of a subject are contained in the upper parts of the hierarchy of a category, and, in transfer of learning; these previously learned coding systems are applied to new events or objects. Figure 3.6 shows a coding system for fractures, with the most general concept at the top, namely fractures, and progressively finer subdivisions or subordinate concepts.

FIGURE 3.6   Coding system for fractures

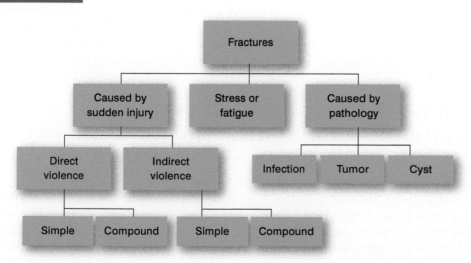

Acquisition of coding systems is influenced by a number of factors, including the learning 'set' of an individual towards a learning task and his or her motivation. In addition, there must be mastery of the specific aspects of a situation before the principles can be combined into a more general or generic coding system, and this acquisition of generic coding systems is enhanced by a variety of learning situations, especially discovery-learning situations.

Discovery learning

Discovery learning involves students in discovering the structure of a subject through active involvement and can be divided into pure discovery and guided discovery. The former is virtually impossible to organize, since it involves no direction whatsoever, so the latter is preferable. The role of the teacher is to pose questions or problems that stimulate students to seek answers in an active discovery way. One of the great obstacles to this kind of learning in nurse education is the pressure on students always to produce the correct answers to questions; this runs counter to the notion of intuitive thinking. Intuition involves making an educated guess about phenomena before one has the complete data and can be very motivating for students because they then have to check whether or not their hypothesis was correct.

Implications for teaching and learning

One implication of Bruner's ideas on the structure of subject matter is that the nurse teacher must ensure that any new material being taught is first explained in terms of its basic structures and principles. It is not helpful to give lots of fine detail in the early stages of encountering a new subject; it is much more sensible to give an outline only. Take the example of microbiology, an important topic for nurses to understand so that they can appreciate the need for asepsis and antibiotics. It would be good practice if the teacher confined the lecture to a general overview of the main principles and concepts of microbiology until the students were well immersed in them. However, it is common to find lectures on microbiology given to first-year students that contain very specific detail about the classification of bacteria, a confusing experience for those students who have not encountered the concepts before.

Discovery learning can be used to good effect in the context of guided discovery; the nurse teacher can ask students to devise a series of questions or problems related to the topic areas and then to try to find answers to those using whatever resources are available. Another discovery approach is to use practical laboratory sessions to generate activities and then to ask students to try to explain why things happened.

GAGNÉ: THE CONDITIONS OF LEARNING AND THEORY OF INSTRUCTION

Robert Gagné does not propose a theory of learning *per se* but focuses on the conditions of learning. Using an information-processing model, he analyzes these conditions and develops a theory of instruction based upon them. Learning is defined as 'a change in human disposition or capability that persists over a period of time and is not simply ascribable to processes of growth' (Gagné, 1985). Thus growth is seen very much as being genetically determined, whereas learning is seen as being mainly under the control of environmental influences that interact with the individual. Any learning situation can be viewed as having a number of elements, namely the student, the stimulus, the contents of the student's memory, and the response or performance outcome. Such a learning situation or occurrence is described as follows:

> 'A learning occurrence, then, takes place when the stimulus situation together with the contents of memory affect the student in such a way that his or her performance changes from a time before being in that situation to a time after being in it. The change in performance is what leads to the conclusion that learning has occurred.'
>
> Gagné (1985, p. 4)

Learning capabilities

Gagné believes that it is possible to make sense of all the different learning outcomes that people make during a lifetime by organizing them into five performance categories, each representing a different kind of learning capability.

- Intellectual skills:
  - discrimination
  - concrete concepts
  - defined concepts
  - rules
  - higher-order rules
- Cognitive strategies
- Verbal information
- Motor skills
- Attitudes

Prototypes of learning

The five varieties of learning capability include some elements that Gagné terms 'prototypes of learning'; these are commonly identified phenomena of learning that constitute basic forms of learning by association. They include:

- classical conditioning;
- operant conditioning;
- verbal-association learning; and
- chaining.

These are seen as basic forms because they comprise only parts of specific capabilities and are insufficient to explain all aspects of complex learning. Hence, association is seen as an important aspect, since its various forms constitute some of the components of the five learning capabilities. Having emphasized the importance of association learning as a basic component of all types of learning, we now examine the five varieties of learning capability in more detail.

Intellectual skills

It is useful to think of intellectual skills as forming a hierarchy in which any particular skill requires the prior learning of those skills below it in the hierarchy, as illustrated in Figure 3.7.

FIGURE 3.7   Hierarchy of intellectual skills

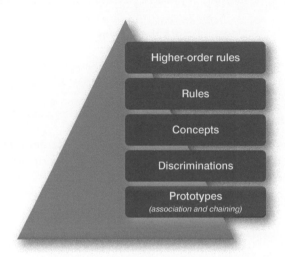

The dependence of intellectual skills on the basic prototypes is shown; each level consists of progressively more complex skills. These intellectual skills are what is referred to as 'procedural knowledge' (i.e. knowledge about how to perform such things as mathematical calculations) and are typified by rule-governed behaviour. Rules state relationships between things and are composed of simpler components called concepts, which in turn depend on the ability to discriminate between various characteristics of things.

Discrimination

Young children learn to respond to collections of things by learning the differences between them, a process called discrimination. Discrimination learning involves perceiving differences in size, shape, colour, texture, etc., and multiple discriminations have to be made when there is more than one stimulus present. Student nurses and midwives may have to learn to discriminate between the various kinds of tissue when using a microscope. This is usually taught by presenting examples and non-examples of a particular tissue, a process called 'contrast practice'. When the student is making multiple discriminations, there is a danger of confusion between stimuli and of interference in the learning of discriminations.

Concrete concepts

Discrimination learning is confined to specific stimuli, whereas concept formation allows the student to respond to collections of things by classifying them into categories sharing common abstract properties. Unlike prototypes and discriminations, concepts are capable of being generalized to other situations and hence they free the student from control by specific stimuli. Once a student nurse has acquired the concept of a 'pressure sore', this can be applied to any example on all areas of the body, provided that the concept adequately represents the range of pressure sores possible. It may be that students have inadequate concepts for some classes of phenomena, so these need to be developed and extended by appropriate instruction.

Gagné describes three stages in the learning of a concrete or observable concept: discrimination, generalization and variation in irrelevant dimensions. The first stage involves the student in discriminating between one object and another, for example a capsule and a tablet. The next stage involves generalization of the discrimination, in which the student discriminates between the capsule and a variety of tablets of various shapes, sizes and colours. The final stage involves variation in the size, shape and colour of the capsules, as well as the variations in the tablets, and, if the student can identify all the capsules, then he or she has acquired the concept of a 'capsule'. This attainment can be tested by showing the student nurse a capsule and a tablet, neither of which have been seen before; if the student nurse can identify the capsule, he or she has attained the concept by identifying a novel instance.

The learning of a concept can be made much easier by the use of language, i.e. verbal cues or instructions; indeed, many of the concepts used in nursing are learned verbally by attending lectures or by reading. Concepts learned in this linguistic manner need to have concrete references to the real world if students really are to understand them. Such concrete reference can be made by the use of practical work in laboratories or clinical settings.

Defined concepts

The previous section looked at concrete concepts, referred to by Gagné as concepts-by-observation; certain concepts, however, can only be learned as definitions, since they do not actually exist as concrete entities, for example, 'health' or 'empathy'. A definition is a statement that expresses rules for classifying objects or events and consists of 'thing-concepts' and 'relational concepts'. The definition of an object consists of four parts:

1. A thing-concept that is superordinate.
2. A set of characteristics of the above.
3. A relational concept indicating the use of the object.
4. A thing-concept that is the object of the verb above.

Figure 3.8 illustrates the components of the definition of the concept of a 'syringe'.

Many concepts are themselves relations and the components of these definitions are slightly different:

1. A relational concept that is already known by the student.
2. A thing-concept that is the object of the above.
3. Modifier words that are the characteristics of the relation.

There is one point of possible confusion between concrete concepts and defined concepts; it is quite common to find that concrete concepts are given definitions, as in the example of syringe, but this does not make them defined concepts. A defined concept cannot be concrete, however, since it is concerned with relations not objects. Defined concepts are taught by pointing out the thing-concepts and the relational concepts to the student and these are then understood, provided that the student has already acquired

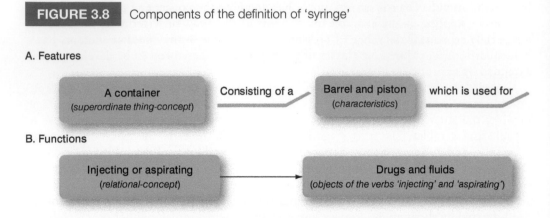

FIGURE 3.8 Components of the definition of 'syringe'

A. Features

A container
(superordinate thing-concept)

Consisting of a

Barrel and piston
(characteristics)

which is used for

B. Functions

Injecting or aspirating
(relational-concept)

Drugs and fluids
(objects of the verbs 'injecting' and 'aspirating')

the relevant component concepts of the definition. For example, the term 'diffusion' can be defined as 'the continual intermingling of molecules in liquids or gases', but for students to understand this concept, they must first understand the component concepts of 'intermingling' and 'molecules'.

Rules A rule is defined by Gagné (1985, p. 118) as 'an inferred capability that enables the individual to respond to any instance of a class of stimulus situations with an appropriate instance of a class of performances'. Rules require, as prerequisites, the component concepts and these are then put in the correct sequence, as in the rules of grammar or mathematics. Rules are often thought of as statements in lay terms, for example the rule book, but it is important to remember that the rule itself is an inferred capability, which is one of the aspects of intellectual skills. However, verbal statements are very useful for learning rules, as in the 'diffusion' example mentioned earlier. Rules are also termed procedures and may consist of long sequences or steps in a particular sequence. Nursing procedure manuals are published that contains a series of rules about the carrying out of various nursing procedures.

Higher order rules We have seen that rules require prerequisite knowledge of the relevant concepts in order to be understood and that such concept attainment is reliant upon the necessary discriminations made by the student, which in turn depend upon associations between stimuli. The increasing complexity of intellectual skill does not stop at rules, but higher order rules may develop as a result of the student's problem solving, resulting in the combination of several rules into a more complex rule. Much learning can be seen to take the form of learning hierarchies, with the simpler rules forming prerequisites for more complex ones, and this implies that there is a cumulative process involved in learning. Hence, simpler rules are transferred to more complex rules, and these higher order rules tend to be more generalizable in their application.

Cognitive strategies

These strategies exert control over the internal mental processes of learning such as thinking, memory and problem-solving and are independent of content. They are involved in the learning of intellectual skills and other learning capabilities and are often referred to as metacognitive processes or 'learning to learn'. Students use cognitive strategies for attending to stimuli, for encoding and retrieving information in memory and for thinking and problem-solving, for example the use of mnemonics and imagery. Cognitive strategies are easily acquired by students and become better with practice, and there is some evidence to suggest that these skills will transfer to other situations.

Verbal information learning

Verbal learning entails 'declarative knowledge', the kind of knowledge involved in telling or verbalizing, and it utilizes sentences or propositions. There are three forms of verbal learning: names (or labels), facts (or single propositions) and organized verbal knowledge:

- *Names or labels*. These are normally learned at the same time as the concept is acquired; hence only one or two labels or names are learnt at any one time. On occasions, however, it is necessary to learn several names at one time, such as when a nurse teacher meets a new student group and has to remember each name, which can be very difficult.

- *Facts or single propositions*. It seems likely that facts are stored in memory as meaningful propositions rather than as verbatim words in some form of semantic network.

- *Organized verbal knowledge*. This refers to collections of propositions that are organized into connected discourse called prose. It is suggested that a student's previous knowledge is a major influence on the learning of new information from prose texts, owing to the previous formation of global schemata for particular situations or events.

Motor skills

Much human learning is to do with movements, and a practice discipline like nursing centres around the learning of motor skills and procedures. There are three dimensions of motor skills: fine/gross performance, continuous/discrete movements and closed/open looped tasks.

Fine versus gross performance   It is possible to distinguish motor skills in terms of the involvement of muscles, gross skills require the use of large muscles, as in the lifting of patients, and fine skills, the use of fingers and wrists, as in the removing of sutures.

Continuous versus discrete movements   These terms are self-explanatory: the former consist of continuous movements such as those of external cardiac massage and the latter consist of single-direction movements, such as the switching off of the nurse call-button.

Closed-looped versus open-looped tasks

The former rely entirely on proprioceptive feedback and can be performed with the eyes closed; the latter involve some kind of external stimulus that influences the movement, such as inflating the cuff on a sphygmomanometer according to the level of the column of mercury.

Motor skills often occur as components of procedures, such as giving a blanket bath or changing a dressing. A procedure consists of a series of rules in sequential order, but also requires certain motor skills in order to be executed. It is therefore incorrect to think of procedures as being motor skills alone; rather they involve both intellectual and motor skills. Practice is a basic requirement for the acquisition of motor skills in order to allow the student to learn from the proprioceptive feedback from his or her own body movements; in addition the student receives feedback both from observing the effects of his or her movements and by augmented feedback from someone else: a teacher or a coach. When attempting to learn a procedure, a student combines a series of part-skills into the total procedure in a particular order; these are known as behavioural chains.

Attitudes

According to Gagné (1985, p. 63), an attitude is 'an internal state that influences (moderates) the choices of personal action made by the individual'. Attitudes are learnt as individuals develop during childhood and adult life. Their relationship to behaviour is not clearly identified, but they serve to predispose the individual to act towards things in a particular way. There are three components of an attitude:

- the cognitive component, which consists of the beliefs that an individual holds about the attitudinal object;
- the affective component, which is concerned with feelings that the individual has about the beliefs that he or she holds about the attitudinal object;
- the behavioural aspect – a predisposition to act in some way – although studies have shown poor correlation between attitudes and behaviour.

A nurse may have a positive attitude towards the older adult, believing that they have a right to be treated with respect and dignity and this belief may be very strongly felt. The nurse may endeavour in his or her behaviour towards the older adult always to ensure that they are treated as individuals and made to feel respected.

The conditions of learning

The learning capabilities outlined above form the cornerstone of Gagné's approach to instruction, since this involves identifying the conditions of learning for each of these capabilities, as well as for the prototypes called association. Gagné suggests that in order to infer that learning has taken place, it is necessary to know not only the changes in performance following instruction, but the capabilities that students already possess prior to instruction. These previously learned capabilities are what Gagné refers to as 'internal conditions of learning', in contrast to 'external conditions of learning', which consist of the stimulus situations outside the student. Both are necessary if learning is to take place, and Gagné has described the internal and external conditions necessary for learning in each of the learned capabilities and prototypes.

Gagné's theory of instruction

Gagné points out that there is a difference between theories of learning and theories of instruction in that the latter utilize a range of theories of learning in order to establish principles of instruction. The events of instruction are different for each of the learning capabilities. Gagné suggests a sequence of instructional events related to internal processes of learning in an information-processing framework:

1. *Gaining attention.* A variety of strategies, including loudness of the voice, gesturing, asking questions or a practical demonstration of something can be used. Attention-getting devices are applicable to all the learning capabilities.

2. *Informing students of the objective.* If students know the objectives of instruction, they will be motivated to learn, so it is important that such objectives are transmitted to them for whichever type of capability might be being taught. These may be stated in the form of behavioural objectives.

3. *Stimulating recall of prior learning.* This is important for all learning capabilities and is commonly done by asking questions of the students.

4. *Presenting the stimulus.* This depends upon what is to be learned and can involve printed materials, the presentation of a problem, a description of a strategy or the demonstration of a motor skill.

5. *Providing learning guidance.* This consists of conveying the meaningfulness of the stimulus by such devices as relating new information to existing knowledge and giving concrete examples of abstract concepts.

6. *Eliciting performance.* Here, the student is asked to demonstrate the application of learning to a novel problem, to ensure that learning has occurred.

7. *Providing feedback.* Feedback as to the correctness or otherwise of a student's performance is important for his or her further learning and this can be achieved by a teacher giving verbal feedback or written comments. Alternative forms can be given by using computers or other technology.

8. *Assessing performance.* This is typically done by means of a test in which the student is given new examples to work on.

9. *Enhancing retention and transfer.* This can be done by giving practice in the relevant capability and by increasing the variety of performance.

Learning is also affected by such variables as the time spent on learning a task and the individual differences in students in terms of motivation, previous knowledge and comprehension.

THE BEHAVIOURIST APPROACH TO LEARNING

John B. Watson is credited with the invention of the term 'behaviourism'. The behaviourist approach to learning is often difficult to grasp initially because of the variety of alternative names used. The behaviourist approach identifies two forms of learning; classical conditioning and operant conditioning, the term 'conditioning' meaning the same as 'learning'.

Classical conditioning: Pavlov

Ivan P. Pavlov (1849–1936) was a Russian physiologist who, in the course of his work on digestive secretions, observed phenomena that are fundamental to stimulus–response theory (Pavlov, 1927). His main interest was the control of salivary and gastric secretions and by careful experimentation he established that salivation relies upon two kinds of stimulation. With the first kind, salivation was an unlearned, physiological reflex that occurred after food was introduced into the mouth of the animal. With the second type, salivation occurred when the animal merely caught sight of the food, i.e. before the food had actually entered its mouth.

This latter type intrigued Pavlov because he had observed that the dogs had begun to salivate immediately he entered his laboratory. Wondering whether this response would occur to other stimuli, he paired a tone on a tuning fork with the immediate delivery of food to the dogs. This pairing was done on a number of occasions and at first the dogs only salivated when food was actually in the mouth, but eventually they salivated after the tone was sounded, but before food had entered the mouth. Pavlov considered that this salivation was a learned response as opposed to an innate reflex and named the process 'conditioning'. Pavlovian conditioning has since been termed 'classical conditioning' to distinguish it from the form of conditioning described by Skinner (see p. 93).

The vocabulary of conditioning requires some explanation, as it is fundamental to the behaviourist approach. In the experiments performed by Pavlov, the first type of salivation was due to an inherent physiological reflex to the presence of food in the mouth of the dog. This is a natural or unconditioned situation, in which the food is said to be the unconditioned stimulus (US) and salivation the unconditioned response (UR). In the second phase of the experiment, the giving of food to the dog was paired with the sound of a tuning fork. After a number of such pairings, the sound of the tuning fork, which had previously been a neutral stimulus, now actually functioned as a stimulus for the flow of saliva. This is now a different situation and is called a conditioned situation, as the tuning fork's sound is said to be the conditioned stimulus (CS) and salivation the conditioned response (CR). Although salivation is the response in both unconditioned and conditioned situations, it is considered that the latter response is a new one: hence the term 'conditioned response'. This response is so called because it is conditional upon the presence of food. If the tuning fork had not been sounded at the same time that food was given to the dog, the conditioned response of salivation would not occur. In other words, the conditioned stimulus (in this case a tuning fork) serves as a signal to the dog that the unconditioned stimulus (in this case food) is about to occur.

Four further terms are used in connection with conditioning: extinction, generalization, discrimination and spontaneous recovery.

Classical conditioning: Watson

John B. Watson (1878–1958) graduated from the psychology school at the University of Chicago, where he had been trained in the skills of animal experimentation. Such experimentation was used to determine the mental qualities of the animals but seldom led to much agreement among psychologists. Watson noted that observations on the animals' behaviour yielded far more objective data than did deliberations concerning an animal's mental state. Watson's position can be summarized in three main statements:

■ Introspective methods have no place in the study of psychology.

■ Observations should be made only on the behaviour of an animal, since this was the object of study in the other scientific disciplines. The emphasis was to be on objective experimentation and replication of results, leaving no place for subjective inquiry.

■ Most behaviour is learned by making an association between a stimulus and a response, hence the term stimulus–response (SR) theory. Experiments in animals can be extrapolated to human beings, as the former differ only in their degree of complexity from man. Watson was convinced that even complex behaviour could be accounted for by this association of stimuli and response, and the publication of Pavlov's work on classical conditioning provided the confirmation that he sought.

Watson became famous for his work with Rosalie Rayner on conditioned fear in humans (Watson and Rayner, 1920). By modern-day standards Watson and Rayner's experiments seem ethically dubious; however, they believed that no permanent harm would be done to the subject of their experiment, a nine-month-old boy called Albert B. (Little Albert). Albert showed no fear when presented with a range of stimuli, including a white rat. He did, however, show a fear reaction to a stimulus consisting of a loud noise behind him, which Watson made by striking a metal bar with a hammer. The conditioning process involved presenting the rat to Albert, then, when he reached towards it, the metal bar was struck loudly behind him, causing him to startle and cry. After repeated pairings of the rat and the noise, presentation of the rat alone caused the child to cry immediately and to crawl away rapidly. His fear of the rat showed generalization to other furry objects, such as a rabbit and a dog. This demonstrated that the Albert had learned to be afraid of the rat through the process of classical conditioning.

Operant conditioning: Skinner

B.F. Skinner has made an important contribution to the study of learning by his work on the form of conditioning known as operant or instrumental conditioning (Skinner, 1938, 1969, 1971). He distinguishes between respondent behaviour and operant behaviour, the former being elicited by specific stimuli and the latter being emitted spontaneously by the organism, such as the random pecking behaviour of pigeons. Classical conditioning involves respondent behaviour and has only limited relevance for the kinds of academic learning with which education is concerned. This is because the conditioned response can have no effect on the environment; in other words, the animal cannot control the events that occur. For example, the dog in Pavlov's experiments made a conditioned response of salivation, but this response in no way affected the speed of delivery of the food. Operant conditioning, on the other hand, operates on the environment, and the learned behaviour is instrumental in controlling events.

The apparatus used for experiments in operant conditioning was the 'Skinner box', a kind of puzzle box containing something that the animal has to manipulate in order to obtain a reward. A great deal of Skinner's work was carried out using pigeons; in a typical experiment the hungry pigeon would be placed in a box containing an illuminated window. In a similar fashion to Thorndike's cat, the hungry bird strutted around in a random manner, pecking here and there until, by chance, it happened to peck at the illuminated window. Immediately, a pellet of food was delivered into a tray beneath the window and was consumed by the bird. Random behaviour was then resumed until the pigeon happened to peck at the illuminated window again and was reinforced with another food pellet. After a number of trials, the random behaviour would cease, and the pigeon would peck at the window immediately it was put into the box. Skinner described the role of the food pellet as a reinforcer of behaviour, in that the window-pecking behaviour was followed by a food pellet that caused the behaviour to be repeated (to the exclusion of non-reinforced behaviour).

This operant conditioning is clearly different from classical conditioning, in that the pigeon's behaviour actually affects the environment by bringing about delivery of the food pellet. Skinner's view of operant conditioning is that it is not a sequence of stimulus–response connections, but rather that behaviour is spontaneously emitted by the organism. He tends to disregard the role of stimuli. There are four principles in operant conditioning: positive and negative reinforcement, punishment and omission of reinforcement.

The central tenet of Skinner's theory is the concept of reinforcement, which he considers to be the main factor in learning. He has done considerable research into patterns of reinforcement and their effects upon the response of the animal, and this has led to the concept of 'schedules of reinforcement'. Skinner has classified these schedules into two main types, continuous and intermittent. In the former type, every response by the animal is reinforced, whereas in the latter only some of the responses are. Intermittent reinforcement can be subdivided into:

■ ratio schedules, which are determined by the rate of the animal's response; and

■ interval schedules, which are determined by the time factor.

In addition, each of these subdivisions may be fixed or variable, giving four possible schedules of intermittent reinforcement.

The importance of these schedules lies in the different rates of response that they produce, ratio schedules giving higher rates than interval ones. This can be explained in terms of the animal's influence over the reinforcement, in that the ratio schedule gives the animal the chance to speed up its response so that reinforcement occurs more often. On an interval schedule, the rate of response has no effect on the delivery because reinforcement is dependent on the passage of time. Variable-ratio schedules bring about the consistently highest response rates, and the ones most resistant to extinction.

'Shaping' is another concept that Skinner has developed in relation to animal behaviour. Shaping implies the incorporation of novel behaviours, which are not part of the animal's natural responses, into its behavioural repertoire. He trained pigeons to play table tennis by selective reinforcement of the desired behaviour. In the first instance, this involved reinforcing the bird when it approached the ball; reinforcement is then given to successive approximations to the desired table-tennis-playing behaviour, such as pecking at the ball, knocking it over the net and, finally, getting it into the opponent's trough.

Animals can be trained to perform complex skills by the use of shaping techniques, but Skinner believes that human behaviour is largely reinforced not by primary reinforcers, such as food or drink, but by secondary reinforcers, such as money and prestige. The effectiveness of secondary reinforcement is well illustrated by behaviour modification techniques that use a token economy in learning disability nursing. Patients can be helped to become independent by the selective reinforcement of desired behaviours, such as washing and dressing, or can be conditioned to modify problem behaviour. Reinforcement in the form of tokens is given for appropriate behaviours, and these can be exchanged for food, cigarettes or other material goods.

Implications for teaching and learning

Behavioural objectives

Another educational application of S–R theory is the behavioural objectives approach. This is an approach to curriculum design that emphasizes the detailed prescription of learning objectives by the educational institution. These objectives must be stated in terms of the observable and measurable behaviours of learners, and the model thus enshrines the principles of behaviourism as defined by Watson.

Programmed learning (programmed instruction)

Programmed learning is based upon behaviourist psychology and the fundamental notions are those of reinforcement and 'chaining'. Programmed learning requires specially prepared materials, which students use for individual study of particular topics.

There are two kinds of programme, linear and branching, which differ in a number of respects from each other.

Linear programmes This kind of programme was devised by B.F. Skinner and consists of a series of closely linked boxes of information called 'frames'. The students are presented with information in frames and are required to supply a missing word at the end of each frame; they can check whether their answer is correct or not before going on to the next frame. The linear programme thus offers information in very small steps, with immediate reinforcement in the form of feedback of correct answers. Each frame is designed to contain material that overlaps with the previous frame as well as the succeeding one, forming a chain of stimulus–response connections. Since it is correct answers that are reinforcing, errors are reduced to a minimum by careful piloting of the programme prior to production.

Branching programmes In contrast to linear programmes, these provide the student with a series of choices rather than allowing the student to supply missing words. In this multiple-choice situation, the student is required to select the answer to a question raised in each frame from a choice of answers supplied. When an answer has been selected, the student is directed to a particular frame, depending on whether the student was correct or not; if the answer was incorrect, the student will be directed to a frame that gives remedial information. It can be seen that this kind of programme has a series of branches that students follow in their progress through the programme, with the slower students taking in more branches than the brighter ones.

Programmed learning can take the form of printed texts such as books, or electronic machines that contain a window and a series of buttons for choosing responses, or computer programs. Branching programmes are rather cumbersome when used in book form, since the reader has to move backwards and forwards through the book in order to follow the branching frames. Students tend to like the programmed-learning format, particularly for topics with largely factual material; the careful formulation of goals for the student and the small steps in learning make it a useful, if sometimes boring, way of studying.

Mastery learning

Mastery learning is another approach that is based on a behavioural objectives model. The method was devised by Benjamin Bloom (1968) and is premised on the assumption that all tasks can be learned by students provided that they are given sufficient time. This key notion of the time taken to learn a task forms the basis for a sequence of instruction called 'mastery learning'. The amount of time taken to learn a task is seen as being dependent on a number of variables:

- the complexity of the task;
- the student's aptitude and experience;
- the ability to understand the material;
- their perseverance; and
- the quality of instruction.

Advocates of mastery learning take the view that individual differences in the achievement of students are not inevitable, and in mastery learning the sequence is designed to ensure that virtually every student will reach the same level of achievement, i.e. mastery level or grade A. The sequence for mastery learning is given in Figure 3.9.

FIGURE 3.9   Sequence for mastery learning

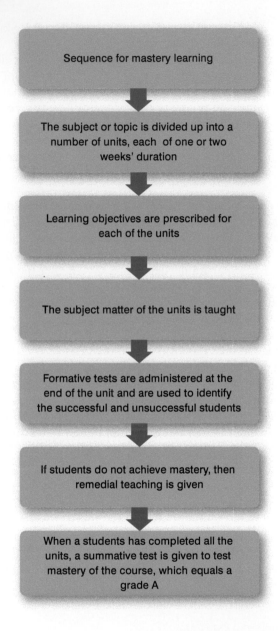

Mastery learning has spread to a wide range of classes and subjects in education and a number of adaptations have emerged. Mastery learning can be used for competency-based learning, humanities and self-development, and it aims to create equality in society by making it possible for all students to attain excellence.

There are, however, a number of criticisms of mastery learning, in particular, its use of specific behavioural objectives and the increased amount of time and resources required for its implementation.

General applications of behaviourism

Classical conditioning is confined to lower-order learning such as a conditioned fear response. However, this may still influence adult learning, as in the case of student nurses who fear written examinations because in the past they have been humiliated by school teachers when their performance has been poor, thus setting up a conditioned fear of examinations. Even though the experience may have been long ago, the emotion can still be very powerful. However, the good news is that conditioned reflexes occur for positive feelings as well as negative, and the learned associations between pleasurable events and feelings can serve to make students enjoy the experience of learning.

One application of classical conditioning that has been used in education is systematic desensitization, a technique commonly used for treating such phobias as fear of spiders or heights. A nurse teacher may encounter a student who has learned a conditioned fear response to participating in small-group discussion or seminar, perhaps due to humiliation in the past. The student could be taught relaxation to counter the effects of anxiety and then the particular stimulus that is causing the fear can be presented in a hierarchy of contact. Having first been taught relaxation, the student would then go through the problem situation in a series of small steps, beginning with discussions with one or two other students only, gradually building up to a full-size group. However, such intervention may be considered to be beyond the competence of a nurse teacher, and systematic desensitization may be more appropriately carried out by a behavioural therapist.

Another way in which students may be helped by classical conditioning is by preventing negative conditioning situations from occurring in the first place. Hence, when student nurses are first introduced to the clinical setting, a concerted effort should be made to make them associate the visit with such positive events as a warm welcome, a sense of *esprit de corps* and a general air of interest and helpfulness.

Operant conditioning offers a greater range of educational applications than classical conditioning. In operant conditioning, reinforcement is a fundamental principle and can be used to provide feedback on learner performance. Knowledge of success is said to act as a reinforcer of behaviour, so it is important to give immediate feedback on performance, in both clinical and classroom settings. Praise may be reinforcing, since it acts as a reward, but it is important to vary the type of reinforcement given, so that the behaviour is maintained. This is more difficult than it sounds, for teachers may appear insincere if they think too much about the way to respond, for example smiling, nodding, praising and the like.

A variable-ratio type of reinforcement produces the highest response rate, so when learning a new response the student should be given reinforcement at frequent intervals, then, as performance improves, less frequently, until eventually only really good performances are reinforced.

A fixed-interval schedule of reinforcement may be effective when reinforcement is given following periodic tests, or by feedback during daily ward reports. As indicated earlier, behaviour modification is a well-tried technique in clinical psychology, where selective reinforcement is used to shape acceptable behaviours in patients/clients. It has been suggested that teachers could use it in class to encourage acceptable behaviours and to discourage negative ones. If the nurse teacher wishes to shape student nurses to answer questions in class, he or she may praise the students each time they answer a question, regardless of whether or not the answer is correct. Gradually, the teacher will begin to praise the students only when the answer is correct. Extinction can be applied to unwanted behaviour such as dominating a lesson or discussion, or coming into class late. If the teacher ignores these behaviours, they may undergo extinction, rather than being reinforced by having attention drawn to them.

Critique of behaviourism

Stimulus–response theories of learning have come in for a great deal of criticism over the years. For example, Skinner's laboratory experiments seem to have little ecological validity when generalized to human beings, i.e. they ignore the importance of human relationships and the social context in which behaviours occur. It is also difficult to see how stimulus–response connections can account for the infinitely complex skills of language. Another difficulty arises when attempting to use S–R theory to explain how individuals learn by imitating the behaviour of other people. Humanistic psychologists find S–R theory distasteful, as it makes the individual merely a puppet, the passive recipient of external forces. In addition, the application of reinforcement theory may lead to a situation where the learner will only consider doing something if there is a reward associated with it, i.e. a 'what's in it for me?' attitude. Another objection concerns the ethical issues surrounding the manipulation of human behaviour, in particular the problem of who has the right to control and manipulate another individual's behaviour.

SOCIAL LEARNING THEORY (OBSERVATIONAL LEARNING THEORY)

Social learning theory has its roots in behaviourism, but, while the basic tenets of behaviourism such as reinforcement are still retained in social learning theory, there is an emphasis on cognitive processes and also on social learning. Social learning is also termed 'observational learning' and 'vicarious learning', and occurs when an individual learns something by observing another person doing it; in other words, it is learning by modelling. According to social learning theory, behaviour is seen as a two-way interaction between an individual and his or her environment, that is, both 'people and their environments are reciprocal determinants of each other' (Bandura, 1977, 1986). Exponents of this theory view the behaviourist approach to learning as one that limits the idea of the potential of individuals and their influence over their own behaviour. According to social learning theory, an individual possesses no inherent behaviour patterns at birth other than reflexes, so must learn everything else. Such learning occurs as a result of observing the behaviour of other people, which allows complex patterns to be acquired in a more efficient way than by trial and error. Indeed, some behaviour such as language can only be learned, according to Bandura, by observation of human models, as it is highly unlikely that mere reinforcement of random vocalization would lead to the complex use of speech that forms the everyday language of an individual.

Learning, then, is envisaged as behaviour acquired by observation of modelling stimuli, providing the learner with a symbolic image of such behaviour, which may serve as a guide. Bandura identifies four processes involved in the observational learning situation: attention, retention, motor reproduction and motivational processes:

1. *Attentional processes* These processes are concerned with the characteristics of the model and of the observer. In the former, some of the factors that influence learning are variables such as:
   a) interpersonal attraction between the model and the observer;
   b) the usefulness of the observed behaviour; and
   c) the distinctiveness, complexity and frequency of contact with the modelled stimuli.

Observer characteristics comprise the level of arousal, capacity to process information, the perceptual set and the amount of previous reinforcement.

2. *Retention processes* It is obviously important to remember the modelled behaviour if one is to learn from it, so the role of such strategies as rehearsal is crucial. The highest level of learning is achieved when the modelled behaviour is first organized and symbolically rehearsed before the behaviour is actually performed.

3. *Motor reproduction processes* The learner must be capable of actually carrying out the observed behaviour and of evaluating it in terms of accuracy.

4. *Motivational processes* Modelled stimuli are more likely to be learned if the observer sees some value in them, but the role of reinforcement in social learning theory is one of facilitation rather than necessity. It may take the form of external reward (such as money) or self-reinforcement, where the learners reward themselves with something when a predetermined behaviour has been achieved. For example, a person may set a number of personal objectives to achieve for a course and, having attained them, may choose to go out to dinner as a reward. The likelihood of the modelled behaviour being learned is increased when the observer sees the model being reinforced for performing that behaviour. This is termed vicarious reinforcement.

Information can be transmitted by the model in a variety of ways, such as an actual physical demonstration, by pictures, words and the mass media. Abstract modelling is the term used for the process whereby the observer elicits the principles of behaviour from a variety of modelled stimuli and applies them to a situation similar to the ones which were observed. Thus, observation of various models performing a nursing procedure would allow the observer to learn the rules of the procedure and these could then be applied to similar situations.

How does social learning theory explain the development of novel or creative responses? Bandura sees the novel response as a utilization of the qualities of many models, to produce a new creative behaviour. There are a number of characteristics of both the model and the observer that make learning more likely. Experiments indicate that persons who possess status, prestige and power are more effective models for those kinds of behaviours. Individuals who are lacking in self-esteem and confidence and those who are dependent tend to be more easily influenced by the behaviours of models who are obviously successful. However, one needs to interpret such results with caution, as many confident people readily adopt the behaviour of those whose actions are seen to be of value.

Implications for teaching and learning

Observational learning is potentially a powerful tool for the nurse teacher in a wide range of applications. One of the important early aspects of nursing which a new student must acquire is the professional role, and this can be fostered by allowing the student to observe a prestigious trained nurse going about their daily work. The student will be able to observe not only clinical skills, but interactions with patients and other members of the health care team, thus learning about professional attitudes as well as techniques. In an early study of modelling in nurse education, Kramer (1972) took students into the clinical areas and had them work in the vicinity, but not actually attached to her. The students thus had the opportunity to see her interacting with patients and giving care, and she acted as a model for their observational learning.

In a British study in an elderly care setting, Raichura and Riley (1985) used modelling as a strategy for teaching trained staff about care of the elderly. The nurse teacher must also act as a professional model when with students, showing enthusiasm about nursing and the ability to do the job skilfully. A good role model must also be a good practitioner if students are to learn the correct roles. It is a useful idea when working with student groups to pair the students so that the weaker ones are working with the more able students and learning by observation. The teacher should ensure that the more able students are given responsibility, since these high-status students are more likely to serve as models for the others. As a facilitator, the teacher should actively include student participation in discussions, identifying innovative ways of implementing change and recognising the need for careful analysis of the environment (Bahn, 2001).

Review questions

1. What are the three domains of cognition?

2. What did Atkinson and Shiffrin define as the main types of memory?

3. What did Bailin *et al*. suggest were the key elements of critical thinking?

4. Define what the Gestalt school of psychology identified as 'learning by insight'.

5. List the three dimensions of motor skills

SUMMARY

- The term cognition refers to the internal mental processes of human beings and encompasses the domains of memory, perception and thinking.

- Memory is the process that allows human beings to store experiences from the past, and to use these in the present.

- Information-processing is an important approach in cognitive psychology; it was developed out of psychologists' interest in the way that computers process information.

- Perception can be defined as an organized process in which the individual selects cues from the environment and draws inferences from these in order to make sense of his or her experience.

- Thinking is a cognitive process consisting of internal mental representations of the world and includes a wide range of activities including problem-solving, reflecting and decision-making.

- Critical thinking is very different from criticism, in that it is basically a positive activity.

- Problem-solving is a good example of the inter-relationship of all the components of an information-processing system of cognition.

- Problem-based learning starts with the problem, and students have to find out what they need to know in order to solve it.

- Decision theory offers an explanation for how people decide to take one kind of action rather than another.

- Motor skills are an extremely important aspect of the practice of nursing, since nursing science is largely a practical endeavour.

- Nurse teachers should try to discourage students from learning material in a rote fashion and, instead, encourage them to learn it meaningfully, by asking them to try to explain the material to a fellow student.

- Discovery learning involves students in discovering the structure of a subject through active involvement and can be divided into pure discovery and guided discovery.

- An attitude is an internal state that influences the choices of personal action made by the individual and is learnt as individuals develop during childhood and adult life.

- The behaviourist approach identifies two forms of learning: classical conditioning and operant conditioning, the term conditioning meaning the same as learning.

- Programmed learning is based upon principles of behaviourist psychology; the fundamental notions are those of reinforcement and chaining.

References

Allen, H. and Murrell, J. (1978) *Nurse Training: An Enterprise in Curriculum Development*. Plymouth: Macdonald and Evans

Anderson, J. and Bower, G. (1973) *Human Associative Memory*. Winston, Washington.

Atkinson, R. and Shiffrin, R. (1971) The control of short term memory. *Scientific American*, 225, 82–90.

Ausubel, D., Novak, J. and Hanesian, H. (1978) *Educational Psychology: A Cognitive View*. Holt, Rinehart & Winston, New York.

Baddeley, A. and Hitch, G. (1974) Working memory. In G. Bowen (ed.) *The Psychology of Learning and Motivation*, Vol. 2. Academic Press, New York.

Baddeley, A. and Lieberman, K. (1980) Spatial working memory. In R. Nickerson (ed.) *Attention and Performance VIII*. Erlbaum, New Jersey.

Bahn, D. (2001) Social Learning Theory: its application in the context of nurse education. *Nurse Education Today* 21: 110–117

Bailin, S., Case, R., Coombs, J.R. and Daniels, L.B. (1999a) Common misconceptions in critical thinking. *Journal of Curriculum Studies*, 31(3), 269–283.

Bailin, S., Case, R., Coombs, J.R. and Daniels, L.B. (1999b) Conceptualising critical thinking. *Journal of Curriculum Studies*, 31(3), 285–302.

Bandura, A. (1977) *Social Learning Theory*. Prentice Hall, Englewood Cliffs, NJ.

Bandura, A. (1986) *Social Foundations of Thought and Action: A Social-Cognitive Theory*. Prentice Hall, Englewood Cliffs, NJ.

Barnes, B. and Clawson, E. (1975) Do advance organizers facilitate learning? *Review of Educational Research.* 45: 637–659

Barrows, H. and Tamblyn, R. (1980) *Problem-Based Learning: An Approach to Medical Education*. Springer, New York.

Bloom, B. (1968) Learning for mastery. *Evaluation Comment*, 1(2) Center for the Study of Evaluation of Instructional Programs, University of California, Los Angeles.

Braungart, M.M. and Braungart, R.G. (2008) Applying learning theories to healthcare practice. In: Bastable SB (Ed) *Nurse as Educator: Principles of teaching and learning for nursing practice* (3rd Edn). Boston: Jones and Bartlett

Brookfield, S. (1987) *Developing Critical Thinkers*. Open University Press, Milton Keynes.

Bruner, J. (1960) *The Process of Education*. Harvard University Press, Cambridge, MA.

Brunt, B.A. (2005) Critical thinking in nursing: an integrated review. *The Journal of Continuing Education in Nursing* 36(2) 60–67

Claxton, G. (1998) Investigating human intuition: Knowing without knowing why. *The Psychologist*, 11(5), 217–220.

Collins, A. and Quillian, M. (1969) Retrieval time from semantic memory, *Journal of Verbal Learning and Verbal Behaviour*, 8, 2407.

Conway, M. (1991) Cognitive psychology in search of meaning: the study of autobiographical memory. *The Psychologist*, 4, 301–305.

Cook, P.R. (2011) Critical thinking in the health professions. In: Bradshaw MJ, Lowenstein AJ (Eds) *Innovative Teaching Strategies in Nursing and Related Health Professions* (5th Edn). Boston: Jones and Bartlett

Cottrell, S. (2011) *Critical Thinking Skills: Developing Effective Analysis and Argument* (2nd Edn). Basingstoke: Palgrave MacMillan

Craik, F. and Lockhart, R. (1972) Levels of processing: a framework for memory research. *Journal of Experimental Psychology*, General, 104, 268–294.

DeYoung, S. (2007) *Teaching Strategies for Nurse Educators* (2nd Edn). New Jersey: Prentice Hall

Driscoll, M. (2004) *Psychology of Learning for Instruction* (3rd Edn). Boston: Pearson

Doyle, W. (1983) Academic work. *Review of Educational Research*, **53**(2), 159–199.

Ebbinghaus, H. (1885) *Memory: A Contribution to Experimental Psychology*. Trans. H.A.

Fitts, P. and Posner, M. (1967) *Human Performance*. New Jersey: Prentice Hall

Gagné, R. (1985) *The Conditions of Learning and Theory of Instruction* (4th edn). New York: Holt, Rinehart and Winston

Howard, D. (1983) *Cognitive Psychology*. Macmillan, London

Köhler, W. (1925) *The Mentality of Apes* Harcourt Brace Jovanovich, New York.

Kramer, M. (1972) The concept of modelling as a teaching strategy. *Nursing Forum*, XI, 59.

Logie, R. (1999) Working memory. *The Psychologist*, 12(4), 174–178.

Meena, V. (1980) The effect of written and graphic comparative advance organizers upon learning and retention from an audio-visual presentation. *Dissertation Abstracts International.* 40: 3713–3714

Miller, G. (1956) The magical number seven plus or minus two: some limits on our capacity for processing information. *Psychological Review*, 63, 81–97.

Minsky, M. (1975) Artificial intelligence. *Scientific American*, Summer, 1975.

Mook, D.G. (1996) *Motivation: The Organization of Action* (2nd edn). London: Norton & Co

Nicholl, G. (1978) The effect of advance organizers on a cognitive social learning group. *Dissertation Abstracts International.* 38: 4475

Nursing and Midwifery Council (2010) *Standards for Preregistration Nursing Education*. London: NMC

Oxendine, J. (1984) *Psychology of Motor Learning* (2nd edn). New Jersey: Prentice Hall

Paivio, A. (1969) Mental imagery in associative learning and memory. *Psychological Review*, 76, 2413.

Pavlov, I. (1927) *Conditioned Reflexes*. Oxford University Press, Oxford.

Popil, I. (2011) Promotion of critical thinking by using case studies as teaching method. *Nurse Education Today* 31: 204–207

Price, B. and Harrington, A. (2010) *Critical Thinking and Writing for Nursing Students: Transforming Nursing Practice*. Exeter: Learning Matters

Pylyshyn, Z. (1973) What the mind's eye tells the mind's brain. *Psychological Bulletin*, 80, 1–24.

Raichura, L. and Riley, M. (1985) Introducing nurse preceptors. *Nursing Times*, 20 Nov

Rosch, E. (1975) Natural categories. *Cognitive Psychology*, 4, 532–547.

Ruger and Bussenius, C.F. (1913). New York Teachers' College, Columbia University, New York.

Rummelhart, D. and Ortony, A. (1977) The representation of knowledge in memory. In R. Anderson, R. Spiro and W. Montague (eds) *Schooling and the Acquisition of Knowledge*. Erlbaum, New Jersey.

Schank, R. and Ableson, R. (1977) *Scripts, Plans, Goals and Understanding*. New Jersey: Erlbaum

Skinner, B.F. (1938) *The Behaviour of Organisms*. New York: Appleton Century Crofts

Skinner, B.F. (1969) *Contingencies of Reinforcement: A Theoretical Analysis*. New York: Appleton Century Crofts

Skinner, B.F. (1971) *Beyond Freedom and Dignity*. Alfred Knopf, New York.

Smythe, M., Morris, P., Levy, P. and Ellis, A. (1987) *Cognition in Action*. Erlbaum, London

Sobocan, J. and Groarke, L. (2010) *Critical Thinking, Education and Assessment: can higher order thinking be tested*? London: The Althouse Press

Thorndike, E. (1911) *Animal Intelligence: Experimental Studies*. Macmillan, New York.

Thorndike, E. (1931) *Human Learning*. New York: Appleton Century Crofts

Tulving, E. (1972) Episodic and semantic memory. In E. Tulving and W. Donaldson (eds) *Organization of Memory*. Academic Press, New York.

Watson, G. and Glaser, E. (1961) *Watson–Glaser Critical Thinking Appraisal*. Harcourt, Brace and World Inc., New York.

Watson, J. and Rayner, R. (1920) Conditioned emotional reactions. *Journal of Experimental Psychology*, 3, 1–14.

Wiggs, C.M. (2011) Collaborative testing: Assessing teamwork and critical thinking behaviours in baccalaureate nursing students. *Nurse Education Today* 31: 279–282

Yuan, H.B., Williams, B.A., Yin, L., Liu, M., Fang, J.B. and Pang, D. (2011) Nursing students' views on the effectiveness of problem-based learning. *Nurse Education Today* 31: 577–581

Further Reading

Brookfield, S.D. (2011) *Teaching for critical thinking: tools and techniques to help students question their assumptions*. Oxford: Wiley-Blackwell

Bowell, T. and Kemp, G. (2010) *Critical thinking: a concise guide* (3rd Edn). London: Routledge

Judge, B., Jones, P. and McCreery, E. (2009) *Critical thinking for education students*. Exeter: Learning Matters

van den Brink-Budgen, R. (2010) *Critical Thinking for Students: Learn the Skills of Analysing, Evaluating and Producing Arguments*. Oxford: How To Books Ltd

PART TWO
LEARNING, TEACHING AND ASSESSMENT

CHAPTER 4
CURRICULUM THEORY AND PRACTICE

THE AIMS OF THIS CHAPTER ARE:

■ To determine the nature of curriculum

■ To consider educational objectives within the cognitive, affective and psychomotor domains

■ To explore the development and design of curricula

■ To examine the importance of equality and diversity within an inclusive curriculum

■ To outline open, distance and flexible learning strategies

KEY TERMS

Curriculum	Validation
Learning outcomes	Student-centred learning
Taxonomy	Learning programmes
Domains	

The term 'curriculum' is used to describe a plan or design upon which educational provision is based; it is the single most important concept in educational delivery, encompassing all the activities normally included under the umbrella terms 'education' and 'training' (Quinn, 1994). Educational provision in nursing takes a variety of forms, from short in-house programmes through to longer formal programmes leading to academic awards.

The two main categories in nursing are pre-registration and post-registration education. The former consists of programmes leading to both an academic award, such as a Bachelor of Nursing degree, and entry to the register of nurses. Post-registration provision, on the other hand, is much more diverse and includes the following:

■ in-house study days for qualified staff, for example intravenous drug administration;

■ discrete modules (courses) for continuing professional development, for example teaching and assessing; and

■ programmes leading to academic awards, such as first degrees and higher degrees.

THE NATURE OF CURRICULUM

Curriculum theory is an established field of study within education, but examination of the literature reveals that the concept is by no means straightforward. There is wide variation between definitions and a number of writers, Lewis and Miel (1972), Tanner and Tanner (1980), Saylor, Alexander and Lewis (1981), have attempted to categorize these. Four main interpretations of the concept emerge:

- *Curriculum as objectives* 'Any statement of the objectives of the school should be a statement of changes to take place in students' (Tyler, 1949).
- *Curriculum as subject matter* 'A curriculum is the offering of socially valued knowledge, skills and attitudes made available to students through a variety of arrangements during the time they are at school, college or university' (Bell, 1973).
- *Curriculum as student experiences* 'Curriculum is all the learning which is planned and guided by the school whether it is carried on in groups or individually, inside or outside the school' (Kerr, 1968).
- *Curriculum as opportunities for students* 'A curriculum is all the educational opportunities encountered by students as a direct result of their involvement with an educational institution' (Quinn and Hughes, 2007).

Skilbeck's (1984) categorization has considerable overlap with the above, but additionally the aspect of culture is introduced:

- curriculum as a structure of forms and fields of knowledge;
- curriculum as a chart or map of the culture;
- curriculum as a pattern of learning activities;
- curriculum as a learning technology.

This categorization has been adapted by Beattie (1987) in his fourfold model of curriculum, described later in this chapter (p. 123). Other writers – Stenhouse (1975), and Saylor, Alexander and Lewis (1981) – take a more generic view of the concept, seeing it as an overall plan or design for learning:

> *'Curriculum is an attempt to communicate the essential principles and features of an educational proposal in such a form that it is open to critical scrutiny and capable of effective translation into practice.'*
>
> Stenhouse (1975)
>
> *'Curriculum is a plan for providing sets of learning opportunities for persons to be educated.'*
>
> Saylor, Alexander and Lewis (1981)
>
> *'Curriculum refers to the learning experiences of students, in so far as they are expressed or anticipated in educational goals and objectives, plans and designs for learning and the implementation of these plans and designs in school environments.'*
>
> Skilbeck (1984)

Quinn and Hughes (2007) offer a definition based upon the principal components of the concept:

> '*A curriculum is a plan or design for education and training that addresses the following questions:*
>
> 1. Who is to be taught? Who will learn? This is the consumer of the curriculum, i.e. the student, course member, colleague, etc., who will experience the curriculum.
> 2. What is to be taught and/or learned? This is about both the intentions and the content of the curriculum. Intentions may or may not be stated overtly, according to the education ideology underpinning the curriculum. Where outcomes, goals, or objectives are overtly expressed, these statements also indicate to some extent the nature of the curriculum content. If the intentions are covert, then content is usually indicated by a list of topics in a syllabus.
> 3. Why is it to be taught and/or learned? This is the ideology of the curriculum, i.e. the beliefs and values that underpin the curriculum approach.
> 4. How is it to be taught and/or learned? This is the process of education, i.e. the teaching, learning and assessment approaches or opportunities available to the consumer.
> 5. Where is it to be taught or learned? This is the context of the curriculum, i.e. the faculty, department, school, college, campus, rooms, etc. It also refers to the place of a given curriculum within the range of awards of the education provider institution.
> 6. When is it to be taught and/or learned? This is the programming/timetabling of the curriculum, i.e. the length, pattern of attendance, etc.'

The concept of curriculum has been further subdivided by some commentators and the more common ones are as follows:

- *official curriculum*, the curriculum laid down in the policy of the institution;
- *actual curriculum*, the curriculum as implemented by teachers;
- *hidden curriculum*, the attitudes and values transmitted by the teachers.

COMPONENTS OF CURRICULUM

The term 'curriculum' encompasses four main aspects of educational provision (see Figure 4.1). These four components are intimately related to each other and the model adopts a rational stance, in that the curriculum design is seen to begin with the formulating of student learning outcomes and then progresses to decisions about what outcomes-related subject matter should be included. Teaching and learning processes are then defined, for example lectures, laboratory work, etc., that will help the student to achieve the learning outcomes, and, finally, the students' achievement of the learning outcomes is assessed using appropriate and relevant assessment methods.

FIGURE 4.1   Components of curriculum

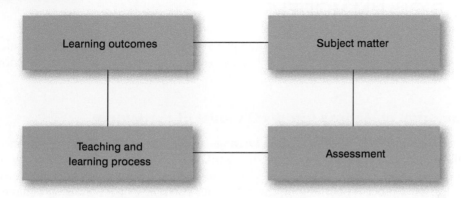

MODELS AND THE CURRICULUM

A model is a physical or conceptual representation of something; physical models are replicas of the things that they represent and may be actual size or built to scale. Architects and town planners build scale models of civic developments that aim to show, in miniature, a replica of the houses and commercial properties that are to be built. In colleges of nursing, students are encouraged to examine models of the organs of the body so as to understand the structure. Other kinds of model do not represent concrete entities, but concepts. Such conceptual models are usually in graphic or mathematical form and attempt to represent abstract concepts.

The term 'model' is used in a variety of ways in relation to curriculum, and there is often confusion between them. There are four main types of model used in curriculum design and development:

- *Curriculum models.* These attempt to represent the nature of curriculum, and reflect the philosophical stance of the originator, for example the behavioural objectives model.
- *Models of learning.* These attempt to represent the nature of learning, and reflect the philosophical or psychological stance of the originator, for example Carl Rogers' humanistic approach.
- *Models of teaching.* These attempt to represent the nature of teaching, and reflect different philosophical beliefs about the nature of the process, for example the transmission model of teaching.
- *Nursing models.* These attempt to represent the nature of nursing, and reflect the philosophical stance of the originator, for example the Roper, Logan, and Tierney model of activities of living.

A given curriculum document may well utilize models from more than one of the above categories. For example, a curriculum for pre-registration nursing might utilize the Stenhouse model of curriculum as an over-arching model, but include Knowles' andragogy approach as a teaching and learning strategy, and the Roper, Logan, Tierney model for nursing theory and practice.

CURRICULUM MODELS

A wide range of models exist which attempt to encapsulate the nature of curriculum, each reflecting the particular ideological stance of the author. Four of the better-known models are described below.

Behavioural objectives (product) model of curriculum

Although having its origins in certain writings at the turn of the century, this model is usually ascribed to Ralph Tyler. In his book *Basic Principles of Curriculum and Instruction*, Tyler (1949) articulated a rationale for effective curriculum, viewing education as 'a process of changing the behaviour patterns of people, using behaviour in the broad sense to include thinking and feeling as well as overt action' (Tyler, 1949, p. 5). He identifies four fundamental questions to be answered in developing a curriculum (1949, p. 1):

1. What educational purposes should the school seek to attain?
2. How can you select learning experiences that are likely to be useful in attaining these objectives?
3. How could you organize learning experiences for effective instruction?
4. How could the effectiveness of learning experiences be evaluated?

This notion of rational curriculum planning was taken up by a number of writers and led to the generic model of curriculum as consisting of four main components:objectives, content, method and evaluation. Hence, the emphasis in this model is on the achievement of objectives by the student. In other words, it is an output model. Tyler stressed the importance of stating objectives in terms of student behaviours: 'any statement of the objectives of the school should be a statement of changes to take place in students' (Tyler, 1949, p. 44). This emphasis on student behaviours was taken up by other proponents of the model and led to a move to limit behavioural objectives to observable, measurable changes in behaviour, leaving no room for such things as 'understanding' or 'appreciation'. The behavioural objectives model has influenced education throughout the world; indeed, in 1977 the then General Nursing Council for England and Wales (1977) issued a circular that espoused the behavioural objectives model for nursing curricula and, by the early 1980s, such objectives were almost universally applied in both classroom and clinical settings.

Educational goal statements

There is no universally accepted terminology with regard to the formulation of educational goals, but the following guide may serve to clarify the concepts involved.

Educational aim   An aim is a broad, general statement of goal direction, which contains reference to the worthwhileness of achieving it. The educational aim is the most important part of the goal system, since all the other objectives are derived from it. The following is an example of an educational aim in nursing: 'Understands the nature of malignant disease, so that he or she may perform skilled nursing care of the patient with such disease.' This statement gives a very general indication of the goal to be achieved, namely the understanding of malignant disease. It does not give details as to what this understanding should consist of, but it does stress the value of achieving this goal, which is the skilled care of the patient. Some authorities subdivide these general goals into immediate and long-term goals and, in nursing, it is likely that teachers will need to state goals for the learner that apply to practice after qualification and so are long-term goals.

Learning outcome   This is the desired end-state of student learning, and describes the knowledge, skills, attitudes and values that a student should acquire as a result of the educational process. Learning outcomes are derived from the educational aims of a programme but are stated in terms of the capabilities that students should attain as a result of instruction. There is a very specific type of learning outcome called a behavioural objective, and this is described below.

Specific behavioural objectives   Also termed instructional objectives or terminal objectives, these are highly specific statements that describe the changes in behaviour that constitute learning. They must always contain a verb that indicates exactly what the learner must do in order to achieve the objective, and this verb should describe an observable action so that achievement can be measured. Behavioural objectives are derived from the secondary goals, for example: 'List five factors which predispose an individual to malignant disease.' The word 'list' describes an observable action on the learner's part, which can be measured simply by asking the learner to write down the list on paper.

If the curriculum uses a behavioural objectives approach to the formulation of goals, then the following guidelines may be helpful:

1. Formulate the educational aims, ensuring that there is some indication of the worthwhileness of achieving them.
2. Formulate the secondary-level goals, which will break down the material into manageable sections for study.
3. Formulate specific behavioural objectives from the secondary-level goals.
4. Formulate any experiential objectives from the secondary-level goals.

Components of a behavioural objective

Behavioural objectives present the most difficulty in formulation, so it is important to examine them in some detail. Most authorities agree with Mager's (1962) suggestion that there are three parts to any objective, namely a verb indicating the learner's observable behaviour, an indication of the conditions under which the achievement will be demonstrated and a standard or criterion by which the performance is evaluated. Let us take each of these and examine them in relation to nursing.

Learner's observable behaviour   Unless the learner's behaviour is observable it is impossible to assess whether or not an objective has been achieved. Take the objective which states:'The learner will understand the structure of bone.' How will the nurse teacher know that the learner has achieved this objective? It is not possible to measure understanding as such, but it can be inferred from certain behaviours. For instance, if learners can write a description of the structure of bone in their own words and without referring to notes or textbooks, then one might safely assume that they have comprehended or understood the material. Thus, it would be much more accurate to state the objective as follows: 'Describe in writing the structure of bone.' The word 'describe' is the action verb, which indicates the learner's observable behaviour. It is important to select verbs that are as unambiguous as possible and which do not rely on the interpretation of the individual who is reading them.

Conditions under which achievement will be demonstrated   Although not always strictly necessary, this can be an aid to clarity in an objective. Conditions are usually such things as time constraints, use of materials or special situations. For example, an objective may state that the condition under which achievement is demonstrated is 'on a patient in bed'. In the example quoted above, the condition is 'in own words, without notes or textbooks'.

Standard or criterion of performance   In the following objective the criterion of performance is 'without danger or discomfort to the patient':'Remove a drain from the wound of a patient using aseptic technique and without danger or discomfort to the patient'. Note that the objective cannot be achieved simply by removing the drain; it must be done according to the criteria.

This objective contains all three components, the action verb 'remove', the condition 'using aseptic technique' and the criterion of 'without danger or discomfort to the patient'. Criteria and standards are useful whenever there is doubt as to the level of performance required in an objective.

In order to perform their role adequately, nurses need a variety of behaviours. They must be able to remember and understand the theoretical aspects of nursing, such as pathophysiology, therapeutics and behavioural sciences. In addition, nurses must possess a wide variety of skills that demand physical ability and co-ordination, such as assisting patients who have difficulty performing activities of living. But the behaviour that is most closely associated with the role of the nurse is the caring aspect, which involves feelings, emotions, attitudes and values, and which puts the nurse in a unique position with regard to helping patients. Of course, most aspects of nursing involve a combination of all three types of behaviour. In order to perform a blanket bath, the nurse must utilize certain theoretical behaviours, such as remembering the patient's condition and relating it to the procedure to be adopted. An assessment of the patient will be needed before commencing. Is the patient in pain? Does the patient require specific help, etc.? Knowledge of the normal and abnormal responses is integrated with information gained from the assessment, to give an overall picture.

The nurse must perform many nursing skills, such as stripping the bed, removing the patient's clothing, altering the patient's position and so on. There is an accepted way of washing and drying a patient that takes a little time to learn. In addition to these 'theoretical behaviours' and 'practical skills', there are the elements of caring, namely interpersonal skills, feelings of empathy, consideration and such. A simple blanket bath is far from simple when analyzed, although it is often argued that anyone with common sense can perform it, as we each take care of our personal hygiene when in normal health. This procedure is often delegated to health care assistants because of this viewpoint, but there is a world of difference between a blanket bath that merely leaves patients clean and one which leaves them clean, un-distressed and with many of their queries or anxieties relieved.

If the role of the nurse requires this wide range of behaviours, then objectives will need to be stated for each of these categories of activity. In addition, it is important that the objectives do not simply require factual recall of information, since nursing involves the ability to apply theoretical knowledge to a practical situation and also to analyze, synthesize and evaluate information.

Bloom's taxonomy of educational objectives

In order to assist the teacher in formulating objectives at different levels and for different kinds of behaviours, Bloom (1956) developed a system of classification called the taxonomy of educational objectives. A taxonomy is a classification, and the best known one is that of Linnaeus, which classifies all living things according to general, and then subsequently more detailed, similarities of structure and function. The taxonomy of educational objectives classifies objectives into three main spheres or domains and each of these is further categorized according to level of behaviour, progressing from the most simple to the highly complex. The levels are arranged in the form of a hierarchy, so that the behaviours at any given level will incorporate those of the levels below.

The three domains are cognitive, which is concerned with knowledge and intellectual abilities; affective, which is concerned with attitudes, values, interests and appreciations; and psychomotor, concerned with motor skills.

The taxonomy for the affective domain was published by Krathwohl *et al.* (1964) and taxonomies for the psychomotor domain have been developed by Simpson (1972) and Harrow (1972).

The cognitive domain Table 4.1 gives the classification of the cognitive domain. There are six levels of objective, each of which is divided into subcategories.

Level 1.00 Knowledge. At this, the most basic, level, all that is required is the bringing to mind of such things as specific facts or terminology, as stated in the subcategories. Typical verbs used to indicate this level are define, describe, identify, label, name, state, list, etc. However, it is important to remember that it is the context of the verb rather than the verb itself that will decide the level, as some verbs can be used at more than one level.

Level 2.00 Comprehension. This refers to understanding, which is usually demonstrated by the learner making limited use of the information. Such activities as paraphrasing a communication whilst maintaining the intent of the original would constitute translation. Interpretation can be observed by the learner summarizing or explaining information in his or her own words, and extrapolation is involved when information is projected beyond the given data. Typical verbs used at this level are paraphrase, translate, convert, explain, give examples.

Level 3.00 Application. The learner is required to apply rules, principles, concepts, etc. to real situations. These should be sufficiently unfamiliar to avoid the mere recall of previous behaviours. Typical verbs used at this level are demonstrate, discover, prepare, produce, relate, use, solve, show.

TABLE 4.1   Taxonomy of educational objectives: Cognitive domain

Level		Category		Subcategory	
1.00	Knowledge	1.10	of specifics	1.11	of terminology
				1.12	of specific facts
		1.20	of ways and means of dealing with specifics	1.21	of conventions
				1.22	of trends and sequences
				1.23	of classifications and categories
				1.24	of criteria
				1.25	of methodology
		1.30	of the universals and abstractions in a field	1.31	of principles and generalizations
				1.32	of theories and structures
2.00	Comprehension	2.10	Translation		
		2.20	Interpretation		
		2.30	Extrapolation		
3.00	Application				
4.00	Analysis	4.10	of elements		
		4.20	of relationships		
		4.30	of organizational principles		
5.00	Synthesis	5.10	Production of a unique communication		
		5.20	Production of a plan, or a proposed set of operations		
		5.30	Derivation of a set of abstract relations		
6.00	Evaluation	6.10	Judgements in terms of internal evidence		
		6.20	Judgement in terms of external criteria		

ADAPTED FROM BLOOM, 1956

Level 4.00 Analysis. This involves the ability to break down information into its component parts, which may be elements of information, relationships between elements, or organization and structure of information. Its purpose is to separate the important aspects of information from the less important, thus clarifying the meaning. Typical verbs are differentiate, discriminate, distinguish.

Level 5.00 Synthesis. At this level the learner is required to combine various parts into a new kind of whole. Creativity is present because the learner produces something unique, such as a plan or design. Typical verbs are compile, compose, create, devise, plan.

Level 6.00 Evaluation. This implies the ability to make judgements regarding the value of material and involves the use of criteria. Typical verbs are compare, contrast, criticize, justify, appraise, judge.

Table 4.2 identifies verbs associated with six levels of objectives.

TABLE 4.2 Verbs associated with six levels of objectives					
Knowledge and understanding			**High level intellectual skills**		
Knowledge	**Comprehension**	**Application**	**Analysis**	**Synthesis**	**Evaluation**
Recalling information	*Explaining information*	*Solving closed-ended problems*	*Solving open-ended problems*	*Creating answers to problems*	*Making critical judgements based on a sound knowledge base*
List	Report	Illustrate	Criticize	Manage	Evaluate
Relate	Review	Schedule	Analyze	Collect	Assess
Record	Translate	Interpret	Question	Propose	Judge
Underline	Describe	Demonstrate	Categorize	Compose	Estimate
Define	Discuss	Apply	Test	Prepare	Compare
Name	Express	Practise	Compare	Arrange	Conclude
Repeat	Identify	Employ	Contrast	Construct	Discriminate
Recognize	Explain	Operate	Debate	Plan	Value
Label	Justify	Prepare	Appraise	Create	Rate
Recall	Summarise	Verify	Experiment	Arrange	Defend

Table 4.3 gives examples of nursing objectives for the cognitive domain.

TABLE 4.3 Examples of nursing objectives for the cognitive domain
Level 1.00 Knowledge
States the four stages of the nursing process.
Defines the term 'psychoneurosis'.
Identifies the functions of the health education officer.
Outlines the three stages of normal labour.
Defines the term 'anaesthesia'.
Names the stages in child development as described by Piaget. It should be noted that all of these objectives are normally to be achieved without reference to notes or textbooks, so it is not necessary to include this in each statement.
Level 2.00 Comprehension
Translates the term 'haematemesis' into its English equivalent.
Summarizes Section 26 of the Mental Health Act 1959.
Gives three examples of the facilities available for the elderly in the community.
Explains in own words the methods available for contraception.
Gives one example of a potential threat to patient safety in the operating department.
Distinguishes between the clean and dirty dressing rooms in the Accident and Emergency department.

(continued)

TABLE 4.3   Examples of nursing objectives for the cognitive domain (*continued*)

Level 3.00 Application

Given the characteristics of ageing, relates these to the needs of the elderly in hospital.

Given the principles of care for a patient with pneumonia, relates these to the care of a particular patient with this condition.

Given the guideline for handling violence in hospital, applies these to the care of a patient with a psychopathic disorder.

Using the rules for calculation of an infant feed, calculates correctly the feed requirements of an infant of given weight and age.

Given the principles of aseptic technique, applies these when preparing trolleys for surgical operations in the operating department.

Level 4.00 Analysis

Given a list of 12 statements about the aetiology of diabetes mellitus, differentiates between those which are factual and those which are assumptions.

From a videotape depicting the performance of a surgical dressing, points out two instances of unsafe technique.

Given a series of 12 assertion–reason statements on psychiatric disorders, identifies at least four in which the reason is inaccurate.

Given a simulated case history of a community patient, distinguishes two inappropriate interventions.

Given a list of surgical instruments for laparotomy, identifies three omissions.

Given a list of nursing interventions in the Accident and Emergency department, discriminates between those that are important and those which are unimportant, in relation to cardiac arrest.

Level 5.00 Synthesis

Writes an original essay on 'The role of the nurse in care of the inpatient with multiple sclerosis'.

Devises a nursing care plan that meets the needs of a patient who has undergone cholecystectomy.

Produces an outline design for an Accident and Emergency department, which allows for the following:

   (1) one-way flow through the department

   (2) prevention of cross-infection

   (3) separate resuscitation area.

Given a list of personnel, designs an off-duty rota for a labour ward, which gives adequate coverage on all shifts.

Writes an original essay on 'The role of behaviourism in psychiatry'.

Devises a plan to meet the needs of a recently discharged lower-limb amputee in the community.

Level 6.00 Evaluation

Evaluates the arguments for and against the use of pertussis vaccine in infants.

Given three methods of contraception, judges which one is best, stating how this decision was reached and what criteria were used.

Justifies the continued use of bottle feeding as opposed to breast feeding in infants.

Compares and evaluates two approaches to the treatment of depression, stating the criteria used.

The affective domain   This domain has particular significance for nursing because it deals with the realm of feelings and attitudes, which constitute the caring functions. It is perhaps useful at this point to clarify what is meant by the terms 'attitude' and 'value'. Both of these are constructs, i.e. terms invented by psychologists to explain things that cannot be observed directly, but which must be inferred from the person's own account or his or her behaviour. 'Values' refer to the person's concept of what he or she considers desirable, and so has a large emotional component. A person's values may include sincerity, compassion, respect, etc. 'Attitudes', on the other hand, are positive or negative feelings about certain things and consist of both cognitive and affective aspects. People who feel that smoking is antisocial and that it endangers health are demonstrating a negative attitude towards smoking.

The affective domain consists of five levels, each of which is subdivided into categories. When writing objectives for this domain, it is essential to include within the written statement both the attitude or value in question, and the behaviour that will indicate the particular value or attitude.

Level 1.00 Receiving (attending) At this level the learner is sensitive to the existence of something and progresses from awareness to controlled or selective attention. It is difficult to tell when a learner is receiving or attending to something, so the best indicator is verbal behaviour. Typical verbs are 'ask', 'choose', 'select', 'reply'.

Level 2.00 Responding This is concerned with active response by the learner, although commitment is not yet demonstrated. The range is from reacting to a suggestion through to experiencing a feeling of satisfaction in responding. Typical verbs are 'answer', 'assist', 'comply', 'conform', 'help'.

Level 3.00 Valuing Objectives at this level indicate acceptance and internalization of the values or attitudes in question. The learner acts out these in everyday life in a consistent way. Typical verbs are 'initiate', 'invite', 'join', 'justify'.

Level 4.00 Organization Having internalized the value, the learner will encounter situations in which more than one value is relevant. This level is concerned with the ability to organize values and to arrange them in appropriate order. Typical verbs are 'alter', 'arrange', 'combine', 'modify'.

Level 5.00 Characterization This is the highest level, and having attained this level the learner has an internalized value system which has become his or her philosophy of life. These are the values that characterize an individual. Typical verbs are 'act', 'discriminate', 'listen', etc. Nurse students, unlike schoolchildren, will have acquired mature attitudes and values systems, because they enter nursing when mature. However, this domain is still most applicable to nurse education, as the learner may have to acquire new attitudes and values, or modify existing ones.

The psychomotor domain   Taxonomies in this domain have been developed by Harrow (1972) and Simpson (1972), the latter having more application to the type of skilled performance involved in nursing.

Level 1 Perception This basic level is concerned with the perception of sensory cues that guide actions and ranges from awareness of stimuli to translation into action. Typical verbs are 'chooses', 'differentiate', 'distinguish', 'identify', 'detect'.

Level 2 Set This is concerned with cognitive, affective and psychomotor readiness to act. Typical verbs are 'begin', 'move', 'react', 'show', 'start'.

Level 3 Guided responses These objectives refer to the early stages in skills acquisition where skills are performed following demonstration by the teacher. Typical verbs are 'carry out', 'make', 'perform', 'calculate'.

Level 4 Mechanism At this level, the performance has become habitual, but the movements are not as complex as the next higher level. Typical verbs are similar to the previous level.

Level 5 Complex overt response This level typifies the skilled performance and involves economy of effort, smoothness of action, accuracy and efficiency, etc. Again, verbs are similar to Level 6.

Level 6 Adaptation Here, the skills are internalized to such an extent that the nurse can adapt them to cater for special circumstances. Typical verbs are 'adapt', 'alter', 'modify', 'reorganize'.

Level 7 Origination This is the highest level, and concerns the origination of new movement patterns to suit particular circumstances. Typical verbs are 'compose', 'create', 'design', 'originate'.

Table 4.4 gives examples of nursing objectives for the psychomotor domain.

TABLE 4.4   Examples of nursing objectives for the psychomotor domain
Level 1. Perception Detects the need for pharyngeal suction in a patient, by listening to the sound of his or her breathing.
Level 2. Set Demonstrates the correct bodily position for lifting a patient.
Level 3. Guided response Performs urine testing as demonstrated by the instructor.
Level 4. Mechanism Sets a tray for an intramuscular injection.
Level 5. Complex overt response Applies with skill a stump bandage to a lower-limb amputee.
Level 6. Adaptation Modifies surgical dressing technique to suit a particular patient's circumstances.
Level 7. Origination Devises an original way of securing a dressing that has tended to come loose soon after application.

A critique of the behavioural objectives model

Although remaining influential in the design of curricula, the behavioural objectives model has been the subject of considerable criticism in the literature. Table 4.5 summarizes the viewpoints of both proponents and opponents of the model.

Perhaps a real-life example may help to show how much of the richness of the learning experience is lost by adhering strictly to a behavioural objectives model. Quinn (2000) describes sitting in on a lecture entitled 'The care of a child with leukaemia'; the teacher's stated objectives for the students were:

1. Recall the normal leucocyte blood picture.
2. State how the blood picture is altered in leukaemia.
3. Deduce some resulting signs and symptoms of leukaemia.
4. Suggest appropriate nursing care for an eight-year-old child undergoing chemotherapy in hospital.
5. Demonstrate an interest in the bone-marrow transplant form of treatment.

TABLE 4.5   Viewpoints of proponents and opponents of behavioural objectives model

Proponents

They provide the student with clear directions as to what must be learnt.

Their use encourages the teacher to examine his or her goals more carefully.

It is relatively easy to assess students' achievements, as behaviours are observable.

They can aid self-instruction.

They are accessible to public scrutiny.

They offer a rational system for curriculum planning.

Students on the whole tend to welcome the clarity that behavioural objectives bring to learning.

They provide a basis for comparison between similar courses in different institutions.

They offer a system for evaluation the performance of the teacher.

Opponents

They act as a set of blinkers that narrow the learning field.

They are difficult to formulate for higher level outcomes and hence encourage trivialization of learning by focusing on lower level outcomes.

They are almost impossible to formulate in the affective domain.

They ignore unanticipated outcomes of instruction.

It is impossible to state objectives for every learning outcome, even if this were desirable.

They are unsuitable for arts subjects such as music, poetry and drama.

They are unsuitable for science subjects, as they emphasize the learning of actual information rather than scientific enquiry.

Their use reflects a training approach rather than an educational one.

They encourage conformity rather than diversity.

It is wrong for one individual, i.e. the teacher, to dictate how another individual, i.e. the student should behave.

They are extremely time-consuming to formulate and require continuous updating.

These objectives seem perfectly acceptable outcomes for the lecture, but such was the skill of the teacher that by the end of the lecture Quinn was feeling a range of emotions that he subsequently wrote down to try to capture their essence:

■ feelings of empathy and caring for those children with leukaemia;

■ admiration for medical science and its new technology, which can offer treatment for children who would have been considered incurable a few years ago;

■ real appreciation of the frightening nature of treatment for leukaemia, especially the necessary isolation of the child during treatment for bone-marrow transplant;

■ feelings of pride for the courage of his fellow humans;

■ understanding of the principle of bone-marrow transplantation; and

■ motivation and a desire to help patients suffering from leukaemia and their relatives (adapted from Quinn, 2000).

It does seem from the list that there were many outcomes that could not have been anticipated by the teacher, yet they were very important results. Quinn suggests that one might argue that in the longer term they are much more important than the behavioural list that the teacher gave to the students, since he was more likely to remember and understand the principles of the lecture because of these feelings.

Stenhouse's process model of curriculum

One of the major critics of the behavioural objectives model was the late Lawrence Stenhouse, who formulated an alternative approach known as the 'process' model. He saw the use of behavioural objectives acting as a filter that distorted knowledge in schools.

> 'The filtering of knowledge through an analysis of objectives gives the school an authority and power over its students by setting arbitrary limits to speculation and by defining arbitrary solutions to unresolved problems of knowledge. This translates the teacher from the role of the student of a complex field of knowledge to the role of the master of the school's agreed version of that field.'
>
> Stenhouse (1975, p. 86)

Requirements for a curriculum

Stenhouse's (1975) minimum requirements for a curriculum are that a curriculum should offer:

1. *In planning:*
   a) principles for the selection of content – what is to be learned and taught;
   b) principles for the development of a teaching strategy – how it is to be learned and taught;
   c) principles for the making of decisions about sequence;
   d) principles on which to diagnose the strengths and weaknesses of individual students and differentiate the general principles (a), (b) and (c) above to meet individual cases;

2. *In empirical study:*
   a) principles on which to study and evaluate the progress of students;
   b) principles on which to study and evaluate the progress of teachers;
   c) guidance as to the feasibility of implementing the curriculum in varying school contexts, pupil contexts, environments and peer-group situations;
   d) information about the variability of effects in differing contexts and on different pupils and an understanding of the causes of the variation; and

3. *In relation to justification:*
   a) a formulation of the intention or aim of the curriculum that is accessible to critical scrutiny.

Stenhouse's position on behavioural objectives

Stenhouse believed that it was possible to organize the curriculum without having to specify in advance the behavioural changes that should occur in students; indeed, he argued that the purpose of education was to make student outcomes unpredictable. Knowledge does not consist of 'known facts' to be remembered, rather, it provides a basis for speculation and conjecture about a discipline. The content of a curriculum can be selected on the basis that it is worthwhile in itself and not merely as the means to achievement of a behavioural objective. Hence, we could argue that the content in a nursing curriculum can be chosen for its worthwhileness in providing examples of the key concepts, procedures and criteria of nursing science. Similarly, teaching methods and learning experiences can be specified in terms of their worthwhileness as learning activities. Stenhouse refers to these statements of worthwhileness as 'principles of procedure' and it is important to note that the principles of procedure for teaching are couched in terms of what the teacher will do rather than what the students will be able to do: for example, 'to encourage students to reflect on their experiences'.

The role of assessment in a process curriculum is very different from that in a product model, with the teacher's role being that of critic rather than marker. The teacher is cast in the role of critical appraiser of the student's work, with the emphasis on developing self-appraisal in the student. According to Stenhouse:

> 'The worthwhile activity in which teacher and student are engaged has standards and criteria immanent in it and the task of appraisal is that of improving students' capacity to work to such criteria by critical reaction to work done. In this sense, assessment is about the teaching of self-assessment.'
>
> Stenhouse (1975, p. 95)

The greatest weakness of the process model is identified by Stenhouse as its dependence upon the quality of the teacher. In this model, the teacher's commitment to professional development is vital; teachers need to see themselves as learners rather than as experts, and to be continually striving to improve their performance and judgement.

Beattie's fourfold model

Beattie's (1987) fourfold model of the curriculum draws upon his experience with nursing curricula. He suggests that there are four fundamental approaches to the task of planning a curriculum for nursing, each with its own particular strengths and weaknesses:

- *The curriculum as a map of key subjects.* As the name implies, this approach consists of mapping out the key subjects in the nursing curriculum, preferably integrating them by means of themes such as 'the human lifespan' to avoid the danger of an isolated collection of topics.

- *The curriculum as a schedule of basic skills.* This approach emphasizes the explicit specification of basic skills of nursing, these skills being culled from recent empirical research into nursing practice. A behavioural objectives approach can be appropriate here, provided that it is not used dogmatically for all aspects of teaching, particularly in relation to the knowledge base for clinical practice.

- *The curriculum as a portfolio of meaningful personal experiences.* This approach puts the students at the centre by organizing the curriculum around their interests and experiences. This is done by using a variety of experiential techniques such as action research, critical incidents, role-play and the like. There will always be a degree of tension between the unpredictability consequent upon student autonomy and the need to ensure sufficient opportunity to cover key areas.

■ *The curriculum as an agenda of important cultural issues.* This approach avoids giving detailed subject matter, focusing instead on controversial issues and political dilemmas in nursing and health care. These issues are chosen because they are open to debate and have no single correct answer, thereby stimulating discussion and enquiry, for example about nurse power or patient power.

How can nurse teachers use these ideas in practical curriculum planning? Beattie suggests that there are three ways of combining the fourfold framework. The first one he calls the 'eclectic curriculum', in which the four approaches are mixed together in some sort of combination. The main problem with this is that the more traditional approaches tend to dominate, leaving only the marginal inclusion of student-centred ideas. Another way is to negotiate each of the key areas with the consumers, the 'negotiated curriculum'. The third way Beattie calls the 'dialectical curriculum', in which the curriculum designer 'goes out to do battle', as it were, to engage in a deliberate, principled and committed struggle to combat, challenge and contest the dominant codes of curriculum (Beattie, 1987, p. 31). In his fourfold model of curriculum, Beattie argues that 'curriculum planners in nursing can and must move beyond simpleminded, 'single-model' approaches and towards complex, multifaceted strategies' (Beattie, 1987, p. 32).

MODELS OF TEACHING

Teaching is a deliberate and purposeful activity directed towards the promotion of learning. It normally comprises two basic elements:the teacher, i.e. the individual doing the promoting of learning, and the student/learner/recipient, i.e. the one whose learning is thus promoted. However, these elements are commonly combined from time to time, as when individuals teach themselves. Teaching can be, and is, carried out by any member of society, for example parents, trainers, etc., but there is also a profession called 'teaching' that includes teachers of children and adults. The element called 'teacher' need not refer exclusively to a human being; there are many non-human teaching resources available, such as computers, video.

A number of models exist that attempt to represent the nature of teaching, and a selection is outlined below.

The transmission model of teaching

This model conceptualizes teaching as a process in which the teacher transmits knowledge, skills and attitudes to the students, who are subsequently considered to have learned these capabilities. This model has been the basis of teaching for centuries and is still very much evident in the lecture method used in higher education. However, the model is not without its critics, who question the relatively passive role of the student in the process. Their reservations are neatly expressed in the aphorism 'the lecturer's notes are transmitted to the student's notes without passing through the brains of either'. Indeed, the model is often termed the 'empty vessel' model, implying that the students are empty vessels waiting for the teacher to fill them up with learning. One eminent proponent of the transmission model of teaching is David Ausubel (see Chapter 3), who argues that the model is the most efficient means of transmitting the culture of a society from one generation to another.

The facilitation model of teaching

In this model, the teacher is seen as a facilitator of learning rather than a transmitter of information, and one of the key originators is Carl Rogers (see Chapter 2). The facilitation of learning requires the setting up of an environment conducive to learning, including interaction between teacher and students in a challenging but non-threatening environment. Proponents of this model emphasize its appropriateness for individual learning and its relevance to life-skills. Opponents cite the time-consuming nature of such activities and the consequent inability to adequately cover the syllabus.

TEACHING TIP

These two models of teaching are at different poles. Have another look at Chapter 2 to see how the learning theories support or otherwise these models. Think about the model of teaching you will try and exemplify.

CURRICULUM DEVELOPMENT

The basic principles of curriculum development apply to both pre-registration and post-registration provision, although there are some differences in approach between these. Pre-registration courses or programmes in nursing and midwifery tend to be offered in both full-time and part-time modes, whereas post-registration continuing education programmes are largely part time.

Since pre-registration programmes form the entry gate to the nursing or midwifery professions they must meet the criteria laid down by the NMC. Post-registration programmes and courses are, on the whole, less constrained by such requirements and provide scope for curriculum designers to be much more flexible and imaginative.

Curriculum development needs to be distinguished from curriculum design at this point:

- *Curriculum development* is a broad concept that encompasses all the processes involved in the production and implementation of a curriculum, from the initial idea through to monitoring and review of its operation.

- *Curriculum design* is a focused activity concerned with questions of structure, content and process, for example curriculum philosophy and model, content-mapping, organization and sequencing of content, etc. It is a subcomponent of curriculum development.

Although nursing curricula within the UK will differ one from another, there will be certain common aspects. For example, the now defunct English National Board describes a documentary analysis of nursing degree curricula undertaken by University College, Suffolk (ENB, 1999) which sets out the similarities and differences between nursing degree curriculum documents from 32 institutions. The ways in which the documents were comparable included:

- The graduate nurse was conceptualized as an innovative leader, flexible, and able to manage change.

- Level descriptors were comparable, but there was difficulty in articulating higher levels of practice.
- Preparation of practice assessors was similar.
- Students were required to undertake a substantial piece of independent work over a period of time.
- For post-registration programmes, there was a common emphasis on flexible delivery.

The documents differed in a number of ways including:

- considerable variation in whether or not practical skills were assessed by direct observation, particularly in post-registration degrees;
- fundamental differences in course structure;
- lack of comparability of distribution of the 360 credits throughout degree programme components;
- no sense of common currency of credits in either learning time or student achievement;
- variation in whether or not students were required to undertake research within their dissertation.

Before proceeding to discuss curriculum development in detail, it may be helpful to highlight the context in which higher education curricula operate, including the important concept of accreditation of prior learning (APL).

Higher education credit schemes in relation to curriculum development

Many higher education institutions use the concept of credit schemes to structure their academic awards. Programmes within a credit scheme are composed of large numbers of discrete, self-contained courses or courses of learning that are designated either core or option. Core courses are compulsory, whereas option courses offer the student a degree of choice. Each course is described in the form of a course specification, and the typical components are shown in Table 4.6.

The complete set of core and option courses will differ from student to student, according to the option courses that they choose. The basic criterion for the inclusion of an option course within a student's programme of study is that he or she must be able to demonstrate its coherence and relevance to the overall programme.

Take the example of a nurse working within the field of sexually transmitted diseases who is undertaking a post-registration degree in nursing studies. This particular nurse may choose to study an option course from a social science degree programme on human sexuality, since this would be relevant to his or her particular professional needs and interests. Similarly, an option course on personnel management from a diploma in management studies may be undertaken so as to improve both knowledge and skills as a departmental manager.

In credit schemes, a specified number of credit points are awarded to the student on successful completion of appropriate learning, and these can be gained in three ways:

- through formal study on a programme;
- from existing qualifications;
- from professional or life experience.

TABLE 4.6 Typical components of a course specification

Course title	Should concisely indicate the nature of the course
Department	
Credit points and learning time	Proportion of a full-time year
Level	Credit level 4, 5, 6, 7, 8
Code	For computer records
Co-ordinator	Individual responsible for delivery
Prerequisite and co-requisite	Courses that must be taken before or concurrently with the course
Rationale	Justifies the inclusion of the course in the programme
Aims	Identify the overall purpose of the course
Learning outcomes	State what the student can do as a result of learning, e.g. 'Analyze the factors which influence the effectiveness of nurse–patient interaction'
Process of learning and teaching	Range of activities to achieve learning
Assessment	Means of testing achievement of learning
Indicative content	List of key topics
Indicative reading	List of representative texts

The system of credit points takes as its standard a three-year full-time undergraduate degree with honours, which is credit rated at 360 credit points, 120 for each of the three years of the course. Each year represents a specific level of learning:

First year = level 4
Second year = level 5
Third year = level 6

There is also a Level M for postgraduate study at Master's degree level. Credit points gained from appropriate learning can accumulate towards a higher education award such as a diploma or degree, and the amount and level of credit normally required for these in England, Wales and Northern Ireland is shown below (QAA, 2009).

■ Certificate of higher education: 120 credit points at level 4
■ Diploma of higher education: 240 credit points, 120 at each of levels 4 and 5
■ Unclassified degree: 360 credit points, of which a minimum of 60 must be at level 6
■ Degree with honours: 360 credit points, of which a minimum of 120 must be at level 6
■ Postgraduate diploma: 70 credit points, of which a minimum of 50 must be at Master's level (level 7)
■ Master's degree: 120 credit points, of which a minimum of 80 must be at Master's level (level 7) and the remainder at level 6.

The system in Scotland differs from that in the three countries above, in that there are 12 levels: SCQF 7, SCQF 8, SSCF 9 and SCQF 10. The first three levels equate with the certificate, diploma and unclassified degree as shown above, but the degree with honours (SCQF 11) requires 480 credit points, where a minimum of 90 are at SCQF level 9 and a minimum of 90 are at SCQF level 10 (SCQF 2012).

Accreditation of prior learning

One of the fundamental principles of credit schemes is that students who have been awarded credit points from one institution can transfer them to studies in another institution. The NMC (2010) advise all higher education institutions to develop their own APL procedures based on best practice in line with the Quality Assurance Agency's current guidelines. The contribution of existing credits, gained outside the awarding institution, towards a higher education award is termed APL (accreditation of prior learning). In order for credit to count towards an award it must be relevant to that award and be at an appropriate level. The length of time since the course was completed also affects its current relevance, so APL is normally confined to courses completed within the previous five years. There is a maximum percentage of APL that can be counted towards an award; for pre-registration programme this is 50 per cent of the total credit required for that award (NMC 2010). In credit schemes a distinction is made between general credit and specific credit, as the following vignette illustrates in Box 4.1.

BOX 4.1

Mitzi was halfway through the second year of a degree in nursing when her husband's company decided to transfer him to the north of England office. She contacted the university nearest to her new address and was told that there was currently no degree in nursing available, but a degree in health studies was well established. Mitzi had earned a total of 240 credit points from her previous nursing degree studies, 120 at each of Levels 4 and 5. However, because the focus was nursing rather than generic health studies, Mitzi was allowed to count only 80 of her Level 5 credit points towards the health studies degree.

Credit awarded to a student for specified learning in one institution is termed general credit and can be transferred to studies in other higher education institutions. The receiving institution, however, may decide that only a proportion of this general credit is actually relevant to its course, and this proportion of the general credit is termed specific credit. If any specific credit matches the learning outcomes of a unit on the course to which the student is transferring, then he or she can be given exemption from that unit.

Deciding the amount of credit

Course leaders in institutions are often faced with the task of deciding how much credit should be allowed for previous qualifications, and this is doubly difficult in the case of courses that do not carry a national credit rating. There are two aspects to be considered when examining sources of evidence about courses:

■ *Quantity of learning* This is based upon a full-time higher education academic year, with adjustment for variations in length of NHS-related courses

- *Quality of learning* In order to appraise the quality of learning, it is necessary to scrutinize:

  a) Level of learning as defined in the scheme definitions; for example, Cardiff University level 6 definition for health schemes is: 'Practitioners who demonstrate an increased level of competence through higher clinical decision-making skills and the delivery of evidence-based care; enhanced knowledge and skills in the interpretation of evidence and its application to care that is clinically effective; and the ability to meet the requirements of contemporary health care with the level of expertise demanded of clinical practice in the 21st century'.

  b) Appropriateness of the aims and outcomes of the course and the relationship between these and the definitions of learning.

  c) Appropriateness of the learning and teaching processes.

  d) Reliability and validity of course assessment in relation to (a), (b) and (c) above.

Accreditation of prior experiential learning

When earlier the concept of APL was discussed, the focus was on learning gained from previous qualifications, but prior learning can also be gained from the day-to-day experience of professional practice or of life generally, as in rearing a child or writing a book. It is important to note that experience alone is insufficient; the student must demonstrate how he or she has learned from the experience. A useful theoretical basis for APEL is given by Kolb (1984) in his experiential learning cycle, which is discussed in Chapter 2. Credit points can be given for such experiential learning provided that it is relevant to the award which the student is seeking to achieve and that a portfolio of evidence for such learning has been presented for accreditation to the awarding institution.

Making an APEL Claim   There are several steps in making a claim for Accreditation of Prior Experiential Learning, which should be supported by a portfolio of written evidence (QAA, 2004; Butterworth, 1993).

- Focus on the area of learning and summarize it in a learning claim. The first step in putting together an APEL claim is for students to decide upon which part of their past experience they wish to base their claim; this can be one large experience or more than one, provided that it is reasonably substantial. It is not usually possible to use many small experiences to build up a claim, as this would lack the necessary coherence.

- Clearly identify and list the learning outcomes derived from the experience. Learning outcomes need to be stated in a precise form rather than in vague, general statements, and must encompass all the knowledge and skills that were learned.

- Check that the learning is relevant and at the right level for the award that is being sought. The claim must be current; i.e. the experience should have been within the last five years, sufficient, and relevant to the award being sought

- Collect sufficient documentary evidence to support the claim, together with at least one suitable testimonial authenticating it. Direct evidence constitutes the student's own work, such as reports, plans, and materials that have been designed, that will demonstrate achievement of the learning outcomes. Indirect evidence refers to testimonials and other evidence from external sources. It is also advisable to include formal certificates or transcripts of qualifications achieved.

- Produce a reflective commentary that describes the experiences and analyses them to show how they produced the learning that is being claimed and the extent to which this learning and/or experience demonstrates the achievement of the programme outcomes/values. This is a very important stage, as it demonstrates the student's ability to reflect upon and conceptualize the experiences.

- Present an outline of APEL portfolio at a formative assessment tutorial. This involves discussion with the APEL advisor about the appropriateness and sufficiency of the claim, and the quality of the reflective commentary.

- Collate all this material and organize it in the form of a portfolio that can be presented to an assessor. The portfolio can be assessed by the APEL advisor or by a 'gatekeeper' who has not been involved with the student's preparation. The portfolio should contain a contents page and each chapter should be clearly labelled.

Stages of curriculum development

There are four stages in the curriculum development process: exploratory, design, implementation and monitoring and review.

Exploratory stage

It is important that education providers liaise closely with service providers to identify gaps in the provision of nursing and midwifery education so that new courses or programmes can be developed to meet those needs. Ideas for new provision should be carefully explored before being either adopted or rejected, and a core team should be set up to this effect. Market research is vitally important to ascertain the views of employers and other interested parties such as statutory bodies. The availability of resources and expertise within the university needs to be explored, and the estimated costs of development will have to be calculated for eventual inclusion in any contract. It is useful to undertake an initial critical path analysis for the development so that a realistic idea of the timescale is gained.

Design stage

If a decision is made to go ahead with the development, a curriculum planning team should be set up to prepare the course or programme for validation and subsequent implementation. The actual process of design and validation is discussed in the next section of this chapter.

Implementation stage

In this stage students have been recruited, all systems are in place, and the curriculum is fully operational. In the early days of implementation, a few teething troubles can be expected until the systems have been fine tuned. For example, the offering of a choice of option courses to students may result in some courses being undersubscribed and others oversubscribed. During the implementation stage, curriculum evaluation is ongoing by means of course evaluation. This does not refer to the assessment of students' achievement of course outcomes, but to the systematic collection of opinions about the quality and usefulness of the courses.

Monitoring and review stage (refer to NMC monitoring)

Although the evaluation of programme courses is an ongoing process, the monitoring and review stage can be usefully seen as a distinct phase in the curriculum. In HE, programme leaders – in consultation with programme committees – are required to produce an annual programme-monitoring report. This report is retrospective for the previous academic year and requires the programme director to reflect upon the quality of the programme using data gathered from a variety of sources such as students' evaluations of courses, external examiners' reports, and the views of employers. This report is scrutinized at a series of meetings before being discussed at a faculty board or academic board. Annual programme monitoring is therefore an important mechanism for ensuring quality on the programme.

When a programme receives approval following validation, a timescale for programme review will be proposed. The length of approval ranges from as little as one year through to indefinite approval, but, regardless of length, continuation of the programme is dependent upon a satisfactory programme review. A review is very similar to a validation event, but the programme team is required to produce a detailed review of the operation of the programme over the prescribed timescale. Proposals for changes must be accompanied by a well-argued rationale and supporting evidence.

CURRICULUM DESIGN

This constitutes the second stage of the curriculum planning process as outlined above. The core team, formed during the exploratory stage to consider the feasibility of the development, now needs to be augmented by a small number of other individuals possessing the required knowledge and experience with reference to the curriculum in question. In curriculum development groups for nursing and midwifery, particularly for pre-registration programmes, the range of representation commonly includes teaching staff, students, and hospital and community service managers. The last group represents the various specialisms of nursing, such as learning difficulties, community nursing, and children's nursing, and are usually chosen to reflect representation from each health district or trust to which the university relates. The curriculum development group should have a chairperson, and it is sufficient to have notes of the decisions made at meetings rather than formal minutes.

Critical path analysis

One of the first issues to be addressed by the group should be a critical path analysis, which identifies deadlines for each aspect of the development. It is useful to work backwards from the proposed date of the validation event, allowing several weeks before the event for the documentation to be available to validation panel members. Other deadlines that need to be included are the first draft of the validation document, the internal validation event, and the printing of the document. A specimen critical path analysis for curriculum development is shown in Figure 4.2

FIGURE 4.2   Specimen critical path analysis for curriculum development

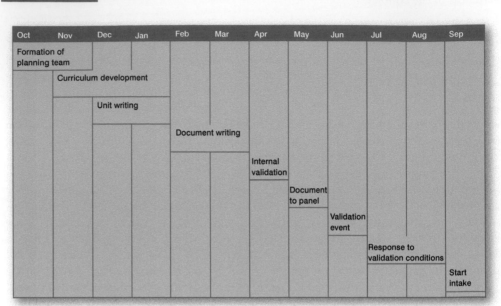

Incorporating statutory body guidelines into the curriculum

Another issue that needs to be addressed early in the development is the question of curriculum 'givens', i.e. the university's regulations on programme development and validation, and the requirements and guidelines of the NMC. For example, the NMC has produced standards for pre-registration nursing education (NMC, 2010) that address a range of domains for each field of nursing including professional values; communication and interpersonal skills; nursing practice and decision making; and leadership, management and team working.

Approval in principle and statement of intent

In 2001, the Nursing Midwifery Order provided legislative powers for the NMC to approve and monitor the standards of educational programmes that lead to entry on to the register and the educational institutions delivering these programmes. Programme approval is jointly undertaken between the NMC, higher education institutions and other stakeholders, which may include clinical placement providers and purchasers of the programme.

Institutions of higher education and statutory bodies both have mechanisms for granting approval in principle, which is normally required before the team can proceed with curriculum development. However, the NMC has no responsibility for the framework of professional development programmes so responsibility for such programmes lies with each individual higher education institution. In the higher education sector, approval in principle normally requires the completion of a planning proposal form which outlines the academic rationale and the resource implications of the proposed programme. The proposal is then considered by the appropriate body at faculty level.

Cardiff University (2009) requirements for the introduction of new programmes of study include the following information:

- Proposing school
- Programme title, type of award and mode of delivery
- Rationale of the proposed programme
- Name of designated programme organizer
- Proposed commencement date
- The likelihood of involvement from other schools within the university
- Name of professional accreditation (if applicable)
- Evidence of local, national, international demand
- Staff resources to support the programme
- Resources to support learning and teaching.

The proposal of a new programme of study is then scrutinized by a number of committees. The School Board approves initial documentation for further development and a proposal cannot proceed without the approval of the Head of School and School Board. The proposal then moves through a series of panels, including the School Advisory Panel, Programme Approval Panel, Academic Standards and Quality Committee before it is finally approved by the Academic Policy Committee.

Writing the validation submission document

Another key component of curriculum development is the validation submission document; the writing of this should, ideally be the responsibility of one person, although informed by the team. The document should be written in parallel with the development so that key aspects are captured as they happen. Higher education institutions differ in their requirements for validation documents, but there is a general structure common to all. The format for programme documentation used in Cardiff University is shown in Table 4.7.

TABLE 4.7 Format for validation submission document (adapted from Cardiff University, 2009)
1. Programme title, type of award, programme manager, length and mode of study
2. Introduction and rationale
3. Admissions policy
4. Level, aims and intended learning outcomes
5. Programme structure, content and delivery
6. Assessment strategy
7. Academic standards and quality assurance
8. Regulations and programme administration
9. Support for students
10. Financial, physical and human resources.

For conjoint validation with the NMC, the validation submission document must address the NMC standards and criteria for programme approval.

Curriculum rationale and model

One of the key sections of the validation document is Section 2, the rationale of the programme. The purpose of the rationale is to outline the philosophy and model upon which the curriculum is based, and all other components of the programme must be congruent with this rationale. For example, the rationale for a nursing curriculum may define the student as an autonomous, reflective individual who is responsible for his or her own learning. Hence, the timetable should provide adequate time for private study and reflection, but if the day is fully programmed with lectures and teaching contact, then there is clearly a mismatch between the rationale and the teaching and learning process. Such incongruence would be seriously questioned at a validation event. The development team may decide to use any one of the curriculum models outlined earlier in this chapter, in their curriculum. On the other hand, they may wish to adapt an existing model to fit their ideas, or devise an entirely new one. Curriculum development teams may be tempted to include a model in their validation document simply because it is expected, but unless the model helps to conceptualize the curriculum it will quickly be detected as irrelevant by the panel.

Organizing and sequencing of curriculum content

The curriculum rationale guides the selection of content, but not the sequencing and organization of that content into some form of logical order. The latter is important if students are to be able to make sense of the programme of study and is achieved by means of a conceptual framework or model. Bernstein (1971) identifies two approaches to content organization in curricula:collection and integration. In a 'collection' curriculum, subjects are taught as separate, isolated entities with clear-cut boundaries, the emphasis being on depth of treatment. In contrast, 'integrated' curricula focus on common themes that unite various subjects, and the emphasis is on breadth of coverage. Collection curricula are typified by timetables containing 'slots' with separate subjects such as 'anatomy' and 'physiology' and 'psychology'. Integrated curricula, on the other hand, consist of broad themes such as 'the individual in pain'. Simmons and Bahl (1992) describe an integrated approach to curriculum development at post-registration level. In nurse education, they see integration having two main meanings: integration of content can be achieved by linking academic disciplines, and also theory and practice; integration also applies to student groups, where students from different branches of nursing, or from other professions, learn together. They describe their PEP curriculum model for post-registration education as developing individual practitioners in three areas: professional development, educational development, and personal development.

Academic validation of curricula

Academic validation is the programme or course approval process used in higher education. It consists of a carefully selected panel of academics that engages the programme team in discussion about the programme curriculum and decides whether or not the programme is approved to run. Validation needs to be distinguished from an allied concept: accreditation. Many programmes and courses in higher education involve professional education and training, and as such are subject not only to university regulations, but also to the requirements for professional recognition by the appropriate professional body. These requirements are safeguarded by the process of professional accreditation, which may consist of scrutiny of the programme documentation alone, or by an accreditation event. The latter is usually combined with a validation event, so that both academic validation and professional accreditation are undertaken at the same time.

In nursing and midwifery, however, there is an additional category called conjoint validation, in which the NMC, higher education institution and other stakeholders are equal partners in the validation process. Once the curriculum development work has been completed the programme can be advertised provided that it states 'subject to validation'.

The validation event is seen as the culmination of the work of the curriculum development team and, if carried out in the right spirit, can be a stimulating academic debate between peers. There are three types of validation: internal, mock and full validation.

- *Internal validation* is a formal component of the quality assurance mechanism of the institution, and consists of a meeting between the curriculum development team and selected members of the institution. The curriculum submission is scrutinized in a similar way to a final validation, using a small panel of internal members of the institution who have no direct involvement with the curriculum in question. Feedback from internal validation is incorporated into the draft validation document, after which it is sent for printing.
- *Mock validation* is the name given to a practice validation event, which is conducted exactly like a real event, the aim of which is to test the team's cohesiveness and ability to defend their curriculum design.
- *Full validation* is a major academic event in which a panel of academic staff is assembled to engage and challenge the programme team on their curriculum design.

Membership of validation panels

The higher education sector has strict guidelines for the choice of panel members, and typical membership is as follows:

- chair – a senior member of staff drawn from the committee responsible for academic standards in the university, who is not from the faculty submitting the programme;
- one academic from the host school, who was not involved in the development;
- one academic from outside the host school;
- an external practitioner who is a practising professional in an appropriate field, or a potential employer of graduates from the programme.

The validation event

Programme development teams usually experience some anxiety when approaching a validation event, since it is important for them to achieve a successful outcome.

However, a validation event is one of the few opportunities that educators have to engage in real academic debate about philosophical and practical educational issues. The programme development team will have received in advance the key agenda issues that the panel wish to cover, but should be prepared also for other issues to be raised during the event. The most important aspect of a programme is the quality of the staff who will be teaching on it, so the programme team must project a confident, informed and cohesive impression. This means that contributions should be distributed amongst the entire team, and not dominated by any one individual. Having said this, it is equally important that the programme director designate should maintain a high profile during the event, and this can be done by taking the lead in some areas of questioning, and by inviting other members of the team to answer particular questions. It is useful to have decided in advance of the event which team member will answer questions on a particular area, such as assessment or admissions. This ensures that no team member should be caught out by not having a satisfactory answer ready. Self-confidence and conviction are the keys to successful validation; the panel are fellow educationalists and peers, so the programme team need not feel intimidated by them. The chair of the event has an important role in keeping the dialogue constructive rather than confrontational, although it is important to encourage an atmosphere of rigorous challenge and debate. There are a number of possible outcomes of a validation event:

- approval for an indefinite length of time, with review at a given time, for example every five years;
- approval for a fixed length of time, for example five years, after which the programme is then subject to review;
- approval that is conditional upon fulfilment of certain requirements within a specified timescale; and
- approval withheld.

Conditional approval is a very common outcome of validation events, and conditions can be imposed for any aspect of the curriculum. For example, the assessment strategy may need to be amended, certain regulations modified, an evaluation carried out by the end of the first year, or a students' handbook produced. Conditional approval will always carry a date by which the conditions must be met, and this can vary from a few weeks to a whole year. The programme development team must make a satisfactory response to the conditions, and this is sent to all panel members. Once the panel has agreed that the conditions have been met, the amendments are incorporated into the validation document, and this then becomes the definitive programme document. This is housed in the library for general access by students and anyone else who is interested in the programme.

Staff development for practice supervisors

Whilst the curriculum group is developing its work, there needs to be a parallel development with the in-service training department to plan for the anticipated training needs of qualified staff who will be involved in the new curriculum. Opportunities must be made available for such staff to spend time in workshops and for study days that relate to specific aspects of the new curriculum.

EQUALITY AND DIVERSITY

Equality of opportunity is a central tenet of modern education, and relates to all aspects of higher education curricula as well as to wider aspects of institutional management. The QAA (2010) recognize that disabled students are integral to the academic community and are entitled to education that meets their individual requirements. They emphasise that accessible and appropriate education should not be viewed as 'additional' but a core element of the overall service that an institution makes available. The entitlements of disabled students need to be managed and have their quality assured in the same way as any other provision. Institutions should be able to address individual cases effectively and also manage their provision in a way that develops an inclusive culture.

The Equality Act [2010] aims to 'protect disabled people and prevent disability discrimination' and provides legal rights for disabled people in terms of:

- employment;
- education;
- access to goods, services and facilities;
- buying and renting land or property;
- functions of public bodies.

The Act defines a disabled person as a person with 'a physical or mental impairment which has a substantial and long term adverse effect on his ability to carry out normal day-to-day activities'. This means that:

- The person must have an impairment that is either physical or mental.
- The impairment must have adverse effects which are substantial.
- The substantial adverse effects must be long-term.
- The long-term substantial adverse effects must be effects on normal day-to-day activities.

The NMC (2010, p. 52) stipulate that providers of nursing and midwifery education tackle essential aspects of equality and diversity and comply with current legislation and state that all students have the right to be treated fairly so programme providers must ensure equality of opportunity, regardless of race, disability, age, gender, religion or sexual orientation. The QAA (2010) have laid down general principles for higher education institutions regarding disabled students (Figure 4.3).

Equality means having the same chances in life as everybody else (HM Government, 2010). Gravells and Simpson (2012, p. 8) define equality as 'the rights of students to have access to, attend, and participate in their chosen learning experience', which is underpinned by the Equality Act (2010) and is regardless of ability and circumstances. The authors further define this meaning in the following sentence:

'In the past, equality has often been described as everyone being the same or having the same opportunities. Now it can be described as everyone being different but having equal rights.'

Gravells and Simpson (2012)

FIGURE 4.3   The general principles for higher education institutions regarding disabled students (adapted from QAA, 2010)

Higher Education providers must enable disabled students to participate in all aspects of the academic and social life of the institution

Senior managers should lead their institution's development of inclusive policy and practice in relation to the enhancement of disabled students' experience across the institution. Information relating to disclosure of impairments is used appropriately to monitor the applications, admissions and academic progress of disabled students

Systems should be in place to monitor the effectiveness of education provision for disabled students, evaluate progress and identify opportunities for enhancement

Continuing professional development should enable staff to enhance their knowledge, reflect upon and contribute towards a fully inclusive institutional culture. Programme details and general information are accessible and include explanations of how the entitlements of disabled students are met

Admissions processes and application of entry criteria include consideration of the duty to promote disability equality. Disabled applicants' requirements are identified and assessed in an effective and timely way. Arrangements for enrolment, registration and induction of new entrants meet the entitlements of disabled students

Assessment of the extent to which the programme is inclusive of disabled students is included in new programmes and the review and/or revalidation of existing programmes

Admissions processes and application of entry criteria include consideration of the duty to promote disability equality. Disabled applicants' requirements are identified and assessed in an effective and timely way. Arrangements for enrolment, registration and induction of new entrants meet the entitlements of disabled students

Assessment of the extent to which the programme is inclusive of disabled students is included in new programmes and the review and/or revalidation of existing programmes

Design and implementation of learning and teaching strategies and the learning environment, recognise the entitlement of disabled students to participate in all activities provided as part of their programme of study

Disabled students are given the opportunity to demonstrate the achievement of learning outcomes and competence standards within assessment practices. Academic support and guidance are accessible and appropriate for disabled students

Institutions have a range of ways in which disabled students can be aided by ICT and to provide students and staff with the information to enable them to make the best use of assistive technologies. Disabled students have access to the full range of student services provided by the institution and that facilities and equipment are as accessible as possible

There are sufficient members of staff with appropriate skills and experience to provide specialist advice and support to disabled applicants and students and to the staff who work with them

Disabled students have access to careers education, information and guidance that supports their progression to employment or further study. All students are able to access the physical environment in which they will study, learn, live and take part in the social life of their institution

Information on all policies and procedures that affect students' ability to complete their studies and assessments is available in accessible formats and communicated to students. Policies and procedures are operated in a way which does not lead to disadvantages to disabled students that arise from the nature of impairment

Diversity is all about valuing and respecting students' differences, regardless of ability, circumstances or any individual characteristics they may have (Gravells and Simpson, 2012). In 2007 the Disability Rights Commission conducted an investigation examining the barriers that disabled people faced when entering, and staying in nursing, teaching and social work. They found that disabled people were discouraged from becoming nurses, social workers and teachers and were sometimes discriminated against before they applied to higher education. The Commission identified particular barriers for students with dyslexia, especially within nursing and made the following profound statement:

> 'There is a common perception that people with dyslexia cannot read and are therefore automatically a risk. However, the nature of dyslexia varies from person to person and many people with dyslexia develop effective coping strategies, including practices and procedures that can enhance safe working for all nurses.'
>
> Disability Rights Commission (2007)

To support this, a research study by the QAA (2009) into the experience of disabled students found that barriers to learning opportunities were still present, whether in physical access to facilities or in inclusivity of teaching methods. Types of disability observed in higher education students can be mainly categorised as a disability that can be seen or one that is considered unseen or invisible as follows:

Seen disabilities

- Physical disability, for example, blindness, lower/upper limb impairment
- Mobility difficulties (with or without the use of mobility aids, for example, walking stick, crutches, wheelchair).

Unseen disabilities

- Medical conditions (long term conditions might include chronic pain, irritable bowel syndrome, rheumatoid arthritis, asthma, epilepsy, bipolar disorder, diabetes or chronic fatigue, which frequently accompanies a long term condition)
- Hearing impairment
- Mental health difficulties
- Specific learning difficulties (this might include dyslexia, dyspraxia, dyscalculia).

There are many barriers to learning for students with both seen and unseen disabilities and whilst the following list only highlights a few, a more comprehensive understanding can be gained from the reference list and further reading section at the end of this chapter.

Barriers to learning

- The location of teaching venues should be accessible and reasonably close together so breaks provide time for students to move between them.
- Students may need to use specialist equipment and this can include assistive software to ergonomic aids so that they can work effectively and comfortably in any learning environment.

■ Some students may need easy access to toilet facilities whilst others may need permission to eat or drink during lectures.

■ Some students may experience difficulty in generating notes during lectures so a trained support worker who can act as note takers can be utilised. Most universities also liaise with outside agencies such as the RNID should a BSL interpreter or speed text operator be required. Support workers can also assist disabled students with mobility difficulties, assist with locating textbooks and using IT equipment, word process student notes and proof reading.

Curriculum provision for students with disabilities

It is important that nurse teachers have an understanding of approaches to disabled students if the latter are not to be disadvantaged so institutions should invest in equality and diversity training for staff in order for them to be able to respond to students' varying needs. Before a programme or module commences some students may disclose a disability or learning difficulty, whilst others may not. It is important to note that 'disability' is a term that some students do not always associate with themselves although they may recognize that they have particular learning needs. Additionally it should be recognized that some disabilities or impairment have not yet been diagnosed or that a student's culture may prohibit them to disclose or seek advice and/or help. Programme specifications should include no unnecessary barriers to access by disabled people (QAA, 2010) and institutions should consider establishing procedures which ensure that:

■ The setting/amendment of academic programme requirements during approval or validation processes includes well-informed consideration of the requirements of disabled students.

■ Programme specifications and descriptors give sufficient information to enable students with disabilities and staff to make informed decisions about the ability to complete the programme (QAA, 2010).

Candidates for nursing or midwifery education are required to possess the physical and mental ability to carry out the demands of the role of nurse or midwife, so this precludes the selection of candidates with severe disabilities. However, candidates may have a degree of disability that does not prevent them from carrying out the role, for example visual impairment, hearing impairment, a physical disability, or dyslexia. Nurse teachers need to take the needs of such students into account during their teaching. For example, they may need to provide paper copies of overhead transparencies for students with visual impairment and ensure that, when talking to students with a hearing impairment, they face the student and speak clearly.

Nurse teachers may encounter students with dyslexia, both diagnosed and undiagnosed; in the latter case, the following indicators may suggest dyslexia:

■ *Reading difficulties* – indicators may include:
  ● slow reading speed;
  ● inability to scan text;
  ● inaccurate reading, omission of words;
  ● loss of place when reading;
  ● difficulty in extracting the main points;
  ● perceived distortion of written words.

- *Writing problems* – indicators may include:
  - spelling difficulties;
  - confusion of small words such as with/which;
  - omission of words;
  - awkward handwriting, slow writing speed;
  - a marked discrepancy between verbal and written performance.

- *Other difficulties* – indicators may include:
  - numeracy – difficulty with mathematical formulae, weak computational skills;
  - oral skills – lack of logical structure in oral presentation, difficulties with mispronunciation and word retrieval;
  - memory – short-term memory may be less effective; inefficient working/short-term memory can cause problems when following instructions;
  - concentration – high levels of distractibility; short attention span; high levels of energy needed to concentrate;
  - organization – poor awareness of time; problems with time management.

Student support mechanisms in higher education

Universities will have a member of staff, such as a learner support co-ordinator who has expertise in dealing with dyslexia, and students should be referred to this individual in the first instance. The student may then be referred for in-house assessment or for psychometric testing by an educational psychologist. Dyslexic students need special help with writing their assignments, and nurse teachers should provide careful feedback on how to construct an essay. It may be necessary to arrange for extra time during examinations, or even to make arrangements for students to be examined by a viva rather than by a written examination. Most dyslexic students benefit from using a computer, and software packages are available to augment standard word-processing software in terms of spelling and syntax.

By making some very simple adaptations to their teaching practice in lectures, seminars and classes, educators can help to ensure that disabled students are not substantially disadvantaged. In other cases, reasonable adjustments will need to be made in response to the particular needs of individual students and to help them overcome their difficulties (RCN, 2010). The QAA (2010) define a reasonable adjustment as a legal requirement for institutions to take reasonable steps to prevent a disabled student from being placed at a disadvantage with regard to his or her learning opportunities. Gravells and Simpson (2012) believe that the Equality Act [2010] presents considerable challenges for lecturers because they are required to anticipate the needs of disabled students and ensure that reasonable adjustments are in place to avoid any disadvantage when compared to a non-disabled student.

The Equality and Human Rights Commission identifies a series of questions to be considered prior to any teaching and learning activity:

- Are lecture theatres and other rooms allocated and timetabled with the needs of disabled students in mind (physical access, lighting and acoustics may be relevant issues to consider)?
- Do lecturers face the front when they speak, including when they are using slides or writing on a board? Amongst others, this assists those who are lip-reading.

- Do lecturers provide their handouts in advance and online? Amongst others, this supports students who are dyslexic.
- Do staff use microphones or allow taping of lectures/classes where this would assist students?
- Do lecturers pace their delivery and where necessary allow brief breaks to enable students and sign language interpreters to keep up?
- Where students have assistants, such as note takers or interpreters, are questions and comments directed to the student rather than to the assistant?
- Are students with communication difficulties, or those who may find presentations difficult for other reasons, supported when preparing presentations?
- Do tutors ensure that only one person speaks at a time during discussions? Amongst others, this assists those who are deaf or hard of hearing.
- In discussions do tutors ensure that all are enabled to contribute regardless of apparent communication barriers?

OPEN, DISTANCE AND FLEXIBLE LEARNING

The educational literature is replete with definitions of open, distance and flexible learning, but little consensus has yet emerged. To be fair, the terms are difficult to pin down because they have more than one meaning; for example, open learning is considered to be both an educational philosophy and a method of delivering teaching. However, it is useful for teachers to have an understanding of the similarities and differences between the terms, and the following section attempts to address these.

Defining open, distance and flexible learning

It is helpful to consider higher education as having four main modes of delivery, as shown in Figure 4.4.

FIGURE 4.4   Modes of delivery in higher education

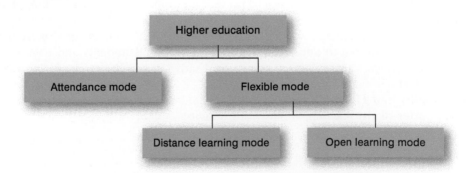

The left-hand box on the diagram shows the traditional delivery pattern in higher education, i.e. students attend the university for their teaching. The right-hand box shows the flexible mode of delivery, a broad category that includes both the distance learning mode and the open learning mode. Given the considerable degree of overlap between the three concepts, it may be helpful to identify the critical attributes that each must possess in order to warrant its title.

Distance learning

In order for a programme to count as distance learning, a significant proportion must be delivered on the basis of a wide geographical separation between the student and the teaching institution responsible for the programme. Distance is normally defined in terms of a student who is more than one hour's travelling time from the institution. Distance, however, is not the only critical attribute; distance learning is invariably delivered by means of text-based learning materials and information and communication technology (ICT), for example email, Internet, video.

Bradley and Cosper (2011) define distance learning as:

> 'an instructional delivery method occurring when learners and educators are separated by time and/or distance during the learning and teaching process'
>
> Bradley and Cosper (2011, p. 354)

Open learning

In order for a programme to count as open learning, there must be a significant element of openness in comparison with traditional attendance programmes. By 'openness' we mean a minimum of restrictions on such things as students' access to programmes, the teaching and learning methods used, the assessment methods, the venue for study, and the timing of study. In reality, absolute openness does not exist; open learning programmes fall somewhere on a continuum, from more or less closed to more or less open. There will always be some kind of restriction imposed upon students in higher education by virtue of validation requirements, quality assurance requirements, and other institutional imperatives.

Open learning is succinctly defined as:

> 'any system where learners work alone, at their own pace, on resources prepared by others, with minimal face-to-face contact either with teachers or other learners.'
>
> Rogers (2001)

Open learning as a philosophical stance   Open learning is also philosophical stance, whose adherents espouse a range of beliefs about the educational process. Hull (1998) includes the following:

- the centrality of student autonomy and self-direction;
- focus on the process of learning rather than the content;
- an emphasis on enquiry, reflection, evaluation and action;
- student ownership of learning, assessment, and reflection processes;
- the integration of theory and practice.

Open learning students normally study at a distance from their educational institution, and their studies utilize text-based learning materials and information and communication technology, e.g. email, Internet, video.

Flexible learning

Flexible learning is the most generic member of the triad of terms, as it covers any strategy that helps to reduce restrictions on students' learning opportunities. It therefore subsumes open learning and distance learning, since both these approaches confer a greater or lesser degree of flexibility upon programmes. Flexible learning also applies to methods used with programmes that have a traditional attendance mode, such as the inclusion of resource materials for self-directed study as part of a course.

The term flexible learning is also used to indicate programmes on which students can combine different modes of study; for example, some courses (modules) could be studied by attending classes at the university, and others by distance learning, using appropriate study materials.

The context of open, distance and flexible learning

Although the origins of flexible learning can be traced as far back as the turn of the twentieth century in the work of writers such as John Dewey, the humanistic educational culture of the 1960s and 1970s provided the real thrust for its further development. The writings of Carl Rogers on client-centred therapy, and its corollary student-centred learning, emphasized the pre-eminence of student empowerment and autonomy, and these ideas found fertile soil in those educators wishing for a more humanistic approach to teaching and learning. During this period there was also a growing interest in the opening up of access to further and higher education using alternatives to traditional entry qualifications, and also flexible methods of delivery. The best known UK example of a mass, open-access, distance learning scheme originating at this time is the Open University.

Race (1993) cites a number of reasons for the move towards flexible learning in higher education, including:

- increasing competition between institutions;
- greater availability of curriculum packages;
- increasing class sizes;
- greater numbers of mature and non-traditional entry students;
- the perception that students in higher education are over-taught;
- the need to foster students' ability to manage their own learning.

In addition to these general factors, nurse education continues to experience severe resource constraints on continuing professional education, with employers placing limitations on the amount of funding available for attendance at courses, and reduced opportunities for study leave. The creation of the NHS internal market gave employers a much greater say in the kind of continuing education provision that they required for their nursing staff, including more flexible approaches to course delivery.

TEACHING TIP

It is always useful to know what alternative courses are available for students; and how they differ from the course you teach. You might glean some new ideas for your own teaching.

Delivery systems for open, distance and flexible learning

Flexible learning workshops

Flexible learning workshops allow students to drop in at a time convenient to them in order to study from specific learning resources, with the additional facility of tutorial guidance if required. Access to the learning workshop may constitute part of a student's normal timetable or simply be available for any learner when he or she happens to require its use. The notion of a learning workshop is different from the commonly encountered resource centre in that it offers more than simple access to learning materials. The tutorial backup needs a more sophisticated system of organization, with a nurse teacher designated as manager of the workshop; the role of the manager is to maintain records of the use of materials, to monitor the functioning of all aspects of the provision and to call upon the appropriate teaching staff to supplement students when required.

There are important differences in the role of workshop tutors compared with the everyday role of a nurse teacher. In a workshop, the tutor is engaged in a one-to-one role as facilitator and consultant and, to be effective in this role, therefore needs the skills of negotiation and diagnosis. The tutor must be able to use the learning materials available in the workshop, and effective management also involves the selection of materials for study. The manager needs to work closely with the library and media resources staff who can provide help with both the classification of materials and with one-to-one support of students.

Remote systems

One of the earliest UK examples of a national remote system is the Open University, which offers undergraduate and postgraduate programmes in a wide range of subject areas. There is also an element of subcontracting within the Open University, with students having access to local educational institutions for tutorial, computing and other support.

Subcontracting systems

There are many universities involved in one of the largest subcontracting systems of flexible learning for nursing within the UK. Emap Healthcare Open Learning has offered educational opportunities and academic awards to nurses and other health care professionals since 1991 to provide academic awards for nurses and other health professionals. The programmes within the scheme are delivered by means of text-based open learning materials, and students receive support within a local university department of nursing. The advantage of this is that students are allowed to learn independently in their own time and at their own pace.

SELECTING, DESIGNING AND WRITING MATERIALS FOR OPEN, DISTANCE AND FLEXIBLE LEARNING

Flexible learning can be introduced into a course or programme in three ways (Race, 1993):

- by using existing materials that match the requirements, for example commercially produced materials such as those from the Open University;
- by adapting existing materials so that they match the requirements;
- by writing new materials to the required specification.

There are clearly advantages and disadvantages with each of these approaches. The use of existing materials means that flexible learning can be introduced quickly, without the need for extensive materials development; however, if such materials do not exactly meet the requirements of the course or programme, it may be better to adapt existing materials. The writing of new materials requires a major resource investment, including staff development costs, design and production costs, and copyright payments. There is also a considerable lead-in time before the materials are ready for use by students.

Selecting existing materials

A wide range of flexible learning materials is available within higher education and nursing. For example, the Open Learning Foundation (OLF) offers materials (at degree and postgraduate level) and services to help universities implement open learning. The OLF service includes the following:

- provision of entire open learning programmes, for example Diploma in Social Work (DipSW);
- development of open learning packages for universities and other education and training organizations;
- teaching and learning materials, and other publications;
- advisory service to institutions.

The Open Learning Foundation also operates a nursing credit scheme to enable nurses to meet the NMC PREP requirements, and the scheme is linked to a series of materials called Healthcare Active Learning. The website address for the Open Learning Foundation is http://www.olf.ac.uk/.

Designing materials

The design of flexible learning materials will depend to some extent on their proposed use:

- They may comprise the teaching and learning material for an entire programme of study.
- They may be a subcomponent of a programme, for example a single course (module) on health promotion.
- They may be entirely free-standing and generic, i.e. not related to a specific programme of study; for example, a flexible learning package on intravenous drug administration.

Whilst there is no hard-and-fast rule about the design of flexible learning materials for each purpose, a useful rule of thumb is that materials for an entire course commonly follow the 'reader and study guide' format, whereas those for a single element normally use the 'learning package' format.

Reader and study guide format

Most programmes of study in higher education are now modular in design, i.e. the components of the programme are broken down into discrete, self-contained units of learning. The 'reader and study guide' format has two sets of flexible learning materials for each course (module), a reader and a study guide.

Reader　　The reader can be thought of as the content of the course, i.e. what the teacher would normally teach in a classroom; hence, the reader could contain extracts from the relevant literature and/or text written by the teacher. The text may be supplemented by pictures and other graphic material.

Study guide　　The study guide is a substitute for the teacher in that it contains the kinds of learning activities that teachers would normally use in a classroom, for example questions, problem-solving exercises, analyses, etc. The guide is designed to relate to each of the sections in the reader, so that students are asked to study a particular section of the reader and are then required to carry out the appropriate activity in the guide.

Some authors like to follow the activities with a commentary, so that students have a basis for comparison between their response and that of the author. However, this may render the activity meaningless, as students may simply read the author's commentary rather than carrying out the activity for themselves.

The learning package format

This format is commonly used for self-contained units of learning; whilst there is no specific formula for writing a learning package, there are some points which can be helpful in clarifying the process. A learning package typically consists of a number of components organized in a logical sequence to help students achieve particular learning goals, as shown in Table 4.8.

TABLE 4.8 Typical components of a flexible learning package	
Rationale	This consists of an introductory statement describing the package and its purpose. It provides an overview of the type of material to be studied and the reasons for each study.
Target population	This identifies the level of programme, or level of experience at which the package will be most suitable. For example, the package may have been designed as a module on the Adult Branch of a Bachelor of Nursing programme, or it may be a component of a master's degree in nursing.
Pre-requisite	If successful completion of the package is dependent on the learner having already achieved certain knowledge or skills, then this knowledge or skill is termed a pre-requisite for the learning package. For example, a pre-requisite for many nursing subjects will be a knowledge of normal structure and function.
Learning outcomes	If the package is linked to a particular model or unit of study, then the learning outcomes will be derived from this. If the package is generic and free-standing, then appropriate learning outcomes will need to be formulated for the package.
Choice of learning activities	If individuals differ in their learning styles, then it is logical to include more than one form of activity by which the learner may achieve the objectives. Activities such as reading, writing, listening, looking and doing should provide sufficient variety in one package to suit the needs of most individuals, who can then select the medium by which they learn best. Further variety can be introduced by the use of different media within these activities, for example the use of video and the Internet.
Optional activities beyond the package	Optional activities may be presented to the learner to enrich the learning experience, but which are outside the confines of the learning package. For example, one suggested activity from a package on 'Nursing the patient with a myocardial infarction' might be that the learner should take the opportunity to visit a patient who has suffered an attack and to discuss with the patient how the condition has affected him or her as a person. It is important that the package contains information about obtaining the necessary permissions to undertake the activity.
Tests	The tests provide feedback to the learner and also serve as a diagnostic tool. They can be divided into three types. (a) Pre-requisite test. This tests the pre-requisite knowledge that the learner must possess before commencing the test. (b) Pre-test. This tests the actual content of the package to determine whether or not the learner needs to proceed through the package. If the pre-test is completed successfully, the implication is that the learner already knows the content of the package and can proceed to a higher level of study immediately. (c) Post-test. This is used to test the learner's achievement of the objective following completion of the learning package. The post-test is very commonly used as a pre-test, the learner initially attempting the test without success and then retaking it after completion of the package. The learner is usually successful the second time and this provides feelings of accomplishment from having visibly learned to pass the test.
Guidance concerning the next step	Successful completion of the learning package should not be the final step; instead, the learner should be directed to the next component in the series, or given advice on the type of learning activities that they should now pursue.

(continued)

TABLE 4.8 Typical components of a flexible learning package (*continued*)	
Teacher's notes	A learning package should contain notes intended for the teacher. It may seem unusual to include these, but one must bear in mind that the intentions of the designer may not always be obvious to a teacher who has not been involved in the production. Such notes might contain details of the feedback received during the pilot study and guidelines for the interpretation of test scores.

The list of components given in Table 4.8 can be considered as a basic list of 'ingredients' for a learning package, so it is useful to examine the 'recipe' for putting these components together. The decision to produce a learning package will commit the institution to a considerable amount of time and effort and, if this expenditure is to reap its benefits, careful planning must be employed from the outset. Table 4.9 illustrates a planning sequence for producing an individualized learning package. This sequence follows a logical order of progression, with each stage designed to eliminate errors and omissions.

TABLE 4.9 Planning sequence for producing a flexible learning package	
Explore the need	Does a similar package exist already? Is a learning package an appropriate medium?
Explore the feasibility of developing a package	Is the development feasible in terms of finance, personnel, resources and time?
Decide the target population	Pre-registration, post-registration or both? Credit level?
Decide the learning outcomes	Are they already prescribed in the programme document, or do they have to be formulated specifically for the package.
Identify prerequisites and co-requisites	Are there other packages/materials/units that should be studied first, or studied in conjunction with the package?
Decide the activities and media for the package	Reading? Writing? Information and communication technology? Experiential? Sequencing? Instructions?
Decide any optional activities	For example, interviews with patients/clients/staff in relation to the theme of the package.
Write the rationale for the package	Write a description of the purpose and structure of the package.
Decide format of pre-test and post-test if used	Teacher or student marked? Where will the answers be found?
Decide format of self-tests	How will student monitor his or her own progress through the package?
Decide content of teacher notes	Write any additional information that teachers might require, e.g. the theoretical assumptions underpinning the approach taken in the package.
Decide format of students' evaluation of the package	How will the user's opinion of the package be solicited?

(continued)

TABLE 4.9 Planning sequence for producing a flexible learning package (*continued*)	
Decide the contents list	Outline the sequence of content but omit page numbers until final draft completed.
Set production deadlines	Realistic, achievable deadlines, including time for any slippage, are needed.
Undertake draft production	Use Desktop Publishing (DTP) if available.
Undertake pilot study	Use a sample of the intended consumers, and obtain detailed feedback on all aspects of the package.
Modify draft package in light of feedback from pilot study	Note 'user-friendliness', clarity, interest and accuracy.
Produce final draft	(a) Text: DTP gives professional finish. Type of cover? Quality of binding? Size of print run? Copyright? (b) Information and communication media:include instructions to user on how to operate the media.
Put package into full use	Include system of monitoring students' use of package, plus evaluation by users.

Writing the materials

The foregoing discussion on designing flexible learning materials seems to make the assumption that teachers can simply sit down and write materials for public consumption. This is very far from being the case; effective authoring of materials requires considerable staff development, and even then some teachers may simply not have the necessary skills to write effectively for this medium. It can be an advantage, when writing flexible learning materials, to have had experience of publishing books or journal papers, because the writer will have been exposed to external criticism as part of the publishing process. Experience of writing books and articles, however, does not necessarily mean that the same style will be appropriate for flexible learning materials, as the target audience is quite different.

THE ROLE OF THE TUTOR IN OPEN, DISTANCE AND FLEXIBLE LEARNING

The skills required in tutoring students on flexible learning programmes encompass generic tutoring skills. However, the nature of flexible learning is such that tutors' interaction with students on a face-to-face basis may occur infrequently, so alternative approaches to tutoring need to be developed.

Tutoring at a distance

Depending upon the nature of the programme of study, distance learning students may meet their tutors on a face-to-face basis every three or four weeks, or as infrequently as once or twice per semester. In either case, the main form of communication will be the telephone and postal service, or electronic forms such as fax and email. The additional roles of the tutor in relation to distance learning students include those described below.

Establishing initial contact with students

It is good practice to send out to students a personal letter of welcome, containing some background details about the tutor, and also the arrangements for contacting the tutor.

Maintaining regular contact

It is very important that tutors maintain frequent contact with distance students, as the students' motivation can quickly fade if they feel isolated and out of touch with their programme. Contact is likely to involve postal, telephone and/or electronic forms of communication; my own preference is for a combination of telephone and electronic communications. It is helpful for students to have some communications in a permanent form, so that they can be referred to again and again. Quinn and Hughes (2007) advocate a series of postal communications, which they refer to as 'Quinformation' sheets; these highlight key aspects of the programme, such as tips on assessments and arrangements for teaching practice assessment visits. This paper communication can be supplemented by telephone calls from time to time to enquire about students' progress, and to offer advice on assessments, etc.

Facilitating student networking

One of the disadvantages of distance learning is that students may feel isolated and alone, so it is important that the tutor encourages students to network with each other. This can be done simply by contacting each student to seek permission to circulate his or her contact details to other students in the tutorial group. Students should be asked to indicate whether or not they are happy to have their home contact details circulated, or whether they prefer their work details to be circulated.

Openness versus emptiness

One of the common issues raised by tutors on open and distance learning programmes concerns those students who make no attempt to respond to communications from their tutor once they have registered on the programme. One viewpoint is that tutors are resources for the student, and if the student chooses not to use them that is perfectly acceptable; in this case, the student could simply enrol on the programme and then submit the assessment at the end, with no communication in-between. This viewpoint seems to be compatible with an adult learning philosophy, in which the students are considered self-directing adults responsible for their own learning.

In a flexible learning programme, it is the student's responsibility to demonstrate to the tutor that he or she is undergoing the process of learning, including critical reflection and analysis of issues and experiences. This requires a certain amount of communication with the tutor in order to monitor the student's progress through this process. Indeed, one of the terms of reference of a programme committee is the monitoring of student progress, and this cannot be fulfilled without a certain amount of interaction between student and tutor.

It is unacceptable for flexible learning students simply to register for a unit of study and then to have no further contact with the institution until they submit an assessment for marking. Even if the students feel that they require no tutorial help with their studies, the tutor will require evidence of engagement with the materials and the literature, and of reflection upon these. The tutor is also required to challenge students' assumptions and conclusions, thus facilitating the development of the students' critical abilities.

Computer-mediated tutoring

One of the most appropriate innovations in tutoring distance students is computer-mediated tutoring or asynchronous conferencing systems, which is defined as:

> *'systems used to join up people and resources, supporting communication and the sharing of information between staff and students, regardless of time and location'*
>
> JISC (2012)

This system often uses Lotus Notes or Outlook software to offer both electronic mail and conferencing databases; email can be used for one-to-one messages and questions, or for one-to-many notices and information. Computer conferencing allows students and tutors to discuss issues in a 'virtual group' but does not take place in real time. Hence, a tutor may initiate activities or ideas onto the server, and the students in the virtual group can respond at any time of the day or night. Students and tutor may initiate and respond to each other's inputs just like a live seminar, but with the advantage of not having to be in the same place at the same time.

MANAGING OPEN, DISTANCE AND FLEXIBLE LEARNING

Flexible learning programmes require specific management structures to ensure the quality of materials and the quality of programme delivery. Quinn and Hughes (2007) identify the following structures based upon experiences with flexible learning programmes.

Editorial board

An editorial board is an essential component of the management structure, and membership would normally consist of the flexible learning manager, the materials editor, the design and layout technician, and representatives of authors. The editorial board is responsible for the commissioning, production scheduling, and review process; commissioning may be done on the basis of payment to the author for the writing, or by including the writing as part of the teacher's normal timetable commitments. It is important that the editorial board maintains oversight of the production schedule, so that action can be taken if there is slippage of deadlines. One of the major quality assurance aspects of the editorial board is organizing the critical review process for materials.

Critical reading of materials

It is essential that all flexible learning materials are exposed to critical reading before the final draft is published. Critical readers should be sought both internally and externally, and should consist of both teachers and students so that the materials are criticized from both perspectives. A guide should be issued so that critical readers have a framework to which they write their critique, and resources need to be made available to pay for the critical reader's services.

Flexible learning administrator

Appropriately skilled administrative support is required to operate distance learning programmes, and this works best if the administrator role is one dedicated solely to the flexible learning operation. The administrator is responsible for mailing of all flexible learning materials, for liaison with the academic registry over issues relating to flexible learning students, and, in conjunction with the appropriate programme leader, organizing the receipt, marking and moderation of students' assessment work.

Structures for flexible learning on a subcontracting basis

It is relatively common within higher education to find that flexible learning is delivered via a system of subcontracting with other educational institutions. These partner institutions offer tutorial support, library and information and communication technology support, and provide a venue for students to meet from time to time. In this system, the following management structures are required.

Partnership liaison tutor

For flexible learning systems that operate on a subcontracting basis, it is necessary to have an academic member of staff who is responsible for liaison with the partner institutions that provide tutoring and other support for students. This individual would visit each partner institution on a regular basis to monitor the quality of support provided for flexible learning students, and to offer advice and staff development to tutors within the partner institution.

Administrative manual

Communication between the parent institution and its partners is of paramount importance for maintaining the quality of the student experience. An administrative manual sets out all the procedures in relation to student support and documentation and provides a basis for monitoring of the partner organizations.

Staffing issues

If the students' experience of flexible learning is to be a quality experience, it requires motivated, committed and, above all, flexible tutors. The staffing of such programmes raises issues not encountered within traditional attendance mode programmes.

Tutor availability outside the working day

One of the most sensitive staffing issues in relation to flexible learning is the availability of tutors outside the normal working day. The majority of students undertake flexible learning programmes because they are fully committed to their employment during the working day. There is therefore little point in offering a tutorial service between the hours of 09.00 and 17.00; rather, the students will want tutorial contact in the evenings or at weekends. To operate such a system requires a fundamental rethink of tutorial staff timetables, if overloading is to be avoided. Ideally, flexible learning tutors should deal exclusively with such programmes, to avoid clashes between teaching times on attendance mode courses.

Tutors working from home

One way of facilitating tutorials for these programmes is to consider a system whereby tutors can use their home as their main work-base. It is relatively easy for staff to be linked electronically to the university via telephone, fax and computer, and this would enable tutors to offer an out-of-hours service to students without having to stay late at work. Some tutors may be happy to offer an evening and weekend service as an alternative to travelling to work every day, but there is the danger that they could end up working a full day at the institution, and then being available out of hours for distance students. There is a growing movement in society towards a working-from-home culture, but some employers feel uneasy about this development, given that employees have to be trusted to do their work without the direct supervision normally available in an institutional setting.

Meeting with students at home

In some systems, tutors of flexible learning students arrange individual and group tutorials in their own homes, as this is much more convenient for evening and weekend meetings, particularly if the tutor lives at some distance from the institution. Whilst this can be a very useful approach, tutors need to be aware of some of the drawbacks; once students are aware of the location of a tutor's home, tutors may be subjected to students 'dropping in' without appointments. They may also be open to accusations by students of improper behaviour, and, whilst this applies also to attendance mode programmes, a defence may be more difficult if the behaviour is alleged to have occurred in the tutor's own home.

Roll-on, roll-off programmes

Another operational implication is that of access to flexible learning programmes. Since flexible provision means that educational provision is available when the student wants it, entry to programmes is commonly on a continuous 'roll-on, roll-off' basis, and this presents a challenge to institutional systems, for example the scheduling of examination boards and the tracking of students.

Cost implications

The cost of development and production of flexible learning materials should not be underestimated:an editorial board is required, writers and critical readers need to be commissioned; permissions to reproduce copyright materials that will be scanned into texts need to be obtained; and materials need to be piloted, all of which have very substantial cost implications. Also, decisions have to be made about design and quality of the materials, as these will influence cost. Materials will not remain up to date forever; therefore, review and updating will need to be scheduled every three to five years, depending upon the nature of the materials. There are also costs involved in the necessary staff development for flexible learning tutors.

On the other side of the equation, there are potential savings to be made from the implementation of flexible learning. The following are examples of such savings:

- Savings can be made on the use of paper materials by downloading the units onto the students' computers.

- In comparison with attendance mode courses, flexible learning does not require classroom space nor is there a need for face-to-face class contact between teachers and students, both of which consume considerable resources.

- By freeing up the tutors from heavy class contact, there may be more time available for staff to undertake research, an increasingly important issue in the light of the research assessment exercise.

- The use of high-quality textual and computer material can be a far more effective learning strategy than poorly delivered lectures, and from a quality assurance point of view are much more open to public scrutiny than the latter.

Library and IT support

Student access to library and IT support facilities is an important aspect for distance learning, since the flexible learning materials need to be supplemented by further reading and inquiry. Whilst the main providing institution can easily monitor the quality of its own libraries, it is more difficult when partner institutions' library provision has to be evaluated.

Student peer support

Open learning can be a lonely experience for distance learning students, so it is important that networking is set up to help them interact with their peers on the same programme.

Use of locally based tutors

Institutions often employ associate tutors who live within the students' locality, so as to facilitate tutoring, but this can present difficulties in ensuring that they maintain good communication with the institution and also with attendance at staff development activities.

Review questions

1. What four main aspects of educational provision does the term 'curriculum' encompass?

2. What are the three domains of Bloom's Taxonomy of educational objectives?

3. What was Lawrence Stenhouse's alternative approach to the behavioural objectives model?

4. What are the four fundamental approaches to the nursing curricula according to Beattie's (1987) model?

5. Describe Bradley and Cosper's (2011) definition of distance learning?

SUMMARY

- The term 'curriculum' is used to describe a plan or design upon which educational provision is based.

- Educational provision in nursing takes a variety of forms, from short in-house programmes through to longer formal programmes leading to academic awards.

- A learning outcome is the desired end-state of student learning and describes the knowledge, skills, attitudes and values that a student should acquire as a result of the educational process.

- The taxonomy of educational objectives classifies objectives into three main spheres or domains, progressing from the most simple to the highly complex; the three domains are cognitive, affective and psychomotor.

- There are four stages in the curriculum development process: exploratory, design, implementation, and monitoring and review.

- Academic validation is the programme or course approval process used in higher education.

- Equality of opportunity is a central tenet of modern education and relates to all aspects of higher education curricula as well as to wider aspects of institutional management.

- The Equality Act [2010] makes it unlawful for higher education institutions to discriminate against students with disabilities and dyslexia.

- By making some very simple adaptations to their teaching practice in lectures, seminars and classes, educators can help to ensure that disabled students are not substantially disadvantaged.

- In order for a programme to count as distance learning, a significant proportion must be delivered on the basis of a wide geographical separation between the student and the teaching institution responsible for the programme.

- Open learning is any system where learners work alone, at their own pace, on resources prepared by others, with minimal face-to-face contact either with teachers or with other learners.

- Flexible learning covers any strategy that helps to reduce restrictions on students' learning opportunities.

References

Beattie, A. (1987) Making a curriculum work. In P. Allan and M. Jolley (eds) *The Curriculum in Nursing Education*. London: Croom Helm

Bell, R. (1973) *Thinking About the Curriculum*. Milton Keynes: Open University Press

Bernstein, B. (1971) On the classification and framing of educational knowledge. In Young M (ed.) *Knowledge and Control: New Directions for the Sociology of Education*. London: Collier Macmillan

Bloom, B. (1956) *Taxonomy of Educational Objectives: The Classification of Educational Goals, Handbook One: Cognitive Domain* New York: McKay

Bradley, K.P. and Cosper, S.M. (2011) Chapter 23 - Distance education: successful teaching-learning strategies. In: Bradshaw MJ, Lowenstein AJ. *Innovative Teaching Strategies in Nursing and Related Health Professions* (5th Edition). Boston: Jones and Bartlett

Butterworth, C. (1993) *Introduction and Self-Assessment Guide to Claiming APEL by Distance Learning*. London: University of Greenwich

Cardiff University (2009) *Programme Approval and Maintenance Handbook* (2nd Edition). Cardiff: Cardiff University

Disability Rights Commission (2007) *Maintaining Standards - Promoting Equality Professional Regulation Within Nursing, Teaching and Social Work and Disabled People's Access to These Professions*. Stratford upon Avon: DRC

ENB (1999) A documentary analysis of nursing degree curricula. *Research Highlights*, 38. English National Board for Nursing, Midwifery and Health Visiting, London

General Nursing Council for England and Wales (1977) *A Statement of Educational Policy*. Circular 77/19. GNCEW, London

Gravells, A. and Simpson, S. (2012) *Equality and Diversity in the Lifelong Learning Sector* (2nd Edition). London: Sage

Harrow, A. (1972) *A Taxonomy of the Psychomotor Domain*. New York: McKay

HM Government (2010) *The Equality Strategy: Building a Fairer Britain*. London: Home Office

HMSO [2010] *Equality Act*. London: The Stationary Office

Hull, C. (1998) Open learning and professional development. In F.M. Quinn (ed.) *Continuing Professional Development in Nursing: A Guide for Practitioners and Educators*. Cheltenham: Stanley Thornes

JISC (2012) Computer-Mediated Conferencing. Available at: http://www.jiscinfonet.ac.uk/

Kerr, J. (1968) Changing the curriculum. In R. Hooper (ed.) *The Curriculum: Design, Context and Development*. Edinburgh: Oliver & Boyd

Kolb, D. (1984) *Experiential Learning*. London: Prentice Hall

Krathwohl, D., Bloom, B. and Masia, B. (1964) *A Taxonomy of Educational Objectives: The Classification of Education Goals, Handbook 2: Affective Domain*. New York: McKay

Lewis, A. and Miel, A. (1972) *Supervision for Improved Instruction: New Challenges, New Responses*. Belmont: Wadsworth

Mager, R. (1962) *Preparing Instructional Objectives*. California: Fearon

Nursing Midwifery Order [2001] Norwich: The Stationary Office

http://www.legislation.gov.uk/uksi/2002/253/made/data.pdf

NMC (2010) *Standards for Pre-Registration Nursing Education*. London: Nursing Midwifery Council

QAA (2004) *Guidelines on the Accreditation of Prior Learning*. Gloucester: The Quality Assurance Agency

QAA (2009) *Academic Credit in Higher Education in England: an Introduction*. Gloucester: The Quality Assurance Agency for Higher Education

QAA (2009) *Outcomes from Institutional Audit: Institutions' Support for Students with Disabilities 2002-2006*. Gloucester: Quality Assurance Agency

QAA (2010) *Code of Practice for the Assurance of Academic Quality and Standards in Higher Education. Section 3: Disabled Students*. Gloucester: Quality Assurance Agency

Quinn, F.M. (1994) The Demise of Curriculum. In Humphreys J, Quinn FM (eds.) *Health Care*

Education: The Challenge of the Market. London: Chapman and Hall

Quinn, F.M. (2000) *Principles and Practice of Nurse Education* (4th Edition). Cheltenham: Nelson Thornes

Quinn, F.M. and Hughes, S.J. (2007) *Quinn's Principles and Practice of Nurse Education* (5th Edition). Cheltenham: Nelson Thornes

Race, P. (1993) *Never Mind the Teaching Feel the Learning.* SEDA Paper 80, Staff and Educational Development Association

Rogers, J. (2001) *Adults Learning* (4th edn). Buckingham: Open University Press

RCN (2010) *Dyslexia, Dyspraxia and Dyscalculia: a Toolkit for Nursing Staff.* London: Royal College of Nursing

Saylor, J., Alexander, W. and Lewis, A. (1981) *Curriculum Planning for Better Teaching and Learning* (4th Edition). New York: Holt, Rinehart and Winston,

SCQF (2012) *Scotland's Framework for Lifelong Learning: a Guide for Learners, Providers and Employers.* Glasgow: Scottish Credit and Qualifications Framework

Simmons, S. and Bahl, D. (1992) An integrated approach to curriculum development. *Nurse Education Today* 12, 310–315

Simpson, E. (1972) The classification of educational objectives in the psychomotor domain. In *The Psychomotor Domain*, Vol. 3. Washington DC: Gryphon House

Skilbeck, M. (1984) *School Based Curriculum Development.* London: Harper and Row

Stenhouse, L. (1975) *An Introduction to Curriculum Research and Development.* London: Heinemann

Tanner, D. and Tanner, L. (1980) *Curriculum Development: Theory into Practice* (2nd Edition). New York: Macmillan

Tyler, R. (1949) *Basic Principles of Curriculum and Instruction.* Chicago: University of Chicago Press

Further Reading

Banks, P., Kane, H., Rae, C. and Atkinson, J. (2012) Support for nursing and midwifery students: A special case? *Nurse Education Today* 32, 309-314

Equality and Human Rights Commission. Available at: http://www.equalityhumanrights.com/

Equality Commission for Northern Ireland Available from: http://www.equalityni.org/site/default.asp?secid=home

Open Learning Foundation. Available at: http://www.olf.ac.uk/

QAA (2010) *UK quality code for higher education. Chapter B4: Student Support, Learning Resources and Careers Education, Information, Advice and Guidance.* Gloucester: Quality Assurance Agency

QAA (2011) *UK Quality Code for Higher Education. Chapter A3: The programme Level.* Gloucester: Quality Assurance Agency

Reid, G. (2009) *Dyslexia: a Practitioner's Handbook* (4th Edition). Oxford: Wiley

Riddell, S., Tinklin, T. and Wilson, A. (2005) *Disabled Students in Higher Education.* London: Routledge

Stainer, L. and Ware, P. (2006) *Guidelines to Support Nursing Learners with Dyslexia in Practice.* Association of Dyslexia Specialists in Higher Education

Storr, H., Wray, J. and Draper, P. (2011) Supporting disabled student nurses from registration to qualification: A review of the United Kingdom (UK) literature. *Nurse Education Today* 31, 29-33

Waterfield, J., West, B. and Chalkley, B. (2006) *Developing an Inclusive Curriculum for Students with Dyslexia and Hidden Disabilities.* Cheltenham: University of Gloucestershire

CHAPTER 5
PLANNING FOR TEACHING

THE AIMS OF THIS CHAPTER ARE:

- To explore a range of teaching strategies used in nurse education

- To examine the process of planning an explanation

- To consider the development and design of questioning techniques

- To illustrate how to develop a teaching plan

- To identify a suitable teaching environment and the range of resources that can enhance the delivery of a teaching session

KEY TERMS

Learning outcomes
Assessment of learning
Concept mapping meta-cognitive
Deductively
Inductively

Health informatics
Expositive
Computer-mediated tutoring
Scheme of work

Professional teaching in nursing, midwifery and specialist community public health nursing is an intentional enterprise that aims to facilitate learning. It is characterized by an acceptance of responsibility for facilitating other people's learning by means of planned and purposeful educational interventions. This is not to say that teaching ignores the possibility of unplanned learning; indeed, there are powerful arguments to support the view that teaching must provide an atmosphere for students in which unpredictable or creative outcomes can emerge. However, even this example shows evidence of broad teaching intentions, namely, the provision of a climate in which unpredictable outcomes are encouraged.

Within nursing, midwifery and specialist community public health nursing there is a wide range of teaching contexts, ranging from the delivery of lectures in a university through to one-to-one teaching sessions with individual students, practitioners, patients and clients. It must also be acknowledged that many teaching encounters in clinical and community settings are opportunistic, arising spontaneously during the day-to-day delivery of care. It is therefore difficult to be specific about what should be included when planning for such a diverse range of teaching, but there are a number of generic factors that might be taken into account, as shown in Table 5.1. However, the relevance of each of these will vary according to the nature of the teaching encounter.

TABLE 5.1   Some factors to be taken into account in planning a teaching session

A. Nature of the teaching encounter

1. Type of learner, i.e. student, qualified practitioner, patient/client

2. Programme-related or non-programme-related teaching

3. One-to-one, small-group or lecture

B. Details of the programme

1. Title

2. Level/year

3. Full-time or part-time attendance

4. Course aims and learning outcomes

5. Indicative content

6. Assessment methods

C. Details of students

1. Number of students

2. Full-time/part-time

3. Relevant prior knowledge and experience

D. Organizational factors

1. Length of teaching session

2. Type of venue, e.g. lecture theatre, classroom, laboratory, workplace, etc.

3. Availability of teaching resources, e.g. whiteboard, overhead projector, computers, etc.

4. Health and safety aspects

5. Equality of opportunity

E. Psychological factors

1. Appropriate sequencing of subject matter

2. Student motivation

3. Individual differences in student ability

4. Individual differences in race, gender, age, etc.

DEFINING THE PURPOSE OF A TEACHING SESSION

The practice of stating aims and learning outcomes is now almost universal within the higher education sector; these are normally of two kinds: general aims and learning outcomes for the programme as a whole, and those for specific modules or units of learning. It is important to state aims and learning outcomes even if the teaching session is not related to an academic programme, since they help the learner to understand the purpose of the session.

Educational aims are broad, strategic statements of intent, which include reference to the value of achieving the aim. For example, 'To assist the students to develop the appropriate knowledge and skills that will enable them to deliver high-quality care to patients suffering from cancer.' Note that no details of the 'knowledge and skills' are given in the aim; fine detail such as this is contained within the learning outcomes. Note also that there is a value included in the aim, i.e. 'enable them to deliver high-quality care'.

Learning outcomes are specific statements about what the student should have achieved by the end of a module or unit and are often stated in terms of student behaviours: for example, 'Defines the terms transient, acute and chronic pain, with reference to the relevant literature.' The behavioural verb here is 'defines', which indicates very clearly what the student is expected to achieve. This would normally be either in written form or by oral explanation. The outcome also contains a criterion for performance, i.e. 'with reference to the relevant literature'.

It would not be sufficient for students simply to be able to 'define the terms'; they must also meet the criterion for performance of the outcome.

Academic level of learning outcomes

Learning outcomes are formulated at the appropriate level for the unit or module in question. Academic levels and definitions vary between higher education institutions throughout the United Kingdom; Table 5.2 gives the levels and definitions in use in Wales, England and Northern Ireland. Levels 4, 5 and 6 correspond to years 1, 2 and 3 of an undergraduate honours degree programme. In Scotland, levels 7, 8 and 9 correspond to years 1, 2 and 3 of an undergraduate honours degree programme.

TABLE 5.2 Definitions of credit levels	
Level 3	Modules, the standard of which is higher than GCSE or its equivalent, which would prepare students for entry to an undergraduate degree
Level HE 4	Modules, the standard of which is higher than modules at level 0, and which are appropriate to the award of a university Certificate of Higher Education
Level HE 5	Modules, the standard of which is higher than modules at level 1, and which are appropriate to the award of a university Diploma of Higher Education
Level HE 6	Modules, the standard of which is higher than modules at level 2, and which are appropriate to the award of an Honours degree
Level 7	Modules, the standard of which is higher than modules at level 3, and which are appropriate to the award of a Master's degree

Learning outcomes and assessment

Learning outcomes and assessment of learning are inextricably linked, in that assessment normally requires the student to demonstrate achievement of the learning outcomes. One advantage of learning outcomes is that they provide learners with clear goals for their studies, but they can shift the focus of study too heavily towards assessment, to the detriment of wider reading.

A learning outcome, as defined by Neary (2000), is what a student should know, understand and be able to do following a period of learning; it includes an indication of the evidence required to demonstrate that learning has been achieved. Whilst each learning outcome should be specific, measurable, achievable, realistic and timed (Hinchliff, 2009) and represent an expectation that the student must learn a different item of knowledge, Welsh and Swann (2002) warn us that too many may create unreasonable expectations. Jarvis and Gibson (1997) point out that learning outcomes result from educators attempting to provide direction for the development of a curriculum at every level. However the desirability of providing such detailed direction is open to considerable question, especially as it proposes a teacher-centred learning approach, which might not be acceptable to educators of adults.

Learning outcomes in nurse education are influenced by the work of Bloom (1956), discussed in Chapter 4 and further on in the chapter, higher-level descriptors (QAA, 2008; SCQF, 2010), and the Nursing and Midwifery Council (NMC, 2008). In terms of meeting these outcomes, Neary (2000) explains that students undergoing an educational programme are assessed on the knowledge and skills that satisfies the governing body of nursing and other professional bodies, to ensure that those individuals are suitable and able practitioners who are fit for purpose.

SELECTING THE SUBJECT MATTER (CONTENT) OF A TEACHING SESSION

It must be acknowledged from the outset that subject matter is not necessarily synonymous with content. The term 'subject matter' is normally attached to the various fields of knowledge that comprise the science and art of nursing, midwifery and specialist community public health nursing, and in this sense it equates with the term 'content'. However, some teaching sessions in nursing and health have as their content a variety of group processes and interactions that are not subject matter per se, but which still require careful planning. This aspect is dealt with in Chapter 6 in the discussion on small-group teaching and experiential learning.

It goes without saying that a teacher should possess a thorough understanding of the subject matter to be taught; in higher education the minimum benchmark for a lecturer is normally the possession of a first degree or equivalent. This level of knowledge does, in itself, present problems in the selection of subject matter for teaching. The more expert a teacher is, the more difficult it is to decide what must go in, and more importantly what has to be left out of, a teaching session.

This may result in the inexperienced teacher cramming far too much information into sessions. The secret of successful teaching is to place severe limits on the amount of content in a given session by the judicious selection of the most important aspects of the topic and the ruthless pruning of other, less crucial material.

Concept mapping

In Chapter 3, the nature of concepts was discussed. When planning teaching sessions, one of the most difficult decisions confronting the teacher is deciding what must go in, what should go in, and what could go in; concept sorting and mapping can be a helpful tool in this regard. Lawless *et al.* (1998, p. 219) offer the following definition:

> 'Concept sorting is a simple, yet powerful, way in which to generate, sort, arrange and rearrange any set of elements, i.e. ideas, concepts, events, statements or procedures, in a visually explicit manner, namely a concept map.'

Hence, the terms have largely the same meaning, but the writers point out that the term 'concept sorting' is used in business and public administration, whereas 'concept mapping' is the preferred term in education because the emphasis is on the relationships between concepts.

Kinchin *et al.* (2008) simplify this definition in the following statement:

> 'Concept mapping is a graphical tool used to represent links between ideas. Ideas are written in boxes and linked with arrows carrying explanatory legends. Concept mapping has been used effectively in a variety of contexts as a classroom technique to enhance learning'

Concept mapping provides a way of prioritizing concepts in a concrete, visual way. The simplest way of making a concept map is to write each concept on a small square of paper and then place the squares on a flat surface. The squares are then arranged in order of their relationship to each other, with the most closely related concepts being placed next to each other. This pattern is then transferred to a diagram, and the relationships between concepts are shown by connecting lines, usually annotated.

Figure 5.1 shows an example of a concept map for the topic 'coronary heart disease'; first-order, second-order and third-order concepts are included. When making a decision about which concepts to include and which to omit, the teacher will need to judge not only the appropriate level of information for the learners in question but also the amount of time available for the session.

When sorting the concepts, lecturers draw upon the relevant literature and their specialist knowledge and experience of the topic, and the end result should be a prioritizing of concepts into key concepts (must be included), second-order concepts (should be included) and third-order concepts (could be included). At the level of the key concepts, selection is usually fairly straightforward; it is at the level of the second- and third-order concepts that the danger of over-inclusion of information is most likely to occur. There are all kinds of fascinating facts and anecdotes attached to the key concepts of nursing and health, and as such these can be important elements in the maintenance of students' interest and motivation.

Problems may arise when the teacher perceives that there are so many key concepts to include that no time is left for these interesting but non-essential aspects of the topic. This dilemma can be lessened if the aim of the session is taken into account. Provided that sufficient book and periodical resources are available in the college, there should seldom be the need for the teacher to attempt to cover all aspects of a topic in detail. By the judicious use of references and further reading, the teacher can limit the number of concepts within the session, and in so doing will free up time for inclusion of anecdotes and other interesting facets of the topic.

FIGURE 5.1   Concept map for coronary heart disease

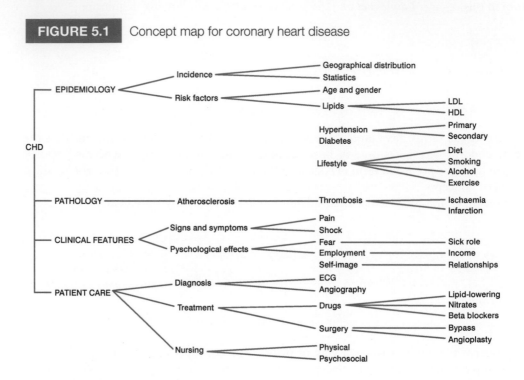

Although the foregoing information has focused on the planning of a single teaching session, concept mapping is equally appropriate for planning a scheme of work for a series of sessions on a broad topic area. It can actually be easier to make a selection from a concept map if more than one session is available, as the time constraints may be less evident.

TEACHING TIP

If necessary use the lecture to motivate students to learn more and for signposting to further information.

SELECTING APPROPRIATE TEACHING STRATEGIES

There is a wide range of strategies available to the teacher and these are discussed in detail in the relevant chapters of this book. Hence, for this section, an overview of the basis on which teaching strategies might be selected will be provided. The starting point for selection of teaching and learning strategies is the broad purpose of the session(s). The strategies must be compatible with the aims of the session; lecturing is very commonly used as a vehicle for conveying subject matter to students, but there may well be more effective ways involving individualized instruction. If the intention of a session is to encourage discussion or debate about issues, student-centred activities should predominate; for skills teaching, demonstration followed by student practice is an appropriate strategy.

Encouraging a deep approach to learning

Evidence suggests that there is over-reliance on those teaching methods involving the transmission of information and that this is often combined with assessment methods that encourage the superficial reproduction of facts.

> 'Students may use learning activities that are of lower cognitive level than are needed to achieve the outcomes, resulting in a surface approach to learning; or they can use high level activities appropriate to achieving the intended outcomes, resulting in a deep approach to learning. Good teaching is that which supports the appropriate learning activities and discourages inappropriate ones.'
>
> Biggs and Tang (2011, p. 16)

The Higher Education Academy compares the characteristics and factors that encourage deep and surface approaches to learning using the work of Biggs and Tang (2011), Entwistle (1990) and Ramsden (2003) in Table 5.3.

Deductive and inductive teaching of concepts

There are two main ways of teaching concepts, deductively and inductively. When teaching a concept deductively, the teacher begins by giving a definition of the concept and then follows this up with a number of examples. Thus, when teaching the concept of 'cell', a definition would be given, followed by a number of examples of various cells such as nerve cells, epithelial cells, and so on. Examples would also be given of non-cells to aid discrimination of the concept.

When teaching a concept inductively, the teacher first gives a number of instances (examples) of the concept and then draws out from the students a definition of the concept. The teacher might begin with illustrations or descriptions of a number of patients, some grossly overweight, some extremely thin, others with specific physical or nervous disorders such as scurvy and bulimia. The students then try to ascertain any factors that are common to all the instances, eventually coming up with a definition of the concept 'malnutrition'.

The following is a useful mnemonic for remembering the difference between inductive and deductive teaching:

- Deductive teaching begins with a definition and then gives instances (examples).
- Inductive teaching begins with instances (examples) and then arrives at a definition.

	TABLE 5.3 Characteristics and factors that encourage deep and surface approaches to learning	
	Deep Learning	**Surface Learning**
Definition	Critically examining new facts and ideas and relating them into existing cognitive structures and making many links between ideas	Accepting new facts and ideas uncritically and attempting to store them as isolated and unconnected items
Characteristics	Looking for meaning. Focussing on the argument or concepts needed to solve a problem	Relying on rote learning. Focussing the formulae needed to solve a problem
	Interacting actively. Distinguishing between argument and evidence	Receiving information passively. Failing to distinguish principles from examples
	Making connections between different modules	Treating parts of modules and programmes as separate entities
	Relating new and previous knowledge	Not recognizing new material as building on previous work
	Linking course content to real life	Seeing course content simply as material to be learnt for an assessment
Encouraged by students	Having an intrinsic curiosity in the subject area. Determined to do well and mentally engaging when completing academic work	Studying a degree for the qualification and not being interested in the subject area. More focus on social and sporting activities than academic work
	Having the appropriate background knowledge for a sound foundation	Lacking background knowledge and understanding necessary to understand academic material
	Good time management allows time to pursue other interests	Excessive workload and lack of time management
	Positive experience of education leading to confidence in ability to understand and succeed	Sceptical view of education, believing that factual recall is what is required
Encouraged by teachers	Demonstrating personal interest in the subject area	Demonstrating disinterest or even a negative attitude towards the subject area
	Concentrating on and ensuring time for discussion around key concepts	Allowing students to be passive during discussions
	Confronting students' misconceptions. Engaging students in active learning	Assessing for independent facts
	Using assessments that require thought, and requires ideas to be used together	Rushing to cover too much material
	Relating new material to what students already know and understand	Emphasizing coverage at the expense of depth of learning
	Allowing students to make mistakes without penalty and rewarding effort	Creating undue anxiety or low expectations of success by discouraging statements or excessive workload

PLANNING AN EXPLANATION

Explanations form the greater part of the teaching of subject matter. When an explanation is given to students, the teacher links what the students already know to the new information that is being given. This principle, despite its age, is nicely captured by Ausubel *et al.* (1978, p. 163):

> 'If I had to reduce all educational psychology to just one principle it would be this: The most important single factor influencing learning is what the student already knows. Ascertain this and teach him accordingly.'

Classification of explanations

Within the literature there are a number of ways in which explanations are classified; for example, Bligh (2000) identifies 11 kinds of explanation, but for everyday practice a much more useful classification is that of Brown and Atkins (1996):

1. Interpretive, i.e. answers the question 'What?'
2. Descriptive, i.e. answers the question 'How?'
3. Reason-giving, i.e. answers the question 'Why?'

Brown and Atkins describe explaining as a three-stage process consisting of:

1. *A problem to be explained (problem identification)* The term 'problem' relates to concepts in the subject matter to be taught to students.
2. *A series of statements (transmission)* These are linked statements made by the lecturer, containing the examples, principles and other material relevant to understanding of the problem, and must be stated at an appropriate level for the students in question. They must be conveyed with clarity, and should arouse students' interest in the explanation.
3. *An understanding of the problem (outcome)* If the explanation is successful, students will understand the problem. If not, the lecturer will have to deliver a new series of statements that offer a different perspective on the problem.

When planning an explanation, the lecturer should initially analyze the topic into its main parts or 'keys' and then establish any links between these, including any rules that might be involved (Davis, 2009; Scales, 2008; Brown and Armstrong, 1984). The particular type of explanation required is identified and incorporated into the teaching plan. In their study, Brown and Armstrong found that better explanations had more keys and a greater variety of cognitive levels of keys, so that lecturers placed more varied demands on the pupils, particularly higher levels of cognitive demand. Better explanations also involved the use of examples, visual aids and rhetorical questions and were more appropriately structured and stimulating.

Sequence for planning an explanation

George Brown (1978) remains one of the few writers to have offered a sequence for planning an explanation:

1. Decide precisely what is to be explained, in the form of a question, for example 'what, why or how?'

2. Identify any hidden variables. These might be prerequisite concepts that, although not immediately obvious in the problem, will influence understanding of the explanation. For example, a hidden variable in the question 'How does oxygen from the air reach the tissues?' would be the concept of diffusion of a gas.

3. State the key points.

4. Design the 'keys'. This involves taking each of the key points and writing each one as a simple statement. Each statement should have one or two examples to illustrate it and also elaborations or qualifications, as appropriate. It is useful to include a restatement or extension of the main point, using different words.

5. Write a summary of the key points, to be used at the end of the explanation.

6. Write the introduction to the explanation. Brown suggests that this is done last so that a motivating and interesting introduction can be devised, which is appropriate to the sequence.

TABLE 5.4 Planning sequence for explaining 'How gallstones cause jaundice'	
Step 1	How do gallstones cause jaundice?
Step 2	Common bile duct conveys bile from liver to intestine via gall bladder Obstruction to bile flow causes jaundice Gallstones block the common bile duct Gallstones cause jaundice
	Hidden variable = gallstones do not always cause jaundice. Thus, the explanation must make clear in what circumstances gallstones cause jaundice.
Step 3	Secretion of bile; storage and passage of bile; formation of gallstones; migration and impaction of gallstone; results of obstruction to flow of bile.
Step 4	(a) Bile is secreted by hepatocyes and conveyed to the gall bladder via the hepatic duct and cystic duct. (b) Bile is stored and concentrated in the gall bladder, from whence it is ejected by muscular contraction, and conveyed by peristalsis into small intestine via cystic duct and common bile duct. (c) In some people, gallstones form from precipitation of bile constituents, for example cholesterol, in gall bladder. (d) Small gallstones may be ejected during contraction of the gall bladder, passing by peristalsis into the common bile duct, where they may impact in the lumen. (e) This implication may cause obstruction to the flow of bile, with resultant rise in back-pressure to the liver. (f) This back-pressure will eventually cause reversal of flow of bile into the bloodstream, raising the serum bilirubin and discolouring the skin and mucous membranes, i.e. jaundice.

ADAPTED FROM QUINN AND HUGHES, 2007

Table 5.4 shows a planning sequence for an explanation, with the problem stated in the form of a question in Step 1. Step 2 shows the attempt to identify hidden variables by stating the relationship between the parts of the question. It can be seen that the explanation needs more than the four points made here, because there is a hidden variable, namely the fact that gallstones do not always cause jaundice. Step 3 is a list of the key points of the explanation, and these are expressed in Step 4 as statements or keys. Each of these keys would need to have some examples to illustrate the point and also elaboration or qualifications. For instance, the teacher might give examples of the kind of people who are likely to suffer from gallstones, possibly including the aphorism 'fair, fat, forty, fertile and flatulent'. Having designed the explanation, all that remains is for the teacher to incorporate it into the teaching plan, taking care to provide a motivating introduction.

DESIGNING EFFECTIVE QUESTIONS

Questioning forms part of the canon of teaching, and it is useful to distinguish between two major types of questions:educational and management questions. Educational questions are those directly concerned with the educational outcomes of the student, such as subject matter, feelings and opinions, whereas management questions are used to organize or control the classroom environment. Examples of the latter might be questions that are really commands, such as 'Would you please stop talking during my lecture?' or 'Would someone like to open a window?' This section focuses on educational questions.

Purposes of educational questioning

The purposes of educational questioning can be grouped under four main headings.

1. *Social purposes:*
   - to promote active involvement of the students during a lesson;
   - to encourage closer relationships between teachers and students;
   - to elicit any special interests or experience from the students.

2. *Motivational purposes:*
   - to develop the student's interest and motivation, e.g. 'How do you think that this problem might be overcome?';
   - to focus attention upon an aspect of the session;
   - to provide a change of stimulus.

3. *Cognitive purposes*
   - to encourage the students to think at varying levels of complexity and in a logical, analytical way.

4. *Assessment purposes:*

- to assess the previous knowledge or skill of a student;
- to assess the student's ability to use the higher levels of cognitive functioning such as analysis, synthesis and evaluation;
- to provide the teacher with feedback on the learning taking place during the course of a lecture.

These four categories emphasize the wide-ranging uses of questioning, but, in practice, it seems that most teachers use mainly factual and closed questions.

Classification of questions

There are many different ways of classifying questions, none of which is entirely satisfactory because questions depend very much on the context in which they are asked. Although none of the following examples is particularly recent, they are probably the most useful ones in the literature.

Bloom's taxonomy classification

In Chapter 4 the work of Benjamin Bloom (1956) is discussed in connection with educational objectives. The taxonomy of educational objectives can be used to formulate questions at different intellectual levels. Bloom classified intellectual or cognitive functions into a hierarchy of levels of increasing complexity, from simple recall of facts to evaluation and judgement of ideas.

The most basic level is called 'knowledge'; questions aimed at this level will ask students to recall a definition or term, state a fact, or identify certain things.

The next level is 'comprehension'; the teacher can test this level by asking questions that require students to restate meanings in their own words or to predict consequences or effects.

The third level is 'application', which requires students to apply rules, methods and principles to specific situations. In a first-aid lecture, for example, the teacher may have already given the rule for casualties, which states that they should be given nothing by mouth. Later in the lecture, the teacher may give a specific example of a casualty with a fractured femur and ask the question, 'How would you deal with the casualty's request for a drink?'

'Analysis', the fourth level, requires questions to be phrased in such a way as to make the student break down concepts or situations into their component parts, whereas the fifth level, 'synthesis', asks the student to do the opposite, i.e. to build up a whole from a series of constituent parts. For example, a question such as 'From what we have done so far, can you tell us what the main areas of your nursing-care plan would be?' is an example of a synthesis-level question. The highest level of intellectual functioning, according to Bloom, is that of 'evaluation' and consists of questions that ascertain from the students their judgements about the best or most effective arguments or courses of action. Table 4.2 in Chapter 4 outlines some of the differences between the six levels of the taxonomy discussed above, although the list of verbs is by no means exhaustive.

Brown and Edmondson's types of questions

Brown and Edmondson (1984) classify questions into two broad categories: 'cognitive' and 'speculative, affective and management'. Cognitive-level questions are arranged in a way similar to Bloom's above, with five subcategories:

1. *Data recall includes* recall of knowledge, tasks, naming, and classifying.
2. *Simple deductions* from data, such as comparing, describing, and interpreting.
3. *Providing reasons,* i.e. causes or motives that have not been taught in the lecture.
4. *Problem-solving.*
5. *Evaluating.*

Speculative, affective and management questions comprise such aspects as speculation, intuitive guesses, expression of emotions, class control, attention and checking understanding.

Kerry's classification

Kerry (1980) has devised a ten-item classification of questions:

1. *Data-recall* questions, i.e. facts are recalled but not used.
2. *Naming* questions, i.e. things are named.
3. *Observation* questions, i.e. what the student observes.
4. *Control* questions, which are part of classroom management.
5. *Pseudo-question,* where the teacher seems to give the impression that a range of answers will be acceptable, but in reality his or her mind is made up.
6. *Speculative or hypothesis-generating* questions, which invite the student to speculate about a hypothetical situation.
7. *Reasoning* questions, which ask for reasons as to why things occur.
8. *Personal response* questions, which ask how the student feels about an issue.
9. *Discriminatory* questions, which look for the points for and against an issue.
10. *Problem-solving* questions, which are geared to finding out about things.

The various classification systems outlined above are not exhaustive, and other types of question have been identified. Probing questions encourage the student to develop his or her first answer, and prompting questions give students hints about the direction that they might take. Convergent questions are those that narrow down to a specific answer, whereas divergent questions open out a number of possibilities.

Making questioning more effective

Questioning is often a rather haphazard affair, with questions being thrown out without too much thought as to their purpose. A number of criteria apply to the formulation of good questions. The question should be short so that it can be remembered by the students whilst they are working out their answers, and it should be stated in language that can easily be understood. The question must also be appropriate to the level of the student, as it is unfair to expect an answer to questions that are at too high a level for his or her particular stage of education. On the other hand, the teacher must try to include questions that require more than simple recall of factual material, by posing questions containing problems that need a thought-out solution.

Needless to say, a question should never be ambiguous and should contain only a single question. For example, it is confusing for a student to be asked a question like 'What are the main points in the pre-operative care of this patient, and why are they important?'

Another example of a poor question is 'Are models of nursing useful in planning patient/client care?' The student need simply say 'Yes' or 'No' to answer the question and the teacher will then have to probe further to elicit the actual 'answer' required.

'Pose, pause and pounce' technique

A useful tip for improving questioning technique is to write out the questions beforehand and include them on the lesson plan. This ensures that the questions have received some careful thought before being included, and so the teacher is less likely to ask poor questions. It is good teaching technique to explain to the students that, whenever a question is posed during a lesson, each of them is to think about the answer and one of them will then be selected by name to answer it. This is sometimes referred to as the 'pose, pause, pounce' technique, and it is useful in that it ensures that each student thinks about the question, just in case it is he or she who is selected. This method is superior to the overhead type of question technique, where the question is posed and students volunteer the answer, because any given student may well decide not to answer the question, leaving the bright members of the audience to vie for the privilege.

The teacher's response to the answers given by students is very important, as the act of questioning is highly threatening from the student's point of view. Teachers often seem unaware of the power that they possess in a lecture; their responses can have a devastating effect on the individual student.

Individuals can be made to feel humiliated by a thoughtless response from the teacher, so sensitivity is needed. Correct answers must be reinforced adequately, and this should also include the correct parts of a partially correct answer. An incorrect answer should not be left but should be followed by another version of the question, rephrased at a lower level. A partially correct answer can usefully be referred to another student for further elaboration.

One problem that requires careful handling is that of the students who do not answer at all. It is tempting to try to relieve their discomfort by moving on to another person, but it is well worth rephrasing the question at a lower level of difficulty so that the reluctant student gains a little success if he or she answers. If the rephrased question still evokes no response, then the best strategy may well be to leave such students for the moment and then to see them privately after the lecture in order to attempt to find a solution to their difficulty. The most common failing of questioning is that the response called for is at a low level of intellectual functioning, such as simple factual recall of information. It is therefore necessary for the teacher to plan for the inclusion of questions that test the higher intellectual functions.

Walsh and Sattes (2011, p. 3) outline that 'quality questioning is not a simple tool for extracting memorised information but a dynamic process through which a teacher intentionally engages students in both cognitive and meta-cognitive practice'. They further outline the intended outcomes of such engagement are to help students with the following:

- Focus their thinking on specific content knowledge.
- Use cognitive processing strategies to developing a deep understanding and long-term retention of content.
- Ask academic questions to clarify or further understanding.
- Monitor process towards learning targets through self-assessment and use of formative feedback.

- Develop personal responsibility by using structural supports for thinking.
- Contribute positively to the creation of a classroom learning community where thinking is valued.

Socratic questioning

Socratic questioning is defined by Elder and Paul (2007) as

'*disciplined questioning that can be used to pursue thought in many directions and for many purposes, including: to explore complex ideas, to get to the truth of things, to open up issues and problems, to uncover assumptions, to analyze concepts, to distinguish what we know from what we don't know, and to follow out logical implications of thought*'.

In other words, 'Socratic questioning is used to promote clarification of issues, probe assumptions, probe reasoning, question evidence, and encourage the student to look for the implications or consequences of their thinking or practice' (Harris, 2008). Elder and Paul (2007) explain that the key to distinguishing Socratic questioning from general questioning is that Socratic questioning is systematic, disciplined, and deep, and focuses on foundational concepts, principles, theories, issues, or problems. Anyone interested in probing thinking at a deeper level should construct Socratic questions and engage in Socratic dialogue. The Critical Thinking Community describe how critical thinking provides a comprehensive view of how the brain functions whereas Socratic questioning takes advantage of that overview to frame questions essential to the quality of that pursuit. Within this in mind, they reveal a list of principles to guide Socratic questioning within the learning and teaching environment and emphasizes that teachers engaged in a Socratic dialogue should:

- Respond to all answers with a further question (that calls upon the respondent to develop his/her thinking in a fuller and deeper way).
- Seek to understand–where possible–the ultimate foundations for what is said or believed and follow the implications of those foundations through further questions.
- Treat all assertions as a connecting point to further thoughts.
- Treat all thoughts as in need of development.
- Recognize that any thought can only exist fully in a network of connected thoughts. Stimulate students — through your questions — to pursue those connections.
- Recognize that all questions presuppose prior questions and all thinking presupposes prior thinking. When raising questions, be open to the questions they presuppose.

The Socratic Method also emphasizes a student-centred approach to teaching and strongly opposes didacticism (Banning, 2005) and according to Oermann (1997) the Socratic method may also be useful within the clinical environment to assess a students' critical thinking.

Drafting a teaching plan

It is interesting to watch how teachers and other public speakers use notes; these are often written on very small cards secreted in the palm of the hand, to which furtive glances are directed from time to time when a prompt is required.

From this behaviour we might conclude that, generally, people feel that they should be able to speak without notes, their use being somewhat akin to cheating! However, it is the needs of the audience, not his or her own prestige, which should be at the forefront of the teacher's mind, and a teaching plan can help to minimize the chances of omitting some vital part of the session and ensure that all the necessary factors have been considered.

Teaching plans need to be distinguished from a closely related concept, that of the teacher's subject-matter notes. Subject-matter notes are used to provide a reminder to the teacher of the actual details of the subject matter during a session and eliminate the possibility of forgetting some crucial aspect. It is quite possible for a teacher to present a teaching session without having teacher's notes, depending on the type of subject matter and the degree of expertise of the teacher. Indeed, many teachers do not use subject-matter notes *per se*, but put the key headings on overhead-projector transparencies, using these as prompts to their memory of the subject matter. It is tempting for newly qualified teachers to write down every word of what they plan to say, but this may well result in their notes being read aloud rather than delivered, and it is also easier for the teacher to lose their place! Even if the teacher is anxious not to omit any detail, it is still possible to include all the major headings and subheading s, with suitable indicators of examples etc., without writing the whole plan in prose form.

Reece and Walker (2007) believe that a lesson plan has two functions:as a strategy or plan for teaching and as a series of cues to be used during the lesson. They also believe that a lesson plan is intended to help teachers to proceed with the teaching session logically; but, even with detailed planning, every eventuality cannot be catered for. A lesson plan is therefore essentially tentative and flexible. In addition to providing structure to a lesson, a lesson plan should identify a sequence of events in the form of an introduction, the progression of the subject material and a conclusion. There are many reasons for the use of lesson plans, and, for them to be effective, many key details should be present:

■ title of session, date, venue, time and duration;
■ details and number of learners;
■ aims and learning outcomes;
■ teaching resources required;
■ layout of venue;
■ sequence and process of session;
■ teacher's initial self-evaluation.

Teachers should focus on planning for effective learning and develop learning outcomes specific to the lesson or scheme of work. Many authors believe that planning for learning involves long-term, medium-term and short-term goals, and in their experience new teachers tend to plan too much content and focus too little on management and organization. They also warn that if teachers try to cover too much material, most of it will not get through to the students (Petty, 2009; Gravells, 2011; Race and Pickford, 2007; Reece and Walker, 2007).

Pro forma for a teaching plan

Table 5.5 shows an example of a completed teaching plan which is written specifically for a classroom teaching situation; Table 5.6 shows an example of a completed teaching plan for a clinical skills session (Dix and Hughes, 2005). The plans each fit on two sides

TABLE 5.5 Example of a teaching plan for a classroom session

Date: January 04   **Time:** 13.30–15.00 hrs   **Group:** Cohort 1   **Subject:** Nursing assessment of the surgical inpatient

Group Number: 60   **Duration:** 1.5 hrs   **Venue:** Lecture Theatre   **Session Style:** Lecture

Previous relevant knowledge:

2nd year pre-registration nursing students who have completed the common foundation unit in year 1 and a 16-week medical module at the beginning of year 2

Aim of the session:

- To apply knowledge base to the safe principles of preoperative preparation for surgical patients

Learning outcomes: at the end of the lesson the students will be able to:

- Demonstrate correctly an understanding of the importance of maintaining a safe environment and ensuring patient safety during the preoperative phase
- Critically examine the theory underpinning the pre-operative check list for surgical patients
- Provide a sound rationale for nursing care which takes into account the social, legal and ethical influences within the peri-operative environment

Time	Duration	Content and development	Method	Rationale	Student activity	AVA	Assessment
13.30	15 mins	• Re-cap on previous session	Quiz	To identify knowledge and understanding from previous session	Student led questions and answering	PowerPoint Slides 1–4	Verbal feedback to indicate prior learning
13.40	5 mins	• Introduction to session • Aims and learning outcomes	Teacher transmission with direct questioning	Signposts where the lesson fits into the perioperative care programme, and highlights structure of the session	Listening with the opportunity to ask questions	PowerPoint Slides 5–7	Allows assessment of prior knowledge
13.45	10 mins	Development 1: QUESTIONS • Why do we assess patients prior to surgery? • Has anyone accompanied a patient to theatre? • Can anyone talk us through the process? • What information is required before the patient leaves the ward area?	Teacher transmission with direct questioning	To assess prior knowledge and understanding To provide feedback on the learning that has taken place during clinical placements	Listening with the opportunity to ask questions Group discussion	PowerPoint Slides 8–11	Allows assessment of prior knowledge

(continued)

Time	Duration	Content and development	Method	Rationale	Student activity	AVA	Assessment
13.50	20 mins	Development 2: • What information does the preoperative checklist comprise?	Practical exercise: Circulation and facilitation while students on task	To foster students' critical thinking abilities	Student Participation Group work to document what the preoperative checklist consists of (4 groups)	PowerPoint Slides 12–13 Acetates and pens	Feedback to the group Assessment of prior knowledge
14.10	30 mins	Development 3: • Examination of preoperative checklist	Teacher transmission with direct questioning	Highlights the importance of patient safety during the preoperative stage and allows the teacher to further expand on the subject	Listening with the opportunity to ask questions	PowerPoint Slides 14–40	Direct questioning will confirm understanding of the subject
14.40	15 mins	Development 4: • Re-cap on today's session • Re-visit learning outcomes and conclusion • Any questions or comments?	Teacher transmission with direct questioning	Ask questions to confirm learning (Diagnostic assessment to gauge learning) Inviting questions and comments provides the opportunity for students to engage in a group discussion	Listening with the opportunity to ask questions	None	Verbal feedback to demonstrate knowledge and understanding
14.50	5 mins	Development 5: Information giving • Reference list • Availability of handouts • Session 3 in the perioperative care programme	Teacher transmission with direct questioning	To provide further reading material for students Handouts are now available on the Web site for students who are absent to access Preparation for next session	Listening with the opportunity to ask questions	PowerPoint Slides 41–42	This session is not formally assessed; however, I will question intermittently to confirm understanding and learning

TABLE 5.6 Example of a teaching session for a clinical skills session

Date: January 13   Time: 13.30–14.30 hrs   Group: cohort 2   Subject: fracture management

Group Number: 20   Duration: 1 hr   Venue: clinical skills laboratory   Session style: clinical skills session

Previous relevant knowledge:
1st year pre-registration nursing students who have completed one theory module

Aim of the session:
• To acquire basic first aid skills in the treatment of people with fractured limbs

Learning outcomes: at the end of the lesson the students will be able to:
• Identify correctly common sites and types of fractures
• Explain how to correctly recognize the signs and symptoms of a fracture
• Describe the appropriate treatment of fractures
• Demonstrate correctly an elevation sling, broad-arm sling and immobilization of lower limbs as per St John Ambulance first aid manual

Time	Duration	Content and development	Method	Rationale	AVA	Assessment
13.30	10 mins	Introduction: aim and objectives Q1. Are there any trained first-aiders in the class? Q2. Has anyone experienced a fracture and is willing to share it with the group?	Teacher transmission with direct questioning	Signposts where the lesson fits into the First aid programme, and highlights structure of the session	PowerPoint Slide 1	Verbal feedback indicates prior level of learning
13.40	10 mins	Development 1 Common sites of fractures – upper and lower limbs Q3. Where are these bones situated in the body? Identify bones on skeleton model	Teacher transmission with direct questioning. Demonstration of skeletal bones using skeleton model	Visualization, aids to retention of learning, better than continuous teacher transmission	Slide 2 and 3 Skeleton model	Allows assessment of prior knowledge
13.50	5 mins	Development 2 Types of fractures Q4. Can anyone identify any types of fractures? Draw identified fractures on flip chart – compare with tutor slide	Teacher transmission with direct questioning Illustrate different fractures on flip chart	Reinforces learning and gives the teacher the opportunity to further expand on subject matter. Visualising the fractures when drawn, aids to retention of learning.	Slide 4 and 5 Flip chart/ pens	Allows assessment of prior knowledge

(continued)

Time	Duration	Content and development	Method	Rationale	AVA	Assessment
13.55	5 mins	Development 3 Signs and symptoms of fractures Q5. What are the signs and symptoms of a fracture? Write student answers on flip chart – compare with tutor slide	Teacher transmission with directed questioning.	Reinforces learning and gives the teacher the opportunity to further expand on subject matter	Slide 6 Flip chart/pens	Allows assessment of prior knowledge
14.00	20 mins	Development 4 Immobilization of upper and lower limb fractures Q6. Can anyone remember where these particular bones are situated? Students to demonstrate application of slings and bandages in pairs	Teacher demonstration of application of slings and bandages Students in pairs to practise skill on each other Circulate and facilitate	Demonstration enhances transmission of information, by the use of tangible equipment. Students are given the opportunity to practise this psychomotor skill in a safe environment	Slide 7 and 8 2nd teacher as a model Slings/bandages	By circulating around the students, allows for visual assessment of the skill
14.20	5 mins	Development 5 Treatment of an open fracture Q7. How do you think an open fracture should be treated – compare with tutor slide	Direct questioning and teacher transmission	Reinforces learning and gives the teacher the opportunity to further expand on subject	Slide 9	Allows assessment of prior knowledge
14.25	5 mins	Development 6 Revisit learning outcomes and conclusion Q8. Any questions or comments?	Teacher transmission	Reinforces lesson content and signposts end of lesson	Slide 10	Allows assessment of what has been learnt and retained during the session

of an A4 sheet and contain spaces for all the essential details and for the actual structure and sequence of delivery.

The column 'Content and development' is for the main headings and the questions that one is planning to ask.

The 'Student activity' column is a useful indicator of the amount of interaction and activity during a lesson and should also include any use of learning resources as well as teacher talk. Although a 'Duration' column is included, the timing is meant to be an approximate guide only, and the plan must be sufficiently flexible to allow for unplanned events.

Space can be allowed also for the teacher's immediate reactions at the end of the session, so that key aspects are recorded whilst fresh in his or her mind; these can then form the basis for later reflection.

Sequencing of subject-matter content

There are many different approaches to the sequencing of subject matter in a teaching plan, but the Herbartian principles are useful as a general approach when considering the sequencing of the session. Johann Herbart was a nineteenth-century German philosopher and educator who formulated a number of principles for teaching, and it is interesting to compare these with Ausubel's assimilation theory of meaningful learning outlined in Chapter 3. The Herbartian principles are as follows:

1. *Teaching should proceed from the simple to the complex.* The sequence should start with the easiest concepts first, so that students acquire the basic building blocks before tackling complex concepts.

2. *Teaching should proceed from the known to the unknown.* The starting point for the sequence should be what students already know about the subject. New material is then introduced to build upon their existing knowledge.

3. *Teaching should proceed from the concrete to the abstract.* Concrete concepts are normally easier to understand than abstract ones, and they are often pre-requisites for abstract concepts. It is therefore useful to teach the concrete concepts first before moving on to the more abstract ones.

Drafting a scheme of work

Within nursing and midwifery education, teachers are normally responsible for the delivery of a specific area of the curriculum, such as a module or unit of study, being of a defined size and duration and consisting of a series of sessions centred on a common theme or topic area. It may be difficult to maintain the overall continuity and coherence of a module if the teacher plans each session individually, so it is preferable to use a scheme of work that encompasses the entire module.

A scheme of work is a document that gives an overview of the key components of each teaching session within the module, and this would normally include the title, goals or learning outcomes, sequence of content, teaching and learning activities, assessment, and media resources. Table 5.7 shows an example of a scheme of work for a course titled 'Teaching research and enquiry skills for staff development of community practitioners.' By considering each of these components for a given session in relation to the others within the scheme, the teacher can ensure integration and coherence of the whole module. The scheme of work is a useful tool for checking on other important

	TABLE 5.7	Example of a scheme of work			

Session	Outcomes	Content	Teaching methods	Assessment
Introduction to research	Understand nature of knowledge	Mutual knowledge, formal knowledge, informed consent, confidentiality	Lecture Issue-centred groups Resource material	Multiple-choice test
Types of research	Understand principles of experimental research Describe the nature of experimental research	Experimental research Non-experimental research	Lecture/discussion Carousel exercise	Nil
Action research	Understand nature of action research Discuss potential projects in own field	Principles: exploratory, practical, problem-centred	Problem-centred groups Case-study material	Quality of feedback from group work
Basic statistics	Awareness of uses and limitations Understanding of basic statistics	Uses and abuses, basic concepts, centrality, variability, correlation, probability, sampling	Activity workshop Handout material	Monitoring of activities
Research critique	Understanding of providing a critique Undertake and elementary critique	Guidelines, academic fraud	Lecture/discussion Practical exercise	Assessment of critiques
Writing a research proposal	Identify sources of funding Write a draft proposal	Sources of funding, DoH, NHS, HEA, etc. Guidelines	Lecture/discussion Workshop on writing a proposal	Assessment of draft proposal Essay assignment on course outcomes

aspects of the module, such as whether or not there is sufficient variety of teaching and learning activities across the module, and the amount of assessment within the module as a whole.

ORGANIZING THE TEACHING ENVIRONMENT

An ideal learning environment is seen as one in which the educational needs of the learners are met (Fretwell, 1985). To assist the andragogical process, adults need a learning environment that does not threaten them (Knowles, 1984), and which supports and encourages them (Kidd, 1973). Despite being considerably dated, these statements still hold true today.

Students should be taught in an environment where learning can be facilitated and encouraged within a non-threatening atmosphere so that they can value and reflect on their experience.

As the poet Robert Burns said, 'the best-laid schemes o' mice an' men gang aft agley', and this is particularly appropriate in the context of organizing the teaching environment. All a teacher's careful planning can be undone if he or she neglects the environment within which the session takes place. The amount of organizing that can be done will depend upon whether the teaching session is in a formal classroom or in the clinical or community areas. It is much easier to organize a classroom than it is to set up a treatment room or consulting room for teaching, and in the latter case all that the teacher may be able to do in advance is to bring some chairs into the room.

When teaching in formal classrooms it is always good practice, wherever possible, to prepare the room in advance of the students' arrival, but this assumes that the previous teacher vacates on time. In reality, sessions often overrun, but even so the incoming teacher should take a few minutes to check the teaching materials and set up any media resources before commencing the actual teaching. The problem may be compounded if the seating arrangements need to be changed, as this can be a time-consuming exercise. However, it can be accomplished more quickly if the students are asked to move their own desks and chairs.

It is useful to switch on the classroom lights, even if the daylight is adequate, since this can have the effect of focusing students' attention; the overhead projector is designed to operate in normal lighting and is therefore not affected.

Sunlight, however, can bleach out the image on the screen if shining directly onto it, so window blinds or blackout curtains need to be closed if this occurs.

Institutions vary in the quality of their resources so teachers should be aware that their carefully prepared teaching plans may be ruined if vital media fail to arrive. Overhead projectors may not be available in every classroom; transparencies may have to be projected onto an adjacent wall if a screen is not available; video-replay facilities may not arrive when ordered and do not always work when they do arrive.

The UK Professional Standards Framework for teaching and supporting learning in higher education (HEA, 2011) and the NMC (2008) Standards to support learning and assessment in practice identify that teachers need to be effective in establishing a productive learning environment and must:

- Act as an advocate for learners in attempting to secure appropriate resources.
- Develop effective learning environments and approaches to student support and guidance.
- Maintain learners' interest in, and engagement with, the learning process.
- Identify and address poor motivation and challenge inappropriate behaviour.
- Engage in continuing professional development in subjects/disciplines and their pedagogy incorporating research, scholarship and the evaluation of professional practices.

The standards also establish that this requires critical understanding and essential knowledge of:

- Specific aspects of effective teaching, learning support methods and student learning.
- The characteristics and purpose of an effective learning environment.
- The value of effective interaction between those involved in teaching and learning.

- What motivates learners and what constitutes acceptable levels of motivation and behaviour.
- Group dynamics and how to manage groups of learners.
- The health and safety requirements applicable to the learning environment.

In addition to this, the NMC (2008) highlight further objectives in relation to the learning environment that nurse teachers should achieve in order to satisfy professional registration. These include:

- Create and develop opportunities for students to identify and undertake experiences to meet their learning needs.
- Provide appropriate peer support.
- Explore and implement strategies for quality assurance.

Finally, one of the most frustrating situations that a teacher can face is that, having prepared the classroom in advance, it transpires that another class has booked the room. Tense negotiations with the other teacher usually follow, taking valuable time away from the lesson and often resulting in a mass move to another room. In these situations, the interpersonal skills of the teachers are severely put to the test, but such events are all part and parcel of the work of teaching.

PLANNING FOR OPPORTUNISTIC ONE-TO-ONE TEACHING

By opportunistic teaching, we mean the kind of spontaneous teaching that occurs as part of everyday professional practice, with students, qualified staff, or patients and clients. Planning for this may seem to be a contradiction in terms, but it is possible to state some general principles that teachers can draw upon whenever opportunities for spontaneous teaching arise.

1. *Initiating spontaneous one-to-one teaching* Whilst accepting that opportunities for teaching during professional practice will arise spontaneously, it is normally possible to predict the broad areas within which such teaching will fall. For example, if the teacher is working on an acute surgical unit, he or she will know the patients' conditions and the nature of their care requirements. Similarly, if the context is a community nursing visit to a client's home, the teaching opportunities will again be broadly predictable. This allows the teacher to do some advance preparation in anticipation of possible teaching opportunities within the specific practice context.

   Teaching opportunities can arise in a number of ways; for example, students may ask the teacher to go through some aspect or procedure with them, or simply ask questions about the care of specific patients. On the other hand, the teacher may initiate teaching by asking questions or by explaining aspects or procedures. Teaching can also be initiated by the teacher if he or she perceives that a student or qualified member of staff is experiencing difficulty with procedures or understanding.

2. *Using appropriate questioning* This has been dealt with in a general way earlier in this chapter, but it is useful to consider questioning with specific reference to spontaneous teaching. It is good practice for teachers to review the types and levels of questions in advance (e.g. Kerry's classification described above), so that they can

select appropriate types and levels for the individuals who are likely to be involved in spontaneous teaching opportunities.

3. *Planning explanations of difficult concepts or procedures* In clinical and community practice contexts there are inevitably concepts and procedures that most people find difficult to grasp, for example biochemistry or pharmacology concepts that are important for the understanding of particular treatments. It is likely that the teacher will encounter again and again requests for an explanation of these concepts, so it is useful to prepare an explanation in advance that can be 'wheeled out' as required. The guidelines on planning an explanation given earlier in this chapter will be helpful in this regard.

4. *Planning ways to assess learning* Assessment is not usually thought of in the context of spontaneous teaching, but there are some situations where feedback on what has been learned is important. This is particularly the case when teaching patients and clients about aspects of continuing care such as long-term drug compliance following discharge, but it is also important for students and qualified staff in some circumstances.

INFORMATION AND COMMUNICATION TECHNOLOGY

> 'Education can play a role in influencing future cultural and social practices with technology'
>
> JISC (2009)

Learning is a necessary part of each individual's growth and development and should, with the assistance of the teacher and the teaching strategies, result in initial teacher-directed approaches gradually giving way to student-centred learning and eventually to self-directed study (Nicklin and Kenworthy, 2000). The need to integrate information technology into nursing education has been recognized and is well documented in the literature. In spite of this, information technology continues to remain a neglected subject in many nursing programmes particularly post-registration nursing programmes.

The higher education agenda stated that the UK needs technological skills to compete in the global market. Modularization, distance and flexible learning and the call for technology to meet these new learning needs have all had an impact on higher education. New teachers should be able to promote learning, enrich the learning environment and enhance the effectiveness of learning through the medium of information and communication technology.

Information and communication technology (ICT) is a term encompassing the full range of teaching and learning resources encountered by students in higher education and nursing. It has replaced former terms such as 'educational technology' and 'media resources'; however, it is important to remember that the new term embraces not only computers, but also more modest media. The field of computing is replete with terminology, and there are two other terms that nurses will encounter in the literature, i.e. health informatics and nursing informatics. Health informatics (HI) is the term used to describe the science of generating, recording, classifying, storing, retrieving, processing, analysing, and transmitting health information (RCN, 2012). Simplified, it is the knowledge, skills and tools which enable information to be collected, managed, used and shared to support the delivery of healthcare and to promote health. Nursing informatics is a sub-category of health informatics and can be seen as 'integrating information and computer science with nursing to enable nurses to record and manage data, process it into information and knowledge, and make knowledge-based decisions about patient care' (RCN, 2012, p. 3).

Information and communication technology is used to promote connections between one learner and other learners; between learners and teachers and between a learning community and its learning resources. The interactions between people in network learning environments can be synchronous, asynchronous or both. The interactions can be through text, voice, graphics, video, shared workspaces or combinations of these forms (JISC/CALT, 2000). Computer-based learning can be said to encompass both the expositive and experiential uses of computers as a teaching tool. It offers students an interactive form of learning, enables self-assessment and supports many different teaching strategies. Students are able to engage in self-paced, self-learning and have some control over the direction of their educational experiences (Hardy *et al.*, 1996). The Joint Information Systems Committee (JISC) champion the use of digital technology to ensure the UK remains world-class in research, teaching and learning. JISC reveal that the use of information and communications technology (ICT) has had a revolutionary impact on research, learning, teaching and educational support services in educational institutions.

JISC is responding to the key concerns of senior managers in Further and Higher Education to help them meet the current and future challenges they face, such as extending the reach of their institution beyond traditional boundaries, creating an agile and sustainable infrastructure, and achieving excellence in education and research.

General issues in the use of ICT

Before moving on to discuss the main applications of ICT in nurse education, it is necessary to make some general points.

Anti-racist and anti-sexist resources

Over the last decade there has been a growing awareness amongst educators of the need to ensure that ICT resources do not perpetuate stereotypes and prejudice. Whilst few teachers would design or select media that were deliberately racist or sexist, they may quite innocently use such materials because they have never thought about their potential to promote stereotyping. When considering resources for teaching, it is useful to check the following aspects:

- Do pictures of social groups actually represent the multicultural nature of society; for example are all the people white?
- Are ethnic minorities portrayed in positions of power, or only white people?
- Does the language used reflect all strata of society, or simply the middle class?
- Are there stereotypes portrayed, for example a male doctor and a female nurse?

The teacher should be familiar with the university's policy in relation to equality; it can be a useful source to help teachers to avoid inadvertent stereotyping.

Manufacturer's instructions for use of ICT

It is of the utmost importance from a health and safety point of view that teachers ensure that they have read the manufacturer's instructions for the use of ICT equipment and, preferably, have received some instruction in their use. It is also important as expensive equipment may be damaged if used incorrectly.

University facilities for ICT production

Universities have sophisticated facilities for the production of ICT, including professional recording studios and graphics departments staffed by skilled technicians. Teachers may simply have to put in a request to these in order to have materials produced by experts in these departments. However, it may not always be convenient or possible to utilize such facilities, so the following sections explain how teachers should set about producing their own media.

Electronic applications for learning and teaching

The generation of students today are seen as 'millennial learners' or the 'Net Generation' because they have been raised in a media-rich environment and live in an information-centric world (Lin, 2012). Opportunities for learning are changing and becoming more numerous and openly available; the nature of knowledge is also changing, so that what counts as useful knowledge is increasingly biased towards what can be represented in digital form, and/or applied to immediate problems and situations (JISC, 2009). Literacy practices are changing where writing has moved from a paper-based to a largely screen-based medium.

Societal demands and expectations in gaining access to information and knowledge anytime, anywhere challenges the established formal styles of teaching. The integration of mobile learning is responsive to a transforming society with an increased demand for more advanced, flexible methods of ICT (Clay, 2011). It is common for students to develop their digital and learning literacies throughout their education programme so innovative uses of technology for learning, such as mobile devices should be used to enhance the flexibility and choice for learners (HEFCE, 2009) and allow the learner to develop new skills in ICT.

Social networking sites such as Facebook are being used by students when planning and completing group work. It is unlikely that an institution would create an e-learning programme within any external application but the use of social networking media could be used to enhance and support an e-learning programme. Groups are private spaces within Facebook for people to discuss common interests i.e. lecture notes. The privacy settings for each group created can be customized so the sharing of information can be controlled.

The chapter takes a Herbartian approach to sequencing, in that it starts with the most basic types of ICT, moving on to progressively more technically sophisticated media and culminating in the latest computer technology for teaching and learning.

FUNDAMENTAL TEACHING AIDS

In UK institutions these fundamental audio-visual aids have largely been superseded by the more sophisticated technology described in the section entitled 'computer mediated teaching aids'. Readers in other countries, however, may still find this section useful.

Using a whiteboard in teaching

The whiteboard or ink board is now the most common type of board in use in higher education teaching rooms. When using a whiteboard for teaching, it is important to have the correct type of marker pen. Most boards use dry marker pens that can be wiped off with a dry cloth; ordinary marker pens cannot be wiped off without the use of some form of spirit. The purpose of the whiteboard is to record, in semi-permanent form, the key points and explanations during a teaching session. This enables the student to see as well as hear the points and to copy them down as a source of reference for the future.

Teachers may feel uncomfortable with silences, so tend to write as quickly as possible, with a resulting loss of legibility. The period spent writing on the board can be used as a mini-break for the students, so that their arousal will increase when the teacher faces them again.

TEACHING TIP

Remember, 'if it's worth writing down, it's worth writing legibly'.

The whiteboard plan

This is a very useful idea for structured teaching sessions and consists of a replica of exactly what the board will look like when the teaching session has been completed. More than one may be required if the teaching session involves a great deal of material, but, if the key points only are written, one plan should suffice. It is important to leave a margin at the side of the board for impromptu explanations and the plan should indicate the indentations and use of colour. A plan ensures that the whiteboard work is of a high standard and has been carefully thought out for maximum impact.

Using flipcharts

Flipcharts are simply large notepads that can be mounted on a stand or over a whiteboard, and marker pens are used to write or draw. When a sheet is completed, it is simply folded over, revealing a clean one. Material can be prepared in advance and revealed at the appropriate time. The guidelines for positioning, illumination and lettering are as for whiteboards. Erasing is not an issue, as the sheets are simply discarded when finished with.

Using an overhead projector

The overhead projector (OHP) is one of the most useful and versatile of educational media; it is a machine that projects large images of clear acetate sheets, called overhead transparencies, onto a screen. The overhead projector is designed for use in daylight, which saves the inconvenience of blackout, and it has the advantage over the whiteboard, in that the teacher faces the audience whilst using it. Transparencies can be prepared from a variety of sources:

- hand-written/hand-drawn by teachers;
- computer-generated by teachers;

■ produced by teachers using a photocopier;
■ produced by commercial publishers.

Overhead projection has another advantage over the whiteboard, in that transparencies can be prepared in advance of the teaching session. They offer the facility for step-by-step presentations, using revelation technique or overlays. On the downside, however, there may be some glare from the bright light of the projector, and the noise of the projector fan can be distracting. During the session, it is important to make full use of the 'off' switch; this should be done whenever a transparency is changed and also if the teacher needs to give a detailed explanation regarding one of the points on the transparency. Switching off the machine will focus the students' attention back to the teacher.

Creating transparencies for overhead projection   Computers are by far the best way to design professional transparencies, and a range of software is available which enables the production of sophisticated transparencies without having to be a computer expert, for example Microsoft PowerPoint, discussed later in this section. If this facility is not available, transparencies can be made by photocopying from paper originals, or by writing or drawing directly onto the acetate sheets.

Projection of silhouettes

The overhead projector will project a silhouette of any solid object on to the screen, such as the shape of an organ or of instruments and drains. For example, the teacher could drawn an outline of a leg onto acetate and then add cardboard silhouettes of the two fragments of a fractured femoral shaft to indicate the displacement and the effects of reduction.

Projection of X-rays and scans

Provided that the lamp is bright enough, any good-contrast X-ray should project onto the screen. An object can be then added, such as a femoral head prosthesis or intercostal drain, to indicate the position in relation to the X-ray structures.

DESIGNING AND USING HANDOUT MATERIAL

Handouts are a common strategy in higher education and consist of a sheet or sheets of paper given to each student for permanent use. Student-teachers often ask, 'What is the best time to distribute handouts?' There is no single answer to this, as it depends on the purpose of the handout. Some lecturers will only distribute handouts at the end of the lecture, because they feel that giving them out during the lecture will distract the students' attention away from what the lecturer is saying.

The problem here is that if the handout is given at the end, it has no current relevance for the student and will probably end up being filed without first being read. Given that higher education students are adults, they should be able to use a handout during the session, provided that the lecturer makes reference to the handout at appropriate points.

Purposes of handouts

The purposes of handouts can be summarized, as follows:

- *To provide information* Handouts can be given to provide information to the students, such as teaching session objectives, facts or statistics and diagrams and charts.
- *As a lecture guide* If the lecture structure is particularly complex, it may be given to the students in the form of a handout that they can follow, adding their own notes.
- *References and further reading* If a lecture contains many references, it is useful to record them on a handout so that the exact details are correct. Further reading can also be suggested.
- *Assessment and questioning* Handouts in incomplete form are commonly used to assess learning during the course of a teaching session. In addition, handouts may be given containing written questions for evaluation at the end of a session.
- *Worksheets and assignments* The student is required to complete the handout, according to the instructions on the sheet; this may require information to be sought or problems to be solved. It is commonly assumed that worksheets should be handed in to the teacher for assessment on completion, but the real role of a worksheet is to put the students in the position of having to gain certain knowledge or skills. These can then be assessed using the conventional methods of assessment, rather than trying to mark the wide variety of responses made to a worksheet.

Petty (2009) describes how handouts can save time for students and teachers if issued at the beginning of a lesson instead of at the end. He advises that teachers talk the students through the handout and encourages them to use it for group work, highlighting important parts of the text; by doing this, he alleges, students become familiar with the content of the lesson, whereas handouts are unlikely to be read later. However, if handouts are distributed at the beginning of a lesson, students' attention might be distracted from what the teacher is saying.

Design of handouts

Students should be encouraged to file handouts, either manually or electronically. The actual layout of text and diagrams will depend upon the nature of the topic, but in general handouts should not be overcrowded with text. Handouts can be designed in a very professional way by using desktop publishing computer packages, which have the advantage of novel designs such as newspaper columns or magazine format.

Methods of reproducing material

In the higher education sector, large-scale reproduction of items such as student handbooks is done by a central printing service. Small-scale reproduction usually consists of photocopying; however, copies are relatively expensive and expenditure on photocopying needs careful monitoring.

Copyright

Copyright laws are designed to protect authors from the wholesale copying of their works, a very real need in view of the ease with which modern copying machines can reproduce materials. However, copying is an important aspect of good teaching, and the licensing scheme operated by the Copyright Licensing Agency (CLA) allows copying without permission within clearly defined limits. In higher education institutions the licence enables teaching, administrative and technician staff, librarians and all students to copy for any one course of study in one academic year. It is a condition of the licence that the number of multiple copies of any one item of copyright material shall not exceed the number needed to ensure that the tutor and each member of a class has one reproduction only. The CLA produces *Guidelines for Users of the CLA Licence*, and a copy should be kept beside the copying machine.

TEACHING TIP

Remember that resources on the internet, such as *You Tube* videos are also may be subject to copyright

The slide projector, audio-cassettes and video-recording in teaching

Using the slide projector

Slide projection is used for showing still pictures to an audience, using 35 mm slides. In order to obtain a clear image it is necessary to operate slide projectors in darkness.

Setting up and using slide projectors As with all equipment, the slide projector should be set up before the teaching session and carefully positioned so that every member of the audience can see the screen. Image size is dictated by the distance of the projector from the screen – the further away it is, the larger the image.

If a remote control lead is being used, it should be tested and then positioned at the teacher's station. Blackout facilities should be operated before the class begins and the lights switched on, as this causes less disruption than doing it during the teaching session. If the slide sequence is spread over different parts of the teaching session with verbal exposition in-between, it is convenient to place an exposed black slide between each of the sequences. This saves the teacher having to keep switching the projector on and off, particularly when teaching in a lecture theatre with a separate projection room.

Slides Slides can be obtained commercially, or teachers can make their own slides using a 35 mm film camera with a close-up facility. When purchasing film for slides, it is important to obtain film for transparencies and not the ordinary film for colour prints.

Using DVD/digital-recordings in teaching

DVD is now firmly established as a major aspect of the entertainment industry, and DVD player-recorders have become a standard feature in most households. Their use in education is similarly established for a wide range of applications. Pre-recorded DVDs are available either as off-air recordings of television programmes, or as commercially produced DVDs; both form an important component of library stock in higher education. The use of pre-recorded DVDs in teaching needs careful thought; lecturers must brief students in advance so that the students understand the DVDs purpose and can jot down relevant notes. Equally important is debriefing after the DVD, to share students' impressions and conclusions.

Making DVD/digital recordings   Digital cameras allow teachers and students to make their own digital recordings, and this enables the reality of society or the workplace to be brought into the classroom, providing authentic material for discussion and analysis. However, students require careful briefing about the use of digital cameras in the hospital or community; permission has to be sought from appropriate authorities, and the public may resent the invasion of privacy.

Closed-circuit television

A less commonly used form of television in education is closed-circuit television; this does not involve recording, but relays live events to other parts of a building via slave monitors. It is useful for observing events where large numbers of observers would be obtrusive or overcrowded, such as in the operating theatre, or for observing interviews without affecting the interaction between participants. It is also used in the clinical skills environment to assess student's skill development

Video-conferencing

Video-conferencing facilities are an increasingly common feature of university campuses, and utilize live video-links between geographically separated campuses. The facility enables groups of students and staff to interact, who would otherwise have to travel long distances to meet together, and can be used for all kinds of meetings. For example, students who live at a distance from a campus are able to register for a programme that is taught at another location; they then participate in the teaching and learning experience by means of video-conferencing. This can help to ensure the viability of programmes that recruit small numbers, by opening them up to students at a distance. Video-conferencing is also useful for conducting tutorial group meetings on programmes where students live in geographically distant locations.

COMPUTER-MEDIATED TEACHING AIDS

Using Microsoft PowerPoint for presentations

This form of visual presentation is tending to replace the overhead projector as the medium of choice for presentations to both large and small groups. Microsoft PowerPoint is a graphics package that is part of the Microsoft Office computer software, and it enables the teacher to produce highly sophisticated slides or overhead transparencies for presentations. It can also create handouts and teacher's notes, and is relatively straightforward to use if the teacher has basic computer skills.

Computer-assisted learning

Computer-assisted learning (CAL) is a type of e-learning or any learning that is mediated by a computer and which requires no direct interaction between the user and a human instructor in order to run. Bloomfield *et al.* (2010) explain that supporters of e-learning champion CAL for its use for greater flexibility, learner autonomy and cost and time efficiency. Courseware, i.e. teaching materials, for CAL can use a single computer or a computer can be used in combination with a range of other media as in multimedia CAL.

With a single-computer approach, the teacher either develops appropriate courseware or it is purchased from manufacturers of educational media. The courseware is selected by the student and loaded into the computer, where it forms the learning experience for the student in whichever mode is appropriate. Computer-assisted learning is only as good as the courseware that goes into it, but computers do have the potential to produce high-quality graphic displays, data storage and retrieval and a host of other effects that would be almost impossible for the individual teacher to emulate in standard teaching situations. Single-computer CAL does have limitations and these can be overcome by the use of multimedia CAL, which consists of a range of media used in the same instructional program, for example sound, pictures, video.

Computer-assisted learning and independent learning

According to Petty (2009), independent learning helps to:

> 'reduce the detrimental effects of having too much content to cover in too little time, and yet provide unique educational gains'

Computer-assisted learning is particularly useful for independent, self-managed learning; students using a computer can take the material at their own pace, referring back to previous sections as and when they deem necessary. They can answer the questions posed by the program in total privacy, without the embarrassment of having their lack of knowledge exposed in front of a group of peers. CAL can help foster the intuitive kind of thinking that is important for discovery learning, by presenting problem-based information about which the student has to make hypotheses, subsequently checking his or her answers against the computer.

Computer-assisted learning can accomplish a number of other teaching functions, such as diagnostic and remedial teaching, in fact most of the activities normally associated with classroom teaching. The great advantage of CAL is that it can offer high-quality instruction that eliminates such variables as poor preparation and presentation by the teacher and problems of timing, fatigue, boredom and loss of attention. Of course, the last three can happen in any medium, but at least with CAL the students can switch off and go for a walk to restore their concentration. Additional computer assisted learning platforms include the use of podcasting, Wiki's, Skype and Textwall and the definitions of these are identified below.

Podcasts   The term 'podcast' is derived from 'iPod' and 'broadcast' and is a presentation or a programme that is available for download as a digital file. The advantage of podcasts from a student's viewpoint is that they can be returned to many times (Haigh, 2010).

Wiki   A wiki is used to create collaborative websites and facilitate note and can be used to facilitate discussion and sharing of information on health related topics (Haigh, 2010).

Skype   Skype is a voice-over internet protocol and software application that allows users to communicate over the internet by voice, video and instant messaging. Skype could be useful for video-conferencing but concerns over security, inappropriate use and excessive bandwidth usage have often prohibited its use within education establishments.

Textwall   Textwall is a web page that learners can send text messages to and is mainly aimed at students for learning and teaching purposes. The messages can be shown on a large screen or interactive whiteboard as part of a lesson for everyone to see. Individuals are not charged for messages but it costs the learner their standard sms charge to send text messages to the Textwall. A Textwall can be used to compose and send bulk text messages to learners for informative, administrative or pastoral purposes. The Web site and further information on Textwall can be obtained from: www.textwall.co.uk.

The Internet and World Wide Web

The term 'Internet' is shorthand for 'International Network of Computers', a network of computers across the world that is connected by high-technology telephone lines. Some companies charge a subscription fee for Internet access, but there is now a growing market of providers who offer free access. Telephone calls to access the Internet are normally charged at the local call rate, which makes browsing the Internet relatively inexpensive if done sensibly. The Internet, usually abbreviated to 'the net', provides users with access to almost limitless amounts of information and also allows them to communicate with other Internet users anywhere in the world.

Electronic mail (email)

Electronic mail or email has brought about a revolution in the way that teachers and students in education communicate with each other. Email has proved to be extremely useful for maintaining tutorial contact with students; it bypasses that bane of teachers' lives, the answering machine (voice mail), allowing the teacher to leave a message without the need to ring back later. Email is particularly useful for tutor's comments on draft assignments, facilitating a very quick turnaround of feedback to the student.

One of the exciting innovations in email tutoring is computer-mediated tutoring (CMT), also termed computer-mediated conferencing, a type of computer conferencing that allows students and tutors to discuss issues in a 'virtual group', but which does not take place in real time. Hence, a tutor may initiate activities or ideas onto the server, and the students in the virtual group can respond at any time of the day or night. Students and tutor may initiate and respond to each other's inputs just like in a live seminar, but with the advantage of not having to be in the same place at the same time.

World Wide Web

The World Wide Web offers information on an astounding range of topics, and almost anything can be purchased from the online shopping stores using a credit card. Teachers in nurse education will normally use their university's Internet service to access the Web, but many teachers will also have their own Internet facilities at home.

INTRANETS AND BLACKBOARD

Intranets

Intranets operate in much the same way as the Internet, but within an institution's own internal computer network (inter = between; intra = within). Hence, intranets are not accessible by the community at large. There is a wide variety of information contained on an intranet, including teaching and learning materials in the form of journal articles, lecture handouts, assignments and revision tips. Intranets are particularly useful for students studying at a distance from the main site, as they can easily access the materials without the need to travel.

Blackboard Content System

The Blackboard Content System is part of the Blackboard Academic Suite; it is a software application that enables institutions to store and manage content more effectively while increasing collaboration. This system is easy to use and has powerful capabilities in three important areas:collection, sharing and discovery of learning content. This application can be used to:

- manage and share files without the need for duplication;
- maintain and track versions of documents;
- provide dedicated file and content storage areas for individuals and groups;
- document academic growth through e-Portfolios; and
- categorize and share learning objects through a Learning Object Catalogue.

Blackboard is a virtual learning environment, used by a large number of universities that enables lecturers to provide online support for teaching and learning by, for example:

- providing online teaching resources (e.g. lecture notes);
- providing students with better tools to navigate learning resources and document their work;
- delivering a secure collaborative environment that enables users to transform information and ideas into powerful learning experiences;
- structuring online class activities (e.g. using discussion groups); and
- conducting online assessments (e.g. creating multiple-choice tests).

Further information on the Blackboard Academic Suite can be obtained from: http://www.blackboard.com.

Review questions

1. Define the differences between Educational Aims and Learning Outcomes.

2. Explain the meaning of 'concept mapping and sorting' and why it is useful in planning teaching sessions.

3. What are the main distinctions between surface learning and deep learning?

4. Describe the differences between deductive and inductive teaching of concepts.

5. What are the key criteria for formulating a good question?

SUMMARY

■ Nursing and midwifery incorporates a wide range of teaching contexts, ranging from the delivery of lectures in a university through to one-to-one teaching sessions with individual students, practitioners, patients and clients.

■ Many teaching encounters in clinical and community settings are opportunistic, arising spontaneously during the day-to-day delivery of care.

■ Learning outcomes and assessment of learning are inextricably linked, in that assessment normally requires the student to demonstrate achievement of the learning outcomes.

■ The secret of successful teaching is to place severe limits on the amount of content in a given session by the judicious selection of the most important aspects of the topic and the ruthless pruning of other, less crucial, material.

■ Concept mapping provides a way of prioritizing concepts in a concrete, visual way.

■ There are two main ways of teaching concepts: deductively and inductively.

■ Explanations form the greater part of the teaching of subject matter; when an explanation is given to students, the teacher links what the students already know to the new information that is being given.

■ There are many different ways of classifying questions, none of which is entirely satisfactory because questions depend very much on the context in which they are asked.

■ A question should be short so that it can be remembered by the students whilst they are working out their answers, and it should be stated in language that can easily be understood.

■ A lesson plan has two functions:as a strategy or plan for teaching and as a series of cues to be used during the lesson.

■ Lesson plans are intended to help teachers to proceed with the teaching session logically, but, even with detailed planning, every eventuality cannot be catered for.

■ Within nursing and midwifery education, teachers are normally responsible for the delivery of a specific area of the curriculum, such as a module or unit of study.

■ A scheme of work is a document that gives an overview of the key components of each teaching session within the module, which includes the title, goals or learning outcomes, sequence of content, teaching and learning activities, assessment, and media resources.

■ Students should be taught in an environment where learning can be facilitated and encouraged within a non-threatening atmosphere so that they can value and reflect on their experience.

■ Information and communication technology is a term encompassing the full range of teaching and learning resources encountered by students in higher education and nursing.

■ Computer-assisted learning is particularly useful for independent, self-managed learning.

References

Ausubel, D., Novak, J. and Hanesian, H. (1978) *Educational Psychology: A Cognitive View* (2nd Edition). New York: Holt, Rinehart and Winston

Banning, M. (2005) Approaches to teaching: current opinions and related research. *Nurse Education Today* 25(7) 502-508

Biggs, J. and Tang, C. (2011) *Teaching for Quality Learning at University: What the Student does* (4th Edition). Maidenhead: Society for Research into Higher Education and Open University Press

Bligh, D.A. (2000) *What's the Use of Lectures?* (6th revised edition). San Francisco:Jossey Bass Publishers

Bloom, B. (1956) *Taxonomy of Educational Objectives:The Classification of Educational Goals, Handbook One: Cognitive Domain*. New York: McKay

Bloomfield, J., Roberts, J. and While, A. (2010) The effect of computer-assisted learning versus conventional teaching methods on the acquisition and retention of hand washing theory and skills in pre-qualification nursing students:a randomised controlled trial. *International Journal of Nursing Studies* 47(3) 287-294

Brown, G. (1978) *Lecturing and Explaining*. London: Methuen

Brown, G. and Armstrong, S. (1984) Explaining and explanation. In Wragg E (ed) *Classroom Teaching Skills*. London: Croom Helm

Brown, G. and Atkins, M. (1996) *Effective Teaching in Higher Education*. London: Methuen

Brown, G. and Edmondson, R. (1984) Asking questions. In Wragg E (ed.) *Classroom Teaching Skills*. London: Croom Helm

Clay, C.A. (2011) Exploring the use of mobile technologies for the acquisition of clinical skills. *Nurse Education Today* 31, 582-586

Davis, B.G. (2009) *Tools for Teaching* (2nd Edition). San Francisco: Jossey-Bass

Dix, G. and Hughes, S. (2005) Teaching students in the classroom and clinical skills environment. *Nursing Standard* 19(35) 41–47

Elder, L. and Paul, R. (2007) *The Thinker's Guide to the Art of Socratic Questioning*. USA: Foundation for Critical Thinking

Entwistle, N. (1990) *Styles of Learning and Teaching* (2nd Edition). New York: Beekman Books Inc

Fretwell, J. (1985) *Freedom to Change: the Creation of the Ward Learning Environment*. London: RCN

Gravells, A. (2011) *Preparing to Teach in the Lifelong Learning Sector* (4th Edition). London: Learning Matters/Sage

Haigh, C. (2010) Legality, the web and nurse educators. *Nurse Education Today* 30(6) 553-556

Harris, M. (2008) Scaffolding reflective journal writing: negotiating power, play and position. *Nurse Education Today* 28(3) 314-326

HEA (2012) Deep and surface approaches to learning. Available from: http://84.22.166.132/learning-and-teaching-theory-guide/deep-and-surface-approaches-learning.html

HEA (2011) *The UK Professional Standards Framework for Teaching and Supporting Learning in Higher Education*. York: Higher Education Academy

HEFCE (2009) *Enhancing Learning and Teaching Through the Use of Technology: A Revised Approach to Hefce's Strategy for E-learning*. London: Higher Education Funding Council for England.

Hinchliff, S. (2009) *The Practitioner as Teacher* (4th Edition). London: Baillière Tindall

Jarvis P, Gibson S (1997) *The Teacher Practitioner and Mentor in Nursing, Midwifery, Health Visiting and the Social Services* (2nd Edition). Cheltenham: Nelson Thornes

JISC (2009) *Learning Literacies in a Digital Age: Briefing Paper*. London: Joint Information Systems Committee

JISC/CALT (2000) *Effective Networked Learning in Higher Education: Notes and Guidelines*. Lancaster: Centre for Studies in Advanced Learning Technology

Kerry, T. (1980) *Effective Questioning*. Nottingham: Nottingham University School of Education

Kidd, R. (1973) *How Adults Learn*. Chicago: Follett

Kinchin, I.M., Cabot L.B, Hay, D.B. (2008) Using concept mapping to locate the tacit dimension of clinical expertise:towards a theoretical framework to support critical reflection on teaching. *Learning in Health and Social Care* 7(2) 93-104

Knowles, M. (1984) *The Adult Learner: A Neglected Species* (3rd Edition). New York: Gower

Lawless, C., Smee, P. and O'Shea, T. (1998) Using concept sorting and concept mapping in business and public administration, and in education: an overview. *Educational Research*, 40(2), 219–231

Lin, C.Z. (2012) Comparison of technology-based cooperative learning with technology-based individual learning in enhancing fundamental nursing proficiency. *Nurse Education Today*, doi: 10.1016/j.nedt.2011.12.006

Neary, M. (2000) *Teaching, Assessing and Evaluation for Clinical Competence: A Practical Guide for Practitioners and Teachers*. Nelson Thornes, Cheltenham

Nicklin, P.J., Kenworthy, N. (2000) *Teaching and Assessing in Nursing Practice: An Experiential Approach*. London: Baillière Tindall

NMC (2008) *Standards to Support Learning and Assessment in Practice: NMC Standards for Mentors, Practice Teachers and Teachers*. London: Nursing Midwifery Council

Oermann, M.H. (1997) Evaluating critical thinking in clinical practice. *Nurse Educator* 22(5) 25-28

Petty, G. (2009) *Evidence-based Teaching: A Practical Approach* (2nd Edition). Cheltenham: Nelson Thornes

QAA (2008) *The Framework for Higher Education Qualifications in England, Wales and Northern Ireland*. Gloucester: Quality Assurance Agency

Race, P., Pickford, R. (2007) *Making Teaching Work: Teaching Smarter in Post-Compulsory Education*. London: Sage

Ramsden, P. (2003) *Learning to Teach in Higher Education* (2nd Edition). London: Routledge

Reece, I., Walker, S. (2007) *Teaching, Training and Learning: A Practical Guide* (6th Edition). Sunderland: Business Education Publishers Limited

RCN (2012) *Putting Information at the Heart of Nursing Care: How it is Revolutionising Health Care*. London: Royal College of Nursing

Scales, P. (2008) *Teaching in the Lifelong Learning Sector*. Maidenhead: Open University Press

Scottish Credit and Qualifications Framework (2010) *SCQF Level Descriptors*. Glasgow: SCQF

Severs, M., Pearson, C. (1999) *Learning to Manage Health Information: A Theme for Clinical Education*. Bristol: NHS Executive

Walsh, J.A., Sattes, B.D. (2011) *Thinking Through Quality Questioning: Deepening Student Engagement*. London: Sage

Welsh, I., Swann, C. (2002) *Partners in Learning: A Guide to Support and Assessment in Nurse Education*. Abingdon: Radcliffe Medical Press

Further Reading

De Gagne, J.C., Bisanar, W.A., Makowski, J.T. and Neumann, J.L. (2012) Integrating informatics into the BSN curriculum: A review of the literature. *Nurse Education Today* 32(6) 675-682

Higher Education Funding Council for England. Available from: http://www.hefce.ac.uk

Higher Education Funding Council for Wales. Available from: http://www.hefcw.ac.uk/home

Higher Education Funding for Northern Ireland. Available from: http://www.delni.gov.uk

Joint Information Systems Committee (JISC). Available from: http://www.jisc.ac.uk/

Scottish Funding Council. Available from: http://www.sfc.ac.uk/home/home.aspx

CHAPTER 6
TEACHING STRATEGIES

THE AIMS OF THIS CHAPTER ARE:

- To identify techniques used for planning and delivering lectures

- To explore the juxtaposition of small-group teaching and experiential learning

- To highlight how role play, simulation, gaming, problem-solving and debate can contribute to effective learning

KEY TERMS

Verbal exposition	Experiential taxonomy
Acrostic	Synectics
Psychomotor skill	Microskill
Proprioceptive feedback	Dyadic
Kinaesthetic feedback	Triadic
Tautological	

THE LECTURE METHOD

It is not surprising that academic personnel in educational institutions are called lecturers, given the predominance of this form of teaching in further and higher education. In lay terms, to lecture someone is to 'go on' at some length about an issue, with the recipient listening either willingly or unwillingly. This is similar to the educational use of the term lecture, i.e. a particular type of educational encounter in which a teacher transmits information to a number of students, with the teacher doing most of the talking and the students mainly listening or writing.

Lecturing is the most common teaching strategy in adult education (Bligh, 1998), but it does tend to polarize teachers' opinions: there are those who love it and those who loathe it. The proponents of the lecture method would argue for its use on two main grounds:

- *A proven track record* The practice of using lectures to transmit the culture of a civilization goes back at least to the ancient Greeks and has therefore stood the test of time. A significant proponent of this viewpoint is the psychologist David Ausubel (Ausubel *et al.,* 1978), who defends the use of lectures for transmission of knowledge. He maintains that it is simply wasteful to ask students to discover everything for themselves, when the transmission mode has been used successfully over generations to transmit the culture of a society. Ausubel's work is described in Chapter 3.

- *Efficient use of resources* In an era of significant resource constraints in higher education, lectures make very efficient use of teachers' time; for example, when giving a lecture to 150 students, the teacher–student ratio is 1:150; this helps to resource small group and laboratory teaching where the ratio may be as low as 1:8. This resource efficiency of lectures is used to good effect in the context of modular programmes. A module is a self-contained unit of learning, and modular programmes are now very common in British higher education. Academic awards are made up of numbers of modules at different academic levels, and efficiency gains can accrue by making a given module available to students from a variety of programmes. For example, an introductory module on psychology could be attended by students from a variety of disciplines, such as nursing, social sciences and humanities. Hence, a single lecture could address several hundred students at the same time, particularly when used in conjunction with closed-circuit television relays or video-conferencing.

The argument about the importance of lectures for the transmission of culture would be disputed by many academics, and is encapsulated in the adage: 'the information from a lecture goes from the lecturer's notes to the student's notes without passing through the brains of either!' Whilst this may be a little overstated, it does raise a serious question about whether lectures actually facilitate students' learning. The argument based upon efficient use of resources would also be challenged by opponents of the lecture method, because it contains the unsupported assumption that lectures actually do make students learn. In fact, the counter-argument is just as powerful; i.e. it might be much more efficient in the long term to use small-group and individual teaching methods, as these may be much more effective in facilitating students' learning.

Uses and shortcomings

Evidence from the literature on the educational use of lectures is summarized below:

- *Purposes* Lectures are as effective as other methods for conveying information, but less effective for the promotion of thinking skills and the changing of attitudes
- *Compulsory attendance* Students who absent themselves from lectures do less well in examinations and tests
- *Time of day* Morning lectures seem superior to afternoon lectures for the recall of information, but this may not apply to the 'evening-type' of learner, whose maximum physiological alertness occurs between 15.00 hours and midnight
- *Length* Attention declines considerably after approximately 20 minutes, with a reduction in the amount of information assimilated and noted

- *Recall* Recall on information from lectures is relatively inefficient, falling to something around 20 per cent recall after one week
- *Delivery* Speed of delivery is closely related to the level of difficulty of the material, and evidence suggests that there is a critical level of difficulty and speed, beyond which the material is delivered with a loss of efficiency

One common criticism of the lecture method is that the information could have been obtained from textbooks just as easily; however, this shows a lack of understanding of the purpose of lectures. Indeed, if they are used only to convey information readily available in other forms such as books, then they are likely to be simplistic or inaccurate due to time constraints. However, used thoughtfully, lectures can complement textbooks by providing:

- up-to-date research information that has not yet reached the textbooks;
- a synthesis of viewpoints from a wide variety of sources;
- clearer explanations of issues and phenomena, with the possibility of demonstration;
- personal involvement of the students by means of activities during the lecture;
- the potential to motivate and inspire students to further study.

TEACHING TIP

Encourage students to read about the subject of the lecture, using their textbooks prior to the lecture.

However, over-reliance on lectures may lead to dependence on the part of the students, who expect all the information to be handed to them 'on a plate'. All too often lectures are long, tedious and poorly organized, whereas with careful planning and practice they can be an effective vehicle for motivating students. The advantages and disadvantages of the lecture method are summarized in Table 6.1.

TABLE 6.1   Advantages and disadvantages of the lecture method

Advantages	Disadvantages
• Efficiency, i.e. one teacher can communicate with a large number of students	• Students' attention may wane
• A well-presented lecture may increase student motivation	• Students are largely passive
• New knowledge may be presented which is not yet in textbooks	• Lectures do not cater for each individual student's needs
• Teachers can integrate the subject matter better than students	• Pace of lecture does not suit all students
• Good for introducing a new topic	• Teacher's bias may be evident
• Useful for giving a framework upon which students can build	• Students obtain material 'second-hand' rather than from primary sources

Lecturing techniques

Lecturing can be seen as analogous to acting, each requiring careful scripting, polished presentational skills, and a certain personal charisma for effective performance. This theatrical performance element may not be present in other forms of teaching and can provide a source of stimulation and job satisfaction for those teachers who enjoy the challenge. The requirements of good lecturing are creativity, well-developed verbal exposition skills, clarity of ideas, an ability to make a subject interesting, enthusiasm and self-confidence. 'Verbal exposition' is the term given to the kinds of talking in which the teacher engages during a lecture, or indeed in any other type of teaching, with the exception of individualized instruction. This 'teacher-talk' can be subdivided into a number of modes, the commonest ones being the stating of facts, the defining and classifying of material, asking and answering questions, giving explanations, comparing and contrasting information, and evaluating material.

Table 6.2 gives guidelines for planning and delivering lectures; it uses an acrostic arrangement under the headings 'before', 'during' and 'after'. In an acrostic, the initial letters of each of the horizontal statements combine vertically to make another word, and

TABLE 6.2   Guidelines for planning and delivering lectures

1. Before the lecture

- Believe in yourself
- Explaining
- Focus on selected aspects
- Over-learn your material
- Rehearse
- Excitement/anxiety

2. During the lecture

- Delivery
- Unusual stimuli
- Recap
- Involve your audience
- Note-taking
- Get out on time

3. After the lecture

- Average/mean performance
- Focus on well-done/less well-done
- Tape the lecture and review
- Experience other people's lectures
- Retain a sense of proportion

this is a simple way to introduce novelty into teaching. Acrostics can also be used as an organizing principle for lecturing on a given topic – any topic – provided that you have the ingenuity to think up appropriate words, and provided that they are not over-used.

COMMENTARY ON THE GUIDELINES FOR PLANNING AND DELIVERING LECTURES

Before the lecture

Believe in yourself

By assuming the role of lecturer, one is, in a sense, claiming to have superior knowledge in comparison with the audience and this may lead to the feeling of vulnerability when facing them. Self-belief is a vital characteristic for successful lecturing; the teacher has an extensive knowledge and experience base which underpins their lectures, and this should provide the confidence to approach the lecture, and the audience, in a positive manner.

Explaining

Explanations are a central activity in most lectures and great care must be taken in their preparation. Explaining is discussed in detail in Chapter 5.

Focus on selected aspects

When planning the lecture it is important to be selective about what to put into it, the temptation being to cram in everything the teacher knows about a topic. Chapter 5 deals with this aspect of planning in more detail.

Over-learn your material

It almost goes without saying that the teacher must know the subject matter of the lecture 'inside-out' if credibility is to be maintained. Students very soon see through any attempts to 'waffle' by a teacher who does not know a particular point or answer. No teacher can know everything about a subject, and it can increase stature if a lack of knowledge is admitted. Needless to say, the teacher who constantly has to say, 'I'm sorry; I don't know', has inadequate background knowledge and this requires attention. If the lecture has been prepared some time in advance, or if it has been given previously, the teacher needs to spend time going over the material again to ensure that he or she has remembered it.

Rehearse

The analogy with acting emerges again here, with the advice that the teacher should spend time rehearsing various elements of the lecture until he or she is satisfied with the likely impact and timing. A digital or audiotape recorder is invaluable for providing feedback on these aspects.

Excitement/anxiety

Lecturing to a large audience is often the main anxiety experienced by those new to teaching, and it largely stems from the fear of making a fool of oneself by 'drying up' or forgetting what to say. The opening of the lecture is often the most nerve-racking part for the inexperienced teacher, but it is common to find that teachers still experience initial nervousness even after years of teaching. Actors often claim that this initial state of high arousal is beneficial, in that it puts an 'edge' on their performance. However, it is useful to distinguish between arousal and anxiety: arousal applies to the state of wakefulness or alertness of the individual, while anxiety applies to a state of arousal above that required for the optimum level of performance. Anxiety, therefore, reduces the performance effectiveness of an individual. What the lecturer is aiming at is a level of arousal sufficient to bring out the best in the performance without tipping over the edge into anxiety, which would reduce his or her effectiveness.

During the lecture

Delivery

On first entering the lecture room, it is important that the teacher takes a couple of minutes to organize the area, check the overhead projector, etc. Very often the students have been sitting in the room prior to the teacher's entry, having already received a previous lecture, and there is a temptation to commence the lecture straight away. So often lecturers begin their session and after a few minutes turn on the overhead projector only to find that it is projecting onto the wall or somewhere other than the screen. It is therefore important to spend a moment or two organizing the area, and to let the audience know so they can feel free to talk to their friends until everything is ready. This should ensure that the lecturer feels confident that all is well prior to commencing the lecture.

The introduction to the lecture is very important in gaining the students' interest and attention, so it is well worth attempting to provide a motivating opening. This could involve asking the audience whether anyone has had experience related to the topic, thus making the session relevant to them. It is also good practice to write out on the chalkboard a plan or outline of the sequence of the lecture, so that students may follow each section without losing track of the explanation.

The aim of a lecture is to communicate certain things to the audience, and the main medium for this communication is the lecturer's voice. There are three components of the vocal apparatus:

- *vocal cords*, which vibrate as the breath passes between them;
- *resonators*, which are the hollow spaces of the mouth, nose and pharynx;
- *speech organs* consisting of the tongue, palate, alveolar ridge, teeth, jaw and lips.

Volume or *loudness* is dependent on the force of the breath striking the vocal cords. Pitch is determined by the length, thickness and tension of the vocal cords, the first two factors being influenced by the size of the larynx. For instance, the small larynx of a child has short vocal cords which give the voice a high pitch. Adult males, on the other hand, possess large larynxes with long cords, producing a low pitch, i.e. a deep voice. Nervous tension will produce a note of higher pitch, and this is often detectable in persons who are anxious. Tone is the result of the air vibrating in the resonating spaces.

One of the most important aspects of speech in the lecture setting is *audibility*. This relies particularly on the careful use of consonants, which ensures clarity, and on the ability of the teacher to project his or her voice. It is good technique to stand up straight and speak from the lungs rather than the throat, ensuring that the lungs are well inflated with each breath. Careful observation of the facial expressions and other non-verbal communication will provide feedback as to whether the rear row of the audience is hearing what is being said.

Expressiveness is another important aspect of speech, as it helps maintain the listeners' interest by providing variety. Variations in intonation are produced by changing the pitch of the voice and also by variations of the volume and rhythm. The use of stress to emphasize important words can make the voice more interesting, and the speed of delivery needs to be at a pace suitable for the students to absorb the material and to write notes. Pausing is a strategy that new teachers need to develop; the tendency is to regard any periods of silence as undesirable, although pauses are a necessity during speech, since they provide the punctuation that makes the words meaningful. It can be useful to take a sip of water periodically, as a way of forcing oneself to pause.

One of the major problems during lectures is the speed of delivery; this can cause loss of attention and is often difficult to judge when inexperienced. The commonest error is going too fast when nervous.

TEACHING TIP

You could keep a card on the desk or lectern with the words 'SLOW DOWN' written on it; this will catch your eye from time to time and remind you to think about the speed of delivery.

The aim of any lecture should be to provide an atmosphere of psychological safety in which the students feel free to volunteer comments or questions. If the teacher conveys the impression of warmth and acceptance towards the group, this, combined with a sense of humour, will go a long way towards establishing the rapport that is so essential to learning. Evidence suggests that interest and enthusiasm are teacher characteristics that are particularly valued by students, and these can be indicated by emphasis and tone of voice, and also by the use of non-verbal signals.

It is difficult to overstate the fundamental importance of non-verbal communication during lectures. Students emit a variety of non-verbal cues and the teacher can gain valuable feedback on his or her performance by observing their facial expressions, which can convey feelings of surprise, puzzlement or astonishment. The teacher also emits non-verbal signals, so it is important to be aware of the role of such signals.

Gesture can play a useful part in explaining concepts, especially those with spatial relationships, but other gestures may prove distracting, such as fiddling with chalk. Head nodding can be a reinforcer of behaviour; if a learner is talking to the teacher and the teacher nods frequently, this can encourage the learner to continue talking. When lecturing, it is also important to engage the students in eye contact periodically, as this indicates interest and confidence. However, it should be noted that the length of time for eye contact should not exceed ten seconds, as longer may provoke anxiety. Honesty is a quality which is not often mentioned in connection with verbal exposition; in this context it implies the willingness of the teacher to admit that he or she does not know the answer to something.

Unusual stimuli

The inclusion of unusual or novel stimuli can be a powerful strategy for maintaining students' arousal and attention during a lecture. Such stimuli could be pictures, music, poems and activities which have an element of surprise or novelty.

Recap

Recapitulation or repetition should be used frequently, so that the learner is exposed to the information on more than one occasion. Provision could also be made for this at the end of the lecture if time allows, as it will help students to retain the information for a longer period of time.

Involve your audience

Adult students are never very happy just sitting listening to lectures; what they like to have is some personal involvement in them. There is a wide variety of strategies for involving students in lectures, even when faced with a large number of students. One effective way is to use buzz groups, in which students form groups of four to six without moving their seats, for example by some swivelling around to face the people behind them. These small buzz groups spend a couple of minutes discussing some aspect of the topic and then feedback is invited. Incomplete handouts offer another way of ensuring student participation; the handout contains only key headings or diagrams and the student is required to fill in the details gleaned from the presentation. A quiz or test given at the end of the lecture may also serve to focus students' attention on the material presented!

Note-taking

This is discussed in detail in Chapter 9, but it is helpful to note a few key points here. There are both advantages and disadvantages in taking notes during a lecture. Taking notes provides a permanent record of the information which is then available for review at a later date. Another advantage is that the information is actively processed and encoded in the student's own words. Bligh (1998) summarizes 29 studies showing that note-taking aids memory, and 20 studies showing that note-taking aids revision. On the negative side, notes may be inaccurate, and students may miss important points whilst writing down previous ones. On balance, however, I favour note-taking if it is done effectively, i.e. recording the key points rather than trying to write down everything word for word. At degree level, it is more important to note key references given in the lecture, so that the original source can be accessed later, avoiding reliance on secondary sources.

Get out on time

It is quite common to find that lectures over-run their allotted time, and this could be thought a cardinal offence! Students find it difficult enough to maintain attention during the normal span of a lecture, and over-running simply compounds the problem. There are also knock-on effects on the students' next class or lunch break, and it delays the next group's access to the lecture room. One of the causes of over-running is an over-ambitious lecture plan for the time available. These lecture plans seem to exert a powerful influence over teachers, who slavishly follow them until the bitter end, often regardless of the time or circumstances. From the teacher's perspective, the lecture plan contains important material that must be covered by the end of the lecture, even if this results in running late in order to do so. On the other hand, the students' perception is quite different, in that the important aspects of their college day are more likely to be the coffee and lunch breaks when they meet with their friends and peers. The teacher should aim to finish five minutes before the official end of the lecture, to give students and themselves a break before starting their next session.

After the lecture

Average/mean performance

Teachers often worry unduly if a lecture does not go as well as they would like, but it is important to see it in the context of their average performance. Some lectures go very well, others we would rather forget; it is not helpful to spend time worrying about a less than satisfying one-off performance. The teacher should aim for a good overall standard of performance but realize that there will inevitably be minor variations from day to day.

Focus on well-done/less well-done

When evaluating a lecture, it is helpful to try to focus on those aspects that were well done and on those that were less well done. By adopting this system the teacher will hopefully avoid distorting the evaluation by agonizing over a single unsatisfactory episode.

Tape the lecture and review

Evaluation of a lecture can be much more effective if the teacher can videotape one from time to time. It is a salutary experience to watch yourself performing as a lecturer, but by and large it is an encouraging activity that can boost confidence considerably.

Experience other people's lectures

Giving lectures can be quite an exciting experience for teachers, but it is easy to forget what it is like from the audience's point of view. It is helpful for teachers to attend lectures from time to time just to remind themselves what it feels like to sit in a lecture, especially if it is not particularly interesting or well presented. Also tips and ideas may well be picked up that can be used in later lectures!

Retain a sense of proportion

The problem with the lecturing/acting analogy is that teachers may feel that they have to produce virtuoso performances in every lecture. Clearly, some teachers have a flair for lecturing, while others are merely competent; the important thing is to be yourself. A sense of proportion is a great asset in lecturing; if the teacher attempts to incorporate every good point of style gained from observation of colleagues, then there will be little room left for the most important quality that the teacher possesses, namely individuality.

VARIANTS OF THE LECTURE

The standard format for the lecture is capable of many adaptations to suit the purposes of the teacher, and three such variants will be discussed: demonstrations, team teaching and dialogue.

The demonstration

A demonstration can be defined as a visualized explanation of facts, concepts and procedures. The purposes of demonstration can be broadly classified into:

- those designed to show the learner how to perform certain psychomotor skills; and
- those designed to show the learner why certain things occur.

In the former, the learner must reproduce exactly the behaviour that is demonstrated; whilst in the latter the behaviour is intended only as a strategy to aid the learner's understanding of a concept or principle. Each of these is now examined in turn.

Demonstrating a psychomotor skill

In Chapter 3, the theory of skills acquisition was discussed, so we will bear these principles in mind when planning a demonstration. There are many teaching strategies available for teaching clinical skills although Reece and Walker (2007) point out that the choice of strategy often relates to two aspects:

- the objective of the session; and
- the number of students in the class.

The strategies adopted for teaching fracture management include demonstration, questioning, small group work and teacher transmission or lecturing. When teaching a lesson that incorporates a psychomotor skill such as fracture management, the demonstration of that skill by a teacher is an essential strategy to ensure student learning (Dix and Hughes, 2005). Table 6.3 gives a checklist for giving a demonstration.

Commentary on Table 6.3

It is good practice to put the sub-skills on the chalkboard in the correct sequence, so this can serve as a guide when the learner is practising the skill. Whatever the purpose of the demonstration, it is imperative that each learner can see what is going on, and this implies very careful arrangement of the room and the lighting. Provision of seating is often considered unnecessary when giving a demonstration, but the students should be comfortable, so that they can give maximum concentration to the demonstration.

Closed-circuit television, if available, can provide a valuable addition to the demonstration, in that the camera can be placed so that it 'shoots' over the shoulder of the teacher, giving a 'demonstrator's-eye view' of the skill. A full-speed total demonstration of the skill, at the commencement of the demonstration, gives the learner

TABLE 6.3 Checklist for giving a demonstration

Before the demonstration

1. Formulate the learning outcomes.

2. Perform a skills analysis.

3. Assess entry behaviours of students, and determine prerequisites.

4. Formulate the teaching plan, with particular reference to:

   a) ensuring optimum visibility;

   b) preparation of all materials.

During the demonstration

5. State the learning outcomes to the students.

6. Motivate them by explaining why the skill is important.

7. Demonstrate the total skill at normal speed.

8. Write the sequence of part-skills on the chalkboard or overhead projector, as a checklist for the step-by-step demonstration.

9. Demonstrate each part-skill slowly, in the correct sequence.

10. Obtain feedback by questioning and observation of non-verbal behaviour.

11. Avoid the use of negative examples and variations in technique.

After the demonstration

12. Provide immediate supervised practice, with adequate time allowance.

13. Provide verbal, rather than physical, guidance.

14. Make the environment psychologically safe by providing a friendly atmosphere and constructive criticism.

15. Remember that initial interest may wane, so provide motivation and encouragement.

16. Remember that students will acquire the skill at different rates, so individualize the planning to cater for the fast and slow learner.

an overall 'gestalt' of the form of the total skill. If the teacher has not demonstrated the skill in class before, or not for some time perhaps, then he or she is well advised to practise the skill a day or so before the class is due. This will have benefits not only from the point of view of the skill itself, but also for the timing. Some teachers like to teach a skill using examples of how not to do it, and others like to include one or two variations of the technique. A common example of this is aseptic technique, which has permissible variations within a framework of principles. However, when teaching a new skill, most authorities would agree that learning is facilitated by teaching only one method of performing the skill and omitting any negative examples. This will minimize the effects of psychological interference that would otherwise arise due to the similarity between the original material and the variations or negative examples. Of course, once the learner has become proficient in the skill, interference from other techniques is unimportant.

It is crucial to formulate the objectives and prerequisites before commencing the lesson plan, just as in preparing any kind of lesson. As we saw in Chapter 3, the skills analysis will provide a detailed breakdown of the types of behaviour that constitute the total skill, and these must then be set out in the correct sequence. This is a very important step, as it is not always appreciated that the learner must not only remember the techniques for each sub-skill, but also the correct sequence of these.

The single most important aspect of the demonstration of a psychomotor skill is the provision of immediate practice for the students. A demonstration can only provide information about the cognitive and affective aspects, and the psychomotor components must be learned through the students' own muscles, i.e. by practice. It is often tempting, when teaching a skill in a clinical setting, to take over from the student in order to 'show' how to do it. Of course, this is quite valid if the student is unsure of the correct technique, but, generally speaking, students must be allowed to learn the skill by doing it themselves. It is thus that students receive the proprioceptive feedback from their own muscles and joints, which in turn modify their performance. No amount of 'showing' by the teacher will provide the necessary kinaesthetic feedback, without which no skill can be learned. Learning a skill can be frustrating and tiring, so it is essential that the atmosphere is friendly and relaxed. Testiness on the part of the teacher will only lead to tension in the students and this in turn will lead to poor performance and an increase in errors. This is why it is so important to allow sufficient time for practice and to bear in mind that not all students will master a skill at the same rate. In this kind of situation, competition between students can be quite counter-productive, so the teacher needs to emphasize that individuals differ in their rates of learning and that it does not matter if some people acquire a particular skill more quickly than others. What is important is that every student actually acquires the skill, not the speed of acquisition.

Demonstrating a principle or concept

Let us take as an example the concept of osmosis, a fundamental concept in medical science, which is readily demonstrated by a simple experiment using two glass beakers, each containing a piece of raw potato. The first jar is filled with plain water and the second with water containing a tablespoonful of salt. After several hours, the potato in the beaker of salt water is seen to be shrivelled and dried up, whilst the potato in the first one remains much the same. If teaching the concept of osmosis in a deductive fashion, then the teacher would first explain and define the term and give examples from human physiology. The demonstration could then follow, as a further example. In the inductive method, however, the demonstration would be presented first and the students put into groups to decide how the findings could be explained. Hopefully, they would arrive at a definition of the phenomenon of osmosis having explored the possibilities. Direct questioning can reinforce the learning that has taken place and can not only stimulate the students but also allow the teacher an opportunity to expand further on the subject being discussed. One disadvantage, however, to this strategy is that only a minority of students may participate; careful planning may be required to avoid this problem.

SMALL-GROUP TEACHING AND EXPERIENTIAL LEARNING

The juxtaposition of small-group teaching and experiential learning within this chapter is no coincidence. These two educational strategies are very much inter-related and interdependent, but it is useful to identify the characteristics of each before going on to explore them in more detail.

Small-group teaching

The term 'small group' is difficult to define. Brown (1996) emphasizes the importance of context in defining what constitutes a small group; i.e. the term can apply equally to three or four students working on a project, or the subdividing of a large lecture group into small groups of twenty or more.

Group size

Clearly, the size of the group will have an effect on the processes occurring within it, particularly with regard to the amount of face-to-face interaction with other group members. With numbers greater than about 25, this becomes impossible and subgroups have to be formed in order to allow for it.

Group size has another important bearing on learning: the larger the group, the less time each individual member will have available for contribution. Let us take a typical one-hour group session: if there are 30 students, each will have a maximum possible contribution time of two minutes; with a group of only ten students, the individual contribution time becomes six minutes. If we assume that not all students contribute to the same extent, it becomes quite probable that certain students will gain at the expense of others; it is interesting to note that none of the above timings includes any input from the teacher and the more the teacher becomes involved, the less time there is for student participation.

Purpose of small groups

The concept of a small group is not defined solely by the numbers of students involved; it also includes the purpose of the group. Broadly speaking, the function of an educational small group is to put the student at the centre of things; to allow opportunities for face-to-face interaction with other group members in order to exchange ideas and feelings; to be challenged by other people's viewpoints – in short, to expand the student's universe of awareness. Brown (1996) suggests that working in small groups can help students to develop interactive and collaborative skills that are necessary for employment and research.

For many teachers, small-group teaching is the essence of education, providing them with the opportunity for more intimate and rewarding engagements with students than is possible in lectures. The term 'small-group teaching' covers a very wide range of strategies and techniques and is one of the main ways in which students learn from and through experience.

Experiential learning

Although experiential learning is not confined to a single teaching or learning method, small-group strategies do provide a major vehicle for many aspects of it: hence the inclusion of both strategies in this chapter.

David Kolb's theory of experiential learning was discussed in Chapter 2 so the present chapter will focus on more practical aspects of experiential learning. At its simplest, experiential learning is learning that results from experience, but, since almost everything in life constitutes experience, this becomes an impossibly global notion. Essentially, experiential learning is learning by doing, rather than by listening to other people or reading about it. This active involvement of the student is one of the key characteristics of this form of learning, together with student-centredness, a degree of interaction, some measure of autonomy and flexibility, and a high degree of relevance.

Kolb (1984) identifies the characteristics of experiential learning:

■ Learning is best conceived as a process, not in terms of outcomes.
■ Learning is a continuous process grounded in experience.
■ The process of learning requires the resolution of conflicts between dialectically opposed modes of adaptation to the world.
■ Learning is a holistic process of adaptation to the world.
■ Learning involves transactions between the person and the environment.
■ Learning is the process of creating knowledge.

From these key characteristics, Kolb offers a working definition of learning:

> 'Learning is the process whereby knowledge is created through the transformation of experience.'
>
> Kolb (1984, p. 38)

The term 'experiential learning' is used in a number of ways in education; some apply it specifically to the learning of 'interpersonal skills', whilst others see it as pertaining to 'field placements' away from the educational institution. It is useful to distinguish between learning from experience and learning through experience (Burnard, 1990). The former involves using past experiences to gain new insights, whereas the latter consists of experiences deliberately planned to facilitate learning. In other words, both 'there and then' and 'here and now' experiences can be useful learning stimuli.

Burnard (1991) describes a study in which nurse teachers were interviewed about their perceptions of experiential learning and experiential learning methods. The range of definitions given by respondents was quite wide-ranging, and included:

■ **tautological** definitions (experiential learning is learning from experience);
■ all-encompassing definitions (any activity could be experiential);
■ time-related definitions (learning from the past and the present);
■ practical definitions (learning from clinical placements);

- personally focused definitions (gaining awareness);
- contrast-with-tradition definitions (less cognitive input).

Although the study used a very small sample, the results graphically illustrate the wide range of perceptions that these nurse teachers have about the concept.

Experiential learning as therapy

In Burnard's study, one of the respondents suggested that for him experiential learning was more like doing therapy, and this view is supported by Rogers (1983) and Heron (1986). It is important, however, that nurse teachers are fully aware of the problems associated with the blending of teaching and therapy. The primary objective of an educational group is the learning of particular aspects of curriculum, whereas the purpose of a therapeutic group is helping group members to 'heal' themselves in a therapeutic setting. Although it is important for students to understand the working of therapeutic groups, the teacher must be careful to avoid running educational groups as therapeutic groups, since there are ethical and moral implications such as informed consent of students.

GROUP DYNAMICS

Whatever the nature of the group, there are a number of fundamental processes that are identifiable; knowledge of these will help the nurse teacher to understand the dynamics of a given group.

Social roles

In any given group, there are many social positions called social roles: the family has roles called 'father' and 'mother'; nurse education has roles called 'teacher' and 'student'; and the individual over time plays many parts. A number of roles are played concurrently, as with a post-registration student who is also a ward manager; others are played sequentially as with the roles of child, adolescent, adult and elderly person.

Types of role

It is useful to differentiate between ascribed roles and achieved roles in society: the former are roles that cannot be altered without difficulty, such as sex roles and social class, and the latter are roles that are achieved by the individual's own volition, such as the roles of husband, engineer and so on. Primary roles are those that are always played, i.e. sex roles and social class; secondary roles are linked to economic awareness and employment, and tertiary roles are occasional ones such as 'captain of the local cricket team'.

Group norms

Group norms are defined as required or expected behaviours and beliefs of group members, which may be covert or overt. Covert or implicit norms are usually typified by the phrase 'it just isn't done', whereas overt norms are usually formulated as explicit rules of behaviour. In nursing, there are explicit rules about the way in which uniform is worn, but, in clinical settings, there may be implicit norms such as 'The ward manager likes it done this way.' It could be argued that norms are simply roles that are applied to all group members rather than to different concepts.

Both roles and norms may be considered as either imposed or emergent. Imposed roles are those that arise from outside the group, such as the appointment of a new head of department; emergent roles are those arising from within a group, such as the election of a chairperson. Such norms may also arise from outside the group as when a nurse teacher lays down the rules for conduct in a small-group session. Alternatively, the group may itself develop norms for behaviour and these are often termed group rules.

Belbin (1997) studied teamwork for many years; he famously observed that people in teams tend to assume different 'team roles'. He defines a 'team role' as 'a tendency to behave, contribute and interrelate with others in a particular way' and named nine such team roles that underlie team success.

The nine team roles are identified in Table 6.4 and are categorized into three groups: action-oriented, people-oriented, and thought-oriented. Each team role is associated with typical behavioural and interpersonal strengths.

TABLE 6.4 Belbin's nine team roles

Action-oriented roles	Shaper, implementer, and completer finisher
People-oriented roles	Co-ordinator, teamworker, and resource investigator
Cerebral roles	Plant, monitor evaluator, and specialist

ADAPTED FROM BELBIN 1997

In addition to team role characteristics (see Table 6.5), Belbin also defined weaknesses that usually accompany the team role and called them 'allowable' weaknesses; these are areas to be aware of and, potentially, to improve.

TABLE 6.5 Belbin's team role characteristics

Action-orientated roles	Shaper	Challenges the team to improve
	Implementer	Puts ideas into action
	Completer finisher	Ensures timely completion
People-orientated roles	Co-ordinator	Acts as a chairperson
	Teamworker	Encourages co-operation
	Resource investigator	Explores outside opportunities
Cerebral rolesW	Plant	Presents new ideas and approaches
	Monitor evaluator	Analyses the options
	Specialist	Provides specialized skills

ADAPTED FROM BELBIN 1997

Bruce Tuckman's classic description of the stages of group development focused on the behaviour of small groups in a variety of environments (Tuckman, 1965). He recognized the distinct phases through which groups develop and suggested that groups need to experience all four stages before they achieve maximum effectiveness. Tuckman further developed the model in 1977 (in conjunction with Mary Ann Jensen), adding a fifth stage:

1. *Forming* Individual behaviour is driven by a desire to be accepted by the others and avoid controversy or conflict. Serious issues and feelings are avoided, and people focus on being busy with routines, such as team organization, who does what, when to meet, etc. But individuals are also gathering information and impressions – about each other, and about the scope of the task and how to approach it. This is a comfortable stage to be in, but the avoidance of conflict and threat means that not much actually gets done.

2. *Storming* Individuals in the group can only remain nice to each other for so long, as important issues start to be addressed. Some people's patience will break early, and minor confrontations will arise that are quickly dealt with or glossed over. These may relate to the work of the group itself, or to roles and responsibilities within the group. Some will observe that it is good to be getting into the real issues, whilst others will wish to remain in the comfort and security of Stage 1. Depending on the culture of the organization and individuals, the conflict will be more or less suppressed, but it will be there, under the surface. When dealing with the conflict, individuals may feel that they are winning or losing battles and will look for structural clarity and rules to prevent the conflict persisting.

3. *Norming* As Stage 2 evolves, the 'rules of engagement' for the group become established, and the scope of the group's tasks or responsibilities is clear and agreed. Having overcome their conflict, group members now understand each other better and can appreciate each other's skills and experience. Individuals listen to each other, appreciate and support each other and are prepared to change pre-conceived views: they feel they're part of a cohesive, effective group. However, individuals have had to work hard to attain this stage, and may resist any pressure to change – especially from the outside – for fear that the group will break up, or revert to a storm.

4. *Performing* Not all groups reach this stage, which is characterized by a state of interdependence and flexibility. Everyone knows each other well enough to be able to work together, and trusts each other enough to allow independent activity. Roles and responsibilities change according to need in an almost seamless way. Group identity, loyalty and morale are all high, and everyone is equally task orientated and people orientated. This high degree of comfort means that all the energy of the group can be directed towards the task in hand.

5. *Adjourning* This is about completion and disengagement, both from the tasks and the group members. Individuals will be proud of having achieved much and glad to have been part of such an enjoyable group. They need to recognize what they've done and consciously move on. Some authors describe Stage 5 as 'deforming and mourning', recognizing the sense of loss felt by group members.

REFLECTION IN SMALL-GROUP AND EXPERIENTIAL LEARNING

One of the most useful strategies for learning in small groups or experiential learning is reflection, and the teacher can assist the student in this process by using a model devised to promote reflection by Boud *et al.* (1985), with a fourth stage added by Johns (1994). The model consists of a series of stages through which the student nurse should progress, having completed an experience. For example, the student may have completed the admission of a patient for surgery and sometime later takes time to reflect on this using the following stages.

1. *Returning to the experience* During this first stage the student is encouraged simply to 'replay' the whole experience over again, describing what happened but not judging it.

2. *Attending to feelings* The aim of this stage is to put students in touch with their own feelings about the experience. They should try to use any positive feelings that they may have about it, such as the pleasure felt by making the patient feel welcomed and reassured. Some feelings can actually form barriers to learning, so these should be removed by such means as laughing about an embarrassing question inadvertently asked during the admission, or by expressing feelings to another person. This removal of obstructing feelings is vital if learning is to take place.

3. *Re-evaluating the experience* The third stage consists of a number of substages, which in essence involve the students in associating the experience with their existing ideas and feelings about admission, and in testing for consistency between them.

4. *Learning* This fourth stage also has a number of substages where students should identify how they feel about the experience. Could they have dealt better with the situation? What was actually learnt from the experience?

This model of reflection needs to be practised until the student feels comfortable with each stage, and this is best accomplished by sharing the reflections with other students.

Developing learners as reflective practitioners

There is a plethora of literature relating to reflection and reflective practice in nursing and as a pioneer of reflection, Schön (1987) has long advocated reflection as a learning and teaching tool and a requirement of promoting professional development. He proposed that professional practice could be enhanced if people are provided with opportunities to reflect on their professional actions rather than relying solely on their acquired technical knowledge. The use of reflection in association with lifelong learning and professional development is explored in Chapter 15 but it useful here to discuss reflection as a strategy for learning and teaching.

All students are required to have a working knowledge and understanding of reflective practice for entry to the professional register.

> *'Newly registered graduate nurses must, through reflection and evaluation demonstrate commitment to personal and professional development and lifelong learning'*
>
> NMC (2010)

Whilst reflection is considered an appropriate vehicle for the analysis of nursing practice, it is gaining credence as a teaching strategy by fostering an understanding of student's work and developing critical approaches essential for providing complex nursing care in clinical and college environments (Duke and Appleton, 2000). Consequently, nurse educators are being called upon to develop nurses who are reflective practitioners (McGrath and Higgins, 2006) in order to link theory with practice.

Examples from the literature

Unravelling the unknowns of reflection in classroom teaching (Scanlan *et al.*, 2002)

In 2002, Scanlan *et al.* explored the meaning and use of reflection in teaching, and how reflection contributes to the development of teaching expertise in the classroom. A small sample of just three nurse teachers were the authors themselves because of their combined interest in reflection as a teaching strategy. The data was collected over two years using five different methods:

1. *Written autobiographies* This included analysing past experiences in order to gain insight and meaning from personal experiences. Each participant completed one written autobiography prior to beginning data collection using other methods. The autobiographies detailed at least one situation experienced by the participants as learners which had a significant impact on teaching practices.

2. *Critical incident journals* Each participant completed six critical incident journal entries relating to their practice throughout the duration of the study and allowed them to focus on significant teaching activities that they vividly remembered

3. *Classroom observations* Each participant was observed twice for a three-hour class by the other two investigators. One observed session was videotaped and each observer independently took field notes regarding the other participant's teaching activities. These observations enabled Scanlan *et al.* (2002) to review and analyze classroom activities individually and then together as a group.

4. *Debriefing following classroom observations* The purpose of the debriefing meeting was to discuss and share their classroom observations and occurred within one week following each classroom observation. The shared observations, coupled with open-ended questions encouraged the investigator who was observed to elaborate on and describe her thinking, thus promoting reflection on action as described by Schön (1987).

5. *Research team meetings* Scanlan *et al.* (2002) identify that research meetings occurred twice during each academic term to discuss the ongoing research, compare notes taken and review autobiographies, debriefing transcripts, and critical incident journals. The aim of such meetings was to challenge their thinking in greater depth about their teaching practices.

The findings of this study should be used with caution given the qualitative design and limited sample. The autobiographies revealed beliefs and assumptions about reflection and its relationship to teaching and focused on narratives that had a tremendous emotional component. The description of the experiences uncovered the emotions associated in our memories with those experiences which they believed had a lasting impact on their teaching. The critical incidents identified beliefs and assumptions about reflection and teaching with one participant commenting:

> '*I believe students learn best when they make the connection between class content and their own personal situations.*'

The analysis of the observed teaching sessions enabled the participants to see if their beliefs and understanding of reflection were applied to their teaching practices and they were able to link their experiences and the abstract concepts related to reflection.

Scanlan *et al.* (2002) suggest that their professional and personal experiences played a profound role in their use of reflection in teaching and that the learning environment for students can be enriched because of this. They imply that reflection is useful in linking lesson content discussed in a classroom setting and students' experiences. An interesting find was the differences in a teacher's ability to use reflection related to experience in teaching in addition to understanding of the content being taught. It appears that the more experienced teachers are more able to engage students. The authors state that:

> *'Personal reflective abilities do not automatically transfer to the use of reflection in the classroom. Time is needed to develop one's confidence in the content and process of teaching before we can use reflection intentionally and meaningfully.'*

Scanlan *et al.* (2002) conclude that participation in the study increased their awareness of their personal use of reflection and that the study supports an examination of one's experiences as a means of understanding reflection and its use in the classroom.

Reflection and the development of reflective practitioners are integral in preregistration nursing programmes (NMC, 2010). Braine (2009) refers to the numerous strategies that can be employed to foster reflection including learning diaries, journaling, critical incident analysis and group discussions but is concerned about the limited literature relating to teaching or assessing reflective practice. She believes nurse lecturers' limited knowledge on how be reflective and how to assist students to reflect is due to a lack of training around the subject. She further states:

> *'If we are to use reflection effectively then we as educators need to understand the concept, its underpinning assumptions, limitations and value. Moreover, we need to be aware that reflection is a highly sophisticated intellectual skill and like all skills, requires learning, and the ability to assess students' acquiescence of these skills.'*

This aim of this mixed-methods study was to explore 11 new lecturers' perception and understanding of reflection and how well they are preparing nurses to be reflective practitioners (Braine, 2009) using the following objectives.

To identify how new lecturers perceive and understand reflective practice:

- Explore how new lecturers facilitate student nurses in developing reflection.
- Clarify the reflective content within the nursing curriculum.
- To understand the perceived preparation for teaching reflective practice amongst new nurse teachers.
- What expectations do the new lecturers have of the Higher Educational Institute in preparing them to teach reflection?

Using a combination of semi-structured questionnaires and focus groups, the findings were discussed within identified five main themes (Braine, 2009):

Perceived lack of efficacy in teaching reflection – Both data collection methods identified a perceived lack of self-efficacy in teaching and facilitating reflection, indicating limited probing questioning by the lecturers during their teaching; this resulted in a reduced stimulation of reflective thinking.

Skills required for reflection – The skills required for reflective practice identified by participants were: self-awareness, critical thinking, problem solving, evaluation, synthesis skills, open mindedness, ability to recall and honesty. Braine (2009) also identified that the experience of the educator was important in relating the theory to practice, along with the individual value that the educator placed on reflection.

Reflection in the curriculum – There was a suggestion that reflection was not explicit within the curriculum, detached from the learning process and that students were not given enough education on the topic. Few participants identified that reflection might occur during lectures and tutorials, personal development plans (PDP), problem based learning (PBL) and during group work.

Strategies used in teaching reflection – Group discussions, the use of critical incidents and questioning skills were the only strategies identified as being used in teaching reflection.

Lecturer preparation – The findings from this theme highlighted that the new lecturers felt inadequately prepared and required support in developing the skills of reflection, primarily due to a lack of knowledge regarding reflection. Barriers to developing reflection in education were identified and included time, number of students, lack of support for students when engaging in reflection and the meta-cognitive skills of the students.

Braine (2009) recognizes that reflection is a complex skill that is cognitively demanding but not that easily developed and recommends that nurse lecturers plan strategies to assist students to develop this skill, which will also further enhance clinical practice. She concludes by stating that lecturers must have knowledge and understanding of reflective practice and reflective writing in order to develop the reflective skills of their students.

Teacher Competences required for developing reflection skills of nursing students (Dekker-Groen *et al.* 2011)

The literature is limited regarding teacher competences required to support the development of reflection skills in nursing students. In competence-based education, teachers need competences to support students' reflection processes so a study by Dekker-Groen *et al.* (2011) aimed to develop a framework of teacher competences required for creating a learning environment for developing student nurses' reflection skills. The authors define reflection as:

> '*a conscious and well-considered process of thinking about and interpretation of situations, events, processes, experiences and emotions, in relation to each other and to already available knowledge, aiming for better comprehension and for learning*'

Dekker-Groen *et al.* (2011) emphasize that thinking activities are comparable to activities in well-known taxonomies of learning objectives and that research into relevant thinking activities during students' reflection processes show that at least eight thinking activities are used (Table 6.6).

TABLE 6.6 Thinking activities during the reflection process

Thinking activity	Description
Describing	Systematically describing or writing about a situation, experience, or emotion that gives rise to the reflection
Analyzing	Clarifying relevant aspects of the description, for example, what the student and other people did, and feelings, what others felt
Structuring	Developing a structure to discover patterns or connections, for example, creating categories or ordering things chronologically
Explaining	Giving reasons for or causes of what happened or what the student did, thought, wanted or felt, in reaction to the situation
Evaluating	Valuing or assessing a situation, experience or emotion by using certain criteria and norms or goals
Concluding	Drawing conclusions about a situation, experience, or emotion in relation to the students' own future thinking and/or performance
Attributing	Attributing aspects or effects to yourself (internal attribution) and/or to outside influences (external attribution) and making it meaningful for other situations
Formulating intentions	Considering what can be learned from the reflection and how it can be applied to a new situation

ADAPTED FROM OOSTERBAAN ET AL. 2011

The framework of teacher competences together with a questionnaire was sent to a sample of 28 participants, including lecturers, researchers and managers deemed experts in reflection, feedback, teaching and nursing education. Participants were issued with information about the competences and the meaning and goals of reflection and were requested to evaluate the framework of competence descriptions according to their importance for teaching reflection skills to student nurse. The framework was adapted according to the participant's feedback (Table 6.7) and the competencies were viewed as were mostly relevant and applicable to teaching reflection.

The framework of teacher competences developed by Dekker-Groen *et al.* (2011) achieved high reliability scores in relation to task domains, task and indicators (Table 6.7) and the authors propose that the framework can be a useful tool in a teacher training programme for reflection training in nursing education.

They further state:

'The framework gives a theoretical input to the description of teacher competences to develop nursing students' reflection skills, by detailed descriptions of teacher competences to improve education in supporting students' reflection skills and by concepts to be used to describe reflection skills in the form of thinking activities.'

TABLE 6.7 Framework of teacher competencies (*Adapted from Dekker-Groen 2011*)

Task Domains	Tasks	Indicators
Preparation of reflection education	*Prepare teaching of reflection skills*	Develop ideas on reflection and feedback, practice reflection skills to students, utilise methods individually and with colleagues
	Acquire competence in thinking activities	Thinking activities are describing, analysing, structuring, explaining, evaluating, concluding, attributing and formulating intentions and provide explanation of these.
	Install competences to evoke reflection	Create a positive learning climate, demonstrate reflection and feedback, suggest learning processes that support reflection, observe and assess reflections
	Stimulate thinking activities	Demonstrate and stimulate thinking activities by asking questions per thinking activity
Learning goals	*Create short term goals*	Demonstrate and link learning questions to thinking activities, prepare learning goals, give reflection tasks to student and support reflection on experiences in practice
	Create long term goals	Teach reflection skills in a safe environment, increase task complexity and decrease teacher control, pay attention to emotions, values and norms in a reflection process, teach students to reflect independently using different methods
Instruction and assignments	*Give instruction about theory and practice of reflection*	Identify content information and skills students need to be able to reflect, apply education and methods to the competence level of students, pay attention to the interaction between theory and practice, give reflection tasks and teach specific skills, show how to reflect, explain and relate reflections to examples of professional development
	Give reflection assignments	Choose or formulate reflection assignments, discuss them with students and attune to their level of development, determine concrete intentions (who, when, on what, how, why) and let students perform them
Coaching reflection skills	*Put in coaching strategies*	Utilise suitable coaching strategies, be a role model, pay attention to communication skills, restraints and resistance of students in the reflection process

(continued)

Task Domains	Tasks	Indicators
TABLE 6.7 Framework of teacher competencies (*Adapted from Dekker-Groen 2011*) (*continued*)		
	Coach the learning process	Stimulate reflection of students through their own reflective attitude, promote an active attitude of students through explanations and examples, coach students while learning to reflect, give and organize feedback in the group which leads to growth and improvement
Development through feedback	Give feedback purposefully	Adjust feedback to the intended development, learning goals, experiences and needs of students, give feedback on different aspects of their functioning in different situations, give tangible feedback on behaviour, request feedback from students about one's own functioning
	Teach how to receive and ask for feedback	Give honest and constructive feedback, explain, show and have students experience how to receive feedback, support interaction about feedback
	Support the use of feedback	Time feedback carefully, speak about the use of feedback, stimulate students to give feedback, relate tasks and results to the students' development, stimulate self assessment
Reflection conversations and assessments	Lead reflection conversations	Use a method, work with an open attitude, apply conversation skills and notice non-verbal signals, discuss reflection patterns, compare theory and practice, confront students with contradictions and formulate strategies for the future
	Assess reflections	Formatively assess content and process in relation to goals, challenge students to reflect deeply, acknowledge how students worked on the reflection tasks, take care of systematic reflection that leads to conclusions for future action

PLANNING AND IMPLEMENTING SMALL-GROUP AND EXPERIENTIAL LEARNING

Small-group teaching and experiential learning is more challenging than many teachers realize, so it is essential to plan carefully for its implementation.

The experiential taxonomy

A helpful framework for planning and implementing small-group and experiential learning is that of Steinaker and Bell (1979). They describe an experiential taxonomy that can be used as the basis for writing learning outcomes for all kinds of small group teaching and learning. The taxonomy can be used for a single lesson or for a complete curriculum course. The taxonomy is shown in Table 6.8, and Table 6.9 shows two applications to nursing for each of the main categories.

TABLE 6.8	The experiential taxonomy (*Adapted from Steinaker and Bell 1979*)	
Taxonomic level		**Description**
1.0	Exposure	Consciousness of an experience
2.0	Participation	Deciding to become part of an experience
3.0	Identification	Union of the learner with what is to be learned
4.0	Internalization	Experience continues to influence lifestyle
5.0	Dissemination	Attempt to influence others

TABLE 6.9	Nursing applications of experiential taxonomy		
Taxonomic level		**Nursing applications**	
1.0	Exposure	(i)	I see an injection given.
		(ii)	I hear about Orem's self-care model.
2.0	Participation	(i)	I administer an injection.
		(ii)	I attempt to use Orem's self-care model.
3.0	Identification	(i)	I become competent in giving injections.
		(ii)	I become adept at using Orem's self-care model.
4.0	Internalization	(i)	Giving injections is now part of my life.
		(ii)	Orem's self-care model is now part of my life.
5.0	Dissemination	(i)	I teach other students to give injections.
		(ii)	I show other students how to use Orem's self-care model.

The physical environment

As with all learning settings, the physical environment should be as pleasant and comfortable as the facilities allow. It is useful if particular rooms are designated as discussion rooms so that students associate them with democratic participation and equality. The main aspect of the physical environment, however, is the arrangement of seating (and desks if used). Some people feel that small-group methods work best when students are seated without desks, as this lends an air of informality to the group. Nevertheless, certain students prefer to have a surface upon which they can jot down key thoughts, especially when the group is working on a specific task that requires writing.

A good rule of thumb is to ensure that whether or not desks are used, every group member has the same facility, including the teacher. It is common to see a group of students sitting in a circle without desks, with a teacher firmly ensconced behind one; this inequality may serve to highlight the differences in status between teacher and students to the detriment of group effectiveness. There is a variety of arrangements for seating during group work, some of the common ones being illustrated in Figure 6.1:

1. The 'U' arrangement is useful for teacher-led discussion, as each member can be seen clearly and, equally, the students can see any material that the teacher may want to show to them.

2. The circle, with or without desks conveys a sense of equality amongst all members of the group; it is particularly intimate when chairs alone are used and even a group of 15 can create a feeling of close personal contact.

3. A number of 'horseshoes', each consisting of a table around which three students are seated, can provide a very effective way of breaking larger groups into subgroups. The seating arrangement ensures that each student can see the teacher during plenary periods; but each 'horseshoe' can work independently, with its members on some aspect of a topic or problem. This arrangement can also capitalize on shortage of space, where a large circle is not feasible.

FIGURE 6.1   Seating patterns for small group teaching (S = student, T = teacher)

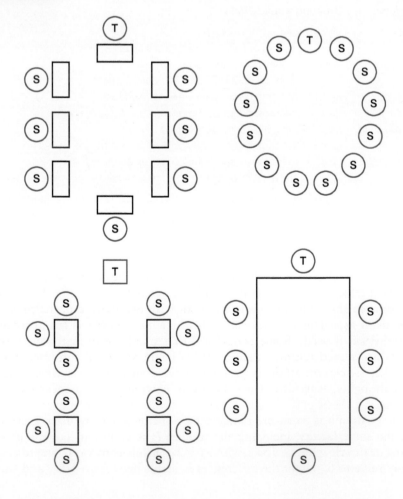

4. The 'committee' arrangement is a useful one for small-group work that has more formal purposes, providing a large surface, in the form of a central table, around which each member is seated. Although each member can engage in eye contact with the rest of the group, the shape of the table can make a big difference to the pattern of interaction. A rectangular table has a natural 'head' at either end, and students occupying these may be seen as the leader or chairperson, whereas a round table has no such natural positions of power. A rectangular table has corners and students occupying these seats tend to make the least contribution to discussions; people generally interact most with those sitting diametrically opposite, again this being more obvious in a rectangle than in a circle.

Re-arranging seating

One of the common errors that inexperienced teachers make is to rearrange seating in the classroom without adequate explanation to the group. Students of all ages tend to be quite sensitive about their personal seat and usually sit in the same place for all sessions. If they suddenly find that the seating arrangements have been altered, they may become resentful; indeed, many an unwitting student teacher has entered a classroom only to find that their carefully planned seating arrangement has been returned to its normal state by the students.

The emotive nature of seating positions is such that the teacher must ensure full and adequate explanation as to why he or she is wishing to rearrange it. A few minutes spent in explaining one's philosophy of teaching and the importance of the students' contributions can save a great deal of trouble later on by giving students rational, sincere reasons for such a rearrangement. Students are usually tolerant of such innovation, provided that they have been consulted before it is implemented.

TEACHING TIP

If a group is particularly resistant to rearrangement, you could leave the seating as it is, but to use a small group activity early in the lesson that requires students to interact with others. This will encourage natural pairing and movement, which can be capitalized on for the remainder of the session.

Psychological environment

The ideal environment for small-group and experiential learning is that which is termed a 'learning community'. This is characterized by a climate of acceptance, support and trust, where each member of the team acknowledges that he or she is still learning and where the needs of students are recognized. This notion of a learning community can apply to the higher education institution and to the clinical or community area and contains an implicit value judgement that students are equal to trained staff in all respects other than those of age and experience. In a learning-community approach, opportunities for learning are made available and professional growth is encouraged by graded responsibility. A large element of negotiation is typical of this approach, where students can determine what they want to learn and the means by which this will be achieved and evaluated.

Establishing trust

The establishment of trust among group members is fundamental to successful small-group and experiential learning. The length of time the small group is likely to be together is an important factor. For example, small-group techniques may be used on a study day, and in this short timescale it would be impossible to develop group identity. On a programme of study, on the other hand, small groups may well remain together for months or years, and it is therefore crucial that the group is given the time and opportunity to foster interpersonal relationships and trust. This means that the teacher must avoid the temptation of setting the group tasks and issues too early. Taking time to facilitate group cohesion will pay dividends later on when the group is able to work effectively without interpersonal conflict and competition.

TECHNIQUES FOR FOSTERING RELATIONSHIPS IN SMALL GROUPS

There are a great many ways in which small groups can be made aware of individual members.

Pairs exercises

One technique is a pairs exercise that aims for maximum interaction. Group members are asked to form pairs, choosing someone they do not know. Each member spends two minutes introducing him- or herself to the other. After this, group members are asked to find another partner whom they do not know, and spend two minutes each on explaining what they hope to gain from the group membership. This pairing continues until all group members have met each other, using topics such as 'my feelings about small group work', and 'problems in my current job'.

In another example, group members are asked to form pairs, and each member must choose a character from literature, theatre, films or television whom they would most like to be. They must explain the reason for their choice, taking up to two minutes to do this.

Developing trust

When members of a small group trust each other, they are able to contribute without fear of being ridiculed if their suggestion seems wrong; indeed, such suggestions may be seen as creative rather than stupid and may lead the group in a new direction. Students need to be able to try out their ideas, and this can only be encouraged in an atmosphere of psychological safety. Where there is trust in a group, each student is free to concentrate his or her energies on learning, rather than wasting them on building up defensive barriers against attacks from other group members. Trust may be developed using techniques which involve the group members in such activities as being led around the room blindfold. Yet another important way in which trust can be developed is the use of group evaluation at the end of each session. The group is asked to allow five minutes at the end for some spontaneous evaluation of the group's performance.

Participation of the teacher

There are many roles that the teacher can adopt in small-group work; he or she may function as the leader, taking the major responsibility for the conduct of the group, or, alternatively, adopt varying degrees of involvement, such as facilitator, resource person and group trainer.

The presence of the teacher is more likely to influence a very small group but be less obtrusive in a larger group. Indeed, the teacher may decide to leave the group entirely on its own during group work, being available close by, but out of sight, should group members feel that they need assistance. If the teacher decides to be involved in the group, there is always the danger that members will see the teacher as the leader, even if it has been made clear that the teacher's function is as facilitator only.

Establishing the right climate

The teacher's role is invested with authority, and it is difficult for students to overcome this barrier. Compare the interaction of a group of student nurses talking in the local pub and their contributions in a small-group learning session. It is obvious that lack of knowledge or interest is not the main factor for the poor response so commonly found in group work; rather, it is the climate of the situation that determines how well students involve themselves in discussions. Presumably, in the local pub there is no danger of humiliation from other people, since it is generally accepted that individuals have the right to express their opinions, however unusual these might be. In addition, the group in the pub is usually made up of friends and a degree of trust is present, which adds to the climate of psychological safety. If this atmosphere could be captured during group work in the college of nursing, there would be fewer problems of participation. Very often it is the teacher's own anxiety that stifles the spontaneous flow of ideas and opinions; the teacher must learn to trust group members to control their own discussion to a large extent, even if he or she is acting as their leader. If the teacher leads the group, then it is vital that he or she avoids evaluating the members, since they may become hesitant about giving their own opinions.

Importance of organization

Many of the dissatisfactions that are experienced with the use of small groups stem from the fact that they have not been properly organized. Because a small group is informal does not mean that it can be conducted in an off-the-cuff manner, and it is sensible to indicate to the students the goals to be achieved and the roles they must assume during the discussion. Each member must be prepared to contribute something to the group, and the importance of this should be explained at the first meeting. The teacher must be aware of attempts to participate by members and, if these are unsuccessful, should assist. A careful watch of non-verbal communication will provide good feedback as to how the students are feeling, and will also reveal such non-productive behaviour as opting out, dominating and seeking sympathy.

BASIC CLASSIFICATION OF SMALL-GROUP TEACHING

The classification of small-group teaching presents a major conceptual problem, in that there is a bewildering array of possible types. It is useful to distinguish between these basic types of small group and the various techniques that might be used with each. For example, role-playing is really a technique that can be used in many types of small group, so it is not included here as a basic type of group. On the other hand, 'syndicate work' seems to have a very specific function and is structured in a particular way, and is thus seen as a basic type of group. The following section explores a number of basic types of small groups in education, and the various techniques that might be used as part of these basic types of group.

Seminar groups

In higher education, a seminar group is mainly concerned with academic matters rather than with individual students and commonly involves the reading of an essay or paper by one group member, followed by a discussion of the topic by the total group. The teacher may decide to be the leader or may delegate leadership to the group. It can be a motivating strategy in nursing, where a student presents a paper on some aspect of nursing and then participates in a discussion with the group. The presentation of a seminar by the student can be counted as an assignment for continuous assessment purposes and this may serve as a motivating factor in ensuring a good-quality seminar.

Tutorial groups

Tutorial groups can take many different forms, and the term is often used synonymously with 'seminar'. It can also mean a one-to-one encounter with a student, an encounter with three or four students and a teacher, or can be synonymous with a controlled discussion. Clearly, the purpose of the tutorial group will largely determine its organization; a one-to-one tutorial is usually related to individual student progress and comments upon specific aspects of the student's work. The same kind of function can be achieved with three or four students together, although this may inhibit some individuals from speaking as freely as they might if they were alone.

Controlled discussion groups

In this form of discussion group, the teacher assumes leadership; its purposes are to clarify points raised during a lecture and to develop the ideas that it contained. Thus it can provide feedback to the teacher on the level of understanding achieved in a lecture and gives an opportunity for further explanation if the students have any difficulties with regard to the subject matter.

Free discussion groups

In contrast to the controlled discussion, this type of discussion is under the control of the group members; the teacher acts merely as an observer and resource person. The topics and direction are decided by the group. This can be a useful method in nursing for developing autonomy in the students, by giving them responsibility for their own learning. In addition, the fact that the topic has been chosen by the students may increase the motivation of the group.

Issue-centred or subject-centred groups

An issue-centred group has as its focus an issue that has no right or wrong answer and which is usually controversial or provocative. Topics such as 'is nursing really a profession?' or 'should resuscitation be carried out on the terminally ill?' provide an opportunity for students' opinions to be questioned and attitudes to be changed. It also provides a forum for public presentation of an individual student's own beliefs and values and gives practice in the efficient presentation of arguments.

Step-by-step discussion groups

A step-by-step discussion group involves a prepared sequence of material designed by the teacher and consisting of key questions or issues that are to be used to draw out the students' own knowledge about the topic. It uses inductive techniques rather than didactic presentation.

Problem-solving groups

In this form of small-group discussion, the students are given a problem to solve and are usually provided with certain sources of information from which to draw their solutions. The problem may be something that requires a single correct answer, or it may involve a number of correct answers, the students being required to decide which one is most appropriate to the situation.

Brown and Atkins (1988) identify four main stages in problem-solving that equate to the following questions:

1. *What is the nub of the problem?* This question gets at the core of the problem, and may identify subproblems, conflicts and contradictions.
2. *Have I met a similar problem before?* By recalling similar problems from past experience, the student may discover that the solution arrived at then will apply to the current problem.
3. *What approaches can I use?* Students may have to resort to trial-and-error experimentation if the solutions in Stage 2 are not successful.
4. *How should I check the solution?* This stage involves checking whether the solution feels right and also reflection upon the strategies used to solve the problem, as part of the development of students' problem-solving skills.

The main purpose of problem-solving groups is to encourage critical thinking by the students, and this method has had considerable success in the teaching of medicine. Nursing faculties have also developed a problem-solving approach to nurse education, using real and simulated patients. A common strategy for problem-solving groups is to present a detailed case history of a patient and then to ask specific questions related to nursing or medical science. The students are required to define the problems and to devise nursing measures that will help to overcome them.

Learning-through-discussion groups

Learning-through-discussion (LTD) groups were described originally by Fawcett-Hill in 1969 and are similar in some respects to the free-discussion groups described above. However, in an LTD group, the topic is decided by the teacher rather than by the students. The teacher's roles in LTD are only those of resource person and group trainer; the teacher does not take part as a group member. The roles normally taken by a teacher or chairperson are seen to be the responsibility of each and every group member. Fawcett-Hill maintains that students have little preparation for involvement in small-group work and so need to have a plan by which to proceed (Fawcett-Hill, 1969). The purpose of this method is to enhance learning of course material by utilizing the skill of each group member.

DeYoung (2007) differentiates between a formal and informal discussion and points out that formal discussions are usually announced in advanced of the session and students are required to prepare for this by reading around certain subject areas or reviewing a DVD or nursing journal feature. Advantages and disadvantages of discussion groups are identified in Table 6.10.

TABLE 6.10 Advantages and disadvantages of discussion groups (*DeYoung 2007*)	
Advantages	**Disadvantages**
An effective teaching strategy for small groups	Time consuming
Assist the teacher to gauge student's understanding to ensure that learning takes place	Inefficient method of communicating information
Misconceptions can be correctly quickly with immediate feedback	Teacher cannot effectively facilitate discussions in large groups
Students are able to learn the process of group problem-solving	Tendency for one or few students to monopolise the discussion
Students gain experience in using critical thinking skills	Students rarely come prepared to contribute to a valuable discussion

DeYoung (2007) believes that good discussions are unlikely to occur spontaneously as they require careful planning but that suitable topics for small group discussions might include controversial issues such as euthanasia, clinical and professional issues, and emotional topics such as death and dying. Once a suitable topic has been identified, DeYoung (2007) advocates the following technique for lecturers to facilitate an effective discussion:

- Make your expectations clear.
- Set ground rules.
- Arrange the physical environment.
- Plan a discussion starter.
- Facilitate, do not discuss.
- Encourage quiet group members.
- Discourage monopolies.
- Direct the discussion among group members.
- Keep the discussion on track.
- Clarify points when confusion arises.
- Tolerate some silence.
- Summarize the discussion points when appropriate.

Syndicate groups

This type of group is valuable for putting students in a position for discovery learning. The total class is given a major topic and then divided into small groups of about six members. Each of these small groups selects one aspect of the major topic and studies this over a period of two weeks or so. Contact with the teacher is maintained intermittently to report progress. When the work has been completed, each group reports its findings to the total group, after which the findings are assessed and interpreted by the teacher and a grade is awarded.

Project groups

The project method can be defined as a unit of purposeful experience in which the educational needs and interests of the student determine the aims and objectives of the activity and guide its process to a conclusion.

Characteristics

The main characteristics of the method are that the students are very much involved in the formulation of the aims and objectives of the project and that they are actively participating in the learning experience. Projects may be done by individuals, but more commonly they are undertaken by a small group of about six members. The main topics can be suggested by the teacher or left completely to the student's imagination, but in both cases it is crucial for the teacher to ensure that the aims of the project are clarified, so that the students are in no doubt as to the purpose of such an exercise. The kinds of aims that a group project can foster are the ability to work co-operatively in groups, collection of information, development of confidence in decision-making and many others.

Motivation and projects

For the project method to be successful it is necessary to have motivated students and this in turn requires subject-matter areas that are seen to be interesting and to contain scope for individuality and imagination. It is common for students to be required to undertake community-based projects, such as a neighbourhood study, and this allows the students scope to be imaginative.

For example, when doing a neighbourhood study, a small group decided to focus their project on access to local facilities by individuals confined to a wheelchair. One of the students sat in a borrowed wheelchair and two other students accompanied him to the local shopping centre. This was an example of experiential learning for the students, as it soon became apparent that it was extremely difficult to withdraw money from a cash point due to the position of the dispenser on the wall of the bank. Similarly, the students tried to gain access to a well-known tourist attraction, but found that it was impossible to do so in a wheelchair. The findings of the students were reported back to the rest of the group, and provided very thought-provoking discussion about life in a wheelchair (Quinn, 2000).

History of the project method

The project method itself is not a new development, having its origins in the 1920s. The method was first described by John Dewey of Columbia University and further developed by his colleague WH Kilpatrick. Dewey's philosophy was that the process of educational thought was more important than the results of such thought; he believed that a child would undergo mental growth if he or she actively participated in solving a problem that he or she saw as real. Use of the project method declined in the 1950s, but, with the advent of the Nuffield Foundation Science Teaching Project and the personal topic in the Certificate of Secondary Education, interest in the method revived.

A number of advantages are claimed for the use of the project method, including greater interest for the student, development of resourcefulness and independence in learning and the opportunity for the student to use important skills such as the identification and analysis of problems and the exploration of solutions. On the other hand, this method has its critics, and the main disadvantages are the time-consuming nature of project work and the difficulty in evaluating the student's achievement.

Planning for project work

When planning to use the project method for the first time, the teacher of nursing should ensure that the exercise is carefully organized. Groups may be allocated by the teacher, or selected by the students according to personal preference. The latter has the advantage of allowing them to work with friends, which may increase motivation and spur their efforts to succeed. As indicated earlier, it is important for the teacher to clarify the purpose of the project so that the enthusiasm and co-operation of the groups are obtained, and it is equally necessary to allocate sufficient time for the work to be accomplished.

When the groups have chosen, or have been allocated, a specific subject area, they decide amongst themselves which objectives and methods of inquiry they will use. The teacher must not control the direction of approach, as this would stifle independence and enthusiasm. The progress of each group's project should be monitored by the teacher, but only to ensure that difficulties are being overcome and that the most efficient techniques of data collection are being used.

The channels for obtaining information from personnel in the hospital or community must be clearly understood by the group. It is important to check that personnel who are likely to be approached by students are willing to spend time talking to them. The form of presentation of the projects should be decided before the students commence their work. All projects should be written up regardless of the form of presentation, and the teacher can negotiate with the group as to whether the projects are presented to the total group or simply submitted to the teacher in written form. Presenting the project to the total group can be seen as the culmination of the students' work and reinforces their feelings of accomplishment and success. Assessment of project work is discussed in Chapter 7.

Small-group projects, then give students the opportunity for more intensive study of a topic, challenging them to seek more widely for resources and giving experience in the skills of problem-solving and decision-making, all of which are important for the changing role of the nurse.

Experiential-learning groups

These groups are characterized by the use of experiential techniques to develop greater expertise in a variety of fields, for example teaching in clinical and community settings.

Focus groups

This is a qualitative research technique that is frequently used in nursing and health research. Rees (2011) points out that a focus group can be conducted with a small group of individuals who are prompted to discuss certain topics and experiences. Focus groups have a degree of acceptability because they tend to capitalize on the most natural form of social communication, the conversation.

TECHNIQUES FOR TEACHING SMALL GROUPS AND EXPERIENTIAL LEARNING

So far we have identified a number of types of educational small group, each having fairly specific purposes or functions. Within any one of these basic types, there are a number of techniques that might be employed to help group members to achieve the purpose of the small group. Again, it is useful to categorize them according to their main purpose, although some techniques have a wide range of application. Table 6.11 identifies the categories.

TABLE 6.11 Categories of techniques for small-group teaching	
Category	Techniques
1 Techniques to maximize group members' interaction with each other	Snowball groups; square-root or crossover groups; buzz groups
2 Techniques to generate creative solutions	Brainstorming; synectics
3 Techniques to generate data	Carousel exercise
4 Techniques to develop group members' self-awareness and empathy	Role-play; simulation; gaming; case study
5 Techniques to develop group members' presentational ability	Debate; seminar; peer-tutoring; microteaching; square-root technique
6 Techniques for applying knowledge and skills to real life	Role-play; simulation; case study; brainstorming
7 Techniques to develop group members' awareness of group processes	Fishbowl technique; peer review; group-interaction analysis

Snowball groups

As the name implies, this technique involves group members in subgroups of ever-increasing size until the total group is involved together. It begins with each individual group member working on a problem and then sharing this information with another student. Each pair then joins with another pair for further work on the problem, and then these tetrads join with each other to form groups of eight. Work continues in this fashion until the entire group comes together to share its ideas in a plenary session. The work can become progressively more detailed as the 'snowball' grows, and this technique is useful for getting every member of the group involved in participation.

Buzz groups

Buzz groups consist of from two to six members and are most frequently used to provide student involvement during a lecture or other teacher-centred session. For example, during a lecture on post-operative nursing care, the large class can be asked to form buzz groups for a three- or four-minute discussion of the complications of surgery. The group leaders then feed back their contributions to the total group. It is often a good idea simply to ask the first row to turn and face the second and the third to turn and face the fourth, and so on. These rows can then be segmented into groups of six students and this system minimizes the reorganization of the room. Buzz groups can be used more than once in any given lecture and provide the students with social activity and involvement, helping to maintain their level of arousal during the lecture. It is often useful to begin a session by asking the students to form buzz groups and write down everything they know about a subject, for example the structure of the heart. This can be fed into the main group and forms the basis of the lecture.

Brainstorming

This is another effective method of obtaining creative solutions to a problem (Osborne, 1993). The idea is for each member to generate as many ideas as he or she can about the problem in question. The emphasis is on free expression of ideas, and no criticism is permitted, however unlikely the suggestions. De Bono (1986) suggests that there are three main features of a brainstorming session: 'cross-stimulation', 'suspended judgement' and a 'formal setting'. Cross-stimulation refers to the effects of other people's ideas on an individual and the fact that these ideas may interact with existing ones to produce creative solutions. As the name implies, suspended judgement means that no criticism of suggestions is allowed, however silly the ideas may seem. It is important that the leader or chairperson be on the lookout for any evaluative comments and stops them immediately. It is not vital to produce entirely new or novel ideas; indeed, it may be that an old idea is the best solution to a difficulty in certain situations.

A formal setting is important so that participants can feel that there is something special about the group and thus be less inhibited about saying things that might seem ridiculous. The organization of a brainstorming group involves a leader or chairperson and someone to make notes of the ideas as they arise; it is helpful to use audiotape recording to ensure that no ideas are lost. The brainstorming activity can take any amount of time up to a maximum of about 30–40 minutes, and frequently lasts only some five to ten minutes.

The activity itself is only a means to an end, so there has to be an evaluation session in order to see what the next steps should be. This evaluation should take place some little time after the brainstorming session itself, and involves the sifting out of all the useful ideas into three categories: those ideas that are of immediate use; those that need further exploration; and those that represent new approaches.

Synectics

Synectics is a system of problem-solving that aims to produce creative solutions by making people view problems in new ways. Creative ideas are seen as involving the making of new connections between ideas, and one way of facilitating this is the use of the 'SES box steps' method (SES Associates, 1986). This method is based on the assumption that all problems contain a paradox or contradiction that can only be solved if new connections can be made. It uses the notions of analogy and metaphor to create these new connections and there are four distinct steps in the process:

1. Identify the paradox, which is the essence of the problem.
2. Develop an analogy or metaphor to provide a creative, different viewpoint.
3. Identify the unique activity associated with the metaphor or analogy.
4. Apply equivalent thinking, in which the unique activity is transferred to the current problem, resulting in a new idea for its solution.

An example will be useful to help understanding of this series of stages. Consider the following problems. A specialist community public health nurse wishes to put on health promotion sessions on the topic of safety in the home, for mothers of young children. Despite local advertising, however, there is a very poor turnout.

1. *Paradox* Health promotion sessions may be perceived by mothers as less attractive than other forms of social interaction, such as visiting friends or attending coffee mornings with other mothers and young children.
2. *Analogy* Sales parties are a well-established strategy for selling all sorts of goods, such as clothes, perfume, and gifts. The salesperson brings the wares to someone's home, and a number of friends, relatives and their children are invited over by the person hosting the party.
3. *Unique activity* The salesperson combines business with a social setting, including company and refreshments.
4. *Equivalent thinking* The specialist community public health nurse must combine the health promotion message with an opportunity for social interaction. This means that he or she must organize the classes as social events, for example by providing refreshments and creating an opportunity for social interaction in an atmosphere of informality.

The carousel exercise

This is an excellent and novel way of generating data from a group of students and also for the development of interviewing skills. The first step is for the teacher to identify a series of topics or subtopics that will be the focus of the session. The group is then divided into two, half of whom will be interviewers and the other half who will be respondents. Each interviewer is given a sheet of paper that is blank apart from a question that is written across the top of the page. The desks are arranged in a circle, with the interviewers seated on the inside facing out and the respondents seated on the outside facing in.

This arrangement ensures that there is a pair of students sitting opposite one another and separated by a desk. At a given signal from the teacher, each interviewer proceeds to ask their respondent to answer the question at the top of their sheet of paper and to answer it as fully as possible. Each interviewer has a different question and five minutes are allowed for each interview, after which time the teacher signals 'all change' and the outer circle of respondents moves round to the next seat on each person's right. The inner circle of interviewers remains in the same position throughout the exercise and every five minutes, a new respondent arrives opposite each of them. They proceed to ask their question to each respondent as they appear, recording the various answers on the same sheet of paper.

Eventually, the entire outer circle will have been interviewed by each of the interviewers and the latter will have a sheet of different responses to their question. These data can then be analyzed to reveal the opinions of those group members who were in the outer circle. It is desirable to then exchange the roles, so that the outer group become the interviewers and vice versa, thus generating twice as much data for analysis.

Simulations

A simulation is an imitation of some facet of life, usually in a simplified form. It aims to put students in a position where they can experience some aspect of real life by becoming involved in activities that are closely related to it. Airline pilots spend time working in flight simulators, which are identical to the flight deck of an aircraft and in which the pilots can gain simulated experience of handling emergencies that cannot (for reasons of safety and/or expense) be gained in any other way. For example, they are able to practise emergency procedures for such things as sudden depressurization, failure of engines, etc., and this experience should transfer to the real-life setting, if it is ever required. The notion of 'transfer of learning' underpins all aspects of simulation, the aim being to use the simulated experience to help the student to learn how to cope with the real thing.

Using simulation in nurse education

Bland *et al.* (2011) describe the aim of simulation as 'engaging students in active learning, creative thinking and high level problem solving'. However they identify concerns that have been identified 'regarding widespread integration of technology-based education tools in nursing education particularly the drift towards technology rather than philosophically-based pedagogy framing curriculum delivery'. In nurse education, a commonly used simulation is that of the cardiac-arrest procedure or 'crash-call'. The teacher organizes the simulation by providing an authentic environment that simulates a ward setting, with a 'patient' in a bed, a locker, charts. Certain staff or students are designated roles such as anaesthetist, sister, relatives and nurses, and the whole scenario of what happens when a patient has a cardiac arrest is enacted. The scenario can be used to give student nurses an insight into how the procedure operates and, in this instance, would serve as a demonstration. Alternatively, students can be asked to take the part of the student who discovers a patient with a cardiac arrest and to imitate the procedures required following such detection. By this means it is possible to give students experience of a situation, without the associated anxiety of learning it initially in the real-life setting. Bland *et al.* (2011) outline the factors that could be attributed to the interest in simulation within nurse education:

- Technological advancements providing opportunities for simulated learning to become available for learning experiences.
- Many students gain exposure to realistic, interactive clinically focused learning strategies.

- Simulation engages all the student's senses as they palpate, listen, observe and synthesise what they see, hear and feel linking with underpinning theoretical concepts.
- Simulated learning takes many forms and spans a spectrum of sophistication from simple reproduction of body parts through to the complex human interactions portrayed by high-fidelity simulators.
- Simulation represents clinical practice through a variety of delivery methods including role play, case studies, software packages, interactive manikins and actors.

Transfer of learning

It is always debatable whether or not there is 'transfer of learning' to the real-life setting, but, at the very least, the students will have had an opportunity to internalize the sequence of procedures required, and to appreciate the urgency of the whole situation. One of the important hallmarks of a simulation is that the students are not required to act out any kind of script; they are expected to behave and react in any way they feel is appropriate. In other words, a simulation involves the students in being themselves and dealing with situations using their normal, everyday behaviour. Whatever the scenario of the simulation may be, the students are expected to be themselves and to deal with the situations presented.

Simulations in first aid

One of the most valuable areas in which simulation can be used is that of first aid. Although this topic has some theoretical basis, the main emphasis is on practical techniques, so it is important to teach first aid in a way that helps students to cope with real-life situations. The first part of each session might introduce the concepts in question and then demonstrate the techniques required. Volunteers are then invited to join in with a simulation, in which they are required to give first-aid treatment to a 'casualty', and the simulation should be as realistic as possible within the limitations of the college setting. With a little imagination and dramatic flair, it is quite possible to create a scenario that simulates to a reasonable extent a first-aid emergency such as a head injury, a fracture, poisoning, and the like. The aim is to create a simulation that is as near as possible to the real-life situation that the student will encounter, so that the established behaviours and procedures can be transferred easily to the new setting.

Simulations and role-play

The term 'simulation' is closely related to the concepts of role-play and gaming; indeed, many simulations will involve an element of role-playing by other people, even though the students in question remain themselves. For example, a teacher may wish to do a simulation involving the admission of a mentally disturbed patient to the admission ward. A student is first identified who will be the admitting nurse, whilst another student or teacher will undertake the role of the disturbed patient. In this scenario, one nurse will be acting out the role of a disturbed patient, i.e. he or she will indulge in role-play; the other nurse, however, will simply behave and react in the way that he or she feels is appropriate in order to carry out the admission, i.e. remaining as him- or herself throughout the simulation.

When carrying out simulations, it is important that the teacher should give full briefing beforehand and allow sufficient time for an adequate debriefing at the end. These aspects are discussed in the next section on role-play.

Role-play

Role-play is derived largely from the work of Moreno on psychodrama (Marineau, 1989) and uses acting and imagination to create insights into the student's own behaviour, beliefs and values, and those of other people. Students are required to take on someone else's identity and to act as they think that person would behave. Although some scripting is essential to delineate the role, this should be kept to a minimum so that the student can act out the role in his or her own way. The use of role play in nurse education is an effective strategy for fostering interpersonal skills and therapeutic relationships and also for engaging students in the method of managing conflict (DeYoung, 2007).

Counter-attitudinal role-play

Role-play can be an excellent way of creating empathy with other people's points of view, particularly if the student is given a role that is opposite to the position or viewpoint currently held. This counter-attitudinal role-play forces students to consider issues and feelings from the other person's point of view and can help them to gain insight into why that person's behaviour is occurring. One of the important points about role-play is that the student, after some initial self-consciousness about the role in question, then quickly settles down to project his or her own character and values into the role. It is this identification with the role that forms the basis for subsequent debriefing and experiential learning. Role-play can be used for almost any social situation and is the method par excellence for exploring interpersonal communication skills. A checklist for organizing role-play is given in Table 6.12.

TABLE 6.12   Checklist for organizing role-play
A **Before the role-play**
1. Organize the room to allow for free interaction
2. Write out the role briefs for each participant
3. Write out instructions for process-observers
4. Do warm-up exercises
5. Do a briefing session, outlining purpose, rules
6. Invite or select participants
B **During the role-play**
7. Enact the role-play
C **After the role-play**
8. Facilitate group discussion and evaluation
9. Re-enact the role-play if required
10. Facilitate group discussion and re-evaluation if re-enacted
11. Explore the implications and applications arising out of role-play
12. Encourage actors to de-role
13. Summarize the original aims and purpose of the role-play
14. Organize group thanks to the actors

Briefing for role-play

As mentioned earlier, briefing and debriefing of participants are vital to the process of role-playing. Briefing is an important preliminary process prior to many kinds of small-group activity and is particularly pertinent to role-playing situations. Briefing involves giving prior guidelines about rules, intentions and goals, and is designed to ensure that participants benefit from the subsequent activities. It is not necessary to declare the outcomes beforehand, particularly if this might 'give the game away'; many role-play activities are designed to allow students to discover things for themselves, so it is important not to pre-empt this.

One of the essential rules of role-play is that no member of the group should be allowed to be a passive observer; any students who are not directly engaged in one of the acting roles should be given the job of 'process observers'. This implies that they are actively observing the role-play, including the verbal and non-verbal signals emitted by the actors. Such process observation is a crucial part of the feedback and debriefing session that follows the role-play.

Debriefing

Debriefing occurs after the activities have been concluded and can be seen as having three stages:

1. A description of what occurred.
2. Sharing of participants' feelings about the activity.
3. The examination of the implications of the activity for future work.

The first stage simply asks participants and observers to describe what occurred during the role-play; this is followed by a sharing of group members' feelings about the activity, and it is important to have an atmosphere of mutual trust for this stage. The final stage involves the application of what has been discussed to the real world of nursing and is where the insights gained can be shared with other students. The actors may receive much useful feedback from the observers about their personal skills of communication, and the group as a whole can benefit from the range of ideas and values generated by the role-play. As a great deal of emotion can be generated during role-play, it is important that the participants are encouraged to de-role at the end, so as to establish contact with reality again. This can be done simply by having students say out loud that they are out of role and that they are their normal selves again.

Game-based learning

Gaming is closely related to simulation and role-play, but gaming differs from simulation in that it has very precise sets of rules and is usually competitive in nature. Unlike simulation, games have no scenario, being complete in themselves, and participants behave as their normal selves. Educational games are simply extensions of recreational games, such as board games, card games and quizzes, and the aim is to create a method of learning that is both enjoyable and beneficial. Game based learning refers to software applications that use games for learning or educational purposes (JISC, 2007) and if used effectively and appropriately, can allow further choice for how the learner can learn and the potential for personalizing the learning experience.

GBL also offers the integration of a range of different learning tools but relies on the following factors:

- The readiness of the learner or learner group to adapt to a new learning tool.
- The correct level of institutional support, for example, technical support, IT lecturing support, resources, curriculum development.

While those institutions already using GBL are satisfied that learning in this way is effective, outstanding issues concerning the level of support needed from the institution do present considerable challenges. However, if the learner group is interested in learning in this way, and if the support structure at the institutional level is sufficient, then the potential of GBL to engage and motivate learners is significant (JISC, 2007).

Problem-based learning

Problem based learning (PBL) is a teaching strategy within the context of enquiry based learning that involves confronting students with real-life problems that provides a stimulus for critical thinking and self-taught content (DeYoung, 2007). Translated to the learning situation, Solomon (2011) describes PBL as follows:

> *'Problem based learning is an educational process where learning is centred around problems as opposed to discrete, subject-related courses. In small groups, students are presented with patient scenarios, generate learning issues related to what they need to learn in order to understand the problem, engage in independent study, and return to groups to apply their new knowledge to the patient problem.'*
>
> Solomon (2011)

The literature appears unanimous in that it generally agrees that students prefer this method of teaching as opposed to traditional methods as it is more effective in structuring knowledge, and students appear to be more cooperative and engaging with the process because they find it more interesting and enjoyable. It is a teaching strategy that lends itself well to the NMC (2010) 'Standards for pre-registration nursing education' where the domains of professional values, communication, decision making and team working underpin the ethos of the PBL process. PBL can also be used for formative and summative assessments.

The concept of PBL has been around for some time and is an effective teaching strategy that has been adopted by many health professions on a global basis. Despite the various components of PBL, Soloman (2011) identifies that the following elements remain constant:

- Small groups of students are issued with a written patient scenario.
- The lecturer's role changes from that of imparter of knowledge to learning facilitator.
- There is emphasis on student responsibility and self-directed learning.
- A written patient scenario is the stimulus for learning with students engaging in a problem solving process as they learn and discuss content related to the problems identified.

Facilitating PBL   The role of the facilitator in PBL is similar to the facilitator of discussion groups and role play as indicated below:

- Establish a good learning environment for the group.
- Be interested and enthusiastic.
- Outline the key skills to be gained from participation in PBL.
- Tolerate silence.
- Facilitate learning – avoid lecturing.
- Ensure learning needs are identified before the tutorial ends.

■ Promote the use of evidence-based resources.

■ Be yourself.

(Solomon, 2011, Fitzgerald, 2008 and DeYoung, 2007)

Resources Solomon (2011) further identifies the number of resources required to effectively facilitate PBL, mainly because learning occurs within small groups. In addition to library and information services, there will be a need for additional small classrooms and also facilitators who are experienced to assume the role of facilitator. The benefits of PBL considerably outweigh the challenges associated with it, and whilst not an exhaustive list, Table 6.13 clearly demonstrates this.

TABLE 6.13   Benefits and challenges of PBL

Benefits	Challenges
PBL can be completed virtually using online and web-based learning interfaces, thus increasing accessibility and reducing the number of facilitators and venues required	Depending on the number of students, facilitating PBL can be costly for educational establishments due to the number of venues and facilitators required
Realistic patient focused content is more relevant and meaningful for students where theory can be applied to practice situations; therefore learning in placed in context and student engagement is likely to be greater	Facilitation in PBL is dependent on the quality of patient scenarios and the capability of problem facilitators to support students
Increased opportunities for shared learning and interprofessional learning	Successful PBL relies on the motivation of students
Increased motivation applied to learning, contributing to a greater experience and student satisfaction	The preparation of patient scenarios and relevant resources is time consuming
Face-to-face contact is inherent in small group teaching and it allows for the development of confidence and interpersonal skills	Some students might feel as though they are 'doing all the work' and frustrations may arise with those who have under-developed independent learning skills
Students enjoy PBL as an interactive teaching strategy as opposed to traditional lecture methods	
PBL promotes critical thinking and encourages a deep approach to learning	
PBL develops skills in decision making, prioritising, team working and presenting new information	
Opportunities for lecturers to enhance their clinical credibility	

Implementing PBL

Below is a series of stages used in the implementation of problem based learning activities.

Stage 1: Launch of PBL and introduction of trigger questions

PBL is usually launched with a cohort of students where background information and purpose of the teaching strategy is discussed. Students are informed that points for further consideration, otherwise known as 'trigger' questions will be put forward at different stages of the PBL. An academic supervisor is often assigned to one or more groups during the PBL tasks; they are responsible for providing support, facilitating group tutorials, and providing feedback at appropriate stages.

A number of ground rules are often established and can take the following format:

- Attendance, professional behaviour, participation and time management of group members is essential.
- Group members should recognize the involvement of others and be mindful of monopolising conversations and contributions.
- Students should be informed of private study time allocated for PBL within timetables and advised to make good use of this.

Stage 2: Explore the problems

- Students are presented with a realistic patient scenario.
- During this stage students are required to discuss the patient scenario in their individual groups and identify the key facts of the situation.
- They explore the main problem(s), brainstorm ideas based on their prior knowledge and highlights gaps in existing knowledge.
- Students often find that they don't know enough to solve the problem but that is the challenge and purpose of problem-based learning.
- Once students have highlighted their learning needs to complete the patient scenario, it is useful at this stage for students to identify their own strengths and weaknesses, develop an action plan and time frame and discuss and agree how to evenly distribute the workload to each group member.
- Students are then advised to identify their learning needs and engage in independent study by working through their allocated tasks, whilst making use of appropriate learning support systems. This can include the library and online resources.

Stage 3: Independent learning process

- During the independent learning process, students will need to collate the necessary information and learn new skills and concepts as they absorb themselves in the problem-solving process.
- Students write up their evidence-based solutions to the problem allocated.
- Research, clinical guidelines and professional standards are essential evidence to support PBL solutions.

- A trigger question may be identified towards the end of this stage.
- Students may be required to submit their completed tasks to the group facilitator prior to the tutorial review; or upload their task to online communities, for example, Blackboard, Dropbox.

Stage 4: PBL tutorial review I

- Following this stage, students return to a PBL tutorial to review group learning and share the information they have retrieved.
- A facilitator can be present during the review and can assist with synthesising the learning materials and information gathered.
- Students should be encouraged to question each other on their contribution and justify the solutions they have identified so they learn from one another. They present their solution to the problem but it is worth remembering that problems can be revisited and edited as new information is discovered, or previous information is discarded.
- A further trigger question may be identified towards the end of this stage.

NOTE: The above stages can be repeated and reviewed as new information becomes available and redefines the problem.

Stage 5: PBL tutorial review II

- The format here is similar to stage 4 but allows discussion of the latest trigger question.
- There are opportunities here to structure the PBL activity prior to presentation, with or without the presence of a facilitator.
- Student can also practice their presentation if they are required to formally present their work.
- Presentations for PBL can take many formats but the most common involve the delivery of a PowerPoint presentation or a poster presentation.

Stage 6: Presentation of PBL

- The purpose of presenting PBL is to disseminate and share knowledge with others and is an opportunity for students to demonstrate what they have learnt.
- If formal presentation is required, many students may feel anxious about presenting to their peers and/or academic staff so practice sessions identified in Stage 5 should be encouraged.
- The presentation of PBL should be structured to include the patient scenario, identification of problems, resources used, problem-solving activities, conclusions and if required, recommendations.
- It may be necessary to reveal any challenges encountered during the PBL process so students should be advised to maintain a constructive and professional approach.
- Students may be challenged on their work so they should be advised to consider and answer questions carefully; if they are unable to answer a question, they can guided to accept it as an opportunity to be explored.

Stage 7: Reflection of PBL

■ Reflecting on the PBL process can be a formative or summative exercise where students are required to self and/or peer assess the group learning activity.

■ This can include individual reflections on the PBL process, contribution of group members, communication, team working, problem-solving ability, learning achieved, challenges encountered.

■ It is also useful to utilize a debriefing session similar to the one used following role play by discussing the process, sharing student's feelings about the activity, and examining the implications of the activity for future work.

Case studies

Case studies are textual descriptions of specific situations that may either be genuine or fictional and that provide a trigger for the discussion of issues and the examination of real-life events. Case studies differ from simulations and PBL in that they offer the student a cognitive view of the event rather than an experiential one. However, it is possible to use a case study as the basis for a simulation, PBL or role-play, with students taking the parts of the characters involved.

Case studies usually entail making decisions about particular courses of action or, alternatively, making judgements about decisions contained within the case study. Case studies can be used to very good effect in bringing theoretical issues closer to the real world of nursing; for example, students may be given a case study of the nursing care of a patient and asked to evaluate the care given in the light of their own knowledge and skills. In some instances, it is useful to use fictional studies to abstract the typical features of issues or problems, but, generally speaking, it is better to use real-life examples, since these are based on actual nursing practice.

Writing a case study

Writing a good case study is time consuming and difficult and Davis (1985) suggests three basic questions that need to be addressed when planning a case study:

1. *What is the major issue or problem?* This needs to be clearly stated along with any subordinate problems related to it.

2. *What facts does the student need?* It is important to include all relevant data required to deal with the problem or issue, but not to overload the case study with superfluous material.

3. *How should the material be presented?* This involves deciding on the sequence of the material, such as background to the case, significant facts, use of the past or present tense, and inclusion of statistics. The writer must avoid putting in personal opinions, keeping only to factual material.

One of the great uses of case studies is to integrate information from a wide range of topics in nursing: in order to solve a nursing-care problem in a case study, the students will need to integrate their knowledge of biological and behavioural science, nursing science and other areas. When using the case-study method the teacher must be very familiar with every detail of the case, so that he or she can be of greatest use to the group during the discussion. The teacher needs to be particularly careful that the group does not skim over the case study too quickly, thereby missing many of the important aspects.

TEACHING TIP

It is very useful to jot down an evaluation of how the session went, so that this is available for reference when the same case study is used again.

The fishbowl technique

This technique is very useful for process observation of group behaviour. The total group is divided into two, and one of these subgroups arranges itself into a circle for discussion and interaction. The other subgroup arranges itself outside the first circle concentrically and can then observe the inner group as though it were in a fishbowl. After the inner group has completed its interaction, the outer group can give feedback and evaluation about the group processes.

Debate

Although commonly thought of as a large-group technique, debate can be used to good effect in small-group teaching. Debate is a formal way of examining issues that can be very exciting to the participants as well as the audience and it has the added advantage of not only raising the students' awareness of issues and values, but also giving them the opportunity to formulate an argument and present it in a public arena.

Debate is quite easy to set up; the teacher can choose a number of issues, or the group may come up with its own list. Four students are required to present their views, two speaking for the motion and two against it. Following the presentations, the issue is opened up to the audience to contribute and then a vote is taken on whether the motion is carried or defeated. Debate is particularly useful for topical, emotive issues and can serve to make students examine their beliefs and values about such issues.

Microteaching

Microteaching is a small-group activity that has many uses in nurse education. Essentially, microteaching consists of a cycle of events. It can be seen that the cycle consists of the performance of some microskill, i.e. some aspect of a social or psychomotor skill such as asking questions, which is recorded on videotape. This recording is then played back to the small group; the performer firstly evaluates his or her own performance, and then the group members contribute their evaluation. The performer then replans the performance using the feedback gained during the analysis. The performance is repeated, incorporating the changes suggested in the analysis, and this is also videotaped. The video is then replayed, further analysis takes place and the cycle is repeated as often as is required until the performance is satisfactory. Microteaching can be a very potent tool for the acquisition of skills, but it does need a fair amount of time in order to allow students the chance to teach and re-teach several times.

Field visits

A well established technique in nurse education, field visits can provide insight when extending students' experience of nursing. Visits can be clinical (to a hospice or specialist centre) or non-clinical (to museums or public utilities). Within programmes for initial registration, it is common to find that students are required to undertake field visits as part of a neighbourhood study, for example to local government offices, sports centres, supermarkets, etc. Briefing and debriefing are important if the maximum learning value is to be gained from the visit.

Exercises

Exercises are particularly common in experiential learning; consisting of structured sequences in which students are actively involved, exercises often contain written instructions. Exercises consist of dyadic, triadic or small-group activities, usually ending in a discussion of participants' feelings about the exercise.

Body movements

Also extensively used in experiential learning, physical contact may or may not be involved in this kind of experience but is common in the various forms of 'warm-up' exercises prior to interpersonal skills sessions. Relaxation also comes under this heading.

Guided imagery and meditation

Guided imagery is being increasingly used in clinical practice, particularly in pain management. For example, a patient might be asked to imagine that he or she has flown to a peaceful island, far away from the pain. In nurse education, these experiential techniques are useful for gaining greater self-awareness. The student sits comfortably relaxed, with eyes closed and with the verbal help of the teacher, imagines being back in a pleasant place of his or her choosing. The student is prompted to involve all the senses in this re-creation.

Meditation is also carried out in a relaxed environment with eyes closed, and there are many techniques for this. One of them consists of simply attending to one's thoughts as they pass through the mind.

Instrumentation

A variety of instruments are used to facilitate activities, the commonest being questionnaires and inventories that direct the student to self- exploration.

COMMON DIFFICULTIES IN SMALL-GROUP AND EXPERIENTIAL LEARNING

The teacher may find that difficulties arise from time to time in a small group, and these require sensitive handling. It is usually better to deal with problems as they arise, but occasionally it may be necessary to have a private word with a group member after the session has finished.

Multi-speak

Commonly in small-group discussion, all the members talk at once (multi-speak), which leads to a chaotic situation where no progress is made. The teacher should exert firm, friendly control to bring the session to order, and a sense of humour is invaluable in keeping the atmosphere informal, while at the same time maintaining order. Very often there is a vocal member of a group who tends to monopolize the session, and it is important not to 'squash' that person, as motivation can easily be lost. Ignoring the contributions may lead to extinction of the response, but it usually makes the student feel hurt and resentful. Possibly the best solution is to remind the student gently that other group members need a chance to air their views also.

Hogging the limelight

A similar problem is that of the student who attempts to engage the teacher in a dialogue, to the exclusion of the rest of the group. This often arises when a student wishes to show that he or she has a particular piece of knowledge or expertise that the other students do not. Again, sensitive handling is required; a particularly useful strategy is deliberately to open out the dialogue to the rest of the group by using such statements as, 'You are raising some interesting points here. Would anyone else like to comment or react to any of them?'

Conflict

Group discussions can become very heated, especially when debating an issue that is emotionally charged, such as abortion. However, conflict is not always undesirable, as productive conflict can be an effective aid to learning. It is useful to reassure the group that disagreement is quite in order, but that it should be the opinion of another group member that is questioned and not that person as an individual. Each group member is respected, but his or her opinions are open to challenge and disagreement.

Emotional outbursts

Occasionally, the teacher may be confronted with an emotional outburst by a group member. One of the most dramatic of all gestures is that of a student walking out of the group, and it is always difficult to know how best to handle such a situation. Resisting the temptation to follow the individual, the teacher should stay with the group and attempt to help them to realize that such behaviour (flight, rather than fight) is one way that people have of coping with anxiety or anger; it is important to convey to the group that this is not a major disaster. However, it is extremely important for the welfare of the group as a whole that the teacher make contact with the distressed student before the next group meeting to discuss the incident with a view to deciding how best to raise it with the group.

Whilst every student has the right to behave in this way when under stress, the teacher cannot ignore the effects of such behaviour on the rest of the group. It might be that at the next meeting the student concerned in the incident should be invited to make a statement to the group about his or her feelings at the time and thus use the incident as a positive learning experience for all concerned.

Unwillingness to participate

Another common problem in small groups is that of the student who is unwilling to participate. Arguably, every individual has the 'right to remain silent' but this obviates the whole purpose of an educational small group. However, the teacher must acknowledge that students will differ in the degree of confidence they possess for making public contributions, and that this may be due to a variety of factors including basic personality, lack of knowledge, feelings of lack of personal worth or inadequate preparation. On the other hand, it may be the teacher's own style that is inhibiting a student; if the climate of the group is not conducive to psychological safety, then it is unlikely that students will risk contributing to discussion, lest they be humiliated or made to feel inadequate in some way.

The previous background and experience of students will also influence their desire to contribute to group discussions; in certain cultures, the teacher is seen very much as an expert who is not to be questioned and this may be difficult to overcome. Childhood experience of teachers who humiliated students may have left scars that ensure that the student tries never again to be put in such a position. Some of these factors may be impossible to change, although the teacher can do a great deal to ensure that the group members are valued and respected. Students can be invited into the discussion by gentle questioning, particularly in areas that rely upon student opinion rather than hard fact, since there is no likelihood of giving an incorrect answer.

It may well be that such reticent students require more specific help in the building up of confidence in public, such as a systematic programme of interaction that begins in pairs and gradually builds up to larger numbers, but such provision has obvious resource implications for the institution.

Review questions

1. Make a list of things that can be done to reduce anxiety before delivering a lecture.

2. How can you ensure that students can achieve the best possible learning outcomes from your lectures?

3. Explain how small-group teaching relates to experiential learning?

4. What are the key aspects you should think about when planning and implementing small group teaching?

5. Create a mind map to show the different techniques for teaching small groups and any relationships between them.

6. What problems can occur in small teaching groups and how can the teacher help to alleviate them?

SUMMARY

- Lecturing is the most common teaching strategy in adult education, but teachers' opinions tend to be polarized: some love it; others loathe it.

- Over-reliance on lectures may lead to dependence on the part of the students, who expect all the information to be handed to them on a plate.

- Lectures are often long, tedious and poorly organized, whereas with careful planning and practice they can be an effective vehicle for motivating students.

- Lecturing can be seen as analogous to acting, each lecture requiring careful scripting, polished presentational skills, and a certain personal charisma for effective performance.

- Recapitulation or repetition should be used frequently, so that the learner is exposed to the information on more than one occasion.

- Adult students are never very happy just sitting listening to lectures; they like to have some personal involvement in them.

- Small-group teaching puts the student at the centre of things, allowing opportunities for face-to-face interaction with other group members in order to exchange ideas and feelings and be challenged by other people's viewpoints.

- Group norms are defined as required or expected behaviours and beliefs of group members, which may be covert or overt.

- A team role can be described as a tendency to behave, contribute and interrelate with others in a particular way.

- The use of small-group teaching has benefits not only in terms of academic learning, but in the development of social skills and confidence in the presence of other people.

- A seminar group is mainly concerned with academic matters rather than with individual students and commonly involves the reading of an essay or paper by one group member, followed by a discussion by the total group on the topic.

- A focus group can be conducted with a small group of individuals who are prompted to discuss certain topics and experiences.

- Group discussions can become very heated, especially when debating an issue that is emotionally charged.

- Technological advancements providing opportunities for simulated learning to become available for learning experiences.

- Many students gain exposure to realistic, interactive clinically focused learning strategies.

- PBL is a popular teaching strategy that promotes critical thinking, encourages a deep approach to learning and develops skills in decision making, team working and presenting new information.

REFERENCES

Ausubel, D., Novak, I. and Hanesian, H. (1978) *Educational Psychology: A Cognitive View*. New York: Holt, Rinehart and Winston

Belbin, R.M. (1997) *Team Roles at Work*. Oxford: Butterworth-Heinemann

Bland, A.J., Topping, A. and Wood, B. (2011) A concept analysis of simulation as a learning strategy in the education of undergraduate nursing students. *Nurse Education Today* 31, 664–670

Bligh, D. (1998) *What's the Use of Lectures?* (5th Edition). Exeter: Intellect

Braine, M.E. (2009) Exploring new nurse teachers' perception and understanding of reflection: An exploratory study. *Nurse Education in Practice* 9(4) 262–270

Boud, D., Keogh, R. and Walker, D. (1985) *Reflection: Turning Experience into Learning*. London: Kogan Page

Brown, G. and Atkins, M. (1988) *Effective Teaching in Higher Education*. London: Methuen

Brown, S. (1996) The art of teaching small groups. *New Academic* 6(**1**), 3–6

Burnard, P. (1990) *Learning Human Skills* (2nd Edition). London: Heinemann

Burnard, P. (1991) Defining experiential learning: nurse teachers' perceptions. *Nurse Education Today* 12, 29–36

De Bono, E. (1986) Brainstorming. In Bligh D (ed.) *Teach Thinking by Discussion*. Guildford: SRHE/NFER-Nelson

Dekker-Groen, A.M., van der Schaaf, M.F. and Stokking, K.M. (2011) Teacher Competences required for developing reflection skills of nursing students. *Journal of Advanced Nursing* 67(7) 1568–1579

DeYoung, S. (2007) *Teaching Strategies for Nurse Educators* (2nd Edition). New Jersey: Pearson Prentice Hall

Dix, G. and Hughes, S.J. (2005) Teaching students in the classroom and clinical skills environment. *Nursing Standard* 19(35), 41–47

Fawcett-Hill ,W. (1969) *Learning Thru Discussion*. Newbury Park, CA: Sage

Fitzgerald, K. (2008) *Instructional Methods and Settings*. In: Bastable S (Ed) Nurse as educator: principles of teaching and learning for nursing practice (3rd Edition). New York: Jones and Bartlett

Heron, J. (1986) *Six Category Intervention Analysis*. Guildford: Human Potential Research Project, University of Surrey

JISC (2007) *Game Based Learning: Briefing Paper*. London: Joint Information Systems Committee

Johns, C. (1994) Nuances of reflection. *Journal of Clinical Nursing* 3(2) 71–75

Kolb, D.A. (1984) *Experiential Learning: Experience as the Source of Learning and Development*. New York: Prentice Hall

Marineau, R. (1989) *Jacob Levy Moreno, 1889–1974*. London: Tavistock/Routledge

NMC (2010) *Standards for Pre-Registration Nursing Education*. London: Nursing Midwifery Council

Oosterbaan, A.E., van der Schaaf, M.F., Baartman, L.K.J. and Stokking, K.M. (2010) Reflection during portfolio-based conversations. *International Journal of Educational Research* 49(4–5) 151–160

Osborne, A.F. (1993) *Applied Imagination: Principles and Procedures of Creative Problem-Solving* (3rd Edition). New York: Creative Education Foundation

Quinn, F.M. (2000) *Principles and Practice of Nurse Education* (4th edition). Cheltenham: Nelson Thornes

Reece, I. and Walker, S. (2007) *Teaching, Training and Learning: A Practical Guide* (6th Edition). Sunderland: Business Education Publishers Limited

Rees, C. (2011) *Introduction to Research for Midwives* (3rd Edition). Oxford: Churchill Livingstone, Elsevier

Rogers, C. (1983) *Freedom to Learn for the 80s*. OH: Merrill, Columbus

Scanlan, J., Care, W.D. and Udod, S. (2002) Unravelling the unknowns of reflection in classroom teaching. *Journal of Advanced Nursing* 38(2) 136–143

Schön, D. (1987) *Educating the Reflective Practitioner: Towards a New Design for Teaching and Learning in the Professions*. San Francisco: Jossey Bass

SES Associates (1986) The SES box method for creative problem-solving. In Bligh D (ed.) *Teach Thinking by Discussion*. Guildford: SRHE/NFER-Nelson

Solomon, P. (2011) Problem based learning. In: Bradshaw MJ, Lowenstein AJ (Eds) *Innovative Teaching Strategies in Nursing and Related Health Professions* (5th Edition). Boston: Jones and Bartlett

Steinaker, N. and Bell, M. (1979) *The Experiential Taxonomy: A New Approach to Teaching and Learning*. New York: Academic Press

Tuckman, B. (1965) Development sequences in small groups. *Psychological Bulletin* 63(3) 384–399

Tuckman, B. and Jensen, M.A. (1977) Stages of small group development revisited. *Group and Organisational Studies* 2, 419–427

FURTHER READING

Barrett, T. and Moore, S. (2011) *New approaches to problem-based learning: revitalising your practice in higher education*. Oxon: Routledge

Clouston, T., Westcott, L., Whitcombe, S., Riley, J. and Matheson, R. (Eds) (2010) *Problem-based learning in health and social care*. London: Wiley-Blackwell

Clynes, M.P. (2009) A novice teacher's reflections on lecturing as a teaching strategy: Covering the content or uncovering the meaning. *Nurse Education in Practice* 9(1) 22–27

Duke, S. and Appleton, J. (2000). The use of reflection in a palliative care programme: a qualitative study of the development of reflective skills over an academic year. *Journal of Advanced Nursing* 32 (6) 1557–1568

McGrath, D. and Higgins, A. (2006) Implementing and evaluating reflective practice group sessions. *Nurse Education in Practice* 6(3) 175–181

Turner, D.S. and Beddoes, L. (2007) Using reflective models to enhance learning: Experiences of staff and students. *Nurse Education in Practice* 7(3) 135–140

CHAPTER 7
ASSESSMENT OF LEARNING

THE AIMS OF THIS CHAPTER ARE:

- To explain the principles and explore the magnitude of assessment

- To consider diverse methods of assessment

- To outline how assessment practices can utilize service users in the workplace

- To highlight the importance of managing the assessment process

KEY TERMS

Structured impressionistic marking
Objective test
Facility index
Discrimination index
Peer assessment
Objective structured clinical
    examination (OSCE)

Portfolios
Profiles
Evidence-based practice
Plagiarism
Moderation

The setting, marking and moderation of students' written assessment work constitutes a very significant part of the lecturers' role in higher education, but in nurse education there is the added dimension of workplace assessment to be considered. Given that both success and failure have important consequences for their future development, students often perceive assessment as the most important aspect of their course or programme, and the one that causes them most anxiety. It is almost inevitable, therefore, that students will see the assessment tasks as the main priority of their studies, to the possible detriment of their wider reading and exploration of topics. This point is nicely made by Brown *et al.* (1997):

> 'Assessment defines what students regard as important, how they spend their time and how they come to see themselves as students and then as graduates. Students take their cues from what is assessed rather than from what lecturers assert is important.'

However, if the assessment has been carefully planned, it will form an integral part of the teaching and learning experience for the student rather than something that distracts from the main business of studying. Brown *et al.* cite examples of studies showing that the type of assessment can influence whether students adopt a reproductive style or deeper strategies of understanding. The UK Professional Standards Framework for teaching and supporting learning in higher education (HEA, 2011) identify the need for teachers to be effective in using an appropriate range of assessment methods that support and underpin student learning.

According to the Quality Assurance Agency for Higher Education (QAA, 2011) assessment provides the means by which students are graded, passed or failed. It provides the basis for the decisions on whether the student is ready to proceed, to qualify for an award or to demonstrate competence to practice. In addition to this, it enables students to obtain feedback on their learning and helps them improve their performance, and it also enables teachers to evaluate the effectiveness of their teaching. The Nursing and Midwifery Council (NMC, 2008a) advocates that nurse educators should contribute to the development and implementation of effective assessment procedures in both practice and educational settings. They must not only support students when receiving feedback and devise subsequent action but also provide advice and support to assessors in the clinical practice setting.

PURPOSES AND AIMS OF ASSESSMENT

Curzon (2003) sees assessment as the process of collecting, measuring and interpreting information relating to students' responses to the process of instruction, whilst Welsh and Swann (2002) defined it as a way in which we determine the extent to which learning has taken place. Neary (2000) believes that there are three reasons why assessment is carried out; these are to ascertain:

- the level of theoretical knowledge;
- the level of practical clinical skills;
- insight into the level of professional attitudes.

Rowntree (1987) highlights six main purposes that assessment serves and argues that in the education of health professionals there should be an element of all these purposes:

- selection;
- maintenance of standards;
- motivation of students;
- feedback to students;
- feedback to the teacher;
- preparation for life.

Assessment can provide valuable feedback to students about their progress, and point out ways in which they could develop further. Also, the successful achievement of a publicly recognized award can enhance an individual's status, and may lead to employment opportunities or confer eligibility to undertake further academic study. There is no doubt that assessment can act as a powerful motivator of study; students expect to be assessed, and they plan their studies accordingly. Assessment also provides feedback to the higher education funding bodies about the effectiveness of an institution, and in that sense is a performance indicator of quality.

Regardless of the type, there are three basic aims of assessment:

- It should assess student performance in relation to the aims of the particular programme in question.
- It should be regarded as an integral component of the teaching and learning process, and not simply a means of measuring attainment.
- It should encourage the students to undertake self-assessment and reflection on their learning.

These aims are set in a context of equality and diversity, and it is a fundamental tenet of higher education that no student is assessed on the basis of their race, religion, politics, gender or sexual orientation.

THE TERMINOLOGY AND DIMENSIONS OF ASSESSMENT

The inclusion of multiple forms of assessment helps students to integrate, synthesize and assimilate the theoretical components of the domain with the clinical application and practical skills involved. Banning (2003) classifies this as a powerful tool as it would not only incorporate strategies to promote critical thinking but would also assess the student's overall performance and ability to reason clinically. One of the most confusing aspects of assessment is the number of different terms used for what is essentially the same thing. Table 7.1 gives the main distinctions between the most commonly used terms.

TABLE 7.1 Terminology of assessment	
Measurement	A quantitative process involving the assigning of a number to an individual's characteristics
Assessment	A term used instead of measurement when a numerical value is not involved, e.g. checklists of behaviours
Evaluation	The process of judging the value or worth of an individual's characteristics obtained by measurement or assessment
Test	An instrument or tool for obtaining measurements or assessments, e.g. an essay
Examination	A formal situation in which students undertake one or more tests under specific rules.

In addition to this basic terminology, it is useful to look at the dimensions of the concept of assessment, as shown in Table 7.2.

TABLE 7.2 Dimensions of assessment	
Formal	Informal
Quantitative	Qualitative
Episodic	Continuous
Formative	Summative
Teacher-centred	Student-centred
Norm-referenced	Criterion-referenced
Achievement	Aptitude/personality
Paper and pencil	Practical/oral

Formal assessment involves the use of tests to obtain data that are then made available to the institution; the data are often subjected to statistical analysis, and comparisons are drawn between students. Examples of formal assessment in nurse education are modular or unit assessments, unseen written components, and clinical practice assessments.

Informal assessment, in contrast, does not involve comparisons with other students; it is essentially private and subjective to the teacher concerned. Such informal assessment is gleaned from the day-to-day observation of students' behaviour, examination of students' notes, and from informal contact and interviews. Informal assessment, then, is for the private use of a particular teacher and forms an essential part of the total assessment process.

Quantitative assessment refers to the use of numerical data in the assessment of students.

Qualitative assessment is concerned with the properties or qualities that an individual possesses. Scores obtained on a written test constitute quantitative data; a student's views on what constitutes effective relationships with a patient would be qualitative data.

There are two dimensions that are concerned with the timing of assessment, the first being 'episodic' versus 'continuous' assessment.

Episodic assessment involves testing the student at specific times or occasions during an educational programme, such as an end-of-year assessment or a number of specific clinical assessments in particular aspects of nursing. One of the major drawbacks of this system is its reliance on a student's 'one-off' performance on the day of the test and this performance may not reflect the student's typical performance over a longer period. In other words, episodic assessment generates data that is based on a very small and possibly unrepresentative sample of a student's behaviour. A further criticism, which relates particularly to the clinical setting, is that of artificiality, in that episodic clinical assessments are often seen as 'set pieces' that the student may rehearse until 'word perfect' and which bear little resemblance to the student's normal working practices.

Continuous assessment as a method of evaluating progress and learning is now well established in many educational institutions, in academic and clinical situations (Neary, 2000). It attempts to overcome the weaknesses mentioned above by sampling all of a student's outputs in a course on a continuous basis. In the college setting, this might involve assessing all of a student's coursework, including tests, projects and seminar presentations. In the clinical setting, continuous assessment samples a student's nursing practice on a continuous basis, so that no particular nursing skill can be said to have been 'passed' on a 'once-and-for-all' basis.

The second time-related dimension is that of 'formative' versus 'summative' evaluation; these terms are used in two distinct ways. First, they can be applied to the assessment of a particular student's achievement and, secondly, to the evaluation of a particular aspect of curriculum design, such as teaching media.

Formative assessment provides feedback about the progress that a student is making whilst the course or unit is being followed, so that modifications can be made to the teaching if necessary.

Summative assessment, on the other hand, takes place at the end of a course or unit to see if the student has achieved the objectives of the programme and is usually done as a formal test covering the content of the course. Many teachers feel that formative assessment should not be graded for assessment purposes, but used only as feedback or diagnosis of student needs.

With regard to the use of these terms for curriculum evaluation, formative evaluation means that instructional material intended for eventual use with students is tested during its formation and modified in the light of these pilot studies. Summative evaluation is the evaluation of such material after it has been used with students in its intended setting.

Another useful dimension to consider is that of '*teacher-centred assessment*' versus '*student-centred assessment*'. Traditionally, the teacher has been the key figure with regard to the assessment of students in nursing, but, with the growth of interest in student-centred learning, there is a move towards much greater involvement of the student in his or her own assessment. Indeed, self-assessment seems to be one of the hallmarks of a professional practitioner in any field, so this is a practice that should be encouraged from the outset.

The next dimension to be considered relates to the interpretation of the results of assessment; there are two main ways that these results can be referenced: norm-referencing and criterion-referencing.

Norm-referenced assessment means that an individual student's score on a test is compared with scores of other students in a given group, and a rank order is assigned. Cut-off points for pass and fail are built into the assessment. In norm-referenced assessment, a student could be in the top 10 per cent of scores in one year, but the same score in the following year may not achieve the top 10 per cent if the scores of the group are generally higher than in the previous year.

Criterion-referenced assessment implies that the score is compared with some criterion or learning task such as achievement of behavioural objectives; it is also termed 'content referenced' or 'domain-referenced' assessment. The main difference between these two forms of referencing is that norm-referenced assessment means that the score obtained by the student is influenced by the performance of the group to which he or she is compared. Criterion-referencing, on the other hand, does not depend on any form of comparison with others, only with achievement in relation to a specific criterion or standard.

Assessment is not only concerned with the measurement of student achievement, but includes such aspects of an individual as attitudes, aptitudes, personality and intelligence. Achievement refers to how well a student has performed in the past; aptitude refers to how well he or she will perform in the future. Assessment of personality and intelligence is usually done using published standardized tests.

A useful distinction can be made between the kinds of tests employed in the assessment of nurses. On the one hand, we have the so-called 'paper-and-pencil' tests, which include essays, objective tests and a host of other kinds of written instruments. At the other end of the scale, there are the practical, clinical forms of assessment and oral examinations. Practical assessment usually involves observation combined with some form of checklist or rating scale to guide the observer. Oral, or *viva voce*, tests rely on the spontaneous answering of questions by the student and allow for follow-up and further elaboration on answers given.

CARDINAL CRITERIA FOR ASSESSMENT

Regardless of the type of assessment employed or the purpose for which it is used, every effective assessment must meet the four cardinal criteria described below.

Validity

This is the most important aspect of a test and is the extent to which the test measures what it is designed to measure. In other words, validity is the relevance of a test to its objectives.

Content validity

Assessments should sample adequately the content of the syllabus and, if this is the case, then the examination is said to have content validity.

Predictive validity

If a test is designed to predict the future performance of a student and it fulfils this function, then it is said to have predictive validity.

Concurrent validity

Concurrent validity is the extent to which the results of a test correlate with those of other tests administered at the same time.

Construct validity

The fourth kind of validity is construct validity. A construct is a quality that is devised by psychologists to explain aspects of human behaviour that cannot be directly observed. For example, such things as attitudes, values and intelligence are constructs. Construct validity is the extent to which the results of a test are related to the data gained from observations of individuals' behaviour with regard to the construct in question.

Reliability

Reliability is the term used to indicate the consistency with which a test measures what it is designed to measure. In other words, it should yield similar results when used on two separate occasions, provided that the other variables remain similar. The main way to assure reliability is to use more than one type of assessment to measure student achievement.

Test–retest reliability

If a test is administered to a group of students and then re-administered, either immediately or after an interval of time, and the scores are similar on both occasions, then the test is said to have high test–retest reliability.

Parallel-form reliability

If the group is given a different test in the retest phase, but one that measures the same thing, a positive correlation indicates parallel-form reliability.

Split-half reliability

To ascertain split-half reliability, the test items are divided into two halves and the correlation between the two sets of scores is calculated.

The importance of validity and reliability is self-evident, but it might be helpful to give an example to show the inter-relationship between them. One of the most common measuring instruments to be found in the home is the bathroom scales. Just like any other assessment tool, the measurement of human weight by the scales must be valid and reliable. To check the validity (accuracy) of the measurement of an individual's weight, it is necessary to record the weight as registered by the scales, and then to check the weight again using different scales, such as can be found in most chemist shops. If the two weights are identical, then the measure is valid, i.e. it is demonstrating accuracy and fitness for purpose.

If the measurement of an individual's weight by the bathroom scales is reliable (consistent) then the scales should register the same weight when the individual weighs themselves again and again (provided, of course, that their weight has remained constant since the last measurement).

It is possible, however, for an assessment test to be valid but not reliable, or reliable but not valid. For example, the bathroom scales may register the same weight each time (reliability), but that weight may be several pounds above the actual weight of the individual (i.e. not valid). Alternatively, the scales may register the correct weight of the individual on some occasions (validity), but the incorrect weight on others (i.e. not reliable).

Discrimination

The purpose of any test is to discriminate between those who answer correctly and those who do not. The term 'discriminate' is used in the sense of 'distinguish between', and not in the equal opportunities sense. If a test makes no discrimination between students, then it has no purpose. The discrimination index will be examined later in this chapter.

Practicality or utility

It is important that a test is practical for its purpose. This implies such factors as the time taken to conduct the test, the cost of using it and its practicality for everyday use.

Transparency

Race (2009, p. 6) refers to transparency as the extent to which learners know where the goalposts are. He argues:

> 'The goalposts are laid down by the intended learning outcomes, matched nicely to the assessment criteria which specify the standards to which these intended outcomes are to be demonstrated by learners, and also specify the forms in which learners will present evidence of their achievement of the outcomes.'

This definition is further explained by Lambert and Lines (2000):

> 'Transparency is used to describe the extent to which students and teachers know what is required of them, know the system by which they will have their work assessed and how the marks are awarded.'

Race (2009) suggests that students remain unclear of where the goalposts lie, despite highlighting learning outcomes in programme/module handbooks, and often experience difficulty with the culture of assessment even though this determines their final award. He believes that students who achieve in assessments have the least problems with transparency. Race also believes that education institutions do not fare well on achieving transparency in assessments and often fail on validity and reliability when considered separately.

PLANNING ASSESSMENTS

Lambert and Lines (2000) identify the purposes of assessment:

- Provide feedback to students and teachers regarding progress in order to provide and support further learning.
- Provide information on the level of students' achievements at certain points during and at the end of programmes.
- Provide the means for selection by qualification; in other words, to determine if students are fit to commence a programme of study.
- Contribute towards information on which judgements are made regarding the quality of students and education establishments.

Further purposes of assessment are identified by Race (2009):

- Assessment is often the driving force which promotes studying.
- To set standards.
- To allow students to make realistic decisions about whether they are up to the demands of a course or module.
- To translate intended learning outcomes into reality.
- To add variety to students' learning experience.
- To lead towards appropriate qualification and a licence to practice, for example, NMC registration.

Given that assessments have significant implications for students, it is essential that considerable time and care is given to their formulation and implementation.

Students' assessment workload

One of the aspects of higher education programmes most commonly highlighted at validation events is the assessment workload of students. Whilst assessment is clearly an important aspect of teaching and learning, over-assessment has a number of undesirable consequences; Brown and Knight (1994) point out that excessive assessment may result in superficial coverage of content rather than understanding in depth. Over-assessment becomes a treadmill for both students and markers, demanding from both parties a considerable commitment of time. There is a danger that students and tutors become subject to assessment fatigue, thereby reducing the quality of the former's assessment work, and the latter's marking. Race *et al.* (2005) suggest seven questions to consider when designing written assessments:

1. What are the outcomes to be assessed?
2. What are the capabilities/skills implicit in the outcomes?
3. Is the method of assessment chosen consonant with the outcomes and skills?
4. Is the method relatively efficient in terms of student time and staff time?
5. What alternatives are there? What are their advantages and disadvantages?
6. Does the specific assessment task match the outcomes and skills?
7. Are the marking schemes or criteria appropriate?

Race *et al.* (2005) believe that assessments should enable the demonstration of excellence and recommend the certain values and principles for their design, as shown in Figure 7.1.

FIGURE 7.1   Values and principles of assessment design

RACE ET AL., 2005

Learning outcomes and assessment

The statement of learning outcomes for programmes and modules is now an almost universal practice in higher education, and these form the basis for planning assessments. It is important that each of the learning outcomes is assessed, although this need not be by formal written assessment for every outcome. The assessment must be appropriate for the level of learning outcome and also for the domain of learning covered by the learning outcome. It is also necessary to bear in mind the general aims of higher education, and to ensure that these are incorporated into assessment strategies. Table 7.3 shows the general aims of higher education.

TABLE 7.3   General aims of higher education
• Engaging with learning, scholarship and research.
• Enabling individual students to achieve their highest intellectual potential
• Promoting creative thinking and analytical skills
• Fostering a commitment to lifelong learning
• Exploring career options
• Developing core skills that include interpersonal skills, problem-solving skills, information technology, time management

QAA 2011

Levels of learning outcomes

Learning outcomes are stated at one of a number of academic levels, and these levels and definitions may vary between higher education institutions. It is important that the assessment takes account of the level of the learning outcome, as the level may not be apparent within the statement itself. In order to ensure that students achieve the outcome at the appropriate level, the assessment must utilize the level-definition of the institution. Learning outcomes are discussed in more detail in Chapter 4.

Domains of learning

Some higher education institutions use Bloom's (1956) taxonomy as a basis for their definitions of the level of learning outcomes. The taxonomy is discussed in detail in Chapter 4 in relation to educational objectives.

ASSESSING KNOWLEDGE AND UNDERSTANDING USING ESSAYS

Essay assessments require learners to supply an answer that is organized in their own words and presented in their own style and, in an examination, handwriting, with few restrictions imposed, and no single correct answer. The term 'essay format' covers a number of forms of written assessment; for example, it is used to describe negotiated coursework as well as formal written examinations.

The use of essay tests

Because of the factors indicated above, essays are inefficient for testing recall of knowledge, but are useful for assessing higher levels of cognitive functioning, such as application, analysis, synthesis and evaluation. There are a number of weaknesses in this form of assessment that may limit its usefulness.

Weaknesses of essay tests

Low content validity

In essay tests, only a small number of questions are answered, hence only a small proportion of the total syllabus is sampled by this method.

Low marker-reliability

Essay tests are notoriously unreliable from the point of view of marking. Every learner knows that some teachers are easy markers and others hard, and the final mark depends to a large extent on the marker. There is often wide variation between markers and between the same markers at different times.

Often ambiguous or unclear

Essay questions are often difficult for the learner to understand because they do not spell out clearly enough exactly what is required.

Marking is difficult

The marking of essay tests is time consuming and often tedious, which may adversely affect the marker's judgement about the quality of the essay.

Student fatigue

This aspect, which is rarely mentioned in connection with essay tests, could be considered a very serious disadvantage. Examinations are commonly timetabled in three-hour slots, so students are required to write for three hours without a break. If a student has a three-hour examination in both the morning and afternoon of the same day, the test may be more a measure of stamina than of academic prowess.

Marks are affected by students' writing ability

The learner's ability to write good prose can influence the mark that is awarded. It is often difficult to separate the content of an essay from the literary style, with the result that a learner may bluff the marker into giving a higher grade than he or she deserves. On the other hand, learners may be penalized for poor grammar or expression, even though they know the content adequately. Of course, the essay must be legible, but under examination conditions, few marks should be taken off for the grammar and spelling. The teacher may draw attention to this aspect by adding a comment in the margin, without this affecting the mark awarded.

Choice is often included

In any essay examination a choice of questions is invariably included, but this practice is open to question on a number of counts. First, it is difficult to construct questions which have the same degree of difficulty, so that in effect a different test is being offered to each learner. This obviously makes comparison difficult between the achievements of students. Secondly, the more able students may well be attracted to the difficult questions and suffer penalties if they fail to do well.

EXAMPLES OF TYPES OF ESSAYS

Interpretive essay

Example: *'The accompanying table relates accidents at work to the type of industry, i.e. manufacturing, construction, railways, coal mining and agriculture. Comment on the relative risk of accidents for the types of industry represented in the table.'*

When answering this type of question, the student has to interpret the table in order to come up with the relative risk for each industry; this requires high-level cognitive functioning.

Hypothesis-formation essay

Example: *'Imagine that you are the chair of a committee charged with making recommendations for the siting of a new home for brain-injury patients in a quiet suburban area of town. Speculate on the likely planning objections to your proposal.'*

In this case, the student has to consider all the relevant facts and come up with a hypothesis about the likely planning objections. This essay cannot be written by a simple reliance on memorized facts; it requires higher-order synthesis.

Questioning-assumptions essay

Example: *'Read this article from the* Journal of Advanced Nursing *and comment on the author's underlying assumptions.'*

This assessment requires the student to explore the article thoroughly and to search for the writer's assumptions. These assumptions may not be obvious, and the student may have to analyze the text deeply before they become apparent.

Inquiry-based assessments

As the name suggests, this type of assessment requires the student to undertake some form of enquiry, the results of which must be written up in the form of a report.

Example: *'Carry out an investigation into the provision for disabled people in terms of access to public buildings within the Cardiff Borough. Write up your findings in the form of a report to go to the Cardiff Borough Council.'*

Assessments requiring synthesis

This kind of assessment requires the student to synthesize information gained by both experiential learning and study in order to identify any gaps between them; it requires high-level cognitive functioning on the part of the student.

Example: *'Select a patient within either a hospital or community setting in consultation with your mentor. Participate in the care for this patient over a period of one week, maintaining a diary of your interactions and interventions. Write a commentary on the care given, within the context of relevant theory from both nursing and social and biological science. Make particular reference to any incongruities between your experiences and your theoretical analyses.'*

MARKING AND GRADING OF ESSAY TESTS

TEACHING TIP

In relation to marking and grading of assessments, it is useful to consider the following helpful points:

- Assessment is a matter of judgement, not simply computation.
- Marks and grades are not absolute values, but symbols used by examiners to communicate their judgement of a student's work.
- Marks and grades provide data for decisions about students' fulfilment of learning outcomes.

Marking and grading criteria

Higher education institutions normally use an institution-wide grading scale for undergraduate programmes, whereas postgraduate programmes tend to be graded on a pass/fail basis or a pass/fail/distinction basis. Grading scales tend to incorporate percentage grading and literal grading, the latter meaning letters such as A, B, C, as illustrated in Table 7.4.

TABLE 7.4 Grading scale for undergraduate assessment

Mark on a 0–100 scale	Comments
70+	Work of exceptional quality
60–69	Work of very good quality
50–59	Work of good quality
40–49	Work of satisfactory standard
0–39	Referral

Undergraduate grading scales are likely to be very similar in other higher education institutions. It is interesting to compare this scale with the percentage equivalents for the class of honours degree, as shown in Table 7.5.

Marks or grades are assigned to students' essays to indicate the degree of achievement that they have attained; there are two systems for assigning grades.

Absolute grading gives the student marks for his or her essay answer, depending on how well the essay has met the assessment criteria, and is usually expressed as a percentage or letter, for example 60 per cent or B.

Relative grading tells the student how his or her essay answer rated in relation to those of other students doing the same test, by indicating whether or not it was average, above average or below average. Relative grading usually uses a literal scale such as A, B, C, D and E

TABLE 7.5 Percentage equivalents for class of honours degree

Percentage	Degree as class	Degree award
0–39%	Fail	Fail
40–44%	Pass	Pass Degree
45–49%	3rd	Third Class Honours
50–59%	2:2	Second Class Honours Division II Second Division
60–69%	2:1	Second Class Honours Division I First Division
70% and above	1st	First Class Honours

However, some teachers would argue that two grades are the best way of marking, so that students are given either a pass or fail grade. This gets over the problem of deciding what constitutes an A or a C grade but does reduce the information conveyed by a particular grade, since no discrimination is made between students who pass with a very high level of achievement and those who barely pass at all.

Analytical method of marking (marking scheme)

When using absolute grading to specific criteria, the analytic method of marking is useful. In this method, a marking scheme is prepared in advance and marks are allocated to the specific points of content in the marking specification. However, it is often difficult to decide how many marks should be given to a particular aspect, but the relative importance of each should be reflected in the allocation.

This method has the advantage that it can be more reliable provided that the marker is conscientious, and it will bring to light any errors in the writing of the question before the test is administered.

Table 7.6 gives an example of an analytical marking scheme for a nursing essay.

Global method of marking (structured impressionistic marking)

The global method, also termed structured impressionistic marking, is best used with relative grading. This method still requires a marking specification, but in this case it serves only as a standard of comparison. The grades used are not usually percentages, but scales, such as 'excellent/good/average/below average/unsatisfactory'. Scales can be devised according to preference, but it is important to select examples of answers that serve as standards for each of the points on the scale. The teacher then reads each answer through very quickly and puts it in the appropriate pile, depending whether it gives the impression of excellent, good, etc. The process is then repeated and it is much more effective if a colleague is asked to do the second reading. This method is much faster than the analytical one and can be quite effective for large numbers of questions.

When marking essay answers it is important to eliminate the 'halo' effect, which is the term used to describe the influence that the preceding answer has on the marker.

TABLE 7.6   Example of an analytical marking scheme for a credit level 3 module assessment

Pressure sores constitute one of the biggest challenges for nursing care. Critically discuss the role of the nurse in risk assessment and prevention of pressure sores (3000 words)

ANALYTICAL MARKING SCHEME

Element		Marks allocated (out of 100)
ELEMENT 1.0: INTRODUCTION (10%)		
1.1	Definitions and prevalence	2
1.2	National context, e.g. DoH targets and strategy	3
1.3	Nursing context	5
ELEMENT 2.0: RISK ASSESSMENT (30%)		
2.1	Factors implicated in pressure sore development, e.g. poor nutrition, immobility, incontinence	10
2.2	Nursing rationale for use of tools for risk assessment, e.g. Norton Scale, Waterlow Scale	10
2.3	Critique of tools, including criteria used for critique	10
ELEMENT 3.0: PREVENTION (30%)		
3.1	Nurse's role in reducing risk factors at home and in hospital	10
3.2	Methods available to nurses, e.g. turning, alternating-pressure mattresses	10
3.3	Critique of preventative measures, including criteria used for critique	10
ELEMENT 4.0: PRESENTATION AND SCHOLARSHIP SKILLS (30%)		
4.1	Spelling, grammar and syntax	3
4.2	Citing and listing references	7
4.3	Coherence of arguments and discussion	10
4.4	Reference for appropriate theoretical perspectives	10

If all the answers from one learner were marked together, then the chances are that this would create an impression, favourable or otherwise, that would influence the marking of the remainder of the answers for that learner. It is thus important to mark all the answers for one question before proceeding to the next. It has been suggested that answers should be shuffled randomly after each question has been marked, so that the position of any paper will not consistently be affected by the quality of the preceding ones.

Anonymous marking helps to eliminate bias, by avoiding the use of students' names; a number is substituted instead. QAA (2011a) stipulate that clear assessment criteria and transparent marking schemes are key factors in assuring that marking is carried out fairly and consistently and identify the following points for consideration when developing policies and procedures on marking and moderation:

■ Ensure that marking and grading is appropriate and comparable. HEIs can suggest the circumstances in which to give precise numerical marks or to use grades or bands of marks when assessing student work.

■ Develop clear guidance about how borderline marks or grades are defined and treated.

■ Identify when double or second marking should be used and what approach should be taken, for example, whether or not the second marker normally has access to the first marker's feedback and highlighting the importance of demonstrating that double or second marking has taken place.

■ Consider the methods to be used when assessments from larger groups are sampled by internal or external examiners.

■ Clearly illustrate the processes governing and recording internal moderation and verification of marks and identify the procedure to be followed when an internal or external moderator disagrees with the original marks.

■ Consider the value of analysing marking and marking trends to facilitate comparisons and provide evidence on standards.

Marking assignments

Consider the following suggestions when marking assessment scripts to maintain fairness to students (Race, 2009; Lambert and Lines, 2000):

■ *Be realistic about what you can do* Marking can become a seriously disliked professional chore and is often subject to repeated procrastination. Marking assignments can be boring and tiring so avoid marking large numbers of scripts in short periods of time. Put scripts for marking into manageable piles.

■ *Avoid halo effects* If you've just marked an outstanding assignment it can be easy to be extra critical if the next assignment you mark is not as good

■ *Watch out for prejudices* There will be all sorts of things which you like and dislike about the style and layout of scripts, not to mention presentation quality. Make sure that each time there is a 'benefit of the doubt' decision to be made, it is not influenced by such factors.

■ *Recognize that your mood will change* Every now and then, check back to scripts you marked earlier, and see whether your generosity has increased or decreased. Be aware of the middle-mark bunching syndrome. As you get tired, your concentration will lapse and it might feel safe and easy to give a middle-range mark. Try as far as possible to look at each script with a clear head.

■ *Remind yourself of the importance of what you're doing* You may be marking a large number of assignments but each individual script may be a crucial landmark in the life of the student concerned. Don't rush the marking process; your verdict may affect a student's degree classification or may affect the rest of their careers.

■ *Make sure you mark objectively* It is important to remember where a student is in terms of their programme stage.

■ *Recognize the needs of second markers* Some universities use a blind double marking system, so you should not annotate assignments in order to avoid prejudicing the judgement of a second marker. You may find it useful to make additional notes or post-its for each assignment so you are able to justify the marks you give at any later stage.

This can save you having to read the assignment again and trying to remember how you arrive at a particular mark.

■ *Provide feedback for yourself and for the module/programme team* As you work through the assignments, note how each student performed. This could assist with the moderation process and inform the moderation report

■ *Keep an overview of the marks you are giving* In a small sample it won't be possible to get a set of results which plot into a normal distribution curve on a graph. However, if you notice that all of your marks are similar or that everyone is getting high marks, this may indicate that something is wrong. It may help you to use a spreadsheet or other visual means to keep track of your marks.

■ *Get help from colleagues* Assistance with and feedback on your marking is invaluable, especially if you're a student teacher or newly qualified teacher. This is relatively straight-forward if your university uses second or double marking, otherwise identify a few assignments, including a strong one, a weak one and an average one, and ask an experienced colleague or two to confirm that they agree with your marks and feedback.

■ *Beware of rising standards* The more experienced you become in marking a subject area, the greater the risk is that you gradually expect or demand higher levels of performance from successive groups of students.

TEACHING TIP

Intermittently revisit the first assignment you marked to make sure you have not become more lenient or harsh in your marking.

Assessing students' written presentation and scholarship skills

Marking an essay assignment involves more than simply checking the content for accuracy; it also requires the marker to make a judgement about the quality of the students' scholarship skills.

Spelling, grammar and syntax

Assessment work in higher education requires students to be able to express themselves adequately in written English. It is therefore important that errors of spelling, grammar, syntax or punctuation are pointed out to the student by markers. Poor use of grammar, syntax and punctuation can interfere with the student's communication of the content of the assessment, preventing it from being fully understood unless an extra effort is made by the marking lecturer. This can adversely affect the final grading of the assessment, since communication is an essential core academic skill.

Citing and listing references

It is standard procedure in higher education that students must adhere to a given format for citing and listing references in their assessment work. Such consistency facilitates the marking and moderation of assessment work.

Scholarship skills

The content of students' assessments in higher education must be appropriate and relevant to the assessment specification. The arguments and discussion must be presented coherently and logically, and in the context of relevant theory.

Giving feedback to students about their presentation and scholarship skills

It is important that, from the outset of their studies, students' attention is drawn to any problems of presentation and scholarship skills. If lecturers ignore such problems this may be perceived by the students as tacit acceptance, reinforcing the likelihood of errors in future assessments. However, it would not be feasible for marking lecturers to point out all the grammatical errors in a student's assessment work, given the length of assessments and the numbers of scripts requiring to be marked. Nevertheless, it is good practice for markers to correct such errors on the first two or three pages of an assessment, and then to note at the end that there are problems in this area. If lecturers identify students with problems in the area of presentation and scholarship skills, they should ensure that such students are made aware of the sources of help available to them within the institution.

VARIANTS OF ESSAYS

The 'seen-paper'

Some essay examinations allow the candidates to see the paper some weeks before the examination and may even allow them to bring notes into the examination (up to 100 words). The test is used to evaluate the candidate's ability to select sources and to organize the information in a meaningful way.

The 'open-book' examination

The candidate is allowed to look up information in a book during the examination. This removes over-reliance on memorizing facts and is closer to the reality of professional behaviour, where information has to be looked up most of the time. Open book testing has demonstrated more consistent and varied study, with students consulting a variety of sources to achieve their desired level of proficiency with regard to learning outcomes. Brightwell *et al.* (2004) suggest several benefits of open-book examinations such as:

- deeper study of course notes;
- development of important professional skills;
- easier marking of exam scripts;
- reduction in students' exam anxiety;
- increased opportunity for student self-evaluation and feedback.

Additionally, the authors identified that open book testing more adequately represents real life situations, where problems are encountered and limitless resources are available for the development of useful solutions to the dilemma.

Using objective tests

The limitations of the essay test led to the development of the objective test, the word 'objective' referring to the marking of the test, which is not influenced by the subjective opinion of the marker. However, the actual writing of the test may be as subjective as setting an essay, depending on the expertise of the writer. In current terminology, an objective-test question is termed an item, and this seems quite logical, as many items are written in the form of statements.

In contrast to essay tests, objective tests have perfect marker reliability, because the answer is predetermined. Content validity is also very high in this form of test, as the large number of items ensures that the syllabus is adequately sampled. Furthermore, the marking can be done very quickly by using hardware such as optical scanners, and items can be kept in a bank and used time after time. The question of student fatigue does not arise, as objective tests take much less time to answer. However, they are very time consuming to write, and tests of the higher levels of intellectual functioning are difficult to formulate. Objective tests are commonly classified into those that require the answer to be selected from amongst alternatives and those that require the answer to be supplied by the learner.

Multiple-choice item

This consists of three parts; the 'stem' containing the problem or statement, the 'key', which is the correct response, and 'distracters', or incorrect responses. There should be at least three options given, to reduce the chances of guessing. Example:

Stem	The type of epithelium that lines the colon is called:
Distractors	a. squamous
	b. cuboidal
	c. transitional
Key	d. columnar

The multiple-choice item is a very versatile test that can measure a variety of levels of functioning. It is less susceptible to guessing, as there is only a one-in-four chance of getting it correct.

Matching item

This consists of two lists in columns, and the learner is required to match items from column A with responses in B. For example:

A	B
1. Yellow discolouration of skin	a) Bile salts
2. Severe itching of skin	b) Unconjugated bilirubin
3. Clay-coloured stools	c) Bilirubinaemia
4. Dark urine with yellow foam	d) Jaundice
	e) Haemolysis
	f) Obstruction

Matching items are useful for testing both knowledge of terminology and specific relationships between facts.

True-false item

True-false items are statements that the learner has to decide are true or false. There is a large risk of guessing in this type of item, and it is often difficult to select items that are categorically true or false. For example:

> *The commonest form of mental illness in Great Britain is schizophrenia. True/false.*

Assertion-reason item

This test presents two statements, an assertion and a reason. The learner is required to decide whether (a) each statement is true and (b) whether the reason is a correct explanation of the assertion. For example:

Assertion	Reason
Pressure in the glomerular capillaries is 70 mm Hg	The efferent arteriole has a smaller calibre than the afferent.

Short-answer (missing word) items

In this item, there is a statement or question that has a missing word that the learner must supply. For example:

> *The part of the brain which contains the visual cortex is called the ....lobe.*

This type is used to test knowledge of terms but is not very useful for higher levels of functioning. Often more than one answer will fit the blank, and this item may encourage rote learning.

Multiple-completion items

This involves the selection of more than one correct response, from a choice of combinations. The learner is looking for the incorrect option, so this item is often termed reverse multiple-choice. For example:

> *Which of the following would indicate occurrence of cardiac arrest?*
> - *Apnoea*
> - *Dilated pupils*
> - *Chest pain*
> - *Absence of pulse.*

GUIDELINES FOR WRITING OBJECTIVE TESTS

Writing multiple-choice items

The stem should include:

- the clearly stated problem;
- only material that is essential for clarity;
- novel material to test higher levels.

The options should:

- be three or more, to limit guessing;
- be in logical or quantitative order;
- be as short as possible, but clear;
- avoid repetition;
- be homogeneous;
- make limited use of negative forms;
- avoid 'all of these' and 'none of these'.

The distractors should be plausible.
The key should be:

- the single best or most likely answer; and
- free of specific determiners.

Specific determiners are clues contained in the item, but not linked to knowledge of content. There are several types to be aware of:

- constant position of key in options;
- length of key in relation to distractors;
- opposite options;
- grammatical inconsistency;
- use of words like 'never' and 'always'.

Students will often see the key as being one of the opposites, as item writers commonly choose statements which are opposite to the one that they have selected. It can be remedied by including another pair of opposites. Table 7.7 provides some examples of tests and comments on their construction.

TABLE 7.7 Worked examples and comments on their construction

Example	Comments
Example 1	
Vitamin B12: a. contains iron b. is absorbed by mouth c. is stored in the liver d. is given for haemolytic anaemia	Stem does not contain the problem

TABLE 7.7 Worked examples and comments on their construction (*continued*)

Example 2

Vitamin B12, one of the water-soluble B group of vitamins, is necessary for: a. prevention of haemolytic anaemia b. formation of haemoglobin c. formation of thrombocytes d. maturation of red corpuscles	Stem contains non-essential material, namely 'one of the water-soluble group of vitamins'

Example 3

A female patient aged 60 is admitted with history of fatigue, dyspnoea on exertion, and fainting attacks. Her vitamin B12 is low and tests reveal achlorhydria. The likely diagnosis is: a. iron deficiency anaemia b. haemolytic anaemia c. pernicious anaemia d. folic acid deficiency anaemia	Stem contains a novel problem, which requires application and synthesis of knowledge

Example 4

The normal range of haemoglobin level for men (g/l) is: a. 320–380 b. 30–80 c. 230–280 d. 130–180	Options should be in rank order

Example 5

A patient's blood pressure when lying down is charted using: a. two black dots joined by an interrupted horizontal line b. two black dots joined by a continuous vertical line c. two black dots joined by a continuous horizontal line d. two black dots joined by an interrupted vertical line	Options are repetitious

Example 6

The inferior boundary of the thoracic cavity is: a. sternum b. thoracic vertebrae c. diaphragm d. peritoneum	Options are not homogeneous; i.e. peritoneum is not part of thoracic cavity.

Example 7

Which of the following are not found in normal urine: a. urea b. albumin c. phosphate d. chloride	Negative should be clearly indicated by capitals or underlining

(*continued*)

TABLE 7.7 Worked examples and comments on their construction (*continued*)	
Example 8	
Which of the following is found in dehydration: a. inelastic skin b. oliguria c. constipation d. all of these	Using 'all of these' is poor; i.e. option (d) can be discarded if student recognizes one wrong option, or two correct ones
Example 9	
The secretion of the sebaceous glands is called: a. cerumen b. sebum c. semen d. sweat	Option c. is implausible
Example 10	
A patient in the ward develops diarrhoea. The nurse's first priority is to: a. increase his fluids b. isolate him c. send stool to laboratory d. commence fluid balance recordings	None of the options is clearly right or best
Example 11	
Hypertension is a state of: a. high blood sugar b. high blood pressure c. low blood sugar d. low blood pressure	Two pairs of opposites are included, to reduce chance of guessing
Example 12	
Diaphragmatic breathing is usually seen when a patient is: a. running b. standing c. sleeping d. in pain	Option d. is grammatically inconsistent

Writing matching items

When writing matching items, there are two specific points to watch out for. The number of choices should always exceed the number of statements, so that guessing is reduced. Also, the longer statements should be used as the premises, so that the student has the shorter responses to scan when searching for the answers.

Writing true-false items

The specific points when writing these are to:

- have an equal number of true and false statements;
- ensure that items are clearly true or false;
- avoid trick questions.

Writing short-answer (missing-word) items

The specific points when writing these are:

- Leave only important words blank.
- Avoid excessive blanks in a statement.
- Ensure that it is factually correct.

ANALYSIS OF OBJECTIVE-TEST ITEMS

One of the more useful characteristics of objective-test items is that they can be stored and used again, but this can only be the case if the item has been validated. Validation is performed after the test has been marked, and two aspects are considered: facility and discrimination. The facility index is the percentage of students who answer the item correctly, and the discrimination index indicates the extent to which an item discriminated between the more knowledgeable and the less knowledgeable students.

Facility index

This is calculated by the following formula:

$$\frac{\text{Number of students who answered correctly}}{\text{Total number of students tested}} \times 100$$

For example, if 40 students take the test, and 20 get the item correct, then the facility index is:

$$\frac{20}{40} \times 100 = 50\%$$

Discrimination index

This is normally calculated by arranging the completed test papers in order from the highest to lowest mark, and then putting them into high and low groups. The top 27 per cent from the high group and the bottom 27 per cent of the low group are used to calculate the index, as follows.

First, work out the number of students in the top 27 per cent who answered the item correctly and subtract the number of students in the bottom 27 per cent who answered the item correctly. Then divide that answer by 27 per cent of the total number of students tested.

The figure of 27 per cent is not rigidly fixed, and if the number of students is less than about 40 it is better to use the top and bottom halves of the group. The index range is from +1.00 to −1.00.

Example: If a batch of 200 test papers is used and the number of correct answers for the top 27 per cent is 40, and for the bottom 27 per cent it is 20, then the calculation will be as follows:

$$\frac{40 - 20}{54} = 0.37$$

Interpretation of indexes

The facility index is generally considered ideal when it is 50 per cent, but the acceptable range is from about 25 to 75 per cent. It is often desirable to include some easy items at the beginning of the test and then make it progressively more difficult.

The index of discrimination ranges from +1.00 to −1.00 and zero indicates no discrimination. Positive discrimination is accepted at 0.3 and above. If the index shows a negative figure, this implies that the less knowledgeable students are getting more correct answers for an item than the more knowledgeable ones and may indicate that the item is ambiguous or that the wrong key has been chosen.

The writing of objective-test items is made easier if regular 'shredding' sessions are conducted, in which three or four lecturers look at new test items to decide whether or not they are suitable for inclusion in pre-testing.

ASSESSMENT OF GROUP PROJECTS

Group projects can take many forms depending upon the subject being studied, but the fundamental principle is that a small number of students work collaboratively on a common problem or task, for example the design and production of artefacts such as a computer program, with each student in the group receiving the same overall grade. Group projects can help students to experience teamwork at first hand, develop interpersonal communication skills and management skills, promote critical thinking, and decreased anxiety. There are also advantages to the teacher, in that the number of assessments to be marked is considerably reduced. There are, however, some disadvantages associated with assessment of groups (Wiggs, 2011):

- In the end, it is students not groups who gain academic awards, so marks have to be awarded to individuals.
- Giving all students in the group the same grade creates the danger that some students will opt out of the work.
- Outstanding students can be dragged down by poor or lazy group members.
- Students felt peer pressure played a role both in preparation for the exam and in being an influence over answers.

One way to overcome the problem of non-contributing group members is for each individual's contribution to the project to be taken into account. The advantage of this is that lazy students do not get the same reward as those who have worked diligently. Race *et al.* (2005) suggest a way of dealing with this issue using a soccer analogy. Students who contribute little to the group project in the early stages are shown a yellow card, and their potential group mark is reduced by 10 per cent. If their commitment does not improve by the end of the project, they are shown a red card and marked at zero!

When attempting to assess projects it is important that a clear set of criteria is used. The nature of the criteria will depend upon the subject specialism; for example, assessment of a project report might use the following criteria:

- identification and context of the issue or problem;
- use of appropriate literature to inform project design;
- design of the project methodology;
- collection and analysis of data/information;
- discussion of findings and implications.

STUDENT SELF-ASSESSMENT

Self-assessment is an important strategy for students to acquire, as it forms the basis of life-skills and lifelong learning. It could be argued that students already engage in self-assessment when, for example, they write successive drafts of assignments until they are satisfied with the quality. Student marking of their own essays can be a very useful way of encouraging self-evaluation. In this method, students are given the opportunity to mark their own essays according to the criteria that the teacher has devised, and then student and teacher discuss their respective marking with each other. Interviews are another useful way of getting students to undertake self-assessment; the teacher can facilitate this by careful use of probing questions that focus attention upon aspects of the student's performance.

Questionnaires provide an alternative method for this and are less time consuming, but both methods are open to distorted reporting by the student. It is best not to grade these self-assessments to ensure honest and unbiased reporting, although the teacher may wish to negotiate with the student about the final grade of work, taking into account these self-assessments. Another method is to keep a self-assessment diary or commentary about progress on a course; this involves the student writing down reflections about his or her experiences and feelings.

PEER ASSESSMENT

Peer assessment is the assessment of a student by his or her peer group and is already familiar to students in the form of quiz assessment, where students exchange answer papers with each other and then mark them correct or incorrect. Essays can be exchanged between students and marked by them prior to returning to the writer, but peer assessment need not be confined to this contentious area. It can be used in a range of other, less sensitive, areas of assessment; for example, it is commonly used to facilitate students' report-writing ability, where peers are invited to comment constructively on draft reports. Similarly, use could be made of peer assessment of students' presentations to an audience; in this case, peer feedback may be more acceptable to the presenters than that provided by the tutor.

Peer-assessment is also useful for assessing practical skills; groups of three or four students are briefed on how to assess their peers' practical skills, and then each student performs the skill whilst the other group members observe. Feedback is given after each performance, and the whole cycle may be repeated so that students can remedy any mistakes or deficits.

There are opportunities for students to enhance their knowledge from peer assessment and to develop an effective strategy in assuring fairness and equity in the grading of group work. McLaughlin and Simpson (2004) found that peer assessment had a positive effect on motivation and was an effective device for encouraging good group management practices by enforcing a degree of discipline for students to engage in meaningful cooperative work.

A problem with any kind of peer assessment is the potential for collusion amongst the students to raise the level of marks. Students might soon realize that if each of them gives a high mark to the other, then the overall marks will be very high for everyone. The teacher needs to be aware of such collusion, especially if the marks are to be taken into account towards a final grade. One solution to this problem is to use peer assessments as feedback rather than as final grading, to ensure honesty of feedback. However, Race *et al.* (2005) emphasize the importance of making peer-assessment marks meaningful, so that students take the issue seriously.

ASSESSMENT AND EVALUATION OF SMALL-GROUP PROCESSES

Assessment of achievement in small groups differs from the assessment of group processes within a group. The following approaches are designed to elicit students' opinions on the interaction processes within their groups.

Individual-response evaluation

Reflective diary

Group members are invited to keep a diary of the events and feelings that they have about the group meetings over a period of time. These comments may be disclosed to the group or the tutor and can give much insight into the group process. However, the fact that the diary may be seen by other people may inhibit students from revealing some aspects of their experiences.

Individual impressions

Students are asked to jot down two aspects of the group that they did not like and two aspects that they did like, for feedback to the tutor, the group or both.

Face-to-face interview

Here, the tutor spends time with a group member discussing his or her perceptions of the group and the usefulness of the process. It can be time consuming but is worthwhile, provided that both parties are sufficiently trusting to be honest and open.

Sociometry

This technique involves individual group members privately writing down the names of other group members with whom they would choose to spend time on a particular activity.

Group-response evaluation

Nominal group technique

There are five stages in this technique as follows:

1. Each group member generates his or her own response.
2. Each group member feeds back his or her response to the group.
3. The group clarifies each member's response.
4. Each group member votes on, and ranks, each response.
5. The group's consensus of opinion is discussed.

Do-it-yourself evaluation

This involves each group member in writing three statements about the group and then 'snowball' groups of two, four and eight people are formed to modify and hone the statements. A plenary is called and the group must edit the list, after which the finished statements are put up on a notice board. Each group member then has to rate each statement on a six-point scale ranging from 'strongly agree' to 'strongly disagree' and record his or her rating in the form of large blobs that can easily be seen. The whole exercise provides a forum for discussion and exchange of feelings.

Group consensus

Group members form 'buzz' groups to ascertain whether they have common likes or dislikes about the group and are required to reach a consensus of opinion.

Group interview

Similar to the face-to-face interview with one group member, this involves the total group in interview with the teacher. Again, this requires skilful handling if it is to be effective and not just tokenism.

'Sculpting'

This is a technique for evaluation that uses physical position to indicate group processes. One member is asked to volunteer to be the 'sculptor' and the rest of the group is asked to remain in any position the chosen member would like to put them in. He or she is asked to 'sculpt' the way that they see relationships within the group; the leader is often put on a chair to indicate elevation above the rest of the group. Trust is essential among members if this is to work well, particularly as some may find themselves in the role of outsider or isolate. Following the sculpting there is group discussion and debriefing about the exercise.

Third-party evaluation

Observation

This can take place during normal group interaction, where a non-group member observes the process of group interaction. The main problem is the Hawthorne effect; i.e. the presence of an observer may alter the natural behaviour of the group.

Video-recording

This can provide a good alternative to a live observer, since it will not interpret the events, only record them. During the analysis playback, group members comment on the process.

ASSESSMENT OF STUDENT PRESENTATIONS TO AN AUDIENCE

It is common practice in project work to require the students to present their projects to an audience of peers or other members of the institution. This can be a useful way of developing students' confidence and skills of public speaking, but it can also provoke a good deal of anxiety. As in other forms of assessment, clear criteria are essential, and it is good practice to involve the students in formulating these. Lecturers need to organize the sequence of presentations very carefully indeed, as timing is crucial if all students are to fit in their presentations.

As a means of reducing anxiety, some tutors prefer not to grade the actual delivery of the presentation, simply using it as feedback to the students concerned. Table 7.8 shows an example of an assessment specification for student presentations on a nurse education programme; in this example the actual presentation is not assessed.

TABLE 7.8   Example of an assessment specification for student presentations

You are required to carry out a ten-minute teaching session to your peer group according to the following criteria:

- You must choose a health topic that you would teach to a patient/client, e.g. healthy eating, giving own insulin

- The session must be based on a plan containing details of aims/goals, sequence of development, content notes, learning aids used, and assessment of learning

- Following the presentation, the plan and materials used must be handed in as part of the assessment

- The plan must also be accompanied by a rationale (1000 words) consisting of the following:

  - An introduction that states why the topic you chose is relevant to the role of the nurse

  - An explanation of the reasons underlying your choice of teaching method and approach. This explanation must make reference to educational theories.

  - A critical self-evaluation of how you felt the lesson went, and any changes you would make in the light of your own and your peer evaluation of your lesson. (Video-recording facilities are available for your presentation.)

(Peer-evaluation consists of brief written feedback by students and tutor following each student presentation)

Please note: the actual presentation of your lesson, although compulsory, does not count towards your grade. You will be graded only on the written materials and accompanying rationale. This decision is to help reduce the stress that inevitably accompanies a student's first formal presentation to a large group.

ASSESSMENT OF LABORATORY PRACTICALS, FIELDWORK AND OBJECTIVE STRUCTURED CLINICAL EXAMINATION (OSCE)

The assessment of practical skills is undertaken in a wide variety of contexts, including laboratory work, fieldwork, objective structured clinical examination (OSCE) and the workplace.

Laboratory practicals

These are usually assessed by means of the student's laboratory reports. These reports are completed by the student after each practical activity, using a standard format. Many laboratories now provide computers so that students can input their reports at the time that they are undertaking the practicals. There must be explicit criteria for assessing the laboratory reports, and examinations should require the students to draw upon their reports when answering examination questions.

Fieldwork

Programmes in nurse education commonly require students to undertake some kind of fieldwork. For example, students commencing a common foundation programme may undertake a survey of food labelling in a local supermarket. Fieldwork is normally assessed by means of students' fieldwork logs and reports, but other artefacts such as video, audio and photography can be assessed.

Objective structured clinical examination (OSCE)

Although originally developed for assessing medical students, objective structured clinical examination (OSCE) have been adapted for use in nursing and allied health professions. Alongside additional methods of assessment, the OSCE is a form of assessment that has evolved over time into a valid and reliable way of assessing student competence (Smith *et al.*, 2012; Gopee, 2010). It consists of a series of work stations where students are required to perform procedures that are assessed by experts using predetermined assessment criteria (Brown and Pickford, 2006). An OSCE requires each student to demonstrate specific skills and behaviours in a simulated work environment with standardized patients. It typically consists of a series of short assessment tasks, each of which is assessed by an examiner using a predetermined, objective marking scheme (Mitchell *et al.*, 2009, p. 399). Common features associated with OSCEs are identified in Box 7.1 and examples of nursing skills that could be assessed using OSCEs are identified in Box 7.2.

During OSCEs, Bloomfield *et al.* (2010) point out that examiners usually assess performance relating to the acronym KMAS:

- *Knowledge*: a student's knowledge and understanding of a particular skill.
- *Motor*: the motor or technical aspects of a skill.
- *Attitude*: the affective aspect or attitude associated with the performance of a skill.
- *Structure*: how a student approaches a skill in terms of a systematic, logical and organizational approach.

BOX 7.1	Characteristics of OSCEs

- Examinations are held in a simulated environment, i.e. clinical skills laboratory.
- They are integral to patient care delivery and management.
- Students/lecturers/manikins can be used in place of real patients.
- OSCEs typically adhere to university examination regulations.
- Examiners are usually university lecturers with occasional use of clinical experts.
- They are judged via a holistic marking guide to enhance both the rigor of assessment and reliability.
- Students are normally required to rotate around a number of clinical assessment stations, allowing assessment of several skills during one examination period.

(Adapted from Creed, 2012; Nulty et al., 2011)

BOX 7.2	Nursing skills that could be assessed using OSCEs

- Monitoring and recording vital signs
- Administration of medicines
- Aseptic technique
- Wound assessment
- Communication
- Patient assessment and history taking
- Cardiopulmonary resuscitation
- Automatic external defibrillation
- First aid
- Bandaging
- Documentation
- Health promotion

As a method of assessment the OSCE offers a number of fundamental advantages:

- promotes student engagement;
- valid examination that can be used formatively and summatively;
- can be used with larger number of students;
- reproducible;
- opportunities for interprofessional collaboration.

Additionally some disadvantages of OSCE have been noted:

- knowledge and skills are tested in compartments;
- the OSCE may be demanding for both examiners and patients;
- time consuming and resource intensive;
- student anxiety.

Developing and examining OSCE assessments has been well published and a list of supplementary material to explore is identified in the further reading section.

ASSESSMENT OF PORTFOLIOS, PROFILES AND EXPERIENTIAL DIARIES

Portfolios, profiles and diaries

Portfolios, profiles and diaries are mainly used within an experiential learning context, including interpersonal skills training, and work-based learning. The terms 'portfolio' and 'profile' are used interchangeably within the literature, and Redfern (1998) identifies the characteristics common to each:

- They value experience as a source of learning.
- They encourage reflective practice.
- They provide a storehouse for information about, and evidence of, experience, learning and achievements.
- They encourage personal and professional development.

Race (2009) defines portfolios as comprising compilations of evidence of students' achievements, including major pieces of work, feedback comments from teachers, and student's reflective accounts; and the most effective way of encouraging students to generate portfolios is to build them into summative assessments. However, he proposes that profiles will be used increasingly in the future to augment the indicators of student's achievements, with portfolios to provide in-depth evidence. Portfolios, profiles and diaries are well established as valuable learning strategies in professional education programmes, but they do present problems in the context of assessment. Institutions differ in their approach to the assessment of portfolios, profiles and diaries; some use them solely as a vehicle for student learning, and do not require them to be assessed, whilst others view them as a component of the learning process. By definition, they are a record of students' thoughts, feelings and reflections on aspects of experience, which are often intensely personal to the student concerned. Although for assessment purposes they cannot be considered to be confidential, they need to be considered with some sensitivity. In addition, it is not easy to define appropriate assessment criteria for learning from reflection. The benefits and challenges of portfolios are highlighted in Table 7.9.

Murrell *et al.* (1998) describe how they assess clinical practice on a stoma care course using portfolios. The assessment involved marking each student's completed portfolio, and also the records of three interviews between the student and her clinical practice supervisor held at the beginning, middle and end of the course. A marking grid was used for the portfolio consisting of five key headings and associated descriptors:

1. Presentation, for example introduction and contents of portfolio.
2. Clinical expertise, for example appropriate and safe **evidence-based practice**.
3. Professional role, for example teamwork, relationships, accountability.
4. Management/education, for example flexible approach to practice and resource allocation.
5. Innovation, for example understanding of change and innovation, ability to promote innovation.

The assessment of portfolio-type material can be assisted if students are given clear advice about how to compile their portfolio, including the need to edit the material that they include, so as to avoid the portfolio becoming too large, and the importance of a

TABLE 7.9 Benefits and challenges of portfolios	
Benefits	**Challenges**
Portfolios reveal more about students than exam results and can include evidence reflecting a wide range of skills and attributes	Portfolios are harder to mark objectively due to difficulties setting assessment criteria which will be equally valid across a diverse set of portfolios.
Portfolios provide evidence of competence; they reflect attitudes and values as well as skills and knowledge, which is beneficial to future employers	The ownership of the evidence can sometimes be in doubt so accompanying portfolios with an oral assessment may substantiate the origin of the contents of portfolios, particularly if the evidence is based on the outcomes of collaborative work
Portfolios reflect progression; they identify areas of good knowledge and areas that require further enquiry	Reviewing portfolios is time consuming; they also take considerable time for students to complete
Portfolios enable theory to be linked to practice and promotes critical thinking	Being critical and honest in reflective writing when it is going to be summatively assessed can prove difficult for some students
Portfolios develop a sense of responsibility for CPD	There should be adequate preparation and support of students, staff and clinical assessors and the model of portfolio used should involve students transforming material into evidence, rather than including material that has not been synthesised

ADAPTED FROM RACE, 2009; TIMMINS AND DUNNE 2009; ENDACOTT ET AL., 2004

contents page and dividers between each section. Portfolios also provide a good vehicle for students to begin to self-assess their work. One of the main uses of portfolios in higher education is for the accreditation of prior learning.

ASSESSMENT OF ACCREDITATION OF PRIOR LEARNING

Accreditation of prior learning has become a significant process within the higher education sector, offering students the opportunity to count relevant, previously acquired learning towards academic awards.

Traditionally it has been divided into two types: learning acquired through successful completion of certificated courses is termed accreditation of prior learning or APL whereas that acquired through uncertificated experiential learning is termed accreditation of prior experiential learning, or APEL.

However, another acronym incorporating both types of prior learning also appears in the literature, AP(E)L. AP(E)L can normally provide the student with advanced standing of not more than 50 per cent of the total credits required for the award that the student is seeking. When a student wishes to claim accreditation for prior learning, his or her claim is subjected to assessment just like any other study component. However, the nature of the assessment will depend upon whether the claim is for APL or APEL.

Accreditation of prior learning (APL)

Assessment for this type is more straightforward, in that certificated learning is assessed against the learning outcomes of the programme on which the student is registered. Certificated learning means any learning gained through study on a formal programme for which a certificate or transcript is provided as evidence of successful completion. Many institutions have a credit tariff of courses that can count as APL against specific programmes, so that assessment is simply a matter of checking that the student's evidence of his or her successful completion of the programme is valid.

Accreditation of prior experiential learning (APEL)

It is important to note that, for an APEL claim to be successful, experience alone is insufficient. The student must demonstrate how he or she has learned from the experience. Credit points can be given for such experiential learning provided that it is relevant to the award which the student is seeking to achieve, and that a portfolio of evidence for such learning has been presented for accreditation to the awarding institution.

Students can be helped to compile a portfolio by asking themselves a series of questions as follows:

1. What past work and training experiences do I have?
2. What have I learned from these experiences?
3. Which of this learning is relevant to this course?
4. Which of the course outcomes can I claim to have already achieved?
5. How can I prove that I have achieved them? What evidence do I have?

AP(E)L portfolios are assessed and moderated according to the same standards as other programme assessments.

Management structures for the operation of APL/APEL

Responsibility for awarding APL or APEL credit resides with the relevant programme board of examiners, but the business of assessing and moderating claims is normally delegated to an accreditation subcommittee. The subcommittee is responsible for monitoring the pathway leader's recommendations for the award of credit for APL and APEL and is also responsible for accrediting courses from external providers. There are two roles that are essential in any APEL system: the APEL adviser and the APEL assessor. The APEL adviser's main role is to assist the claimant to formulate his or her learning claim in accordance with the procedures of the institution. Because of this close involvement in the process, the actual assessment of the claim is undertaken by the APEL assessor or gatekeeper, someone who has had no previous involvement with the claimant in relation to the learning claim.

Reliability and validity of AP(E)L assessment

Higher education institutions approach the assessment of prior learning in a variety of ways, and nurse education has been at the forefront of developments in this area.

A number of key points in relation to AP(E)L in health education programmes is identified by QAA (2011, 2004):

- AP(E)L assessment appears to be as valid and reliable as other forms of assessment in higher education.
- Although portfolios are the main method of assessment for AP(E)L, higher education providers should consider a range of assessments to consider claims for prior learning.
- APEL is not normally graded, nor does it count towards the degree classification.
- Reflection is an important aspect of portfolio construction.
- Applicants should be fully informed of the nature and range of evidence considered appropriate to support a claim for the accreditation of prior learning.
- The AP(E)L adviser role is a crucial one in ensuring the quality of the system.
- The assessment of learning derived from experience should be transparent and open to internal and external scrutiny and monitoring within institutional quality assurance procedures.

ASSESSMENT IN THE WORKPLACE

Work-based or placement learning in nurse education is usually undertaken as part, or whole, of a programme of study. The QAA (2007) outline the purpose of a well-designed assessment strategy:

> 'A well-designed assessment can help to reinforce the relevance of the work-based or placement learning to other parts of the programme and vice versa, and give students a range of opportunities to demonstrate achievement of their learning. In designing assessment for contexts where the learning and/or the assessment takes place 'off campus', it is important that any assessment tests the intended learning outcomes both accurately and fairly.'

Race (2009) points out that increasing use is being made of assessments based on students' performance and competence in the workplace; and offers a few advantages and disadvantages associated with this.

Advantages

- Work-based learning can balance the assessment picture. Future employers are likely to be equally interested in students' competence and academic performance, and assessing work-based learning can give useful information about students' competences beyond the curriculum.
- Assessing placement learning helps students to take placements seriously.

Disadvantages

- The reliability of assessment is difficult to achieve. Placements tend to be highly individual, and students' opportunities to provide evidence which lends itself well to assessment can vary greatly from one placement to another.

■ Some students will have much better placements and experiences than others so will have the opportunity to achieve predetermined competences and demonstrate their potential, while others will be constrained into relatively routine work practices.

The following points may assist in achieving a balance between validity and reliability when assessing work-based learning (NMC, 2010; Race, 2009; QAA, 2007):

■ Explore how best you can involve employers, professional regulators and colleagues.

■ Ensure the purpose of the assessment and the proportion of students' overall assessment that will be derived from their placement is clear.

■ Expect placements to be very different.

■ Ensure that the mentor is qualified to assess.

■ Decide carefully whether to tutor-assess during workplace visits.

■ Consider including the assessment of a work log or reflective journal.

■ Help to ensure that assessment does not blind students to their learning on placement.

Assessment within clinical practice is further explored in Chapter 11.

THE USE OF SERVICE USERS IN ASSESSMENT

The Standards for preregistration nursing education (NMC, 2010) advocate the involvement of service users and carers in the assessment of preregistration nursing students. The NMC (2010) define service users and carers as follows:

> 'Service users are people of any age using any health or social care services in any sector who require the professional services of a nurse or midwife; and include in-patients, outpatients, clients, residents and all similar categories. Nurses also work with other individuals and groups to which the service user belongs or is closely connected. These include partners, families, significant others, carers, interest groups, communities, networks and populations. The term 'service users and others' encompasses any category that fits in with the service user's needs and circumstances.
>
> A carer is an individual providing personal care for a person or people who, due to illness, infirmity or disability, are unable to care for themselves without this help.'

Davies and Lunn (2009) explain how the main role of service users in the clinical teaching environment has traditionally been to act as a subject for clinical assessment, diagnosis and treatment by students, under the guidance of clinicians, at different stages of the students' educational programme. They further explain how the service users' role has developed to undertake teaching responsibilities by discussing their medical condition and how it impacts on their families, carers and quality of life; however, their teaching role has further developed into the assessment of students.

Davies and Lunn (2009) investigated a new system of formative assessment in the clinical environment on students' perceptions of their communication skills, by recruiting patients to assess the student who provided their treatment on a given day. They also aimed to investigate the potential for the involvement of service users and their carers in the assessment of students. A communication assessment tool was developed using 12 communication statements accompanied by scoring the experience they received from zero to ten, with ten being the best experience received. Students were assessed in terms of:

- introduction to the patient;
- maintaining eye contact during conversation;
- information gathering;
- clear and concise terminology;
- listening skills;
- feedback on patient's treatment;
- involving patients in decision making;
- caring ability;
- attention to patient;
- patient sensitivity;
- verbal explanation of health care advice;
- written explanation of health care advice.

A total of 102 students were involved in the study where 44 students were considered to be experienced students, and 58 to be novice students. It is not clear exactly how many service users were involved by the authors reveal that a small number declined to take part, citing a number of reasons: did not have their reading glasses so were unable to read the questions; confusion and capability regarding their role.

A large number of students felt their communication skills had improved as a result of being assessed by patients; they were comfortable with the formative assessment process and felt it was a fair reflection of their abilities. Nonthreatening and non-judgemental real-life feedback was identified as an additional benefit for the student. Service users were found to be responsive to the assessment and reported that they had enjoyed their contribution towards student assessment at the same time as receiving treatment.

Students were invited to research and produce an information leaflet for newly diagnosed patients with inflammatory bowel disease, which were informally assessed and graded by an expert panel of patients and carers. Munro *et al.* (2012) aimed to highlight how service users from a national support group can be involved in both undergraduate nurse education and in NHS service planning and delivery.

A sample of 52 students were required to develop an evidence-based leaflet for patients newly diagnosed with inflammatory bowel disease that was to include relevant background information relating to aetiology, signs and symptoms, prognosis, treatment and support. An expert patient panel involved in the assessment comprised three patients and three carers and was chaired by the husband of one of the patients. The findings revealed that the expert panel of service users took their role seriously and conducted the assessment in a professional manner. They enjoyed the experience and were impressed with the effort and research undertaken by the students. However, the feedback that students received could be viewed as a little too direct and the Chairman highlighted a concern that this may affect a students' self-esteem.

Students positively evaluated the evidence-based learning activity and felt they were forced to achieve a higher level of work because they were being assessed by experts. A more accurate account of the prospect of surgery, dietary advice and a clear explanation of medical terms were recommendations offered by service users.

Munro *et al.* (2012) emphasized that students and service users highlighted presentation and language as key to designing effective patient information leaflets.

In conclusion, the authors believe that engaging an expert panel to assess the undergraduate students demonstrates that service users are able to become partners in developing nursing education to suit their own needs.

Issues with service user involvement in assessment

Despite the positive experiences highlighted above, Stacey *et al.* (2012) advise caution when considering service user involvement in assessing student nurses and make the following comment:

> 'What is noticeable in the NMC's requirement for involvement is the lack of acknowledgement that meaningful involvement may be problematic. What has become evident in our research is that this laudable initiative should be carefully contemplated before being implemented; in fact we question whether it should implemented at all without the required evidence-base.' (p. 482)

Although the NMC (2010) insist that valid and reliable assessments must be evidence-based, Stacey *et al.* (2012) highlight the lack of guidance offered by the governing body to involve service users in the assessment of student nurses. They advise against this involvement until the appropriate evidence base is established and the NMC provide the necessary direction. They are rightly concerned that the lack of guidance may lead to the exploitation of service users, which is supported by Webster *et al.* (2012, p. 137) in the following statement:

> 'It would be remiss to attempt to assess the impact on the practice of volunteer patients giving feedback without first striving to prepare them to deliver meaningful constructive feedback and to ensure they felt comfortable to do so.'

In addition to the lack of preparation and feedback skills, Stacey *et al.* (2012) identify further issues with service user assessment; they explain that if a patient were to provide negative feedback to a student there is the potential for them to receive a reduced quality of care, which is not only in direct conflict with the NMC (2008b) Code, but can also place a service user in a vulnerable position due to their health status and dependence on healthcare provision at that time.

MANAGEMENT OF THE ASSESSMENT PROCESS

All the foregoing discussion about ensuring the validity and reliability of assessments can be rendered meaningless if the management of the assessment system is inadequate.

Assessment regulations

One of the most important aspects of assessment is the assessment regulations; these act as an absolute guide to the whole assessment system for a given course or programme and should be followed meticulously. Although assessment regulations will be specific to a given course or programme, there are some generic aspects that apply to most:

■ *Student referral* The first time a student is unsuccessful in an assessment is commonly termed 'referral'. There would normally be one opportunity for retrieval for each unit assessment, and there is usually a maximum grade that can be obtained, which is less than the highest grade possible.

■ *Compensation* This refers to a situation where a good grade in one assessment can compensate for a weaker grade in another. Some courses allow this; others do not.

■ *Submission date for assessments* There should be a published date for submission of assessments, after which the student will be deemed to have been referred. In exceptional circumstances, the student may be granted an extension. A request for such an extension must normally be made in writing and received by the institution before the original due date for submission.

■ *Failure on re-submission of assessment* In the event of students being referred and then failing upon being re-assessed, they would normally be counselled to reconsider their programme of study. The failed unit may then be retaken only at the discretion of the institution.

■ *Suspected cheating and plagiarism* All higher education institutions will have a policy on suspected cheating and **plagiarism**, and this should be available to students via the student handbook for each programme. Cheating is self-explanatory; it includes taking unauthorized material into examinations with the aim of gaining an unfair advantage. Plagiarism is using other people's work and passing it off as the student's own; it includes using published references without acknowledging the source. The procedures for dealing with these normally involve a series of stages, depending upon whether the offence is considered to be minor or serious. For a first or minor offence, the student would normally be warned by the head of department, and a record kept. For significant offences, the student may be referred to an assessment offences panel, which will decide the appropriate penalty.

Students with additional assessment requirements

Students often have special assessment requirements, which may require extra time and encouragement to achieve their true potential. The following is a list of some specific requirements:

■ religious beliefs, for example, if students were fasting, or if a situation in which they were working caused ethical or moral dilemmas;

■ physical disabilities, for example, deafness, arthritis, migraine, etc. that might interfere with the student's performance;

■ the student might be very shy or nervous;

■ the workload that the candidate is dealing with might be too excessive;

■ the student may find difficulty in writing, owing, for example, to dyslexia, and other avenues of producing evidence must be explored, such as oral questioning, written evidence and simulation;

■ the student might require extra study time because family commitments make it difficult for them to study at home

Presentation of students' assessment work

It is good practice to impose a degree of uniformity on the presentation of students' assessment work, by issuing and reinforcing standards for presentation. Students are expected to word-process their assessment work and their work should normally be submitted in an appropriate lightweight folder or file. Exceptions to the latter are allowed for portfolio and similar assessments, where the amount of material is such that a more extensive binder is required.

Submission of assessments

The handing-in procedures for unit assessments are very important. Students must be made aware of the correct procedures for the handing-in of assessments, and no deviations should be allowed. Programmes will vary in their handing-in procedures; Table 7.10 shows a typical example.

TABLE 7.10   Example of a handing-in procedure for assessments
• Assignments must be handed-in to the designated office by the close of day on the deadline date for submission
• Assignments are not normally handed in to teaching staff
• A receipt is normally issued to the student as proof that the assessment has been handed in
• If assignments are posted, they should be sent by recorded delivery
• Students should keep a copy of all their assessments, in case of loss

Extensions to the deadline for submission of assessment

Students may request an extension to the unit assessment deadline in the case of exceptional circumstances such as prolonged illness, bereavement or severe domestic problems. Requests should be made in writing to the course leader in advance of the submission deadline, giving the reasons for the request and providing supporting evidence, for example a medical certificate. Alternatively, some institutions require the request to be sent directly to the academic registry, which then forwards it to the appropriate programme leader. If a request for extension is not granted, students should note that work submitted after the deadline will lead to the assessment being referred. They should also note that everyday pressure of work would not normally be grounds for an extension.

STUDENT CONDUCT DURING ASSESSMENTS

'Institutions should encourage students to adopt good academic conduct in respect of assessment and seek to ensure they are aware of their responsibilities.'

QAA (2011a)

QAA (2011a) emphasize the importance of ensuring that students receive information and guidance about their responsibilities as active participants in assessment, and provide the following examples:

■ The implications of academic misconduct must be clear. Policies and procedures should be applied consistently across an institution, to avoid the possibility of students in different departments or schools being treated differently for similar contraventions of rules covering cheating. The effects on students of academic misconduct may be harsher in some academic disciplines than others, especially where programmes involve fitness to practice.

■ Higher education institutions should promote sound academic practice and emphasize the importance of understanding and avoiding plagiarism.

■ Higher education institutions should implement administrative procedures to prevent fraudulent activities in formal examinations, for example, impersonation and the submission of work that is not that of the student.

■ Students must be aware of the different definitions of academic misconduct in respect of assessment and the associated penalties incurred. This can include any form of cheating, including plagiarism, collusion, impersonation and the use of prohibited material (including any material that breaches confidentiality, or that is downloaded from electronic sources without appropriate acknowledgement).

Conduct of formal written examinations

The room should be prepared the evening before, with desks spaced evenly and the appropriate materials distributed. Clocks must be clearly visible and synchronized, and a room plan with seat numbers should be displayed outside the room. Before the commencement of the examination the teacher should provide water to drink, in case a student gets a coughing spasm. The lighting and ventilation will need careful monitoring during the examination.

The name of each candidate should be checked before entry to the room or hall, and personal property should be stored separately in a cupboard or at the rear of the hall. Candidates should bring no books or paper unless specifically requested to do so. If there are a large number of candidates, a microphone and public-address system may be required.

At the commencement of the examination, the invigilator should read out any instructions, such as beginning each answer on a fresh page, and he or she should point out the procedure for leaving the room for purposes of visiting the toilet. The examination papers can then be distributed, face down on each desk and the candidates requested not to turn them over until instructed. The invigilator asks them to turn the paper over and to check that they have the correct one. The instructions at the top of the paper are read out and the candidates are told when time checks will be given. The word is given to commence the examination, and the invigilators are responsible for observing the candidates throughout the examination.

Time is called at the end, and candidates are requested to put their pens down. They check each question to see if they have numbered it correctly and are then dismissed. The invigilators collect and arrange the papers in order, checking them against the attendance register.

MARKING AND MODERATION OF STUDENTS' ASSESSMENT WORK

The programme leader is responsible for distributing the assessment work to the appropriate members of the team for marking; marking tutors should also be given a deadline for the return of the marked work and the appropriate marking record forms for completion. The latter constitute an important official record of the marks awarded to each student and form the basis of information subsequently input into the institution's academic information system.

When the marked work has been returned the programme leader will need to organize an internal moderation meeting at which the range of assessment work is sampled and scrutinized by the programme team.

MODERATION OF MARKED ASSESSMENT WORK

Before marked work is handed back to the students, it undergoes two kinds of moderation, internal and external. The purpose of moderation is to ensure consistency and fairness of marking amongst the unit markers. Inter-marker reliability, i.e. consistency, is notoriously low, and internal moderation seeks to expose marked papers to a second scrutiny so as to determine the consistency of marking standards between different unit markers. External moderation is carried out by the external examiner appointed to the programme, and the aim here is also to monitor consistency and standard of marking to ensure that students are being assessed fairly. In addition, the external examiner can compare the standard of work with that on similar courses nationally.

Internal moderation

Internal moderation can be carried out in a number of ways, but the principles remain the same, i.e. to ensure fairness and consistency of marking across the programme. Internal moderation normally consists of the scrutiny of a sample of students' work across the range of marks.

Internal moderation and double-marking (second-marking)

It is important to distinguish internal moderation from double marking. Double or second marking is a process whereby two tutors independently mark a student's work and come to an agreement about the final mark awarded. However, this process has limited value: as it focuses on the work of individual students it does not tell us anything about the overall consistency of a given marking tutor across their entire range of marking. Moderation, on the other hand, involves one marker evaluating another marker's judgement.

Internal moderation process

One effective way to carry out internal moderation is to select from each marking teacher a sample of marks that they have awarded at each grade or percentage band. Of course, it is important that markers avoid moderating their own work. The moderators will have a sample of each grade or percentage band for every marking teacher and are then in a position to ascertain the degree of consistency between markers for each grade or percentage band. If only one unit is being assessed, the internal moderation will sample only in relation to that unit.

For example, each teacher is asked to provide a 10 per cent sample from each of the grade or percentage bandings that they have used in their marking. For a typical programme using a literal grading system, this might involve three or four papers marked at Grade A, and a similar number from each of Grades B to D, including all borderline and referred papers. This is a resource-intensive activity and as such requires careful planning. Whatever system is used, it will have to be agreed by the programme committee and the board of examiners.

One point that is often contentious is whether or not internal moderators should alter individual student marks. Generally speaking, moderators should only adjust student marks if all the assessments within a category have been moderated, for example all borderline or referred papers. Since moderation involves only a sample of the students' assessments, there will be many students whose work is not moderated. If the moderators were to alter individual student marks, this could give an unfair advantage or disadvantage to those students whose work was sampled.

When internal moderation has been completed, a sample of assessments should be sent to the external examiner for further scrutiny.

External moderation

External moderation is undertaken by the external examiner, who will inform the programme leader of the procedures that he or she would like to adopt for this. Normally, the external examiner would receive all referred papers and all papers awarded the highest grade, as well as a sample of papers from each grade or percentage band. The programme leader needs to ensure that the external examiner has a timescale sufficient for adequate scrutiny of the papers.

Once the moderation system has been completed, assessment work can be returned to students. Assessments are made available for collection at the departmental office. Students should note that any mark awarded is provisional at this stage. The final mark is determined when the board of examiners meets, and a unit pass list is sent to each successful student as soon as possible after that meeting. Students who were unsuccessful are informed individually by letter.

EXTERNAL EXAMINERS

The external examiner plays a crucial role in the assessment process and must be present at any meeting of the board of examiners where conferment of awards is recommended. A decision of the external examiner is normally taken as final, except in extreme cases such as disagreement between external examiners, when the matter would be referred to the academic board of the institution. External examiners should be experts in the relevant subject area and be experienced in the assessment of students at the level of the programme in question. Their judgements must be impartial and not influenced by previous association with either students or staff of the institution. Table 7.11 gives the typical responsibilities of an external examiner (QAA, 2011b):

TABLE 7.11 Typical responsibilities of an external examiner

- Approve proposed examination papers and other assessments
- Consider and, if appropriate, agree proposed changes to assessment regulations
- Undertake moderation of students' assessment work, including scrutiny of all students' work proposed for the highest and referred grades
- Compare students' assessment performance with that of students on comparable courses elsewhere
- Report on the consistency and standard of internal marking
- Attend meetings of the board of examiners at which recommendations are made for conferment of academic awards
- Provide reports to the institution on the assessment process

BOARDS OF EXAMINERS

Table 7.12 gives the typical composition of a board of examiners, and Table 7.13 outlines its responsibilities.

One of the responsibilities of the programme leader is making arrangements for meetings of the board of examiners, in consultation with the chair and the external examiner; these arrangements include room booking and catering. He or she must also arrange the production of all papers, including draft results lists and pass lists, for each meeting and be prepared to comment on individual students' performance. When required to do so by the board, the programme leader should be prepared to comment on any mitigating circumstances affecting student performance.

Following the meeting of the board of examiners, the programme leader must arrange for the mailing of pass lists and referral/fail letters to students, and also send copies to the registry for the academic information system.

TABLE 7.12 Typical composition of a board of examiners

- Appropriate senior manager (chair)
- Other senior managers with involvement in the programme
- Programme leader
- Representative of staff teaching on the programme as internal examiners
- External examiner(s)
- A representative from the academic registry will normally attend meetings to record the proceedings and to offer advice regarding regulations

TABLE 7.13 Typical responsibilities of a board of examiners
• Oversight of assessment procedures
• Ensuring students are assessed fairly
• Maintenance of the standard of awards
• Ensuring compliance with assessment requirements
• Making decisions about student progression and reassessment
• Recommending students for academic awards

Subject assessment panels

Some higher education institutions allow boards of examiners to delegate responsibility for the assessment of groups of units to subject assessment panels. The chair of such panels is normally the head of the school that houses the majority of units, and membership consists of internal examiners, i.e. staff who taught the units under consideration, and external examiner(s).

Subject assessment panels consider and approve assessments for units in the panel's subject area, submit marks and recommendations to the relevant board of examiners and notify the board in relation to students' extenuating circumstances.

Chairing the board of examiners

The board of examiners is normally chaired by the head of department or his or her nominee, and the approach should be formal and rigorous. Each meeting should be numbered, for example 'fifth meeting of the board of examiners'; this facilitates review of decisions taken at previous meetings.

The chair should never take the minutes of the meeting, as this would distract him or her from conducting the meeting in an appropriate manner. The minutes should be headed 'Confidential', and recorded by an experienced administrator who should identify the chair and the secretary by name. Each agenda item should be numbered according to the number of the meeting, for example 5.1. Sub-items should be numbered similarly, for example 5.1.4. Where an agenda item requires action, the minutes should indicate clearly and boldly the individual(s) responsible for undertaking the action, so that completion may be checked at a subsequent meeting of the board of examiners.

It is customary for the chair to read aloud the name of each candidate whose results are being considered. When the board has confirmed the results of the cohort, the chair and the external examiner should sign the master copy of the examination results. All copies should be numbered, so that when they are collected back from board members at the end of the meeting, the administrator can check that all have been returned. This measure is designed to maintain the confidentiality of the proceedings.

In the event that a student is given a fail grade, the chair would normally ask if there are any mitigating circumstances in relation to the student concerned. If the board considers that the mitigating circumstances were such that the student's performance in the assessment was adversely affected, the board has the authority to allow the student to do the assessment again.

Appeals against a decision of the board of examiners

All institutions have procedures for appeals by students, and the grounds of appeal are carefully defined (QAA, 2011c). Students may not appeal against the academic judgement of the markers as ratified by the board of examiners. The grounds upon which an appeal may be based are normally:

- illness or other factors which the student claims affected his or her performance, but which he or she was unable or unwilling, for legitimate reasons, to make known to the board of examiners before it made its decision;
- the occurrence of an administrative error or other irregularity affecting the assessment;
- the assessment was not carried out in accordance with the regulations for the programme.

Appeals are conducted by an appeals committee whose typical composition includes a deputy vice-chancellor, the dean of faculty, a head of department from a different faculty, a member of the academic board of the institution, and a student nominee of the students' union. No member of the committee should have had previous involvement with the student in matters regarding the appeal.

Review questions

1. Explain the terms validity and reliability in terms of assessment.
2. Compare and contrast the analytical method of marking (mark schemes) with the global method of marking (structured impressionistic marking).
3. What are the advantages and disadvantages of group work?
4. Describe what an Objective Structural Clinical Examination (OSCE) consists of and discuss the advantages and disadvantages of this method of assessment.
5. Describe the benefits of using patients (service users) in the assessment process and the drawbacks.
6. Why is it so important to manage the assessment process?

SUMMARY

- Setting, marking and moderating students' written assessment work constitutes a very significant part of the lecturers' role in higher education, but in nurse education there is the added dimension of workplace assessment to be considered.

- A carefully planned assessment can form an integral part of the teaching and learning experience for the student rather than something that distracts from the main business of studying.

- Assessment can provide valuable feedback to students about their progress, and point out ways in which they could develop further.

- The inclusion of multiple forms of assessment helps students to integrate, synthesize and assimilate the theoretical components of the domain with the clinical application and practical skills involved.

- Norm-referenced assessment means that an individual student's score on a test is compared with scores of other students in a given group, and a rank order is assigned.

- Criterion-referenced assessment implies that the score is compared with some criterion or learning task such as achievement of behavioural objectives.

- Assessment is not only concerned with the measurement of student achievement but includes such aspects of an individual as attitudes, aptitudes, personality and intelligence.

- Essay assessments require the learner to supply an answer that is organized in his or her own words and presented in his or her own style and, in examinations, handwriting, with few restrictions imposed, and no single correct answer.

- Marking an essay assignment involves more than simply checking the content for accuracy; it also requires the marker to make a judgement about the quality of the students' scholarship skills.

- Formative feedback is that which is given to students during the process of preparing their work for assessment.

- Feedback needs to be adapted to students' differing levels of confidence and experience.

- Group projects can help students to experience teamwork at first hand, and also to develop interpersonal communication skills and management skills.

- Work-based assessment is not controlled entirely by academic staff from the institution; employers, supervisors and workers may all be involved to some extent in the context of the assessment.

- One of the most important aspects of assessment is the assessment regulations; these act as an absolute guide to the whole assessment system for a given course or programme, and should be followed meticulously.

References

Banning, M. (2003) The use of structured assessments, practical skills and performance indicators to assess the ability of pre-registration nursing students to apply the principles of pharmacology and therapeutics to the medication management needs of patients. *Nurse Education in Practice* 3, 1–7

Bloom, B. (1956) *The Taxonomy of Educational Objectives: The Classification of Educational Goals, Handbook One: The Cognitive Domain*. New York: McKay

Bloomfield, J., Pegram, A. and Jones, C. (2010) *How to Pass Your OSCE: A Guide to Success in Nursing and Midwifery*. Harlow: Pearson Education Limited

Brightwell, R., Daniel, J.H. and Stewart, A. (2004) *Evaluation: is an Open Book Examination Easier?* York: Higher Education Academy

Brown, G., Bull, J. and Pendlebury, M. (1997) *Assessing Student Learning in Higher Education*. London: Routledge

Brown, S. and Knight, P. (1994) *Assessing Learners in Higher Education*. London: Kogan Page

Brown, S. and Pickford, R. (2006) *Assessing Skills and Practice: Key Guides for Effective Teaching in Higher education*. Abingdon: Routledge

Creed, F. (2012) Chapter 1 - An introduction to OSCE assessments. In: Caballero C, Creed F, Gochmanski C, Lovegrove J (Eds) *Nursing OSCEs: A Complete Guide to Exam Success*. Oxford: Oxford University Press

Curzon, L.B. (2003) *Teaching in Further Education: an Outline of Principles and Practice* (6th Edition). London: Continuum

Davies, C.S. and Lunn, K. (2009) The patient's role in the assessment of students' communication skills. *Nurse Education Today* 29(4) 405–412

Endacott, R., Gray, M.A., Jasper, M.A., McMullan, M., Miller, C., Scholes, J. and Webb, C. (2004) Using portfolios in the assessment of learning and competence: the impact of four models. *Nurse Education in Practice* 4(4) 250–257

Gopee, N. (2010) *Practice Teaching in Healthcare*. London: Sage

HEA (2011) *The UK Professional Standards Framework for Teaching and Supporting Learning in Higher Education*. York: Higher Education Academy

Lambert, D. and Lines, D. (2000) *Understanding Assessment: Purposes, Perceptions, Practice*. London: Routledge

McLaughlin, P. and Simpson, N. (2004) Peer assessment in first year university: how the students feel *Studies in Educational Evaluation* 30(2) 135–149

Mitchell, M.L., Henderson, A., Groves, M., Dalton, M. and Nulty, D. (2009) The objective structured clinical examination (OSCE): Optimising its value in the undergraduate nursing curriculum. *Nurse Education Today* 29(4) 398–404

Munro, J., Whyte, F., Stewart, J. and Letters, A. (2012) Patients assessing students' assignments; Making the patient experience real. *Nurse Education Today* 32(2) 139–145

Murrell, K., Harris, L. and Tomsett, G. (1998) Using a portfolio to assess clinical practice. *Professional Nurse* 13(4) 220–223

Neary, M. (2000) *Teaching, Assessing and Evaluation for Clinical Competence: A Practical Guide for Practitioners and Teachers*. Cheltenham: Nelson Thornes

NMC (2008a) *Standards to Support Learning and Assessment in Practice*. London: Nursing Midwifery Council

NMC (2008b) *The Code: Standards of Conduct, Performance and Ethics for Nurses and Midwives*. London: Nursing Midwifery Council

Nulty, D.D., Mitchell, M.L., Jeffrey, C.A., Henderson, A. and Groves, M. (2011) Best practice guidelines for use of OSCEs: maximising value for student learning. *Nurse Education Today* 31(2) 145–151

QAA (2011a) *UK Quality Code for Higher Education Chapter B6: Assessment of Students and Accreditation of Prior Learning*. Gloucester: Quality Assurance Agency

QAA (2011b) *UK Quality Code for Higher Education Chapter B7: External Examining*. Gloucester: Quality Assurance Agency

QAA (2011c) *UK Quality Code for Higher Education Chapter B9: Complaints and Appeals*. Gloucester: Quality Assurance Agency

QAA (2007) *Code of Practice for the Assurance of Academic Quality and Standards in Higher Education. Section 9: Work-based and Placement Learning*. Gloucester: Quality Assurance Agency

QAA (2004) *Guidelines on the Accreditation of Prior Learning*. Gloucester: Higher Education Academy

Race, P. (2009) *Designing assessment to improve Physical Sciences Learning*. York: Higher Education Academy

Race, P., Brown, S. and Smith, B. (2005) *500 Tips on Assessment* (2nd Edition). London: Routledge

Redfern, E. (1998) The power of the professional profile. In Quinn FM (Ed.) *Continuing Professional Development in Nursing: A Guide for Practitioners and Educators*. Cheltenham: Nelson Thornes

Rowntree, D. (1987) *Assessing Students: How Shall We Know Them?* (2nd Edition). London: Kogan Page

Smith, V., Muldoon, K. and Biesty. (2012) The Objective Structured Clinical Examination (OSCE) as a strategy for assessing clinical competence in midwifery education in Ireland: A critical review. *Nurse Education in Practice* 12 242–247

Stacey, G., Stickley, T. and Rush, B. (2012) Service user involvement in the assessment of student nurses: A note of caution. *Nurse Education Today* 32(5) 482–484

Timmins, F. and Dunne, P.J. (2009) An exploration of the current use and benefit of nursing student portfolios. *Nurse Education Today* 29(3) 330–341

Webster, B.J., Goodhand, K., Haith, M. and Unwin, R. (2012) The development of service users in the provision of verbal feedback to student nurses in a clinical simulation environment. *Nurse Education Today* 32(2) 185–189

Welsh, I. and Swann, C. (2002) *Partners in Learning: A Guide to Support and Assessment in Nurse Education*. Abingdon: Radcliffe Medical Press

Wiggs, C.M. (2011) Collaborative testing: Assessing teamwork and critical thinking behaviours in baccalaureate nursing students. *Nurse Education Today* 31 279–282

Further Reading

Corry, M. and Timmins, F. (2009) The use of teaching portfolios to promote excellence and scholarship in nurse education. *Nurse Education in Practice* 9(6) 388–392

Elliott, N. and Higgins, A. (2005) Self and peer assessment – does it make a difference to student group work? *Nurse Education in Practice* 5(1) 40–48

Harden, R.M. (1990) Twelve tips for organizing an Objective Structured Clinical Examination (OSCE). *Medical Teacher* 12(3/4) 259–264

Jones, A., Pegram, A. and Fordham-Clarke, C. (2010) Developing and examining an Objective Structured Clinical Examination. *Nurse Education Today* 30(2) 137–141

Merriman, C. and Westcott, L. (2010) *Succeed in OSCEs and practical exams: an essential guide for nurses*. Maidenhead: Open University Press

Rhodes, C.A. (2012) User involvement in health and social care education: A concept analysis. *Nurse Education Today* 32(2) 133–138

Rush, S., Firth, T., Burke, L. and Marks-Maran, D. (2012) Implementation and evaluation of peer assessment of clinical skills for first year student nurses. *Nurse Education in Practice* 12(4) 219–226

Sowter, J., Cortis, J. and Clarke, D.J. (2011) The development of evidence based guidelines for clinical practice portfolios. *Nurse Education Today* 31(8) 872–876

Speed, S., Griffiths, J., Horne, M. and Keeley, P. (2012) Pitfalls, perils and payments: Service user, carers and teaching staff perceptions of the barriers to involvement in nursing education. *Nurse Education Today*, doi: 10.1016/j.nedt.2012.04.013

Stickley, T., Stacey, G., Pollock, K., Smith, A., Betinis, J. and Fairbank, S. (2011). Developing a service user designed tool for the assessment of student mental health nurses in practice: a collaborative process. *Nurse Education Today* 31 (1) 102–106

CHAPTER 8
STUDENT FEEDBACK

THE AIMS OF THIS CHAPTER ARE:

- To discuss the context of feedback and feeding forward

- To illustrate the benefits and barriers to effective feedback

- To outline the principles of effective feedback

- To consider the needs of students when writing summative feedback comments on assessments

KEY TERMS

Feedback
Annotation

THE CONTEXT OF FEEDBACK AND FEEDING FORWARD

The National Student Survey (NSS) forms part of the quality assurance framework for higher education and highlights that feedback is generally the lowest performing category across the majority of UK institutions. The design of the survey has been open to some criticism but the results are taken very seriously. As a result of the annual NSS, institutions have developed effective methods of using survey data as part of an annual review and evaluation of programmes to inform their continuous quality improvement process. Institutions have been aware of students' experience of feedback for some years and have undertaken various strategies to improve student satisfaction in this area (Williams and Kane, 2008).

Meaningful feedback on assessed academic work forms a crucial part of student's development and is an important contributor to the quality of the student experience (Race, 2009; Beaumont *et al.*, 2008; Irons, 2008; Lizzio and Wilson, 2008; Nicolans MacFarlane-Dick, 2006; Yorke, 2003). The Quality Assurance Agency (2011) states:

> *'institutions must provide appropriate and timely feedback to students on assessed work in a way that promotes learning and facilitates improvement but does not increase the burden of assessment'*

Feedback is a key learning and teaching strategy (Duncan, 2007; Carless, 2006), and one of its primary aims is to indicate how the student can develop in respect of future work. Gibbs and Simpson (2004) argue that feedback to the students on their assignments is the single most powerful influence on student achievement.

> *'**Feedback** is any information, process or activity which affords or accelerates student learning based on comments relating to either formative or summative assessment activities'*
>
> (Irons, 2008)

Sadler (1989) highlighted that feedback is the 'key element' in formative assessment but can only serve as a formative function when it is used to alter the gap between current and the required/expected levels of understanding, an element under student control. Irons (2008) supports this by emphasizing that feedback should attempt to provide students with an indication of where they are in relation to achieving learning outcomes, where they need to progress to and how they will be able to reach the expected level. In order for this to be effective the feedback should be based on understood goals which the student believes are achievable and valuable. The purpose of effective feedback is discussed by Spendlove (2009) who identified that it assists a student to shape and direct the next phase of learning; and the key to effective feedback is through causing deep thinking, increasing reflection and providing guidance on how to improve (feed-forward).

In meeting the needs of students for feedback on their progression and attainment, the QAA (2011) offer the following points and suggest that institutions consider:

- providing feedback at an appropriate time in the learning process, and soon after the student has completed the assessment task;
- specifying the nature and extent of feedback that students can expect and whether this is to be accompanied by the return of assessed work;
- the effective use of comments on returned work, including relating feedback to intended learning outcomes and assessment criteria, in order to help students identify areas for improvement as well as commending them for achievement;
- the role of oral feedback, either on a group or individual basis, as a means of supplementing or replacing written feedback;

■ providing guidance about the point in the module or programme where it is no longer appropriate for a member of staff to continue providing feedback to a student on his/her work; this is normally when a student is approaching a submission date for summative assessment, for example two weeks.

Aside from identifying what a student has done well and not so well, feedback should also identify how a student can improve for a future assessment; this is known as feeding forward.

> *'Feeding forward is a strategy for enabling students to make effective use of assessment feedback by using feedback from one assessment to assist with the completion of a future assessment.'*
>
> (Gopee, 2010)

Race (2009) advises that lecturers should check that adequate 'feed-forward' is offered, rather than merely feedback on what has already been done. He also emphasizes the importance of helping students to differentiate between feedback and feed-forward, to review the latter carefully, and regard it as the most useful part, and consciously build upon it as their assessment work progresses. Feeding-forward in assessments are designed with a built-in opportunity for students to put the feedback to immediate use (Carless, 2007).

The literature is replete with the benefits and barriers of effective feedback and a synopsis of these are listed in Table 8.1 and Table 8.2 respectively (Carless *et al.*, 2011; Ferguson, 2011; Handley and Williams, 2011; NUS, 2011; Race, 2009; Irons, 2008; Duncan, 2007).

TABLE 8.1 Benefits of effective feedback

- Feedback can be meaningful in terms of achievement and progression
- There are opportunities to improve learning
- Creates opportunities for clarification and discussion
- Emphasizes progress rather than failure
- Feedback may enhance future grades
- Methods of feedback can be dictated by student
- There are opportunities for individual and group/cohort feedback
- Feedback causes deep thinking
- Feedback provides guidance on how to improve
- Feedback increases reflection and encourages development of self-assessment and peer evaluation and assessment
- Promotes a learning journey and encourages greater achievement
- Foster greater levels of self-esteem, confidence and motivation which, in turn, can result in greater progress
- Enable tutors to realign their teaching content and teaching methods in response to learners' needs
- Encourages effective dialogue between students and lecturers

TABLE 8.2   Barriers to effective feedback

- Students more concerned with mark than qualitative feedback
- Feedback can be vague, lacks guidance, and unrelated to the assessment criteria
- Comments are sometimes negative, demotivating, lack clarity and are difficult to act upon
- Comments written academically and not in student language
- Inconsistency in feedback amongst academic staff
- Lecturer time constraints – may rush feedback
- Lack of value and engagement placed on feedback
- Students not trained or informed about how to use feedback
- Lack of understanding of assessment criteria that guides feedback

PRINCIPLES OF EFFECTIVE FEEDBACK

The general principles that guide effective feedback to students remain paramount; that is, feedback should be constructive, consistent, actionable and student focussed.

The ten principles of feedback (Figure 8.1) are intended to guide and enhance feedback practice for the benefit of students and lecturers and have been adapted from the work of many authors (Ferguson, 2011; NUS, 2011; QAA, 2011; HEA, 2010; Race, 2009; Spendlove, 2009; Beaumont *et al.,* 2008; Irons, 2008; Lizzio and Wilson, 2008; Poulos and Mahony, 2007; Taylor, 2007; Nicol and Macfarlane-Dick, 2006; Orrell, 2006; Race *et al.,* 2005; Juwah *et al.,* 2004).

Principle 1: *Feedback should be for learning, not just of learning*

Feedback should be primarily used as a learning tool and therefore positioned for learning rather than as a measure of learning. We believe that assessment feedback should be at the heart of the learning process. Feedback is often given at the end of an assignment to simply record a student's achievement. This approach fails to utilize it as a learning tool and therefore does not provide any developmental advice which will allow a student to progress. The use of assessment for learning techniques or formative assessment, encourages this as it involves the completion of tasks whereby the assessment itself, and subsequent feedback is a learning tool. Ideally feedback should only consist of constructive comments with marks or grades; particularly for any that counts towards a summative end of course assessment released after the comments have been acted upon. We have seen that an over reliance on marks and grades can impede learning as students may come to focus too much emphasis on performance goals rather than learning goals. Feedback where a mark or grade replaces constructive comments has been shown to have a negative effect on the self-esteem on low ability students.

Principle 2: *Feedback should be progressive and facilitate self-assessment and reflection in learning*

A member of academic staff, for example, the personal teacher should be responsible for monitoring a students' academic progress throughout their programme of study. Reflection on learning will link to self-assessment and will identify key areas for development.

FIGURE 8.1 Principles of effective feedback

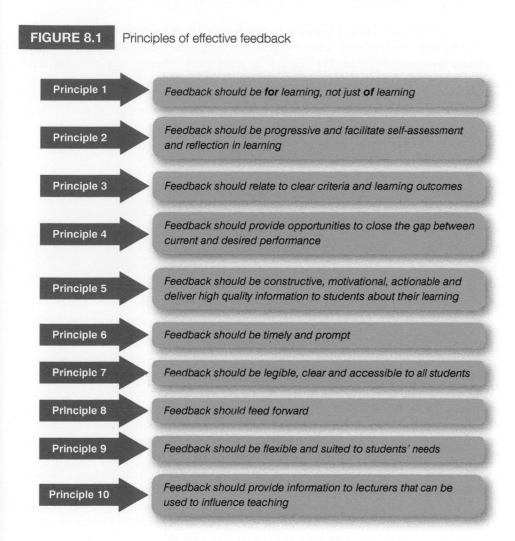

Principle 1 — Feedback should be **for** learning, not just **of** learning

Principle 2 — Feedback should be progressive and facilitate self-assessment and reflection in learning

Principle 3 — Feedback should relate to clear criteria and learning outcomes

Principle 4 — Feedback should provide opportunities to close the gap between current and desired performance

Principle 5 — Feedback should be constructive, motivational, actionable and deliver high quality information to students about their learning

Principle 6 — Feedback should be timely and prompt

Principle 7 — Feedback should be legible, clear and accessible to all students

Principle 8 — Feedback should feed forward

Principle 9 — Feedback should be flexible and suited to students' needs

Principle 10 — Feedback should provide information to lecturers that can be used to influence teaching

Feedback from self-assessment practices can play a powerful role in learning by encouraging reassessment of personal beliefs, attitudes and interpretations. Enabling students to assess their own learning can be influential to personal and professional development and can encourage progression. Rather than a one-off event after assessment, feedback should be part of continuous guided learning and an integral part of the learning experience. Students should be expected and encouraged to reflect on feedback from previous summative assessments and the personal teacher could be instrumental in assisting students in identifying strategies to address areas for improvement in future assessments. Assessment practices need to enable students to receive feedback on their progress which they can use to aid their progression. Many simple mistakes, particularly referencing, grammar and syntax can be addressed if a student's progression is under constant review.

Principle 3: *Feedback should relate to clear criteria and learning outcomes*

Assessment guidelines, marking grids and criteria/learning objectives should be student-centred and written in a language that students understand. This allows understanding of what is required in assessments. Research has indicated that lecturers and students often interpret assessment guidelines differently and such differences can occur when standards are based or interpreted on tacit knowledge and assumptions, which are often complex to articulate and communicate. Therefore it is crucial that these issues are overcome, perhaps by illustrating exemplars of good and poor performance, and there is a clear and common understanding between lecturers and students about the meanings behind assessment guidelines and assessment criteria. Group tutorials or seminars on feedback and assessment practices may also enhance students' understanding of assessment. It is vital that assessment feedback is given solely in relation to agreed and fully understood criteria and no other.

TEACHING TIP

Clearly communicate to the student what they did well against the assessment criteria, what they did less well and where improvements can be made.

Principle 4: *Feedback should provide opportunities to close the gap between current and desired performance*

A students' actual performance in an assessment should be highlighted on written feedback sheets and also highlighted on electronic marking grids if applicable. It should be clear to the student what he/she has done well. Desired performance can be linked to areas for improvement. Areas for improvement/desired performance should be clearly identified on all written feedback sheets. They can also be emphasized to students during face-to-face feedback tutorial sessions if required. Feedback should measure the student's current learning state but also be used as a means for closing the gap between the student's learning state and the learning objectives. The QAA (2011) advise caution with language when giving feedback to students and stress the importance of using 'final language' such as weak or poor as this can cause irretrievable breakdowns in the communication between assessor and student. They also recommend avoiding words such as excellent, as this can also cause problems when a student only receives good or very good in subsequent assessments. They suggest that assessors only praise exactly what was very good or excellent in a little more detail, rather than take the short cut of just using the adjectives themselves.

Principle 5: *Feedback should be constructive, motivational, actionable and deliver high quality information to students about their learning*

Feedback should be student-centred, meaning that it must be understandable to students and should be high quality and effective in its guidance. There are sometimes differences in the quality and quantity of feedback received from different markers, and students can be disadvantaged if they follow suggestions made by one marker and find that another marker interprets the criteria differently (Taylor, 2007). Feedback needs to be concise, focused and meaningful if it is going to be constructive for students and it must be individualized to fit each student's achievement and directly related to the particular piece of work. The feedback must be tailored to justify an accompanying assessment grade or mark and manageable for students. Receiving too much feedback can result in students not being able to sort out the important feedback from the routine feedback, reducing their opportunity to benefit from the feedback they need most. Vague comments such as 'could do better', without explaining how they could actually do so, are not productive forms of feedback. Receiving feedback can sometimes be difficult as students often think it will be negative or critical and students often view negative feedback as a reflection on him/her personally. This can serve to damage motivation and self-esteem while doing little to help actual learning. If students come to fear what feedback they could receive it may prevent them from picking up their feedback and speaking directly to the lecturer. It is important that comments are not overly negative so feedback needs to contain a certain amount of positive comments, for confidence and motivation purposes. The inclusion of positive components, including praise and encouragement in a feedback session contributes to reinforcing correct responses, but also to address the potentially adverse effects of constructive feedback on self-esteem and motivation. Empowering feedback should strengthen and consolidate learning but whilst the QAA (2011) stress that this is easier to ensure when feedback is positive, the provider of feedback must carefully consider critical feedback can be equally empowering to learners. It is essential that students are provided with the opportunity to discuss their feedback on a face-to-face basis with their academic supervisor or a member of the academic team. This should ideally occur within a week of the results being published in order to facilitate timely feedback.

Principle 6: *Feedback should be timely and prompt*

Feedback should be provided in a timely and prompt manner, allowing students to apply it to future learning and assessments. If feedback is returned in an untimely fashion, particularly after submission dates of subsequent assignments, students are prevented from fully developing and progressing in their learning. It is important that students are aware of how long to expect the turnaround to be so they have realistic expectations. If this is not done it might result in unnecessary student dissatisfaction. The timing of feedback should also vary, because whilst feedback is traditionally offered at the end of the learning process, this is often too late. Therefore, midway feedback to students can be much more productive.

Principle 7: *Feedback should be legible, clear and accessible to all students*

Feedback should be written in plain language so it can be easily understood by all students, enabling them to engage with it and support future learning. There should be little use of jargon, abbreviations or acronyms that some students may struggle to understand. This is particularly important for students whose first language may not be English. A common complaint of is that hand-written feedback can often be illegible. Some students do misinterpret comments and suggestions and fail to understand potentially valuable points. Not all students are full-time and so different methods/ technologies should be utilized to ensure all students have easy access to their feedback. Not all students retrieve their feedback on assessments so more flexible mechanisms through which to disseminate feedback should be explored. This could be via email or through online discussions. It is essential that feedback practices serve the needs of all students, not just those whose needs are easily met within current common structures.

Principle 8: *Feedback should feed forward*

Feeding-forward can provide generic feedback to students in ways that help them to improve their individual performance by learning from the cohort as a whole. Students can learn from the feedback on mistakes or inadequacies of other students' work, and find out about difficulties which were commonly encountered. Students should be able to act on such feedback and take that forward to future assessments. Students should be able to refer to the feedback again and again, and continue to learn from it. To do this the feedback should highlight both what went well in the work and prioritize what needs to be improved to do better next time. Markers should offer suggestions on how to improve the next element of the work, so that adjustments can be made in an ongoing manner.

Principle 9: *Feedback should be flexible and suited to students' needs*

Students learn in different ways and therefore feedback is not 'one size fits all'. Students should be offered feedback in various formats depending on their needs, for example, some students may prefer to discuss their written feedback face-to-face from the marker, whilst other students are content to receive feedback electronically.

Verbal feedback can occur in person or via telephone or podcast. Verbal feedback provides an ideal opportunity for student/ supervisor engagement and should provide the student with insight into the appropriateness of their written product. Group feedback is often valued by students where a lecturer could reveal typical areas that were done well and areas for general improvement. Online discussions could examine assessment feedback in general, which gives students the opportunity to comment. Within reason students should have the opportunity to receive feedback in ways that would be most productive to their learning. This would be optimum in an environment where there was positive and frequent peer to tutor dialogue.

Principle 10: *Feedback should provide information to lecturers that can be used to influence teaching*

Good feedback practice is not only about providing accessible and usable information that helps students improve their learning, but it is also about providing good information to teachers. Lecturers need to know how students are progressing in order to produce feedback that is relevant and informative. One method of doing this to integrate the learning outcomes of the module and assessment within teaching sessions and then using questioning and observation method to identify student difficulties with subject matter. Frequent questioning can help teachers generate information about students' levels of understanding and skill so that they can adapt their teaching accordingly. Students could be asked in groups to identify 'a question worth asking', based on prior study that they would like to explore for a short time at the beginning of the next tutorial. This may aid deeper learning and allow discussion of difficult concepts. The benefits for lecturers are likely to be heightened awareness about student misconceptions, improved attendance and more engaged students.

Annotation

In meeting the needs of students for feedback on their progression and attainment, it can be helpful to consider the effective use of comments on returned work. Annotation is described as a summary made of information in a book, document, or other information. In academia this is commonly used in draft documents, where a marker has written notes about the quality of a students' assignment or perhaps just underlined or highlighted certain text. This is not dissimilar to the use of 'Track changes' within a word document where changes made to a document are tracked, including insertions, deletions and formatting changes.

Annotated bibliographies, give descriptions about how each source is useful in constructing a paper or argument. Ball *et al.* (2009) describe annotation as indicating areas for development and also areas of good scholarly style within the text of an assignment, whilst others believe annotation to be just notes on a page. Annotation describes the augmentation of text with additional content and is a visual instrument designed to actively engage with text (Ball, 2010). As a means of facilitating feedback to students, annotation can be used in a number of ways (Ball *et al.*, 2009).

A survey by Ball *et al.* (2009) facilitated the collection of standardized information from a random sample of students' scripts (n = 40) and analyzed for annotation quotes and symbols in respect of content, difference, length, approach and clarity. A questionnaire was also distributed to a convenience sample of 323 participants utilizing students (n = 249) and lecturers (n = 72) with experience of annotation from the feedback process. A total of 124 questionnaires were completed by the student sample and only 14 questionnaires were returned by the staff sample. In view of the low staff response rate, additional information was retrieved via the use of three focus groups. Table 8.3 outlines annotation quotes and symbols from a number of sampled scripts within the study.

TABLE 8.3 Annotation quotes and symbols

• !!	• Why is all this necessary?
• -----------------------	• *
• What is this?	• Who says?
• On what basis?	• Why and how? Why??
• Would you expect there to be?	• ??
• How?	• No
• Simplistic	• Yes
• ⟲	• Which, which
• √	• S

BALL ET AL., 2009

Staff participants were asked to comment on a number of issues associated with the annotation of scripts e.g. what annotation achieves, is it useful and does it improve knowledge and assignment writing. A synopsis of the pros and cons of annotation is broken down in Table 8.4.

Annotation appeared to be viewed in a more positive light by the student participants who stated that annotation:

■ Provides an opportunity to reflect on criticism.
■ Improves work for future performance.
■ Sets new goals.
■ Can be used as a guide to develop skills.
■ Enables resubmission more confidently or more successfully.

TABLE 8.4   Pros and cons of annotated feedback

Pros	Cons
• Helps to inform the next assignment • Provides specific feedback • Provides accurate feedback • Identifies strengths and weakness of assignment • Aids learning • Corrects errors • Identifies areas for change • Encourages reflection on ways to improve work/learning • Provides balanced remarks • Enhances student-centred approach to learning	• Not always written in a way that motivates students • Tone of annotation can undermine confidence • Does not help to improve future work • Makes students focus on negative feedback • Can be difficult to read and/or interpret • It is time consuming • Staff say they are marking twice – once on the essay and once on the feedback sheet

BALL ET AL., 2009

Ball *et al.* (2009) make a number of recommendations in the process of annotating students' assessments:

1. Wording should be sensitive, constructive and aware of tone being used.
2. Annotation should not be standardized.
3. Stand-alone comments such as ticks or lines are helpful to students.
4. Annotations should link to the comments on the student feedback sheet.
5. Annotation should not occur during second marking as too much annotation can confuse students.
6. Cryptic signs in the margins lead to interpretive difficulty.

Additionally, the authors also identify points of good practice that are borne out of the literature and the results of the research study:

■ Treat students' work with respect.
■ Ensure feedback and annotation is written with a helpful attitude and tone.
■ Provide balanced comments by identifying good points and areas of weakness.
■ Phrase some comments in the form of questions.
■ Give an explanation and justification of grade/mark awarded.

Guidance and feedback

A guidance and feedback loop was developed by Hounsell *et al.* (2008) and identifies a number of processes within assessment feedback which can promote discussion between lecturers and students. The model (Figure 8.2) depicts a six-staged illustration of the processes and influences upon the students' expectations of assessment feedback including:

1. students' prior experiences of assessments;
2. preliminary guidance;

3. ongoing clarification;
4. feedback on performance/achievement;
5. supplementary support;
6. feed-forward.

FIGURE 8.2   Guidance and feedback loop

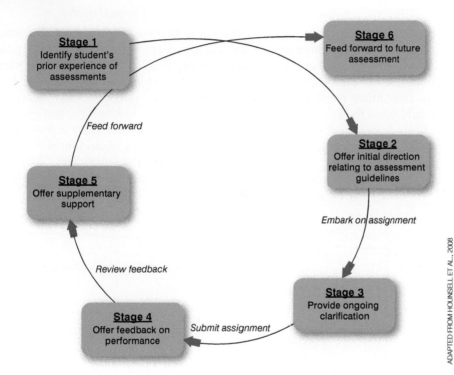

The loop highlights the concerns of students about the guidance they have received prior to writing up an assignment, while they are writing it, and after submission (Hounsell, 2008). The loop is understood as a reminder that the feedback received by the students is closely linked to the guidance they are given in advance, as well as while they work on their assignments (Hounsell, 2008, p. 4).

Giving formative feedback to students

Formative feedback is that which is given to students during the process of preparing their work for assessment, i.e. prior to their handing in the final draft. It is important that a clear policy exists with regard to the provision of formative feedback to students about their assessments. It is appropriate that students should be able to seek advice about their assessments, but the danger exists that the teacher may influence the subsequent draft to such an extent that the assessment is no longer the student's own work, but a collaborative effort of both student and teacher.

TEACHING TIP

Teachers should not accept written drafts of entire assignments from students for formative comments; it is, however, appropriate to comment on outline assignment drafts, or one section of an assignment.

Writing summative feedback comments on students' assessments

Formal summative examinations are designed solely to assess students' achievement, so feedback comments are not often offered and the papers are not returned to the students, which is in conflict with the National Union of Students (2011). However, in assessment by coursework it is common practice to provide written as well as verbal feedback. The question of how much feedback to give is a difficult one, since for some answers the teacher would have to write out the entire essay again to indicate the improvements required. In addition, feedback is time consuming, whereas it is fairly easy simply to assign a mark without comments. However, feedback is very important for students' learning, provided that they review such feedback rather than just filing their essays away. It is often better to return marked essays to the student during a tutorial so that the main feedback points can be discussed.

- *Start with the positive* Most people need encouragement and to be told when they are doing something well.

- *Offer alternatives* If negative feedback is given, it is important not to criticize but to suggest what the student could have done differently. Turn a negative into a positive suggestion.

- *Own the feedback* It is important to own the feedback. Beginning the feedback with 'I' or 'in my opinion' is a way of avoiding the impression of being the giver of 'cosmic judgements' about the other person.

- *Leave the student with a choice* A teacher may invite resistance if the feedback given demands change. Skilled feedback will offer students information about themselves in a way that leaves them with a choice about whether or not to act on it. It can help to examine the consequences of any decision to change or not to change, but it does not involve making change mandatory.

- *Ask the student* It is often helpful to ask students how they think they have performed; it will enable them to feel involved in the assessment process.

- *Do not labour what went wrong* It is only necessary to get the student to recognize and accept what went wrong and to identify how it can be corrected.

- *Empathize* Be sensitive about how students feel about their performance and try to put yourself in their position.

A standardized method of introducing feedback has been highlighted as an effective practice by Williams and Kane (2008) where feedback is provided in relation to pre-defined criteria, that is, the summative marking criteria; providing corrective advice, not just information on strengths/weaknesses; and prioritising areas for improvement. Some of the perceived benefits of standardising formative assessment feedback for students (Table 8.5) and lecturers (Table 8.6) appear to outweigh the challenges as highlighted below, although it could be argued that some points are idealistic.

TABLE 8.5 Perceived benefits and challenges of formative assessment for students	
Benefits for students	**Challenges for students**
<ul><li>Detailed and appropriate feedback</li><li>Feedback is taken more seriously</li><li>Demystifies the assessment process</li><li>Guidance on how to improve their performance</li><li>Areas of concern are clearly identified</li><li>Areas for improvement are clearly identified</li><li>Improved student performance</li><li>Formative assessment is more focussed</li><li>Students have a better understanding of what is expected of them and seeing how to get there</li><li>Assists students to identify areas of difficulty</li><li>Students see assessment criteria clearly and are aware that no preferential treatment is given to any student ensuring parity across the provision of formative assessment</li><li>Learning about how to accept constructive criticism and get an insight into developing their work</li><li>Students are more motivated to learn</li><li>Students take responsibility for their own learning</li><li>Consistent and transparent assessment practices</li></ul>	<ul><li>Non-engagement with formative assessment</li><li>Timing issues – many students leave work until the last minute and are often out of time for formative feedback</li><li>Students can become confused if feedback raises more questions than it answers</li><li>The academic supervisor providing formative feedback will not be the lecturer who marks the final assignment</li></ul>

TABLE 8.6 Perceived benefits and challenges of formative assessment for lecturers	
Benefits for lecturers	**Challenges for lecturers**
<ul><li>The making of judgements is much more transparent and informative</li><li>Formative assessment is more focussed</li><li>Students have a better understanding of what is expected of them and seeing how to get there</li><li>Teachers are able to determine what standards students already know and to what degree</li><li>An efficient method of giving detailed feedback</li><li>Positive feedback from students on the process</li><li>More engaged students</li><li>Criteria and course aims are brought into the forefront of students' minds</li><li>Provide opportunities to close the gap between current and desired performance</li></ul>	<ul><li>Staff resistance and non-compliance with formative assessment</li><li>Eschewing subjectivity: being explicit about criteria and standards</li><li>A new process could be time consuming initially</li><li>Further time challenges if all students engage with the process</li><li>Students may not read and pay attention to feedback</li></ul>

It is important to ensure that feedback is congruent with student expectations, and that student expectations are congruent with good learning practices (Poulos and Mahony, 2007) so consideration could be given to developing an assessment guide for students, separate to a university assessment and feedback strategy.

Review questions

1. Describe the role of feedback in student assessment.

2. How does feeding forward help students learn?

3. Give five tips for providing effective feedback.

4. Compare the 'pros' and 'cons' of verbal feedback with written feedback.

SUMMARY

- Meaningful feedback on assessed academic work forms a crucial part of student's development and is an important contributor to the quality of the student experience.

- The purpose of feedback is to assist a student to shape and direct the next phase of learning.

- Feedback should be constructive, consistent, actionable and student focussed.

- Feedback should be primarily used as a learning tool and therefore positioned for learning rather than as a measure of learning.

- Enabling students to assess their own learning can be influential to personal and professional development and can encourage progression.

- Feedback should be used as a means for closing the gap between the student's learning state and the learning objectives.

- Feedback should be provided in a timely and prompt manner, allowing students to apply it to future learning and assessments.

- Annotation describes the augmentation of text with additional content and is a visual instrument designed to actively engage with text.

- A guidance and feedback loop can identify a number of processes within assessment feedback which can promote discussion between lecturers and students.

- It is important to ensure that feedback is congruent with student expectations, and that student expectations are congruent with good learning practices.

References

Ball, E.C. (2010) Annotation an effective device for student feedback: a critical review of the literature. *Nurse Education in Practice* 10(3) 138–143

Ball, E., Franks, H., Jenkins, J., McGrath, M. and Leigh, J. (2009) Annotation is a valuable tool to enhance learning and assessment in student essays. *Nurse Education Today* 29(3) 284–291

Beaumont, C., O'Doherty, M. and Shannon, L. (2008) *Staff and Student Perceptions of Feedback Quality in the Context of Widening Participation*. York: Higher Education Academy

Carless, D., Salter, D., Yang, M. and Lam, J.(2011) Developing sustainable feedback practices. *Studies in Higher Education* 36(4) 395–407

Carless, D. (2006) Differing perceptions in the feedback process. *Studies in Higher Education* 31 (2) 219–233

Duncan, N. (2007) Feed-forward: improving students' use of tutors' comments. *Assessment & Evaluation in Higher Education* 32(3) 271–283

Ferguson, P. (2011) Student perceptions of quality feedback in teacher education. *Assessment & Evaluation in Higher Education* 36(1) 51–62

Gibbs, G. and Simpson, C. (2004) Conditions under which assessment supports students' learning. *Learning and Teaching in Higher Education* 1 (1) 3–31

Handley, K. and Williams, L. (2011) From copying to learning: using exemplars to engage students with assessment criteria and feedback. *Assessment & Evaluation in Higher Education* 36(1) 95–108

HEA (2010) *Feedback - Make it Work for You: Three Steps to Get the Best Out of Feedback*. York: Higher Education Academy

Hounsell, D., McCune, V., Hounsell, J. and Litjens, J. (2008) The quality of guidance and feedback to students. *Higher Education Research and Development* 27(1) 55–67

Irons, A. (2008) *Enhancing Learning Through Formative Assessment and Feedback*. Oxon: Routledge

Juwah, C., Macfarlane-Dick, D., Matthew, B., Nicol, D., Ross, D. and Smith, B. (2004) *Enhancing Student Learning Through Effective Formative Feedback*. York: The Higher Education Academy

Lizzio, A. and Wilson, K. (2008) Feedback on assessment: students' perceptions of quality and effectiveness. *Assessment & Evaluation in Higher Education* 33(3) 263–275

Nicol, D.J. and Macfarlane-Dick, D. (2006) Formative assessment and self-regulated learning: a model and seven principles of good feedback practice. *Studies in Higher Education* 31(2)199–218

NUS (2011) *Charter on Feedback and Assessment*. London: National Union of Students

Orrell, J. (2006) Feedback on learning achievement: rhetoric and reality. *Teaching in Higher Education* 11(4) 441–456

Poulos, A. and Mahony, M.J. (2007) Effectiveness of feedback: the students' perspective. *Assessment and Evaluation in Higher Education* 33(2) 143–154

QAA (2011) *UK Quality Code for Higher Education Chapter B6: Assessment of Students and Accreditation of Prior Learning*. Gloucester: Quality Assurance Agency

Race, P. (2009) *Designing Assessment to Improve Physical Sciences Learning*. York: Higher Education Academy

Race, P., Brown, S. and Smith, B. (2005) *500 Tips on Assessment* (2nd Edition). London: Routledge

Sadler, D.R. (1989) *Formative Assessment and the Design of Instructional Systems*. Instructional Science 18: 119–144

Spendlove, D. (2009) *Putting Assessment for Learning into Practice*. London: Continuum International Publishing Group

Taylor, C. (2007) *Feed-Forward to Improve Academic Writing*. Centre for Bioscience Autumn Bulletin. York: The Higher Education Academy

Williams, J. and Kane, D. (2008) *Exploring the National Student Survey: Assessment and Feedback Issues*. York: Higher Education Academy

Yorke, M. (2003) *Formative Assessment in Higher Education: Moves Towards Theory and the Enhancement of Pedagogic Practice*. Higher Education 45(4) 477–501

Further Reading

Duers, L.E. and Brown, N. (2009) An exploration of student nurses' experiences of formative assessment. *Nurse Education Today* 29(6) 654–659

Feito, J.A. and Donahue, P. (2008) Minding the gap: annotation as preparation for discussion. *Arts and Humanities in Higher Education* 7(3) 295–307

O'Donovan, B., Price, M. and Rust, C. (2004) Know what I mean? Enhancing student understanding of assessment standards and criteria. *Teaching in Higher Education* 9(3) 325-335

Orsmond, P., Merry, S. and Reiling, K. (2005) Biology students' utilization of tutors' formative feedback: a qualitative interview study. *Assessment & Evaluation in Higher Education* 30(4) 369–386

Tang, L. (2012) *Engage in assessment for learning and feedback for undergraduate dissertations*. York: Higher Education Academy

Weaver, M.R. (2006) Do students value feedback? Student perceptions of tutors' written responses. *Assessment & Evaluation in Higher Education* 31(3) 379–394

Whitelock, D., Gilbert, L. and Gale, V. (2011) *Technology-Enhanced Assessment and Feedback: How is evidence-based literature informing practice*? York: Higher Education Academy

CHAPTER 9
INFORMATION LITERACY AND STUDY SKILLS

THE AIMS OF THIS CHAPTER ARE:

- To highlight the levels of study in higher education
- To discuss the importance of effective reading and note-taking
- To explore strategies of effective studying

KEY TERMS

Self-reinforcement
Mathemagenic behaviours

Students commencing a programme of study in higher education have two characteristics in common: they are adults with a greater or lesser amount of life experience, and they have had the benefit of some ten years of compulsory schooling. It would seem safe, therefore, to assume that they had accrued a range of study skills over that period of time, but experience with higher education students shows that they often have considerable weaknesses in this area.

The inclusion of study skills training is now an important feature of higher education; the diminishing resource base for teaching, combined with the ideology of student-centred-learning, has led to an increase in self-directed learning in most curricula for professional education. Also, many students entering nurse education are mature individuals who may not have undertaken any study since leaving school, and even those students who enter with previously acquired qualifications may find that the approach to teaching has shifted considerably since they qualified. Without the support of study-skills workshops and advice, students may find it very difficult to pursue independent study in an efficient and effective manner.

LEVELS OF STUDY IN NURSE EDUCATION

It is self-evident that students need to be able to undertake independent study at a level appropriate to the award that they are pursuing. Within nurse education there is the full spectrum of academic awards, from Diploma of Higher Education through to Doctor of Philosophy, but there are also in-house CPD programmes that may or may not carry academic credit. One of the characteristics of the progression from certificate level through to doctoral level is an increase in students' independence and autonomy. Table 9.1 shows the characteristics of a range of levels of study descriptors in higher education and how they correspond to the:

- Credit and Qualification Framework for Wales (CQFW) used in Wales;
- Scottish Credit and Qualifications Framework (SCQF) used in Scotland;
- Framework for Higher Education Qualifications (FHEQ) used in England and Northern Ireland;
- National Framework of Qualifications in the Republic of Ireland (NFQI) used in the Republic of Ireland.

TABLE 9.1 Characteristics of levels of study in higher education

| Award | Characteristics | Credit levels | | | |
		CQFW	SCQF	FHEQ	NFQI
Certificate of Higher Education (Cert HE)	First stage of higher education study	4	7	4	6
Diploma of Higher Education (DipHE)	Extends and reinforces theoretical and practical aspects of knowledge	5	8 or 9	5	6 or 7
Bachelor's degree with honours	Requires a capacity for sustained, independent, high-quality work	6	9 or 10	6	7 or 8
Master's degree	Requires ability to reflect on significance and inter-relationship of knowledge, and to formulate original ideas and innovative proposals, all with a fair degree of autonomy	7	11	7	9
Doctoral degree (PhD)	Requires ability to produce an independent and original contribution to the field of knowledge	8	12	8	10

INFORMATION LITERACY

Information literacy is becoming one of the major fundamental skills for students undertaking higher education programmes and is defined as a cluster of skills needed to locate, retrieve, analyze, utilize and apply information (Holman-Rector and Aggarwal, 2007), and such skills enable students to use information in order to succeed in their studies and to be effective lifelong learners. Information literacy is the ability to know when there is a need for information, and to be able to identify, locate, evaluate, interpret and apply information (RCN, 2010); this is also mimicked by the NMC (2010) Standards for pre-registration nursing education who identify a requirement for nurses and midwives to have access to support and skills development in relation to finding, managing, evaluating and applying information and evidence.

The RCN (2010) identified seven information competencies mapped to the Skills for Health competences and KSF dimensions that can be utilized by nurses and midwives who need to develop skills to support their practice:

1. identifying why information is needed;
2. identifying what information is needed;
3. carrying out a search to find information;
4. evaluating how the information meets the identified need;
5. using information and knowledge inclusively, legally and ethically;
6. managing information;
7. creating new information or knowledge.

The RCN (2010) states that each of the seven competences are intended to be used as a framework that supports a nurses' thinking about the information required to inform activities of varying complexity. The amount or complexity of information required will influence which competences and related knowledge should be applied in any situation.

MAKING EFFECTIVE USE OF THE LIBRARY

Since one of the main characteristics of undergraduate and postgraduate study is the ability of the student to work independently, the library is the single most important educational resource for this and should be treated as integral and active parts of the educational process. If they are to benefit from their studies, students need to develop a thorough understanding of all the facilities afforded by a library.

Registration and induction

Library registration usually takes place at the same time as general registration for a programme, and the student identity cards that are issued incorporate library access. In higher education, it is common practice for the library to provide an induction programme for new students, complemented by written guides to the various library facilities. The induction covers such aspects as the opening hours, the borrowing rights of students, any system of fines that may be in operation, and photocopying facilities. In addition, it should be pointed out that no food or drink is allowed into the library, and conversation is reduced to the bare minimum to avoid disturbing other people's study.

Most libraries in higher education have a security system, which is activated if a book is taken out of the library without the appropriate authorization. Multidisciplinary libraries are common within the health service and combine the resources for a wide range of health professions such as nursing, midwifery, medicine, and the professions supplementary to medicine. The periodicals or journals stock is usually very extensive in multidisciplinary libraries.

Classification systems

The Dewey classification scheme (Dewey decimal system) is the system favoured by university libraries to classify resources. It is divided into ten main classes (Table 9.2).

Within this main classification, there are more specific ones; for example, nursing is classified at 610, anatomy and physiology at 612, psychology at 150–159, and education at 370. The Dewey classification is used not only for the main book stock, but for reference books, periodicals, oversize materials, pamphlets, and audio-visual media. When searching for specific subjects, students tend to concentrate on books, and they may need reminding to look at the other resources, such as academic journals shelved in different areas of the library.

TABLE 9.2   Dewey decimal system

000	Generalities and computing	500	Natural sciences and mathematics
100	Philosophy and psychology	600	Technology
200	Religion	700	Arts
300	Social sciences	800	Literature
400	Language	900	Geography and history

Reading lists

Distributing a module or programme reading list to the university library can help to ensure relevant resources are available to students at the right time. Librarians prefer to receive the reading list a few months before the commencement of a module and/or semester and often request that the following information accompanies them to determine the number of copies required:

- whether a text is deemed to be essential reading or background reading;
- other recommended reading per module/programme (this can include journals, websites, policy documents);
- anticipated number of students per module/programme.

Most librarians can assist lecturers checking and/or updating reading lists and can also add live links to electronic resources and library catalogue records. Additionally, the following services can also be offered within copyright and licensing constraints:

- Create live links to items from a virtual learning environment.
- Purchase eBooks.
- Make items available for short-loan.
- Add items to the photocopy collection.

EFFECTIVE READING SKILLS

The student may gain a great deal of information by simply handling a book and noting some of its features. An idea of its content can be ascertained from reading the publicity description found on the back of the book or the flaps of the dust jacket. In addition, a preface or foreword will indicate the target audience and often the aim of the author, but it should be remembered that a foreword by an eminent writer, although usually a good recommendation, should not be taken as the sole criterion for the excellence of a book.

A glance at the bibliographical page will indicate the author, title and date of publication; if the book is into a second or subsequent edition, this may indicate success. The contents page can be scanned for an idea of the main sequence of the book, and it is important to examine the index to see the kind of content included.

Approaches to reading

In the past, researchers have discovered a mutual relationship between students' academic reading skills and academic success. Hermida (2009) believes that students and lecturers take the learning of this skill for granted and because of this, some students tend to use a surface approach to reading academic materials. Students will approach reading in different ways, depending upon its purpose. Glendinning and Holmström (2004) Brown and Atkins (1988) identify the approaches:

- *Scanning*–this approach is used to find a specific piece of information.
- *Skimming*–this is used to obtain an overall impression of an article or chapter.
- *Surveying*–this is used to ascertain the overall structure of an article or chapter.

- *Light study reading*–this is reading with no specific purpose other than general background study.
- *Directed reading*–this is focused reading for a specific purpose, for example to grasp concepts, theories.
- *Deep study reading*–this is active reading in depth for example to discover meanings, to consider and evaluate arguments.

Pre-reading and follow-up reading

If at all possible, it is very useful for students to do some relevant reading prior to each group meeting. They will be in a much better position to contribute during the session and will also have a good insight into the topic under discussion. It is equally valuable to do some follow-up reading each week after the unit meeting, as this will help students to consolidate their learning, and it also offers further perspectives on the topic.

EFFECTIVE NOTE-TAKING

Bligh (198) in a review of studies on note-taking as an aid to memory concludes that the evidence supports the position that note-taking during a lecture does aid students' memory of the lecture content. He also notes the evidence that note-taking for revision can improve performance. Therefore, on balance it appears that note-taking is to be recommended if it is done effectively, i.e. recording the key points rather than trying to write down everything word for word. At degree level, it is more important to note key references given in the unit, so that the original source can be accessed later, avoiding reliance on secondary sources. Table 9.3 gives some advantages and disadvantages of note-taking.

TABLE 9.3 Advantages and disadvantages of note-taking	
Advantages of note-taking	**Disadvantages of note-taking**
Provides a permanent record for later review	May be inaccurate
Material is encoded in student's own words	Student may miss part of lecture whilst writing notes
Aids memory of lecture points	May inhibit student's own processing activities if structured by teacher
Aids performance in revision	

Some teachers prefer to give notes in the form of handouts, so that accuracy is ensured and nothing is missed during the lesson. On the other hand, giving printed notes means that the students do not have a chance to encode material in their own words, a major disadvantage. It also means that the student's own unique processing activities are suppressed. Perhaps the best compromise is for the teacher to use incomplete handouts that contain the key headings and subheadings of the lecture and leave sufficient space for the students to write in their own notes.

Systems for note-taking

If students wish to take notes from teaching sessions, there are a number of systems for this.

The standard system

The standard system consists of writing down the key headings and subheadings, with outline descriptions under each one as in Table 9.4.

The pattern system

The pattern system uses only main concepts, which are connected by lines showing the interrelationships, as in Figure 9.1.

Taylor (2003) and Bligh (198) offers advice to students on effective note-taking:

- Abbreviations should be used, and you should develop your own system of shorthand for frequently occurring concepts.
- Layout should be neat and flexible. Plan your notes so that information from other sources can be added later.
- Note questions and problems rather than facts.
- Keep a notebook for thoughts and ideas about the subject, for use anytime.
- Review notes immediately after the lecture and add any further points.
- Familiarize yourself with the subject before attending the lecture, so that your mind is prepared.

TABLE 9.4	Standard system of note-taking: Rheumatoid Arthritis
Definition	**RA is an autoimmune disease that causes joint inflammation**
Incidence	• Second most common form of arthritis in the UK; affects around 400,000 people in the UK; can affect adults at any age, but most commonly starts between the ages of 40 and 50 • About three times as many women as men are affected. • Genes inherited from parents may affect the likelihood of developing RA, but genetic factors alone do not cause rheumatoid arthritis.
Aetiology	Some evidence that lifestyle factors may affect risk of developing RA - is more common in people who: • smoke, eat a lot of red meat, drink a lot of coffee RA is less common in people who: • have a high vitamin C intake, drink alcohol in moderation
Pathology	• Immune system starts attacking the body's own tissues instead of germs and viruses, which causes inflammation • Inflammation normally ceases fairly quickly but in RA it becomes a long-term (chronic) process; unsure what starts the inflammation in RA • Genes inherited from parents don't cause disease but may increase chances of developing it
Clinical features	Common symptoms include: • painful, swollen joints, stiffness, tiredness (fatigue), depression and irritability • anaemia, feeling generally unwell, hot and sweating flu-like symptoms Less common symptoms include: • weight loss, eye inflammation, rheumatoid nodules • inflammation of other parts of the body
Investigations	• Physical assessment, blood tests (ESR, CRP), x-rays • MRI, CT and ultrasound scans
Management	• Drugs (analgosia, steroids, anti-inflammatory drugs, disease modifying anti-rheumatic drugs) • Physical therapies (physiotherapy, occupational therapy) • Surgery (joint replacement, tendon release)
Prognosis	• 75 per cent of people will continue having some joint pain, swelling and flare-ups • 20 per cent will always have very mild rheumatoid arthritis • 5 per cent will develop severe disease with extensive disability • Slightly greater chance of having a heart attack or stroke - risk is probably reduced by controlling the disease

SOURCE: ARTHRITIS RESEARCH UK, 2011

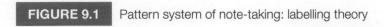

FIGURE 9.1   Pattern system of note-taking: labelling theory

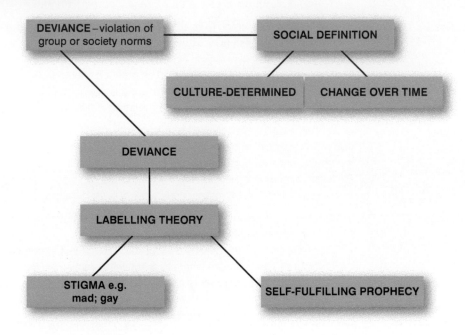

PARTICIPATING IN GROUP DISCUSSION AND SEMINARS

A key aim of units at undergraduate and postgraduate level is to foster students' critical-thinking abilities, and one way of doing this is to encourage students to participate actively in discussion and debate. Students should be encouraged to venture opinions to the group, even if they are not entirely sure of their knowledge. The value of participation lies in stimulating other members of the group to challenge contributors' ideas, and students should try to keep an open mind about the issues that they confront, even if they feel strongly one way or the other; this will allow them to evaluate the issue more objective. Not everyone likes group work, and students may feel that the same few people always dominate the discussion, so that others cannot get a word in. Unit leaders need to be alert to this and be prepared to take steps to encourage the more silent members to contribute. Students must be encouraged to participate in group discussions during the units; it really is important that they experience the process of constructive criticism. Seminar presentation involves speaking to the group on a particular topic, either chosen by the student or allocated by the tutor. Students may feel that this is a nerve-racking experience, especially if they have not done anything like it before! Tutors can give guidance and tips to help students with seminar presentations, as shown in Figure 9.2.

FIGURE 9.2   Guidance for students' seminar presentations

Prepare your material carefully, i.e. ensure that any visual materials are written large enough to be seen

Make a brief plan of the presentation so that you have the sequence in front of you (*it is very disconcerting for you to lose your place*)

Ensure that you have thoroughly understood the content of your material; you may be questioned about it by group members!

Prepare the classroom carefully beforehand, i.e. make sure that everyone can see the chalkboard/screen, etc.; ensure that the overhead projector is aligned carefully, with a full-size image on the screen (*if unsure how to do this, ask your tutor*)

Remember, the aim of the seminar is that the group *learns* something from your presentation, i.e. do not bombard them with masses of information; use overhead projector or handouts for key points; allow sufficient time for note-taking

Allow opportunities for *discussion,* i.e. the seminar is *not* about giving information, but should stimulate thinking and debate; keep formal information to a minimum; posing questions for the group to answer can stimulate debate

Try to make your presentation serve two purposes, i.e. for the seminar and also as the basis of your unit assessment. This will ensure that you take the necessary care over the reading and preparation of the topic

TEACHING TIP

Although induction usually occurs on commencement of a programme, a handout that reinforces the importance of information literacy procedures, library systems, effective reading and note-taking skills would be helpful for students.

PLANNING TO STUDY

Studying at higher education level needs to be carried out frequently and regularly in order to achieve the required learning outcomes of the programme. This is easier said than done, particularly where studying is done on a part-time basis. Study time often conflicts with work responsibilities and family commitments, and there may well be associated guilt if studying is seen to take students away from their children. It is therefore very important to plan carefully for study, so that a sensible balance is struck between these conflicting demands.

Planning study time

Like most other activities in life, studying is facilitated by planning. A carefully prepared plan of study can eliminate the somewhat haphazard approach that tends to be common among students. To be really effective, study must be seen as a natural part of the student's life, just like meal times and other routines. Another aspect is the temptation to escape from the chore of study by using certain devices that may or may not be unconscious. For example, daydreaming is a common occurrence during study as are frequent trips to make coffee, or some other ploy that takes one away from the 'unpleasant' situation. Boredom is another problem against which the student must fight, and it is good advice to suggest that he or she uses a pencil to make notes at regular intervals, thus aiding concentration and providing a feeling of 'getting somewhere'. Joining with a small group of students to examine a common problem can be a motivating activity from time to time and gives different perspectives on an aspect of study.

When planning for study it is important to include regular breaks so that fatigue is avoided. Stretching one's legs every hour or so will help keep concentration and make the subsequent study more efficient. It is unlikely that a period of study longer than about three hours will be useful at any one time and even this length may prove difficult. An interesting suggestion is given by Bandura (1977), which he terms 'self-reinforcement'. It involves setting oneself certain study goals and allocating a reward that is conditional upon attainment of these goals. For example, students might decide to study a particular section of a textbook until they could describe its content in their own words. The reward that they allocate could be a walk in the park, which can be taken only when the objective has been achieved.

Organizing the environment for study

It is important that books and materials can be left lying in the same place, since having to put them away, and then take them out on another occasion, can be very demotivating. A comfortable chair, with good support for the lumbar spine, is crucial, and the room should be at a comfortable temperature with adequate ventilation to offset fatigue. Daylight is the best form of illumination, but in the evenings it is good to have two light sources with adequate shading to prevent glare. Many students automatically switch on music when commencing study, as this makes the task less of a chore. However, music is a source of distracting input that will interfere with studying, so it is better to save music for the five-minute breaks in studying that are taken every hour or so.

STRATEGIES FOR EFFECTIVE STUDY

There are a number of strategies that can help students to study more effectively, including rehearsal, mnemonics, and self-assessment.

TEACHING TIP

You will hopefully find these strategies useful for your own study but remember to share them with your students.

Rehearsal

This is the silent repetition of sentences or words over and over again as a way of remembering them. It is a particularly important metacognitive strategy for retention of material, and there are two closely related concepts: review, which involves going back over material that one has previously read, and recitation, which is actually saying the material out loud.

Mnemonics

These are memory aids that involve mental strategies; the best-known ones involve rhymes, such as 'Thirty days hath September, April, June and November ...'

Mnemonics can be visual, as in the case of imagery. Evidence suggests that by forming a mental picture or image we can remember items much better. For example, one can form a picture in which items for recall are associated with aspects of the home; one item may be hanging in the hall, another on the sofa. A more practical example in nursing is the use of images of patients one has nursed in the past. The student should try to recall a patient who had nursing problems and picture the care given. Narrative is a closely related idea and consists of making up a story that links all the words one wishes to remember.

Self-testing

Self-testing can be a useful strategy for increasing retention of material, and evidence for this is offered by Rothkopf (1970) and Rothkopf and Johnson (1971). Rothkopf maintains that learning from written materials involves two processes, the first one being the study and inspection behaviours of the student. He calls these 'mathemagenic behaviours', i.e. behaviours that give birth to learning. The second process is the actual acquisition of learning of the subject matter. Rothkopf maintains that the study habits of students are fluid and can be constantly modified during study. He tested these ideas in a series of experiments involving the use of questions inserted into texts and found that the greatest facilitative effect on learning occurred when the questions were inserted after the material to which they related, i.e. post-questions. The implication for students is that the regular testing of study materials by the use of post-questions may well enhance learning.

TACKLING ASSESSMENTS AND EXAMINATIONS

Assessments and examinations tend to be perceived by students as the most important aspects of a programme of study, and this is understandable, given the consequences of failure. Advice about tackling assessments and examinations can help relieve some of the anxiety that students experience and possibly improve their performance.

Approaching coursework assessment tasks

The most important single step in tackling the assessment is to read the assessment specification carefully. It is, unfortunately, a relatively common occurrence to find that a student has been referred on an assignment because he or she has not conformed to the assessment specification for that unit. No matter how scholarly or erudite an assignment is, it will not gain a pass grade unless it meets the specification for the unit. It is no good having 'the right answer to the wrong question'. When students have thoroughly understood the assignment brief (if in doubt, it can be checked with the unit leader), they should ask themselves the following questions:

1. Assuming that there is a choice of assignments, is it sufficiently motivating to pursue in preference to other relevant topics?
2. Is it manageable in terms of time and resources available to meet the deadline for handing in?
3. Are there sufficient references available to be able to demonstrate skilful use of the literature?

Reading for the assessment

When writing assignments it is vital to demonstrate the ability to use the literature with insight. Textbooks provide an overview of the topic and are a good starting point. Students should always check the date of publication, especially in books that have been reprinted several times. It is easy to misinterpret a current reprint date and assume that the book is quite new, whereas it may be several years old and therefore possibly out of date. Journals offer up-to-date articles on specific aspects of a topic and usually contain an abstract from which the students can quickly tell whether or not the article is relevant to their study. Journal articles are also important as a source of criticism of other articles or theories. Journals often run consecutive editions containing 'blasts and counter-blasts' from contributors with opposing viewpoints, and these provide fascinating insights into critical, analytic argument. The literature of philosophy is often overlooked by nursing students but can be extremely useful in providing insights into issues such as values, beliefs, judgements, freedom of choice. The mass media, i.e. newspapers, radio and television, are also a useful source of reference. There are many excellent articles and programmes relating to health matters, and these tend to address current, controversial issues.

Effective writing for coursework assessments

It is the coursework assessments, along with clinical assessments and examinations that enable students to demonstrate achievement of the learning outcomes of their programme. Most students will require some help with the formulation of their assignments, particularly if they have not had recent experience of study.

Composing an essay-type assignment

Composing an essay involves four main processes (Burns, 2008; Humes, 1983):

1. *Planning* This takes more time than any other process, and includes not only the initial planning before commencement of writing, but the constant planning that goes on throughout the composition. Planning includes the organization and generation of content and the sequencing of goals.

2. *Translating* This is the transformation of thoughts into written form and consists of complex mental activities, such as attending to syntax and structure.

3. *Reviewing* Writers engage in retrospective activities to check if their written ideas are actually what were intended. It also serves to re-orientate the writer for the next section.

4. *Revising* This covers editing of the written material and usually results in the production of a second draft, although much editing can occur during the initial draft.

Figure 9.3 outlines the assignment writing process within an 'easy to follow' flowchart approach.

Essay-type assignments vary enormously in their approach, from the standard essay question to case studies and problem-centred assignments. However, it is possible to draw a few general guidelines for students to consider. Essays must be written in prose, not in note form, with sentences of appropriate length and the sensible use of paragraphs. Great store is attached to legibility and clarity of expression in all educational systems, so careful planning is required beforehand. Even under examination conditions it is important to do a brief plan before attempting to write an answer to ensure that all the main aspects have been considered for inclusion.

One method for planning assignments has been used for many years but remains an effective system even today. Spider diagrams can allow you to make connections and construct logical arguments from what would otherwise be just a series of notes. They also allow the student to visualize the overall content and structure of work in the form of diagrammatic reasoning, in other words, brainstorming or mind-mapping. According to Burnard (2004), brainstorming involves giving the imagination free rein around a given topic; notes or associations related to the question are written down in any order. Figure 9.4 gives an example of a spider diagram that focuses on an assignment relating to accountability within the perioperative environment.

The length of an assignment must be clearly indicated by the teachers and any minimum and maximum length strictly adhered to. It is quite unfair to state that an assignment has a maximum of 3000 words and then to accept ones that are perhaps twice this long. Students who stuck to the limit are then, in effect, penalized as the others will have included much more material in their work. Students should state the word count of their assignment on the title page of the submission. New penalties for excessive word counts have been introduced in many institutions and should be strictly adhered to.

Word counts for all summative assignments should usually fall within plus or minus 10 per cent of the wordage specified in the assessment guidelines. This means that, for example, if the wordage for a summative assignment is 4000 words, the work must have a word count of no less than 3600 words and no more than 4400 words, although few penalties are generally used for under-wordage. Words that form part of the word count include all words in the text that comprises the introduction, main body, recommendations and conclusion, with the exception of tables and diagrams.

Strict attention must be paid to the wording of the assignment; there is an ever-present temptation to interpret the question or title in the way the student would

FIGURE 9.3 Assignment writing process

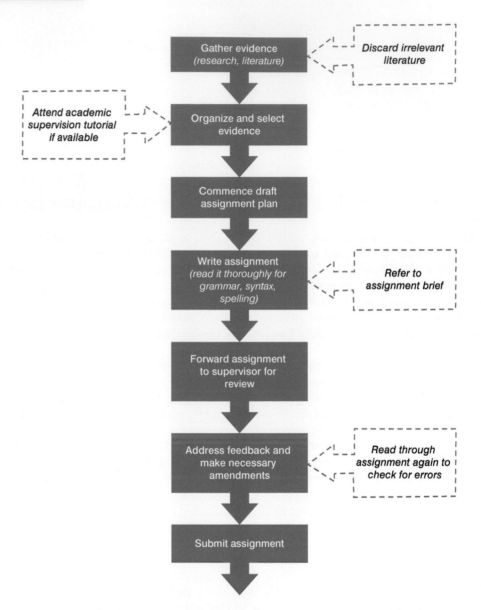

like it to be phrased, rather than how it is actually phrased. Students should use fluorescent highlighter pens to identify the key words in the question or title, since these dictate the form of response required. Table 9.5 gives a list of common terms and their meaning.

It is well worth spending time initially on designing the overall structure of the assignment, as a good assignment can be weakened by a poor or incoherent structure. Whilst there is no ideal or standard structure, it may be helpful to offer the student a basic pattern as shown in Figure 9.5.

FIGURE 9.4   Spider diagram example

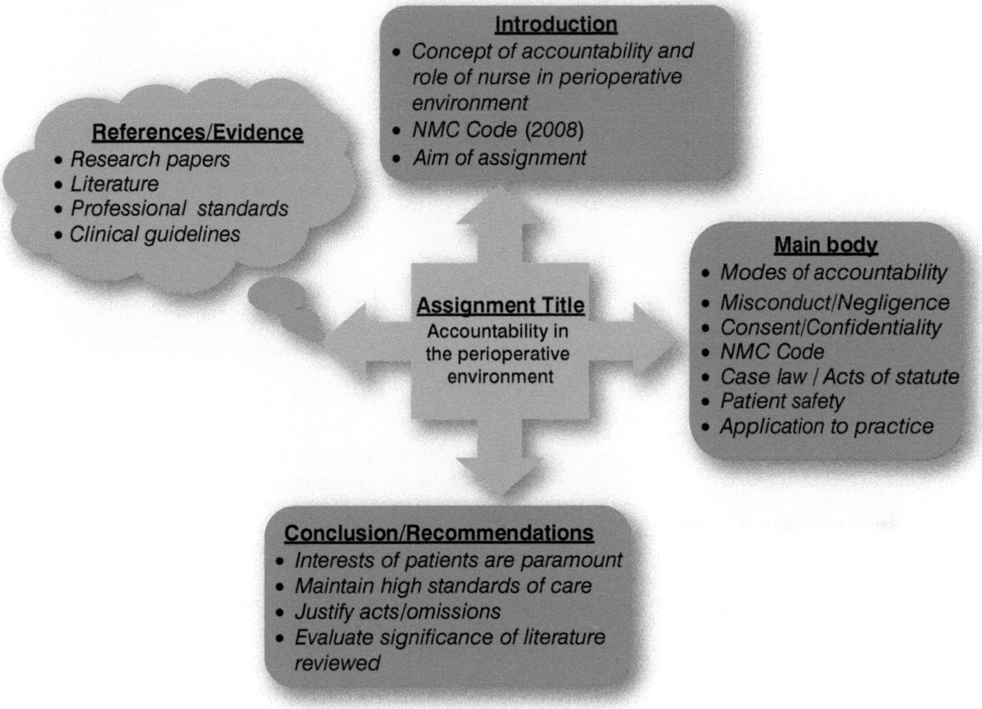

Introduction
- *Concept of accountability and role of nurse in perioperative environment*
- *NMC Code (2008)*
- *Aim of assignment*

References/Evidence
- *Research papers*
- *Literature*
- *Professional standards*
- *Clinical guidelines*

Main body
- *Modes of accountability*
- *Misconduct/Negligence*
- *Consent/Confidentiality*
- *NMC Code*
- *Case law / Acts of statute*
- *Patient safety*
- *Application to practice*

Assignment Title
Accountability in the perioperative environment

Conclusion/Recommendations
- *Interests of patients are paramount*
- *Maintain high standards of care*
- *Justify acts/omissions*
- *Evaluate significance of literature reviewed*

TABLE 9.5   Common terms used in assessments

ANALYZE	Literally, breaking up the issue into its constituent parts and describing them in detail
ASSESS	Estimate the pros and cons of the issue and give a judgement on these
COMPARE AND CONTRAST	Show the similarities and differences between the concepts
DEFINE	Show the exact meaning of the concept
DESCRIBE	Give a picture of an object or event without judgement
DISCUSS	Give viewpoints from both sides and then round off with own conclusion based on these
LIST	Write down in tabular form with minimum words
OUTLINE	A general overview without fine detail
STATE	Present the points briefly without elaboration

FIGURE 9.5   Typical structure of an essay assignment

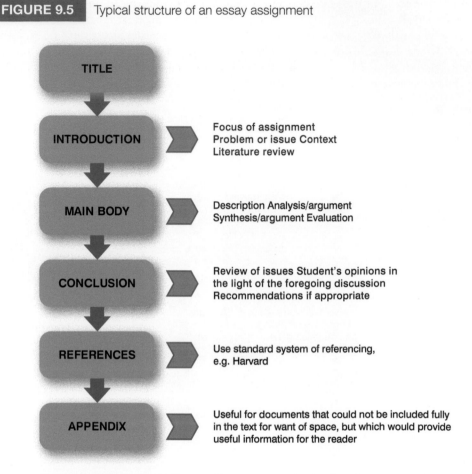

Failing an assignment

Some students are likely to experience the failure of an assignment, and one of the most common reasons is that the students have not tried as hard and performed as well as they are able. Other reasons for failure are likely to include illness, personal circumstances, learning difficulties and plagiarism. Although all institutions have systems in place to support students who fail, Mardell and Moore (2005) offer some very useful advice on how actually to fail an assignment. Whilst by their own admission it is relatively 'tongue-in-cheek', it is worth drawing students' attention to it as a reminder of the pitfalls associated with academic writing. They identify key areas that students often dismiss when studying, which include planning, plagiarism and referencing.

Plagiarism

There are now a number of Internet sites that offer to write students' assignments for them. Apart from the obvious plagiarism that occurs, the issue relating to trustworthiness has huge implications for students and qualified nurses. The NMC (2008) demands that we uphold the reputation of the profession; if a nurse sees nothing wrong in paying for an assignment to be written or in passing off a pre-written assignment as his or her own, then it can be assumed that the same person is capable of being untruthful in issues relating to general nursing practice. This might include a drug error that poses severe consequences for a patient. In circumstances such as this, the whole issue of fitness for purpose must be explored.

In 2001 the Joint Information Systems Committee (JISC) was launched to address student plagiarism and is funded by all the UK post 16 and higher education funding bodies and Research Councils. Their mission is:

> 'To provide world-class leadership in the innovative use of Information and Communications Technology to support education, research and institutional effectiveness.'
>
> (JISC, 2011)

Park (2003) expressed concern that plagiarism in the UK is becoming more common so the Plagiarism Advisory Service is in place to issue advice and guidance on all aspects of plagiarism prevention and detection to institutions, academics and students (JISC, 2011). It uses a UK version of an American electronic detection service known as 'Turnitin' and provides an online plagiarism detection service that can help identify cases of unfair practice in written work. Submitted assignments are checked against its database of previously submitted papers and millions of web pages, highlighting found matches and returning a colour-coded 'originality report'.

The Turnitin website identifies plagiarism as an 'act of fraud' and considers all of the following as plagiarism:

- submitting another person's work as your own;
- copying words or ideas from another person without giving credit;
- failing to put a quotation in quotation marks; and
- changing words but copying the sentence structure of a source without giving credit.

JISC (2005) further emphasize:

> 'Most cases of plagiarism can be avoided by citing sources and simply acknowledging that certain material has been borrowed, and providing the information necessary to find that source is usually enough to prevent plagiarism.'

Revising for examinations

Examinations are virtually confined to pre-registration programmes in nursing and midwifery education and are often perceived by students as the most stressful aspect of a course. It is crucial that students commence revision as early as possible if stress is to be minimized, and the regular review of lecture notes will help. Again, planning is the key to effective revision, with objectives and deadlines for each week, but, in the case of examination revision, motivation is of paramount importance. Revising in study groups can provide excellent motivation and, in addition, the presence of other students who feel equally ignorant can be very reassuring. Frequent changes of stimulus can help combat staleness, and the use of a learning resources centre with audio-visual aids may provide a welcome change from reading. It cannot be overemphasized that cramming is a very inefficient and risky business, as the high levels of stress that develop close to the examination act to impair the learning performance.

Examination technique

Sitting for an examination requires a degree of self-control, since panic can so easily undermine an otherwise well-prepared candidate. If the examination consists of an unseen paper, the candidate will not be allowed to take any resources into the examination room other than those for writing and drawing. The instructions for filling in the answer book should be noted. On the first scan of the paper, the student should carefully note the number of questions to be answered, the parts from which they should each be selected if relevant, and the amount of time to be allocated to each. It is wise to allocate an equal amount of time to each question, including an allowance at the end of the examination to go back over and check the answers. The students should be advised to scan the questions and to select the one that they feel most confident about. Once writing begins anxiety levels should fall, and the students will be able to choose subsequent questions in a more rational frame of mind. Students should be advised to make a brief plan before commencing a question, as this can ensure that all necessary elements of the answer have been considered. This plan can then act as a prompt when the writing begins to flow. It is important that a careful watch is kept on the time, as it is all too easy to overrun on the easier questions, leaving a shortfall for the more difficult ones. During the last five minutes or so, the student should read through all answers, adding brief points that were missed the first time. As a final check, the student should ensure that all papers are properly identified according to the instructions.

During the last ten years a plethora of literature has been published relating to study skills with particular emphasis on searching library catalogues, books, periodicals, databases and other library resources. Much of the literature has also focused considerably on searching the literature and discussing the purpose of bibliographies, abstracts and indexes. Rather than explore comprehensively and repeat the sound advice offered by other published works, a 'further reading' list at the end of this chapter will guide the reader to alternative sources. This will include literature that focuses on the following elements in further detail:

- essential skills for students who are returning to study;
- time management and working with deadlines;
- conducting a literature search;
- principles of a literature searching strategy;
- finding, using and managing information;
- critically reviewing the literature;
- academic writing and using literature to demonstrate critical analysis;
- essay planning;
- creating arguments;
- avoiding plagiarism in academic writing;
- referencing systems.

Review questions

1. Suggest how teachers can help students structure their note-taking during lectures.

2. Explain three strategies that could help students study more effectively.

3. List five tips to help students revise more effectively for their examinations.

4. If you were planning a study skills workshop for some new undergraduates for half a day what would it include? List the sessions with a brief description.

SUMMARY

- The inclusion of study-skills training is an important feature of higher education.

- Without the support of study-skills workshops and advice, students may find it very difficult to pursue independent study in an efficient and effective manner.

- Students need to be able to undertake independent study at a level appropriate to the award they are pursuing.

- One of the main characteristics of higher education study is the ability of the student to work independently.

- Students should be encouraged to undertake relevant reading prior to each group meeting, as they will be in a much better position to contribute during the session and will also have a good insight into the topic under discussion.

- Some teachers prefer to give notes in the form of handouts, so that accuracy is ensured and nothing is missed during the lesson.

- A key aim of units at undergraduate and postgraduate level is to foster students' critical-thinking abilities, and one way of doing this is to encourage students to participate actively in discussion and debate.

- A carefully prepared plan of study can eliminate a haphazard approach that tends to be common among students.

- There are a number of strategies that can help students to study more effectively, including rehearsal, mnemonics, and self-assessment.

- When writing assignments it is vital to demonstrate the ability to use the literature with insight.

- Spider diagrams can enable a student to make connections and construct logical arguments from what would otherwise be just a series of notes.

- Revising in study groups can provide excellent motivation and, in addition, the presence of other students who feel equally ignorant can be very reassuring.

References

Arthritis Research UK (2011) Rheumatoid arthritis. Available from: http://www.arthritisresearchuk. org/arthritis-information/conditions/ rheumatoid-arthritis.aspx

Bandura, A. (1977) *Social Learning Theory*. Englewood Cliffs, NJ: Prentice Hall

Bligh, D. (198) *What's the Use of Lectures?* (5th Edn). Exeter: Intellect

Brown, G. and Atkins, M. (1988) *Effective Teaching in Higher Education*. Methuen, London

Burnard, P. (2004) *Writing Skills in Healthcare*. Cheltenham: Nelson Thornes

Burns, D. (2008) The write stuff. *Nursing Standard* 23(3) 66

Glendinning, E.H. and Holmström, B. (2004) *Study Reading: A Course in Reading Skills for Academic Purposes*. Cambridge: Cambridge University Press

Hermida, J. (2009) The importance of teaching academic reading skills in first-year university courses. *The International Journal of Research and Review* 3 20–30

Holman-Rector ,L. and Aggarwal, A.K. (2007) A Modular Approach to Information Literacy. *Information Management* 20(3/4) 18–21

Humes, A. (1983) Research on the composing process. *Review of Educational Research*, 53(2) 201–216

JISC (2005) Deterring, detecting and dealing with student plagiarism. Available from: http://plagiarismconference.org/documents/resources/JISC-BP-Plagiarism-v1-final.pdf

JISC (2011) JISC strategic objectives. Available from: http://www.jisc.ac.uk/aboutus/strategy.aspx

Mardell, A. and Moore, C. (2005) How to fail an assignment. *Nursing Times* 101(37) 44–45

Nursing Midwifery Council (2008) *The Code: Standards for Conduct, Performance and Ethics*. London: NMC

Nursing and Midwifery Council (2010) *Standards for Preregistration Nursing Education*. London: NMC

Park, C. (2003) In other (people's) words: plagiarism by university students – literature and lessons. *Assessment and Evaluation in Higher Education*, 28(5), 471–488

Rothkopf, E. (1970) The concept of mathemagenic activities. *Review of Educational Research* 40: 325–336

Rothkopf, E. and Johnson, P. (1971) *Verbal Learning Research and the Technology of Written Instruction*. New York: Teachers College Press

RCN (2010) *Finding, Using and Managing Information: Nursing, Midwifery, Health and Social Care Information Literacy Competences*. London: Royal College of Nursing

Taylor, J. (2003) *Foundations in Nursing and Health Care: Study Skills in Health Care*. Cheltenham: Nelson Thornes

Further Reading

Anderson, I. (2009) Avoiding plagiarism in academic writing. *Nursing Standard* 23(18) 35–37

Carnwell, R. and William, D. (2001) Strategies for the construction of a critical review of the literature. *Nurse Education* Today 1: 57–63

Cottrell, S. (2008) *The Study Skills Handbook* (3rd Edn). Basingstoke: Palgrave

Craig, C. (2009) *Study Skills for Health and Social Care Students*. London: Sage

Dobinson-Harrington, A. (2006) Personal tutor encounters: understanding the experience. *Nursing Standard* 20(50) 35–42

Duffy, K., Hastie, E., McCallum, J., Ness, V. and Price, L. (2009) Academic writing: using literature to demonstrate critical analysis. *Nursing Standard* (23) 47 35–40

Gimenez, J. (2011) *Writing for Nursing and Midwifery Students* (2nd Edn). Basingstoke: Palgrave

Hart, S. (Ed) (2010) *Nursing: Study and Placement Learning Skills*. Oxford: Oxford University Press

Hendry, C. and Farley, A.H. (2006) Essential skills for students who are returning to study. *Nursing Standard* 21(6) 44–48

Knowles, J. and McGloin, S. (2007) Developing critical analysis skills in academic writing. *Nursing Standard* 21(52) 35–37

Lloyd, M. (2007) Developing academic writing skills: the PROCESS framework. *Nursing Standard* 21(40) 50–56

Maslin-Prothero, S. (Ed) (2010) *Baillière's Study Skills for Nurses and Midwives* (4th Edn). Edinburgh: Baillière-Tindall Elsevier

NHS Education for Scotland. Towards even better practice: The healthcare practitioner booklet from the Better Informed for Better Health and Better Care series Available from: http://www.infoliteracy.scot.nhs.uk/media/1923912/healthcare.pdf

Timmins, F. and McCabe, C. (2005) How to conduct an effective literature search. *Nursing Standard* 20(11) 41–47

Younger, P. (2010) Using Google Scholar to conduct a literature search. *Nursing Standard* 24(45) 40–46

CHAPTER 10
QUALITY AND EVALUATION

THE AIMS OF THIS CHAPTER ARE:

- To explore the concept of educational quality assurance
- To discuss how quality issues are applied across the continuum of higher education
- To highlight key quality frameworks that promote best practice in learning and teaching

KEY TERMS

Cybernetic
Accreditation
Validation
Scrutineer

QUALITY IN HIGHER EDUCATION

The purpose of the Quality Assurance Agency for Higher Education (QAA) is to safeguard standards and improve the quality of higher education in the United Kingdom by offering advice, guidance and support to help universities, colleges and other institutions provide the best possible student experience of higher education. The Quality Assurance Agency also offers guidance on maintaining and improving quality assurance processes and developing programme delivery, and acts as an advisor to the Government on the merits of applications for degree awarding powers or the 'university' title (House of Commons, 2011).

The QAA Code of practice for the assurance of academic quality and standards in higher education provides guidance on maintaining quality and standards for universities and colleges. It is made up of 10 sections and revisions of individual sections are continually being updated. The UK Quality Code for Higher Education (2012a) sets out the Expectations that all providers of UK higher education are required to meet and is used to:

> *'assure the standards and quality of higher education in the United Kingdom and is developed and maintained by the QAA for Higher Education (QAA) through consultation with the higher education sector and is used by individual higher education providers to ensure students have the high-quality educational experience they are entitled to expect' (p. 2).*

EDUCATIONAL QUALITY ASSURANCE

Quality assurance is now a major consideration for providers of goods and services in today's society, and this includes the two large 'service industries' of higher education and the health service. Consumers of goods and services are more informed nowadays about quality issues and their statutory rights, and this applies also to 'consumers' of higher education and the health service.

Evaluation is a common feature of our everyday lives. When purchasing goods and services our opinions are commonly sought as part of the process. For example, travel companies issue questionnaires to solicit clients' opinions about the quality of their holiday arrangements; car showrooms evaluate the degree of satisfaction experienced by purchasers of new cars. Whether or not this is good for the consumer will depend on what use the provider makes of the feedback; cynics might suggest that it is merely a marketing ploy designed to encourage continuing purchaser loyalty. The evaluation of a range of aspects of educational provision, such as the evaluation of teaching, is one of the cornerstones of institutional quality assurance. The maintenance of quality in higher education and nursing education is a corporate responsibility, involving both academic and support staff. Educational quality assurance operates at four levels in higher education:

1. individual lecturer level;
2. programme level;
3. institution level;
4. external quality monitoring.

As with any hierarchy, each level subsumes the one below, and there is inevitably some overlap between levels, but even so it will provide a useful conceptual framework for the discussion.

The quality concept

When discussing quality assurance in education the obvious starting point is a definition of the term 'quality'. This is no easy task because quality is a philosophical concept and, like beauty, is in the eye of the beholder. The literature is replete with debates about its fundamental nature, and these do not necessarily shed light on the nature of quality in higher education. Quality is normally thought of as a positive concept; i.e. it is a good and desirable thing to which individuals and institutions should aspire in their provision of goods and services. However, we also talk of goods and services as being of poor quality, and, if quality equates to goodness or excellence, this constitutes a contradiction in terms. Definitions of academic quality and quality assurance by QAA (2012a) are identified below.

> '**Academic quality** is how well your higher education provider supports you in your learning: the teaching, the support available, how you are assessed, and the resources available.'
>
> '**Quality assurance** is the process for checking that the standards and quality of higher education provision meet agreed expectations.'
>
> (QAA, 2012a)

A helpful contribution to the debate is made by Green (1994), who describes six ways in which the term is used in higher education:

- *Traditional concept of quality* The term implies excellence, i.e. a product or service that is special or exclusive, and produced to very high standards. In higher education terms, this would apply to the 'Oxbridge' institutions.
- *Quality as conformance to specifications or standards* This approach is derived from manufacturing industry, where the quality of a product is measured by its conformance to a specification or standard. A process of quality control is used, and products that fail to measure up are rejected.
- *Quality as fitness for purpose* In this approach, quality is judged on the basis of whether the product or service fulfils its purpose.
- *Quality as effectiveness in achieving institutional goals* This is a variant of the fitness-for-purpose approach; the quality of an educational institution is the extent to which it fulfils its own mission and goals.
- *Quality as meeting customer's stated or implied needs* In this approach, the focus is on satisfying the needs of customers or clients both in the design and delivery of the product or service.
- *Pragmatic definition of quality* This is really not a definition at all, but reflects an acceptance that it is not possible to come up with a unitary definition of quality that is appropriate for all the various stakeholders in higher education. Lecturers, students and employers each have different priorities, so what constitutes quality for one group will not be so for others. Therefore, quality is only meaningful in the context of the needs of each stakeholder.

We could add a further definition to Green's list, namely 'quality as value for money', i.e. as a return on investment made. It is possible to produce goods or services that satisfy both fitness for purpose and customer need, but which do not represent good value for money.

Boyle and Bowden (1997) offer an interesting perspective on the quality debate:

> 'Our view is that in recent years most progressive thinkers and those whose are motivated by positive practical outcomes, have moved on from the endless esoteric debates on concepts of 'quality'.
>
> In fact, healthy 'learning organizations' (not just educational institutions) are tending to view the need for having a comprehensive approach to maximizing how well things are done as the best reason for adopting a practical meaning for the notion of quality.'

Within education, evaluation is occasionally used interchangeably with assessment but Wood and Dickinson (2011) recognize the two words as distinct and different:

> '**Assessment** is the process of measuring a student's performance within a formal or informal task designed to evidence what has been learnt and to what level.
>
> **Evaluation** is the considered judgement about the quality of a product, a process and/or experience.'

Evaluation is undertaken at all levels; by internal and external stakeholders because it has been established as a method to sustain quality assurance and where necessary, to drive quality improvement.

QUALITY ASSURANCE

Quality assurance (QA) was originally developed for the manufacturing and service industries, and the approaches used in higher education are derivations of these systems, with suitable modifications for educational contexts. However, definitions of quality derived from manufacturing industry do not necessarily transfer easily into the higher education context. For example, if educational quality is seen as fitness for purpose, the question then arises as to whose purpose we are talking about, i.e. students', lecturers', employers' or the states? Similarly, if it is defined as customer satisfactions, who are the customers of higher education: students, employers, or society at large?

The term 'assurance' implies an action taken by one party towards another in order to convey sureness or certainty about something. Hence, quality assurance literally means that the provider of products or services tells the consumers that they can be sure of the quality of such products or services. In the industrial context, this is often given in the form of a guarantee, warranty or customer charter. In 1993 Ellis described a set of characteristics of quality assurance in whatever context it occurs that is supported by Biggs and Tang (2011) and Wood and Dickinson (2011) and that is still relevant today:

1. The specification of standards for whatever is conceived as the product or service.

2. The identification of critical functions and procedures that will be necessary to achieve these standards.

3. Constant recourse to the consumer to set and monitor the accomplishment of standards.

4. Documented clarity with regard to both the standards to be achieved and the procedures that must be followed to achieve these standards.

5. A **cybernetic** approach to standard and procedure setting, which involves monitoring that standards are being met and procedures followed, and taking action to remedy or rectify shortfalls coupled with a regular review of the appropriateness of standards and procedures.

6. The total involvement of all personnel and a commitment to development and training.

It may be helpful at this point to offer a working definition of educational quality assurance (EQA):

> '*Quality in higher education is the extent to which the education provided by an institution consistently meets the standards defined by that institution in relation to its goals and mission.*'

Hence, educational quality is defined in terms of the congruence between an institution's stated standards and its performance in achieving these.

Quality assurance and accountability

Quality assurance has become established in all aspects of the public sector, and it is argued that the need for accountability has been the driving force behind its development. Winch (1996) argues that accountability is not only a political issue, but a moral one; when an individual or organisation contracts to provide a service to a customer, it has a moral obligation to do so to the best of its ability.

Accountability in relation to education has become a key issue in our society, and a number of authors identify historical pressures that have contributed to this (Hoecht, 2006; Huisman and Currie, 2004; Winch, 1996):

- the public's expectations that education will promote cultural continuity, moral order and economic growth;
- the rise of neo-liberalism, which believes that market forces are the best way of ensuring freedom of choice, quality of service, and transparency of accountability;
- a decline in the public's deference towards professionals, and less willingness to assume that professionals know best.

Public accountability covers not only finance, but also time and other resources. Public awareness of accountability has been raised by the publication of various charters relating to the quality and standards of service in the public sector, examples being the Students' Charter, and the Patients' Charter.

The idiom of quality assurance

At this point it may be useful to define a range of other concepts used in the context of educational quality assurance.

- *Quality control* is an industrial process in which products are checked against a specification and discarded if not up to standard. Quality control can only detect defective products; it cannot prevent them from being manufactured. This contrasts with quality assurance, which is designed to prevent poor quality service, thus obviating the need for quality control.
- *Quality management* refers to the system of management of quality within the institution, i.e. the design, structure and functioning of the quality system.
- *Quality audit* refers to the evaluation of an institution's quality assurance and quality management systems, undertaken either internally or by external agencies.
- *Quality assessment* involves assessing the standards of an institution against external criteria: for example, an external examiner assesses the quality of students' work in an institution against that of students on similar courses in other institutions.
- *Standards* are desired and achievable levels of performance against which actual performance in practice is compared.
- *Performance indicators* are measures of the progress made by an educational institution towards achieving its mission and goals. They are usually quantitative, for example statistics, ratios, costs, etc., and cover the 'three Es': efficiency, effectiveness and economy. This provides a basis for comparison between higher education institutions.
- *Value added* refers to the enhancement of a student's learning and experience as a result of pursuing an educational programme.

Three of these concepts, performance indicators, value added and standards warrant further explanation.

Performance indicators

The term 'performance indicator' or PI gives an impression of something tentative, rather than precise or exact measures that are used to guide decisions about quality. Performance indicators are actions or approaches that higher education providers have agreed reflect sound practice and the Higher Education Statistics Agency (HESA, 2012) produce these on behalf of all the UK funding bodies. Performance Indicators provide comparative data on the performance of institutions in widening participation, student retention, learning and teaching outcomes, research output and employment of graduates. PIs are usually classified as the three Es: efficiency indicators, effectiveness indicators, and economy indicators, and these are applied to educational inputs, processes, and outputs. Performance indicators, then, are used help judge the quality of education within an institution and are applied to a wide range of general attributes of the system.

Cave *et al.* (1991) highlight some of the problems in using PIs in higher education. Those PIs that are difficult to measure may be given a lower priority; for example, teaching is a much more difficult activity to measure accurately than research, and this could lead to a shift in emphasis from teaching towards research. Performance indicators may also result in pressure upon academics to publish material in journals, possibly resulting in quantity rather than quality of publication.

Value added (added value)

Some aspects of higher education, such as examination success rates, lend themselves more readily to quantitative measurement, whereas it is apparent that others, such as 'value added', are very difficult to quantify. Traditionally, students' attainment has been judged by their qualification or degree classification and has taken no account of the differences in individual students' abilities at the start of their course. Many educationalists believe that the real importance of education lies in the value that it adds to the student as a result of undertaking it. The concept of value added can therefore be applied even if the student fails to complete the programme. One measure of value added is the relationship between input, i.e. entry qualifications, and output, i.e. degree classification.

Standards

The stating of standards and associated criteria is becoming common practice within many sectors of education. Standards are desired and achievable levels of performance against which actual performance in practice is compared. Commonly, they comprise two elements: a standard statement describing the goal or outcome to be met, and the criteria necessary to achieve the standard.

QUALITY ASSURANCE AT INDIVIDUAL LECTURER LEVEL

This could be considered to be the most important level of quality assurance. Individual lecturers are the people in the 'front line' when it comes to the delivery of teaching and personal tutoring and are thus in the best position to influence the quality of the students' teaching and learning experience. When discussing quality assurance at individual lecturer level, there are two main aspects to consider: quality in relation to teaching and quality in relation to the lecturer's continuing professional development.

Quality of teaching

In discussions about education, the words 'teaching' and 'learning' are invariably linked together, the assumption being that teaching promotes learning. In practice, however, a cause-and-effect relationship is difficult to demonstrate. It is quite probable that some teaching results in student learning, but it is equally probable that some teaching prevents student learning. An example of the latter could be as follows: a teacher's intimidating manner might engender in students a fear of the subject, which in turn interferes with their learning of that subject.

However, quality assurance of teaching is premised on the assumption that teaching influences learning and that poor quality teaching has a negative effect on student learning. The importance of teaching quality is endorsed by the Government in its response to the Dearing Report (DfEE, 1998):

> 'The Government's long-term aim is to see all teachers in higher education carry a professional qualification, achieved by meeting demanding standards of teaching and supervisory competence through accredited learning or experience.'

The Higher Education Academy and the NMC quality standards are discussed further on in the chapter.

Evaluating the quality of teaching

The literature contains many examples of ways in which the quality of teaching can be assessed and assured, each reflecting the particular stance of the originator. Bligh (1998) offers a number of principles for evaluating teaching:

- Lecturers should initiate and be involved in the process.
- The purpose of evaluation needs to be made explicit.
- Evaluation needs to be 'tailor-made' to achieve its purpose.
- Evaluation should be individualized, not a pre-packaged process.
- Improvement of teaching should take priority over personnel and funding decisions.
- Evaluation of teaching should consist of sampling over time and on different courses.
- It should employ a variety of methods.
- It should contain some open-ended questions.
- Caution should be employed when evaluating opinions.
- Evaluation should take place early enough to allow for remedial action.

Methods of evaluating teaching include evaluation tools for completion by self, students or peers, and other performance indicators such as the standards attained by students, degree classification, withdrawal rates, and employment rates.

Self-evaluation of teaching

Evaluation of teaching is often included as part of a wider evaluation of a module or unit. An example of a checklist for self- and peer-evaluation is given in Table 10.1.

TEACHING TIP

Reflection is an important part of teaching as well as nursing practice. The above form will help you reflect on how well you are performing in different aspects of your teaching and which areas you could improve on. It would also be useful to reflect on particular incidents that may have gone particularly well or not so well, see p xxx to find out more on reflection.

Peer-evaluation of teaching

Peer-evaluation of teaching remains a contentious issue in higher education; lecturers have traditionally enjoyed complete autonomy in the classroom, and when assessment has occurred it has largely been in the form of written evaluation by students. However, the advent of staff appraisal in higher education has raised the profile of teaching quality, as it constitutes one aspect of the appraisal process for lecturing staff. Some observational assessment takes place as part of both internal and external audit, but only affects small numbers of staff and occurs infrequently. The evaluation form shown in Table 10.2 is appropriate for either self- or peer-evaluation of teaching.

TABLE 10.1	Checklist for self-and peer-evaluation of teaching				
Item		**Highly satisfactory**			**Weak**
A	*Lesson plan*				
1.	Learning outcomes defined	1	2	3	4
2.	Organization and sequence	1	2	3	4
3.	Variety	1	2	3	4
4.	Student activity	1	2	3	4
5.	Learning aids	1	2	3	4
6.	Learning checks	1	2	3	4
7.	Timing	1	2	3	4
B	*Delivery of lesson*				
8.	Audibility of voice	1	2	3	4
9.	Clarity of speech	1	2	3	4
10	Expressiveness of voice	1	2	3	4
11.	Speed of delivery	1	2	3	4
12.	Use of pauses	1	2	3	4
13.	Confidence	1	2	3	4
14.	Enthusiasm	1	2	3	4
15.	Warmth	1	2	3	4
16.	Psychological safety	1	2	3	4
17.	Sense of humour	1	2	3	4
18.	Non-verbal communication	1	2	3	4
19.	Accuracy of content	1	2	3	4
20.	Content up to date	1	2	3	4
21.	Research quoted	1	2	3	4
22.	Clarity of explanations	1	2	3	4
23.	Level of lesson appropriate	1	2	3	4
24.	Quality of media resources	1	2	3	4
25.	Technique for using media resources	1	2	3	4
26.	Use of questioning	1	2	3	4
27.	Student participation	1	2	3	4
28.	Opening of lesson	1	2	3	4
29.	Closing of lesson	1	2	3	4

TABLE 10.2   Teacher evaluation form for completion by students

The purpose of this questionnaire is to help me to adapt my teaching to your needs as a student. Please indicate your opinion of my teaching during the course you have just completed by putting a tick in the appropriate box.

X	X applies	Marked tendency to X	Some tendency to X Y	Marked tendency to Y	Y applies	Y
Content relevant to nursing						Content not relevant to nursing
Organization of subjects good						Organization of subjects poor
Subjects made interesting						Subjects made rather dull
Presented with clarity						Presented in a confusing manner
Audibility and speech good						Audibility and speech poor
Speed of delivery ideal						Speed of delivery too fast or too slow (underline appropriate one)
Amount of information ideal						Amount of information too much or too little (underline appropriate one)
Level of subject ideal						Level of subject too high or too low (underline appropriate one)
Visual presentation good						Visual presentation poor
Good rapport with class						No rapport with class
Good student participation						No student participation
A lot of learning took place						Very little learning took place
Good feedback given on student progress						No feedback given on progress
Irritating and distracting mannerisms (please specify)						
Comments						

Students' evaluation of teaching

Given the fact that students are the primary consumers of teaching, it is very important to ascertain their opinions of teaching. However, it is more useful to ask them to evaluate a course of lessons rather than individual ones (provided that the teacher has had more than one encounter with the students). There are two reasons for this, the first being that the response rate from students may drop dramatically if they have to complete a large number of evaluations and, secondly, the teacher then obtains a more average response to his or her teaching rather than the specific points from a single session. Table 10.2 shows an example of a teaching evaluation form to be completed by students.

QUALITY ASSURANCE AT PROGRAMME LEVEL

Higher education is delivered via programmes or courses leading to academic awards, with each programme having a programme team responsible for its day-to-day operational management. Whilst team members are responsible for the quality of their own teaching on the programme, the team has collective responsibility for the quality of the programme curriculum.

Quality of curriculum

The first check on the quality of curriculum occurs at the validation event for the programme, and checks continue in the form of programme monitoring and programme review. As stated earlier, the term curriculum encompasses the four main aspects of educational provision, which are intimately related to each other and the model adopts a rational stance, in that the curriculum design is seen to begin with the formulating of student learning outcomes and then progresses to decisions about what outcomes-related subject matter should be included. Teaching and learning processes are then defined, for example lectures, laboratory work, group work, discussions, debate, self-directed learning, that will help the student to achieve the learning outcomes, and, finally, the students' achievement of the learning outcomes is assessed using appropriate and relevant assessment methods.

The Quality Assurance Agency (2011a) offers the following criteria for a quality curriculum:

1. *Relevance*, relates to present and anticipated future needs.
2. *Aims and objectives*, explicit and carefully focused.
3. *Time constraints*, effective use of time for individual subjects and their arrangements.
4. *Content*, a body of knowledge which offers breadth and depth and is state of the art and well balanced.
5. *Progression*, cumulative knowledge and skills which allows for planned progression.
6. *Sequencing*, coherent sequencing of subjects and subject matter.
7. *Integration*, different aspects of the curriculum allow for integrated working.
8. *Core skills*, relevant balance of all core skills.
9. *Accreditation*, appropriate **accreditation** of the programme from professional bodies, other colleges.

Programme evaluation

Programme evaluation needs to be distinguished from evaluation of teaching, the latter being just one component of the former. Although evaluation of teaching contributes useful information, it is insufficient in itself as an indicator of course quality because it does not cover other aspects such as organization and resources. Overall course evaluation is particularly important in credit schemes, where pathways consist of many modules. In this case, module evaluation will not provide evidence of the overall aspects of the pathway, so provision needs to be made for this before students leave the pathway. Institutions may have a standard format for course evaluation forms, or they can be designed specifically for the course in question. Indicator 7 of the QAA (2011a) quality code for programme design and approval refers to higher education institutions having the means of assessing the effectiveness of their programme design, approval, monitoring and review practices. It states that evaluation of processes can provide a focus for enhancement and will allow institutions to consider:

- The benefits gained by the institution, staff, students and other stakeholders from the approval activities undertaken.
- How the outcomes of methods promote enhancement of students' learning experiences.
- The internal and external identification and dissemination of effective practice.
- Opportunities to make approval practices more effective and efficient.
- Whether the institution is managing risk appropriately and proportionately for its portfolio of programmes.

Student evaluation of the curriculum

Evaluation of the programme curriculum by students is now established throughout the higher education sector, and forms an important aspect of educational quality assurance. Given that students are the most obvious consumers of higher education, it seems self-evident that their opinions about the quality of their modules and programmes should be given serious consideration by the institution. When designing student evaluation forms, institutions need to decide the breadth and scope of coverage; some institutions focus mainly on the quality of the teaching, and some include such aspects as the quality of pre-entry information, induction, and tutorial support. In addition to this, other institutions might question library and IT support, teaching venues and domestic arrangements. QAA (2012b) outline in Figure 10.1 how student involvement in quality can influence the development and delivery of the student learning experience in terms of the key aspects of higher education provision:

Although QAA (2012b) acknowledge that all should be involved in quality assurance and enhancement processes, they recognize that this is not always possible but maintain that higher education institutions must create a culture and climate that promotes student engagement and offers all students an opportunity to be involved. For such an environment to be effective, they believe that higher education institutions should:

- Be aware of the importance of feedback from students.
- Ensure that nomination and election of student representatives are agreed with the student body using transparent mechanisms.
- Provide induction and ongoing support for students and staff appropriate to their roles.
- Monitor and review the effectiveness of their policies and processes for engaging students in their quality processes.

FIGURE 10.1   Student involvement in quality assurance

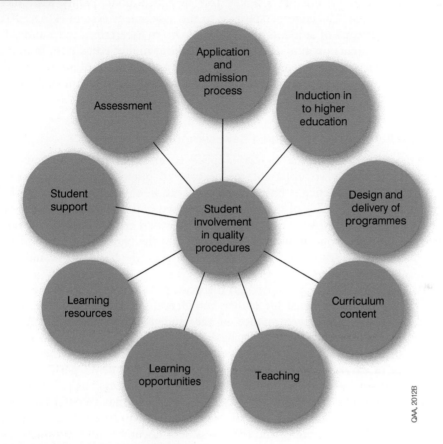

QAA, 2012B

Quality of student assessment

Of all the aspects of the higher education curriculum, assessment is the area that is subject to the most rigorous quality assurance mechanisms. Whilst some of these mechanisms operate on an institution level, others operate at programme team level, hence the inclusion of the quality of assessment in this section. The QAA (2011b) offers the following principles in relation to the quality of student assessment:

- Institutions should ensure that information and guidance on assessments are clear, accurate and consistent and accessible to all staff, students, practice assessors and external examiners.

- Assessment practices should be explicit, valid and reliable and applied consistently across each institution. All staff involved in the assessment of students must be competent to undertake their roles and responsibilities and be offered opportunities to update and enhance their expertise as assessors.

- Boards of examiners and assessment panels have an important role in overseeing assessment practices and maintaining standards, and institutions should develop policies and procedures governing the structure, operation and timing of their boards/panels.

- Institutions should have effective mechanisms to deal with breaches of assessment regulations, and the resolution of appeals against assessment decisions.

Role of the external examiner in assuring the quality of assessment

The external examiner system plays a key role in educational quality assurance by bringing in an external, objective perspective to the assessment system (QAA, 2011c). The role involves scrutiny of students' assessment work to ascertain if the standards are comparable with students on similar courses throughout higher education. In addition, the external examiner can comment on the consistency and standard of internal marking, and make suggestions for improvements to the assessment system. The role of the external examiner is discussed in detail in Chapter 7.

Ensuring quality of practice-based assessment

It is interesting to note that the rigidity applied to ensuring the quality of written assessments is not nearly so apparent in the case of practice-based assessments in nursing. Assessment of practice is based upon observation of students in the workplace and is largely the responsibility of qualified nurses based in the practice setting to which the student is allocated. Unlike written assessments, which constitute a single episode, practical assessment is a continuous process throughout the placement. The decision on whether to pass or fail a student will therefore be made on the basis of that individual's overall progress during the placement.

Moderation of written work is based on the principle of sampling, i.e. the student's written work is only a sample of his or her knowledge, whereas practical assessment attempts to assess the total performance of the student during the placement. This suggests that the assessment of theory is based upon a different paradigm from that of practical assessment, the latter being more like staff appraisal than assessment per se. A moderator or external examiner cannot scrutinize the student's performance, nor moderate the assessor's judgement, because the assessment process has taken place over a period of several weeks. It is therefore very unusual to find that an external examiner has had any involvement in the practical assessment of student nurses, apart from scrutinizing the student's portfolio, and the assessment documentation produced by the assessor despite recommendations made by the NMC.

QUALITY ASSURANCE AT INSTITUTION LEVEL

So far in this chapter the role of the individual lecturer and the programme team in quality assurance has been examined. We now turn our attention to the institution's overall quality-assurance system that impacts on all aspects of the work of the institution.

Aims, characteristics and spectrum of institutional quality assurance

It is essential that all the staff of the institution have a clear understanding of the quality assurance system. This information should be available in the form of a quality assurance handbook or manual and should include a statement of the aims and characteristics of the quality assurance system. In order to assure the quality of the totality of the educational experience of its students, the institution's quality assurance system must cover all aspects of its work, and not just the educational programmes. Table 10.3 illustrates the spectrum of institutional quality assurance, under the headings of inputs, processes and outputs. These can form the basis for the development of performance indicators, allowing comparison with other higher education institutions.

TABLE 10.3 Spectrum of institutional quality assurance

A	Inputs	
1.	College organization and policy	Quality of leadership Institutional philosophy Mission statement Vision Management structure Relationships with staff Financial management Staff development policy Public relations and publicity Equal opportunities policy Quality assurance systems
2.	Personnel	Teaching staff and library/support staff – Qualifications – Motivation – Morale Staff–student ratio Staff development opportunities Individual performance review
3.	Library and support services	Adequacy of book stock and periodicals Opening hours Student support Information technology and media resources Secretarial and administrative support
4.	Enterprises	Teaching accommodation Halls of residence Security arrangements Ground maintenance Catering Car parking Recreation Child care
5.	Students	Admission and access Entry qualifications Motivation
B	Processes	
6.	Curriculum	Relevance Employer-focus Planning Validation, monitoring and review
7.	Teaching	Preparation Delivery Assessment Teacher–student relationships

(continued)

TABLE 10.3 Spectrum of institutional quality assurance *(continued)*		
8.	Research and consultancy	External funding Publication in refereed journals Citations Client satisfaction with consultancy
9.	Student guidance and counselling	Guidance and counselling by teachers Availability of a college counselling service
C	Outputs	
10.	Student achievement	Assessment/examination success rates Employment rates Progress to further study Value added
11.	Course monitoring/evaluation	Annual monitoring reports Quinquennial review

Programme validation, monitoring and review

There are three closely related concepts involved in the quality assurance of programmes and courses, i.e. programme validation, programme monitoring and programme review.

1. Programme validation is the process by which a proposal for a new course or programme is examined to assess its suitability for inclusion in the institution's portfolio.
2. Programme monitoring involves the continuous ongoing appraisal of the course or programme by the course director and course team, and the production of an annual course or programme monitoring report for the institution.
3. Programme review is a periodic investigation to see if the course or programme is still meeting its objectives, and whether appropriate monitoring and evaluation is taking place.

Programme validation

The purpose of validation is to ensure that the course or programme is of a standard comparable to similar awards elsewhere within higher education. The peer-review procedure involves initial scrutiny by a panel of the course or programme documentation prior to the validation event, so that key issues can be identified and conveyed to the chair of the event for inclusion in the agenda for the meeting. During the event, the panel will engage the course or programme team in dialogue and debate on the issues identified, and at the end of the meeting a decision will be made on whether or not the course or programme should be approved to run. A report of the meeting and decisions is circulated to the course or programme team shortly after the event.

The composition of the validation panel should provide for a rigorous examination of the course and the course team, thus ensuring the quality of the course. Membership is drawn from a wide range of individuals, including members from the proposing institution, subject experts from other institutions, members from the relevant industry or profession, service users, students and members with understanding of the processes of higher education.

Programme monitoring

This involves the continuous appraisal of the course or programme by the course director and course team, and the production of an annual or periodic monitoring report for the institution.

Annual or periodic monitoring reports The programme director and programme committee are responsible for the production of an annual or periodic monitoring report which is sent to the college or department faculty board or equivalent. The monitoring report is one of the key mechanisms for quality assurance, and provides data about a range of aspects of educational delivery. Table 10.4 gives the issues that annual or periodic programme monitoring reports should consider.

Some institutions use a scrutineer system for monitoring. A scrutineer is a member of academic staff assigned to a particular course or programme, who scrutinizes the monitoring procedure. There is dialogue between the scrutineer and the course director about the draft monitoring report and how it might be made more effective. The scrutineer also speaks to the report at the faculty board, and the system provides added rigour to the process of quality assurance.

TABLE 10.4 Considerations for annual or periodic monitoring reports
1. Evidence on student performance and progression
2. Responses to annual programme review and evaluation of the previous year and actions undertaken as a consequence
3. Evaluation of programme changes (including admissions and selection policies, student intakes, entry qualifications, continuing viability of programmes and market demand and employment prospects)
4. Noteworthy practice in teaching, learning and assessment
5. Evidence sources utilized in the conduct of the Annual Programme Review and Evaluation (including staff/student panels, student feedback, National Student Survey data, peer review of learning and teaching)
6. Feedback from external sources (including external examiners and professional accreditation bodies)
7. Feedback from former students and their employers
8. Material available to students such as programme specifications, student handbooks and websites

QAA 2011D

Programme review

Quinquennial review is a periodic investigation, usually five-yearly, to see if the course or programme is still meeting its objectives and whether appropriate monitoring and evaluation are taking place. It follows a similar process to that of validation, including peer-review by a panel constituted in the same way as that for a validation event. However, three additional aspects are required for a review event:

■ a critical appraisal of the strengths and weaknesses of the programme, including recommendations for changes in the light of the critical appraisal;

■ a sample of current and past students invited to attend to offer their opinions on their experience of the programme;

■ a sample of marked student assessments to indicate the standard of work achieved on the programme.

> ## TEACHING TIP
>
> It is a good idea to make yourself familiar with the monitoring and review procedures of the programmes that you are involved in; as well as the reports. You can then see how you can contribute to the overall excellence.

Internal quality audit

Internal quality audit is undertaken periodically by an institution to assure itself and others that its quality assurance systems are appropriate for maintaining the standard of its academic awards, and that its development activities are enhancing the quality of teaching and learning.

Internal quality audit covers the range of quality assurance mechanisms in the institution, including its validation, monitoring and review processes, the appointment of external examiners, the procedures of committees and boards and partnership arrangements.

All institutions have their own policies, procedures and systems of internal quality audit, so information relating to this should be sought from each individual's institution.

EXTERNAL QUALITY MONITORING LEVEL

In this final level in the hierarchy of quality assurance, we turn our attention to those quality assurance agencies external to higher education institutions. There is a wide range of such external agencies; including government agencies, accrediting bodies, and professional bodies, all of which exert considerable influence on the quality assurance mechanisms of higher education institutions.

Institutional scrutiny and subject review

The QAA provides independent verification of the quality of programmes of study throughout higher education, by a process of scrutiny of institutions and review of subject units. In order to avoid duplication of effort, the scrutiny process should engage with the institution's internal validation and review cycle and also with any professional or statutory accreditation process, where relevant. The cycle is six years in length; and in each year academic reviewers review a number of programmes, culminating in reports on outcome standards and on quality of learning opportunities.

Quality Assurance Agency guidelines for institutional audit

The QAA has produced guidelines for institutional audit across all four countries within the United Kingdom (QAA Scotland, 2012; QAA, 2009a; QAA, 2009b) in which there are seven audit sections, each subdivided into specific categories within which dimensions and focus are identified. Each area has a quality statement relating to the area of the institution, and evidence of performance is described for each category.

Section 1: Introduction and background

The quality statement is: 'the institution sets the context for the audit, with an outline of developments since the previous audit and action taken on the outcomes of the previous audit'.

- the institution and mission;
- the information base for the audit;
- developments since the previous audit.

Section 2: Institutional management of academic standards

The quality statement is: 'the institution should outline the approach taken to make sure that its academic standards are secure and fit for purpose'.

- the institution's framework for managing academic standards with reference to the learning and teaching strategy;
- external examiners;
- approval, monitoring and review of award standards;
- academic infrastructure and other external reference points;
- assessment policies and regulations;
- progression and completion statistics.

Section 3: Institutional management of learning opportunities

The quality statement is: 'the institution should make sure that the learning opportunities for students help them make good use of those opportunities'.

- the institution's framework for managing the quality of learning opportunities;
- external examiners;
- approval, monitoring and review of award standards;
- academic infrastructure and other external reference points;
- role of students in quality assurance;
- links between research or scholarly activity and learning opportunities;
- modes of study;
- resources for learning;

- admissions policy;
- student support;
- staff support.

Section 4: Institutional approach to quality enhancement

The quality statement is: 'the institution should take deliberate steps to enhance students' opportunities for learning and reflect upon the effectiveness of this approach in improving the quality of the learning opportunities available to students'.

- the institution's approach to managing quality enhancement;
- external examiners;
- approval, monitoring and review of award standards;
- academic infrastructure and other external reference points;
- role of students in quality enhancement;
- dissemination of good practice;
- staff development and reward.

Section 5: Collaborative arrangements

The quality statement is: 'the institution should outline its approach to the management of its collaborative provision including flexible and distributed learning (including e-learning)'.

- the institution's approach to managing its collaborative arrangements;
- external examiners in collaborative provision;
- approval, monitoring and review of award standards;
- academic infrastructure and other external reference points;
- management information.

Section 6: Institutional arrangements for postgraduate research students

The quality statement is: 'the institution should outline its approach to maintaining the academic standards and quality provision of postgraduate research programmes and reflect upon the effectiveness of this approach'.

- institutional arrangements and the research environment;
- selection, admission, induction and supervision of research students;
- progress and review arrangements;

- development of research;
- feedback arrangements;
- assessment of research students;
- representations, complaints and appeals arrangements for research students.

Section 7: Published information

- the institution's approach to ensuring accuracy and completeness of published information;
- students' experience of published information and other information available to them.

The Higher Education Academy

The Teaching Quality Enhancement Committee (TQEC) was established in 2002 by the HEFCE, Universities UK (UUK) and the Standing Conference of Principals to review the support of enhancement of quality in learning and teaching in higher education. The TQEC published its final report in January 2003, which proposed the creation of a single, central body to support the enhancement of learning and teaching in higher education – the Higher Education Academy (HEA). The Academy was formed in 2004 from a merger of the Institute for Learning and Teaching in Higher Education (ILTHE), the Learning and Teaching Support Network (LTSN) and the TQEF National Co-ordination Team (NCT).

The HEA's mission is to help institutions, discipline groups and all staff to provide the best possible learning experience for their students; its strategic aims and objectives are as follows:

- to be an authoritative and independent voice on policies that influence student learning experiences;
- to support institutions in their strategies for improving the student learning experience;
- to lead, support and inform the professional development and recognition of staff in higher education;
- to promote good practice in all aspects of support for the student learning experience;
- to lead the development of research and evaluation to improve the quality of the student learning experience;
- to be a responsive, efficient and accountable organization.

In February 2006, the HEA announced the launch of the first ever National Professional Standards Framework for standards in teaching and supporting learning in higher education. This framework was developed following consultation with the sector and recognized:

> *'the distinctive nature of teaching in higher education and respect for the autonomy of higher education institutions. It also recognizes that the scholarly nature of subject inquiry and knowledge creation, and a scholarly approach to pedagogy, are unique features of higher education in the UK.'*
>
> (HEA, 2006)

A new edition of the standards framework was published in 2011 (HEA, 2011) and its aims are as follows:

- Supports the initial and continuing professional development of staff engaged in teaching and supporting learning.
- Fosters dynamic approaches to teaching and learning through creativity, innovation and continuous development in diverse academic and/or professional settings.
- Demonstrates to students and other stakeholders the professionalism that staff and institutions bring to teaching and support for student learning.
- Acknowledges the variety and quality of teaching, learning and assessment practices that support and underpin student learning.
- Facilitates individuals and institutions in gaining formal recognition for quality enhanced approaches to teaching and supporting learning, often as part of wider responsibilities that may include research and/or management activities.

The NMC quality assurance framework

Higher education programmes that relate to practice within the professions have been accredited by the relevant statutory or professional body, such accreditation often being a requirement for courses leading to entry to a given profession. Within the UK, all programmes leading to entry to the professional register held by the Nursing Midwifery Council for Nursing, Midwifery and Specialist Community Public Health Nursing was until 2002 accredited by the appropriate National Board for Nursing, Midwifery and Health Visiting. Since the disbandment of the four UK boards, the NMC now has statutory responsibility for midwifery supervision and the quality assurance of educational programmes.

The Nursing and Midwifery Order 2001 provided legislative powers for the NMC to approve and monitor the standards of educational programmes that lead to entry on to the register and the educational institutions delivering these programmes. Hence, the NMC has powers to take appropriate action to ensure that such standards are met. The quality assurance framework (NMC, 2011) provides a 'risk-based approach' to quality assurance that supports public protection through the application of professional standards.

The framework encompasses key activities aimed at ensuring the quality of approved NMC provision across the UK. These include approval, re-approval, endorsement, modification and monitoring. Although the main principles are common, the NMC (2011) is keen to point out that the ways in which they are undertaken in each country within the UK do differ.

NMC UK-wide quality assurance and enhancement standards

The quality assurance standards were published in 2011 and provide additional guidance to those involved in the process of approval/re-approval to ensure that regulatory requirements are fully understood and have been met. It is recommended that they are read in conjunction with the standards for preregistration nursing education (NMC, 2010) or any other nursing education programme that requires validation, for example, standards for preregistration midwifery education (NMC, 2009), standards of proficiency for nurse and midwife prescribers (NMC, 2006). The standards must be achievable and are research based or evidence based where possible. There are ten standards for preregistration programmes, each elaborated further by required activity criteria (Figure 10.2). Table 10.5 shows an example of the standard and some of the associated criteria for programme approval/re-approval.

FIGURE 10.2   Quality assurance standards for preregistration programmes

STANDARD 1: Safeguarding the public
Nursing and midwifery education must be consistent with The code: Standards of conduct, performance and ethics for nurses and midwives (NMC, 2008)

STANDARD 2: Equality and diversity
Nursing and midwifery education must address key aspects of equality and diversity and comply with current legislation

STANDARD 3: Selection, admission, progression and completion
Processes for selection, admission, progression and completion must be open and fair

STANDARD 4: Support of students and educators
Programme providers must support students to achieve the programme outcomes, and support educators to meet their own professional development needs

STANDARD 5: Structure, design and delivery of programme
The programme must be structured, designed and delivered to meet NMC standards and requirements

STANDARD 6: Practice learning
Practice learning opportunities must be safe, effective, integral to the programme and appropriate to programme outcomes

STANDARD 7: Outcomes
The programme outcomes must ensure that NMC standards for competence are met and that students are fit for practice and fit for award on completion

STANDARD 8: Assessment
Programme outcomes must be tested using valid and reliable assessment methods

STANDARD 9: Resources
The educational facilities in academic and practice settings must support delivery of the approved programme

STANDARD 10: Quality assurance
Programme providers must use effective quality assurance processes in which findings lead to quality enhancement

NMC, 2011

TABLE 10.5 Standard statement and required activity criteria for programme approval/re-approval

STANDARD 4
Support of students and educators: **Programme providers must support students to achieve the programme outcomes, and support educators to meet their own professional development needs**
Required activity criteria:
1. Programme providers must ensure that programmes include an induction period that includes an explanation of the requirements of the curriculum.
2. Programme providers must ensure that students are allocated to an identified mentor, practice teacher or supervisor during practice learning placements.
3. Programme providers must ensure that those who supervise students in practice are appropriately prepared and supported in that role.
4. Higher education institutions must ensure that support facilities, including learning support, are available to all students enrolled on educational programmes.
5. Programme providers must give students access to pastoral support, occupational health facilities and disability specialists.
6. Programme providers must ensure that learning time is protected as specified in the NMC (2010) standards for preregistration nursing education.
7. Programme providers must provide nursing and midwifery teachers with time for professional development to enable them to remain up to date in their field of practice.

ADAPTED FROM NMC, 2011

National Student Survey

The National Student Survey (NSS) has been conducted at higher education institutions across the UK since 2005 and requests that undergraduate students in their final year evaluate their experience of their programme. The survey is conducted across all publicly funded higher education institutions in England, Wales, Northern Ireland, and participating institutions in Scotland. Further Education Colleges with directly funded higher education students in England have also been able to participate since 2008. It was commissioned by HEFCE and is administered by Ipsos MORI. The NSS is launched at the beginning of each year, January – February, and closes at the end of April; students are requested to answer 23 core questions, relating to eight elements of the student learning experience: Table 10.6 identifies the statements that accompany each element of the NSS.

Student feedback from the NSS is used to compile year on year comparative data within higher education institutions, departments, and the education sector. NSS data is likely to be used in a number of ways:

- League tables are use to rank institutions and programmes according to student satisfaction along with additional data from the higher education statistics agency.
- To identify differences in student experience on programmes within a higher education institution.
- To identify areas of higher education that could facilitate best practice and enhance the student learning experience.
- To influence prospective students' choice of university or programme.

TABLE 10.6 Statements that accompany each element of the NSS

Teaching	• Staff are good at explaining things • Staff have made the subject interesting • Staff are enthusiastic about what they are teaching • The course is intellectually stimulating
Assessment and feedback	• The criteria used in marking have been clear in advance • Assessment arrangements and marking have been fair • Feedback on my work has been prompt • I have received detailed comments on my work • Feedback on my work has helped me clarify things I did not understand
Academic support	• I have received sufficient advice and support with my studies • I have been able to contact staff when I needed to • Good advice was available when I needed to make study choices
Organisation and management	• The timetable works efficiently as far as my activities are concerned • Any changes in the course or teaching have been communicated effectively • The course is well organized and is running smoothly
Learning resources	• The library resources and services are good enough for my needs • I have been able to access general IT resources when I needed to • I have been able to access specialised equipment, facilities, or rooms when I needed to
Personal development	• The course has helped me to present myself with confidence • My communication skills have improved • As a result of the course, I feel confident in tackling unfamiliar problems
Overall satisfaction	• Overall, I am satisfied with the quality of the course
Student's Union	• I am satisfied with the Students' Union at my institution

Review questions

1. In a higher education institution, at what levels should there be quality assurance measurements?
2. How can higher education institutions encourage student involvement in quality assurance?
3. What assumption is the quality assurance of teaching based on?
4. What problems are there with quality assurance in assessment of practice?
5. What role has the Quality Assurance Agency (QAA) have in quality assurance in higher education and how does this differ from the role of the NMC?

SUMMARY

- Meaningful Academic quality refers to how well a higher education provider supports students in their learning.

- Quality assurance is the process for checking that the standards and quality of higher education provision meet agreed expectations.

- Evaluation is the considered judgement about the quality of a product, a process and/or experience.

- The purpose of the Quality Assurance Agency for Higher Education is to safeguard standards and improve the quality higher education.

- The Quality Assurance Agency offers guidance on maintaining and improving quality assurance processes and developing programme delivery.

- The evaluation of a range of aspects of educational provision, such as the evaluation of teaching, is one of the cornerstones of institutional quality assurance.

- Quality assurance has become established in all aspects of the public sector, and it is argued that the need for accountability has been the driving force behind its development.

- Quality assurance of teaching is premised on the assumption that teaching influences learning and that poor quality teaching has a negative effect on student learning.

- Methods of evaluating teaching include evaluation tools for completion by self, students or peers.

- Programme evaluation needs to be distinguished from evaluation of teaching, the latter being just one component of the former.

- Evaluation of the programme curriculum by students is now established throughout the higher education sector, and forms an important aspect of educational quality assurance.

- Student assessment is the area that is subject to the most rigorous quality assurance mechanisms.

- The external examiner system plays a key role in educational quality assurance by bringing in an external, objective perspective to the assessment system.

- The purpose of programme validation is to ensure that the course or programme is of a standard comparable to similar awards elsewhere within higher education.

- The Higher Education Academy helps institutions, discipline groups and all staff to provide the best possible learning experience for their students.

- Higher education programmes that relate to practice within professional programmes are accredited by the relevant statutory or professional body.

- The National Student Survey evaluates final year undergraduate students' experiences of their programme.

References

Biggs, J. and Tang, C. (2011) *Teaching for Quality Learning at University: What the Student Does* (4th Edition). Maidenhead: Open University Press

Bligh, D. (1998) *What's the Use of Lectures?* (5th Edition). Exeter: Intellect

Bloom, B. (1956) *Taxonomy of Educational Objectives: The Classification of Educational Goals, Handbook One: Cognitive Domain* New York: McKay

Boyle, P. and Bowden, J.A. (1997) Educational quality assurance in universities: an enhanced model. *Assessment and Evaluation in Higher Education* 22(2) 111–121

Cave, M., Hanney, S. and Kogan, M. (1991) *The Use of Performance Indicators in Higher Education*. London: Jessica Kingsley Publishers

DfEE (1998) *Higher Education for the 21st Century: Response to the Dearing Report*. London: HMSO

Green, D. (Ed) (1994) *What is Quality in Higher Education?* Buckingham: Society for Research into Higher Education/Open University Press

HEA (2006) *The UK Professional Standards Framework for Teaching and Supporting Learning in Higher Education*. York: Higher Education Academy

HEA (2011) *The UK Professional Standards Framework for Teaching and Supporting Learning in Higher Education*. York: Higher Education Academy

HESA (2012) *Performance Indicators in Higher Education in the UK*. Cheltenham: Higher Education Statistics Agency

Hoecht, A. (2006) Quality assurance in UK higher education: issues of trust, control, professional autonomy and accountability. *Higher Education* 51(4) 541–563

House of Commons (2011) Government reform of higher education: Twelfth Report of Session 2010–12 (*Volume I). London: The Stationary Office*

Huisman, J. and Currie, J. (2004) Accountability in higher education: bridge over troubled water? *Higher Education* 48(4) 529–551

NMC (2006) *Standards of Proficiency for Nurse and Midwife Prescribers*. London: Nursing Midwifery Council

NMC (2008) *The Code: Standards of Conduct, Performance and Ethics for Nurses and Midwives.* London: Nursing Midwifery Council

NMC (2009) *Standards for Pre-Registration Midwifery education*. London: Nursing Midwifery Council

NMC (2010) *Standards for Pre-Registration Nursing Education*. London: Nursing Midwifery Council

NMC (2011) *Quality Assurance Handbook*. London: Nursing Midwifery Council

Nursing Midwifery Order [2001]. London: The Stationery Office

QAA (2009a) Handbook for institutional audit: England and Northern Ireland. Gloucester: Quality Assurance Agency

QAA (2009b) Handbook for institutional review: Wales (2nd Edition). Gloucester: Quality Assurance Agency

QAA (2011a) *Code of Practice for the Assurance of Academic Quality and Standards in Higher Education: B1: Programme Design and Approval*. Gloucester: Quality Assurance Agency

QAA (2011b) *UK Quality Code for Higher Education Chapter B6: Assessment of Students and Accreditation of Prior Learning*. Gloucester: Quality Assurance Agency

QAA (2011c) *Code of Practice for the Assurance of Academic Quality and Standards in Higher Education: B7: External examining*. Gloucester: Quality Assurance Agency

QAA (2011d) *Code of Practice for the Assurance of Academic Quality and Standards in Higher Education: B8: Programme Monitoring and Review*. Gloucester: Quality Assurance Agency

QAA (2012a) *The UK Quality Code for Higher Education: A Brief Guide*. Gloucester: Quality Assurance Agency

QAA (2012b) *Code of Practice for the Assurance of Academic Quality and Standards in Higher Education: B5: Student engagement*. Gloucester: Quality Assurance Agency

QAA Scotland (2012) *Enhancement-Led Institutional Review Handbook* (3rd Edition). Glasgow: Quality Assurance Agency for Scotland

Winch, C. (1996) *Quality in Education*. Oxford: Blackwell

Wood, J. and Dickinson, J. (2011) *Quality Assurance and Evaluation in the Lifelong Learning Sector*. Exeter: Learning Matters

Further Reading

QAA (2011) *Code of Practice for the Assurance of Academic Quality and standards in Higher Education: A1: Setting and Maintaining Threshold Academic Standards*. Gloucester: Quality Assurance Agency

QAA (2011) *Code of Practice for the Assurance of Academic Quality and Standards in Higher Education: A2: The Subject and Qualification level*. Gloucester: Quality Assurance Agency

QAA (2011) *Code of Practice for the Assurance of Academic Quality and Standards in Higher Education: A3: The Programme Level*. Gloucester: Quality Assurance Agency

QAA (2011) *Code of practice for the Assurance of Academic Quality and Standards in Higher Education: A4: Approval and Review*. Gloucester: Quality Assurance Agency

QAA (2011) *Code of Practice for the Assurance of Academic Quality and Standards in Higher Education: A5: Externality*. Gloucester: Quality Assurance Agency

QAA (2011) *Code of Practice for the Assurance of Academic Quality and Standards in Higher Education: A6: Assessment of Achievement of Learning Outcomes*. Gloucester: Quality Assurance Agency

Turner, D.A. (2011) *Quality in Higher Education*. Rotterdam: Sense Publishers

PART THREE
SPECIFIC TEACHING CONTEXTS

CHAPTER 11
PLACEMENT LEARNING

THE AIMS OF THIS CHAPTER ARE:

- To explore the theoretical underpinning of work-based learning

- To outline potential difficulties associated with work-based learning

- To explain the process and purpose of educational audit

- To highlight support mechanisms for students and qualified staff in the work place

- To provide an overview of learning and teaching strategies in the work place

KEY TERMS

Socialization	Mentor
Deviance	Preceptorship
Stress	Competence
Educational audit	A competency
Clinical competence	Central-tendency error

Nursing, midwifery and specialist community public health nursing practice is carried out in a range of workplace settings, including hospital wards and departments, community health centres, GP surgeries, schools, nurseries, day centres, residential homes and industry. It is therefore self-evident that these settings constitute important learning environments; indeed, experiential learning is based on the premise that learning gained through experience is more meaningful and relevant than that acquired in classrooms.

Some people prefer to use the term 'learners' to describe individuals who are pursuing an education or training programme in the workplace, but given that everyone is now meant to be a 'lifelong learner', the term 'student' seems a more appropriate distinction. Within a given workplace setting, a variety of individuals can be classed as students at one time or another:

- *Pre-registration student* These are students undertaking an educational programme in a higher education institution leading to an academic award and registration as a nurse or midwife. Their presence in the workplace is on the basis of a placement, i.e. they spend a given amount of time in a range of workplace settings but are not part of the workforce of those settings.

- *Post-registration students* These are qualified registered nurses or midwives who are undertaking either:

  - An educational programme in a higher education institution leading to an additional academic and/or professional award; or
  - An in-house programme of professional development.

Most of these are in-service students, i.e. they are undertaking their studies on a part-time or flexible basis, whilst maintaining their responsibilities as members of the workforce in a given workplace setting. However, some post-registration programmes, such as specialist community public health nursing, lead to a further professional registration and are therefore classified as being both pre- and post-registration. These programmes require full-time attendance, and the students undertake placements in a range of community workplace settings.

- *National Vocational Qualification (NVQ) students* These are normally health care assistants who are undertaking an NVQ programme at a college of further education leading to an NVQ award. These are part-time in-service programmes with an emphasis on workplace learning and assessment.

From the foregoing discussion, it can be seen that workplace settings in nursing, midwifery and specialist community public health nursing provide the learning environment for a whole range of personnel, including those undertaking formal programmes, and those receiving informal, and often spontaneous, teaching as part of their day-to-day practice. Hence, this environment for learning becomes a crucial factor in the success or otherwise of the personnel involved, so it behoves nurse teachers to appreciate the social dynamics of the workplace. Chapter 6 contains a detailed discussion of group dynamics, but selected aspects relating to the workplace are included below.

GROUP DYNAMICS AND THE WORKPLACE

The workplace does not simply provide an environment for learning the knowledge and skills required for practice; it also serves as a vehicle for pre-registration students' socialization into the profession of nursing or midwifery.

Socialization

From early infancy, individuals learn the values, knowledge and patterns of behaviour that make them a member of their particular society; the process by which an individual undergoes induction into these expected behaviours or roles is termed 'socialization', and is a lifelong process involving transmission of culture.

Primary socialization

This begins in infancy and is mediated through the immediate family; sex roles, social class morals and manners are all part of this early socialization process.

Secondary socialization

This begins once the child commences school and is influenced not only by teachers but also by peers; the latter exert a powerful effect as the child moves into adolescence, when peer-group pressure may result in behaviour at variance with the child's family or society.

Occupational socialization

This is a particular kind of secondary socialization, which involves induction into specific occupational roles after leaving school. Nursing culture has a powerful influence on new members, socializing them into the role of nurse, with all its attendant values and behaviours. In the past, there was great emphasis on conformity and obedience to superiors and a very rigid code of personal and professional behaviour. Socialization may begin in anticipation of future rules, and this anticipatory socialization is important in facilitating the eventual uptake of such roles. Many girls are socialized into nursing from an early age by means of play, especially that associated with hospitals and caring, whilst boys are raised to conform to the male gender role. The mass media are a powerful influence on such socialization and may well be responsible for sex-role stereotyping and racism. Television, newspapers and even children's books may portray nursing as being the exclusive preserve of women; indeed, women are commonly depicted in occupations such as nursing, teaching, domestic work and catering, whereas men are commonly depicted in roles such as engineering, medicine, fire fighting or policing.

The public nature of work-based teaching

One of the major differences between classroom teaching and workplace-based teaching is that the latter is a much more public endeavour. In the classroom, the teacher is normally alone with the students; in contrast, the workplace is populated by a wide range of people including:

- nursing and medical staff
- practitioners from the professions allied to medicine, for example physiotherapist, occupational therapist, medical laboratory technicians;
- support workers and administrators
- patients, clients, relatives and friends
- counsellors, ministers of religion.

It is very likely that much of the teaching will take place in this public arena, so it may be helpful to explore the effects of an audience on human performance. The mere presence of an audience may facilitate or hinder behaviour, the so-called 'audience effect'. For example, many actors and athletes feel that they need an audience in order to perform to their fullest ability. On the other hand, the presence of others can exert an inhibitory effect on behaviour and this has been demonstrated in a number of interesting studies.

TEACHING TIP

When teaching students in the workplace, look out for behaviour that might indicate nervousness, for example flushing and clumsiness. It might help if you engaged yourself in another task, working beside the student, until he or she relaxes around you.

Latané and Darley (1968) showed the effect of the presence of other people on an individual's reaction to emergency situations. They conclude that people are less likely to intervene in an emergency if other people are present and that this can be explained by diffusion of responsibility. If a person encounters an emergency when alone, that person is solely responsible for his or her actions. If, however, other people are present, each individual may feel that his or her own responsibility is reduced and this makes the person less likely to become involved.

Roles and norms

Within the workplace setting, roles and norms exert a significant influence. Roles are actions within a given status, such as the leadership role of the ward manager. Norms are standards or values of behaviour, which may be formal or informal. Formal norms in a workplace setting are imposed by the organization, such as a requirement for practice to be evidence based. Informal norms develop from within the group as a result of interaction; for example, one ward may have a norm involving a particular way of organizing the daily workload. Individuals tend to conform to the prevailing norms of the workplace, and there is evidence that norms may develop over a short period. In a classic study on group norms, Sherif (1936) demonstrated the rapid convergence to a group norm of individuals' opinions regarding the extent of apparent movement of a spot of light in a darkened room. Hence, individuals who join a workplace setting will be expected to adhere to the norms, or risk alienation or ostracism.

Labelling theory and expectancy effect

Another aspect of group dynamics that has significance for workplace settings is that of labelling and expectancy effect. In sociological terms, labelling is the assigning of an individual to a category as a means of classifying his or her behaviour or state. Hence, 'ill' is a label used to distinguish people who are not healthy; 'vandal' is a label that distinguishes people who exhibit antisocial behaviour involving damage to property.

Labelling, then, involves classifying people who deviate from what is considered to be normal; the term 'deviance', however, is used to indicate a negative social evaluation.

Primary deviance

This is the assigning of a label to particular behaviours or states judged by society as deviant; these behaviours are socially defined and will vary between different cultures. The behaviours that a society considers deviant may change over the course of time; in the UK, it used to be considered deviant to attempt suicide or to live as a couple without being married, whereas nowadays these behaviours are seen in a quite different light.

Secondary deviance

Once society has assigned a label to an individual, certain consequences may occur. When a person is labelled 'deviant', he or she becomes stigmatized or disgraced in the eyes of society; depending upon the nature of the deviance, the individual may be shunned or worse – this is particularly true for labels such as 'rapist'. Many diseases, however, can stigmatize the sufferer, especially mental illness, epilepsy, Aids and even such problems as deafness or blindness. Indeed, it can be argued that the diagnosis of such conditions in itself constitutes labelling of primary deviance, setting in train a series of predictable social consequences.

The 'self-fulfilling prophecy'

A second major effect of labelling is that of changes in the individual's self-concept; as a result of social reactions to the original label, the affected person begins to respond in a way that is compatible with that label. In other words, they come to believe that they are what the label says they are and produce stereotyped behaviour that accords with it. This phenomenon has been termed the 'self-fulfilling prophecy' – a prophecy that comes true solely because it has been made. For example, a ward manager labels a student nurse as 'lazy' and people begin to react to the student according to this label; eventually, the nurse begins to accept the label and the students' behaviour becomes lazy. Obviously, there must have been an initial episode that led to the label, but it may have been a 'one-off' incident entirely untypical of the individual.

The notion of self-fulfilling prophecy has been explored in education, where it is known as 'teacher-expectancy effect'. There is a good deal of evidence about the effect of people's expectations on certain outcomes; experimenters have to be cautious when interpreting results because such results may be due to the 'Hawthorne effect' – a variation in people simply due to the fact that they are being observed. The presence of an observer may have either positive or negative effects on the performance of students that are totally unrelated to the style of teaching given.

In a classic study by Rosenthal and Jacobson (1968), carried out in an American school, teachers were given false information about some of the children in their classes; these children were purported to have unusual academic potential and were called 'spurters', but in reality they were randomly selected from the total class. The children were given tests of non-verbal intelligence at the start of the experiment and again at four months and eight months and results showed that the 'spurters' had gained significantly more in terms of IQ than the other children. This was ascribed to the fact that teachers' expectations of the 'spurters' had acted as a self-fulfilling prophecy, which made them achieve more. The study has been criticized on methodological grounds, but there is some support from other studies for the view that teacher-expectancy can influence learning.

THE WORKPLACE LEARNING ENVIRONMENT

The qualified staff are a key factor influencing the learning environment in hospital placements, the role of ward manager being particularly influential. Not only do they have control of the management of the area, but they also serve as role-models for nursing practice. The leadership style and personality of the ward manager are important determinants of an effective learning environment, as demonstrated in a series of classic surveys in the 1980s (Pembrey, 1980; Orton, 1981; Ogier, 1982, 1986; Fretwell, 1983).

Characteristics of a workplace environment conducive to learning

The following summarizes the main perceptions of students in these research studies with regard to the characteristics of a good clinical learning environment.

A humanistic approach to students

Qualified staff should ensure that pre-registration students are treated with kindness and understanding and should try to show interest in them as people. They should be approachable and helpful to students, providing support as necessary, and try to foster the students' self-esteem. In the case of colleagues undertaking post-registration programmes, qualified staff should be sensitive to their study needs, a point easily overlooked when a colleague has been working in the clinical area for some time as a full-time practitioner.

Team spirit

Qualified staff should work as a team and strive to make the student feel a part of that team. They should create a good atmosphere by their relationships within the team.

Management style

This should be efficient and yet flexible in order to produce good-quality care. Teaching should have its place in the overall organization, and students should be given responsibility and encouraged to use initiative. Nursing practice should be consistent with that taught in the university.

Teaching and learning support

Qualified staff should be encouraged to act as supervisors, mentors, preceptors, and assessors as appropriate. Opportunities should be given for students to ask questions, attend medical staff rounds, observe case conferences and new procedures and have access to patients'/clients' records. Non-nursing professionals such as doctors, physiotherapists, occupational therapists, dieticians and chaplains can also contribute to the learning environment provided that they are made to feel part of the total team. It is important for the ward manager to spend a little time with new non-nursing colleagues in order to explain the ethos of the ward or department in relation to learning, thus encouraging them to see themselves as a resource for student learning.

It is not always appreciated that students themselves are very much a part of the learning environment and not merely the passive recipients of its influences. An effective environment will encourage the students to take responsibility for their own learning and to be active in seeking out opportunities for this. Critical thinking and judgement are fostered in an atmosphere where the student can question and dissent without feeling guilty or disloyal.

An important part of the learning process is experimentation, in which the student can try to apply concepts and principles in different ways; this implies that the student will need to adopt different approaches to patients and be innovative. There may be other students in a clinical area, and this peer support can be invaluable. Planning for two students to work together can offer substantial benefits for both, provided that they take time to discuss approaches and decisions and their underlying rationale.

The learning environment in community nursing

So far we have discussed learning environments with reference to hospital settings, but the environment is equally important when students are in community placements. Prior preparation in advance of a student placement is vital to ensure that the student gains the most from it. It is good practice to establish empathy with the student many weeks before the actual placement, for example by the mentor giving the student his or her work and home telephone numbers so that they can discuss expectations and 'housekeeping' issues such as transport arrangements.

The physical environment is clearly very different from that of a hospital, particularly when it involves domiciliary visits to patients in their own homes. Nursing staff are guests in this situation, with no right of entry and, consequently, much of the teaching will occur by observation, with discussion following later after leaving the patient's home. Much of this discussion takes place in the practitioner's car in a one-to-one setting, calling for very good interpersonal skills on the part of the teacher. The practitioner needs to put the student at ease and treat him or her as an equal. The effects of a strained relationship are much more difficult to cope with when there are only two people involved.

Clinics and post-natal groups provide another community learning environment for students. When running a well-baby clinic the mentor can combine tutorials for both student and parent, since the information is common to both. In community placements, media resources tend to be less readily available than in hospital settings, and hence the mentor places greater reliance on discussion and role-modelling strategies.

Stress and the workplace learning environment

Work-related stress has become a major issue for employers and employees, evidenced by the increasing number of claims for compensation arising out of work-induced, stress-related illness. Indeed, the term has now become a normal part of our everyday experience of living, exemplified in the expression, 'I'm really stressed-out'. There can be few work settings that have more potential for stress than hospitals or community health settings; the very nature of the work involves staff in close contact with patients who are themselves often distressed and traumatized.

The nature of stress

Stress is a difficult concept to pin down, but it is generally thought of as consisting of two components:

- *Stressors* These are events in our lives that threaten our physical or mental well-being.
- *Stress responses* These are our reactions to the stressors we encounter.

The reaction of the individual to stressors occurs in three well-defined stages termed 'the general adaptation syndrome' (Selye, 1956):

1. *The alarm reaction* This is a short-term reaction characterized by changes in physiology, such as increased heart rate, respiration, endocrine activity and sympathetic-nervous-system activity. This combination is commonly referred to as the 'fight or flight' reaction.

2. *Resistance to stress* In this stage the body processes return to normal and the individual adapts to the stress.

3. *Exhaustion* This rarely occurs in psychological stress, although it is common in extreme physical conditions such as severe exposure. Here, the individual has used up all the resources for coping, and death may occur.

This adaptation syndrome is non-specific, in that it occurs when the person encounters any form of stress, of whatever severity. One approach to stress is called 'person–environment fit theory' (Caplan, 1983), in which stress is defined as either:

- demands that exceed the individual's capability to fulfil, i.e. he or she is overwhelmed; or
- an individual's capability exceeds the demands upon her or him, i.e. he or she is underwhelmed. This is typified by the case of an individual whose work does not sufficiently 'stretch' his or her capabilities.

Effects of stress upon the individual

The impact of stress can be classified into two main categories: the effects of stress on students' performance in the workplace, and the effects of stress on the health of students and staff in the workplace.

Effects of stress on students' performance in the workplace

An individual's level of emotional arousal has a significant effect on his or her subsequent performance, including cognitive as well as physical performance (Hebb, 1972). Each individual has an optimal level of arousal at which that person performs at his or her best; under-arousal or over-arousal results in deterioration in performance of learning tasks, particularly complex ones.

The effects of stress on the health of students and staff in the workplace

The reaction to stress will vary from individual to individual, with some experiencing feelings of anger and aggression, and others apathy and depression. Relationships can be affected, and some individuals may find solace in alcohol or drugs. Anxiety is another common symptom of stress, and there is evidence that it can impair the response of the immune system, leading to illness. There is also evidence of a link between stress and heart disease, especially in relation to the 'Type A personality' (Friedman and Rosenman, 1974).

Sources of stress in the workplace

The categorization of sources of stress in organizations by Cooper and Marshall (1976) is adapted below in Table 11.1 to provide a framework for thinking about sources of stress in the clinical and community workplace.

Numerous stressors that are specific to healthcare environment are identified in Figure 11.1 by a number of authors (Healy and Tyrrell, 2011; McVicar, 2003; Burnard *et al.*, 2000; Cooper, 1999).

Coping with stress in the workplace

Many of the stressors encountered in the workplace will be beyond the individual practitioner's power to change. The organization carries a responsibility for the health and safety of its employees, and the increasing incidence of litigation on the grounds of stress-induced illness is forcing organizations to look more seriously at workplace stressors.

TABLE 11.1	Sources of stress in the workplace
Job-related stressors	• Too much work to get through in the time available • Insufficient staff to support practitioners • Inadequate availability of equipment or resources • Little opportunity to use higher-level skills
Role-related stressors	• Role ambiguity, e.g. lack of clarity about boundaries of role • Role conflict, e.g. between role as practitioner and manager • Inadequate staff development for role • Role conflict between work and family
Relationship-related stressors	• Conflict with superiors • Conflict with subordinates • Difficulties with colleagues from other health disciplines
Career-related stressors	• Pressures of continuing professional development • Expectations of promotion • Fear of redundancy
Organization-related stressors	• Inadequate communication • Internal politics • Secrecy and lack of trust

ADAPTED FROM COOPER AND MARSHALL, 1976

FIGURE 11.1	Sources of stress in the healthcare workplace

Working environment and perceived workload	Excessive paperwork and administration	Patient related issues and emotional cost of caring
Leadership and management style	Volume of patients	Professional conflict
Fluctuating shift patterns	Lack of time for education	New technology

One of the most important elements of coping is being able to recognize the signs of stress in oneself, and to attempt to identify the main stressors involved. This enables coping strategies to be mobilized at a relatively early stage before the stress gets to a more serious level. The following coping strategies are commonly identified in the literature:

■ Avoid taking on more work than you can cope with, by developing your assertive ability to say no to requests.

■ Delegate jobs to other colleagues where possible.

■ Always ensure that breaks are taken outside of the workplace area; for example, go to the staff dining room for coffee and go outside to the shops at lunch time.

■ Undertake relaxation techniques, such as physical-relaxation techniques and meditation, at appropriate times.

■ Suggest to management that stress-reduction programmes should be made available for staff.

■ Try setting up a stress support group in the workplace, where colleagues can share their experiences.

■ Use the individual performance review/appraisal system to bring to the attention of management the workplace stressors that you have identified, for example lack of staff development for your role; inadequate resources, etc. This will ensure that they are formally recorded with the organization, an important point if evidence is needed at a later date.

■ Report to your GP if your symptoms of stress are severe; not only may treatment be provided, but a formal record is made which may be important evidence if needed at a later date.

Managing emotion in the workplace

Clinical and community settings are, by their very nature, places of intense emotions. These encompass positive emotions, such as excitement, joy, elation, and also negative emotions, such as anger, frustration and fear. It is interesting to note that both positive and negative emotions can equally disrupt normal functioning in an individual, including the person's relationships with others and his or her ability to make judgements and take decisions. It may be necessary for nurses, midwives and specialist community public health nurses to manage other people's disruptive emotions in the workplace, be it those of colleagues, patients or clients, and a number of principles of good practice for managing the emotions of others are suggested by Ostell *et al.* (1999):

1. *Deal with the emotional reaction before attempting to resolve the problem.* The individual's disruptive level of emotion needs to be reduced so that he or she can begin to consider the problem rationally, and the authors suggest two approaches to this. Apologizing to the individual can be helpful if there is a justifiable grievance of some kind: for example if a patient has to wait in the accident and emergency department for a long time, or if the recipient of the outburst is responsible in some way for the circumstances provoking the outburst. An alternative approach is to use reflective statements such as 'I can see that you are unhappy about …' These may help to defuse the emotion but may well have the opposite effect if perceived as a statement of the obvious.

2. *Avoid behaviour that heightens adverse emotional reactions.* When responding to disruptive emotional outbursts it is self-evident that one should avoid any behaviour that might exacerbate the other person's emotional state. Hence, any form of confrontation should be avoided, and it is important not to become angry when dealing with an angry person, as this will simply fuel his or her emotional reaction.

3. *Employ behaviours likely to dissipate adverse emotional reaction.* It seems normal to offer sympathy to individuals who demonstrate disruptive emotional reactions, but this can often reinforce the adverse emotional reaction by seeming to agree with the person's view of the circumstances. It is preferable to use empathy to show that the person's circumstances are understood, and this can be done by reflecting his or her views back and by non-judgemental questioning.

4. *Recognize differences between emotions.* The authors point out that all emotional reactions should not be treated in the same way, because different emotions tend to be stimulated by different patterns of thinking: for example, anger commonly arises when an individual's demands have been denied; anxiety when individuals anticipate unpleasant consequences that they perceive to be beyond their control.

5. *Where appropriate, attempt to find a solution to the underlying problem.* Finding a solution to the underlying problem can only occur once the disruptive emotional reaction has subsided. It is important to find a solution in order to prevent similar outbursts when the circumstances are encountered again. A counselling approach can be useful here, but advice and instructions are also helpful in some cases.

6. *Learn to 'actively accept' reality.* Some problems that cause adverse emotional reactions are not capable of solution, for example bereavement and redundancy; in such cases, the individual must learn to accept reality by letting go of unattainable desires. However, this may take considerable time, and the help of a professional counsellor may be required.

Auditing the workplace learning environment

In order to be considered an appropriate placement for pre-registration students, there must be adequate governance of practice learning and evidence of effective partnerships between education and service providers (NMC, 2011). The workplace must meet the standards and principles for practice learning laid down by the NMC (2010) as identified in Table 11.2.

TABLE 11.2 Standards and principles of practice learning
Standard: Practice learning opportunities **Practice learning opportunities must be safe, effective, integral to the programme and appropriate to programme outcomes**

1	Students and those supporting practice learning must be provided with information that includes dates, outcomes to be achieved, and assessment documents for each period of practice learning
2	Mentors and practice teachers must meet the relevant requirements within the *Standards to support learning and assessment in practice* (NMC, 2008a)
3	Local registers of mentors and practice teachers must be maintained according to *Standards to support learning and assessment in practice* (NMC, 2008a), including sign-off status of mentors, record of updates and date for triennial review
4	Programme providers must use objective criteria and processes for approving new practice learning environments, and audit them at least every two years
5	Audits of practice learning environments must demonstrate how the nature, scope and quality of the learning experience supports programme outcomes
6	Students must have access to a range of practice learning opportunities sufficient to meet programme outcomes
7	Programme providers must ensure that the 2300 hours of practice learning gives students the opportunity to learn in direct contact with healthy and ill people and communities. Students are required to use this experience to organize, deliver and evaluate their nursing care on the basis of the knowledge and skills they have acquired. Simulation may be used for up to 300 hours of practice learning
8	Practice learning opportunities must occur across a range of hospital, community, and other settings
9	Programme providers must ensure that practice learning throughout the programme provides students with experience of 24-hour and 7-day care
10	A risk assessment must be completed before anyone under 18 can enter a practice learning environment

Educational audit

Educational audit is a process that ensures collaboration between higher education institutions and health care providers on an ongoing basis. It is seen as the assessment of a placement completed by a link lecturer for that clinical area. The NMC (2011) states that audits should be completed every two years and serve to ensure that placements are appropriate learning environments for student nurses. Hughes (2004) outlines an example of information retrieved from an educational-clinical audit of an operating theatre environment:

- *Section 1* outlines the general details and skill mix within the placement.
- *Section 2* identifies the regular educational opportunities available to students during the placement. In addition to working within the realms of anaesthetics, recovery and scrub, the perioperative environment might offer other learning environments that include visits to:
  - pre-assessment clinic
  - endoscopy unit
  - surgical day ward
  - sterile supplies unit
  - lunchtime teaching tutorials
- *Section 3* demonstrates how the placement supports and facilitates the learning environment and how the skills and knowledge of students can be developed. The placement must indicate how it can involve students in assessing, planning, implementing and evaluating the delivery of patient care and provide evidence of sound educational standards in relation to support and supervision for students.

The audit document may require a named link lecturer who will provide learning and educational support for students and staff in the practice setting. A link lecturer is a lecturer allocated to a clinical placement who is the first point of contact for health care providers regarding student issues, see later in this chapter for more information. It is usual for a named clinician to liaise with the link lecturer to ensure that the relationship between the university and the placement is effective.

The encouragement of continuing professional development must be visible in the placement area and staff enabled to fulfil the requirements of professional registration. There must also be evidence of opportunities available for clinical supervision within the operating theatre environment.

- *Sections 4 and 5* provide a summary of previous student evaluations of the placement; an action plan is identified for any areas of improvement with an appropriate timescale for completion.

PLACEMENT SUPPORT SYSTEMS FOR STUDENTS AND STAFF

Clinical practice placements

Practice placements are a vital component of the student nurse experience, so it is important that they reflect both the nature of the provision of care to meet health care needs and the demands of professional registration (Hughes, 2003). Students have the right to expect support from key individuals within each placement to enable them to identify learning opportunities. They must be able to make sense of their practice through the application of theory, feedback and reflection on their clinical practice experience. Back in 1997, the English National Board (ENB) called for greater emphasis on the assessment of practical skills in the workplace to ensure a competent workforce and the delivery of quality care. Part of the increased focus on the development and assessment of clinical competence was to improve public protection (UKCC, 2000). This increased the responsibility of clinical mentors in relation to the accurate assessment of clinical competence (Watson 2000). Therefore, adequate preparation of mentors to undertake this role was crucial to ensuring that student nurses were 'fit for practice, purpose and award' at the end of education programmes (Hughes, 2003).

The importance of practice placements in the education of health care professionals was emphasized in *Making a Difference* (DH, 1999) as part of the Government's drive to modernize the NHS and to ensure that education for health care professionals was strengthened and focused on the services needed by patients. A subsequent development was *Placements in Focus* (ENB/DH, 2001), which was published to enhance guidance and standards for student placements and practice experience and to enable local standards to be developed within a national framework. This document recognized the importance of staff as good role models within the practice learning environment and advocated, as part of their ongoing learning, students should experience the positive culture of clinical governance, where an evidence-based approach to practice was fundamental.

The NMC (2010) standards for pre-registration nursing education document acknowledged that pre-registration programmes must meet certain requirements and provide a clear, ongoing set of outcomes for commissioning bodies, higher education institutes, NHS trusts, mentors and students. These all have a responsibility for ensuring that, at the point of initial registration, student nurses must be fit to practice.

Practice learning teams

According to Chapple and Aston (2004), practice learning teams involve a group of nursing practice staff and lecturers who work collaboratively to make a significant contribution to supporting student learning and assessment within a designated clinical area or group of clinical areas. Furthermore, they explain, such teams lead the development and maintenance of the clinical learning environment and provide support and guidance to mentors and assessors, and to others who contribute to ensure that students meet their clinical learning outcomes and develop appropriate competencies.

Practice learning teams were also introduced by Brooks and Moriarty (2006), following concerns raised by students that clinical placements were not addressing their learning needs; mentors had also expressed concern, as they were feeling overwhelmed by the large numbers of students in practice and the difficulty in providing appropriate levels of support. Having identified examples of good practice already in existence, the authors developed numerous initiatives to improve the mentoring process for nursing students. These included:

- student communication boards
- student information days
- exit questionnaires
- mentor information packs
- student 'drop-in' sessions.

Strategies to ensure that students experience a positive clinical placement have been clearly recommended by Twentyman *et al.* (2006) and by Morgan (2005). They encourage clinical staff to ensure that students are welcomed and made to feel part of the team and make the following recommendations:

- Orientate the students to the ward, routine and staff that they are likely to encounter during placement.
- Ensure that students receive appropriate handover and are allocated tea breaks with other team members.
- Encourage students to be involved in every aspect of patient care.
- Collaborate with students and involve them in the decision-making and problem-solving process.
- Use a variety of teaching strategies within practice placements.

Student induction to the clinical setting

On commencement of the clinical placement, it is important to identify students' learning needs during the induction process (see Table 11.3) and discuss any concerns and anxieties that the student may have (Hughes, 2003). A useful way of organizing this is through a learning agreement or contract (Welsh and Swann, 2002). Whilst such a learning contract is not totally binding, Neary (2000) suggests that it should specify what the student will learn, how it will be achieved and the criteria for measuring success. The standards for competence is determined through staged achievement within the following four domains (NMC, 2010).

Domains of competence

- *Professional values*
- *Communication and interpersonal skills*
- *Nursing practice and decision making*
- *Leadership, management and team working*

(NMC, 2010)

These domains can be applied to all nursing specialities and serve to produce realistic and achievable learning objectives.

TABLE 11.3   Student nurse induction process

- Liaise with education co-ordinator.
- Orientation of department and introduction to key people.
- Meet with mentor and discuss opportunities for working together.
- Identify learning needs and agree learning outcomes.
- Discuss concerns and anxieties relating to clinical placement.
- Discuss philosophy of care, health and safety issues, policies and procedures, sickness and absence, working hours, lunch breaks.
- Establish lines of communication and emergency communication, e.g. cardiac arrest call, fire.
- Discuss ethical and moral issues relating to clinical speciality.
- Discuss roles and responsibilities of multiprofessional team.
- Discuss respect for dignity, religious and cultural beliefs of patients.
- Identify available learning resources.
- Identify other specialities specific to the department.
- Identify link lecturer and clinical teacher/practice facilitator for clinical placement and contact details.

ADAPTED FROM HUGHES, 2003

MENTORSHIP

The concept of mentoring in nurse education is not a new one. The original concept of mentoring is well documented and is said to have originated in the United States (Morle, 1990; Clutterbuck, 1991). It started to appear in the nursing literature in the early 1980s, having traditionally been linked to professions such as medicine, law and business, and has resulted in a wealth of published literature. Although mentorship has assumed respectability in professional education, Jarvis and Gibson (1997) maintain that it remains a term that is not easily defined, as numerous articles have debated what the term actually means. However evidence suggests that mentoring is primarily associated within clinical settings, and to lesser extent educational establishments (Sword *et al.*, 2002). The terms 'mentor' and 'mentorship' have received considerable attention in the last decade within nurse education and the mentoring role is summarized by the NMC (2008a, p. 19) as follows:

> *'An NMC mentor is a registrant who, following successful completion of an NMC approved mentor preparation programme – or comparable preparation that has been accredited by an AEI as meeting the NMC mentor requirements – has achieved the knowledge, skills and competence required to meet the defined outcomes. A mentor is a mandatory requirement for pre-registration nursing and midwifery students'*

Mentorship is seen by many writers as being a long-term relationship that extends throughout a student's programme, whereas others limit the concept to a relationship within a specific placement. In some systems, students are encouraged to choose their own mentors, and in others the mentor is assigned to the student. The former is preferable if possible, because it increases the likelihood of compatibility between mentor and student, an important factor in the relationship.

Qualities of a mentor

The personal qualities of a mentor and the nature of the relationship between the mentor and student are central to the success of the mentorship process (Pulsford *et al.*, 2002), and from the literature (Gopee, 2010; Davies *et al.*, 1994; Darling, 1986) it can be surmised that the attributes of a good mentor include:

- Trust, openness, generosity of time.
- Clinical, content and pedagogical knowledge.
- Approachable, motivated to teach, good communication skills.
- Patient, kind, good listener, sound practitioner, academic nurse, good teacher.

In contrast, a qualitative study of effective mentoring by Gray and Smith (2000) indicated that students quickly lose their idealistic view of their mentor and over time develop an insight into the qualities of a poor mentor. Poor mentors were identified as promise breakers, lacking in knowledge and expertise, unapproachable and intimidating to students. Characteristics of a good and poor mentor are listed in Table 11.4, although it is worth noting at this point that all registered nurses, midwives and specialist community public health nurses have a duty to facilitate students to develop their competence (NMC, 2008b). Therefore it could be argued that many of the characteristics of a poor mentor contravene the NMC (2008b) Code.

TABLE 11.4 Characteristics of a mentor

Characteristics of a good mentor	Characteristics of a poor mentor
Approachable	Intimidating to students
Knowledgeable and motivated to teach	Promise breakers
Supporting	Lacking in knowledge and expertise
Good listener and trustworthy	Unapproachable
Patient and friendly	Poor communicator
Experienced and enthusiastic	Lack of time for students
Demonstrates interest in students	
Committed to the mentoring process	

Morle (1990) describes a mentor as someone who smoothes progression up the career ladder as they are primarily selected because of their professional powers and personal characteristics. Whilst this is a likely notion in the business setting, it appears to bear little resemblance in nursing, although some practitioners might dispute this. Morle

(1990) also questioned whether or not the term 'mentorship' was really appropriate within nursing educational systems and perhaps the term 'preceptorship' should be given serious consideration, and as a consequence, this has been debated by many authors (Donovan, 1990; Armitage and Burnard, 1991; Lloyd-Jones *et al.*, 2001).

Following the recommendations of the Fitness for Practice report (UKCC, 1999), and since then the NMC (2008a) published standards to support learning and assessment in practice. Aimed at lecturers, practice teachers and mentors, these standards promote the integration of theory and practice, which only serves to ensure the support of students. Table 11.5 identifies the mandatory standards for mentors and mentorship.

TABLE 11.5 The developmental framework for mentors to support learning and assessment in practice

DOMAIN	STANDARD
Establishing effective working relationships	• Demonstrate an understanding of factors that influence how students integrate into practice settings • Provide ongoing and constructive support to facilitate transition from one learning environment to another
Facilitation of learning	• Use knowledge of the student's stage of learning to select appropriate learning opportunities to meet individual needs • Facilitate the selection of appropriate learning strategies to integrate learning from practice and academic experiences • Support students in critically reflecting upon their experiences to enhance future learning
Assessment and accountability	• Foster professional growth, personal development and accountability through support of students in practice • Demonstrate a breadth of understanding of assessment strategies and the ability to contribute to the assessment process as part of the teaching team • Provide constructive feedback to students and assist them in identifying future learning needs and actions • Manage failing students so that they may enhance their performance and capabilities for safe and effective practice • Be accountable for confirming that students have met, or not met, the NMC competencies in practice • As a sign-off mentor confirm that students have met, or not met, the NMC standards for pre-registration nursing education (NMC, 2010) and are capable of safe and effective practice
Evaluation of learning	• Contribute to evaluation of student learning and assessment experiences • Participate in self and peer evaluation to facilitate personal development

Create an environment for learning	• Support students to identify learning needs and experiences that are appropriate to their level of learning • Use a range of learning experiences, involving patients, clients, carers and the professional team, to meet defined learning needs • Identify aspects of the learning environment which could be enhanced Act as a resource to facilitate personal and professional development of others
Context of practice	• Contribute to the development of an environment in which effective practice is fostered, implemented, evaluated and disseminated • Set and maintain professional boundaries that are flexible for providing interprofessional care • Initiate and respond to practice developments to ensure safe and effective care is achieved and an effective learning environment is maintained
Evidence-based practice	• Identify and apply research and evidence-based practice to their area of practice • Contribute to strategies to increase or review the evidence-base used to support practice
Leadership	• Plan learning experiences that will meet students defined learning needs • Be an advocate for students to support them accessing learning opportunities Prioritize work to accommodate support of students within their practice roles • Provide feedback on the effectiveness of learning/ assessment in practice

ADAPTED FROM NMC, 2008A

Whilst emphasizing the difference between theory and practice, Benner (1984) recommended that it was the role of experienced nurses in the clinical environment to facilitate the transition from novice to competent practitioner. Burnard (1990) also refers to a mentor as an experienced practitioner whose role is to guide and look after the student whilst Neary (1994) defines a good mentoring relationship as '*a dialogue between two people committed to improvement*'. In general, a mentor is usually someone who is experienced, frequently more senior than the learner and who provides support, encouragement and guidance.

The need for a mentor

Due to the strong workplace tradition of mentorship, Neary (2000) points out that students or new recruits are often assigned to more experienced people who can induct them into clinical settings and assist on skill development, understanding and attitudes. She also points out the numerous 'gains' that can be achieved for the mentor, the mentee and the employing institution (Table 11.6).

TABLE 11.6   Gains achieved during the mentoring process

Gains for the mentor:

- Improved job satisfaction
- Increased recognition within the establishment
- Improved communications between the mentor and other staff
- Opportunity for accredited training
- Membership of a new and wider network of other mentors and trainers
- Introduction to lifelong learning

Gains for the mentee:

- Improved self-confidence and motivation
- Becoming more familiar with the ways of working of the establishment
- Fuller and better use of existing resources
- Personal and career development
- Specific help with meeting the outcomes of the institution
- Help in ensuring that the support of education is relevant to their work

Gains for the employing institution:

- Improved communication between individuals at different levels
- Increased motivation of staff as interest is shown in their professional input
- Skills of staff are recognized more quickly
- Higher calibre staff are attracted
- A contribution to staff development across the whole institution
- The establishment of a body of mentors for general use with new students

NEARY, 2000

One of the controversial issues in mentoring is whether or not mentors should also act as assessors in relation to their students. Anforth (1992) argued that the role of mentor is incompatible with that of assessor, as it presents a moral dilemma between the guidance and counselling role and the judgmental assessment role. However, it is difficult to understand why there should be a dilemma between these two aspects, since assessment should constitute an important teaching and learning strategy and not simply a punitive testing of achievement. If the mentor has an open, honest and friendly relationship with the student, assessment can provide a rich source of feedback and dialogue to further the student's development. The term 'mentor' is used to describe a qualified and experienced member of the practice-placement staff who enters into a formal arrangement to provide educational and personal support to a student throughout the period of the placement. This support may involve a range of functions including teaching, supervision, guidance, counselling, assessment and evaluation. However, the mentor is not the only member of the practice-placement staff who carries out these functions, and other staff will undertake these according to the needs of the student and the practice area.

Preceptorship

From the foregoing discussion it is apparent that there is much overlap in the literature between the concepts of mentor and preceptor. Burke (1994) sees preceptors and students as having a short-lived, functional relationship for a specific purpose in a practice setting.

Given the definition of mentorship above, preceptorship can be seen as a specific teaching and learning strategy rather than as a generic support system for students. Therefore a definition of a preceptor can be as follows:

> *'an experienced nurse, midwife or specialist community public health nurse within a practice placement who acts as a role model and resource for a student who is attached to him or her for a specific time span or experience'*

> *'A preceptor is a registered nurse who helps newly qualified nurses develop confidence and reinforce their knowledge and skills after their initial registration.'*
>
> (NMC, 2010)

Preceptorship uses the principle of learning by 'sitting next to Nelly' but in a more systematic and planned way. A student is attached to the preceptor for a relatively long period of time, such as a day or a week, and 'shadows' the preceptor throughout. The student's role is to observe the various interactions and decisions that the preceptor is involved with in the course of his or her work, and then time is made available for the student and preceptor to meet privately to discuss the events that have occurred. During these meetings, there is two-way dialogue about the various approaches adopted and the decisions made by the preceptor, and the student can ascertain the basis for such decisions. Clearly the person chosen to be the preceptor needs to have the confidence and interpersonal skills to be questioned about why one course of action was taken rather than another, and equally the student needs to have sufficient confidence not to be overawed by the power differential. In management training, the preceptorship is often conducted in an institution other than the one in which the trainee works, and this has the advantage of avoiding a 'boss' relationship between preceptor and student. Preceptorship offers not only benefits to the students, but also to the preceptors because the system helps the preceptors to clarify their reasons for making particular decisions or taking certain courses of action.

The sign-off mentor

The criteria for sign-off mentor are identified in the NMC (2008a) Standards to support learning and assessment in practice, which states that:

> *'Nurses and midwives who make judgements about whether a student has achieved the required standards of proficiency for safe and effective practice must be on the same part or sub-part of the register as that which the student is intending to enter. Only sign-off mentors and practice teachers that are on the same part of the register and in the same field of practice may confirm that students have met the relevant standards of proficiency for the particular programme leading to registration or a qualification that is recordable on the NMC register.'*
>
> (NMC, 2008a)

Clinical placement providers must ensure that a nurse or midwife designated to sign-off proficiency for a particular student at the end of a programme is (NMC, 2008a):

- Working in the same field of practice as that in which the student intends to qualify.
- Clinical currency and capability in the field in which the student is being assessed.
- Knowledge and understanding of programme requirements and practice assessment strategies.
- An in-depth understanding of their accountability to the NMC for the decision they must make to pass or fail a student when assessing proficiency requirements at the end of a programme.
- Been supervised on at least three occasions for signing off proficiency by an existing sign-off mentor.

Triennial review of mentors and practice teachers

The Nursing and Midwifery Council (NMC) requires that in order to remain on the local register of mentors all mentors and practice teachers must produce, at a formal review held every three years, evidence that they have:

- Mentored at least two students (practice teachers to have supervised at least one student) within the three-year period.
- Supervisors of midwives are required to mentor at least one student undertaking a supervisor of midwives programme during the three-year period relating to triennial review.
- Participated in annual updating.
- Explored the validity and reliability of judgements made when assessing practice in challenging circumstances.
- Mapped ongoing development in their role against the current NMC mentor/practice teacher standards.
- Been deemed to have met all requirements needed to be maintained on the local register as a mentor, sign-off mentor or practice teacher.

Managing failing students

Throughout pre-registration education programmes mentors and practice teachers are responsible for assessing clinical competence and confirming that students are capable of safe and effective practice. They are required to consider the practice evidence to make a judgement that all competencies have been met and that the student is considered proficient (NMC, 2008a). One of the key competencies and outcomes for a mentor is to manage failing students so that they may enhance their performance and capabilities for safe and effective practice or be able to understand their failure and the implications of this for their future. They are accountable for confirming that students have met, or not met, the NMC competencies in practice.

The NMC (2010) standards for practice learning placements reveal the following requirements when concerns with students are highlighted:

> 'Programme providers must ensure that processes are in place to address issues or concerns about a student's progress, and that these are dealt with full and quickly.
>
> Programme providers must help students deal with any issues and concerns using a clear, time-limited development plan within or across periods of practice learning.'

The study by Duffy (2003) highlighted the problems inherent in clinical practice when mentors 'failed to fail' students whose clinical competence was under debate. Her qualitative study aimed to uncover mentors' and lecturers' experiences regarding the issue of students passing clinical assessments when not having demonstrated sufficient competence. Duffy (2003) confirmed that students were passing assessments when doubt about their clinical competence was suggested; a key concerned revealed that some students achieved registration despite such misgivings. One of the key issues was that mentors did not always identify and address problems early enough in the student's placement and did not follow the appropriate procedure when it came to a fail scenario; this meant that lecturers could not always support the mentors' decision. Duffy suggested that there were significant practice implications of mentors' reluctance to fail students, notably the potential of compromising professional standards, patient safety and protection of the public.

Indicators to the possibility of failing students have been widely documented (Carr *et al.*, 2012; Carr *et al.*, 2010; Gopee, 2010; McGregor, 2007; Duffy and Hardicre, 2007):

- Lack of underpinning knowledge.
- Inconsistent clinical performance.
- Lack of insight into weaknesses so unable to change following constructive feedback.
- Unsafe practice.
- Not responding appropriately to feedback.
- Lack of interest or motivation.
- Absence of professional boundaries or poor professional behaviour.
- Experiencing personal issues such as ill health.
- Unreliability, persistent lateness/absence.

Carr *et al.* (2012) report that mentoring student nurses who fail to reach the required standard of practice can be distressing for all who participate in assessment whilst Duffy (2003) uncovered a number of reasons why mentors failed to fail students.

- Lack of knowledge about the assessment process and unsure whose role it is to fail the students.
- Reluctance to fail students early in their programme thinking their competence may develop with time.
- Previous mentors 'passing the buck' or giving students the 'benefit of the doubt'.
- Perceived personality clashes with the mentors, undermining mentors with threats of further action.
- Reluctance to be responsible for ending a student career at the end of their programme.

Having reflected on experiences with failing students, Carr *et al.* (2010) made a number of recommendations to optimize the student and mentor experience:

- Access appropriate mentor training programmes and updates which will include a systematic approach to maximise skills. For example, peer review and observation, portfolio evidence of mentorship.

- Trust your judgement and intuition. If there are concerns that a student's practice is unsatisfactory there is usually a foundation for concern.

- Do not be apprehensive about discussing concerns with the link lecturer; the sooner an issue is identified the better chance of maximising a students' opportunity to succeed.

- Remember your wealth of personal experience and do not be afraid to be open and honest with the student about concerns.

- Do not leave discussions until the end of a placement; it will not enable the student to succeed and will cause personal distress if a student has not had the opportunity to improve.

- Use the recognized procedures, guidelines and necessary paperwork to record assessments and discussions with students; ask the link lecturer to attend to provide additional support.

- Try to facilitate the procedure of failing in positive terms; use the feedback to succeed in the future; build confidence.

- If a situation becomes uncomfortable and non-productive it is acceptable to take time out, reflect, seek advice and support to ensure that discomfort and distress to all is minimized and an opportunity to help a student succeed is not lost.

- Share concerns with colleagues.

- Set time aside to reflect or engage in clinical supervision to enrich learning and provide an even more exceptional standard of mentorship.

THE ROLE OF THE PRACTICE TEACHER/PRACTICE EDUCATOR

At one time in nursing, there were two types of nurse teacher: the nurse tutor, whose primary responsibility lay in classroom teaching, and the clinical teacher, whose primary responsibility was teaching in practice placement settings. These roles have been unified under the title of practice teacher or practice educator, a qualified teacher who has retained clinical competence and whose responsibilities include teaching, supervision and assessment of students. Additionally some practice teachers also undertake part-time roles in the clinical practice and education settings by acting as module leaders for post-registration modules.

The literature has identified a number of key roles for teachers in practice settings (Brown *et al.*, 2012; Sayer, 2011; Gopee, 2010; Gerrish, 1992)

- *Educational support for practice-based staff* This includes advice about dealing with supernumerary students on pre-registration programmes, and support for staff acting as mentors to students.

- *Tutoring students* This includes facilitating the development of students' autonomy as students; enabling the acquisition of knowledge and skills and professional values; feedback; and their skills with regard to reflective practice.

- *Facilitating good practice* This includes awareness of current practice, providing a resource to unit staff, promotion of research-mindedness, and fostering a critical approach to practice.

- *Developing interpersonal relationships* This includes building sound relationships and providing reassurance and experiences that could reduce the student's anxiety

Gerrish suggests that teaching in practice placements requires a commitment by the teacher, collaboration between education and service staff, and staff development for teachers on their new role in relation to practice.

Staff development for mentors and preceptors

The careful selection of practice-placement staff for these important roles is crucial, and Burke (1994) suggests that personal characteristics, clinical expertise, teaching skill, and motivation are important. Courses of preparation may take the form of recognized courses such as teaching and assessing in clinical practice or a Post Graduate Certificate in Education course. On the other hand, they may be specifically designed in-house courses of preparation, and these need careful joint planning between education and service, and also ongoing monitoring and quality assurance.

Encouraging student autonomy means a 'hands-off' approach, which some experienced practitioners may find uncomfortable. There is also the potential for perceived threat on the part of practitioners who qualified some time ago, when supporting undergraduate students. This may result in barriers arising between mentor and student, to the detriment of learning.

TEACHING TIP

A very useful strategy for staff development is networking between practice-placement support staff. Networking can be formal or informal, and it functions in much the same way as self-help groups by providing mutual support and sharing of experiences.

Clinical supervision

Clinical supervision is peer-support for practitioners in clinical and community settings; it is defined by the Department of Health (DH) as:

> '*a formal process of professional support and learning which enables the individual practitioner to develop knowledge and competence, assume responsibility for their own practice and enhance consumer protection and safety of care in complex clinical situations*'
>
> (DH, 1993)

Clinical supervision is described by the NMC as:

> '*an important part of clinical governance and allows registrants to develop their skills and knowledge and helps them to improve patient/client care*'
>
> (NMC, 2006)

Although it does not advocate any particular model of clinical supervision, the NMC (2006) has defined a set of principles that should underpin any system of clinical supervision used; these include the following:

- Clinical supervision supports practice, enabling registrants to maintain and improve standards of care.
- Clinical supervision is a practice-focused professional relationship, involving a practitioner reflecting on practice guided by a skilled supervisor.
- Registrants and managers should develop the process of clinical supervision according to local circumstances. Ground rules should be agreed so that the supervisor and the registrant approach clinical supervision openly, confidently and are aware of what is involved.
- Every registrant should have access to clinical supervision, and each supervisor should supervise a realistic number of practitioners.
- Preparation for supervisors should be flexible and sensitive to local circumstances. The principles and relevance of clinical supervision should be included in pre-registration and post-registration education programmes.
- Evaluation of clinical supervision is needed to assess how it influences care and practice standards (NMC, 2006).

Clinical supervision is carried out in two main ways: one-to-one supervision and group supervision.

One-to-one clinical supervision This is the most common form of clinical supervision, in which an experienced nurse acts as the clinical supervisor for a less-experienced colleague.

Practitioners normally choose someone with whom they have a good relationship to be their clinical supervisor, usually a colleague from the same area of work.

Group clinical supervision   In this approach, one supervisor is designated for the group, and the advantages claimed are that it exposes supervisees to alternative modes of helping and fosters an appreciation of the widespread nature of their concerns.

Implementing one-to-one clinical supervision   The introduction of clinical supervision is a very sensitive issue, and it may be regarded with scepticism or suspicion by some practitioners. For example, prospective supervisors may see it as an unnecessary, time-consuming activity that diverts resources from direct patient/client care. Supervisees may be suspicious of the motives of managers in introducing clinical supervision, seeing it as a covert means of disciplining staff for inadequate practice.

Some practitioners may consider it naive to disclose openly and honestly important aspects of their professional practice to a clinical supervisor, particularly if they feel that such disclosure might adversely affect their future employment prospects. It is also possible that some models of clinical supervision may give staff the impression that it is a counselling intervention or, at worst, some kind of amateur psychotherapy. Hence, one of the most important aspects of clinical supervision is the relationship between supervisors and supervisees. Mutual trust is required, and this could take some time to develop, particularly if there was no choice in the selection of the supervisor (Table 11.7).

TABLE 11.7   Characteristics of clinical supervision

Purpose

- Professional support and learning and development of knowledge and competence
- Responsibility for own practice
- Enhance consumer protection
- Help practitioner to examine and validate his or her practice and feelings
- Pastoral support
- Formative assessment
- Ensuring standards of clinical and managerial practice
- Maintain and support standards of care
- Improve quality of patient care and staff performance
- Reduce stress and burn-out

Process

- A formal process
- A practice-focused professional relationship that should be developed according to local circumstances
- Every practitioner should have access
- Preparation for supervisors is important and should be included in pre- and post-registration programmes
- Evaluation is needed and should be determined locally

ADAPTED FROM BOND AND HOLLAND, 2010, GRANT AND QUINN, 1998

Negotiating the supervision contract   The first meeting between the clinical supervisor and supervisee tends to be the most difficult, since both parties may be unsure about how to proceed. It is helpful if this first meeting focuses on negotiating the supervision contract, as the process of negotiation will itself help to encourage the development of rapport between the two parties. Since the contract contains tangible aspects such as practical arrangements and record-keeping, it provides a less-threatening focus for discussion in the initial phase of the meeting when the parties are at their most anxious. A supervision contract is a useful way of clarifying the working agreement, as well as making for an easier relationship, since everyone knows where they stand. Table 11.8 shows the components normally included in a supervision contract (Milne, 2009; Grant and Quinn, 1998).

TABLE 11.8   Elements of a supervision contract
• Practical arrangements, i.e. time, place, frequency and length of meetings
• Record-keeping arrangements
• What will happen in the case of missed sessions?
• Confidentiality
• What will happen in the case of incompetent practice?
• What communication, if any, will there be between the supervisor and the supervisee's manager?
• What access, if any, will the supervisee have to the supervisor between sessions?

Practical aspects of supervision meetings   Practical arrangements for clinical supervision may not always be straightforward. For example, offices are rarely appropriate for clinical supervision, as constant disturbance can be expected from telephones and visitors. White (2009) reported that all members wanted to get away from their immediate working environment in order that privacy could be ensured and distractions minimized.

Difficulty may be experienced in finding a suitably private room that is not already booked, particularly if several clinical supervision meetings are taking place on the same day. Over-running of a previous meeting is a common occurrence, resulting in erosion of the time available for the next meeting; one hour is a reasonable time allocation, but timing will vary depending on local circumstances. The problem of room bookings is further compounded where supervision for practice nurses and specialist community public health nurses takes place in rooms in GP surgeries, because the use of such rooms may be chargeable and this will impact on the overall resource provision for clinical supervision.

Given that both parties to clinical supervision are busy practitioners, it is likely that one or both will arrive late from time to time. When negotiating the supervision contract, it is useful to allow a margin for late arrival; for example, the parties might agree to wait up to half an hour for the other to arrive. This margin can help reduce panic reactions, such as driving too fast to get to the meeting on time. The time of day in which the meeting takes place will vary according to local circumstances, but many supervisors and supervisees prefer the end of the day, when patient/client demand may be less. The frequency of meetings varies widely in the literature, ranging from weekly to three-monthly.

Keeping records of supervision It is important that both supervisor and supervisee keep records of clinical supervision for their personal professional profile, as evidence of professional development. Whilst these records are confidential to the individuals concerned, it is also necessary to keep a managerial record of clinical supervision which contains the minimum amount of information required by management in order to be able to confirm that supervision has occurred, and to enable the time to be costed. This would normally be the names of the supervisor and supervisee, the dates on which supervision took place, and the reasons for any cancellation. In cases of litigation by patients or clients, such records can provide evidence of the ongoing professional development of the practitioner involved.

Cassedy (2010) emphasizes that clinical supervision is not personal counselling or therapy and that counselling skills can be utilized in clinical supervision to provide support with the focus clearly on the supervisee's performance, ability and effectiveness in their work setting.

Role of the link lecturer

The integration of nurse education with higher education has highlighted an uncertainty over the clinical role of nurse lecturers (Hughes, 2004). Although beliefs have been identified from lecturers maintaining strong links with clinical practice, the evidence has previously suggested that nurse lecturer preparation in practice areas was limited (Murphy, 2000). Following the move into higher education and the demise of the clinical teacher, Camiah (1998) argued that an effective model for nurse lecturers in practice no longer existed.

The concept of link lecturer emerged following the demise of the two-tier system of clinical teacher and lecturer in favour of one level of teacher to work in both the clinical and educational environment. As a result, Ramage (2004) points out that all teachers were assigned to clinical areas in which they were to facilitate the development of an educational milieu to support student learning in practice.

Around the 1990's the teaching and support of student nurses in the practice setting was a shared responsibility between clinical staff, clinical nurse teachers and to a lesser extent, nurse lecturers (Chapple and Aston, 2004). The Peach Report (UKCC, 1999) emphasized the importance of clinical learning for students and the importance of the role of the link lecturer in supporting them. The link lecturer role is defined as:

> 'A lecturer allocated to the clinical placement area who liaises with placement staff on student issues, and is the first point of contact for the health care provider who assists the mentors in practice in the facilitation of a supportive, creative learning environment and will provide support throughout the clinical assessment.'
>
> (WG, 2005)

There appears to be a plethora of terms associated with the link lecturer role, which can sometimes include:

■ clinical teacher;
■ teacher/practitioner;
■ lecturer/practitioner;
■ clinical facilitator;
■ practice educator;
■ practice education facilitator.

However, it must be acknowledged that whilst the role of the link lecturer does resonate with some of the experiences of the above roles, its primary role in practice (Welsh Government, 2005) is to:

■ Monitor the effectiveness of the mentorship system in their allocated clinical areas.
■ Provide support to students, mentors, clinical managers and education co-ordinators.
■ Provide appropriate feedback to clinical areas following student evaluations (Murphy, 2000).

There are four key elements of the clinical role of nurse teachers, which include liaison, teaching, clinical practice and research (Collington *et al.,* 2012; Price *et al.,* 2011; Murphy, 2000). Figure 11.2 identifies many other aspects of the role that link lecturers identify with.

FIGURE 11.2 Aspects of the link lecturer role

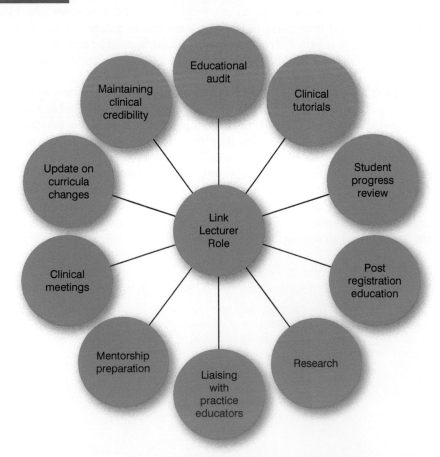

The multi-faceted roles of the link lecturer that are most utilized within the clinical setting include the following areas:

- student support;
- educational audit;
- mentorship;
- clinical credibility;
- research.

Pre-registration student support

One of the most important aspects of the link lecturer role relates to supporting students in practice. Following the recommendations of the FFP report (1999), the NMC (2008) published revised standards for the preparation of teachers of nursing, midwifery and specialist community public health nurses. These standards, aimed at lecturers, practice educators and mentors, promote the integration of theory and practice which only serves to ensure the support of students (Hughes, 2004).

While nurse educators are striving to respond to changes in education the dichotomy between the theoretical input taught in the classroom and what is practiced or experienced in the clinical area remains a problem for some (Hughes, 2004). As an example, to address this issue, pre-registration students at a university in Wales are now more prepared for their operating theatre experience, which is integrated within the second year of the programme. During the theory block, students receive 11 hours of taught perioperative nursing sessions all relating to different specialist areas within theatre; all of which can be applied to the clinical setting. These include:

- Understanding the principles and nurse-led practices of pre-assessment, primarily associated with day surgery.
- Nursing assessment of surgical in-patients, focusing mainly on the rationale for the checking and completion of the preoperative check list.
- Principles and practice of anaesthesia addressing mainly the methods and triad of anaesthesia; role of the anaesthetic nurse; patients with special needs; nursing care during the peri-anaesthesia period.
- Intraoperative nursing care highlights relevant issues that include caring for patients during the intraoperative phase; patient positioning; surgical diathermy and the roles of the scrub and circulating nurse.
- Postoperative nursing care is delivered as a half taught didactic lecture illustrating the principles of this vulnerable perioperative stage and using a student centred learning approach by means of patient scenarios and problem-based learning.
- The final taught session focuses on postoperative complications of anaesthesia and surgery and again utilizes patient scenarios completed as student group work.

A study by Hughes (2006) evaluated the operating theatre experience of pre-registration nurses. Using a non-randomised convenience sample of 150 second-year students over a nine month period, students were issued with a questionnaire of 25 questions at the end of their theatre placement. Although only 57 per cent of questionnaires were returned, the majority of students (76 per cent) felt adequately prepared for their clinical placement in terms of the above theoretical content.

Clinical credibility

What exactly is clinical credibility and how is it generally defined? In terms of the critical care environment, does it mean that a lecturer should be able to walk into an intensive care unit and prepare the environment appropriately for a ventilated patient? Then act in a competent manner and assist the anaesthetist for the duration of the shift? Anecdotal evidence suggests that six weeks away from any clinical area renders a nurse as 'deskilled' (Hughes, 2004).

A study by Aston *et al.* (2000) explored the role of the link lecturer in the practice setting, which overall highlighted a lack of strategic management of the practice role by educational institutions. Interestingly, whilst they found that clinical credibility was of great importance for lecturers, both clinicians and lecturers felt that this was a broad term and that clinical credibility was understood to mean an awareness of current issues and changes in the practice setting. Maintaining clinical credibility was seen as a broader issue in a study by Collington *et al.* (2012). A number of lead midwives for education listed a range of activities that were acceptable in facilitating lecturers being up to date but there was a general belief that engaging in 'hands-on' midwifery practice was essential to supporting lectures in university. However there was an acknowledgement that maintaining clinical practice was becoming more difficult in some universities.

To overcome the obstacles of maintaining clinical credibility there are several strategies that have been adopted to enhance the link lecturer role. The experiences of Maslin-Prothero and Owen (2001) identify that nurse lecturers should consider their current knowledge, skills and expertise to develop an individualised practice-based role that enables them to keep in touch with current clinical developments. They suggest a number of realistic, pragmatic approaches that nurse lecturers can use to enhance both clinical competence and credibility, and to ensure that their teaching is up-to-date and grounded in the realities of clinical practice. Some of these include:

- Developing the learning environment.
- Involvement in practice development.
- Developing links with local trusts.
- Involving clinicians in teaching in the college environment.
- Clinically orientated research.

The debate surrounding the clinical credibility of nurse lecturers was discussed by Ousey and Gallagher (2010) who state that balancing the competing demands of a clinical role and a teaching role is too difficult to achieve. They further state that nurse lecturers do not have to be clinically credible to successfully facilitate the learning of students; but what the nurse lecturer must achieve is the development of strong partnerships between service and education to ensure that students are suitably prepared to meets the needs of the clinical areas.

Research

Since the integration of nursing education into higher education in the 1990s, growing numbers of nurse educators are now required to undertake research, or supervise students who are undertaking research, as an integral part of their role. Universities now demand that lecturers pursue research and scholarship in their individual disciplines (Maslin-Prothero and Owen, 2001), in addition to their teaching and learning commitments. A lecturer in mental health may consciously choose to develop one of his research interests within the clinical environment as a means of keeping in touch with current developments in mental health practice. This provides an invaluable opportunity to keep in touch with current issues, concerns and developments. Thus link lecturers can contribute to the development of professional practice and actively be involved, and advance their own knowledge base through research activities and regular contact with experts in practice (Maslin-Prothero and Owen, 2001). Meskell *et al.* (2009) support this view and believe that collaborative research is the means by which close links between clinical and education should be developed.

TEACHING AND LEARNING STRATEGIES IN THE WORKPLACE

The principles of teaching and learning that have been expounded in this book are applicable to teaching and learning in the workplace. However, some teaching strategies are more appropriate for the workplace environment than others, and this section will explore a range of these.

Teaching on a one-to-one basis

Teaching on a one-to-one basis demands skills quite different from those used in the classroom setting; both teacher and student are more exposed to each other and the encounter takes place in the presence of other staff, patients and visitors. The need to appear competent and credible to all these groups, including the student, can add considerably to the pressure on the teacher, making it more difficult to allow the student to make decisions or to try out new approaches. On the other hand, there can be great personal satisfaction in helping to provide good-quality nursing care whilst at the same time facilitating the growth of nursing skills in the student.

Much one-to-one teaching is opportunistic, i.e. the kind of spontaneous teaching that occurs as part of everyday professional practice, with either students, qualified staff, or patients and clients. Opportunistic teaching can arise in a number of ways; for example, students may ask the teacher to go through some aspect or procedure with them, or simply ask questions about the care of specific patients. On the other hand, teachers may themselves initiate teaching by asking questions or by explaining aspects or procedures.

Teaching can also be initiated by teachers if they perceive that a student or qualified member of staff is experiencing difficulty with procedures or understanding. Within a given workplace setting there will be some concepts that most students find difficult to understand, and the teacher is asked time and time again to explain these to each new student. It is a useful strategy to prepare an explanation in advance that can be 'wheeled out' as required, preferably using some kind of visual material. Feedback on student learning is important, even in spontaneous one-to-one teaching.

TEACHING TIP

Use questioning to elicit the student's understanding of any explanations you have given.

Case conferences

Ideally these should involve all members of the nursing team in discussion and evaluation of the nursing care of a particular patient. Medical staff have long used the case-presentation method as a learning tool for students and qualified doctors, and the same principles apply to the use of nursing-care conferences. There is no standard format for such a conference, but it is usual for one nurse to present the patient's case and then for the whole team to be involved in the discussion. This helps the student to feel part of the nursing team, as well as providing the skills required in a public presentation of 'self'. Such conferences provide a useful holistic view of the patient and his or her problems, together with an opportunity to analyze critically the care that has been received, to the mutual benefit of both nurses and patients.

Handover report

Many qualified practitioner nurses view the handover report as a valuable opportunity to do some teaching. Handover is done normally in two ways:

- verbal handover, involving the entire nursing team meeting together in a room for a reasonable period of time during the day;
- non-verbal handover, conducted at patients' bedsides using documents.

Verbal handover can be a useful teaching strategy if the ward manager or staff nurse often takes time to ask questions about aspects of patients' conditions and care, and if the atmosphere is relaxed and informal. There are important trade-offs from a ward report in addition to the actual report itself, namely the fostering of team spirit and the development of public-speaking ability and confidence in presenting information to peers. However, there are disadvantages, including nurses' reliance on memory, the amount of time consumed, and the fact that nurses are often called away before the handover is complete.

Kennedy (1999) reports on a study of non-verbal bedside handover in an elderly care setting. Using non-participant observation, the study investigated the early-to-late shift handover; the key components of handover were identified as venue, grade of nurse, documents used, patient involvement, content of handover, whether the person handing over was the care-giver, and whether unnecessary people were present. The main findings were as follows:

- Handover was quicker; staff were available on the ward for other patients if needed.
- Support workers played little part in the handover.
- Staff were not confident about using care plans for the handover, as these could not be relied upon.

The study recommended that all qualified nurses should attend planning workshops, that bedside handover should continue and that patients should be included wherever possible, and that the role of the support worker should be reviewed in relation to communication and documentation.

Clinical rounds

Students can gain a great deal from accompanying a doctor or nurse on a clinical round. The former is useful for gaining insight into the role of the medical team in patient care, and it is interesting to listen to the discussion with regard to treatment. Students may find it valuable to accompany a nurse teacher on a similar round and to make comparisons of the needs of patients with similar conditions, and also to look at the difference in attitudes between such patients. Examples of pathology can be pointed out, for example oedema or inflammation, and the reasons discussed at the end of the round. Students should always carry a notebook to write down any queries or observations, but single sheets of paper must not be allowed, as they can easily be lost and other patients may read the confidential details.

Reflective practice diary

Reflective diaries or records are one of the key strategies in experiential learning and consist of brief written descriptions of situations that can be used as the basis for reflection later. The following examples are from the reflective diary of a specialist community public health nurse who is undergoing training as a mentor.

Situation 1: Student's first day on community placement

The first day of the student's placement was spent in discussion and negotiation of her learning contract in the light of my case-load requirements. Since child protection is a major facet of my work, I made it clear to the student that this aspect must by law take priority over all other matters. Before commencing their community placement students are required to complete a community profile so that they have insight into the area. However, the student in question arrived at my office having completed a community profile on a completely different area to the one in which I work. This meant that the student had no information whatsoever about the area, so we had to negotiate a series of sessions in which I could explain the key aspects of the placement community. I also contacted her personal tutor in the university to emphasize how important it is for students to undertake a community profile that relates to their placement.

Situation 2: Student's first visit to a client's home

One of the items on my student's learning contract was to visit a family with a new baby. By accompanying me on the visit, the student was able to see and understand exactly what a specialist community public health nurse does in such a visit. During a prior briefing discussion, I explained the official standard for a new-birth visit and asked the student to pay particular attention during the visit to how I taught the mother to look after the baby, and to compare my performance with that of the official standard. I wanted her to focus particularly on my use of verbal and non-verbal communication with the family, since interpersonal relationships are fundamental to the specialist community public health nurse role.

On arriving back at the surgery following the visit, we had a debriefing session in which I challenged the student by asking her to evaluate my performance against the official standards, and how she would now approach her next new-birth visit in the light of what she had learned.

Situation 3: Developmental assessment in the clinic

At age 18 months infants come to the clinic for assessment of physical and behavioural development, and this involves a variety of tests, for example hearing, speech, vision, motor movements, etc. I acted as a role model for the student, in that she was asked to observe and record carefully my relationships and involvement with the clients, with particular emphasis in this case on the practical aspects of testing. One of the objectives in the student's learning contract was to develop the skills of developmental assessment of infants, so I planned the learning environment with this goal in mind. During the clinic, the student was asked to observe me performing the developmental assessment on a number of infants, and was then encouraged to participate in the assessment of a number of infants. Once I was satisfied that she had grasped the essential points, I allowed her to conduct an assessment in partnership with me, but she was asked to take the lead, and to treat me as her student, showing me what to do. This was a very effective way of teaching, as it showed the student aspects which she needed to study further.

Critical incident technique

Critical incident technique (CIT) is a useful tool for identifying aspects of practice which the student felt were particularly positive or negative (Flanagan, 1954). These critical incidents can then be reflected upon and analyzed to give new insights into practice. Critical incident technique was used by Benner (1984) in her study of acquisition of nursing skill; she identified critical incidents as any of the following:

- those in which the nurse's intervention really made a difference in patient outcome;
- those that went unusually well;
- those in which there was a breakdown;
- those that were ordinary and typical;
- those that captured the essence of nursing;
- those that were particularly demanding.

Participants were asked to include the following information in their description of critical incidents:

- the context;
- a detailed description;
- why the incident was critical to the participant;
- what the participant's concerns were at the time;
- what he or she was thinking about during the incident;
- what he or she felt about it afterwards;
- what he or she found most demanding about it.

Learning contracts

Learning contracts are an effective tool for developing student autonomy in practice placements. It is useful to meet with students prior to the placement to begin the initial contract negotiation, and this can be modified as required once the placement has commenced. The theory and components of a learning contract are discussed in Chapter 2.

Teaching a motor skill

Although it is possible to teach some motor skills by simulation in a nursing laboratory, such learning will still need to be consolidated in the workplace setting. Teaching motor skills involves the same principles as any other form of teaching, namely, an atmosphere conducive to learning that is free from threat or stress. There must be opportunity for feedback and analysis of the performance, and teachers must appreciate that learning a skill requires time and that individual students will differ in the amount of time that they require. One point to be borne in mind is that nursing procedures involve more than motor skills; Gagné (1985) classifies procedures as intellectual skills or rules for determining the sequence of actions, and thus students need to learn the procedural rules as well as the motor-skills aspects.

When planning to teach motor skills, the teacher will have to consider the level at which the student must learn the skill. It is obvious that students cannot achieve the highest level of proficiency for every skill they learn; indeed, experienced nurses will vary in their relative degree of skill amongst the nursing procedures that they practise. There will be some motor skills that students must learn to the highest level and others where an intermediate level is acceptable. A useful point of reference for levels of skills is the notion of taxonomies of motor skills. In Chapter 4, the taxonomy of Simpson (1972) is outlined in relation to curriculum objectives, and this can provide guidance for the teacher. The taxonomy has seven levels as follows:

1. Perception – concerned with perception of sensory cues.
2. Set – concerned with readiness to act.
3. Guided response – skills performed under guidance of instructor.
4. Mechanism – performance becomes habitual.
5. Complex overt response – typical skilled performance.
6. Adaptation – skills can be adapted to suit circumstances.
7. Origination – creation of original movement patterns.

It would seem that many nursing skills learned by students will be geared at levels 3 or 4 and that the higher levels may only be reached when the student has practised as a qualified nurse for some time. Skills at level 3 are commonly taught in specialist areas, where the student is allowed to perform under guidance having first been shown how to do a procedure. For example, the skills of dialysis may be taught at this level during a student's allocation to a renal clinical area, but there is no expectation that the student nurse will achieve a highly skilled performance during the brief allocation period. The same can be said for other clinical specialisms such as intensive-care units, neonatal units and the like.

The teaching of motor skills involves the provision of information and the opportunity for practice under supervision. Table 11.9 gives a checklist for teaching a motor skill, and the key points are further elaborated below.

The provision of an atmosphere conducive to learning has already been discussed and its importance noted. Skills analysis is a useful way of identifying the part-skills that comprise the total motor skill. Table 11.10 shows a task analysis for the motor aspects of the procedure for performing a surgical dressing.

These motor skills are further subdivided into part-skills and elements, and it can be seen that the elements consist of many previously learned entry behaviours, such as moving the bed table and pulling curtains. Determining the sequence of the procedure is important, and it may be forgotten that students must remember this as well as the motor skills. Entry behaviours need to be identified, because they are already learned and hence do not need to be taught again.

The skill is normally modelled by an actual demonstration, but in the classroom setting it can also be done by video, and it gives the students an overall impression of the skill they are aiming at.

TABLE 11.9 Checklist for teaching a motor skill

1. Provide an atmosphere conducive to learning
2. Carry out a skills analysis to determine part-skills and elements
3. Determine the sequence of the procedure
4. Assess entry behaviours of students – these need not be taught again
5. Model the skill by demonstration at normal speed
6. Teach the sequence of the procedure
7. Teach the motor skill by either whole-learning or part-learning method
8. Allocate sufficient time for practice
9. Provide augmented feedback on performance
10. Prompt student to use intrinsic feedback
11. Encourage transfer of existing similar skills by pointing out similarity

TABLE 11.10 The procedure of performing a surgical dressing

Total motor skill	Part-skills (tasks)	Elements*
1.0 Preparation of work area	1.1 Clearing space	1.11 Pushing locker away
		1.12 Moving bed table
	1.2 Screening	1.21 Holding curtain and pulling it round
	1.3 Closing windows	1.31 Pulling window cord
	1.4 Positioning patient	1.41 Asking if possible to lie recumbent
		1.42 Removing pillows
		1.43 Folding bedclothes
		1.44 Loosening clothing
		1.45 Covering with blanket
2.0 Preparation of equipment and trolley	2.1 Hand-washing	
	2.2 Cleaning trolley	
	2.3 Collecting equipment	
	2.4 Setting trolley	
	2.5 Taking to bedside	
3.0 Performance of dressing	3.1 Opening bags	
	3.2 Loosening dressing	
	3.3 Hand-washing	
	3.4 Opening packs	
	3.5 Removing dressing	
	3.6 Cleaning wound	
	3.7 Applying dressing	

4.0 Organization of trolley	4.1 Closing pack 4.2 Closing bags 4.3 Securing bags
5.0 Ensuring patient's comfort	5.1 Attending to position
6.0 Clearing of trolley and equipment	6.1 Removing from bedside 6.2 Disposal of soiled dressings 6.3 Disposal of instruments 6.4 Hand-washing 6.5 Clearing equipment 6.6 Cleaning trolley 6.7 Hand-washing
7.0 Returning to patient	7.1 Assist with clothing 7.2 Assisting with position 7.3 Offering drink, newspaper, 7.4 Removing screens 7.5 Returning tables, lockers
8.0 Recording and reporting	8.1 Writing report 8.2 Reporting verbally to nurse in charge 8.3 Comparing report with previous one

*Elements are stated only for Section 1.0 of the total motor skills

There is some controversy as to whether skills should be taught in their entirety (whole-learning), or divided into part-skills, with each part being taught separately first and then combined into a whole–part-learning. The disadvantage of whole-learning is that it may be difficult to comprehend large units of procedures if taught together. However, part-learning may waste time because the student has to learn the part-skills first and then learn to combine them together. It may also be boring for the student if the part-skills are simple. The advantages of whole-learning are that it may be:

- more meaningful, as perceived as whole;
- more efficient, as students can identify the aspects that need further practice within the whole;
- more effective for students who already have a background in the skill;
- better for highly motivated students;
- better for older students.

The advantages of part-learning are that it may:

- help to motivate students, as each part-skill provides immediate achievement
- by its small-step nature act as reinforcement for learning
- be better for younger students
- be better for students lacking a background in the skill
- help to improve specific responses for part-skills.

Another area of controversy is that of massed practice versus spaced practice; massed practice involves continuous practice until the skill is learned, whereas spaced practice may spread the practice over a period of time, with rest in between. There is no evidence that one is better than the other, but there are obvious pitfalls associated with massed practice, such as boredom and fatigue. As we have seen earlier, feedback is a crucial aspect of motor-skills learning, without which no improvement can occur. The teacher needs to encourage students to become aware of the intrinsic feedback from their own muscles and joints, which informs them about the position of limbs and the action of movements. Information gained from their own observation of their actions will also help the students to learn a skill and here again the teacher may use questioning to ascertain whether each student is able to self-evaluate outcomes.

The main role of the teacher is in providing augmented feedback in the form of verbal guidance both during and on completion of the motor performance. The nurse teacher can teach for transfer of learning by using a variety of techniques to make the student understand the principles underlying the skill. Existing skills must have been well learned if they are to transfer positively to the new skill, and the similarities need to be pointed out to the students.

Benner's model of skill acquisition in clinical nursing practice

Patricia Benner's book *From Novice to Expert* (1984) has become one of the most frequently quoted research studies in nurse education. Benner conducted paired interviews with beginners and experienced nurses about significant nursing situations that they had experienced in common, in order to identify any characteristic differences between their descriptions of the same situation. Additionally, she carried out interviews, critical incident technique, and participant observation with a sample of experienced nurses, new graduates, and senior students, to ascertain the characteristics of performance at different stages of skill acquisition.

Using an adaptation of the five-stage model of skill acquisition developed by Dreyfus and Dreyfus (1980), Benner described the characteristics of performance at five different levels of nursing skill: novice, advanced beginner, competent, proficient, and expert (Figure 11.3). During his or her passage through these stages, the student relies less upon abstract rules to govern practice and more on past experience. Nursing situations begin to be seen as a unified whole within which only certain aspects are relevant, and the nurse becomes personally involved in situations rather than a detached observer. It is important to note that Benner uses the term 'skill' in its widest sense to mean all aspects of nursing practice, and not simply psychomotor skill performance.

FIGURE 11.3   Novice to expert framework

Stage 1: Novice

This level is characterized by rule-governed behaviour, as the novice has no experience of the situation upon which to draw, and this applies to both students in training and to experienced nurses who move into an unfamiliar clinical area. Adherence to principles and rules, however, does not help the nurse to decide what is relevant in a nursing situation and may thus lead to unsuccessful performance

Stage 2: Advanced Beginner

Unlike principles and rules, aspects are overall characteristics of a situation that can only be identified by experience of that situation. For example, the skills of interviewing a patient are developed by experience of interviewing previous patients, and the advanced beginner is one who has had sufficient prior experience of a situation to deliver marginally acceptable performance. Advanced beginners need adequate support from supervisors, mentors and colleagues in the practice setting

Stage 3: Competent

This stage is characterized by conscious, deliberate planning based upon analysis and careful deliberation of situations. The competent nurse is able to identify priorities and manage his or her own work, and Benner suggests that the competent nurse can benefit at this stage from learning activities that centre on decision-making, planning and co-ordinating patient care

Stage 4: Proficient

Unlike the competent nurse, the proficient nurse is able to perceive situations holistically and can therefore home in directly on the most relevant aspects of a problem. According to Benner, proficient performance is based upon the use of maxims and is normally found in nurses who have worked within a specific area of nursing for several years. Inductive teaching strategies, such as case-studies, are most useful for nurses at this stage

Stage 5: Expert

This stage is characterized by a deep understanding and intuitive grasp of the total situation; the expert nurse develops a feel for situations and a vision of the possibilities in a given situation. Benner suggests that critical incident technique is a useful way of attempting to evaluate expert practice, but she considers that not all nurses are capable of becoming experts

BENNER, 1984

ASSESSMENT IN THE CLINICAL ENVIRONMENT

Within the UK, practice-placements constitute 50 per cent of the total hours of study on programmes for pre-registration nurse education, so work-based assessment is a major component of the overall assessment strategy (NMC, 2010). The sequencing and balancing between university and practice-based study should be planned to promote an integration of knowledge, attitudes and skills. The NMC (2010) standards for pre-registration nursing education specifies that practice-centred standards essential in nursing are directly linked to the wider goals of achieving clinical effectiveness within health care teams, with the ultimate aim of achieving high-quality health care. A further stipulation is that assuring the quality of nursing care is one of the fundamental underpinnings of clinical governance and must be addressed within all programmes of preparation. Clinical practice placements should provide opportunities to enable students to develop understanding of users' experiences of health care, and that the length of such placements should be sufficient to achieve the standards of proficiency required.

However, work-based assessment presents a challenge to nurse educators in terms of the validity and reliability of the assessment methods used to determine students' competence. Unlike classroom assessment, work-based assessment is not controlled entirely by academic staff from the institution; employers, supervisors and workers may all be involved to some extent in the context of the assessment. Clients, patients and relatives also form part of this context, and this presents a very different assessment scenario from, for example, essay assessments in the higher education institution.

Competence

The term 'competence' has a range of meanings according to the context within which it is discussed. The term has several dimensions such as task competence, job competence, functional competence, occupational competence, and vocational competence. Eraut (1998) suggests that common usage of the term applies to two kinds of situation. In the first, an implicit binary scale operates; i.e. an individual is either competent or not competent. This is the meaning of competence as used in competence-based assessment systems such as the National Vocational Qualifications (NVQ) framework. In the second situation, competence means 'adequate but not excellent', and this view is reflected in the expression 'mere competence', which indicates mediocrity.

The terms 'competence' and 'competency' are defined by the RCN (2005) and NMC (2008a) below:

> *'Competence is taken to represent the overall ability of an individual to perform effectively within a role. This includes the knowledge, skills, attitudes and experience to undertake a whole role to the standard expected of like persons within a similar environment.'*
>
> (RCN, 2005)

> *'A competency describes the skills and abilities to practise safely and effectively without the need for direct supervision. Competencies are achieved incrementally throughout periods of practice experience during a programme. At the end of the final period of practice experience or supervised practice it is the evidence of achievement of all competencies that enables sign-off mentors or practice teachers to decide whether proficiency has been achieved.'*
>
> (NMC, 2008a)

Assessment by observation

By far the most common, and valid, method of assessment for work-based learning is observation by the assessor. However, the mere presence of an observer is often sufficient to raise students' anxiety levels so that the quality of their performance is adversely affected. On the other hand, the presence of an observer can, in some circumstances, enhance performance. One of the weaknesses of assessment by observation is the subjectivity of the observer, so it is of paramount importance to have specific assessment criteria in the form of a checklist or rating scale that serves as a guide for the assessor and allows a second observer, when present, to assess the same aspects as the first.

Checklists

A checklist is simply a list of student behaviours associated with a particular aspect of practical work, with a space for the assessor to check or tick off whether or not that particular behaviour occurred. There is no means of indicating how well behaviour was carried out, and this limits the usefulness of checklists. A checklist normally contains only the desired behaviours, but it can include the behaviours that constitute poor performance. Table 11.11 shows an example of a checklist.

Categories or descriptions of nursing behaviours are notoriously difficult to write with any precision, as many interventions involve value judgements about quality and will vary between assessors.

There are many ways that a nurse can establish rapport with a patient and it may be that the only sure way of telling whether or not it has occurred is to ask the patient

TABLE 11.11 Checklist for assessment of 'admission of patients from waiting list'	
Assessor should place a tick or a cross in each box depending upon whether or not the behaviour was observed	
Prepares bed and locker area in advance	
Greets patient (and companion)	
Introduces him or herself	
Conducts patient to bed	
Ensures privacy whilst patient is unpacking	
Introduces patient to adjacent patients	
Shows patient the ward layout	
Allows ample opportunity for questions	
Gives only essential explanations initially	
Makes appointments for further explanation and discussion	
Employs appropriate procedures with regard to patient's property	

whether he or she felt that a rapport existed. Even then, the patient may be reluctant to say that rapport did not exist; the patient might feel this would be letting the nurse down, or that such a comment might influence the quality of care received for the rest of the hospital stay.

Rating scales

Rating scales provide an indication of the degree or amount of a particular characteristic and use either numbers or descriptions. Fearon (1998) describes a six-point rating scale used to indicate the level of achievement on a given competence. The scale extends from zero (novice) through to six (expert) and the following rating descriptions are used:

0. Cannot perform this activity satisfactorily to participate in the clinical environment.

1. Can perform this activity but not without constant supervision and some assistance.

2. Can perform this activity satisfactorily but requires some supervision and assistance.

3. Can perform this activity satisfactorily without assistance and/or supervision.

4. Can perform this activity satisfactorily without assistance and/or supervision with more than acceptable speed and quality of work.

5. Can perform this activity satisfactorily without assistance and/or supervision with more than acceptable speed and quality of work and with initiative and adaptability to special problem situations.

6. Can perform this activity satisfactorily without assistance and/or supervision with more than acceptable speed and quality, with initiative and adaptability and can lead others in performing this activity.

TABLE 11.12 Examples of descriptive rating-scales

A. Bipolar description

X	X applies	Marked tendency to X	Some tendency to X Y	Y applies	Y
Work shows a consistently high standard of attention to detail and finish					Work does not always show sufficient attention to detail and finish

B. Single-word category

Gives a full explanation to patient prior to commencing a procedure	Always	Usually	Occasionally	Never

C. Phrase description

Working in partnership with another nurse	Takes a leading role	Shares equal responsibility with partner	Allows partner to lead most of the time

Critical incident technique

One way of generating behavioural descriptions is critical incident technique or CIT (Flanagan, 1954). This involves the observation of competent practitioners as they practise, noting down any particular desirable or undesirable incidents. These particularly critical incidents are written down as descriptions of behaviours rather than as evaluative comments and then large numbers of these incidents are classified by experts to see if there is agreement about whether or not they represent particularly good or bad practice. The incidents that are agreed by the experts are then used to provide descriptions of effective or ineffective job performance and can be used as checklists for observational assessment.

SOME PROBLEMS WITH ASSESSMENT BY OBSERVATION

The assessor

Accurate assessment requires care and effort if it is to be objective, and there may be a lack of time and interest for this. An assessor may be biased in his or her perception of the performance, and this bias can take a number of forms. The 'halo' effect occurs when the assessor is influenced by the general characteristics of the student: if the assessor forms a good impression of the student, the latter is likely to be rated highly on the performance – and if the impression is unfavourable, then the reverse will occur. Another common factor is the central-tendency error, in which the rater gives everybody an average mark.

The generosity error occurs when the rater gives a higher score than is warranted; the explanation for this is the tendency to feel that our nursing role is to care for students, so this the assessor does unconsciously. In addition to the above factors, assessors will be subject to the same influences on their interpersonal perception as everyone else, namely past experience, motivation and personality.

The student

The main factors that influence assessment from the student's point of view are state of preparation, level of anxiety and the presence of others. The first point is self-evident, in that the student must have prepared adequately for the aspects that are being assessed. Anxiety has the effect of degrading decision-making, which could make a difference to an assessment in which decisions are required. The presence of others, i.e. the assessor, may have the effect termed diffusion of responsibility (Latané and Darley, 1968), which might account for a student's indecision in the assessment.

The methodology

The criteria chosen for the observation schedule will have implications for reliability and validity, and it is exceedingly difficult to formulate objective criteria for checklists or rating scales. The problem is that most criteria are fairly general; this may be necessary because it is impractical to state them in a more precise way.

These examples illustrate the dilemma referred to earlier about trying to make accurate descriptions of nursing behaviours. One solution is to give more detailed criteria; for example, 'Describes the action, dosage, route of administration, unwanted side effects and contraindications of a given drug, to the level indicated in the current edition of the *British National Formulary*.' This criterion is certainly more specific and does give the student an idea as to the kind of level of questioning to expect. However, it is rather lengthy, and one can imagine a checklist of skills required for a medicine round being stated in several pages of text.

Another problem is that, although such objectives are reasonably meaningful when applied to knowledge or motor skills, how do we go about writing criteria for the interactional elements of a drug round? We could try 'Displays warmth and friendliness towards patients during the drug round.' This is certainly an important aspect of nursing care, but the difficulty lies in the assessor's interpretation of the behaviours that are considered to be warm and friendly. At first glance it may seem fairly straightforward, until we begin to wonder what the borderline is between friendliness and familiarity and between humour and offence.

One way round the problem would be to adopt a stance advocated by Stenhouse (1975) who suggests that the teacher, as an expert in the field of nursing, can judge the quality of what is observed without having to define what that quality might consist of in advance. In other words, a competent teacher-practitioner can tell whether a student has done a satisfactory drug round or not without having to go through any kind of checklist. The problem arises when different assessors hold different views on competence, but perhaps it is naive to expect any real consensus in nursing, or in any other social-science endeavour, since there are so many variables to be considered. In the world of the arts, an art critic makes judgements about the merits of a work of art without having to specify in advance what the work of art should look like.

Many teachers are often asked by students: 'How should I approach this topic in order to get an A grade for my assignment?' All one can say in reply is, 'I can't tell you in advance what an A assignment will look like, but I will recognize one when I see it.'

ASSESSMENT OF ATTITUDES

The term 'attitude' is used in two senses within the nursing and teaching professions: in one sense it is used to describe someone who exhibits undesirable characteristics, as in 'he was giving me a lot of attitude', and, in another sense, it describes a human psychological phenomenon. The balance between university- and clinical-based education should be planned not only to promote integration of knowledge and skills but also to promote an integration of attitudes. The All Wales document for pre-registration nursing highlights that appropriate action should be taken if a student indicates unsatisfactory performance in terms of professional behaviour/attitude (WG, 2005). Consequently, consistent or repeated unsatisfactory professional attitude will result in the students' discontinuation from the course. Professional attitudes are assessed in terms of students' individual needs, communication and teamwork and rating scales are completed by both the student and mentor in clinical practice. A scoring system is employed between 1 (lowest) and 7 (highest) and students should achieve 3 or above in each criterion statement. A score below 18 will require discussion with the student's personal teacher and referral to a senior educational manager. An example of an assessment of professional attitudes in relation to teamwork is demonstrated in Table 11.13.

TABLE 11.13 Assessment of professional attitudes for team working						
Always waits to be told to do things			Looks for work and carries it out within own ability			
1	2	3	4	5	6	7
Reluctant to take responsibility			Prepared to take responsibility appropriate to stage within the course			
1	2	3	4	5	6	7
Works as an individual, shows no awareness of team responsibilities			Works well as a team member			
1	2	3	4	5	6	7
Needs supervision to see that work is being done			Can always be trusted to carry out allocated work			
1	2	3	4	5	6	7
Is unable to accept constructive criticism			Always prepared to accept constructive criticism			
1	2	3	4	5	6	7
Shows little interest in learning, e.g. never asks questions			Always well motivated to learn, e.g. asks questions regarding new experiences			
1	2	3	4	5	6	7

ADAPTED FROM WG, 2005

Attitudes as undesirable characteristics of an individual

Experienced practitioners and teachers can often 'feel' that a student has the wrong attitude towards aspects of nursing work; it may be exhibited in a general lack of enthusiasm in the workplace, or a manner that 'rubs up' colleagues in the wrong way. These characteristics are often difficult to pin down to specific incidences, and assessors are naturally cautious about commenting on a student's negative attitude, as the requirement for transparency in assessment decisions means that specific examples must be recorded. If a student's attitude gives an assessor cause for concern, it is important that additional opinions are sought from other professionals who have experience of the student.

Attitudes as a human psychological phenomenon

Attitudes are commonly described as having three components: a cognitive component or belief, an effective component or feeling, and a motor component or tendency to action. Attitudes predispose an individual to act in a certain way towards stimuli and are thus powerful influences on learning and behaviour. Some people may adopt an anti-smoking attitude; this would consist of a set of beliefs about smoking plus a set of related feelings of disgust, bafflement or aggression towards smokers. The third component is the action tendency, which would make the individual react to smokers in a typical way, probably avoidance or confrontation.

Measurement of attitudes

A note of caution is required here; the methods of assessing attitudes outlined below include a wide range of techniques, most of which require a qualified psychologist to administer and interpret.

Self-report

In this approach, the students are asked to write down their attitudes towards something, either anonymously or otherwise, depending on the degree of trust and the honesty of the respondent.

Published inventories

These are standardized scales for measuring attitudes to various things, such as attitudes towards college. They are more useful than home-made tests because they claim to have high validity and reliability, but they may not meet individual teachers' exact requirements.

Likert scaling

In this technique, a pool of items is devised to cover the attitude in question, and then a scale is drawn up that rates each item under five points, ranging from 'strongly agree' to 'strongly disagree'. These five points are scored from one to five, and the teacher can choose whether the high score of five is to mean a favourable or unfavourable attitude towards the statement in question. Once this has been decided, the inventory is given to respondents, who are asked to tick the appropriate response for each item, and then the total score is calculated. This score gives an indication of the respondent's attitude towards the thing in question: favourable, unfavourable or neutral. Table 11.14 shows an example of a Likert scale for attitude measurement.

TABLE 11.14 A Likert scale for attitude measurement					
	Strongly agree 5	Agree 4	Uncertain 3	Disagree 2	Strongly disagree 1
1. Nursing gives me a great deal of job satisfaction					
2. Academic nurses don't make good practical nurses at the bedside					
3. Enrolled nurses are the best bedside nurses					

The semantic differential

This kind of rating scale consists of a number of bi-polar rating scales, each with seven points between them. At either end of the scales there are adjectives that are the opposite of each other, such as black–white, and respondents are each required to select a point on the scale that they feel represents their feelings about the item in question.

Projective techniques

The most famous of these is the 'ink-blot' test, but others include the word-association test and the thematic apperception test (TAT). Projective techniques aim to reach behind the mask that people put up consciously or otherwise to prevent access to awareness. In the ink-blot test respondents are required to study patterns to see what they represent. In the word-association test, the respondent has to respond very rapidly to the experimenter's prompt words by saying a word that comes into his or her mind that is associated with the first word. In the TAT, the respondent is shown a picture and asked to make up a story about what he or she thinks is going on.

Review questions

1. What are the main differences between classroom and work-based learning?

2. What are the potential problems associated with work-based learning?

3. What is the purpose of educational audit?

4. What problems are associated with a mentor's 'failure to fail' an incompetent student?

5. What support mechanisms are available for students and qualified staff in the workplace?

6. What problems are there with validity and reliability with assessment in practice?

SUMMARY

■ Workplace settings in nursing and midwifery education provide the learning environment for a whole range of personnel, including those undertaking formal programmes and those receiving informal, and often spontaneous, teaching as part of their day-to-day practice.

■ The workplace does not simply provide an environment for learning the knowledge and skills required for practice, it also serves as a vehicle for pre-registration students' socialization into the profession of nursing or midwifery.

■ One of the major differences between classroom teaching and workplace-based teaching is that the latter is a much more public endeavour.

■ Within the workplace setting, roles and norms exert a significant influence.

■ Labelling involves classifying people who deviate from what is considered to be normal; the term deviance is used to indicate a negative social evaluation.

■ Qualified staff are a key factor influencing the learning environment in hospital placements.

■ Qualified staff should ensure that pre-registration students are treated with kindness and understanding and should try to show interest in them as people.

■ Qualified staff should be encouraged to act as supervisors, mentors, preceptors and assessors.

■ The process of mentorship facilitates learning opportunities, supervises and assesses students in the practice setting.

■ Terminology frequently used to describe a mentor includes teacher, supporter, coach, facilitator, assessor, role model and supervisor.

■ An important part of the learning process is experimentation, in which the student can try to apply concepts and principles in different ways.

■ Work-related stress has become a major issue for employers and employees, evidenced by the increasing numbers of claims for compensation arising out of work-induced, stress-related illness.

■ The impact of stress can be classified into two main categories: the effects of stress on students' performance in the workplace and the effects of stress on the health of students and staff in the workplace.

■ Educational audit is a process that ensures collaboration between higher education institutions and health care providers on an ongoing basis.

■ Practice placements are a vital component of the student nurse experience, so it is important that they reflect both the nature of the provision of care to meet health care needs and the demands of professional registration.

■ Clinical supervision is a formal process of professional support and learning.

References

Anforth, P. (1992) Mentors, not assessors. *Nurse Education Today* 12, 299–302

Armitage, P. and Burnard, P. (1991) Mentors or preceptors? Narrowing the theory-practice gap. *Nurse Education Today* 11: 225–229

Aston, L., Mallik, M., Day, C., Fraser, D., Cooper, M., Hall, C., Hallawell, R. and Narayanasamy, A. (2000) An exploration into the role of the teacher/lecturer in practice: findings from a case study in adult nursing. *Nurse Education Today* 20(3) 178–188

Benner, P. (1984) *From Novice to Expert: Excellence and Power in Clinical Nursing Practice*. California: Addison-Wesley

Bond, M. and Holland, S. (2010) *Skills of Clinical Supervision for Nurses: a Practical Guide for Supervisees, Clinical Supervisors and Managers* (2nd Edition). Maidenhead: McGraw-Hill

Brooks, N. and Moriarty, A. (2006) Development of a practice learning team in the clinical setting. *Nursing Standard* 20(33) 41–44

Brown, J., Stevens, J. and Kermode, S. (2012) Supporting student nurse professionalisation: The role of the clinical teacher. *Nurse Education Today* 32(5) 606–610

Burnard, P. (1990) The student experience: adult learning and mentorship revisited. *Nurse Education Today* 10: 349–354

Burnard, P., Edwards, D., Fothergill, A., Hannigan, B. and Coyle, D. (2000) Community mental health nurses in Wales: self-reported stressors and coping strategies. *Journal of Psychiatric and Mental Health Nursing* 7(6) 523–528

Burke, L. (1994) Preceptorship and post-registration nurse education. *Nurse Education Today* 14, 60–66

Camiah, S. (1998) Current educational reforms in nursing in the United Kingdom and their impact on the role of nursing lecturers in practice: a case study approach. *Nurse Education Today* 18(4) 368–379

Caplan, R. (1983) Person-environment fit: past, present and future. In Cooper C (Ed.) *Stress Research: Issues for the Eighties*. Chichester: Wiley

Carr, J., Walker, W., Carr, M. and Fulwood, D. (2012) Reflect for success: use of mentor recommendations to help failing students. *British Journal of Community Nursing* 17(5) 226–228

Carr, J., Heggarty, H., Carr, M., Fulwood, D., Goodwin, C., Walker, W. and Whittingham, K. (2010) Reflect for success: recommendations for mentors managing failing students. *British Journal of Community Nursing* 15(12) 594–596

Cassedy, P. (2010) *First Steps in Clinical Supervision: a Guide for Healthcare Professionals*. Maidenhead: McGraw-Hill

Chapple, M. and Aston, E.S. (2004) Practice learning teams: a partnership approach to supporting students' clinical learning. *Nurse Education in Practice* 4(2) 143–149

Clutterbuck, D. (1991) *Everyone needs a mentor: Fostering Talent at Work* (2nd Edition). London: Institute of Personnel and Development

Collington, V., Mallik, M., Doris, F. and Fraser, D. (2012) Supporting the midwifery practice-based curriculum: The role of the link lecturer. *Nurse Education Today* doi: 10.1016/j.nedt.2011.09.017

Cooper, J. (1999) Managing workplace stress in outpatient nursing. *Professional Nurse* 14(8) 540–543

Cooper, C. and Marshall, J. (1976) Occupational sources of stress. *Journal of Occupational Psychology* 49, 11–28

Darling, L. (1986) Cultivating minor mentors. *Nurse Educator* 11(4) 24–25

Davies, B.W., Neary, M. and Philips, R. (1994) Final report. *The practitioner-Teacher. A Study on the Introduction of Mentors in the Pre-Registration Nurse Education Programme in Wales.* Cardiff: UWCC, School of Education

DH (1993) *Vision for the future*. London: The Stationary Office

DH (1999) *Making a Difference: Strengthening the Nursing, Midwifery and Health Visiting Contribution to Health and Health Care*. London: The Stationary Office

Donovan, J. (1990) The concept and role of mentor. *Nurse Education Today* 10: 294–298

Dreyfus, S. and Dreyfus, H. (1980) A five-stage model of the mental activities involved in directed skill acquisition. Unpublished report supported by the Air Force Office of Scientific Research, University of California, Berkeley

Duffy, K. (2003) *Failing Students: a Qualitative Study of Factors that Influence the Decisions Regarding Assessment of Students' Competence in practice*. London: Nursing Midwifery Council

Duffy, K. and Hardicre, J. (2007) Supporting failing students in practice 1: assessment. Nursing Times 103(47) 28–29

ENB (1997) *Standards for Approval of Higher Education Institutions and Programmes*. London: English National Board for Nursing Midwifery and Health Visiting

ENB/DH (2001) *Placements in Focus: Guidance for Education in Practice for Health Care Professions*. London: English National Board/ Department of Health

Eraut, M. (1998) Concepts of competence. *Journal of Interprofessional Care* 12(2) 127–39

Fearon, M. (1998) Assessment and measurement of competence in practice. *Nursing Standard* 12(22) 43–7

Flanagan, J. (1954) The critical incident technique. *Psychological Bulletin* 51, 327–358

Fretwell, J. (1983) Creating a ward learning environment: the sister's role. *Nursing Times Occasional Papers* 79(34) 42–44

Friedman, M. and Rosenman, R.H. (1974) *Type A Behaviour and your Heart*. New York: Knopf

Gagné, R. (1985) *The Conditions of Learning and Theory of Instruction* (4TH Edition). New York: Holt, Rinehart and Winston

Gerrish, K. (1992) The nurse teacher's role in the practice setting. *Nurse Education Today* 12, 227–232

Gopee, N. (2010) *Practice Teaching in Healthcare*. London: Sage

Grant, P. and Quinn, F.M. (1998) Clinical supervision. In Quinn FM (Ed.) *Continuing Professional Development in Nursing: a Guide for Practitioners and Educators*. Cheltenham: Stanley Thornes

Gray, M.A. and Smith, L.N. (2000) The qualities of an effective mentor from the student nurse's perspective: findings from a longitudinal qualitative study. *Journal of Advanced Nursing* 32(6) 1542–1549

Healy, S. and Tyrrell, M. (2011) Stress in emergency departments: experiences of nurses and doctors. *Emergency Nurse* 19(4) 31–37

Hebb, D.O. (1972) *Textbook of psychology* (3rd Edition). Philadelphia: Saunders

Hughes, S.J. (2003) Student nurse theatre placements: the new curriculum. *British Journal of Perioperative Nursing* 13(9) 366–373

Hughes, S.J .(2004) The role of the link lecturer in the perioperative environment. *British Journal of Perioperative Nursing* 14(10) 458–462

Kennedy, J. (1999) An evaluation of non-verbal handover. *Professional Nurse* 14(6) 391–394

Latané, B. and Darley, J. (1968) Group inhibition of bystander intervention in emergencies. *Journal of Personality and Social Psychology* 10, 215–221

Lloyd-Jones, M., Walters, S. and Akehurst, R. (2001) The implications of contact with the mentor for pre-registration nursing and midwifery students. *Journal of Advanced Nursing* 35(2) 151–160

Maslin-Prothero, S.E. Owen, S. (2001) Enhancing your clinical links and credibility: the role of nurse lecturers and teachers in clinical practice. *Nurse Education in Practice* 1(4) 189–195

McGregor, A. (2007) Academic success, clinical failure: struggling practices of a failing student. *Journal of Nursing Education* 46(11) 504–511

McVicar, A. (2003) Workplace stress in nursing: a literature review. *Journal of Advanced Nursing* 44(6) 633–642

Meskell, P., Murphy, K. and Shaw, D. (2009) The clinical role of lecturers in nursing in Ireland: Perceptions from key stakeholder groups in nurse education on the role. *Nurse Education Today* 29(7) 784–790

Milne, D. (2009) *Evidence-Based Clinical Supervision: Principles and Practice*. London: Wiley-Blackwell

Morgan, R. (2005) Practice placements for students: a literature review. *Nursing Times* 101(30) 38–41

Morle, K.M.F. (1990) Mentorship - is it a case of the emperor's new clothes or a rose by any other name? *Nurse Education Today* 10(1) 66–69

Murphy, F.A. (2000) Collaborating with practitioners in teaching and research: a model for developing the role of the nurse lecturer in practice areas. *Journal of Advanced Nursing* 31(3) 704–714

Neary, M .(1994) Teaching practical skills in colleges. *Nursing Standard* 27: 35–38

Neary, M .(2000) *Teaching, Assessing and Evaluation for Clinical Competence: a Practical Guide for Practitioners and Teachers*. Cheltenham: Nelson Thornes

NMC (2008a) *Standards to Support Learning and Assessment in Practice*. London: Nursing Midwifery Council

NMC (2008b) The Code: *Standards of Conduct, Performance and Ethics for Nurses and Midwives*. London: Nursing Midwifery Council

NMC (2006) *A–Z Advice Sheet: Clinical Supervision*. London: Nursing Midwifery Council

NMC (2010) *Standards for Pre-Registration Nursing Education*. London: Nursing Midwifery Council

NMC (2011) *Quality Assurance Handbook*. London: Nursing Midwifery Council

Ogier, M. (1982) *An Ideal Sister*. London: RCN

Ogier, M. (1986) An 'ideal' sister – seven years on. *Nursing Times Occasional Papers* 82(5) 54–57

Orton, H. (1981) Ward learning climate and student nurse response. *Nursing Times Occasional Papers* **77**(17)

Ostell, A., Baverstock, S. and Wright, P. (1999) Interpersonal skills of managing emotion at work. *The Psychologist* 12(1) 30–34

Ousey, K. and Gallagher, P. (2010) The clinical credibility of nurse educators: Time the debate was put to rest. *Nurse Education Today* 30(7) 662–665

Pembrey S (1980) *The Ward Sister – Key to Care*. London: RCN

Price, L., Hastir, L., Duffy, K., Ness, V. and McCallum, J. (2011) Supporting students in clinical practice: Pre-registration nursing students' views on the role of the lecturer. *Nurse Education Today* 31, 780–784

Pulsford, D., Boit, K. and Owen, S. (2002) Are mentors ready to make a difference? A survey of mentors' attitudes towards nurse education. *Nurse Education Today* 22: 439–446

Ramage, C. (2004) Negotiating multiple roles: link teachers in clinical nursing practice. *Journal of Advanced Nursing* 45(3) 287–296

Rosenthal, R. and Jacobson, L. (1968) *Pygmalion in the Classroom*. New York: Holt, Rinehart and Winston

RCN (2005) *Guidance for Mentors of Nursing Students and Midwives: an RCN Toolkit*. London: Royal College of Nursing

Sayer, L. (2011) Strategies used by experienced versus novice practice teachers to enact their role with community nurse students. *Nurse Education Today* 31(6) 558–563

Selye, H. (1956) *The Stress of Life*. New York: McGraw Hill

Sherif, M. (1936) *The Psychology of Social Norms*. New York: Harper

Simpson, E. (1972) The classification of educational objectives in the psychomotor domain. *The Psychomotor Domain*, Vol. 3. Gryphon House, Washington, DC

Stenhouse, L. (1975) *An Introduction to Curriculum Research and Development*. London: Heinemann

Twentyman, M., Eaton, E. and Henderson, A. (2006) Enhancing support for nursing students in the clinical setting. *Nursing Times*, 102(14) 35–37

UKCC (1999) *Fitness for Practice: The UKCC Commission for Nursing and Midwifery Education*. London: United Kingdom Central Council for Nursing, Midwifery and Health Visiting

UKCC (2000) *Requirements for pre-registration nursing programmes*. London: United Kingdom Central Council for Nursing, Midwifery and Health Visiting

Watson, S. (2000) The support that mentors receive in the clinical setting. *Nurse Education Today* 20, 585–592

WG (2005) *Fitness for Practice All Wales Initiative: Assessment of Clinical Practice*. Cardiff: Welsh Assembly Government

Welsh, I. and Swann, C. (2002) Partners in learning: a guide to support and assessment in nurse education. Abingdon: Radcliffe Medical Press

White, E. (2009) Implementation of Clinical Supervision: educational preparation and subsequent diary accounts of the practicalities involved, from an Australian mental health nursing innovation. *Journal of Psychiatric and Mental Health Nursing* 16(10) 895–903

Further Reading

Cochrane, D., Palmer, J., Lindsay, G., Tolmie, E., Allan, D. and Currie, K. (2009) Formulating web-based educational needs assessment questionnaire from healthcare competencies. *Nurse Researcher* 16(2) 64–75

Duffy, K. and Hardicre, J. (2007) Supporting failing students in practice 2: management. Nursing Times 103(48) 28–29

Felton, A., Sheppard, F. and Stacey, G. (2012) Exposing the tensions of implementing supervision in pre-registration nurse education. Nurse Education in Practice 12(1) 36–40

Helyer, R. (2010) *The Work-Based Learning Student Handbook*. Basingstoke: Palgrave

Garnett, J., Costley, C. and Workman, B. (Eds) (2009) *Work Based Learning: Journeys to the Core of Higher Education*. Middlesex: Middlesex University Press

CHAPTER 12
INTERPROFESSIONAL EDUCATION

THE AIMS OF THIS CHAPTER ARE:

■ To highlight the key features of interprofessional education

■ To discuss interprofessional education within an historical perspective

■ To explain the drivers that underpin interprofessional education

■ To illustrate the main principles that are central to interprofessional education

Interprofessional education is a considerable subject area and one that is much explored in the literature. On that basis, this chapter seeks only to provide an overview of this important aspect of learning and teaching and discuss the key elements associated with it. For a more in-depth exploration, the reader is encouraged to refer to the reference and further reading section. It has long been established that professions that work together should learn together (UKCC, 1999) and that collaboration and co-operation across health care disciplines is fundamental to maintaining high-quality care. Interprofessional education (IPE) was introduced in health and social care 40 years ago in North America and Europe and was endorsed 20 years later by the World Health Organization (Barr, 2009). Barr (2009) cites the work of the World Health Organization and states that IPE can:

■ develop the ability to share knowledge and skills collaboratively;

■ enable students to become competent in teamwork;

■ decompartmentalise curricula;

■ integrate new skills and areas of knowledge;

■ enhance interprofessional communication;

■ generate new roles;

■ promote interprofessional research;

■ permit collective consideration of resource allocation according to need;

■ ensure consistency in curriculum design.

HISTORICAL PERSPECTIVE OF IPE

On behalf of the Department of Health, Barr (2007) outlined a 30-year historical account of interprofessional education in the UK from 1966 to 1996, which was supplemental to the 'creating an interprofessional workforce' document published by the Department of Health (DH, 2007). He grouped IPE initiatives in to three 'mutually reinforcing subsidiary movements': work-based, pre-qualifying and qualifying (Barr, 2007, p. 3). Barr (2007) reports on work-based IPE initiatives such as seminars and short courses that were typically isolated and small in scale and often 'one off' events.

The 1980s saw a growing interest in shared learning and a rolling programme of workshops were instigated. Barr (2007) describes how barriers between professions reduced as workshops became more prevalent and a unit of skilled and experienced facilitators was established. Such initiatives became less pre-occupied with interprofessional relationships, and more committed to service improvement and health promotion. Topics covered by the workshops included needs-led assessment and care planning, meeting the needs of service users and carers, working in partnership, cross-cultural communication, discharge planning and protecting vulnerable adults.

The end of the 1980s and early 1990s saw the introduction of multiprofessional courses in health and social care at Master's level, primarily aimed at nurses, social workers, physiotherapists and occupational therapists to compensate for limitations in their pre-registration education; and to complement practice experience with a grounding in the social sciences and research skills. Towards the end of the 1990's, interprofessional programmes at Master's level were fairly well established in post registration education particularly collaboration of the allied health professions.

Barr (2007) points out that 'medicine, dentistry and pharmacy have enjoyed a relatively secure and established status with no need for comparable educational movements, although lack of them may be one reason for their relative isolation from subsequent developments in IPE' (p. 8).

A joint working group was later established for IPE at preregistration and post registration level between students preparing for the Certificate in Social Service and the specialized mental handicap nursing register. Only two pre-registration programmes took off initially but neither survived major reforms in nurse and social work education, but two similar programmes, Project 2000 and the Diploma in Social Work, were later established linking the new qualifying systems (Barr, 2007). There were reports of shared learning in undergraduate studies across England but questions were raised as to whether such learning was truly interprofessional.

In the North of England, interprofessional education was introduced into pre-registration programmes for physiotherapists, radiographers, occupational therapists and chiropodists based on common skills and utilizing problem based learning methods. Additionally, meetings, seminars, joint home visits and a residential weekend were organised where students in general practice, nursing and social work on placement compared perspectives and explored ways to overcome barriers in their clinical practice.

In the South of England, some medical, nursing and physiotherapy students were required to spend approximately two weeks undertaking practice learning together in the department for older people. Games role-play and debates were IPE methods utilized in Scotland.

The Centre for the Advancement of Interprofessional Education later completed a survey of IPE in the UK and found 455 examples of IPE. Topics cover were life stages from maternity to palliative care, chronic illnesses, collaboration, primary care, counselling, disabilities, education and training, management, ethics and mental health (Barr, 2007).

Whilst it is generally recognized that IPE can never be more than part of an undergraduate programme (Barr, 2005), the Department of Health (2007) supports the view that IPE should not be a mere add on to a uniprofessional programme, but should be central to all programmes and be mandatory and assessed.

Whilst students of nursing, medicine and professions allied to health have different learning needs and levels of attainment, Saunders (1997) recognized that some curriculum content was common to all professions and therefore lends itself to multiprofessional-based learning.

Even though skills and content may be similar across professional healthcare programmes, there is generally limited interaction between students in each profession and few opportunities for faculty development in the area of IPE. According to Salfi and Solomon (2011), this lack of attention to IPE could lead to undervaluing or misinterpreting each profession's contributions, with the potential of impairing communication, collaboration and teamwork in the clinical environment. The popularity of interprofessional education as a means of preparing the workforce has challenged teams to rethink ways of learning and teaching in the clinical practice setting (Ridley, 2009).

DEFINING IPE

The importance of IPE has been well documented in the literature during the last decade and one of its key advocates is the Nursing Midwifery Council, as stipulated within the standards for preregistration nursing:

> '*Programme providers must ensure that students have the opportunity to learn with, and from other health and social care professionals in practice and academic settings in order to enhance the experiences of patients.*'
>
> (NMC, 2010, p. 75)

Defining the term 'interprofessional' has proved problematic for almost a decade, and there still does not appear to be a sound consensus of definition. Scholes and Vaughan (2001) believe that the terms interprofessional, multiprofessional, multidisciplinary and interdisciplinary are regularly used interchangeably without careful consideration as to their underpinning meanings. Scholes and Vaughan define interprofessional working as interactions between team members, whilst multiprofessional working involves a group of people from different health and social care professions who do not necessarily interact. The authors refer to multidisciplinary working as practitioners who share the same professional background but practise within different specialities.

Masterson (2001) also distinguishes between multiprofessional and interprofessional working: multiprofessional work is seen as a co-operative enterprise in which traditional forms and divisions of professional knowledge and authority are retained, whilst interprofessional work is seen as a willingness to share and to give up exclusive claims to specialized knowledge and authority if other professional groups can meet patient needs more efficiently and appropriately.

The Centre for the Advancement of Interprofessional Education (CAIPE) based in the UK endorses the term interprofessional education as used by Freeth *et al.* (2005a) to include all learning that takes places in academic and work based settings before and after qualification:

> *'Interprofessional Education occurs when two or more professions learn with, from and about each other to improve collaboration and the quality of care.'*
>
> (CAIPE, 2002)

The NMC offers the following similar definition:

> *'An interactive process of learning which is undertaken with students or registered professionals from a range of health and social care professions who learn with and from each other.'*
>
> (NMC, 2010)

DRIVING IPE FORWARD

The need for interprofessional education is driven by the recognition that the British healthcare system promotes effective interprofessional learning and collaboration with the aim of optimizing patient care and patient outcomes. In 2001, the Department of Health emphasized the need for core skills elements in learning programmes for all health care students, which would provide the basis for interprofessional learning, and has since been high on the health care agenda. The prevalence and scope of interprofessional education is highlighted by Gopee (2010) and suggests that it is beneficial in many ways. He also refers to a strong policy commitment to IPE in the UK in both pre-registration and post-registration programmes. Whilst IPE can present organisational challenges, it offers the opportunity for students to gain further insight in to the role of other professions in order to prepare them for effective joint working in clinical practice (DH, 2009).

In 2007, the Department of Health funded the development of a programme focusing on creating an interprofessional workforce (CIPW) for health and social care in England, in partnership with CAIPE and NHS South West. The CIPW Framework identifies examples of good practice in interprofessional education, learning, teaching and development and supports the development of an interprofessional workforce, which can collaborate to:

- Improve patient/service user safety and quality of care.
- Support integrated, holistic services for services users and carers.
- Enhance workforce capacity and improve overall system efficiency.

■ Reduce professional and organisational barriers to eliminate duplication and waste and foster innovation and improvement.

■ Improve job satisfaction.

More recently, the World Health Organization (WHO) recognized interprofessional collaboration in education and practice as an innovative strategy that will play a pivotal role in mitigating the global health workforce crisis by strengthening health systems and improving health outcomes. In 2010, they developed a framework for action on interprofessional education and collaborative practice (WHO, 2010), with the aim of providing strategies and ideas that will help health policy-makers implement the elements of interprofessional education and collaborative practice that will be most beneficial in their own area of practice.

After nearly 50 years of investigation, the World Health Organization acknowledges that there is sufficient evidence to indicate that effective interprofessional education enables effective collaborative practice and that this is a necessary step in preparing a 'collaborative practice-ready' health workforce that is better prepared to respond to local health needs. They define a 'collaborative practice-ready' health worker as one who has learned how to work in an interprofessional team and is competent to do so.

Although WHO (2010, p. 7) acknowledge that mechanisms that shape interprofessional education and collaborative practice are not the same in all health systems, health policy-makers are advised to utilize a range of mechanisms that are most applicable and appropriate to their own local or regional context. These include:

■ supportive management practices;

■ identifying and supporting champions;

■ the resolve to change the culture and attitudes of health workers;

■ a willingness to update, renew and revise existing curricula;

■ appropriate legislation that eliminates barriers to collaborative practice.

To capture interprofessional activities from a global perspective, the WHO Study Group on Interprofessional Education and Collaborative Practice conducted an international environmental scan in order to determine the current status of interprofessional education globally, identify best practices and highlight examples of successes, barriers and enabling factors in interprofessional education.

A total of 396 respondents from 42 countries responded to the survey and results noted that IPE occurs in many different countries and healthcare settings and involves students from a broad range of disciplines including nursing, midwifery, allied health, medicine and social work. Interestingly interprofessional education was found to be compulsory for the majority of respondents and that student engagement occurred mainly at undergraduate level. Additionally, it was reported that many educational and health policy benefits were experienced from IPE as identified below.

Educational benefits

■ Students have real world experience and insight.

■ Staff from a range of professions provide input into programme development.

■ Students learn about the work of other practitioners.

Health policy benefits

- Workplace practices and productivity are improved.
- Patient outcomes are improved.
- Staff morale is raised.
- Patient safety is improved.
- There is better access to health-care.

Collaborative practice was found to decrease patient complications, length of hospital stay, hospital admissions, clinical incidents and mortality; whereas in community mental health settings collaborative practice was found to increase patient and carer satisfaction, promote greater acceptance of treatment, reduce duration and cost of treatment, reduce the incidence of suicide, increase treatment for psychiatric disorders and reduce outpatient visits.

PRINCIPLES OF INTERPROFESSIONAL EDUCATION

Barr and Low (2011) outline principles of IPE in Figure 12.1 based on values, process and outcomes, which can be considered by those who are engaged in commissioning, designing, delivering and evaluating interprofessional education.

PLANNING INTERPROFESSIONAL EDUCATION INITIATIVES

The WHO (2010) emphasize that developing interprofessional education curricula is a complex process, and may involve staff from different faculties, work settings and locations; sustaining interprofessional education can be equally complex and requires:

- Supportive institutional policies and managerial commitment.
- Good communication among participants.
- Enthusiasm for the work being done.
- A shared vision and understanding of the benefits of introducing a new curriculum.
- A champion who is responsible for coordinating education activities, highlighting the benefits and identifying barriers to progress (Figure 12.2).

It can be a challenging experience to teach students how to learn about, with and from each other but careful preparation of instructors for their roles in developing, delivering and evaluating interprofessional education is essential. The WHO (2010) suggest that for interprofessional education to be successfully embedded in curricula, the early experiences of staff must be positive to ensure continued involvement and a willingness to further develop the curriculum based on student feedback.

FIGURE 12.1   Principles of IPE

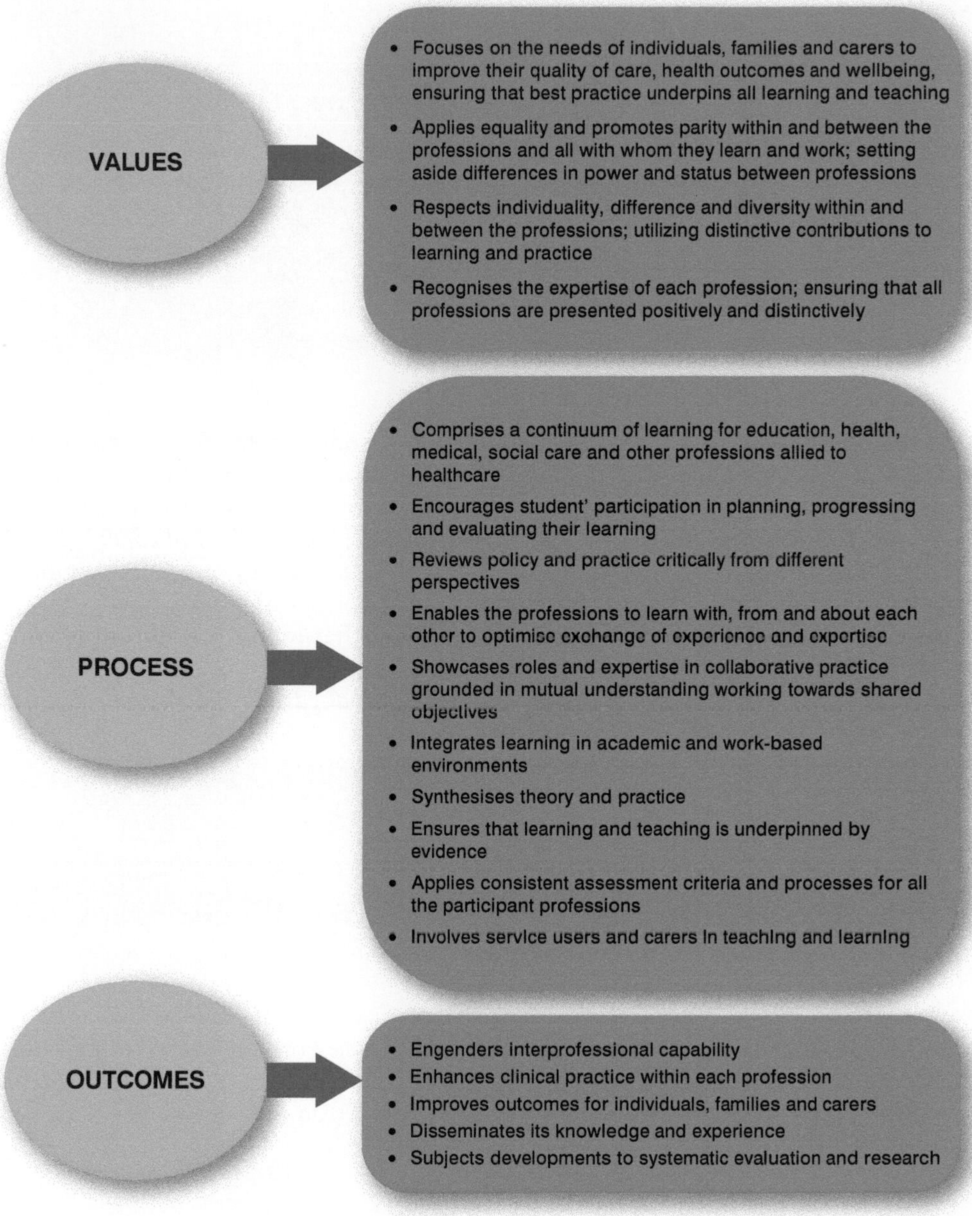

VALUES

- Focuses on the needs of individuals, families and carers to improve their quality of care, health outcomes and wellbeing, ensuring that best practice underpins all learning and teaching
- Applies equality and promotes parity within and between the professions and all with whom they learn and work; setting aside differences in power and status between professions
- Respects individuality, difference and diversity within and between the professions; utilizing distinctive contributions to learning and practice
- Recognises the expertise of each profession; ensuring that all professions are presented positively and distinctively

PROCESS

- Comprises a continuum of learning for education, health, medical, social care and other professions allied to healthcare
- Encourages student' participation in planning, progressing and evaluating their learning
- Reviews policy and practice critically from different perspectives
- Enables the professions to learn with, from and about each other to optimise exchange of experience and expertise
- Showcases roles and expertise in collaborative practice grounded in mutual understanding working towards shared objectives
- Integrates learning in academic and work-based environments
- Synthesises theory and practice
- Ensures that learning and teaching is underpinned by evidence
- Applies consistent assessment criteria and processes for all the participant professions
- Involves service users and carers in teaching and learning

OUTCOMES

- Engenders interprofessional capability
- Enhances clinical practice within each profession
- Improves outcomes for individuals, families and carers
- Disseminates its knowledge and experience
- Subjects developments to systematic evaluation and research

ADAPTED FROM BARR AND LOW, 2011

FIGURE 12.2 Barriers and benefits of IPE

Benefits of IPE

- Students gain real life experience and insight
- Fosters respect and students learn about the work of other professionals
- Learning and teaching input from a range of professions
- Students strengthen their professional identify
- Students gain knowledge and skills of complex conditions
- Breaks down professional barriers
- Opportunities for innovation and creativity

Barriers of IPE

- Complex, time consuming with rigid curricula
- Incompatible clinical skills and timetables
- College interest and expertise
- Professional rivalry and not all staff value IPE
- The threat of increased workload for lecturers

The literature describes that making attendance compulsory, developing flexible scheduling and innovative learning and teaching strategies can enhance effective interprofessional collaboration and enhance the development of clinical practice and service improvement (Bennett *et al.*, 2011; WHO, 2010; Hammick *et al.*, 2007; Freeth *et al.*, 2005a). The literature also advocates using the principles of adult learning in terms of problem-solving, appreciative enquiry and action learning sets, involvement of students, and utilizing learning and teaching methods that reflect real life experiences of students in order to ensure that interprofessional education is more effective (CAIPE, 2012; WHO, 2010; Bluteau and Jackson, 2009; Hean *et al.*, 2009; Freeth *et al.*, 2005a).

TEACHING TIP

To ensure interprofessional education make attendance compulsory and develop flexible scheduling and innovative learning and teaching strategies.

All interprofessional initiatives should utilise a framework for effective planning, implementation and evaluation purposes. Planning collaboratively with personnel from other health care professions is likely to have an impact on the success of the project (Figure 12.3).

Learning and teaching approaches to IPE

The theoretical underpinnings of IPE practice has progressed well over the last five years and is no longer the atheoretical discipline it has been accused of in the past (Hean *et al.*, 2009; Clark, 2006). Interprofessional education is grounded in adult learning theory (Barr, 2005) (see Chapter 2) so it is essential that educationalists and researchers underpin their practice with sound theoretical frameworks, first to improve the quality of their curriculum development and evaluative practice (Hean *et al.*, 2009).

FIGURE 12.3 Framework for planning IPE

What are the external/internal drivers influencing the development of this programme?

• *Consider professional standards, Government policies, clinical guidelines*

Who are your potential partners?

• *Other schools, colleges, universities, health boards*

What is the overall goal of this activity at the interdisciplinary and discipline-specific levels?

• *Consider attitudes, skills development, team building*

What are the opportuniites within the current learning context?

• *Consider the student population, education establishments, disciplines of students and level of training, the scheduling, length of programme*

What barriers/difficulties do you anticipate?

• *How might you overcome them?*

Who are the main people involved in designing this intervention ?

• *Consider their involvement, roles and responsibilites, building group trust and cohesiveness, ensuring sound communication, and resolving conflict*

What are the main aims of the IPE activity?

• *Consider IPE content*

What teaching methods and tools will you use to operationalise the aim?

• *Consider PBL, workshops, debate*

How will the IPE be evaluated?

• *Consider student satisfaction, learning and results*

How can IPE be sustained?

• *Consider the academic culture and climate, finance and human resources*

ADAPTED FROM OANDASAN AND REEVES, 2006

In 2005, Barr speculated on a theoretical framework for IPE that could be identified as follows:

> 'the application of principles of adult learning to interactive, group-based learning that relates collaborative learning to collaborative practice within a coherent rationale informed by understanding of interpersonal, group, inter-group, organizational and inter-organizational relations and processes of professionalization.'
>
> (p. 23)

IPE introduces a pedagogical approach with its own classification that aims to re-contextualize traditional and distinct bodies of professional knowledge into the knowledge of professional collaboration (Salfi and Solomon, 2011). This contemporary method of teaching can overcome the traditional ways of knowing about how to be a professional practitioner and has the potential to result in more effective relationships with other healthcare teams.

The power of PBL in professional and interprofessional learning is well testified, but relying on any one method is unnecessarily restrictive and may unintentionally devalue those drawn from other fields of education (Barr, 2009). Learning approaches frequently used in IPE have been recognized by a considerable number of authors, many of which are listed in Figure 12.4 (WHO, 2010; Barr, 2009; Bluteau and Jackson, 2009; Hean *et al.*, 2009; Pulman *et al.*, 2009; Payler *et al.*, 2008; Hammick *et al.*, 2007; Clarke, 2006; Barr, 2005; Barr *et al.*, 2005; Freeth *et al.*, 2005a; Cooper *et al.*, 2001).

FIGURE 12.4   Learning and teaching approaches to IPE

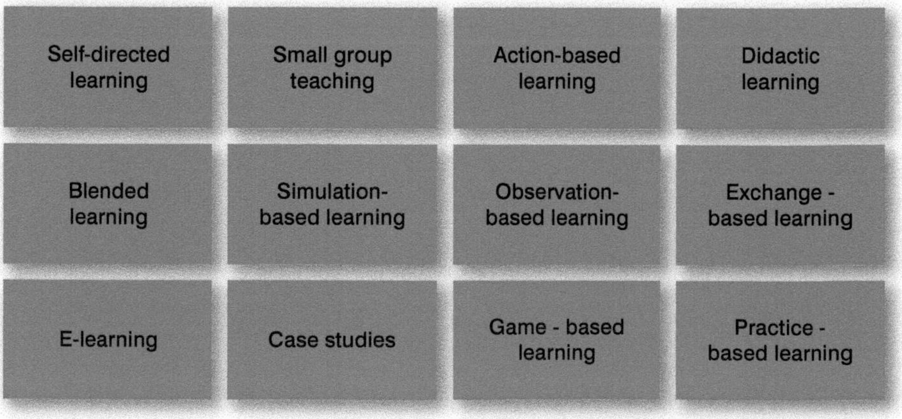

Self-directed learning	Small group teaching	Action-based learning	Didactic learning
Blended learning	Simulation-based learning	Observation-based learning	Exchange - based learning
E-learning	Case studies	Game - based learning	Practice - based learning

Clark (2006) discussed the purpose of IPE theory, which involves identifying a major concept to guide the development of programme structures and processes; specify learning objectives and effective methods for achieving them, suggesting appropriate roles for students in the educational process, and evaluating the outcome and impact of IPE programmes. The practicalities of theoretical underpinnings were revealed as essential, because it integrates and explains knowledge, predicts what is not yet known or observed, and helps to develop interventions to address problems. Following this, a number of potential theoretical approaches were highlighted:

- Cooperative, collaborative, or social learning; experiential learning.
- Epistemology and ontology of interdisciplinary inquiry.
- Cognitive and ethical student development.
- Reflection.

TEACHING TIP

Interact and collaborate with teachers in other healthcare professions, interprofessional working at this level will facilitate interprofessional education for your students.

Shared learning

Much of the literature on interprofessional teamwork has addressed increasing collaborative practices through interprofessional and shared-learning programmes. Scholes and Vaughan (2001) explain that, whilst this can occur in higher education settings, it also needs to centre on learning from one another in practice if it is to be most effective.

> 'Shared learning, also identified as multiprofessional learning refers to opportunities for learning between students from different fields of nursing, and between nursing students and those from other professions.'
>
> (NMC, 2010)

Traditionally each profession has provided a different approach to health care from a different educational base, and Masterson (2001) notes that professional education and assessment of competence has been traditionally uni-disciplinary. She also argues that service and role developments require a readiness to cross traditional boundaries not only in practice but also in education; as the work of health professionals continues to change, significant changes will also be required in the types of education and training that are provided. Following reforms in education and service, Masterson (2001) expects to see greater emphasis on work-based systems of learning, which aim to encourage the student to be an autonomous learner (Chapman, 2006) and mean moving away from a model in which the teacher imparts knowledge towards one where the teacher is a facilitator of learning (Chapman and Howkins, 2003).

Educators and policy makers have argued that interprofessional education breaks down some of the traditional and unhelpful demarcations between the health and social care professions, facilitates cultural change and promotes successful team working (Masterson, 2001). It is thought to provide opportunities for health and social care professionals to learn with, from and about each other, which, according to Masterson (2001), includes developing knowledge, skills and attitudes required for collaboration.

Shared learning for undergraduate students

Cooper *et al.* (2001) undertook a systematic review to explore the feasibility of introducing interdisciplinary education within undergraduate health professional programmes. As many authors have previously identified, including Scholes and Vaughan (2001) and Masterson (2001), Cooper *et al.* (2001) found that considerable conceptual confusion remains regarding clarification of the terms interprofessional and multiprofessional when associated with shared learning.

They discovered that the majority of reviews used two different professional student groups, nursing and medical students, although a variety of health professionals were involved at student and faculty level; some of these included students of:

- dentistry;
- physiotherapy;
- occupational therapy;
- operating theatre practice;
- dietetics;
- audiology;
- pharmacy;
- social work;
- psychology;
- speech therapy;
- chiropody.

Cooper *et al.* (2001) reported that the majority of educational interventions occurred in non-clinical environments using academic classrooms for teaching, although there was significant variation in both the quality and the type of educational interventions used. The authors point out that those educational interventions addressed a variety of topics and that a range of teaching methods were utilized. Cooper *et al.* (2001) categorized the outcomes of the review according to Kirkpatrick's (1967) classification system, using four stages of educational evaluation: reaction, learning, behaviour, results.

Within each of these categories, a number of themes emerged. The reaction category identified themes relating to evaluation of interprofessional learning experiences, timing of courses and teaching methods. Each of these themes demonstrated the value placed on the learning experience with early learning experiences enhancing participation in interdisciplinary activities. This category also identified that strong administrative support and experienced faculty members were required to plan and facilitate the course. However, Cooper *et al.* (2001) found that obstacles to the success of interprofessional learning were lack of time, scarce financial resources, assignments specific to each professional group, varying educational schedules and discipline-specific requirements for registration. Not surprisingly, the nursing students found the interprofessional experience more useful than the medical students did.

The behaviour category highlighted practical experiences valued by the students as enhancing interdisciplinary learning; whilst from the final category, results, it was discovered that student perceptions of actual co-operation and sharing of resources within and across professional boundaries had significantly improved after interdisciplinary learning. Although the literature identified a lack of educational or psychological theory guiding the development of interprofessional education, Cooper *et al.* (2001) suggest that the outcomes indicate the necessity of a fundamental approach to interprofessional education, one that integrates the best external evidence with educational expertise and students' choices. To conclude the systematic review, Cooper *et al.* (2001) stipulated that:

> '*as the need for interdisciplinary teamwork evolves with the increasing complex needs of service users and changes in the boundaries of professional practice, so the need for formal preparation for this way of working becomes more important. Professional education, as it stands, does not appear to equip practitioners with these skills. However, if teaching on an interdisciplinary basis is seen as an educational approach rather than a subject in itself, then it can only provide additional benefits which have been shown to relate to changes in knowledge, attitudes, skills and beliefs.*'

Although not exhaustive, health topics that lend themselves to IPE are featured in Figure 12.5.

FIGURE 12.5   Subjects suitable for interprofessional education

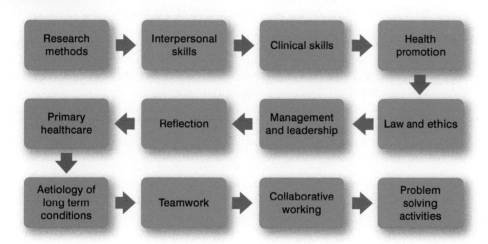

Distance and blended learning

With the development of e-learning, Harden (2009) reports that distance learning has increased in popularity in undergraduate, postgraduate and continuing education. He refers to the 'CRISIS' criteria for effective continuing education, which was developed in the context of distance learning and acknowledges the potential advantages inherent in independent learning:

- *Convenience* for the student in terms of pace, place and time.
- *Relevance* to the needs of the healthcare practitioner.
- *Individualization* to the needs of each student.
- *Self-assessment* by the student of his or her own competence.
- *Interest* in the programme and motivation of the student.
- *Systematic* coverage of the topic or theme for the programme.

Blended learning comprises a combination of multiple approaches to learning where learning is facilitated by a combination of different modes of delivery, models of teaching and styles of learning, and founded on transparent communication amongst all parties involved with a course. The use of 'blended' virtual and physical resources can include a combination of technology-based materials and face-to-face sessions used together to deliver instruction. A blended learning approach can also be adopted where e-learning is combined with face-to-face learning to create an integrated learning experience.

Evaluating interprofessional education initiatives

The value of evaluating interprofessional education initiatives is widely recognized. The main aim of evaluation is to identify strengths and areas for improvement for future IPE activities; particularly, evaluation can confirm the strengths of the initiative and highlight the challenges that need to be addressed (Gaudet *et al.*, 2007). Mackay (2004) cautions that many IPE initiatives are not evaluated rigorously and few are written up and published. He believes that to promote IPE evaluations it is valuable to have 'off the shelf' evaluation tools to reduce the time taken to develop and validate tools relevant to the IPE evaluation being undertaken; this could also prove to be a catalyst for publication.

The effectiveness of IPE can be evaluated in many ways. For example, Stone (2006) outlines that programme evaluation measures may focus on whether there is credible evidence that educational outcomes have been achieved or whether IPE leads to better interprofessional practice (IPP). The quality and specifically the validity of any IPE program evaluation can only be as good as its individual level measures, that is, the evidence that is collected to investigate what students learn during a program (or do not). Hence Stone (2006) believes that the purpose of evaluating a programme, module and/or learning activity is to:

- Ensure quality assurance and improvement.
- Develop and trial instruments, procedures and methods for evaluating IPE.
- Build on the existing knowledge base with respect to IPE.
- Provide evidence of the feasibility and effectiveness of IPE to help influence or underpin policy.

Trochim and Donnelly (2006) further highlight the purpose of evaluation:

- Celebration of success.
- Accountability for resources.
- Impact and efficiency assessment.
- Fine tuning.
- Informing decisions on the roll-out from pilot projects.
- Assessing transferability of programmes from one context to another.
- Learning about processes present in interprofessional education.

There are many different types of evaluations depending on the object being evaluated and the purpose of the evaluation (Table 12.1).

TABLE 12.1 Types of evaluation	
Needs assessment:	May be used to determine the need for the programme, justify it, and design it
Efficiency evaluation:	Compares the costs and benefits of the programme
Utilization evaluation:	Evaluates whether the evaluation itself was used. Many good evaluations are not used for reasons unrelated to the evaluation itself
Programme monitoring:	Determines whether the programme was implemented as planned and how it was delivered and received
Context evaluation:	Examines the political, social, financial, and other contexts for the programme and the evaluation
Formative evaluation:	Uses information collected during the early stages of the program to modify the later stages. The most encompassing difference is the one between evaluation during the development of a programme and those done on completion of the programme
Summative evaluation:	Determines whether the objectives of the programme were met

Perhaps the most important basic distinction in evaluation types is that between formative and summative evaluation (Trochim and Donnelly, 2006). Formative evaluations strengthen or improve the object being evaluated—they help form it by examining the delivery of the programme, the quality of its implementation, and the assessment of the organizational context, personnel, procedures and input.

In contrast, summative evaluations examine the outcomes of an object by describing what happens following the delivery of a programme; assessing whether the object can be said to have caused the outcome; determining the overall impact of the causal factor beyond only the immediate target outcomes; and, estimating the relative costs associated with the object (Solomon and Salfi, 2011; Freeth *et al.*, 2005b; Mackay, 2004; Kapborg and Fischbein, 2002; Luecht *et al.*, 1990).

Formative evaluation includes several evaluation types as identified by Trochim and Donnelly, 2006) below:

- *needs assessment* determines who needs the program, how great the need is, and what might work to meet the need;
- *evaluability assessment* determines whether an evaluation is feasible and how stakeholders can help shape its usefulness;
- *structured conceptualization* helps stakeholders define the program or technology, the target population, and the possible outcomes;
- *implementation evaluation* monitors the fidelity of the program or technology delivery;
- *process evaluation* investigates the process of delivering the program or technology, including alternative delivery procedures.

Summative evaluation can also be separated:

- *outcome evaluations* investigate whether the program or technology caused demonstrable effects on specifically defined target outcomes;
- *impact evaluation* is broader and assesses the overall or net effects — intended or unintended — of the program or technology as a whole;
- *cost-effectiveness and cost-benefit analysis* address questions of efficiency by standardizing outcomes in terms of their dollar costs and values;
- *secondary analysis* re-examines existing data to address new questions or use methods not previously employed;
- *meta-analysis* integrates the outcome estimates from multiple studies to arrive at an overall or summary judgement on an evaluation question.

Mackay (2004) also proposes that the availability of quality tolls can lead to a good quality IPE evaluation and refers to and several examples available that are designed to measure IPE outcomes. One such tool, a questionnaire by Leucht *et al.* (1990), was designed specifically to measure outcomes of interdisciplinary education, with good validity and reliability data and known as the Interdisciplinary Education Perception Scale. This is a questionnaire that comprises of 18 items and uses a Likert type response claiming to measure the professional perceptions of students exposed to interdisciplinary settings (Table 12.2). The instrument is designed to:

- clarify the four attitudes of professional competency and autonomy;
- identify perceived needs for professional co-operation;
- provide perception of actual co-operation and resource sharing within and across professions;
- allow understanding of the value and contributions of other professionals.

Trochim and Donnelly (2006) provide further advice when defining evaluation questions and suggest that consideration be given to the following questions:

- Who do I need to negotiate with?
- Who are the key stakeholders and what are their interests in this specific instance of interprofessional education?
- Who are the other evaluators and what are their interests and expertise?
- What resources are available for the evaluation?
- What is the allocated timeframe?
- What is the purpose and scope of evaluation?

Barr *et al.* (2004) point out that evaluation at one point in time does not give a complete picture of the education to be evaluated; but to achieve a complete picture, they further point out that several evaluations with different aims, using varying methods and tools, are required.

TABLE 12.2 Interprofessional education perception scale

Descriptor	Strongly Disagree	Moderately Disagree	Somewhat Disagree	Somewhat Agree	Moderately Agree	Strongly Agree
Individuals in my profession are well trained	1	2	3	4	5	6
Individuals in my professions are able to work closely with individuals from other professions	1	2	3	4	5	6
Individuals in my profession demonstrate considerable autonomy	1	2	3	4	5	6
Individuals in my profession need to cooperate with other professions	1	2	3	4	5	6
Individuals in my profession must depend on the work of other professions	1	2	3	4	5	6
Individuals in other professions think highly of my profession	1	2	3	4	5	6
Individuals in my profession trust each other's professional judgement	1	2	3	4	5	6
Individuals in my profession are competent	1	2	3	4	5	6
Individuals in other professions often seek the advice of my profession	1	2	3	4	5	6
Individuals in my profession have a higher status than people in other professions	1	2	3	4	5	6

Review questions

1. Why is interprofessional education important?

2. How can interprofessional education be embedded into the nursing curriculum?

3. What are the teaching approaches you can use for effective interprofessional education?

4. What are the outcomes of a successful interprofessional education programme?

SUMMARY

■ Professions that work together should learn together and that collaboration and co-operation across health care disciplines is fundamental to maintaining high-quality care.

■ The popularity of interprofessional education as a means of preparing the workforce has challenged teams to rethink ways of learning and teaching in the clinical practice setting.

■ Interprofessional education is an interactive process of learning which is undertaken with students or registered professionals from a range of health and social care professions who learn with and from each other.

■ Developing interprofessional education curricula and sustaining it is a complex process.

■ Interprofessional initiatives should utilize a framework for effective planning, implementation and evaluation purposes.

■ Interprofessional education is grounded in adult learning theory.

■ Shared learning refers to learning between students from different fields of nursing, and between nursing students and those from other professions.

■ Blended learning comprises a combination of multiple approaches to learning where learning is facilitated by a combination of different modes of delivery.

■ The main aim of evaluation is to identify strengths and areas for improvement for future IPE activities.

■ The quality and specifically the validity of any IPE program evaluation can only be as good as its individual level measures.

■ Formative evaluations strengthen or improve the object being evaluated.

■ Summative evaluations examine the outcomes of an object by describing what happens following the delivery of a programme.

References

Barr, H. (2005) *Interprofessional Education, Today, Yesterday and Tomorrow.* York: Higher Education Academy

Barr, H. (2007) *Interprofessional Education in the UK: Some Historical Perspectives - An Education and Training Framework for Health and Social Care in England.* London: The Stationary Office

Barr, H. (2009) Chapter 24 - Interprofessional education. In: Dent JA, Harden RM (Eds) *A Practical Guide for Medical Teachers* (3rd Edition). London: Churchill-Livingstone

Barr, H., Koppel, I., Reeves, S., Hammick, M. and Freeth, D.S. (2005) *Effective Interprofessional Education: Argument, Assumption and Evidence*. London: Wiley-Blackwell

Barr, H. and Low, H. (2011) Principles of interprofessional education. Available from: http://caipe.org.uk/resources/principles-of-interprofessional-education

Bennett, P.N., Gum, L., Lindeman, I., Lawn, S., McAllister, S., Richards, J., Kelton, M. and Ward, H. (2011) Faculty perceptions of interprofessional education. *Nurse Education Today* 31(6) 571–576

Bluteau, P. and Jackson, A. (Eds) (2009) *Interprofessional Education: Making it Happen*. London: Palgrave Macmillan

CAIPE (2002) Defining IPE. Available from: http://caipe.org.uk/resources

CAIPE (2012) *Interprofessional Education in Preregistration Courses*. Fareham: Centre for the Advancement of Interprofessional education

Chapman, L. (2006) Improving patient care through work-based learning. *Nursing Standard* 20(41) 41–45

Chapman, L. and Howkins, E. (2003) Work-based learning: making a difference in practice. *Nursing Standard* 17(34) 39–42

Clark, P.G. (2006) What would a theory of interprofessional education look like? Some suggestions for developing a theoretical framework for teamwork training. *Journal of Interprofessional Care* 20(6) 577–589

Cooper, H., Carlisle, C., Gibbs, T. and Watkins, C. (2001) Developing an evidence base for interdisciplinary learning: a systematic review. *Journal of Advanced Nursing* 35(2) 228–237

DH (2001) *Working Together, Learning Together: a Framework for Lifelong Learning for the NHS*. London: The Stationery Office

DH (2007) *Creating an Interprofessional Workforce: Report of the CIPW Working Group*. London: The Stationery Office

DH (2009) *Education Commissioning for Quality*. London: The Stationery Office

Freeth, D.S., Hammick, M., Reeves, S., Koppel, I. and Barr, H. (2005a) *Effective Interprofessional Education: Development, Delivery and Evaluation*. London: Wiley-Blackwell

Freeth, D., Reeves, S., Koppel, I., Hammick, M. and Barr, H. (2005b) *Evaluating Interprofessional Education in Health and Social Care: a Self-Help Guide*. York: Higher Education Academy

Gaudet, J., Shekter-Wolfson, L., Seaberg, R., Stulla, D., Cohoon, C., Kapelus, G., Goldman, J. and Reeves, S. (2007) Implementing and evaluating interprofessional education for health sciences students: early experiences from a Canadian college. *Journal of Interprofessional Care* 21(4): 459–461

Gopee, N. (2010) *Practice Teaching in Healthcare*. London: Sage

Hammick, M., Freeth, D., Koppel, I., Reeves, S. and Barr, H. (2007) A best evidence systematic review of interprofessional education: BEME Guide no. 9. *Medical Teacher* 29, 735–751

Harden, R.M. (2009) Chapter 21 - Independent learning. In: Dent JA, Harden RM (Eds) *A Practical Guide for Medical Teachers* (3rd Edition). London: Churchill-Livingstone

Hean, S., Craddock, D. and O'Halloran, C. (2009) Learning theories and interprofessional education: a user's guide. *Learning in Health and Social Care* 8(4) 250–262

Hopkins, D. (1989) *Evaluation for School Development*. Buckingham: Open University Press

Kapborg, I. and Fischbein, S. (2002) Using a model to evaluate nursing education and professional practise. *Nursing and Health Science* 4 25–31

Luecht, R.M., Madsen, M.K., Taugher, M.P. and Petterson, B.J. (1990) Assessing professional perceptions: design and validation of an Interdisciplinary Education Perception Scale. *Journal of Allied Health* 19(2) 181–191

Mackay, S. (2004) The role perception questionnaire (RPQ): a tool for assessing undergraduate students' perceptions of the role of other professions. *Journal of Interprofessional Care* 18(3) 289–302

Masterson, A. (2001) Cross-boundary working: a macro-political analysis of the impact on professional roles. *Journal of Clinical Nursing* 11(3) 331–339

NMC (2010) *Standards for Pre-Registration Nursing Education*. London: Nursing Midwifery Council

Oandasan, I. and Reeves, S. (2005) Key elements of interprofessional education. Part 2: Factors, processes and outcomes. *Journal of Interprofessional Care* May Supplement 1 39–48

Payler, J., Meyer, E. and Humphris, D. (2008) Pedagogy for interprofessional education: what do we know and how can we evaluate it? *Learning in Health and Social Care* 7(2) 64–78

Pulman, A., Scammell, J. and Martin, M. (2009) Enabling interprofessional education: The role of technology to enhance learning. *Nurse Education Today* 29(2) 232–239

Ridley, C.A. (2009) Team preparation. In: Smith A, McAskill H, Jack K (Eds) *Developing Advanced Skills in Practice Teaching*. Basingstoke: Palgrave Macmillan

Rossi, P.H., Lipsey, M.W. and Freeman, H.E. (2004) *Evaluation: A Systematic Approach* (7ᵗʰ Edition). London: Sage

Salfi, J. and Solomon, P. (2011) Chapter 17 - Interprofessional education. In: Bradshaw MJ, Lowenstein AJ (Eds) *Innovative Teaching Strategies in Nursing and Related Health Professions* (5ᵗʰ Edition). Boston: Jones and Bartlett

Saunders, D. (1997) Multi-professional learning. *Practice Nursing* 8(7) 3

Scholes, J. and Vaughan, B. (2001) Cross-boundary working: implications for the multiprofessional team. *Journal of Clinical Nursing* 11(3) 399–408

Stone, N. (2006) Evaluating interprofessional education: The tautological need for interdisciplinary approaches. *Journal of Interprofessional Care*. 20(3): 260–275

Trochim, W.M.K. and Donnelly, J.P. (2006) *Research Methods Knowledge Base* (2ⁿᵈ Edition). Buffalo: Atomic Dog Publishing

UKCC (1999) *Fitness for Practice: The UKCC Commission for Nursing and Midwifery Education*. London: United Kingdom Central Council for Nursing, Midwifery and Health Visiting

WHO (2010) *Framework for Action On Interprofessional Education and Collaborative Practice*. Geneva: World Health Organization

Further Reading

Mann, K., Sargeant, J. and Hill, T. (2009) Knowledge translation in interprofessional education: what difference does interprofessional education make to practice? *Learning in Health and Social Care* 8(3) 154–164

Patton, M.Q. (2011) *Developmental evaluation: applying complexity concepts to enhance innovation and use*. New York: The Guilford Press

Williams, B., McCook, F., Brown, T., Palmero, C., McKenna, L., Boyle, M., Scholes, R., French, J. and McCall, L. (2012) Are undergraduate healthcare students ready for interprofessional learning? A cross-sectional attitudinal study. *The Internet Journal of Allied Health Sciences and Practice* 10(3) 1–11

Williams, B., Brown, T., McCook, F., Boyle, M., Palermo, C., Molloy, A., McKenna, L., Scholes, R., French, J. and McCall, L. (2011) A pilot study evaluating an interprofessional education workshop for undergraduate health care students *Journal of Interprofessional Care* 25(3) 215–217

CHAPTER 13
TEACHING PATIENTS, CLIENTS AND THEIR FAMILIES

THE AIMS OF THIS CHAPTER ARE:

■ To explore the context of teaching patients, clients and families

■ To Identify effective strategies for teaching patients, clients and families

■ To illustrate examples of teaching patients, clients and their families in a range of contexts

KEY TERMS

Health promotion
Health education

Facilitation
Assessment of learning

Previously a range of 'consumers' of nurse education were identified, including pre-registration students, post-registration students, health care support workers, and practitioners receiving informal, spontaneous teaching as part of their day-to-day professional practice. However, there is another significant group of people who do not come under the banner of nurse education, but for whom teaching by nurses, midwives and specialist community public health nurses is an important part of their care, namely patients, clients and their families.

Each of the chapters in this book has focused on a particular aspect of nurse education, with a strong emphasis on a range of teaching strategies. These teaching strategies are essentially generic, in that they can be used for teaching adults in any educational setting, and with any subject matter, so this means that they should be equally applicable to the teaching of patients, clients and their families. However, there are some important differences between the teaching of students and that of patients, clients and families, and this chapter will explore a range of issues relating to the teaching of the latter group.

ISSUES AND CONTEXT

When considering the teaching of patients, clients and their families, it is useful to clarify what is actually meant by 'teaching'. Nurse–patient interactions involve a wide range of activities subsumed under the umbrella term 'communication', and these include social conversation, information-giving, asking and answering questions, explaining, and demonstrating skills. It is only social conversation that would not normally be included in the concept 'teaching', so it seems sensible to consider teaching as a fairly generic activity encompassing a variety of interaction activities that often overlap with the concept of 'professional practice'.

One of the similarities between teaching students and teaching patients, clients and their families is that both involve a wide range of contexts, including hospitals, clinics, GP surgeries, nursing homes, and patients'/clients' homes. Hence, the principles of teaching students in clinical and community settings will be useful as a basis for teaching patients, clients and their families.

Sources of professional guidance

The NMC Code governs the practice of every nurse, midwife and specialist community public health nurse. According to the standards of the Code, the practitioner is personally accountable for his or her own practice, which means that individual practitioners are answerable for their actions and omissions, regardless of advice or directions from another professional, and they must recognize and respect the role of patients and clients as partners in their care and the contribution they can make to it (NMC, 2008).

This applies to all aspects of care, including the teaching of patients, clients and their families, and it is interesting to compare it with the humanistic philosophy of adult education, which shares the same beliefs about openness, fostering independence and student involvement.

Furthermore, the NMC Code (NMC, 2008) identifies standards about information-giving that can be applied to the teaching of patients, clients and their families, including:

- the importance of giving clear information on which the patient/client can make informed choices;
- the importance of using language that is familiar to them, which should be accurate, truthful and presented in such as way as to make it easily understood; and
- the need to ensure that patients/clients understand the information they are given.

The NMC also says that:

- Written communication is as important as verbal communication.
- Patients/clients have a legal right to information about their condition, and registered practitioners providing care have a professional duty to provide such information.
- A patient/client who wants information is entitled to an honest answer, although selective information may be appropriate in rare circumstances.
- You always need to obtain the explicit consent of patients/clients before disclosing specific information.

This last point about confidentiality becomes an important issue when teaching members of a patient's/client's family about aspects of their loved one's care. The patient/client may not wish certain details to be disclosed to members of the family, so the teacher will need to ensure that confidentiality is maintained, and prepare his or her approach should the confidential issue be raised by the family.

Differences in assumptions underpinning the teaching of students and patients/clients

The teaching of students in nurse education is premised on a number of assumptions, and it is interesting to see if these assumptions are necessarily valid for the teaching of patients, clients and their families. Table 13.1 identifies a range of common assumptions that it would normally be appropriate to apply to nurse education students. Of course, there will be individual student variations within these categories, but we can expect that these assumptions would be more or less valid for most nurse education students. Similarly, the assumptions on the right-hand side would not be appropriate for all patients and clients, but they will be valid for many.

Table 13.1 is designed to ensure that nurse teachers clearly understand the assumptions that they make about the people whom they are teaching. It is all too easy to transfer the assumptions of student-teaching into the teaching of patients, clients and their families, and the consequences could be distressing for both parties. For example, a patient who is left with a colostomy following surgery will need a considerable amount of teaching in order to be able to cope with the condition after he or she is discharged home. However, the patient may well react with disgust when seeing the colostomy working for the first time and develop a negative attitude towards any kind of teaching about it. Unless the nurse is sensitive to the underlying reason for this attitude, he or she may feel that the patient is ungrateful for the teaching efforts.

TABLE 13.1 Contrasting assumptions about nurse education students, and patients, clients, and their families

Students	Patients/clients and their families
Highly motivated to learn	May not be motivated to learn, e.g. may be in denial, or depressed, etc.
Ready to learn in order to register and practice	May not be ready to learn, as could still be coming to terms with the condition
Attention span and memory normal	Attention span and memory may be low due to illness and fatigue
Understand the technical terminology of nursing and health	May need technical terms translating into everyday language
A high level of prior educational attainment	A wide range of prior educational attainment, with some patients, clients, or family members having learning difficulties
Expect formal assessment of learning	May be anxious or feel threatened by assessment of learning

This situation presents a challenge to the teaching skills of nursing staff, since they cannot simply ignore the situation; they must use tact and sensitivity to try to help the patient to come to terms with his or her condition.

TEACHING TIP

One possible strategy is to introduce the patient to another person who has successfully adapted to life with a colostomy, so that the problem can be viewed from a longer-term perspective, enabling the patient to begin the process of adaptation.

PATIENT-TEACHING AND HEALTH PROMOTION

One of the interesting issues about teaching patients, clients and their families is the extent to which such teaching can be considered to come under the umbrella term of health promotion. The concept of health can be viewed in various ways, as one individual's definition will differ from another's. Until a few years ago, health promotion used to be called health education although within the nursing literature, the terms seem to be used interchangeably; so it may be helpful to look at a number of definitions of each of these terms.

Scriven (2010) believes that the main aim of health promotion is 'for people to have more control over the health aspect of their lives, essentially to empower them'. Whilst Naidoo and Wills (2009) and Green and Tones (2010) share very similar views:

'Health promotion refers to a group of activities that help to reduce the incidence of disease and improve health and well-being.'

'Health promotion is the name given to all those activities which are intended to prevent disease and ill-health and to increase well-being in the community.'

These terms embrace a very wide range of activities including:

- environmental health, for example food hygiene, sewage, health and safety at work, housing;
- personal protection, for example seat-belt legislation, immunization;
- health education, for example safe-sex campaign, healthy lifestyle awareness;
- illness prevention, for example screening for cervical cancer, coronary heart disease;
- political activity, for example lobbying politicians for health legislation.

Government policy and health promotion

Health promotion takes place in a context of government health initiatives, and there are many government documents that are important in this context.

> *'Healthy lives, healthy people: our strategy for public health in England'*
>
> (Department of Health, 2010)

The white paper aims to create a wellness service and to strengthen national and local leadership. It outlines Government's commitment to protecting the population from serious health threats; helping people live longer, healthier and more fulfilling lives; and improving the health of the poorest, fastest. In terms of health and wellbeing, Government identifies an intention to enable local communities to improve health throughout people's lives and reduce inequalities by:

- Taking a sound approach to different stages of life and key transitions as opposed to tackling individual risk factors in isolation. Mental health is a key element of this with the imminent publication of a new mental health strategy.
- Providing all children with the best start in life with a commitment to reducing child poverty, by increasing the number of health visitor and refocusing Sure Start Children's Centres for those who need them.
- Making it pay to work by creating new jobs.
- Designing communities for active ageing and sustainability.
- Working collaboratively with business and voluntary sector through the Public Health Responsibility Deal with networks focusing on food, alcohol, physical activity, health at work and behaviour change.

> *'A healthier future: a twenty year vision for health and wellbeing in Northern Ireland 2005-2025'*
>
> (DHSSPSNI, 2004)

A Healthier Future is a strategy for health and wellbeing for the people of Northern Ireland. It presents a vision of how health and social services will develop in Northern Ireland between 2005 and 2025 and focuses the following themes:

- promoting health and wellbeing.
- protecting and caring for vulnerable people.
- delivering services effectively and efficiently with the available resources.
- establishing close working relationships between the people and organizations that influence health and wellbeing.
- improving quality.

A considerable amount of ill health is due to smoking, drug misuse, excessive alcohol intake, obesity and a lack of physical activity. One of the main aims of this policy is to improve the physical and mental health and social wellbeing of the people of Northern Ireland. Government acknowledge that people are living longer and enjoying better health in their old age and attribute this to the success of public health measures as well as new medical treatments.

Better health, better care: action plan (Scottish Government, 2007)

The Scottish Government believe that the health strategy 'Better health, better care' is a significant step towards making the people from Scotland healthier and identify three main components:

- Health improvement.
- Tackling health inequality.
- Improving the quality of health care.

Some of the aims of this strategy are to:

- Increase healthy life expectancy in Scotland.
- Break the link between early life adversity and adult disease.
- Reduce health inequalities, particularly in the most deprived communities.
- Reduce smoking, drug misuse and excessive alcohol consumption.
- Promote a balanced diet and healthy weight, and encourage physical activities across the lifespan.
- Promote the sexual health strategy. (Scottish Government, 2005).

Together for health (Welsh Government, 2011)

The Welsh Government highlight challenges that the NHS faces that include financial constraints and the growing number of people with long term conditions. Their vision for the future health of people in Wales is that more children will have a better start in life, the gap between those with best and worst health will narrow and people will be enjoying more years of high quality life. The Welsh Government aim to take a more active role in supporting children's health and, through annual health campaigns, tackle the biggest priorities facing public health:

- alcohol;
- obesity;
- smoking;
- teenage pregnancies;
- drug abuse.

In addition to the UK Governments' strategies for health and wellbeing, the National Institute of Health and Clinical Excellence (NICE) have developed a range of public health guidance around health promotion:

- Promoting physical activity for children and young people (NICE, 2009).
- Preventing harmful alcohol consumption (NICE, 2010).
- Preventing skin cancer (NICE, 2011).
- Promoting smoking cessation (NICE, 2008).
- Obesity guidance on the prevention, identification, assessment and management of overweight and obesity in adults and children (NICE, 2006).

STRATEGIES FOR TEACHING PATIENTS, CLIENTS AND THEIR FAMILIES

There are three main types of teaching intervention, depending on who does the initiating:

- *Nurse-initiated teaching* This has two components:
  - teaching that the nurse believes the patient requires, for example how to administer his or her own insulin; and
  - teaching that the nurse believes the family requires, for example how to carry out eczema dressings on their child, or how to deal with an elderly patient following discharge home. This is termed 'carer education'.
- *Patient/client-initiated teaching* This is teaching that the patient/client requests, for example 'How can I maintain my weight loss after I have been discharged home?'.
- *Family-initiated teaching* This is teaching that the family requests, for example 'How can my husband reduce the risk of a recurrence of his heart attack?'.

These categories can present dilemmas, such as whether the nurse should teach a seven-year-old directly, or teach the parent instead. In some circumstances, family members need to be taught how to supervise their loved ones in such activities as taking their medication, or ensuring that they do their exercises. This is not the only example of 'carer education'; some children are the sole carers for ill or disabled parents, and in this case the child needs to be taught how to care for the parent.

The issue of confidentiality is important in terms of teaching the carer; the nurse must ensure that the patient/client identifies what information may be divulged to the carer, and that information must remain confidential.

Planning for teaching

When teaching patients, clients and their families, the teaching can be either planned in advance, or spontaneous, depending upon the context. Advance planning is always preferred, since it helps to eliminate errors and omissions. However, even spontaneous teaching can incorporate an element of advance planning; the principles of planning for teaching are discussed in detail in Chapter 5.

Giving information and explanations to patients, clients and families

When giving information to patients, clients and their families, the following tips may be helpful:

- Ascertain what they already know about the subject or issue, and then build upon that knowledge (this is the principle of Ausubel's assimilation theory of meaningful learning, described in Chapter 3).

- Deal with the most important aspects of the topic or issue and add those of lesser importance later.

- In order to avoid overloading the patient/client/family with information, proceed in a sequence of small steps, checking their understanding at each step (this is based upon the work of Skinner described in Chapter 3).

- Avoid the use of medical terminology as far as possible, by translating it into layman's language.

- Observe learner(s) closely for signs of puzzlement and, if detected, help to clarify the point of concern.

- Observe learner(s) closely for signs of fatigue or distress and, if detected, discontinue the session.

- At the middle and end of the teaching session, ask the patient/client/relative to repeat back to you, in his or her own words, the gist of the information that you have given.

A detailed discussion of planning an explanation can be found in Chapter 5.

Using questioning with patients, clients and families

Questioning is an important strategy when teaching patients, clients and their families; types and purposes are outlined below:

- *Open questions* These are phrased so as to allow the patients to respond in any way they like and are particularly useful for ascertaining the patient's feelings.

- *Probing questions* These are used to follow up a previous response by the patient and allow the teacher to explore the response in more depth. However, their use requires skill and sensitivity on the part of the teacher, as this type of question may provoke anger or distress in some situations.

- *Factual questions* These are used to check whether patients have understood the teacher's points, and consist simply of asking them to repeat back certain items of information.

A detailed discussion of questioning can be found in Chapter 5.

One-to-one teaching with patients and clients

This is the most common form of teaching with patients and clients in hospital, and its success depends to a large extent on the interpersonal skills of the teacher. The pace of the teaching has to be judged carefully to ensure that the patient is keeping up with the information, and the atmosphere needs to be informal and relaxed. Patients with some conditions will tire easily, so the sessions should be kept short. Some of the advantages and disadvantages of one-to-one teaching are outlined in Table 13.2.

TABLE 13.2 Advantages and disadvantages of one-to-one patient teachings	
Advantages	**Disadvantages**
Patient gets the undivided attention of the teacher	Patient may feel under the spotlight
Rapport can be established more quickly with just one patient	Patient may miss the support of other patients
Progress can be quicker with just one patient	Patient may feel that the teaching is going too fast for him or her
Teacher can check learning more easily with just one patient	Patient may feel embarrassed if he or she does not learn quickly

Teaching small groups of patients and clients

Small-group teaching can be a very useful strategy for teaching patients, clients and their families, and it is used extensively in health promotion in the community. Group size is an important variable, and for maximum effect the number of patients should not be more than ten. Groups can be used for a variety of purposes, including collective exercise sessions, classes on a specific topic, discussions of health issues, and demonstrations of particular skills. Small-group teaching requires a good understanding of group dynamics on the part of the teacher, as well as skills of facilitation. The principles of small-group teaching are discussed in detail in Chapter 6.

Using information materials for teaching patients, clients and their families

Patient education has featured prominently in both the professional literature and policy communications recently and is widely recognized as an important component of the nurse's role (Black, 2009). Patient education is defined as 'any combination of learning experiences designed to improve patients 'behaviours' and is usually undertaken using a structured educational programme (one-to-one or group) and written material, for example, leaflets (Makelainen *et al.*, 2009). One-to-one patient education is the method most commonly used and has been reported to be effective because of its flexibility and the nurse's opportunity to focus on an individual patient's needs of information and support. Through education, patients can be made aware of their illness and potential treatment options and it is important to have an open and honest discussion with patients in order to assess their current knowledge and understanding and to identify their needs and expectations.

One of the important principles of teaching patients, clients and their families is the need to back up verbal teaching with written and pictorial materials. These enable patients to review the information that they have been taught, and to refer to it again and again as required. It is also useful to have the same topic explained in more than one way, as this aids understanding. Information materials are available in a wide range of formats, from the simple pen-and-paper format produced by the teacher, through to the very polished materials available from health promotion departments. Information materials are often designed locally by groups of professionals to meet a specific local need, but it is important to ensure that the design and layout is reader friendly and easy to understand.

Coulter *et al.* (1999) carried out an evaluation of patient information provided by a range of organizations including self-help groups, consumer and voluntary organizations, professional bodies, health authorities and NHS trusts, drug companies, and private health insurers. The materials covered ten common conditions or treatments and were reviewed by patients and academic specialists. The patients had personal experience of the health problems, and the academics were familiar with the research evidence. Focus groups were used to elicit the patients' opinions about the materials; the academic specialists used a checklist to review the materials independently, and the publishers of the materials were sent a questionnaire. The findings included the following:

- Very few of the materials met patients' information needs adequately.
- Very few publishers had researched patients' information needs before they started.
- Specialists identified many inaccuracies and misleading statements, the most common fault being an over-optimistic view that emphasized benefits and glossed over risks and side effects.
- Many materials were too basic and introductory, and some were too technical.
- Many materials contained advice that was not supported by evidence, with only two being based on systematic reviews.
- One-third of the materials did not include a publication date, and the specialist reviewers found that many were out of date.
- Focus-group participants preferred a facilitative rather than prescriptive style, the use of picture and diagrams, a clear structure and headings, and important sections highlighted.
- Participants preferred materials that actively engaged them, such as space to write down questions, or symptom diaries.

The authors offer the following checklist for the content of patient information materials:

- Use patients' questions as the starting point.
- Ensure that common concerns and misconceptions are addressed.
- Refer to all relevant treatment or management options.
- Include honest information about benefits and risks.
- Include quantitative information where possible.
- Include checklists and questions to ask the doctor.
- Include sources of further information.
- Use non-alarmist, non-patronizing language in active rather than passive voice.
- Design should be structured and concise with good illustrations.
- Be explicit about authorship and sponsorship.
- Include reference to sources and strengths of evidence.
- Include the publication date.

The provision of patient information is an important part of health care. Garner *et al.* (2012, p. 283) argue that all patient information leaflets require evaluation, and that evaluation to date has mostly been relating to readability. They propose a framework for evaluation that reflects the role of the patient perspective in communication and uses methods for evaluation based on simple linguistic principles.

The framework has three elements that give rise to three approaches to evaluation:

- *Readability of the text* This may be assessed using well established procedures.
- *Comprehensibility of the text and reader* This may be assessed using multiple-choice questions based on the lexical and semantic features of the text.
- *Communicative effectiveness of the reader* This explores the relationship between the emotional, cognitive and behaviour responses of the reader and the objectives of the information leaflet.

The Department of Health has certified a scheme for producers of health and social care information by means of an information standard quality mark. The organisations that meet the criteria of 'The Information Standard' will be entitled to place a quality mark on their information materials so people searching for health and social care information can easily identify it as coming from a reliable, trustworthy source.

Assessing patients, clients and their families' learning

Assessment of learning is an intrinsic component of the teaching process, regardless of the context in which the teaching takes place. However, when teaching patients, clients and their families, there are issues of which the teacher needs to be aware. When teaching students, there is an expectation on both sides that student learning will be assessed from time to time; indeed, the student has no choice in the matter. Patients, clients, and their families are not students, and this needs to be taken into account when considering how to assess their learning following a teaching session. The most common method of assessing patients' learning is oral questioning, and this can usually provide sufficient feedback on their understanding. It is less common to find that patients' understanding is assessed by written methods, although the use of novel materials such as a quiz, may well be quite acceptable to patients, clients and their families.

Assessment of learning is discussed in detail in Chapter 7.

EXAMPLES FROM THE LITERATURE

In this section, examples of teaching patients, clients and their families have been selected from the literature to illustrate patient, client and family education in a range of contexts.

Teaching patients with Parkinson's disease

Parkinson's disease is a progressive neurodegenerative disease that is usually diagnosed in older adults over the age of 70. It has also been known to be diagnosed in adults under the age of 40. O'Maley *et al.* (2005) point out that, although Parkinson's disease is not a curable disease, treatment should be aimed at symptom control to maintain quality of life. The authors explain how conducting education sessions, regarding the use and side effects of medications, is a strategy that can be used to assist in maintaining quality of life.

O'Maley *et al.* (2005) believe that a sense of empowerment over their symptoms is often experienced by patients through educational sessions. Such sessions for patients with Parkinson's disease are delivered by a variety of methods, including one-to-one and group sessions. Group teaching and individual teaching sessions were discussed earlier in this chapter; O'Maley *et al.* (2005) identify difficulties that are often encountered in both methods:

- Group teaching:
  - lack of privacy
  - individual needs are not always addressed.
- One-to-one teaching:
  - time is required
  - specialist knowledge is required by the nurse
  - patient-support mechanisms should be ongoing to optimize the session outcomes.

There are many special considerations that O'Maley *et al.* identify, which should be addressed when teaching patients with Parkinson's disease:

- The time of the session should be planned with the patient.
- The location should be convenient and accessible.
- Carers and/or family members should be invited to attend.
- The patient should be assessed for cognitive impairment as the delivery of information may need to be adapted.
- The session should be planned during a period when the patient is in the best physical condition.
- Facilities for the patient should be appropriate to his or her needs; for example, there should be enough room to move around, and seating and toileting needs should be recognized.
- Educational material should be readable and easily understood.

In order to promote interest and motivation, O'Maley *et al.* advocate that all information provided within an educational session should be relevant to the patient's needs and explained in a way that the patient is able to understand. Discussing problems that the patient experiences on a daily basis will develop an 'interactive exchange', thus ensuring that the patient's priorities are the main focus (O'Maley *et al.*, 2005).

The authors emphasize the importance of evaluation following a one-to-one or group teaching session, to justify the nursing time required to facilitate the educational process. They stress that evaluating a session should ensure that the patient with Parkinson's disease is:

- aware of his or her current medication;
- aware of the dosage and timing of medication;
- aware of potential side effects;
- able to utilize appropriate coping mechanisms to deal with the symptoms of the disease if the medication proves ineffective; and
- confident to deal with Parkinson's disease medication.

Teaching and support for the breastfeeding family

The early predictions of breastfeeding problems and ways in which such problems can be rectified were discussed by Dann (2004). Problems with breastfeeding are often encountered by new mothers but, according to Dann, it is all about a good latch at the breast. She highlights that 'the gold standard for proof of milk transfer from the breast to the infant is audible swallowing' but emphasizes that repetitive swallowing deep in the infant's throat ensures that milk is being received.

Problems with breastfeeding can include pain, bleeding and nipple tenderness, all of which are signs that the latch is incorrect; even though the infant might be swallowing milk. Dann (2004) notes that symptoms predictive of poor breastfeeding might include:

- increased infant weight loss;
- hypoglycaemia; and
- infrequent feeding.

When real problems are identified, Dann advocates a lactation consultation or lactation teaching session by a midwife, during which adequate education can be provided for the mother and her partner. Whilst acknowledging that new mothers are often tired and overwhelmed, Dann explains that the midwife should allow adequate time for the mother to 'move comfortably through the lactation assessment' and that both parents should be involved in this process to 'solidify each parent's role as caregiver of a new baby'.

The lactation session should preferably be conducted in a comfortable environment as information will be more forthcoming and also more easily absorbed by the mother. Dann suggests using a logical strategy to retrieve relevant information and solve problems during the session; this might entail:

- listening to the mother's opinion about the infants' feeding;
- carefully examining the infant and noting its current weight and the weight at birth, alertness, hydration, and presence of jaundice;
- examining the infant's tongue, palate and lingual frenulum;
- questioning the mother regarding breast changes during pregnancy and since delivery of the infant;
- noting the condition of the mother's breasts, checking for the presence/absence of milk and nipple damage;
- assessing the latch by listening for audible swallowing and observing the mother's comfort levels;
- assisting the mother to position the infant comfortably for feeding; and
- allowing adequate time for the mother to demonstrate feeding following instruction.

Dann (2004) advises that follow-up of the mother is essential to ensure that the problems are resolving and that written instructions to reinforce the teaching should be provided as a point of reference for the mother. Different strategies and methods to achieve effective latch-on are recommended by Dann, but she warns that 'no matter how perfect the mother's breastfeeding might be, the infant is primarily responsible for a good latch and effective breastfeeding.'

Supporting patients with psychosis

Houghton *et al.* (2006) focused on a two-day workshop for mental health workers, which aimed to assist workers to think about how they can work effectively with patients distressed by their psychotic experiences. The authors point out that the workshop:

'moves beyond the traditional narrow view of psychotic experiences as primarily a symptom of illness treated by medication, to a broader approach which incorporates many different ways of understanding psychosis.'

The authors also point out that the workshops encourage a fresh approach by prioritizing and including user-led sessions and involvement as a part of the training. The workshops were conducted over a two-day period and facilitated by service-users, user development workers and clinical psychologists. The content of the programme included:

- understanding psychosis using various frameworks;
- the contested nature of mental health;
- perspectives of professional, public and service users;
- the causes and cultural context of psychosis;
- fighting discrimination;
- psychological interventions;
- medication and approaches to promoting recovery.

Houghton *et al.* (2006) explain that much debate occurred over what participants felt was important in helping people who were distressed by their psychotic experiences. They identified a number of key themes that emerged from such discussions:

- *Being human* Participants discussed the importance of human qualities such as listening, being friendly, and that these are easily forgotten but are beneficial in assisting recovery.
- *The importance of small talk* Having conversations with service users using everyday language was therapeutic.
- *Shrinking the gap between us and them* This theme stressed the need to work collaboratively and to avoid distancing themselves from service-users.
- *The value of user views* The distressing experiences of service-user trainers were highlighted, and this was seen as inspirational by participants.
- *The importance of activities* Participating in meaningful activities was identified as an important role for mental health workers as these can assist with the recovery process.
- *Combating discrimination* Discrimination towards people with mental health difficulties was discussed by workers, who identified the importance of addressing discrimination in their own establishments and services.
- *Encouraging hope* The importance of encouraging a positive outlook was stressed within this theme by focusing on service-users' strengths as opposed to their difficulties.
- *The meaning of psychotic experiences* Workers were encouraged to talk to clients regarding their psychotic experiences.

By evaluating the workshops using qualitative and quantitative methods, Houghton *et al.* (2006) found that the majority of participants gained further understanding of service-user perspectives on psychosis; identified ways to work more effectively with psychotic patients; enhanced practice and developed greater awareness of psychological and social understanding of psychosis.

The facilitators also benefited from the workshops and believed that tremendous value can be gained from:

'providing a space where broader understandings of psychotic experiences and service receipt can be safely explored and shared; examples of good practice can be exchanged within a learning environment where all are encouraged to contribute.'

The authors maintain that collaboration between workers and service-users was well received by staff attending the programme as it helped to learn about service-user involvement in the training process and also assisted in creating conditions for a positive experience for the service-user. Houghton *et al.* (2006) emphasize that this approach to psychosis sees learning from the service-user as vital in informing and developing practice and that 'developing collaborative relationships encourages a positive and more hopeful outlook towards recovery'.

Teaching parents to administer subcutaneous methotrexate

Livermore (2003) highlighted problems within a paediatric rheumatology unit where families were experiencing difficulties accessing treatment by injection for their children on a weekly basis. She describes how a teaching package, specifically prepared for parents and children to administer methotrexate was designed and implemented.

The work of numerous authors is cited by Livermore (2003): collectively they identify that methotrexate is an agent of choice in the management of paediatric rheumatology; it has profound anti-inflammatory and immunosuppressive effects with minimal toxicity when given in small doses; and the drug can be administered orally, intramuscularly, intravenously or subcutaneously.

Livermore points out that whilst methotrexate is essentially a cytotoxic drug; it is classed as a 'dangerous drug', which is why families and their children are required to travel weekly to hospital to receive the drug. She highlights many disadvantages in respect of regular travel and its implications for families and children: time off work and school, long waiting times in hospital and increasing anxiety for children are just a few. However, the benefits of administering methotrexate at home are quite evident: increased flexibility, reduced disruption for the family and children, minimizing the 'sick role', and the development of a teaching pack for families.

Prior to the development of a teaching pack, certain issues had to be resolved with consideration to:

- safe storage, handling and disposal of sharps and methotrexate in the home environment;
- precautions that families would need to adhere to;
- advice for families such as teaching sessions and information booklets referring to pregnancy, breastfeeding and latex allergies;
- the design of a teaching package and the venue of teaching sessions; and
- the recommended injection technique to teach parents and children. (Livermore, 2003)

Livermore explains that a teaching package was developed by nursing staff, a paediatric consultant rheumatologist and a ward pharmacist and reviewed by a drugs and therapeutics committee. The teaching sessions were conducted over a three-week period and focused on subcutaneous injection technique using oranges for practice, the availability of methotrexate prescriptions locally, acquiring sharps and disposal of equipment, and administering methotrexate under supervision. Once the staff were satisfied with the parent's/child's competence, drug administration could then be undertaken at home, although the hospital could be contacted for further support and guidance if necessary.

Evaluation of the teaching package provided mostly positive responses with the main objective of enhancing family life achieved. Livermore (2003) concludes by emphasizing that:

> *'this programme has demonstrated how a simple intervention can have a major positive impact on family life; education and safety issues were paramount in the structuring of the programme and central to addressing the fears and concerns of everyone involved.'*

Teaching stoma patients to self-care

Black (2009) discusses how residential care homes can help older stoma patients to be self-caring but the successful rehabilitation of the stoma patient following discharge is dependent on a number of factors:

- Demonstrating knowledge and understanding of the type of stoma a patient has and whether it is temporary or permanent.
- Understanding the correct appliance for the patient to use but also being knowledgeable of alternative appliances if the original is found to be difficult or causes skin problems.
- Solving common problems that are sometimes seen after stoma surgery.
- Understanding ageing issues.

The role of the carer is seen as vital in supporting the patient perioperatively by being able to answer questions about their care effectively and Black (2009) believes that such carers should possess anatomical knowledge in order to be able to answer such questions, for example, where the disease is, and where the stoma will be located on the patient. She emphasizes the importance of the patient's practical and emotional needs postoperatively and advocates the involvement of a stoma care nurse to provide ongoing education and assist the patient and carer with key aspects of care provision.

Black (2009) recognizes that the involvement of carers in discharge preparation is well established but their training needs and understanding of stoma care are often overlooked; she explains that involvement of the stoma care nurse will ease the transition from hospital to residential care whilst providing continuity for the patient and the carer at the same time. Teaching should be straightforward and supported by aide memoires such as wipe-down picture cards for stomas, which may be positioned upright and numbered consecutively so a patient may follow the regime of appliance change effectively. Black (2010) advocates an eight point co-ordinated and progressive teaching approach that includes the following elements:

1. preparation of the equipment;
2. preparation of the patient (physically and psychologically);
3. removal of used appliance;
4. skin care;
5. skin protection;
6. preparation of new appliance;
7. application;
8. disposal of used appliance.

Black (2010) reminds us that time is essential for the patient to assimilate new skills and adjust to the change in for example bowel function; so patience and repetition is vital. Further guidelines for teaching stoma self-care for older patients are identified in Table 13.3.

TABLE 13.3   Guidelines for teaching stoma self-care
Make sure the patient has the correct glasses, hearing aid or other necessary appliance before starting
Identify pre-existing conditions or barriers that may affect learning
Plan multi-sensory teaching; for example, written material, demonstration, DVDs
Give adequate time for recovery after surgery
Motivate by stressing the importance of being independent
Choose the best time of day for teaching (older people may take longer to 'get going' in the mornings and thus to absorb new information)
Keep to a routine
Set realistic targets of attainment for each day, being aware that repetition of the same skill may be required for several days
If the patient uses a wheelchair, make sure there is enough room for patient and carer to manoeuvre in the washroom area
Repeat teaching procedures until the patient is confident

ADAPTED FROM BLACK, 2010

It is important to also evaluate patient learning and this can be undertaken as follows:

- *Questioning* – simple questioning of a patient's understanding of what they have learnt is usually enough to ascertain that learning has taken place.
- *Observation* – watch the patient undertake the task to ensure the correct technique is being maintained.

Expert Patient Programme Community Interest Company (EPP CIC)

The Expert Patients Programme (EPP) was originally piloted by the NHS in 2002–2004 and based on a long-term condition self-management programme. The expert patient programme community interest company (EPP CIC) was established in 2007 and provides and delivers courses aimed at helping people who are living with a long-term health condition to better manage their condition on a daily basis.

The courses are free and provide opportunities for people to learn new coping skills, with the aim of improving quality of life. The EPP recognizes that many long-term conditions can be disabling; these can include arthritis, chronic heart failure, chronic bronchitis, glaucoma and depression. There are some conditions that cause severe pain, such as endometriosis, arthritis and ulcerative colitis, whilst others can cause embarrassment, for example psoriasis, incontinence, stigma, epilepsy and schizophrenia.

Available to anyone aged 18 and over, the course is run over a six-week period, and patients are taught about managing their condition by dealing with pain and tiredness; coping with feelings of depression; healthy eating; relaxation techniques and exercise; communicating with family, friends, carers and health professionals; and planning for the future.

Patients are taught by trained tutors who also have a long-term health condition. Whilst the programme does not provide health information or treatment, it does aim to provide patients with the confidence to take responsibility for their own care, and share experiences with others. Whatever the long-term condition, the EPP can enable patients to be less dependent on health and social care programmes.

Looking after me

There is also an expert patient programme called 'Looking after me' and a 'young carer's programme', which is aimed at adults and young people who care for someone with a long-term condition or disability. This course is also free of charge and led by trained tutors who have experience of caring for a friend/relative. Although the course itself does not address topics such as carer's rights and benefits, and skills such as moving and lifting, this information is freely available on a resource table.

Teaching carers in the home environment

Following discharge from hospital, many patients require looking after by relatives or friends, and this is no easy task for people who are not professionally trained. Nurses need to be aware of the carer's need for information about the role, and also about the support services available in the community. It is very important when caring for relatives that carers look after their own health, as caring for sick or elderly relatives can be physically and emotionally exhausting.

Carers UK

Carers UK is a registered charity that operates in Scotland, Wales, Northern Ireland and England and was set up to improve the lives of carers. According to Carers UK, the term 'carer':

> *'is used to distinguish those who provide care for others on an unpaid basis ... from those who are paid (care workers, home helps and people employed by someone with a disability).'*
>
> (Carers UK, 2012)

Carers UK aim to improve the lives of carers by:

- transforming the understanding of caring so that carers are free from discrimination and are valued by society;
- mobilizing carers, decision-makers and the public to bring about the changes that make a real difference to carers' lives; and
- informing carers of their rights, the help available and how to challenge injustice so that they can lead fulfilled lives.

The Action for Carers and Employment (ACE) national partnership, which is led by Carers UK, works to support the inclusion of carers in training and work. Carers UK point out some staggering statistics regarding carers:

- One in eight adults are carers equating to approximately six million people
- Fifty-eight per cent of carers are women and 42 per cent are men.
- Over 1 million people care for more than one person.
- Carers save the economy £119 billion per year, an average of £18 473 per carer.

- Over 3 million people juggle care with work, but the demands of caring mean that one in five carers are forced to give up work altogether.
- People providing high levels of care are twice as likely to be permanently sick or disabled.
- 625 000 people suffer mental and physical ill health as a direct consequence of the stress and physical demands of caring.
- 1.25 million people provide over 50 hours of care per week.

The Carers (Equal Opportunities) Act 2004

The Carers (Equal Opportunities) Act was successfully passed through the House of Commons in 2004; currently it extends only to Wales and England. This Act amends many of the sections of the Carers (Recognition and Services) Act 1995 and the Disabled Children Act 2000. Its main aim is to provide carers with more choice to lead a more fulfilling life, by ensuring that:

- carers receive information about their rights;
- assessment of carers considers leisure, lifelong learning and work opportunities;
- local authorities enlist the help of housing, education and health in supporting carers.

Carers UK (2012) offer a number of broader benefits of the legislation:

- It increases the employability of carers who wish to return to work.
- More carers are able to juggle work and care and remain in employment.
- There are more opportunities for carers to access learning and training programmes.
- There are more opportunities for carers to lead a more fulfilled life.

Benefits of home care

Home care can confer benefits on both the carer and the relative being cared for (Voluntary Aid Societies, 1997):

1. For the relative:
   - Being cared for at home confers a degree of independence greater than that in an institutional environment.
   - A much more personal type of care can be given, as the carer knows the relative's personal likes and dislikes.
   - The home environment contains all the familiar home comforts, such as favourite books, pictures and furniture.

2. For the carer:
   - Providing support for the relative may enhance a closer relationship.
   - There is pride and satisfaction in knowing that the relative is receiving good care.
   - Looking after a relative develops organizational skills, such as prioritizing and time management.

Carers' needs

Carers need to be helped to recognize emotions, such as anger and guilt, and to identify the underlying reasons for them. They need also to be aware of the dangers of becoming isolated and lonely, and the need to make the effort to maintain friendships and outside activities. It is essential that carers are made aware of the wide range of care professionals with whom they may have contact, including GP, social services, community nurses, chiropodist, and ambulance personnel. They will also need information on the types of benefits available to home carers, including Invalid Care Allowance (ICA), and disability benefits for the relative.

The majority of registered charities now produce information booklets relating to specific diseases. For example, the Arthritis Research Campaign (ARC, 2011) has produced a comprehensive guide for caring for a person with arthritis. It explains how a carer can help someone with arthritis; what arthritis means; how to communicate effectively with the person who has arthritis; how to offer practical help with treatment, and how a carer can access further information, advice and support.

Caring for relatives dying at home

It is natural for most people who are terminally ill to want to be cared for at home, and whether or not this is feasible will depend upon the commitment of the carer, the suitability of the home environment, and the availability of local support services. Home care of a dying relative is very demanding, and the advice given earlier about the health of the carer is very much applicable here. In some areas, a care attendant is available to sit with the relative for a few hours; a 'tuck-in' service may be available to help get the relative to bed, or a live-in helper may be available to provide continuous care. Other short-term care is provided by day centres and day hospitals, and longer term care by nursing homes or hospices.

Carers will need to understand the needs of a dying person and the fears that they may have about dying, including fear of pain, suffocation or losing control over their lives (Mares, 2003). When the relative dies, the carer will need to know the procedures to follow, for example calling the doctor, contacting a funeral director, contacting other relatives and friends, contacting a minister of religion where appropriate, and registering the death with the Registrar of Births, Marriages and Deaths.

TEACHING PATIENTS, CLIENTS AND FAMILIES ABOUT SUPPORT GROUPS

Support groups or self-help groups are formed of people who join together because they have some life experience in common, such as problems with alcohol, experience of a particular disease or disability, or experience of bereavement or stillbirth. Support groups can help not only those who have experienced these events but their carers also. Contact details for support groups can be found in the local press, internet and in local libraries. The kinds of activities that take place in support groups include the following (be.Macmillan, 2012):

- provision of information, for example by producing or obtaining literature, by inviting speakers, by forming a library;
- social activities, for example dances, trips out;
- fund-raising;
- campaigning, for example publicity, lobbying health authorities;
- provision of services, for example volunteer helpers or physiotherapist.

Table 13.4 gives an indication of the range of support groups that exist in the community with accompanying websites.

TABLE 13.4 Support groups	
UK Patient Support	www.patient.co.uk
Alzheimer's Society	www.alzheimers.org.uk
National Autistic Society	www.autism.org.uk
Cancer Backup	www.cancerbackup.org.uk
Diabetes UK	www.diabetes.org.uk
Down's Syndrome Association	www.downs-syndrome.org.uk
KIDS (working for children with special needs)	www.kids.org.uk
MENCAP (Royal Society for Mentally Handicapped Children and Adults)	www.mencap.org.uk
Age Concern	www.ageconcern.org.uk
CRUSE (bereavement care)	www.crusebereavementcare.org.uk
SANDS (Stillbirth and Neonatal Death Society)	www.uk-sands.org
British Heart Foundation	www.bhf.org.uk
Carers UK	www.carersuk.org
ARC (Arthritis Research Campaign)	www.arc.org.uk
Pain Concern	www.painconcern.org.uk
Gender Trust	www.gendertrust.org.uk
Stroke Association	www.stroke.org.uk
APEC (Action on Pre-eclampsia)	www.apec.org.uk
Mental Health Foundation	www.mentalhealth.org.uk
Cystic Fibrosis Trust	www.cftrust.org.uk
Asthma UK	www.asthma.org.uk
Meningitis Research Foundation	www.meningitis.org
Gingerbread	www.gingerbread.org.uk
RNIB (Royal National Institute for the Blind)	www.rnib.org.uk
Spinal Injuries Association	www.spinal.co.uk
MIND	www.mind.org.uk
Parkinson's Disease Society	www.parkinsons.org.uk
OUCH UK (cluster headache support)	www.clusterheadaches.org.uk
Haemophilia Society	www.haemophilia.org.uk
Positively Women (HIV/AIDS support)	www.positivelywomen.org.uk
Terrence Higgins Trust	www.tht.org.uk
Leonard Cheshire (disabled care and support)	www.leonard-cheshire.org

Review questions

1. Describe some of the assumptions which the teaching of students in nurse education is premised on.

2. What is meant by the term 'health promotion'?

3. What are the three main types of teaching intervention strategy when teaching patients, clients and their families?

4. Outline some different types of questioning suitable to use when teaching patients, clients and their families.

5. Provide some examples of how written and pictorial materials can be used effectively to support verbal teaching when teaching patients, clients and their families.

SUMMARY

- Health education is a subcomponent of health promotion and is the term that is most appropriate for the teaching of patients, clients and their families.

- When teaching patients, clients and their families, the teaching can either be planned in advance or spontaneous, depending upon the context.

- Teaching in small groups can be a very useful strategy for working with patients, clients and their families, and it is used extensively in health promotion in the community.

- Patients, clients, and their families are not students, and this needs to be taken into account when considering how to assess their learning following a teaching session.

- Nurse-patient interactions involve a wide range of activities subsumed under the umbrella term 'communication'; these include social conversation, information-giving, asking and answering questions, explaining, and demonstrating skills.

- The concept of health can be viewed in various ways, as individuals will have different definitions of the term.

- One of the main aims of health promotion is for people to have more control over the health aspect of their lives; essentially it is to empower them.

- The NHS and local government have taken the lead together in promoting health by helping individuals make informed, healthy lifestyle choices and giving them the practical support and motivation to achieve this in a way that reflects the reality of their lives.

- When caring for relative, it is very important that carers look after their own health, as caring for sick or elderly relatives can be physically and emotionally exhausting.

References

ARC (2011) Caring for a person with arthritis: an information booklet
Available from: http://www.arthritisresearchuk.org/arthritis-information/arthritis-and-daily-life/caring-for-a-person-with-arthritis.aspx

Be.Macmillan (2012) Handbook for self-help and support groups. Available from: http://be.macmillan.org.uk/be/p-19960-handbook-for-self-help-and-support-groups.aspx

Black, P. (2009) Teaching stoma patients to self-care. *Nursing and Residential Care* 11(11) 546–9

Black, P. (2010) Teaching stoma patients the practical skills for self-care. British *Journal of Healthcare Assistants* 4(3) 132–135

Carers UK (2012) The voice of carers
Available from: https://web.carersuk.org/

Coulter, A., Entwistle, V. and Gilbert, D. (1999) Sharing decisions with patients: Is the information good enough? *British Medical Journal*, 318, 318–322

Dann, M.H. (2004) The lactation consult: problem-solving, teaching and support for the breastfeeding family. *Journal of Paediatric Health Care* 19(1), 12–16

DH (2010) *Healthy Lives, Healthy People: Our Strategy for Public Health in England*. London: The Stationery Office

DHSSPSNI (2004) *A Healthier Future: A Twenty Year Vision for Health and Wellbeing in Northern Ireland 2005–2025*. Belfast: Department of Health, Social Services, and Public Safety

Garner, M., Zhenye Ning, M.A. and Francis, J. (2012) A framework for the evaluation of patient information leaflets. *Health Expectations* 15(3) 283–294

Green, J. and Tones, K. (2010) *Health Promotion: Planning and Strategies* (2nd Edition). London: Sage

Houghton, P., Shaw, B., Hayward, M. and West, S. (2006) Psychosis revisited: taking a collaborative look at psychosis. *Mental Health Practice* 9(6) 40–43

Livermore, P. (2003) Teaching home administration of sub-cutaneous methotrexate. *Paediatric Nursing* 15(3) 28–32

Makelainen, P., Vehvilainen-Julkunen, K. and Pietila, A.M. (2009) Rheumatoid arthritis patient education: RA patients' experience. *Journal of Clinical Nursing* 18(14) 2058–2065

Mares, P. (2003) *Caring for Someone Who is Dying* (3rd Edition). London: Age Concern

Naidoo, J. and Wills, J. (2009) *Foundations for Health Promotion* (3rd Edition). London: Baillière Tindall, Elsevier

NICE (2006) *Obesity Guidance on the Prevention, Identification, Assessment and Management of Overweight and Obesity in Adults and Children*. London: National Institute for Health and Clinical Excellence

NICE (2008) *Smoking Cessation Services in Primary Care, Pharmacies, Local Authorities and Workplaces, Particularly for Manual Working Groups, Pregnant Women and Hard to Reach Communities*. London: National Institute for Health and Clinical Excellence

NICE (2009) *Promoting Physical Activity for Children and Young People*: guidance. London: National Institute for Health and Clinical Excellence

NICE (2010) *Alcohol Use Disorders - Preventing Harmful Drinking: Guidance*. London: National Institute for Health and Clinical Excellence

NICE (2011) *Skin Cancer Prevention: Information, Resources and Environmental Changes*. London: National Institute for Health and Clinical Excellence

NMC (2008) *The Code: Standards of Conduct, Performance and Ethics for Nurses and Midwives*. London: Nursing Midwifery Council

O'Maley, K., O'Sullivan, J., Wollin, J., Barras, M. and Brammer, J. (2005) Teaching people with Parkinson's disease about their medication. *Nursing Older People* 17(1) 14–20

SG (2007) *Better Health, Better Care: Action Plan*. Edinburgh: Scottish Government

Scriven, A. (2010) *Ewles and Simnett: Promoting Health a Practical Guide* (6th Edition). London: Baillière Tindall, Elsevier

WG (2011) *Together for Health*. Cardiff: Welsh Government

Further Reading

Boyde, M., Tuckett, A., Peters, R., Thompson, D., Turner, C. and Stewart, S. (2009) Learning for heart failure patients (The L-HF patient study). *Journal of Clinical Nursing* 18(14) 2030–2039

Friedli, L. and Parsonage, M. (2007) Mental health promotion: building an economic case. NIAMH: http://www.niamh.co.uk/

Macleod, S.H., Elliott, L. and Brown, R. (2011) What support can community mental health nurses deliver to carers of people diagnosed with schizophrenia? Findings from a review of the literature. *International Journal of Nursing Studies* 48(1) 100–120

Matthews, C. (2007) *The carer's handbook: essential information and support for all those in a caring role* (2nd Edition). Oxford: How To Books Ltd

Scottish Association for Mental Health (2006) *What's it worth? The social and economic costs of mental health problems in Scotland*. Glasgow: SAMH

PART FOUR
CONTINUING PROFESSIONAL EDUCATION

CHAPTER 14
PREPARATION FOR AN EDUCATION POST

THE AIMS OF THIS CHAPTER ARE:

- To outline the criteria for a nurse lecturer's post

- To highlight the challenges of becoming a new lecturer

- To characterize the contemporary roles associated with clinical/academic careers

- To discuss the development of probationary objectives

- To identify the process of achieving qualified teacher status

KEY TERM

Clinical academic

Teaching and learning are subjects that involve all qualified nurses. They live in a constantly learning profession where the teaching and facilitation of students features greatly in their day-to-day working life. The Nursing and Midwifery Council demands that registered nurses and midwives maintain their professional knowledge and competence by regularly taking part in learning activities (NMC, 2008a). They are also required to facilitate students of nursing and midwifery and others to develop their clinical competence. This chapter focuses on preparation for a nurse education post in higher education. The terms 'teacher' and 'lecturer' will be used interchangeably but will refer to the same position.

CRITERIA FOR NURSE LECTURER ROLE

Teaching in higher education is very demanding but, like nursing in clinical practice, it is also very rewarding. The mandatory requirements for a post in nurse education are:

- registration with the Nursing Midwifery Council;
- master's degree or working towards a PhD.

Having a postgraduate certificate in education is not always essential when applying for a teaching position, but it is essential to undertake study for this qualification once in a post. The NMC (2010) outlines that teachers who make a major contribution to educational programmes must hold appropriate experience and be working towards an NMC recordable teaching qualification.

Table 14.1 identifies many of the essential and desirable criteria for a nurse lecturer role; however, the list is not exhaustive, and criteria are set by each individual university.

MAKING THAT STEP INTO HIGHER EDUCATION

Making a step into higher education often proves difficult for many nurses in practice for a variety of reasons. They do not know if they will be suited to the environment or if the environment will be suited to them. We have already established that teaching in practice differs greatly from teaching in the education setting, but there are also many similarities. Working in a team to ensure the best possible learning environment for students is something with which all nurses are familiar, as is the necessity to maintain professional development. To address areas of uncertainty and to confirm the move is the right one, it might prove beneficial to follow some or all of the following:

- Make links with a School of Nursing and Midwifery through a link lecturer who will be able to provide details of pre- and post-registration programmes, teaching practice.
- In the absence of a link lecturer, consider making contact with the director or deputy director of a specific nursing branch that applies to you, i.e. adult, mental health, child branch (both these steps above can demonstrate your enthusiasm and sometimes strengthen any future application).
- Gain practical teaching experience in the classroom environment. It is sometimes more appropriate to start teaching post-registration students as these groups tend to be smaller in number, so less daunting for new teachers.
- Apply for a secondment to the school for 6–12 months; during this time you will be able to assess your suitability for the job.

Clinical academic careers

In 2005–2006, the four UK chief nursing officers established an agenda for updating nursing careers, which forms part of a working programme focusing on all the main health care professionals. The document, *Modernising Nursing Careers: Setting the Direction* (DH, 2006), highlighted that nursing and health care is changing and that, as a

TABLE 14.1   Criteria for a nurse lecturer role

Essential criteria

- Current registration with the Nursing Midwifery Council
- Master's degree or PhD in nursing or other related subject
- Clinical practice experience in a specific setting (*timescale differs enormously between five and ten years*)
- Excellent communication skills with the ability to present complex information to others using a range of media
- Effective teaching skills with the ability to deliver high-quality lectures and tutorials, develop own teaching materials and methods and meet defined learning objectives at both UG and PG level
- Specialist knowledge of key issues and debates in teaching, learning, curriculum planning, pedagogy and assessment
- Knowledge and understanding of current issues in nurse education
- An understanding of strategic issues in nursing and midwifery health care contexts
- An understanding of health and social care policies
- Ability to work autonomously and as part of a team
- Ability to adapt to change
- Ability to influence others
- Excellent organizational skills and ability to effectively manage and prioritize own workload
- Critical thinking skills
- IT skills

Desirable criteria

- Post-graduate certificate in education
- Experience of research
- Evidence of scholarly activity
- Evidence of presenting at conferences
- European Computer Driving Licence (ECDL)

dynamic profession, nursing is responsive and adapting to meet the needs of patients and the public. The four elements of a nurse's role link to the core and specific dimensions of the NHS knowledge and skills framework. These four elements are:

- practice;
- education, training and development;
- quality and service development;
- leadership, management and supervision.

The DH (2006) identified the following four key priority areas that must be addressed in order to create modern nursing careers that were fit for purpose:

- developing a competent and flexible nursing workforce;
- updating career pathways and career choices;
- preparing nurses to lead in a changed health-care system;
- modernizing the image of nursing and nursing careers.

The lack of a clinical academic careers framework for midwives and nurses was further highlighted in the 2007 report, *Developing the Best Research Professionals* (UKCRC, 2007) and examined the role of nurses as educators and researchers and the barriers that were preventing them from reaching their full potential in these areas. The report promoted a flexible career structure in order to develop the clinical academic role with a principal focus on the development of the research dimension of a clinical academic career. The UKCRC (2007) defines a clinical academic nurse as:

'A nurse who is engaged in both clinical and academic duties; the academic duties may include research, teaching or both. The substantive contract of employment may be held by an NHS Trust or a Higher Education Institution. Honorary contracts are held with the non-substantive host.'

The Council of Deans for Health (2012) define a clinical academic practitioner as follows:

'A clinical academic is a health professional who is engaged concurrently in both clinical and academic activities and can provide clinical leadership in the pursuit of excellent evidence based healthcare. Activities will include research, scholarship and clinical practice, and will also involve contribution to teaching. The substantive employment contract may be held with an NHS trust or other provider organization or a higher education institution. Honorary contracts are held with the non substantive host.'

The Department of Health (2012) points out that clinical-academic roles are usually joint appointments between a higher education institution and healthcare provider. One organization will hold the substantive contract of employment and will establish honorary contracts to facilitate working across organisational boundaries.

Clinical academic careers provide opportunities for clinically credible practitioners to contribute to the education of midwives and nurses. They are often a service user's first point of contact and are able to make a unique contribution to health research and scholarship. However, the literature has revealed that clinical nurses, who undergo role transition, are often inadequately prepared for the role in which they are entering (Dempsey, 2007).

Dempsey (2007) explored the experiences of six female clinical nurses from different universities in Ireland who have transitioned to the role of nurse lecturer. All participants were educated to Master's level and had 6–18 years clinical experience before they transitioned to the nurse lecturer role. Semi-structured interviews were conducted in order to gain an understanding of their experiences of role transition. Five themes emerged from the findings:

1. *Feelings experienced during the transition* A negative experience was reported by all participants during the early stages of their new role and highlighted feelings such as being frightened, daunted, fear of the unknown and experiencing a sense of loss for the clinical area. One participant explained the fear she felt when standing up in front of a class for the first time, which Dempsey (2007) attributes to low self-confidence in their ability to perform their role successfully. However, once the participants had been in post for a while and had gained some experience with the education environment and lecturing, their feelings of negativity towards the role transition changed to a positive one.

2. *Educational preparation for the role* Participants received educational preparation for the role of nurse lecturer and found this beneficial. However, they were not prepared for the administrative role of the lecturer, coupled with the lack of marking experience and inadequate practical application of theoretical content to classroom teaching.

3. *Actual and potential support structures available* One of the main sources of support that participants found in valuable was from their colleagues but a mentoring programme to guide and orientate new staff would have been beneficial. Participants further commented that to ease them in to the new role, they would have preferred to observe the role of a lecturer before transferring to higher education.

4. *Hindering factors of the role* Factors that affected participant's development or role transition included a lack of confidence in their teaching ability, being burdened with a heavy workload, inadequate amounts of time, and orientation to their new role and to the university structure; difficulties experienced in organizing workload and having to deal with a new found independence also hindered role development.

5. *The overall transition experience* Despite the above difficulties, participants revealed that their transition to higher education had been a challenging but positive experience and were happy to move to an academic environment.

Dempsey (2007) concludes that the negative feelings and experiences initially encountered by participants were found to decrease as they accepted and gained experience in their new role, and became more familiar with their work environment. She believed that nurse lecturers will understand more about the expectations and demands of university life, and develop necessary coping skills and de-stressors to face adverse conditions over time.

The experiences of nurses appointed as lecturers in higher education were investigated by Boyd and Lawley (2009) using semi-structured with nine participants. Previously experienced and successful nurses and clinical experts found themselves to be 'newcomers' and aware of their lower status within their higher education institution. Feelings similar to the study by Dempsey (2007) were revealed but additionally, feeling 'thrown in the deep end' regarding learning and teaching strategies and level of autonomy within higher education were identified.

Boyd and Lawley (2009) outlined that new lecturers 'expressed a view of the student audience as being focused on clinical practice and valuing credibility as a clinical nurse practitioner rather than for example credibility as a scholar or researcher'. Difficulties encountered during the initial stages of the new role are identified as follows:

- Prepping teaching sessions in terms of applying theory to clinical knowledge.
- Time management in general.
- Lack of ability to say 'no' to requests for their time.
- Assessment procedures and marking student work was reported as difficult and time-consuming.
- Awareness of organization and administration procedures were reported as challenging.
- Reluctance to keep asking for help because of colleagues' heavy workload.

The benefits during the initial stages of the new role are viewed as being clinically credible and the support received through structured mentoring. Overall, the new lecturers in nursing expressed a determination to develop and demonstrate competence in their new role by 'seeking credibility through knowing'. Boyd and Lawley (2009) point out that participants focused mainly on the student audience and on the context of teaching in order to establish this credibility. Their aim, at least in the early stages of their new role, was on establishing credibility as a nurse.

A qualitative, grounded theory study of 20 nurse lecturers by Schoening (2009) was used to describe the process of how nurses make the transition to the role of nurse educator. The findings of this study provide insight into the process that occurs during the transition from nurse to nurse educator. Schoening (2009) revealed the following reasons why clinical nurses choose an academic career:

- *Wanting to make a difference* Participants felt that nursing education was a way to make their mark on the profession by influencing the next generation.
- *Lifestyle* The demanding nature of clinical practice became difficult to manage for some participants especially for those with children and other family/external commitments. Therefore the academic environment provided an escape route from weekends, evenings, and holidays spent away from family. The enhanced autonomy enjoyed by university lecturers allowed the participants greater flexibility in how they spent their time.
- *The thing to do at the time* Some participants revealed that an education career was a natural progression following achievement of a higher degree.

However, during the course of the study some tensions with new role became apparent:

- *Stranger in a strange land* Whilst the participants entered nursing academia to teach and liked working with students, they had little understanding of what working in a university setting really entailed.
- *No roadmap* All participants felt as though they had not been adequately prepared or oriented to their new role as a nurse educator and the 'sink or swim' experience was unsettling and unexpected, which resonates with the findings of Boyd and Lawley (2009).
- *No guide* A considerable number of participants did not have a mentor to support them in the early stages of their new role. The main arrangements consisted of meeting with a named person at the beginning of the semester to 'learn the ropes'. None of the participants reported having regular observation or feedback on their teaching in the classroom or clinical setting and subsequently reported feeling as though they had no real direction.
- *Fear of failure* More than half of the participants described fear of failure in some way and their biggest fear was being unable to answer a student's question. Fear also arose from a lack of confidence and self-doubt in their teaching ability.

As participants became more familiar with the academic environment they described a strategy, '*Making it your own*' as a way of taking ownership of their new role. It was a process that allowed them to find their own teaching style and was accomplished by individualizing their classroom and clinical activities to fit that style. Eventually the participants described reaching a place where they felt 'comfortable' or 'effective' in their new role. Schoening (2009) describes embracing this new identity as feeling like a teacher, but not forgetting that they were a nurse.

Interestingly, gradual acceptance of responsibility in order to adapt to their new roles came only after two to three years; as they became more comfortable in their new role, they began to think that being a teacher is less about being an invincible authority and more about helping their students learn to think for themselves. Schoening (2009) stipulates that a big part of making this transition was letting go of the need to have all the answers.

Developing probationary objectives

Once employed in a school of nursing and midwifery, new lecturers are usually required to set objectives for the probationary period. The probationary period for new employers is set by each individual university, although the average timescale is three years. New lecturers are also offered a programme of induction activities and are assigned a mentor for the duration of their probationary period. The induction process will usually involve meeting colleagues, programme managers, and directorate managers in all nursing branches; it might also include attending education committees and examination boards and observing teaching strategies.

The mentor is usually a senior member of academic staff who is able to offer support and advice during the induction and probationary process. He or she will usually undertake regular probationary reviews in order to identify the new lecturer's progress. This can include how the new lecturer is progressing in terms of:

- knowledge and teaching skills;
- lesson planning;
- professional development needs;
- dealing with students;
- relationships with colleagues;
- coping with administration;
- maintaining work–life balance.

The mentor will also assist the new lecturer to develop probationary objectives. If there are doubts about performance, an extension of the probationary period may be offered. Table 14.2 offers a list of objectives that could be considered during the probationary period. They are again not exhaustive and will differ according to institution.

ACHIEVING QUALIFIED TEACHER STATUS

Completing the PGCE and achieving qualified teacher status is a mandatory requirement of all lecturers in higher education (NMC, 2008b). Although mandatory completion of a course can be de-motivating for some people, there are tremendous benefits to be gained from the PGCE course that are not experienced in other courses. Group-based learning enhances the learner's ability to compare and contrast the needs of self and others; group dynamics also facilitate the development of strategies for advancing the learning process and overcoming problems. A number of authors point out that learning in groups can often be much more fun than learning singly and can facilitate

TABLE 14.2 Objectives for the probationary period

Meet and greet

During the induction and probationary period, the new lecturer will:

- Meet with colleagues, programme managers and directorate managers and understand their roles and responsibilities
- Meet with library, IT and AVA staff and understand their role and the services they provide
- Meet research staff and learn about the school research strategy
- Join a research group that is of interest

Policies and protocols

During the induction and probationary period, the new lecturer will:

- Obtain and read the nursing curriculum
- Read and understand the university referencing guidelines and plagiarism document
- Observe the process of undergraduate interviews
- Attend recruitment and selection training
- Attend exam board for undergraduate and post-graduate courses
- Read and understand the policy relating to personal teacher arrangements
- Understand the process of supervizing distance learning students

Teaching

During the induction and probationary period, the new lecturer will:

- Aim to become a qualified teacher
- Develop a range of teaching strategies
- Gain experience of teaching in lecture theatres, classrooms and small group teaching
- Plan a series of teaching sessions
- Engage in teaching for pre-registration and post-registration students
- Utilize the peer review process for feedback on teaching strategies
- Determine the availability of IT support and access appropriate training, i.e. ECDL
- Assist in the facilitation of pre-registration and/or post-registration module(s)
- Participate in curriculum development
- Gain understanding of evaluation processes and stages of evaluation during academic courses
- Supervize pre and post-registration students
- Engage with first/second marking and moderation

(continued)

TABLE 14.2   Objectives for the probationary period (*continued*)

Clinical practice setting

During the induction and probationary period, the new lecturer will:

- Engage with the clinical educational audit process
- Identify allocated clinical link areas in practice
- Understand school guidelines on the role of the link lecturer
- Visit and make introductions to clinical link areas
- Observe the clinical educational audit process
- Complete clinical educational audit unsupervised

Professional development

During the induction and probationary period, the new lecturer will:

- Commence/complete PGCE
- Undertake Master's module for mentoring
- Attend annual/bi-annual mandatory training
- Access higher degree

the continuation of learning once the formal session has ended. They note that students may continue to discuss ideas outside the classroom and apply themselves creatively to group tasks. This is an aspect of the course that is particularly enjoyable and motivating, especially when a group is engaged in developing a teaching package for presentation to the rest of the students (Solomon, 2011; Armitage *et al.*, 2007; DeYoung, 2007; Reece and Walker, 2007)

It is always comforting to work and learn with people of the same educational and professional background, but it is also beneficial to learn and teach with people from differing professions. During the early stages of a teaching career, many lecturers wish that they had embarked on a PGCE course years before, as it could have eased progression into higher education. Although there is no hard-and-fast rule here, one of the main advantages of completing this course 'in post' is the opportunity to combine educational theory and practical teaching in tandem.

Whilst working in clinical practice, however, completing all aspects of the PGCE might on occasions prove difficult, particularly in relation to understanding and implementing relevant issues relating to classroom management, curriculum planning and development, and higher education professional education. Limited links with higher education institutions can hinder progress within the course, and students have often to rely on written information in academic journals and textbooks.

The PGCE provides an enhanced level of knowledge and understanding of the essential aspects of teaching and learning. The transition from being a nurse in the clinical environment to being a teacher within higher education has been described as a process of losing one's identity and entering a personal and professional limbo (MacNeil, 1997). Schoening (2009) and Dempsey (2007) argue that such nurses are removed from the clinical environment but are not yet part of the educational establishment, and the transition phase for a novice teacher can be fraught with anxiety and insecurity.

The interesting study by MacNeil (1997), 'From nurse to teacher', presents the views of teachers encountering their first experience of classroom teaching, regarding the preparation and support offered by colleagues. The majority of new teachers appeared to learn by copying how other teachers taught. MacNeil found that teaching sessions were delegated on the basis of which students were in college at a given time and that new teachers were allocated what they regarded as the 'less academic' teaching and the teaching sessions that nobody else wanted to teach.

PGCE curriculum

Whilst the PGCE provides both personal and professional development at postgraduate level, it also enables new teachers to respond effectively to the needs of adult learners in a rapidly changing higher education sector. The knowledge and understanding that is usually gained during a PGCE is clearly outlined by Neary (2002, p. 237) and relates to a number of realistic learning opportunities that a PGCE can provide (Table 14.3).

COMPILING A TEACHING PORTFOLIO OF EVIDENCE

All teachers learn to be increasingly competent throughout their teaching careers; however, many authors believe that the teacher in training needs to be more systematic about this process (Reece and Walker, 2007; Rogers, 2007). They discuss many ways in which new teachers can accomplish this; these revolve mainly around the generation of evidence to demonstrate competence in a particular aspect of teaching. To do this, the authors suggest the use of a paper-based or electronic portfolio to record accurately not only teaching and learning activities but also reflections on those activities. Neary (2002) identifies further ways to record learning, advocating the use of journal writing to facilitate appropriate attitudes towards practice and encourage a habit of reflective practice. One of the purposes of this, she adds, is to develop the meaning of experiences by relating unique experiences to established theory or by developing one's own theories. Another strategy for considering professional development needs involves keeping a record of professional experience in and outside the college and could take the form of a portfolio that includes a combination of examples of work with students and accounts of our development as teachers (NMC, 2011b). Table 14.4 identifies the possible components of a teaching portfolio that new lecturers may be required to complete as part of their induction process in an education role or as a requirement of a PGCE.

TABLE 14.3   The purpose of a PGCE

- Make the transition from being an expert in a subject to becoming a professional teacher in the post-16 sector
- Acquire knowledge of relevant educational theories of the post-16 system
- Study teaching within the social, psychological and philosophical context and relate these to changes in the provision of education and training
- Develop the strategies, tactics and expertise necessary for planning, preparing, implementing and evaluating teaching and learning activities for the subjects and classes that he or she is expected to teach
- Identify barriers faced by learners in education and training, such as disability, age, race and gender, and promote professional practice that recognizes and values diversity
- Respond to the educational needs of the older adolescent and adult learner
- Develop confidence in your professional knowledge; develop a personal philosophy of education and commitment to and critical awareness of professional situations
- Plan teaching and learning to meet students' needs
- Use a range of information technologies, media and methods to support teaching and promote learning
- Assess student learning and achievement, using an appropriate range of assessment techniques
- Practise and develop a range of professional skills and techniques associated with an effective teacher
- Demonstrate effectiveness as a specialist teacher and reflective practitioner
- Use opportunities to enhance own learning and develop skills and strategies to facilitate other people's learning
- Investigate an aspect of an organization and understand the context in which education takes place
- Be enterprising and respond positively and effectively to change
- Evaluate own effectiveness and students' learning experiences

ADAPTED FROM NEARY, 2002

TABLE 14.4   Components of a teaching portfolio

Section 1 *Background*	• Introduction to educational background of university/school • Student biography
Section 2 *Observed teaching activities*	• Lessons 1, 2, 3, 4, 5, 6, associated lesson plans, lesson handouts • Assessments of practical teaching • Reflections on teaching and assessment process

Section 3 *Teaching evaluations*	• Selection of evaluation forms • Students' comments
Section 4 *Teaching environment*	• Layout of typical classroom environment • Layout of typical lecture theatre environment
Section 5 *Presentations*	• Teaching appraisals • Approaches to teaching and learning
Section 6 *Assessment and marking*	• Formative and summative assessment guidelines • Assessment marking grids • Examples of students' assignments (consent required) • Examples of feedback marking sheets
Section 7 *Practical teaching*	• Record of practical teaching hours and those completed • Appraisal of personal performance
Section 8 *Reflections*	• Personal reflections on practical teaching experience
Section 9 *Probationary objectives*	• Probationary objectives and methods of achievement • Additional evidence to support teaching/learning activities
Section 10 *Teaching curriculum*	• Extract from pre/post-registration curriculum • Extract from post-registration module(s)

Research activity

Increasingly, many lecturers are active in the field of research and are also engaged in individual and departmental projects that enrich and enliven their teaching; they are producing publications and developing a profile in the research culture of the university (Hinchliff, 2009). There is increasing pressure for nurse lecturers in higher education to become research active, and the PGCE can often provide an ideal opportunity to engage for the first time in a small research project. This can increase motivation to incorporate research into teaching methods and can lead to further involvement in research activity within education.

BECOMING AN IDEAL TEACHER

During a nursing and teaching career the majority of new teachers will experience many conflicting feelings, which are both positive and negative in nature. Some aspire to the qualities of a good teacher, reflecting the standards set by the Nursing Midwifery Council, Quality Assurance Agency and Higher Education Academy. Teaching on a one-to-one basis in the clinical environment can enhance feelings of confidence, as the individual uses his or her experience and ability to share knowledge of the clinical and theoretical aspects of specialist practice.

There is probably no such thing as 'an ideal teacher' as we all have strengths and weaknesses both in and outside the classroom environment. However, Reece and Walker (2007) describe their version of an ideal teacher as having the following characteristics:

- expert in own subject;
- expert in the teaching role, well organized and prepared;
- confident and open to suggestions and other viewpoints;
- flexible and approachable, interested in students and spends time with them;
- fair, even-tempered, friendly with a sense of humour;
- knows the students as individuals including their strengths and weaknesses;
- communicates well in a variety of modes;
- leads well with an appropriate pace;
- flexible and willing to change approach;
- gives feedback within an appropriate timescale.

Additionally, it is often perceived that a good teacher, particularly in nurse education, is both educationally and clinically credible and able to make clear links between theory and practice; talks to students and not at them in a language that is easily understood; is adaptable to their situation and surroundings; is considerate of students' needs and disabilities and is not easily distracted by disruptions in a classroom or lecture theatre environment. Although realistically it is inconceivable to think that teachers can achieve all of the above qualities, aspiring to achieve the majority would possibly satisfy today's adult learners.

From the student's perspective, an effective teacher is one who gains credibility from competence, character and intention, is honest and fair, is qualified by experience to know what he or she is talking about and is concerned about the students as well as him- or herself (Burns, 1982). In contrast, Hinchliff (2009) believes that ineffective teacher behaviour is often linked to poor interpersonal skills and an inability to respect and value the student; although some people seem to be born teachers, the complexity of behaviours that constitute teaching can be learned and developed over time.

All nurse teachers will recall being a student, qualifying as a nurse and undertaking many courses of study throughout their career. Being in a classroom and observing the different mannerisms of teachers, teaching strategies, presentation skills, class control and imparting knowledge will provide awareness of what is considered to be a good or bad teacher. It becomes evident who is able to deliver the content of the lesson effectively; who is interesting to listen to; who is understandable; who captures and maintains attention; and who is not intimidating or threatening.

As a teacher in the clinical environment, there are now specific guidelines and quality standards to guide the teaching process (QAA, 2012; NMC, 2011a; NMC, 2008b). Teaching on a one-to-one basis, or to small groups of students, allows assessment of a student's understanding of a subject area and for that subject to be revisited, if necessary, to 'fill in' knowledge gaps. Teachers in practice are able to evaluate sessions almost immediately in order to improve on the quality of teaching and learning.

As a new nurse lecturer in a School of Nursing you will become more aware of what good teaching qualities should be and how you should teach and facilitate adult learners in higher education. Commencing a Post-graduate Certificate in Education (PGCE) is an ideal opportunity to learn the theories of teaching and learning and be able to apply them in practice instantaneously. In some respects, this is referred to as learning 'on the job'.

THE CHALLENGES OF BEING A NEW TEACHER

No teaching takes place in a vacuum, and Armitage *et al.* (2007) point out that, even though teaching may be seen as a partly planned and partly spontaneous act, approaches to it are shaped by a variety of factors. They also highlight that these factors include personal belief systems, our own experience of being taught, our personality and our theoretical understanding of the teaching and learning process. Learning to teach is a complex, challenging, and, often, a painful experience, and student teachers repeatedly begin their teaching experience with a simplistic and idealistic understanding of their role, the relationship that they may have with students and the nature of learning and teaching (Furlong and Maynard, 1995).

Having taught in the clinical environment, most teachers would report that it compares very little to the experiences and realities in a higher education establishment. Approaches to teaching in practice are seldom considered as it is often delivered on an ad hoc basis. During a teaching career, all teachers will experience conflicting feelings and emotions that are both negative and positive in nature. Concerns are often associated with teaching a large audience and controlling student behaviour.

Teaching a large group

A new nurse lecturer provides an example of an early teaching session in a university:

> '*During one of my first days of teaching, I was faced with students, admittedly a minority, who sat with their backs to me for most of the day, would not participate in group work, and one student who sat at the back of the classroom read a tabloid newspaper quite blatantly. I remember thinking "What do I do about this?" and feeling out of my depth as I wasn't prepared for this kind of behaviour. I experienced emotions such as anger and frustration and questioned their motives for learning in higher education? Why were they here? Do they want to learn? I was later informed that I should have asked the student(s) to leave the classroom and that I was entitled to do this. However, I was uncomfortable with this, probably because I was an inexperienced visiting teacher.*'

It is probably fair to say that the above example and the issues associated with it are often regarded as reality shocks and critical incidents. These experiences can be meaningful because they are completely new, and they can be both challenging and thought provoking; to some extent, they bring home the reality of teaching adults. Student behaviour can be poor at times, and their attitude is often fundamental in shaping a new teacher's approach to teaching. However it is the feeling of trepidation when facing a larger audience that new teachers are likely to remember most often, and finding a solution to managing such a situation is often difficult. Concern about facing a large audience can stay with a new teacher for some time, but there are some that might argue that this is not a recurring feature associated with teaching. In other words, a fear of teaching large audiences should disappear quite soon after starting a teaching career. Drawing on conversations with carefully selected colleagues can often prove reassuring, enabling the new teacher to come to an understanding of how to control anxiety and respond effectively.

TEACHING TIP

Remember that as a new teacher, or even as a teacher in training you are more knowledgeable and experienced than students. You should use this to your advantage to promote and encourage learning in students.

Whilst a new teacher might struggle to overcome anxieties related to teaching to a large audience, being anxious can be advantageous; it can help the new teacher to settle into the new role and function effectively, and it can also nourish and strengthen a new identity. It provides motivation to learn and assists conceptualization of how the different learning and teaching experiences can influence teaching strategies. Certain beliefs and expectations can either enhance or militate against teaching, and teachers will often need advice and guidance throughout their career to appreciate the complexities associated with education processes.

Student behaviour

An aspect of teaching that is not often considered is identified by Hinchliff (2009) who argues that, although teachers may be nervous when teaching, the students may also be afraid to speak. Welsh and Swann (2002) remind us not to underestimate the anxiety that students may experience in learning situations; they say that care should be taken to alleviate this and to assist students to progress towards their goals. A possible reason for students' reluctance to speak and ask questions in class is that increased group size could often be intimidating and adversely affect communication. Armitage *et al.* (2007) point out that students' behaviour can sometimes be irritating, disturbing or destructive, and that the kind of behaviour that is acceptable in the classroom will depend on the tolerance levels of the teacher on that particular day. They also point out that teachers frequently establish a set of rules and set boundaries for behaviour patterns but these rules are not often communicated because of their association with the teaching of children.

Furlong and Maynard (1995) believe that a disruptive class or student can be an extremely unsettling experience for student teachers and that classroom control is essentially related to confidence. On the other hand, Reece and Walker (2007) argue that careful planning of teaching sessions – ensuring that students are challenged appropriately with relevant learning activities – should increase motivation and reduce class disruption. They do, however, acknowledge that some post-16 students are not mature enough to respond fully to this situation; and, when this happens, they suggest the use of a protocol.

TEACHING TIP

Communicate your expectations to students and also endeavour to provide them with challenging and relevant learning activities to minimize bad behaviour in your classroom.

TABLE 14.5 Effective classroom management

Effective classroom management

- Set standards of behaviour and apply rules firmly and fairly
- Students often try to see 'how far they can go'. Be prepared for this and be consistent and clear
- All classes present problems; success is achieved by the way we deal with problems

In general:	In the classroom:
• Do not ignore misbehaviour • Avoid confrontation • Listen and establish facts • Judge only when all facts are known	• Know your subject • Begin on time and be prepared • Encourage student contributions • Keep students occupied and interested • Motivate all students

Try to avoid:	Try to:
• Humiliation – students resent it • Shouting – it diminishes you • Over-reacting – the problem will grow • Sarcasm – it damages you	• Use humour – it builds bridges • Listen – it earns respect • Be positive and build relationships • Be consistent and confident

ADAPTED FROM REESE AND WALKER, 2007

In order to learn about student behaviour and class control, it is often beneficial to observe an experienced lecturer in the teaching environment, perhaps someone who is known for their zero tolerance of bad behaviour. By using one's powers of observation and recognizing teaching practices that are congruent with one's own beliefs, strategies can slowly be adopted so that the new teacher is able to respond effectively when faced again with bad behaviour. Having expert help to develop these teaching skills is an important part of the learning process, and the coaching activities of peers who are prepared to share their knowledge and experiences should be valued.

PROFESSIONAL DEVELOPMENT FOR NEW TEACHERS

Some of the immediate professional development needs of new teachers are often covered in the university's development programme. Mandatory updates that include fire-hazard awareness, health and safety, equality and diversity, basic life support, and recruitment and selection of students are sometimes completed annually or bi-annually. There are also opportunities for academic staff to access a range of study days and short courses. Although many universities now insist that new lecturers already possess a Master's degree, if this is not the case, some might wish to pursue a higher degree such as a research degree, which can include a Master of Philosophy, MSc in Research Methods or PhD.

Other areas that would enhance personal growth and development in the nurse lecturer's role include further development of learning and teaching methods, for example experimenting with computer-assisted learning programmes and problem-based learning. There are also opportunities to satisfy clinical demand, with the development and introduction of distance learning packages which would be of enormous benefit to post-registration students.

CAREER PATHWAY

The majority of lecturers in higher education pursue their own areas of research and develop these in order to contribute to the wider research activities of their directorate/ university. Although the working hours tend to be around 35–37 per week, all lecturers are expected to work the hours necessary in order to fulfil their responsibilities; administrative activities can take up a significant amount of a lecturer's time as can marking assignments, so long working hours are not uncommon. During the first year, new lecturers tend to concentrate on developing their teaching and research skills and experience, and on mentoring undergraduate students. Early responsibility is common, and most lecturers are given a high degree of autonomy; but, as their career progresses, further responsibility can be given in teaching, research or administration and, in some cases, a combination of all three.

Promotion to more senior levels will depend on willingness to undertake further responsibility, professional development and continued research activity. Progression to senior posts may be possible for lecturers who build continually on this expertise; however, promotional prospects vary amongst higher education institutions. Senior posts can include:

- senior lecturer;
- reader;
- directorate manager;
- deputy head of school;
- head of school.

Having embarked on a career that ensures lifelong learning, teaching in higher education can provide what can only be described as 'emancipatory' feelings. It appears that the more a person does and achieves, the more that person is motivated and wants to progress, and teaching in higher education offers opportunities to equip students with the necessary tools for continued professional development and lifelong learning.

Review questions

1. Identify some of the essential and desirable criteria for a nurse lecturer role.

2. List some typical probationary objectives agreed between a new lecturer and their mentor.

3. Explain how the Council of Deans for Health (2012) defined a clinical academic practitioner.

4. What have Reece and Walker (2007) identified as some of the characteristics of an ideal teacher?

5. Explain some teaching techniques you might use to minimise bad behaviour in the classroom.

SUMMARY

- It is evident from the literature and with hindsight from personal experiences that planning for effective teaching and learning is the key to a teacher's success.

- In order to achieve this, accessing an appropriate course of study can ensure that novice teachers gain the necessary knowledge and understanding of educational processes to influence their teaching and learning strategies.

- The PGCE can assist new teachers to develop key skills and understanding of the theories of learning, curriculum planning, lesson planning, preparation of the learning environment, and the management of students in the classroom environment.

- Teaching and learning is about flexibility; it is about learning how to learn; it is about problem solving, and it is about growth.

References

Armitage, A., Bryant, R., Dunnill, R., Flanagan, K., Hayes, D., Hudson, A., Kent, J., Lawes, S. and Renwick, M. (2007) *Teaching and Training in Post-Compulsory Education* (3rd Edition). Maidenhead: Open University Press

Boyd, P. and Lawley, L. (2009) Becoming a lecturer in nurse education: the work-place learning of clinical experts as newcomers. *Learning in Health and Social Care* 8(4) 292–300

Burns, R. (1982) *Self-concept development and education*. London: Holt, Rinehart and Winston

Council of Deans of Health (2012) *Clinical Academic Careers for Nursing, Midwifery and the Allied Health Professions: Position Statement*. London: CoDH

DH (2006) *Modernising Nursing Careers: Setting the Direction*. London: The Stationery Office

DH (2012) *Developing the Role of the Clinical Academic Researcher in the Nursing, Midwifery and Allied Health Professions*. London: The Stationary Office

Dempsey, L.M. (2007) The experiences of Irish nurse lecturers role transition from clinician to educator. *International Journal of Nursing Education Scholarship* 4(1) 1–12

DeYoung, S. (2007) *Teaching Strategies for Nurse Educators* (2nd Edition). New Jersey: Pearson Prentice Hall

Furlong, J. and Maynard, T. (1995) *Mentoring Student Teachers: The Growth of Professional Knowledge*. London: Routledge

Hinchliff, S. (2009) *The Practitioner as Teacher* (3rd Edition). London: Churchill Livingstone

MacNeil, M. (1997) From nurse to teacher: recognising a status passage. *Journal of Advanced Nursing* 25 634–642

Neary, M. (2002) *Curriculum Studies in Post-Compulsory and Adult Education: A Teacher's and Student Teacher's Study Guide*. Cheltenham: Nelson Thornes

NMC (2008a) *The Code: Standards of Conduct, Performance and Ethics for Nurses and Midwives*. London: Nursing Midwifery Council

NMC (2008b) *Standards to Support Learning and Assessment in Practice*. London: Nursing Midwifery Council

NMC (2010) *Standards for Pre-Registration Nursing Education*. London: Nursing Midwifery Council

NMC (2011a) *Quality Assurance Handbook*. London: Nursing Midwifery Council

NMC (2011b) *The PREP Handbook*. London: Nursing Midwifery Council

QAA (2012) *Code of Practice for the Assurance of Academic Quality and Standards in Higher Education: B3: Learning and Teaching*. Gloucester: Quality Assurance Agency

Reece, I. and Walker, S. (2007) *Teaching, Training and Learning: A Practical Guide* (6th Edition). Sunderland: Business Education Publishers Limited

Rogers, J. (2007) *Adults Learning* (5th Edition). Maidenhead: Open University Press

Schoening, A.M. (2009) *The Journey From Bedside to Classroom: Making the Transition From Nurse to Nurse Educator*. Lincoln: University of Nebraska

Solomon, P. (2011) Problem based learning. In: Bradshaw MJ, Lowenstein AJ (Eds) *Innovative Teaching Strategies in Nursing and Related Health Professions* (5th Edition). Boston: Jones and Bartlett

UKCRC (2007) *Developing the Best Research Professionals*. London: UK Clinical Research Collaboration

Welsh, I. and Swann, C. (2002) *Partners in Learning: a Guide to Support and Assessment in Nurse Education*. Abingdon: Radcliffe Medical Press

Further Reading

DH (2008) *Towards a framework for post-registration nursing careers*. London Department of Health

Scottish Executive (2008) *Advanced Practice Toolkit*. Edinburgh: Scottish Executive

WG (2009) *Post registration career framework for nurses in Wales*. Cardiff: Welsh Government

CHAPTER 15
LIFELONG LEARNING

THE AIMS OF THIS CHAPTER ARE:

- To briefly highlight the historical context of lifelong learning

- To discuss key policies and standards that promote lifelong learning

- To explore reflective practice within the context of lifelong learning

- To illustrate strategies for teaching reflective practice

KEY TERMS

Continuing professional development
Lifelong learning
Critical thinking

Self-directed learners
Reflective practice

Given the constantly changing nature of subject areas and education, it is imperative that staff continue to build upon and develop the knowledge and skills acquired during their initial teacher training. Continuing professional development (CPD) continues to be the favoured term and has appeared in a number of different guises over the years, including staff development, continuing education, professional development and lifelong learning. Regardless of the term used, the aim is to ensure that the knowledge and skills of lecturers and practice educators are kept up to date and remain relevant, both in terms of subject and educational expertise. Awareness of the importance of CPD has received a considerable boost with the publication of several significant reports and documents relating to it.

HISTORICAL CONTEXT

The Dearing Report

The terms of reference of the Dearing Report (Dearing 1997) were:

> 'To make recommendations on how the purposes, shape, structure, size and funding of higher education, including support for students, should develop to meet the needs of the United Kingdom over the next 20 years, recognizing that higher education embraces teaching, learning, scholarship and research.'

Recommendations 9, 13, 14, 15, 47 and 48 refer specifically to staff development; the three main aspects covered are:

- The need for institutions to review, update and make available to all staff their policies with regard to staff development.
- The need for institutions to review the impact of communications and information technology on the role of staff, and ensure that the necessary support and training is made available.
- That an Institute for Learning and Teaching in Higher Education (ILT) be established for the purpose of accrediting programmes of teacher-training, the commissioning of research into teaching and learning, and the encouragement of innovation. All new full-time academic staff should undertake an accredited teacher-training course as part of their probationary period of employment.

Government response to the Dearing Report

In February 1998, the Government published its response to the Dearing Report, *Higher Education for the 21st Century* (DfEE, 1998). It welcomed the recommendations on the need for institutions to review and update their staff development policies, and to make these available to staff, and encouraged institutions to follow up these recommendations. The Government also welcomed the recommendations on the need for training and support of both staff and students in communications and information technology, and identified the importance of the now defunct Institute for Learning and Teaching (ILT) in the kite-marking and development of these materials. The Higher Education Academy, which replaced the Institute for Learning and Teaching in 2004, is discussed in Chapter 4.

Teacher training for higher education

The issue of accredited teacher-training was also welcomed:

> 'Government's long-term aim is to see all teachers in higher education carry a professional qualification, achieved by meeting demanding standards of teaching and supervisory competence through accredited learning or experience.'

This aim was welcomed by many people inside and outside the higher education sector. Indeed, most members of the public would have been unaware that higher education lecturers can be employed as teachers without possessing a teaching qualification. Most higher education institutions now require all newly appointed lecturers to undergo teacher training as a condition of employment, the most common routes being a postgraduate certificate in education. It is interesting to note that, in this area, nurse education is leading the way; the NMC, has always required teachers of nurses to hold a recognized teaching qualification.

In 2003, the Department of Health published the White Paper, *The Future of Higher Education* (DH, 2003), which set out Government's plans for radical reform and investment in universities and higher education colleges. A year later saw the introduction of the Higher Education Act 2004 intended to assist the implementation of a number of policies set out in the above white paper. This has since been superseded by the Higher Education Act [2011].

The higher education White Paper published by Government in 2011, identified major changes to the way the higher education system in England will be funded and regulated. In particular, additional public funding for teaching will be routed through the student loan system and less through HEFCE, who will have a greater role in regulation and protecting the interests of current and potential students.

The Further and Higher Education Bill in Wales [2012] sets out the Welsh Government's legislative proposals in relation to further and higher education reform and will introduce powers for the Welsh government to fund universities directly, bypassing the council. Some of the key proposals are to:

■ review quality assurance and enhancement of higher education provision;
■ strengthen the learner voice, access arrangements and dispute resolution procedures in higher education.

All UK Governments, through educational reform focus on 'widening access', a term referred to as the aspiration of increasing the proportion of students from under-represented groups entering and completing higher education (House of Commons, 2011; DELNI, 2011; Scottish Government, 2011; Welsh Government, 2012). Changes to the funding for higher education could significantly reduce opportunities for potential students to access learning and development. The House of Commons (2011) emphasize the importance of recognizing the significant work experience of older workers and their ability to do the job to encourage learning and progression.

LIFELONG LEARNING – AN OVERVIEW

The lifelong learning, otherwise known as career-long professional learning sector is large and diverse and includes those who work in further and higher education and work-based learning across the United Kingdom (LLUK, 2011).

> 'Lifelong learning is defined as 'all learning activity undertaken throughout life, with the aim of improving knowledge, skills and competence, within a personal, civic, social and/or employment-related perspective.'
>
> (ESAE, 2012)

Lifelong learning has long been linked with evolving patient care delivery and management and is complemented by a commitment towards lifelong education and development. Lifelong learning is therefore about:

- *Acquiring and updating all kinds of abilities, interests, knowledge and qualifications from pre-school years to postretirement* Lifelong learning promotes the development of knowledge and competence that will enable an individual to adapt to the knowledge-based society and actively participate in all aspects of social and economic life, taking more control of his or her future.
- *Valuing all forms of learning including* Formal learning, such as a degree programme undertaken at university, and informal learning such as vocational courses and skills acquired within the workplace. (ESAE, 2012).

UK Governments have dedicated substantial investment to equip NHS staff with the skills and knowledge to improve careers.

Liberating the NHS: Developing the Healthcare Workforce – From Design to Delivery (DH, 2012)

The Government is committed to supporting a world class healthcare education and training system and published a policy framework for a new approach to education and training in 2012 titled '*Liberating the NHS: Developing the Healthcare Workforce – From Design to Delivery*'. This policy framework aims to empower healthcare employers and national and local clinical leaders to take a leading role in planning and developing the workforce. It is advocated that healthcare providers employ staff with the skill mix appropriate to deliver a high quality service to patients in every circumstance. Objectives of this framework are:

- Ensuring security of supply; this means having people with the right skills in the right place at the right time.
- Ensuring quality education and training that supports safe, high quality care and greater flexibility.
- Ensuring value for money and widening participation.

Additionally the framework highlights the need for sustainable and transparent investment in education and training and strong partnerships with universities and education providers, to make the most effective use of the skills of educators. Table 15.1 refers to an education and training outcomes framework in development that sets outcomes for the education and training system; this will enable the allocation of education and training resources to be linked to quantifiable, quality outcomes (DH, 2012).

The policy framework also reviews education and training for nurses and midwives and acknowledges that nurses are the largest single profession within the health service and critical to providing care of the highest standard (DH, 2012). There is a requirement to allow nurses, midwives and specialist community public health nurses to use their professional judgment about what is right for patients and families by providing them with the necessary skills and confidence to work effectively in an increasingly complex working environment and take on specialist roles. Continuing personal and professional

TABLE 15.1 Education Outcomes Framework Domains

Excellent education: Education and training is commissioned and provided to the highest standards, ensuring learners have an excellent experience and that all elements of education are delivered in a safe and appropriate environment for patients, staff and students.

Competent and capable staff: There are sufficient healthcare staff educated aligned to service and changing care needs, to ensure that people are cared for by staff that complete a suitable induction, trained and qualified, who have the required knowledge and skills to do the jobs the service needs, whilst working effectively within a team.

Adaptable and flexible workforce: The workforce is educated to be responsive to changing service models and responsive to innovation and new technologies with knowledge about best practice, research and innovation, that promotes adoption and dissemination of better quality service delivery to reduces variability and poor practice.

NHS values and behaviours: Healthcare staff have the necessary compassion, values and behaviours to provide person centred care and enhance the quality of the patient experience through education, training and regular CPD, that instils respect for patients.

Widening participation: Talent and leadership flourishes free from discrimination with fair opportunities to progress and everyone is able to participate to fulfil their potential, recognising individual as well as group differences, treating people as individuals, and placing positive value on diversity in the workforce and there are opportunities to progress across the five leadership framework domains.

DH, 2012

development is seen as 'shared responsibility' between the nurse and their employer with opportunities for CPPD across disciplines to be maximized.

Graduating to success: a higher education strategy for Northern Ireland (DELNI, 2011)

The Higher Education Strategy for Northern Ireland provides a strong strategic focus for the future, and a framework for further developing a dynamic, high quality, world-renowned higher education sector. DELNI (2011) explain that higher education must:

- deliver a high quality learning experience that is underpinned by a fit-for-purpose quality assurance framework;
- provide opportunities for students to improve their employability skills;
- maintain a supportive learning environment.

The higher education strategy also proposes that all students should have the opportunity to develop a distinctive range of skills, attributes and experiences that will enhance their employability and set them apart from their peers.

> *'Lifelong learning must be at the heart of the system and new routes into, and through, higher education must be developed.'*
>
> (DELNI, 2011)

The Northern Ireland Government's vision about lifelong learning is clearly evident in this framework; they believe that learning should be valued, recognized, recorded and accredited wherever possible. Furthermore, they advocate a more flexible lifelong learning environment for students, meaning that higher education must be flexible in delivery and in funding (DELNI, 2011). The Strategy aims to create a lifelong learning system to:

- increase part-time and postgraduate capacity within higher education;
- provide the further education sector with an augmented role in the delivery of intermediate higher education provision;
- continually review the curriculum to ensure that it remains relevant and current;
- provide greater support for economically relevant subjects.

Flexible provision of higher education will require a flexible funding policy and the strategy aims to enhance the funding arrangements in order to foster a lifelong learning ethos.

Standards for the lifelong learning sector: a user guide (Lifelong Learning UK Council, 2011)

The 'Standards for the lifelong learning sector' highlights the different standards available and demonstrates how they can be used as tools to support individuals and organisations. It includes a number of examples which outline how to make the most of these resources that are freely available and easily accessible. LLUK (2011) discuss how the provision of lifelong learning has a direct impact on the economic and social wellbeing of the UK and that 'there is a constant drive towards improving the sector's performance, in terms of its responsiveness, effectiveness and efficiency' (p. 5). Despite the poor financial climate that has affected the UK for a number of years, there remains a need to deliver a valuable high quality service. The lifelong learning standards can be used to support personal development by:

- Providing a framework for collating evidence of work performance.
- Helping to ensure that work reflects good and best practice by supporting activities associated with self-appraisal, benchmarking and identifying role related development needs.
- Supporting recognition of achievement and performance, by providing evidence towards meeting relevant competency frameworks and professional development schemes.
- Creating a bridge between current roles and related occupations to support wider career opportunities.

The standards for lifelong learning support continuing professional development (CPD) activities in a number of ways particularly in terms of:

■ Planning for CPD.
■ Identifying professional development needs to achieve CPD related goals.
■ Organizing professional development activities to meet identified needs.
■ Recording and reviewing CPD activities.

LLUK (2011) emphasize that there is an intention for these standards to complement and not to compete with, or replace, professional registration standards or competency frameworks that are appropriate or required for some roles; they are able to support the CPD process, but they do not have to be used in isolation.

LIFELONG LEARNING AND CPD

Lifelong learning is also perceived as an essential aspect of post-registration education and practice, which according to Gopee (2001) is seen as central to professional self-regulation in nursing. He claims that, although lifelong learning is very much apparent in nurse education, various other forms of informal learning occur all the time. Informal learning can also take place in formal settings, such as modules and courses at diploma, degree and higher degree level, study days and half-day shorter programmes (Gopee, 2001).

The Department of Health (2012) supports the identification of professional and service needs in a personal development plan, which should identify different learning preferences, highlight where team or multi-professional learning offers the best solution and take full advantage of opportunistic learning on the job. It emphasizes that CPD does not necessarily mean going on a course. Gopee (2001) points out that lifelong learning has evolved consistently over the last few decades at conceptual level; however, obstacles remain, and these are mainly at organizational level. Obstacles to lifelong learning are identified in Figure 15.1.

Critical thinking and clinical actions empower the professional nurse, and continuing education may be the key to promoting and maintaining competency, strengthening the profession and improving quality care (Griffitts, 2002). In order to promote nurses' professional development, Griffitts (2002) advocates making their education a priority and suggests the following strategies:

■ Partner with expert staff to promote professional accountability through periodic self-evaluation and ongoing education.
■ Invite staff to share what they have learnt at continuing education activities.
■ Encourage staff to choose continuing education opportunities of interest, which will promote attendance and professional accountability.
■ Make educational opportunities available at more than one time and allow participants to choose which time to attend.
■ Constantly seek and praise good work.

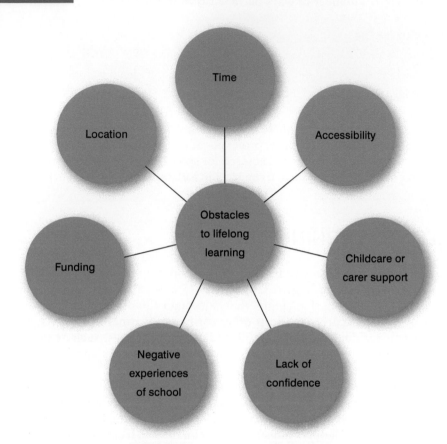

FIGURE 15.1   Obstacles to lifelong learning

Promoting lifelong learning

Jarvis (2005) believes that, in order to create lifelong learners, changes must be made in nurse education and managerial practice; contentiously, he suggests that if lifelong learning were actually fostered in nursing then continuing education might be less necessary. Jarvis (2005) defines lifelong learning as:

> *'any planned series of incidents at any time in the lifespan, having a humanistic basis, directed towards the participants' learning and understanding.'*

However, he does acknowledge that it may be necessary to assist self-directed learners to be more effective in their quest for knowledge because they may still need to acquire study skills. Study skills should be an integral part of professional preparation in order that professionals become lifelong learners.

What is interesting is that Jarvis (2005) explains how learners should be given the opportunity to develop into self-directed learners rather than become teacher dependent; they may then acquire a problem-solving attitude that would equip them better for their career. Following this, nurse educators might see changes in their own role, moving away from providing packaged knowledge to enable learners to pass their qualifying examinations to becoming educators preparing professionals for a lifetime of service (Jarvis, 2005).

Because lifelong learning is increasingly being appreciated as an essential ingredient for ensuring high-quality patient care, Gopee (2002) advocates the need for sensitivity by both employer and employees to nurture all mechanisms that can facilitate this. He believes that sensitivity issues should be acknowledged to facilitate lifelong learning in the clinical setting and also that clinical managers should recognize the communities of their workforce.

A study by Ryan in 2003 aimed to identify the factors that influenced motivation to participate in CPD among three groups comprising qualified nurses, occupational therapists, and physiotherapists. A questionnaire derived from the literature was used to determine the differences between lifelong learning and CPD in a sample of 300 participants; 182 questionnaires were returned. When asked for their understanding of lifelong learning, the three groups gave similar responses. Some of these responses included:

- personal development encompassing all aspects of daily life;
- ongoing acquisition of knowledge and skills in a personal, professional and social context;
- the ability to continue self-development by having access to education throughout the lifespan;
- PREP, reflection, maintaining best standards;
- learning on a continuous basis to update knowledge and experience.

The participants in Ryan's (2003) study were also asked for their understanding of CPD; all three groups provided identical answers:

- updating knowledge and skills in line with the requirements of a professional body; and
- the need to prove that one is keeping abreast of professional issues relating to one's own area of work or professional interest.

It appears from the study that the most influential factor for undertaking CPD was to increase professional knowledge. The least influential factor was the desire to achieve a higher educational qualification; students who previously had poor education did not feel that this was a reason for undertaking CPD. Other factors include:

- updating existing qualifications;
- increasing the status of the profession;
- demonstrating professional competence;
- fulfilling statutory requirements of governing body;
- increasing self-esteem; and
- obtaining further qualifications for promotion purposes.

Interestingly, Ryan (2003) found no difference between the intrinsic or extrinsic motivational factors amongst the group, although some participants showed a willingness to undertake a CPD course with partial study leave; others were prepared to pay for CPD courses, and some were prepared to complete a CPD course without study leave. She concludes that:

> *'continuous professional development is a fundamental component that lies along the continuum of lifelong learning.'*

A sequential triangulation study by Hughes (2005) aimed to investigate nurses' perceptions of the value of CPD in the NHS and private sector. The study also aimed to analyze the factors that influence these perceptions and any potential barriers to successful CPD. A questionnaire was designed from the literature to establish nurses' feelings in relation to CPD with the results used to highlight themes for further exploration at interview. Semi-structured interviews took place to explore the link between professional development and reflection and were used to determine if the nurses' ability to reflect affected their personal values as well as the challenges to CPD. The results indicated that, in the majority of nurses in both public and private sectors, professional development had a positive influence on practice. However, Hughes (2005) acknowledges that although there were similarities in the responses, there was a clear difference between responses of nursing-home and NHS staff concerning career prospects and being sent on particular study activities. The results suggested that nurses in the NHS value professional development as a means of career progression; whereas nurses in the private sector may experience difficulty accessing and undertaking professional development activities, owing to lack of availability or because it is their employer who decides if they should go.

Hughes (2005) also identified that reflective practice was not seen as a major benefit of professional development and few participants acknowledged reflection as a means of improving practice. She suggests that there is an inherent problem in developing professionally if nurses find critical reflection difficult and concedes that, if some nurses are unable to reflect on their own learning, not only is the learning process incomplete, but they cannot be expected to improve their practice as a result of studying. Hughes (2005) claims that this illustrates that nurses are disassociating PREP from lifelong learning and may be choosing study activities that meet the PREP requirements as opposed to CPD, which can improve practice. She concludes that, if nurses continue to undertake study activities without reflecting on their learning needs, then resources will continue to be misdirected and PREP will continue to be a futile exercise for some.

REFLECTION

Reflection embraces the concept of Lifelong learning and is recognized as an essential aspect of continuing professional development and is seen as a fundamental process in improving the quality of learning and teaching. The concept of reflective practice is mainly associated with the idea of reflection on experience (Johns, 1996); however, Watson (2002) believes reflection to be an accurate representation of the students' practice and that gaps in knowledge and/or skill competence can be identified quickly and rectified. This is encapsulated nicely by Jasper (2013):

> *'Reflective practice is considered to be the way in which professionals learn from their experiences, create practice theory and develop expertise.'*

Spouse (2001) argued that for many years the theory-practice gap has dominated approaches to preparing students for their future role, with an increased emphasis on work-based learning. However, Jasper (2013) further emphasizes how the learning that is achieved using reflective strategies is different from the theory that provides the knowledge underpinning practice. In other words, reflective practice bridges the gap between theory and clinical practice by providing a strategy that helps to develop both understanding and learning.

Dix and Hughes (2004) recognize that a considerable number of learners benefit from reflective practice. Johns (1995) argued that, to enable learners to understand and learn through lived experiences, they should take congruent action towards developing increasing effectiveness, within the context of what is understood as desirable practice. Many nursing students are expected to keep reflective journals whilst on clinical placements, and some are required to submit a reflective essay during each module of the programme (Dix and Hughes, 2004).

The nature of reflection

Reflection is essentially a psychological construct that is closely related to a range of other internal mental (cognitive) processes such as thinking, reasoning, considering and deliberating (Gregory, 1997). The term is used in two ways:

- in a general sense, as synonymous with thinking and deliberating; and
- in a specific sense, as the recollection of past experiences and mental states by retrospection, i.e. 'looking back'. (The word 'reflection' is derived from the Latin *reflectere*, meaning to bend back.)

The nature of reflective practice: Schön's approach

Perhaps the single most influential interpretation of reflective practice is that of Donald Schön, whose approach has influenced thinking about professional practice in a number of professions, not least those of teaching and nursing.

The publication of *The Reflective Practitioner: How Professionals Think in Action* (Schön 1991) and *Educating the Reflective Practitioner: Towards a New Design for Teaching and Learning in the Professions* (Schön, 1987) had considerable impact on both the teaching and the nursing professions, providing, as the books do, an alternative rationale for professional practice.

Schön's focus is the relationship between academic knowledge as defined in universities and the competence involved in professional practice. He argues that professional practice is based upon a technical rationality model that makes erroneous assumptions about the nature of practice and in so doing reduces its importance in relation to theory. Technical rationality views professional practice as the application of general, standardized, theoretical principles to the solving of practice problems; in other words, professional practice is problem-solving. This top-down view puts general theoretical principles at the top of the hierarchy of professional knowledge and practical problem-solving at the bottom, leading to what Schön termed the pre-eminence of theory and the denigration of practice.

Problem-setting

Within the technical rationality model, professional practice is viewed as a process of instrumental problem-solving, with the assumption that problems are self-evident. Schön, however, argues that in reality practitioners are not presented with problems per se, but with problem-situations. These must be converted into actual problems by a process of problem-setting, i.e. selecting the elements of the situation, deciding the ends and means, and framing the context. Technical rationality also fails to take account of the fact that problems encountered in professional practice are rarely standard or predictable.

Knowing-in-action

Schön uses this term to describe the intuitive or tacit 'knowing' that is embedded in professional actions. Intuition is a mental process, commonly termed the 'sixth sense', and refers to a process by which an individual comes to a conclusion about something in the absence of sensory inputs and without consciously thinking about it. For example, skilled practitioners constantly make intuitive judgements about situations without being able to specify exactly the criteria on which they base those judgements; this is often termed 'thinking on your feet'. Schön maintains that, although this intuitive 'knowing' is implicit within our actions, it is possible for practitioners to access this by reflecting on what they are doing while they are doing it.

Reflection-in-action

Reflection-in-action occurs when the practitioner is confronted by a novel puzzle or problem-situation that he or she attempts to resolve. This resolution occurs when the problem is 're-framed', i.e. seen differently during the actions. It is the process of reflecting upon the intuitive 'knowing' that is implicit in a practitioner's actions, whilst at the same time carrying out those actions, that constitutes reflection-in-action.

It is important to emphasize that the reflection is inherent in the action itself and not in any thinking going on at the same time. Reflection-in-action is non-rational and non-linear and is embedded in the action. Richardson (1990) succinctly captures this phenomenon: 'Schön found intelligence in the act itself rather than in attempting to make the act seem intelligent.' Schön suggests that reflection-in-action is triggered more commonly by surprising results, whereas anticipated results are less likely to be thought about. Reflection-in-action occurs within what Schön terms the action-present, i.e. the timescale in which any action by the practitioner can still influence a situation.

Reflection-on-action

This is the type of reflection that is referred to in the models of reflection discussed in the previous section of this chapter and involves retrospection on past experiences, the aim of which is to generate knowledge for future practice. Reflection-on-action contrasts markedly with reflection-in-action, the latter occurring whilst the practitioner is engaged in actions rather than thinking about it later.

Knowledge-in-action

This is practical professional knowledge and develops by the process of reflection-in-action. It does not rely on a series of conscious steps in a decision-making process; instead it is inherent in the action itself. It is not possible to ascertain this knowledge-in-action by talking to a practitioner, as it is not a conscious process, but expert knowledge can be elicited by observing the practitioner reflecting-in-action.

Characteristics of reflective practitioners

This notion of the reflective practitioner, according to Schön, contrasts markedly with the prevailing model of professional practice, the technical rationality model.

According to Schön, the reflective practitioner is characterized by a range of personal qualities and abilities, such as the ability to engage in self-assessment to criticize the existing state of affairs, to promote change and to adapt to change, and the ability to practise as an autonomous professional. He also distinguishes between the effective and the ineffective practitioner: the former is able to recognize and explore confusing or unique events that occur during practice, whereas the latter is 'burned-out', i.e. confined to repetitive and routine practice, neglecting opportunities to think about what he or she is doing.

Although Schön's ideas on reflective practice have been widely accepted within the nursing profession, his approach has been criticized because of a lack of empirical support. Interestingly, Muncie and Russell (1989) point out that there is 'virtually no elaboration of the psychological realities of reflection-in-action': for example, What makes it begin? What happens when it begins? How do we know when it is occurring?

A qualitative study by Smith and Jack (2005) aimed to ascertain whether students found reflection to be a meaningful activity and if there are perceived benefits associated with reflective practice. A sample comprising 50 students was invited to take part in the study to determine their views on whether reflection is a useful tool for learning; however, only eight students volunteered to take part. A semi-structured focus-group interview, which lasted for one hour, was guided by open questions relating to reflective practice. A Web-based learning environment discussion board was used as a forum for posing questions relating to the benefits of reflection.

Smith and Jack (2005) discovered that some of the findings corroborated the literature. Many of the students agreed that keeping a reflective diary was beneficial once they had mastered the art of reflective writing and were able to be critical and analytical in their approach. The students completed a learning styles inventory by Honey and Mumford (1992) to diagnose their learning style; and those who identified their style as being reflective in nature found reflecting on practice more useful. Therefore, Smith and Jack (2005) conclude that students' learning styles are pertinent to their perception of the usefulness of the reflective process.

Price (2005) emphasizes that reflection is not seen as a learning style but as a skill that students should be encouraged to master if lifelong learning is to become a reality. Interestingly, he assumes that there are divergent and strongly held views in university departments on what reflection relates to; Burnard's (2005) experience supports this.

STRATEGIES FOR TEACHING REFLECTIVE PRACTICE

Boud, Keogh and Walker's model of reflection

A number of models of reflection have been used – accurately and not so accurately – within nurse education. A model by Boud *et al.* (1985) to which Johns (1995) added a fourth stage could be acknowledged as being one of the clearer models; with only four stages, it allows less room for irrelevant material (Figure 15.2).

FIGURE 15.2   Model of reflection

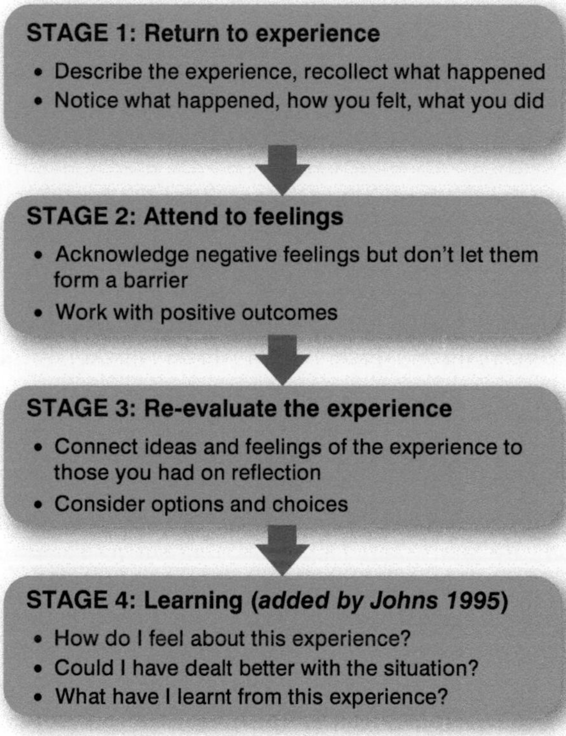

STAGE 1: Return to experience
- Describe the experience, recollect what happened
- Notice what happened, how you felt, what you did

STAGE 2: Attend to feelings
- Acknowledge negative feelings but don't let them form a barrier
- Work with positive outcomes

STAGE 3: Re-evaluate the experience
- Connect ideas and feelings of the experience to those you had on reflection
- Consider options and choices

STAGE 4: Learning (*added by Johns 1995*)
- How do I feel about this experience?
- Could I have dealt better with the situation?
- What have I learnt from this experience?

ADAPTED FROM BOUD ET AL., 1985; JOHNS, 1995

The purpose of Stage 1 is to stand back from the experience, clarify perceptions and focus on it again with the benefit of time and concentration. Stage 2 is intended for noting any positive or negative feelings; these might include pleasure, anger, frustration, elation, annoyance or a sense of achievement. Stage 3 is re-evaluation of the experience, and Stage 4 allows for identification of learning and professional development.

> 'The Boud, Keogh and Walker (1985) model demonstrates a relatively rational approach to the process of reflecting upon experience, and as such as been adopted widely in nursing as a tool for teaching practitioners how to reflect. It is worth noting, however, that Boud et al. (1993) emphasize that systematic reflection is not the only way in which individuals learn from experiences: What we can say is that learning from experience is far more indirect than we often pretend it to be. It can be prompted by systematic reflection, but it can also be powerfully prompted by discrepancies or dilemmas which we are "forced" to confront.'

'They go on to conclude: *Much as we may enjoy the intellectual chase, we cannot neglect our full experience in the process. To do so is to fool ourselves into treating learning from experience as a simple, rational process.*'

Whilst acknowledging the feelings of self and others enhances self-awareness and is an important aspect of health care, this stage could be, and often is, incorporated within the experience/situation narrative, thus reducing the need for unnecessary subheadings. However, as with Gibbs (1988) and Atkins and Murphy (1993) a section for feelings still remains.

The Johns model of structured reflection

Johns (1992) uses the concept of guided reflection to describe a structured, supported approach that helps practitioners learn from their reflections upon experiences. The approach involves using the model of structured reflection, one-to-one or group supervision, and the keeping of a structured reflective diary. The model of structured reflection uses a series of questions which help structure the practitioner's reflections. In addition to one core question there are five sets of cue questions, as shown in Table 15.2.

The Johns model is more detailed than any of the models outlined, and there are both advantages and disadvantages to this. The nursing literature indicates that nurses need to be taught how to reflect, and the detailed questions that practitioners are required to ask of themselves in the Johns model certainly provide a comprehensive checklist for reflection. The disadvantage of such a detailed structure is that it imposes a framework

TABLE 15.2 The Johns model of structured reflection

Cue questions	
Aesthetics	• What was I trying to achieve? • Why did I respond as I did? • What were the consequences for the patient, others and me? • How was this person (were these people) feeling? • How did I know?
Personal	• How did I feel in this situation? • What factors were influencing me?
Ethics	• How did my actions match with my beliefs? • What factors made me act in incongruent ways?
Empirics	• What knowledge did or should have informed me?
Reflexivity	• How does this connect with previous experiences? • Could I handle this better in similar situations? • What would be the consequences of alternative actions for the patient, others and me? • How do I now feel about this experience? • Can I support myself and others better as a consequence? • How has this changed my ways of knowing?

ADAPTED FROM JOHNS, 1992

that is external to the practitioner, leaving little scope for inclusion of his or her own approach. It is also open to criticism on the grounds of complexity, although other models can be criticized on precisely the opposite grounds, i.e. that they may appear simplistic and self-evident.

Driscoll's model of reflection

Pre- and post-registration students should be able to use a reflective model that does not impact on their learning and restrict their writing skills. They should be able to guide the reflection and have overall control over their learning process. Too often, students use a model of reflection that inhibits their creativity and detracts from the situation or experience. To avoid confusing students and forcing them to write about irrelevant issues, a model of reflection should have a minimum number of headings with clear guidelines for each. By the time a student has addressed all of the questions under each heading of a reflective model, there is sometimes little or no wordage remaining to allow creativity or independent thinking. Although Borton's (1970) framework comprises an acceptable three stages, the headings 'What?', 'So what?' and 'Now what?' adopted by Driscoll (2000) imply a flippancy that might not influence a student to consider the exercise seriously, thereby distracting from the learning situation (Table 15.3).

A model of elementary reflection

An interesting argument from Jones (1999) appears to corroborate this reasoning; it states that models of reflection are generally inadequately used, incompletely implemented and misunderstood by practitioners. Burnard (2005) discovered that student reflections can sometimes be 'wrong' and that it is possible to fail a student's reflective activity. He describes how failed activities are often sent back to students to be done again, and he questions, quite justifiably, if we really believe that students can re-reflect on what they have written? This leads to another contentious argument, i.e. that a large number of students' reflective accounts are fictitious (Burnard, 2005).

A short and clear model of reflection would allow for freedom of expression and could incorporate three steps (see Figure 15.3).

Step 1: The learning experience Anecdotal evidence suggests that many students believe that they should reflect on a negative aspect of their practice when, in fact, that is not the case. Reflecting on a learning situation can be a positive or negative experience, although a model with the heading 'If I encountered the situation again, what would I do

TEACHING TIP

Consider 'teaching' reflection as a group activity; to make this less personal it could be done as a role play with a fictitious scenario.

TABLE 15.3 Driscoll's model of reflection
What? Returning to the situation
• What is the purpose of returning to this situation?
• What exactly occurred?
• What did you see? What did you do?
• What was your reaction?
• What did other people do? E.g. colleague, patient, relative.
• What do you see as key aspects of this situation?
So what? Understanding the context
• What were you feeling at the time?
• What are you feeling now? Are there any differences and, if so, why?
• What were the effects of what you did (or did not do)?
• What good emerged from the situation, e.g. for self, others?
• What troubles you, if anything?
• What were your experiences in comparison to your colleagues?
• What are the main reasons for feeling differently from your colleagues?
Now what? Modifying future outcomes
• What are the implications for you?
• What needs to happen to alter the situation?
• What are you going to do about the situation?
• What happens if you decide not to alter anything?
• What might you do differently if faced with a similar situation again?
• What information do you need to face a similar situation again?
• What are your best ways of getting information about the situation should it arise again?

ADAPTED FROM DRISCOLL, 2000

differently?' does suggest to students that the experience should be regarded as a negative one and that they acted inappropriately.

Step 2: Evaluation   We all evaluate the actions of other people and form opinions about how effectively they do things. We also judge our own performance by being aware of what we did well, or less well. Learners should be encouraged to analyze the situation, and their involvement in it, and to draw lessons from this for their future practice (Price, 2005).

FIGURE 15.3 A model of elementary reflection

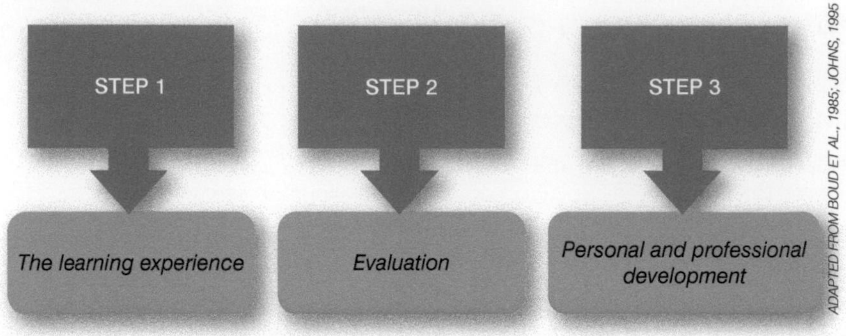

Step 3: Personal and professional development   An important aspect of reflective practice is to learn from personal and professional experience. Through reflection, a person is able to engage in an ongoing dialogue with the self, which enhances self-awareness (Scanlon and Chernomas, 1997), and is then able to come to a personal understanding of his or her own practice, facilitating further development of professional expertise. In essence, reflection can help to clarify thoughts and emotions, to work out strategies and to focus on professional development and progress (Cottrell, 2008).

A framework for reflection should be simple and straightforward to allow a student to make progress through each stage with relative ease. Some might argue that a reflective exercise should be completed and then closed, but this could have implications. Reflection should not only allow a student the freedom to work through a positive or negative experience, but it should also be used to inform future learning and clinical practice and enhance personal and professional development. Therefore, to forget or close the experience at any point could be seen as imprudent.

Review questions

1. How would you define lifelong learning?

2. List five of the key obstacles to lifelong learning.

3. What did Ryan's study identify as the main motivational factor for undertaking CPD training?

4. How does Jasper define reflective practice?

5. Explain the differences between 'reflection-in-action' and 'reflection-on-action'

SUMMARY

- The knowledge and skills of lecturers and practice educators are kept up to date and remain relevant, both in terms of subject and educational expertise.

- Most higher education institutions now require all newly appointed lecturers to undergo teacher training as a condition of employment, the most common route being a postgraduate certificate in education.

- Lifelong learning is the term often used to refer to the learning that occurs throughout the working life of an individual and which may be planned or not.

- CPD programmes should meet local service needs and also those of individual professionals.

- Clinical governance must be underpinned by a culture that values lifelong learning and recognizes the key part that it plays in improving quality.

- Lifelong learning is seen as an essential aspect of post-registration education and practice and is central to professional self-regulation in nursing.

- Critical thinking and clinical actions empower the professional nurse, and continuing education may be the key to promoting and maintaining competency, strengthening the profession and improving the quality of care.

- Learners should be given the opportunity to develop into self-directed learners rather than become teacher dependent.

- Reflective practice has been identified as one of the key ways to learn from experiences, and education recognizes it an as essential tool for helping health care students to make links between theory and clinical practice.

- Reflection is essentially a psychological construct that is closely related to a range of other internal mental (cognitive) processes, such as thinking, reasoning, considering and deliberating.

- Reflection-in-action occurs when the practitioner is confronted by a novel puzzle or problem situation that he or she attempts to resolve.

- The reflective practitioner is characterized by a range of personal qualities and abilities, such as the ability to engage in self-assessment, to criticize the existing state of affairs, to promote change and to adapt to change, and the ability to practise as an autonomous professional.

- A model by Boud et al. with a fourth stage added by Johns could be acknowledged as one of the clearer models of reflection; with only four stages, it allows less room for irrelevant material.

- A short and clear model of reflection would allow for freedom of expression and could incorporate three steps: the learning experience, evaluation, and personal and professional development.

References

Atkins, S. and Murphy, K. (1993). Reflection: a review of the literature. *Journal of Advanced Nursing* 18 1188–1192

Borton, T. (1970) *Reach, Touch and Teach*. London: Hutchinson

Boud, D., Keogh, R. and Walker, D. (Eds) (1985) *Reflection: Turning Experience into Learning*. London: Kogan Page

Burnard, P.(2005) Reflections on reflection. *Nurse Education Today* 25, 85–86

Cottrell, S. (2008) *The Study Skills Handbook* (3rd Edition). Hampshire: Palgrave Macmillan

Dearing, R. (1977) *Higher Education in the Learning Society: The Report of the National Committee of Inquiry into Higher Education*. Norwich: HMSO

DELNI (2011) *Graduating to Success: A Higher Education Strategy for Northern Ireland*. Belfast: The Stationary Office

DfEE (1998) *Higher Education for the 21st Century: Response to the Dearing report*. London: HMSO

Dix, G. and Hughes, S.J. (2004) Strategies to help students learn effectively. *Nursing Standard* 18(32) 39–42

DH (2003) *The Future of Higher Education*. London: The Stationery Office

DH (2012) *Liberating the NHS: Developing the Healthcare Workforce – From Design to Delivery*. London: The Stationary Office

Driscoll, J. (2000) *Practising Clinical Supervision*. Edinburgh: Ballière Tindall

ESAE (2012) European Commission's memorandum on Lifelong Learning: http://ec.europa.eu/education/policies/lll/lll_en.html

Gibbs, G. (1988) *Learning by Doing: A Guide to Teaching and Learning Methods*. Oxford: Oxford Polytechnic

Gopee, N. (2001) Lifelong learning in nursing: perceptions and realities. *Nurse Education Today* 21(8) 607–615

Gopee, N. (2002) Human and social capital as facilitators of lifelong learning in nursing. *Nurse Education Today* 22(8) 608–616

Gregory, R.L. (1997) (Ed) *The Oxford Companion to the Mind*. Oxford: Oxford University Press

Griffitts, L.D.(2002) Geared to achieve with lifelong learning. *Nursing Management*, 33(11) 22–25

Honey, P. and Mumford, A. (1992) *The Manual of Learning Styles* (Revised edition). Maidenhead: Peter Honey

House of Commons (2011) *Government Reform of Higher Education*: Twelfth Report of Session 2010–12 (Volume I). London: The Stationary Office

Hughes, E. (2005) Nurses' perceptions of continuing professional development. *Nursing Standard* 19(43) 41–49

Jarvis, P. (2005) Lifelong education and its relevance to nursing. *Nurse Education Today* 25(8) 655–660

Jasper, M. (2006) *Reflection, Decision-Making and Professional Development: Vital Notes for Nurses*. London: Wiley-Blackwell

Johns, C. (1992) The Burford nursing development unit holistic model of nursing practice. *Journal of Advanced Nursing* 16, 1090–1098

Johns, C. (1995) Framing learning through reflection within Carper's fundamental ways of knowing in nursing. *Journal of Advanced Nursing* 22(2) 226–234

Johns, C. (1996) Using a reflective model of nursing and guided reflection. *Nursing Standard* 11(2), 34–38

Jones, K.N. (1999) Reflection: an alternative to nursing models. *Professional Nurse* 14(12) 853–855

Lifelong Learning UK Council (2011) *Standards for the Lifelong Learning Sector: A User Guide*. London: LLUK

Muncie, H. and Russell, T. (1989) Educating the reflective teacher: an essay review of two books by Donald Schön. *Journal of Curriculum Studies* 21(1) 71–80

Price, B. (2005) Self-assessment and reflection in nurse education. *Nursing Standard*, 19(29) 33–37

Richardson, V. (1990) The evolution of reflective teaching and teacher education. In Clift T, Houston W, Pugach M (eds) *Encouraging*

Reflective Practice in Education. New York: Teachers College Press

Ryan, J. (2003) Continuous professional development along the continuum of lifelong learning. *Nurse Education Today* 23(7) 498–508

Scanlon, J.M. and Chernomas, W.M. (1997) Developing the reflective teacher. *Journal of Advanced Nursing* 25(6) 1138–1143

Schön, D. (1987) *Educating the Reflective Practitioner: Towards a New Design for Teaching and Learning in the Professions*. San Francisco: Jossey Bass

Schön, D. (1991) *The Reflective Practitioner: How Professionals Think in Action*. Aldershot: Ashgate Arena

Scottish Government (2012) *Putting Learners at the Centre: Delivering our Ambitions for Post-16 Education*. Edinburgh: The Stationary Office

Smith, A. and Jack, K. (2005) Reflective practice: a meaningful task for students. *Nursing Standard* 19(26) 33–37

Spouse, J. (2001) Bridging theory and practice in the supervisory relationship: a sociocultural perspective. *Journal of Advanced Nursing* 33(4) 512–522

Watson, S. (2002) The use of reflection as an assessment of practice: can you mark learning contracts? *Nurse Education in Practice* 2, 150–159

Welsh Government (2012) *Further and Higher Education (Wales) Bill*. Cardiff: Welsh Government

Further Reading

Avis, J., Fisher, R. and Thompson, R. (Eds) (2009) *Teaching in lifelong learning: a guide to theory and practice*. Maidenhead: Open University Press

Gravells, A. (2012) *Preparing to teach in the life-long learning sector* (5th Edition). London: Learning Matters

Morgan-Klein, B. and Osborne, M. (2007) *The concepts and practices of lifelong learning*. Oxon: Routledge

Rolfe, G., Jasper, M. and Freshwater, D. (2010) *Critical reflection in practice: generating knowledge for care* (2nd Edition). Palgrave Macmillan

CHAPTER 16
CONTINUING PROFESSIONAL DEVELOPMENT: THE UNIVERSITY CONTEXT

THE AIMS OF THIS CHAPTER ARE:

- To explore continuing professional development for lecturers within higher education

- To illustrate the multi-faceted role of nurse lecturers

- To highlight development needs within the realms of teaching and learning, research and management

- To outline research and scholarly activity that informs learning and teaching

KEY TERMS

Open learning
Appraisal

Humanistic concept
Peer review

Within all sectors of education, continuing professional development is acknowledged as being essential for maintaining and improving the quality of educational provision. It is not therefore the exclusive province of individual teachers but must take into account the goals and strategies of the department and the institutions in which they work. Hence, there will be variations in the nature of continuing professional development (CPD) according to the priorities of the teacher's department; for example, some departments may see their main priority as developing more staff as active researchers; others may wish to develop open and distance learning materials for their programmes. It is normally the case that funding for staff development is linked to these departmental/institutional priorities, and in this way teachers are 'encouraged' to undertake appropriate staff development within the stated priority areas. The importance of CPD to the work of the institution is underlined by its inclusion in the agenda of annual staff appraisal interviews.

The terminology related to CPD can be confusing, as a variety of terms are in current use for what is essentially the same concept: continuing professional development, staff development (SD), continuing professional education (CPE), and lifelong learning. The first three are normally applied to formal learning in an institution, whereas the latter is a more generic term that includes learning outside the formal education system. There are two main reasons why CPD is an important concept for nurse teachers:

■ The design and delivery of CPD programmes and activities are significant areas of work in nurse education.
■ Nurse teachers are required to maintain their own continuing professional development.

The NMC (2008a) Code sets out standards for conduct, performance and ethics, and states that registered nurses, midwives and community public health nurses are required to:

■ protect and support the health of individual patients and clients;
■ protect and support the health of the wider community;
■ act in such a way that justifies the trust and confidence the public have in them;
■ uphold and enhance the good reputation of the professions.

Continuing professional development has a major role to play in maintaining this requirement, and Standard 6 of the NMC code relates specifically to CPD: 'maintain and improve your professional knowledge and competence'.

The teacher's role in nursing, midwifery and health visiting is performed in two distinct, yet inter-related contexts, i.e. the university department and the workplace. The requirements for CPD cover both these settings, and for the sake of clarity the former is addressed in this chapter and the latter in Chapter 17.

Although CPD was acknowledged in association with lifelong learning in Chapter 15, the current chapter explores a range of university-focused CPD strategies, including staff appraisal, the Higher Education Academy, research and scholarly activity, the research exercise framework, and writing for publication.

CPD IN NURSING, MIDWIFERY AND SPECIALIST COMMUNITY PUBLIC HEALTH NURSING

Obviously, CPD has important implications for professional nurses and for the general public. The public has a right to be safeguarded against malpractice and to be protected from charlatans, and members of the public expect nurses to possess up-to-date knowledge and skills appropriate to the specialism in which they practice.

A nurse's motivation to undertake continuing professional development may arise from a range of different needs. The most obvious one that springs to mind is the NMC (2011) PREP standards, to which all registered nurses must conform if they are to continue on the register of nurses. The PREP standards are discussed in detail in Chapter 17.

There are also more altruistic motives, such as a desire to improve the standard of practice, and other less altruistic ones, such as gaining further qualifications to enhance promotion prospects or a desire to increase personal status by the acquisition of masters or doctoral degrees. There is even the possibility that some nurses may see CPD as providing evidence of safe practice in cases of litigation by patients or clients.

Many qualified practitioners can be classified as post-registration students, as they are pursuing formal courses as part of their CPD. For the majority of these nurses, studies will be undertaken whilst they are in full-time employment. The position with regard to study leave and funding for CPD continues to worsen, and partial funding is the best that many can expect to gain. Study leave to attend formal courses is even more difficult to obtain, and in cases where it is granted the demands of service mean that it may not always be possible to take the leave. Hence, the demand for more flexible approaches to study has led to the development of distance and open learning programmes which allow post-registration students to study in their own time and without the need for attendance at an institution.

Another development in the delivery of CPD for nurses is the accreditation of prior learning (APEL); this has enabled experienced practitioners to identify learning gained within the workplace, to provide evidence of such learning in a portfolio, and to use the credit thus gained to contribute towards the final award. For many nurses, this has meant a considerable reduction in the time taken to gain a higher education award.

Nurse lecturer roles in higher education

Teacher's roles are extremely varied and diverse and, if we asked two nurse lecturers to describe their work, we are likely to gain two completely different accounts of its emphasis, of time allocation and of ways of working. However, both lecturers are likely to say that they undertake the following activities:

- teaching;
- curriculum planning;
- administration.

Figure 16.1 illustrates the multi-faceted role of nurse lecturers.

FIGURE 16.1   Role of the nurse lecturer in higher education

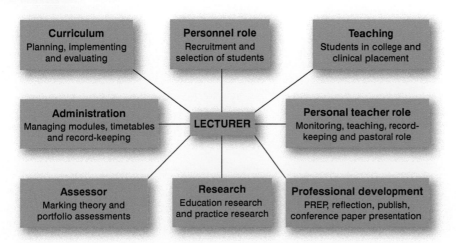

According to the NMC (2008b) nurses and midwives who intend to take on the role of teacher must fulfil the following criteria:

■ Their teaching role will be supported by appropriate professional and academic qualifications and ongoing research, education and/or practice development activity to provide an evidence base for their teaching.

■ The NMC requires all NMC teachers to maintain and develop their knowledge, skills and competence as a teacher through regular updating.

■ Those teachers employed in approved educational institutions will need to meet the requirements of their employers for scholarly activity.

■ For teachers who also have a clinical role, the NMC also requires that they ensure their knowledge and skills of practice are up to date.

Teachers should be prepared to demonstrate to their employers, and NMC quality assurance agents, how they have maintained and developed their knowledge, skills and competence as teachers. The NMC (2011) PREP guidelines offer a suggested format for recording learning (Table 16.1).

TABLE 16.1	Recording learning activity (*NMC, 2011*)
Section	**Guideline**
I	A list and a description of your work place or organization and role for the last three years
	You should record your work place(s) and your work or role(s) that relate to the learning activity you describe
	If you have worked in various places, but in essentially the same role, you may want to group this type of work together and summarise it in this section
	If you were not working, we suggest you put 'not working'.
II	The learning activity – what did you do? You should record the learning activity related to the work you identified for the last three years
	You should state the date when this learning activity took place and state how many hours the learning activity took
III	Description of the learning activity – what did it consist of?
	Provide a detailed description of what the learning activity consisted of, why you decided to do the learning or how the opportunity came about, where when and how you did the learning and what you expected to gain from it
IV	Outcome of the learning activity – how did the learning relate to your work?
	You should record the effect it has had on the way in which you work or intend to work in the future and an action plan for follow-up learning that you may plan in the future.

FIGURE 16.2 CPD activities for nurse lecturers

Figure 16.2 shows some of the CPD activities for nurse lecturers.

STAFF APPRAISAL/INDIVIDUAL PERFORMANCE REVIEW

We spend about one-third of our adult lives at work and, as well as providing money for living, work also functions as an important vehicle for the expression of our individuality. There is little doubt that it is social relationships that make or break the working environment, rather than the nature of the job per se, and it is a sad reflection on the management style of senior personnel that so many people fail to derive job satisfaction from their work. It is important to appreciate the holistic nature of work to the individual; it is intimately related to self-development, social position and identity, and is not simply a collection of performances to be evaluated.

The concept of staff appraisal needs to be carefully defined in order to be distinguishable from other related concepts such as assessment and review of performance. Appraisal, in its literal sense, is the estimation of value or quality, and it is this emphasis on value that makes it more global than assessment. Appraisal can be seen as being a humanistic concept in which individual's aspirations, perceptions and needs are considered, as well as his or her performance in the job. Hence, performance evaluation is a necessary part of appraisal, but there is much more to it than that.

Purposes of appraisal

Appraisal is used for a variety of purposes within educational management, and these can be broadly classified into those that are aimed at the person being appraised and those that are aimed at management. In the former category, appraisal is used to encourage staff development, self-evaluation, team awareness and review of performance. From the management point of view, appraisal is used to clarify the organization's objectives, to improve communication, to develop staff resources and to evaluate the performance of the organization. An appraisal can be thought of as a system in which staff can provide feedback to management and management can provide feedback to staff, in terms of ambitions, growth and development and perceived needs. The process of appraisal centres around two questions:

- Are you contributing to the growth and development of the organization?
- Is the organization contributing to your own growth and development?

There is one purpose that has been omitted, but which is commonly suggested, namely discipline. Indeed, appraisal may be a euphemism for a procedure that ends in disciplinary action, but it should not be used as a system for disciplinary action, since this undermines the whole purpose of appraisal, i.e. the development of the individual. Clearly, disciplinary action may be required in some cases, but the procedure should be distinct from appraisal. Equally, an appraisal interview should not form the basis for an employer's reference, as this may inhibit free and frank discussion during appraisal.

Implementing appraisal

To have maximum benefit for appraisee and appraiser, the appraisal interview needs planning, and confidentiality must be ensured. The following sequence may be useful:

Preliminary reflection

A week or two before the appraisal interview, each party should take time to complete an initial form that focuses on key aspects of the appraisal such as those illustrated in Table 16.2. This ensures that each party has given consideration to the various aspects of appraisal and should mean that the interview itself can be used to best advantage.

The appraisal interview

When carrying out an appraisal interview. sufficient time must be allowed, so that two-way feedback can occur without a feeling of having to move on quickly. Considering that the appraisal interview may be the only time that the appraisee has the opportunity for in-depth interaction with the manager, it is not unreasonable to allocate an entire morning or afternoon. There must be no interruptions by telephones or callers, and instructions must be given to this effect. Provision of refreshment is useful, as it avoids the loss of continuity occasioned by a visit to the common room for this purpose.

The appraiser must approach the appraisal with as much objectivity as possible; it is often difficult to discuss the weaknesses of a respected colleague. On the other hand, the appraiser must be able to accept criticism of his or her own management of a team without becoming defensive. It is important to ensure that the appraiser actually knows the performance of the person being appraised. If the appraisee is a teacher, then the appraiser may wish to observe the appraisee's teaching. However, peer observation of teaching is a sensitive area, and may be resisted by the appraisee's professional organization or trade union. Nevertheless, with the advent of the Higher Education Academy (see below), it is likely that peer observation of teaching will become more established in higher education as it is accepted as a necessary and appropriate mechanism to facilitate professional development. The career development aspect of appraisal is important, and time should be given to the discussion of the CPD of the appraisee.

TABLE 16.2   Elements of appraisal

Section 1: Appraisee self-evaluation

Teaching and learning

- Identify personal goals for the previous year and explain how these were achieved
- Identify new skills acquired or new projects completed
- List aspects of the role that you do well
- List aspects of the role that could be improved upon, e.g. training and development/peer/manager support
- Provide details of undergraduate programmes that you contribute towards or are responsible for
- Provide details of postgraduate/post-registration programmes that you contribute towards or are responsible for
- Identify other teaching and learning activities that you contribute towards, e.g. recruitment and admission of students/staff, module management, curriculum development and validation processes
- Identify the number of students that you supervise at undergraduate level, postgraduate/post-registration level and research level

Research

- Provide details of research completed since the last appraisal (this can include publications, publications in press, conference papers)
- Provide details of research that is currently in progress
- Identify future research plans

External activities

- Provide details of activities that you undertake outside the university (this can include journal reviewer; editorial responsibilities; book proposal reviewer; representing the university on external bodies, e.g. HEA, QAA, HEFCW; clinical activities, e.g. link lecturer responsibilities; member of institutions, e.g. HEA; commercial activities, committee work).

The coming year

- Provide details of objectives for the coming year
- Identify personal and professional development activities, which are required to meet personal objectives, e.g. research, conferences, study days and short programmes, higher degrees, secondment opportunities
- Identify which of these activities would be your highest priority

Section 2: Appraiser evaluation

The appraiser evaluation might invite comments in relation to the appraisee's:

- quality of work
- productivity
- use of initiative
- teamwork
- tasks/projects that have been completed
- areas of work that require support/training

Section 3: Personal and professional development plan

This section of the appraisal should identify training or development activities, highlighting each activity in priority order. This should then be agreed upon by both appraisee and appraiser.

TEACHING TIP

Think about how you would like to develop your career carefully, the problems you have encountered and what training needs you have to address these problems. Think of your appraisal as an opportunity!

The action plan

At the end of the interview both parties should agree on an action plan for the appraisee that clearly states the actions which are to be undertaken over the coming year with regard to job performance and personal or professional development. This may involve taking further courses of study, gaining new experiences, attempting new techniques for teaching, or undertaking research. When the appraiser has completed the appraisal form, both parties should sign it. One copy is given to the appraisee and forms the basis of the following year's appraisal. A further copy is retained by the human resources department.

When an appraisal system is in development, there can be great anxiety amongst staff, particularly if they are suspicious of the motives for its introduction. Indeed, it has been referred to as 'an overt system of espionage by consent' and this indicates the fear that information will be used against the provider. Separating appraisal from discipline and references can go a long way towards reducing anxiety, but in the final analysis the system will be judged by the personal qualities and skills of the appraiser, including his or her sensitivity and trustworthiness. As stated above, the appraisal record should be agreed and signed by both appraisee and appraiser with a copy retained by each. In the event of a disagreement between the appraisee and appraiser in relation to performance or personal and professional development, the areas of disagreement should be recorded on the appraisal form. The appraisee can then seek an interview with the appraiser's line manager.

THE HIGHER EDUCATION ACADEMY

The Higher Education Academy (HEA) defines personal development planning as a:

'Structured and supported process undertaken by an individual to reflect upon their own learning, performance and/or achievement and to plan for their personal, educational and career development'

(HEA, 2012)

The HEA emphasizes that personal development planning (PDP) embraces a range of approaches to learning that link planning PDP, completing PDP, recording thoughts, ideas and experiences, and reflecting on experiences and the results of learning. One of the HEA's aims is to lead, support and inform the professional development and recognition of staff in higher education. The Higher Education Academy (HEA) has developed a National Professional Standards Framework for Teaching and Supporting Learning in Higher Education (HEA 2011) on behalf of the higher education sector across the UK. The framework, based upon applying areas of activity, core knowledge and professional values, provides a descriptor-based approach for higher education institutions to determine their own criteria in the application of the standards framework. These areas are applied to learning outcomes and assessment activities within professional development programmes in order to demonstrate application of the standards. The HEA supports the continuing professional development of staff engaged in teaching and supporting learning and states that lecturers should:

> *'Engage in continuing professional development in subjects/disciplines and their pedagogy, incorporating research, scholarship and the evaluation of professional practices'*
>
> (HEA, 2011)

The Framework's central purpose is to help those seeking to enhance the learning experience of their students, by improving the quality of their learning and teaching support (HEA, 2011). Additionally, it could be used to:

- Promote the professionalisation of teaching and learning support within the HE sector.
- Foster creative and innovative approaches to learning and teaching.
- Enable HE staff to gain recognition and reward for developing their capabilities as teachers and supporters of learning.
- Facilitate and support the design and delivery of initial and continuing education development programmes and activities.
- Demonstrate to students and other stakeholders the professionalism that staff and institutions bring to teaching and support for student learning.
- Support senior staff seeking to:
  - develop policies and systems for the recognition and reward of teaching and learning support staff;
  - promote a strong culture of teaching and learning support.

In order to demonstrate application of each of the standards, six areas of activity, core knowledge and professional values are applied to learning outcomes and assessment activities within the higher education institution's professional development programme (see Table 16.3). Higher education institutions can be accredited for their use of the new standards with the support of the HEA.

TABLE 16.3   The standards framework (*adapted from HEA, 2011*)

Areas of activity

- Design and planning of learning activities and/or programmes of study
- Teaching and/or supporting student learning
- Assessment and giving feedback to students
- Developing effective environments and student support and guidance
- Undertake continuing professional development in subjects and their pedagogy, whilst utilising research, scholarship and the evaluation of professional practices

Core knowledge (and understanding of)

- The subject material
- Appropriate methods for teaching and learning in the subject area and at the level of the academic programme
- How students learn, generally and in the subject
- The use of appropriate learning technologies
- Methods of evaluating the effectiveness of teaching
- The implications of quality assurance and enhancement for professional practice

Professional values

- Respect for individual learners
- Commitment to incorporating the process and outcomes of relevant research, scholarship and/or professional practice
- Commitment to development of learning communities
- Commitment to encouraging participation in higher education, acknowledging diversity and promoting equality of opportunity
- Commitment to continuing professional development and evaluation of practice

Staff development programmes

All higher education institutions are committed to providing relevant training and development opportunities and offer short programmes for staff development. The annual appraisal review identifies the training and development needs of staff, which are usually structured under the themes of teaching and learning, research and management. Some of the short programmes offered by universities are listed below:

Programmes related to teaching, learning and assessment:

- lecturing skills;
- small-group teaching;
- personal tutoring;
- creating an inclusive environment;
- designing teaching sessions and modules;
- strategies for assessment;
- enhancing feedback to students.

Programmes related to research:

- coaching and mentoring students;
- getting grant funding;
- getting a journal article published;
- preparing a book proposal;
- research governance and ethics;
- supervizing research students;
- academic career path.

Programmes related to management:

- time management;
- managing meetings;
- leading and managing teams;
- handling conflict;
- appraisal training;
- negotiating skills.

Personal and professional development:

- rapid reading;
- objective setting;
- problem solving.

RESEARCH AND SCHOLARLY ACTIVITY

As part of their contract of employment, academic staff in higher education are required to engage in research and scholarly activity (RSA); this generic term covers a range of activities contributing to the continuing professional development of staff members. RSA takes place in two main ways:

- as ongoing activity throughout the teaching year;
- as self-managed activity separate from time-tabled teaching weeks and annual leave entitlement.

Research and scholarly activity should inform the individual's teaching, so the nature of the activity is normally negotiated between the staff member and his or her manager. However, during the annual staff appraisal process, teachers are normally required to demonstrate how they have used their RSA time. Figure 16.3 identifies typical RSA activities.

The most significant imperative for undertaking research and scholarly activity is the research excellence framework (REF).

FIGURE 16.3　Research and scholarly activities

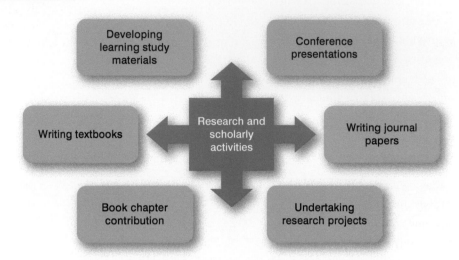

RESEARCH EXCELLENCE FRAMEWORK

The Research Excellence Framework (REF) is the new system for assessing the quality of research in UK higher education institutions (HEIs); it replaces the Research Assessment Exercise (RAE) and will be completed in 2014. The REF will be undertaken by the four UK higher education funding bodies; managed by the REF team based at the Higher Education Funding Council for England (HEFCE) and overseen by the REF Steering Group, which consists of representatives from the four funding bodies:

- Department for Employment and Learning (DELNI);
- Higher Education Funding Council for England (HEFCE);
- Higher Education Funding Council for Wales (HEFCW);
- Scottish Higher Education Funding Council (SHEFC).

The primary purpose of the REF is to produce assessment outcomes for each submission made by higher education institutions:

- The funding bodies intend to use the assessment outcomes to inform the selective allocation of their research funding to HEIs, with effect from 2015–16.
- The assessment provides accountability for public investment in research and produces evidence of the benefits of this investment.
- The assessment outcomes provide benchmarking information and establish reputational yardsticks.

Through the research excellence framework, REF (2011a) state:

'the UK funding bodies aim to develop and sustain a dynamic and internationally competitive research sector that makes a major contribution to economic prosperity, national wellbeing and the expansion and dissemination of knowledge.'

The REF is a process of expert review where higher education institutions are invited to make submissions in 36 units of assessment, which are assessed by a sub-panel of experts for each unit of assessment, working under the guidance of four main panels. Sub-panels apply a set of generic assessment criteria and level definitions, to produce an overall quality profile for each submission. Institutions will be invited to make submissions to each unit of assessment and assessed in terms of:

- *The quality of research outputs* This will continue to be the primary factor in the assessment. Sub-panels assess the quality of research outputs in terms of their 'originality, significance and rigour' with reference to international research quality standards.
- *The wider impact of research* Sub-panels assess the 'reach and significance' of impacts on the economy, society and/or culture that were underpinned by excellent research conducted in the submitted unit, as well as the submitted unit's approach to enabling impact from its research.
- *The vitality of the research environment* Sub-panels assess the research environment in terms of its 'vitality and sustainability', including contribution to the wider vitality and sustainability of the wider discipline or research base.

The final weightings attached to each of these areas are:

- research outputs – 65%;
- impact – 20% (may increase in subsequent REFs);
- environment – 15%.

The outcomes of the overall assessment will identify excellence; panels will produce a sub-profile for each element (outputs, impact and environment), to be combined into an overall excellence profile. The profiles will show the proportion of submitted work at each point on a five-point scale (1* to 4* plus Unclassified). The definitions of overall quality levels and definitions of starred levels, which apply to the 2014 REF, are identified in Table 16.4.

TABLE 16.4	REF definitions of quality levels (REF, 2011b)
Four star	Quality that is world-leading in terms of originality, significance and rigour
Three star	Quality that is internationally excellent in terms of originality, significance and rigour but which falls short of the highest standards of excellence
Two star	Quality that is recognized internationally in terms of originality, significance and rigour
One star	Quality that is recognized nationally in terms of originality, significance and rigour
Unclassified	Quality that falls below the standard of nationally recognized work. Or work which does not meet the published definition of research for the purposes of this assessment

RESEARCH GOVERNANCE

In 2005, the Department of Health (DH) published the *Research Governance Framework for Health and Social Care'*. The document sets principles, requirements and standards for clinical and non-clinical research undertaken by the DoH, NHS, social care agencies, industry, charities, research councils and universities within the health and social care system. The framework seeks to:

> *'promote improvements in research quality and involves bringing general performance in line with those at the leading edge; it provides a context for the encouragement of creative and innovative research and for the effective transfer of learning, technology and best practice to improve care.'*
>
> (DH, 2005)

The standards of the framework apply to the domains of ethics, science, information, health and safety, employment, and finance and intellectual property. It sets out clearly the responsibilities of participants, researchers, investigators, research funders and research sponsors. It also sets out the key responsibilities of:

- universities and others employing researchers;
- organizations providing care;
- care professionals;
- research ethics committees.

Further principles of the framework are identified in Table 16.5 and research governance frameworks for Northern Ireland, Scotland and Wales are identified in the further reading list.

WRITING FOR PUBLICATION

Publications are an important form of continuing professional development, as well as a significant generator of funds and kudos for the educational institution. Publications will enhance an individual's curriculum vitae and will possibly influence short-listing and employment prospects. The term 'publication' encompasses a wide range of activities:

- sole authoring of books;
- editorial authorship of books involving a number of contributors;
- writing chapters in edited books;
- writing journal papers or articles;
- writing open, distance and flexible learning study materials;
- writing material for electronic media, for example CD-ROM, Internet.

TABLE 16.5   Research governance (*adapted from DH, 2005*)

Research governance

- Defines mechanisms of delivering the principles, requirements and standards within the framework
- Describes monitoring and assessment arrangements
- Improves research and safeguards the public by:
  - Enhancing ethical awareness and scientific quality
  - Promoting good practice
  - Reducing adverse incidents and ensuring lessons are learnt
  - Forestalling poor performance and misconduct
- Is for all those who:
  - Design research studies
  - Participate in research
  - Host research in their organization
  - Fund research proposals or infrastructure
  - Manage research
  - Undertake research
- Is for managers and staff in all professional groups, no matter how senior or junior
- Is for those working in all health and social care research environments, including:
  - Primary care
  - Secondary care
  - Tertiary care
  - Social care
  - Public health

Writing and editing books

Publishing is a commercial enterprise and, like any other commercial enterprise, profitability is a major consideration. When presented with a book proposal from a prospective author, publishers have to estimate the market and projected sales targets. Hence, a proposal must have something special that makes it capable of attracting sales in a very competitive market, and it is more likely to be accepted for publication if it meets one or more of the following criteria:

- It addresses a need that has developed out of some professional policy decision, for example clinical supervision or clinical governance.
- It addresses an aspect of nurse education not previously addressed in the literature, i.e. a 'first in the field'.
- It adopts a different or novel approach to the subject, making it more attractive to potential readers than existing titles.
- It contains contributions by acknowledged experts in the field, i.e. it includes 'star names'.
- It is written by an author who already has one or more successful publications with the same company.

If a teacher is interested in writing a book, the first consideration is whether he or she will be the sole author or the editor for a number of contributors. In both cases, the work can be shared with one or more authors/editors. However, the more authors/editors that are involved, the less any individual's royalty payments. Royalties are paid on the sales of a book, usually 10–12 per cent, and are paid each year at the end of the tax year.

At first glance, becoming the editor of a book seems a fairly easy way of getting into print; the idea is quite seductive, that you simply need to find a few people who will each contribute a chapter on some aspect of the book's theme, add an introductory chapter yourself, and you have a book under your belt! However, the reality is very different; most authors would rather write a dozen sole-authored books than be the editor of one multi-contributor text!

The editor's job requires a combination of characteristics, including vision, literary skills, administrative skills, and above all interpersonal communication skills. Vision is required if one is to come up with an idea for an edited book that will make a significant contribution to professional knowledge or debate, and at the same time more or less guarantee sufficient sales to meet the publisher's targets. It is also required when deciding the structure of the book and the decisions about who should be invited to contribute a chapter or chapters. Editing a book is a complex business, and good administrative skills are essential to maintain communication with the contributing authors. The more contributors one has in a book, the more difficult the task of editing becomes. The very fact that contributors are chosen for their expertise will inevitably mean that they have other priorities that get in the way of manuscript deadlines, and one of the most frustrating aspects of editing is the chasing-up of chapter drafts from contributors. This is where interpersonal communication skills come in; a mixture of friendliness, respect and assertiveness will go a long way in encouraging recalcitrant authors to submit their manuscripts, but as a last resort the editor can always enlist the assistance of the publisher to send a more formal reminder to them.

Writer's block

One of the problems encountered by professional writers from time to time is the so-called 'writer's block', a psychological state in which an experienced writer becomes unable to write, sometimes for considerable periods of time. This phenomenon is more likely to occur in the case of sole-authored works, where the workload is considerably greater than that involved in contributing one or two chapters to an edited volume. The everyday workload of teachers in nurse education makes major demands on their time and commonly spills over into their private time in evenings and weekends. Hence, the added demands of authoring a book can be very stressful, particularly as deadlines approach and slippage occurs. This stress can be compounded by feelings of guilt about neglecting family responsibilities, and the demands of writing may mean that insufficient time is available for recreational pursuits that are so important for 're-charging the batteries'.

TEACHING TIP

Remember to make some time to look after yourself; if you become ill and/ or exhausted you will not be able to meet any of the demands mentioned above.

There are a number of strategies that may help prevent or eliminate writer's block. It is important to ensure that, wherever possible, writing is done when you are fresh and alert. Writing is a creative activity, and it is very difficult to be creative if you are exhausted in the evening after a heavy day's work. Maintaining regularity of writing is also important, because the more one slips behind in the writing schedule, the more pressure and guilt we feel; this in turn may cause further blocking, so writers should try to do even a small amount of writing each day if possible.

Some publishers prefer to meet with their authors on a regular basis throughout the period of writing, so as to maintain contact and to monitor the author's progress. Whilst this may not be welcomed by every author, meetings with the publisher once per term serve as mini-deadlines that help to maintain focus and ensure that the schedule is adhered to.

Writer's rights

Given the ubiquity of photocopying, authors and editors of books need to know their rights in relation to their intellectual property. Chapter 5 discusses the legal position with regard to photocopying of books and journal articles and identifies the restrictions on the amount and type of material that can be copied. The Authors' Licensing and Collecting Society (ALCS) exists to collect fees for photocopying and to pass 50 per cent of these on to those authors who are members; the other 50 per cent goes to the publisher. Membership involves a small annual fee. ALCS has issued a declaration of academic writers' rights (ALCS, 2012) that covers the following areas:

- It acknowledges the role of the academic author as a communicator.
- It emphasizes the academic author's aspiration to be a full partner in the communication process with academic employers, publishers, libraries and users.
- It emphasizes that a fair balance needs to be struck between the needs of academic authors, educational institutions, publishers, learned societies.
- A contract should be used to specify the uses of an academic author's work, and the author should not be made to transfer copyright.
- Most academic authors wish to get a fair share of revenues for their work.
- The moral rights of authors are important, for example the right of the author to be identified as the author of the work, and the right to prevent the work being altered or amended without permission.

Prior to 1997, fees for photocopying only applied to books, but it is now possible for authors of journal articles to receive 25 per cent of the photocopying fee, provided that the publisher does not own less than 90 per cent of the photocopying rights.

Writing for professional journals

Writing an article for a professional journal is usually the first step that teachers take into the world of publication. Unlike book publications, journals are rated according to the degree of prestige they carry, so the most prestigious journals are also the most difficult ones in which to get an article published. Indeed, the REF takes the title of the journal into account when rating publications in higher education institutions. Most journals offer a guide for contributors that covers such aspects as word length, submission process, referencing format, illustrations and charts, and information about the review process.

Trouble-shooter's checklist for prospective authors

Alton-Lee (1998) offers the following checklist for prospective authors, based upon the critical feedback given to authors by reviewers. Although a little dated, the checklist, which remains relevant today, identifies 13 weaknesses demonstrated by prospective authors, and these are given in rank order of occurrence, from most common to least common, in the 142 studies researched.

1. Lack of methodological transparency, adequacy, or rationale: insufficient information given.
2. Unjustified claims: based on insufficient evidence, or in spite of evidence.
3. Shortcomings in format: title, abstract, presentation of data, style.
4. Theoretical shortcomings: failure to provide, articulate or develop theoretical perspectives.
5. Data analysis problems: inadequate or lacking in substance.
6. Inadequacies in literature reviews: insufficient, dated, not linked to subsequent studies.
7. Insufficient clarify of focus: focus not clear at outset, focus changed, no statement of research question or purpose of study.
8. Conceptual confusion: need to take more care with definitions, and use of metaphor.
9. Parochial blinkers: ensure that local contexts, policies and practices are made meaningful to readers in different regions or countries.
10. Does not add to the international research literature: need to ensure that the manuscript extends or develops the international literature in the area of study.
11. Failure to link findings to the research literature: authors had not linked their findings to the relevant research literature.
12. Lack of critical reflections on implicit assumptions: authors are challenged to focus critically on unexamined issues implicit in their manuscripts such as gender, political and economic resource issues.
13. Victory claims: reviewers rejected overly optimistic outcomes and achievements as lacking in credibility.

An interesting study that surveyed the views of editors of nursing journals about the process for submission and review of articles is described by Wildman (1998). Data were received from 22 journals, 16 of which routinely submitted articles to referees or reviewers. In terms of the quality of papers submitted, the data showed that there were two main aspects that made a manuscript immediately appealing to editors: relevance and presentation. There were three main grounds that would cause editors to immediately reject a manuscript: irrelevance, poor presentation, and failure to adhere to guidelines.

The most common problems with manuscripts included poor academic work, poor use of English, non-adherence to guidelines, inappropriate references, poor presentation and unaltered coursework. The points most frequently raised with authors about the suitability of their manuscripts for publication included a requirement for better editing to improve understanding, amendments to meet journal requirements, attention to writing style, a need to be more critical, and an alteration of the title. Based upon the study, and the literature, the author offers a checklist for successful publication that includes the following helpful points.

Prospective authors should:

- Consider discussing their work with the journal editor before submitting it for publication.
- Use a 'critical friend' to read the article before submission.
- Be prepared to accept constructive criticism from editors and reviewers.
- Celebrate when the article is accepted, but be prepared for a long wait before it is published.

In support of the studies undertaken by Alton-Lee (1998) and Wildman (1998), Shattell *et al.* (2010) also highlighted factors that influenced a reviewer's recommendation for publication; namely writing style and grammar, professional significance, methodology used and theoretical significance.

Refereeing journal papers

Refereeing journal papers is used to determine the suitability of an article for publication. All journal papers should seek to inform and educate the potential reader, and they are usually assessed for knowledge and understanding, attitude, skills, application and synthesis. All prospective authors are encouraged to follow the 'author guidelines' required by individual journals and these guidelines should be followed explicitly.

Burnard and Hannigan (2001) reflect on the process of reviewing journal papers submitted for publication and acknowledge that for those working in higher education, 'getting work published is an essential activity'. The authors focus on the range of problems often associated with the reviewing process, particularly individual reviewers' motivation, mood, time availability, and their preferences and prejudices and identify that there are many other contributing factors that impact on the overall variability of the reviewing process. Additionally, the issue of anonymity is also addressed; some journals reveal the reviewer's identity, whereas most do not.

When discussing the process of peer review, Burnard and Hannigan (2001) point out that reports of submitted articles can vary considerably; sometimes with little regard given to how prospective authors might feel when reading the report, especially if the reviewer has offered less than favourable comments. The authors argue that bluntness by the reviewer can impact on motivation and can discourage prospective authors from developing their work for publication; reviewers are advised to give careful consideration to the tone and manner in which their comments are conveyed.

In light of this, Burnard and Hannigan (2001) believe that the current reviewing process should be 'reviewed' and make the following comments:

- the reviewing process is not uniform across journals;
- the methods of reviewing differ considerably (e.g. tick-boxes, detailed report);
- there is a lack of clarity and reason for anonymous reviewing;
- guidelines should be available to reviewers to ensure that their comments are 'concrete' and to avoid disparaging remarks.

The authors remind us that, like students, prospective authors are also learning a craft, so reviewing journal papers should be a supportive and encouraging process.

An online survey by Freda *et al.* (2009) examined the experiences of 1675 nursing peer reviewers who reviewed manuscripts for professional nursing journals. They identified issues with training and support for reviewers in terms of feedback on reviews and concluded that journal editors could consider instituting programmes of orientation, training, and support. Freda *et al.* (2009) also revealed that reviewers should consider discussing these issues with editors to make their needs for feedback and training known as this could ultimately strengthen the nursing literature in the future.

Presenting papers at conferences

Presenting papers at conferences is considered to be an essential component of continuing professional development in higher education. Conferences are advertised a long time in advance, accompanied by a request for submission of papers. Guidelines on the length of papers are issued by the conference organizers, and if a paper is accepted it is allocated a slot in the conference timetable. Papers are usually read by the presenter, but there is no hard-and-fast rule about the style of presentation. Conference organizers often make conference papers available to delegates on registration, or, alternatively, the papers are published soon after the event.

Writing open, distance and flexible learning study materials

The foregoing discussion about writing books and academic articles will apply to a greater or lesser extent to the writing of open, distance and flexible learning study materials, depending upon whether or not the materials are written for a commercial publisher or for an academic institution. In the former case, they can be considered to be like any other commercial publication, but in the latter there are a number of significant differences from ordinary publishing.

Copyright issues

The employing institution holds the copyright of any open, distance and flexible learning study materials produced by staff in the course of their employment, even though individuals are named as the author of such work. Hence, all such materials must carry the copyright symbol and text in the recommended form of words to ensure full protection of the copyright.

Corporate identity rules

All higher education institutions have corporate identity rules whose purpose is to ensure that business stationery, business cards and promotional and other material produced by the institution conform consistently to the correct image. The rules include such aspects as the institution's crest, logo and corporate colours; the corporate typeface, front and back covers, and the corporate house style for letters, memoranda and facsimile.

Issues relating to the writing of open, distance and flexible learning materials are discussed in Chapter 4.

Review questions

1. Explore opportunities for continuing professional development (CPD) as a nurse lecturer.

2. What are the different aspects of a nurse lecturer role and what skills are required for each aspect?

3. What should the outcomes of an appraisal be?

4. Why is research and scholarly activity important for a nurse lecturer?

SUMMARY

- Within all sectors of education, continuing professional development is acknowledged as being essential for maintaining and improving the quality of educational provision.

- The importance of CPD to the work of the higher education institution is underlined by its inclusion in the agenda of annual staff appraisal interviews.

- The demand for more flexible approaches to study has led to the development of open and distance learning programmes which allow post-registration students to study in their own time, and without the need for attendance at an institution.

- Nurse teachers' roles are extremely varied and diverse but usually involve teaching, curriculum planning and administration.

- Teachers need to contribute effectively to the continuous improvement of quality by evaluating their own practice, by identifying opportunities for personal and professional development, and by participating in programmes of professional development.

- Staff appraisal can be seen as being a humanistic concept in which the individual's aspirations, perceptions and needs are considered, as well as his or her performance in the job.

- Appraisal is used to encourage staff development, self-evaluation, team awareness and review of performance.

- Appraisal, from the management point of view, is used to clarify the organization's objectives, to improve communication, to develop staff resources and to evaluate the performance of the organization.

- Personal development planning is a structured and supported process undertaken by individuals to reflect upon their own learning, performance and/or achievement and to plan for their personal, educational and career development.

- All higher education institutions are committed to providing relevant training and development opportunities and offer short programmes for staff development.

- Academic staff in higher education are required to engage in research and scholarly activity.

- REF is a mechanism for allocating research funding to institutions based upon the quality of their research and is conducted by the four UK higher education funding councils every four to five years.

- Research governance sets principles, requirements and standards for clinical and non-clinical research.

- Publications are an important form of continuing professional development, as well as a significant generator of funds and kudos for the educational institution.

- Writing an article for a professional journal is usually the first step that teachers take into the world of publication.

- All journal papers should seek to inform and educate the potential reader and are usually assessed according to knowledge and understanding, attitude, skills, application and synthesis.

References

Alton-Lee, A. (1998) A trouble shooter's checklist for prospective authors derived from reviewers' critical feedback. *Teaching and Teacher Education* 14(8) 88–90

Authors' Licensing and Collecting Society (2012) *Academic Writers and Rights*. London: ALCS

Burnard, P. and Hannigan, B. (2001) Reviewing the review process: towards good practice in the peer review of manuscripts submitted to nursing journals. *Nurse Education Today* 21(3) 238–242

DH (2005) *Research Governance Framework for Health and Social Care* (2nd Edition). London: The Stationery Office

Freda, M.C., Kearney, M., Baggs, J.D., Broome, M.E. Dougherty, M. (2009) Peer reviewer training and editor support: results from an international survey of nursing peer reviewers. *Journal of Professional Nursing* 25(2) 101–108

HEA (2011) *The UK Professional Standards Framework for Teaching and Supporting Learning in Higher Education*. Available from: http://www.heacademy.ac.uk/ukpsf

HEA (2012) *PDP: Personal Development Planning*. Available from: http://www.heacademy.ac.uk/resources/detail/pdp/pdp

NMC (2008a) *The Code: Standards of Conduct, Performance and Ethics for Nurses and Midwives*. London: Nursing Midwifery Council

NMC (2008b) *Standards to Support Learning and Assessment in Practice*. London: Nursing Midwifery Council

NMC (2011) *The PREP Handbook*. London: Nursing Midwifery Council

REF (2011a) Research Excellence Framework sector impact assessment. Available from: http://www.ref.ac.uk/background

REF (2011b) Assessment framework and guidance on submissions. Available from: http://www.ref.ac.uk/media/ref/content/pub/assessmentframeworkandguidanceonsubmissions/02_11.pdf

Research Excellence Framework. Available from: http://www.ref.ac.uk

Shattell, M.M., Chinn, P., Thomas, S.P. and Cowling, W.R. (2010) Authors' and editors' perspectives on peer review quality in three scholarly nursing journals. *Journal of Nursing Scholarship* 42(1) 58–65

Wildman, S. (1998) Publishing your work in nursing journals. *Professional Nurse* 13(7) 419–422

Further Reading

Department for Employment and Learning Northern Ireland (DELNI). Available from: http://www.delni.gov.uk

DHSSPSNI (2009) *Research governance framework for health and social care*. Belfast: Department of Health, Social Services and Public Safety

Freda, M.C. and Kearney, M. (2005) An international survey of nurse editors' roles and practices. *Journal of Nursing Scholarship* 37(1) 87–94

Higher Education Funding Council for England (HEFCE). Available from: http://www.hefce.ac.uk

Higher Education Funding Council for Wales (HEFCW). Available from: http://www.hefcw.ac.uk

Kearney, M. and Freda, M.C. (2005) Nurse editors' views on the peer review process. *Research in Nursing and Health* 28(6) 444–452

SG (2009) *Research governance framework for health and community care* (2nd Edition). Edinburgh: Scottish Government

Scottish Higher Education Funding Council (SHEFC). Available from: http://www.sfc.ac.uk/home/home.aspx

WG (2009) *Research governance framework for health and social care* (2nd Edition). Cardiff: Welsh Government

CHAPTER 17
CONTINUING PROFESSIONAL DEVELOPMENT: THE CLINICAL CONTEXT

THE AIMS OF THIS CHAPTER ARE:

- To explore continuing professional development for nurses in clinical practice and the requirements of professional regulation

- To illustrate methods of self-directed and assisted CPD activities

- To discuss the key elements of staff appraisal

- To outline how learning and development needs can be identified by means of personal development planning

KEY TERMS

Clinical audit
PREP

In Chapter 16, continuing professional development (CPD) was discussed in the context of the university, but there are also important CPD issues relating to clinical and community practice that have a bearing on the role of the nurse teacher. This chapter addresses the NMC PREP standards; resources for CPD; staff appraisal, personal development planning; clinical governance; the National Institute for Health and Clinical Excellence (NIHCE); clinical effectiveness and evidence-based practice; clinical audit and self-assessment.

POST REGISTRATION EDUCATION AND PRACTICE (PREP)

The RCN (2003a) emphasizes not only that all nurses must embrace and engage in the principles of continuing professional development and lifelong learning but also that professions that work together should learn together. Standard 6 of the NMC Code of Professional Conduct (2008) tells us that we must maintain our professional knowledge and competence. It further states that all registrants:

> *'Must keep skills and knowledge up to date throughout their working life and take part in appropriate learning and practice activities that maintain and develop competence and performance.'*

Post-registration education and practice (PREP) standards are designed to keep nurses up to date with new developments in practice and encourage us to reflect for ourselves. It provides an excellent framework for CPD and, although not a guarantee of competence, it is a key element of clinical governance. Within the nursing profession, CPD is a mandatory requirement, which must be met in order for registration to be renewed, and nurse lecturers are not exempt from this.

The NMC (2011) PREP handbook identifies two PREP standards that affect a practitioner's registration. These are:

- the PREP (practice) Standard; and
- the PREP (continuing professional development) Standard.

The PREP (practice) Standard

This standard requires nurses, midwives and specialist community public health nurses to have completed a minimum of 450 hours of practice during the three years prior to renewal of registration. If registrants do not meet this requirement, they are expected to complete an approved return to practice course before registration can be renewed.

The PREP (CPD) Standard

The NMC (2011) points out that this standard requires a commitment from registrants to undertake continuing professional development and:

- undertake at least 35 hours of learning relevant to practice during the three years prior to renewal of registration;
- maintain a personal professional profile of learning activity;
- comply with any request from the NMC to audit how these requirements have been met.

The PREP standard can be met in a variety of ways, and *The PREP Handbook* (NMC, 2011) provides a template for recording evidence of CPD learning: i.e. evidence of where the registrant was working; the nature of the learning activity; a description of the learning activity and how the learning activity informed and influenced the work of the registrant. Table 17.1 outlines a suggested template for recording evidence of PREP.

TABLE 17.1 Template for recording evidence of PREP (*adapted from NMC, 2011*)

CPD PERIOD – the three year period to which this learning applies

From: To:

WORKPLACE – where you were working when the learning activity took place

Name of organization:
Brief description of your work/role:

NATURE OF THE LEARNING ACTIVITY

Date:

Briefly describe the learning activity, for example, reading a relevant clinical article, attending a course, observing practice:

State how many hours this took:

DESCRIPTION OF THE LEARNING ACTIVITY

Describe what the learning activity consisted of, for example, why you decided to do the learning activity, how the opportunity presented itself and what you expect to gain from it

OUTCOME OF THE LEARNING ACTIVITY

How did the learning activity inform and influence your work? Do you intend to follow-up the learning?

It could be argued that all nurses should receive some assistance from their employers for CPD, but the primary responsibility for maintaining competence to practice remains with the individual. Continuing professional development ensures that the practitioner remains not only fit to practise but also develops the knowledge and competence needed to advance practice and progress through clinical and other career pathways (RCN, 2004). However, the RCN (2004) acknowledges realistically that employers wanting to access government finance and individual nurses seeking CPD support from their employers face many obstacles. In an attempt to overcome this, the RCN suggests an increase in collaboration between clinicians and nurse teachers to facilitate work-based learning, which should be research focused and educationally grounded.

The DoH (2008) fosters the belief that post-registration education and CPD should be grounded in clinical governance and draw on clinical audit. Clinical effectiveness findings enable the development of a research-aware workforce. The clinical governance framework is an umbrella term for everything that helps to maintain and improve high standards of care for patients and the RCN (2003b) emphasizes how education, training and development are an integral component of this framework.

RESOURCES FOR CPD

There are many different ways in which CPD can be accomplished and not just through undertaking post-registration courses. Figure 17.1 shows how CPD can be achieved; Figure 17.2 gives examples of self-directed CPD, and Figure 17.3 shows CPD activities that require support.

FIGURE 17.1   Examples of CPD activities

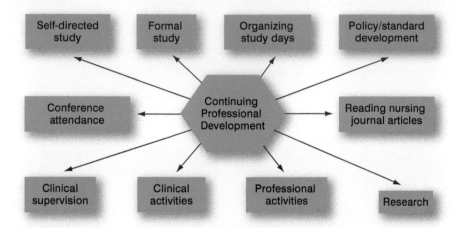

FIGURE 17.2   Examples of self-directed CPD activities

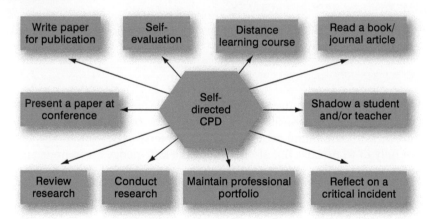

FIGURE 17.3   Examples of assisted CPD activities

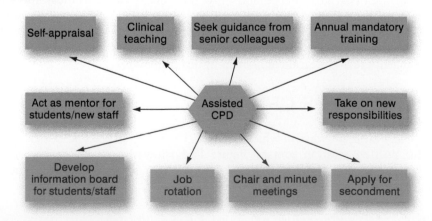

In its 'learning zone' section, the *Nursing Standard* provides a weekly CPD article; ten multiple-choice questions linked to the article give readers the opportunity to assess their knowledge and understanding of the article. Readers are encouraged to answer the questions and record the time that it takes to complete them. Once the self-assessment has been completed, it can be included in a professional portfolio and used towards the PREP requirements. Additionally, readers can gain a certificate of learning by reading a *Nursing Standard* 'learning zone' article and writing a practice profile of between 750 and 1000 words. The journal provides a framework for reflection for completing the practice profile and offers a number of prompts for readers to consider before submitting their profile:

1. What have I learnt from this article and how does it relate to my practice?

2. To what extend were the intended learning outcomes met?

3. What can I apply immediately to my practice or patient care?

4. Is there anything I did not understand, need to explore or read further to clarify my understanding?

5. What else do I need to do to extend my professional development in this area?

6. What other needs have I identified in relation to my professional development?

7. How might I achieve the above?

STAFF APPRAISAL

Although the fundamental principles associated with staff appraisal were discussed in Chapter 16, staff appraisal in the clinical setting is equally relevant and important. Until recently, there was little emphasis or, indeed, literature focused on appraisal in practice. Very often, documentation to support appraisal or individual performance review (IPR) consisted of one page identifying the following elements:

■ objectives for the coming year;

■ training and development needs;

■ resources required;

■ how the objectives would be measured.

This is in considerable contrast to the appraisal system undertaken in higher education; but the CPD requirements of clinicians are vital to ensure professional development and the future needs of patient care delivery and management. The Care Quality Commission believes that staff appraisal in practice should be based upon the principle that all staff have three fundamental rights:

■ the right to know what is expected of them;

■ the right to know how they will be measured;

■ the right to know how they are doing.

According to the NHS Staff Council (2010) a good appraisal system should include the following:

■ the agreement of clear objectives at the start of the appraisal cycle – these should be SMART, i.e. specific, measurable, achievable, realistic and timed;

■ the agreement of a related personal development plan to ensure that the staff member is assisted to develop any skills necessary to achieve the objectives (as well as development for career progression);

■ regular reviews to assess and discuss progress where honest and objective feedback is provided;

■ the giving of quality feedback to ensure that there are no surprises at the annual performance review discussion.

To fulfil all of the above:

■ managers and supervisors should be trained to undertake appraisal properly;

■ all internal monitoring systems should cover implementation and equity.

Table 17.2 demonstrates key elements of the staff appraisal system.

TABLE 17.2 Staff appraisal system
Part A: Taking stock
What do you see as the purpose of your job?
Last year's objectives
• Summarize your main objectives last year • Note your successes, personal achievements, difficulties and changes
Skills and strengths
• What do you feel are your skills and strengths in your current job? • Do you have skills and abilities that are not fully used and which you would be interested in developing? • What hinders full effectiveness in your job and what can be done about it (e.g. lack of information, communication issues, resources, management style, systems)? • Are there any issues relating to equality and diversity that you wish to raise (e.g. working hours, health issues, which may be impacting on your working life)? • Are there any issues relating to health and safety that you wish to raise?
Part B: Planning ahead/action plan
• What will be the key objectives in your job for the next year (objectives should be SMART)? • Medium- and long-term development. (In the longer term, what career developments, personal ambitions or changes in duties could be considered?)
Part C: Planning ahead/action plan
• Appraisee: identify priorities for discussion • Appraiser: identify additional points for discussion
Part D: Agenda: to include objectives and target date

PERSONAL DEVELOPMENT PLANNING

The implementation of *Agenda for Change* (DH, 2003) and the process of personal development review are becoming the accepted means of turning learning into improvements in care and services. Harding and Salmon (2005) recognize that most activities in the workplace can be regarded as opportunities for self-directed learning, for teaching others, or for strengthening and enhancing knowledge and skills. The authors maintain that most professional learning is experiential or reflective in nature, occasioned by events and experiences at work. They define on-the-job learning and development as follows:

- participating in specific areas of work;
- project work;
- secondments;
- reflective practice;
- professional and clinical supervision;
- mentoring;
- work shadowing;
- acting-up into senior posts.

Most people disregard learning that does not involve an academic course, but Jenkins (2006) stresses that flexible approaches to learning and a willingness to accept new technologies are vital. She suggests that learning is beneficial because:

- it encourages you to direct your own life;
- it stimulates you to see alternative approaches;
- it helps you maintain an interest in your career;
- new skills can be offered to employers and patients;
- learning helps to remove age barriers to career development.

Knowledge and skills framework

The NHS Knowledge and Skills Framework (KSF) demands that participation in annual appraisal is undertaken by all staff, leading to the production of a personal development plan (PDP).

According to the Department of Health (DH, 2004), one of the key purposes of the NHS KSF is:

'to facilitate the development of services so that they better meet the needs of users and the public through investing in the development of all members of staff.'

The framework also serves to:

'support the effective learning and development of individuals and teams – with all members of staff being supported to learn throughout their careers and develop in a variety of ways, and being given the resources to do so.'

The DH (2004) emphasizes that the KSF is designed to form the basis of a development review process; it is intended to be an 'ongoing cycle of review, planning, development and evaluation for all staff' that makes links between the needs of the organization and the development needs of individual staff members. Figure 17.4 demonstrates the development review process.

FIGURE 17.4 Development review process (*Adapted from DH, 2004*)

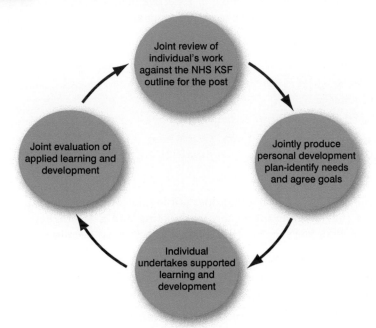

The DoH (2004) development review process consists of:

■ reviewing how individuals apply their knowledge and skills to meet the demands of their current post and identifying whether they have any development needs;

■ developing a personal development plan for the individual outlining the learning and development to take place;

■ learning and development for the individual supported by the reviewer;

■ evaluating the learning and development and reflecting on how it has been applied to work.

The DH (2004) explains that the review process benefits individuals by:

■ enabling them to be clear about the knowledge and skills that they need to apply in their post;

■ enabling them to access appropriate learning and development;

■ showing how their work relates to the work of others in their immediate team and beyond;

■ identifying the knowledge and skills that they need to learn and develop throughout their careers;

■ providing a structure and process for the NHS to invest in individuals' learning and development throughout their working life in the NHS.

Personal development planning identifies the learning and development needs of individuals and also identifies how these needs are taken forward. As in the appraisal system, PDP should be recorded and copies retained by the individual and by the reviewer. Some of the main points to be considered when developing a PDP are outlined by the DH (2004):

- The learning and development requirements of each individual must be identified in order to develop and apply knowledge and skills in the short and long term.
- The learning and development must be prioritized through considering:
  - statutory and regulatory requirements;
  - the individual's strengths and weaknesses.
- The individual's preferred method of learning must be identified.
- A person who has responsibility for taking the different aspects of the learning and development forward should be identified.
- A date for the next formal review should be arranged.

All CPD and PDP must be evaluated to identify the learning that has occurred. The purpose of the evaluation stage within the development review process is to enable individuals to reflect on the effectiveness of their learning and development, and identify how learning has improved their application of knowledge and skills in their post; it is also to provide feedback to the organization, highlighting areas for improvement.

CLINICAL EDUCATION CO-ORDINATOR/FACILITATOR

Students undertaking a practice placement within the clinical setting are supported by a range of qualified and unqualified personnel, and support mechanisms for qualified staff have already been established. The primary personnel actively involved in supporting pre-registration students include qualified nurses with mentor status and education co-ordinators or clinical facilitators (Hughes, 2006). There appears to be a plethora of terms associated with the role of education co-ordinators in the clinical practice setting, including:

- teacher/practitioner;
- clinical teacher;
- education facilitator;
- practice educator;
- practice development nurse/facilitator;
- educator/practitioner (Hughes, 2006);
- liaison lecturer.

These education co-ordinators plan practice placements, allocate students to appropriate learning situations and provide personal support to students, mentors and all qualified and unqualified staff. Practice-based teaching is not new, and Koh (2002) believes that it is often seen as a means of enhancing student learning and enriching the clinical learning environment. To support students and qualified staff in practice, effective educational activities within the clinical environment should be available.

Clinical education facilitators are responsible for the selection and organization of training and development in practice settings. McCormack and Slater (2006) explain that the facilitators' role can be seen as contributing to cultural change within an organization. The authors go on to explain how the clinical education facilitator is in a good position to lead the development of a learning culture through a work-based learning model; the role is a respectable and valued one, allowing facilitators to influence learning developments in the workplace.

Some of the benefits of an education co-ordinator/practice educator in practice are identified by Hughes (2006):

- helps with problems and advice;
- supportive;
- available if needed;
- approachable;
- aids in achieving skills;
- provides introductions to relevant staff;
- assists with documentation.

Training needs analysis

One of the many roles of the education co-ordinator is to identify the training and development needs of qualified and unqualified staff. Training needs analysis (TNA) is defined as:

> *'a training and educational strategy that meets the continuing professional needs of healthcare staff, both qualified and unqualified.'*

It is also seen as a means of improving service delivery (Gould *et al.*, 2004). Pedder (1998) refers to the TNA as a systematic consultation and identification of the learning or training of the key people involved; she describes six stages associated with TNA at organizational level (see Table 17.3).

Pedder (1998) also refers to a 'learning needs analysis (LNA)', which is completed less formally by an individual during individual performance review. The LNA links well to the PDP described by the DoH (2004) and involves highlighting learning objectives and developing an action plan with a time frame identified for its completion.

TABLE 17.3   Key stages of training needs analysis (*adapted from Pedder 1998*)
Stage 1:
Identify competence, skill, learning or knowledge required, which may be simple or require a complex level of research
Stage 2:
Identify key people or stakeholders involved, which will include staff, patients, managers, purchasers, providers or those commissioning services
Stage 3:
Consider the best means of ascertaining the knowledge of the key people in stage 2; identify what they need to know, or do, to achieve stage 1
Stage 4:
Consult all groups identified in stage 2 and check their understanding
Stage 5:
Analyze data, using valid systematic methods and match against what needs to be known or what skills are required to find the gaps in the present knowledge or skill – this will identify a training need
Stage 6:
Present to management with a plan of how to meet identified need

Whilst education co-ordinators/practice educators are often responsible for completing the TNA, anyone with an educational interest or remit, including managers, can be involved in this process. However, as with most things, there are, as Table 17.4 shows, benefits and drawbacks associated with TNA.

TABLE 17.4 Benefits and challenges of TNA (*adapted from Pedder 1998*)	
Benefits	**Drawbacks**
• Realistic objectives are set within a timescale • Improvements are seen in staff knowledge • Scarce resources are targeted towards identified developments, knowledge or skills • Principles underpinning corporate governance may be demonstrated • The need for clinical updating is evidenced within an organization	• The process is time consuming • It is difficult to target specific areas • Communication on education and training may fail, unless a multidisciplinary approach is taken • Only those who attend identified courses will be able to use the knowledge gained and pass it on to colleagues

CLINICAL GOVERNANCE

The Government White Paper *The New NHS: Modern, Dependable* (DH, 1997) introduced a new quality initiative called clinical governance, which has important implications for professional practice and teaching.

Clinical governance is a framework that unites a range of quality initiatives including clinical effectiveness, evidence-based practice, reflective practice, and quality improvement processes such as clinical audit. The aim of clinical governance is to assure and improve clinical standards at local level throughout the NHS.

The White Paper also created a new quality body called the National Institute of Clinical Excellence, whose purpose is to appraise new and existing interventions, and to disseminate evidence-based guidance. It may be helpful at this stage to offer a range of definitions of the term 'clinical governance', in order to identify its key components. 'Governance' means 'the act of governing', and hence clinical governance means that clinicians become responsible for the act of governing the service. The following definitions expand on this.

Definitions of clinical governance

> 'Clinical governance is an umbrella term for everything that helps to maintain and improve high standards of patient care. It covers a whole range of quality improvement activities that many nurses are already doing – for example, clinical audit and practice development. It also provides a framework to draw these activities together in a more co-ordinated way.'
>
> (RCN, 2004)

> 'Clinical governance describes the structures, processes and culture needed to ensure that healthcare organisations – and all individuals within them – can assure the quality of the care they provide and are continuously seeking to improve it'
>
> (DH, 2012)

> 'Clinical governance is a framework designed to help registrants and other health care professionals to continuously improve quality and safeguard standards of care; the principles of clinical governance apply equally within the independent and private sectors, as supported by the Care Standards Act 2000.'
>
> (NMC, 2006)

The NMC (2006) specifies that clinical governance is underpinned by:

- professional self-regulation;
- strong leadership;
- effective communication;
- being patient focused;
- a commitment to quality;
- valuing each other;
- continuing professional development.

Activities relating to clinical governance

The main activities relating to clinical governance are outlined by RCN (2003) and the NMC (2006):

- Research and development:
  - primary research;
  - implementing research findings;
  - critical appraisal of research evidence.
- Risk management:
  - health and safety assessment;
  - clinical risk assessment;
  - staff training;
  - policy/procedure/protocol development.
- Quality initiatives:
  - continuous professional development;
  - standard setting;
  - complaints handling and critical incident reporting;
  - user/patient involvement;
  - evidence-based practice;
  - clinical supervision.
- Clinical effectiveness:
  - standard setting;
  - evidence reviews;
  - identification/production of clinical guidelines.
- Clinical audit:
  - criterion-based audit;
  - significant-event audit.

All nurses need to acquire the skills to carry out these elements of clinical governance, including auditing skills, disseminating good practice, and appraising research findings. The application of these principles provides an environment in which clinical excellence can flourish and high standards of patient care can be provided (NMC, 2006).

The implementation of clinical governance differs somewhat between NHS trusts and primary care groups (PCGs). In the former, the chief executive is responsible for ensuring that the trust is meeting its quality responsibilities; in the latter, a senior professional member takes responsibility for planning and implementation throughout the PCG.

As mentioned earlier, the clinical governance framework brings together a number of quality initiatives, some of which are already well established, and others that are new. The following sections will address a selection of these initiatives.

NATIONAL INSTITUTE FOR HEALTH AND CLINICAL EXCELLENCE

The National Institute for Health and Clinical Excellence (NICE) is an independent organization responsible for providing national guidelines on promoting good health and preventing and treating ill health. It produces guidelines in the following three areas of health:

- *public health* guidance on the promotion of good health and the prevention of ill health;
- *health technologies* guidance on the use of new and existing medicines, treatments and procedures within the NHS; and
- *clinical practice* guidance on the appropriate treatment and care of people with specific diseases and conditions within the NHS.

The guidelines are developed in association with the NHS and the wider health care community, including NHS staff, health care professionals, patients, carers, industry and academic staff.

CLINICAL EFFECTIVENESS AND EVIDENCE-BASED PRACTICE

These two concepts, although often discussed as separate entities in the literature, are effectively the same and focus on the importance of evidence as the basis for practice.

Clinical effectiveness is very much part of the clinical governance framework; it emphasizes the need for practitioners to be clinically effective in their practice. This development reflects the shift in culture consequent upon the white paper, from the quantity-focused provision of care towards a quality-focused, evidence-based approach to health care. (Clinical effectiveness is discussed in more detail below.)

Evidence-based practice is a term derived from evidence-based medicine (EBM), and is also referred to as evidence-based nursing (EBN). Rees (2011) nicely sums up this approach:

> 'Evidence-based practice is a philosophy of encouraging clinical activity to be founded on sound evidence. Research, particularly in the form of randomised controlled trials, is a highly regarded source of such evidence. It should also take account of professional consensus of opinion and client acceptance. The aim is to follow best practice for each person receiving health care support.'

According to the RCN (2003b), practising from an evidence base usually involves five stages, detailed in Table 17.5.

TABLE 17.5 Five stages of evidence-based practice (*adapted from RCN, 2003*)	
Stage 1:	Identifying areas of practice that are viewed as problematic
Stage 2:	Identifying best available evidence
Stage 3:	Using the identified evidence to define best practice
Stage 4:	Putting this evidence into practice
Stage 5:	Measuring performance against expected outcomes through peer review or clinical audit

Clinical effectiveness

Adams (1999) outlines the requirements for clinical effectiveness:

'To be clinically effective involves primarily ensuring that your practice is based on the best available evidence of effectiveness and meets your clients' requirements. Furthermore, that you implement any change to practice within a framework of review and evaluation. Once you have achieved clinically effective practice it is important to share your experiences with others so that they may also benefit from it.'

Stages in achieving clinical effectiveness

Adams (1999) describes a practitioner's achievement of clinical effectiveness as involving six stages:

1. *Question your routine practice* This involves selecting an aspect of clinical practice and then asking specific questions such as: 'What evidence is there for the way I currently practise this aspect?' 'Could it be performed more effectively?'

2. *Find the best evidence* This stage involves searching for the best evidence for the chosen aspect of practice. Such evidence can be acquired from colleagues, journals and books, electronic databases, such as the Cochrane database of systematic reviews, and the Internet.

3. *Interpret your evidence* This stage involves a critical appraisal of the sources of evidence acquired in Stage 2. This requires a thorough understanding of research principles and methodology, and skills in interpreting the evidence.

4. *Put your evidence into practice* The evidence is applied in the practitioner's day-to-day practice.

5. *Evaluate clinical change* This involves determining the impact of the change on patient/client care, for example audit.

6. *Disseminate successful outcomes* It is important to make known to other professionals any successful outcomes, so that good practice is disseminated.

An alternative model for nurses to use to evaluate their clinical effectiveness is offered by McClarey (1997); it also consists of six steps:

1. *Is there any research available which could be used? Is this the highest level of evidence available?* This involves the identification of an area of practice, and investigating whether or not it is based on evidence or tradition. Step 1 involves searching databases and other sources of evidence.

2. *Is this a practice that should be research based?* This requires a consideration of whether or not the chosen area of practice is, or should be, research based. If no evidence is available, the practitioner should bring this to the attention of those in the service with responsibility for prioritizing research.

3. *Has the research been incorporated into a systematic review?* If the identified evidence is in the form of a systematic review, it has greater credibility. A systematic review brings together a range of research focusing on a given topic.

4. *Are there guidelines, standards or consensus statements for implementing this evidence?* Although evidence may be available, there may be no guidelines or standards. If this is the case, the latter will need to be developed at local level.

5. *How can I implement a proposed change in practice?* Successful implementation requires collaboration, consultation and multi-professional agreement, using publicity, conference presentations, and forums.

6. *Is anything else needed to ensure that care is clinically effective?* Auditing should be carried out to ascertain the impact of the change on patient/client care, and there should be continuation audit to ensure that the improvement is maintained.

Clinical audit

NICE (2012) defines clinical audit as:

> '*a quality improvement process that seeks to improve patient care and outcomes through systematic review of care against explicit criteria, and the implementation of change. Aspects of the structure, processes and outcomes of care are selected and systematically evaluated against explicit criteria.*'

Clinical audit is the component of clinical governance that offers the greatest potential to assess the quality of care routinely provided for NHS users; the principles for best practice in clinical audit are identified below:

- it provides the mechanisms for reviewing the quality of everyday care provided to patients with common conditions;
- it builds on a long history of nurses, doctors and other health care professionals reviewing case notes and seeking ways in which to serve their patients better;
- it addresses quality issues systematically and explicitly, providing reliable information;
- it can confirm the quality of clinical services and highlight the need for improvement.

Critical incident analysis

Critical incident technique (Flanagan, 1954) provides a useful strategy for helping practitioners to reflect; Benner (1984) identified critical incidents in nursing as comprising any of the following:

- those in which the nurse's intervention really made a difference in patient outcome;
- those that went unusually well;
- those in which there was a breakdown;
- those that were ordinary and typical;
- those that captured the essence of nursing;
- those that were particularly demanding.

Benner's study provides a useful framework for reflecting upon and analyzing critical incidents, leading to new insights into practice; descriptions of critical incidents should cover the following:

- the context of the incident;
- a detailed description of it;
- why the incident was critical to the practitioner;
- what the practitioner's concerns were at the time;
- what the practitioner was thinking about during the incident;
- what the practitioner felt about it afterwards;
- what the practitioner found most demanding about it.

Wood (1998) offers a four-stage model for analyzing critical incidents:

1. description of what took place during the incident;
2. analysis of communication skills used and clarification of the underpinning moral values;
3. exploration of potentially effective alternative strategies to those skills actually employed, including moral justification for proposed alternatives;
4. identification of implications for practice.

Critical incident technique is not without its problems; Rich and Parker (1995) explore the morality of using critical incident technique as a teaching and learning tool. They point out that if students' critical incidents contain reference to dangerous behaviour or unprofessional conduct, the tutor or lecturer may be deemed to be in breach of the NMC code of conduct if he or she does not report the behaviour to the appropriate authorities.

SELF-ASSESSMENT

Self-assessment is the process of identifying your strengths, weaknesses, opportunities and threats (SWOT); it can also identify your interests, personality, traits and values and can be used in order to make an informed career choice or to assess your current career role.

The most common personality inventory is the Myers-Briggs, which identifies attitudes, needs, individual traits and motivation (available from the Myers-Briggs Foundation:

www. myersbriggs.org). However, for the purposes of this chapter, we will focus on self-assessment and SWOT analysis of professional development.

A SWOT analysis is aimed at discovering certain characteristics about you and/or your job. By recognizing your strengths, weaknesses, opportunities and threats, you are in a position to uncover your talents and abilities and put your weaknesses and threats into perspective. A SWOT analysis can be undertaken for a number of reasons, for example, within the change management process when considering a change in current practice. It is also used for assessing one's suitability for promotion or a career change.

Self-assessment and SWOT analysis have many benefits, allowing each individual to:

- become more independent;
- become more motivated;
- become more responsible for his or her own learning;
- be able to recognize the next steps in learning and development.

It is well known, especially in nursing, that it is far easier to criticize ourselves than it is to comment on our good points, although generally the strengths should outweigh the weaknesses and threats. Redfern (1998) explains that self-appraisal is about identifying both sides of what she terms 'a positive-improvement' equation; by this she means that we are all good at some things and we all have areas which could be improve upon.

A SWOT analysis can be undertaken from a personal perspective or from a professional perspective, i.e. job related. However, it is probably more accurately undertaken from both perspectives. Although a relatively simple concept, a SWOT analysis is quite difficult to complete on one's own. One of the misconceptions associated with this process is that should be completed by an individual alone; it should be completed in association with a colleague and/or manager as he or she will see you quite differently from where you see yourself. The person is also in a better position to identify your strengths in terms of teamwork, professionalism, candour, consideration. Table 17.6 identifies a SWOT analysis template for a possible career change or promotion.

TEACHING TIP

To help create a SWOT analysis with views from other people, ask five people who know you well or have worked with you to list five of your strengths and five things you could do better and send them to another trusted person. This person collates the responses, so they are anonymous and gives them back to you.

Example of SWOT analysis in practice

Oliver is currently employed as a practice educator in an operating theatre, which forms part of a surgical directorate. He is informed of a lecturer's post teaching surgery and perioperative nursing at the local university and would like to apply; the only problem that Oliver identifies is that he does not think that he has the necessary experience required to work in the higher education sector. His direct line-manager, Olwen, suggests that Oliver undertakes a SWOT analysis, and she offers to provide a managerial and collegial perspective.

A SWOT analysis of Oliver's current and possible future role is demonstrated in Table 17.7.

TABLE 17.6 SWOT analysis template

Strengths	Weaknesses
• What do you do well? • What are your good qualities? • What are your achievements? • What are you confident about? • What do others see as your strengths • Which of your strengths can open up opportunities?	• What could you improve? • What are your weak points? • Is anything or anyone holding you back? • What do others see as your weaknesses? • How can you change your weaknesses into strengths?
Opportunities	**Threats**
• What good opportunities or learning opportunities are available to you? • What is happening within the profession? • What do others see as your opportunities? • How can you turn your strengths into opportunities?	• What might stop you developing: i.e. what obstacles do you face? • Does anything worry you about your job/profession? • Do you fit into the professional structure: i.e. is your job changing? • What do others see as your threats? • What threats do your weaknesses expose you to?

TABLE 17.7 Oliver's SWOT analysis

Strengths	Weaknesses
• Bachelor degree • Specialist practitioner – NMC • Excellent interpersonal skills and works well within a team • Outstanding organizational skills • Adapts well to change • High standard of achievement • Ability to build relationships • Very supportive, approachable, reliable, trustworthy, competent, confidential and professional. • Honesty (can also be a weakness) • Sense of humour • Motivated and good motivator • Works well under pressure • Enjoys challenges • Experience of teaching in practice • Some experience of teaching students in university • Identifies own limitations – need for support	• Lack of teaching qualification • Time management • Difficulty saying 'no' • Impatient (can also be a strength) • Stubborn • Honesty (can also be a strength)
	Opportunities
	• Further career • Professional development is actively encouraged in HE • PGCE: to gain credibility as a qualified teacher • Higher degree – masters and/or PhD • Recruitment – student nurse placements • Improve time management
	Threats
	• Time • Lack of confidence in ability to perform the role of the lecturer • Rheumatoid arthritis disease and uncertainty regarding the future

Review questions

1. Make a list of self-directed continuing professional development (CPD) activities that a nurse in clinical practice and a nurse lecturer could partake in.

2. What are the main points to consider when developing a personal development plan (PDP)?

3. Summarise the main responsibilities of a clinical educational coordinator.

4. How does evidence-based practice impact on clinical effectiveness?

SUMMARY

- All nurses must embrace and engage in the principles of continuing professional development and lifelong learning.

- Post-registration education and practice standards are designed to keep nurses up to date with new developments in practice and to encourage reflective practice.

- All nurses should receive some assistance from their employers for CPD, but the primary responsibility for maintaining competence to practice remains with the individual.

- CPD ensures that the practitioner remains not only fit to practice but also develops the knowledge and competence needed to advance practice and progress through clinical and other career pathways.

- Staff appraisal in practice should be based upon the principle that all staff have three fundamental rights: the rights to know what is expected of them, how they are doing, and how they will be measured.

- *Agenda for Change* (DoH, 2003) and the process of personal development review are becoming the accepted processes for turning learning into improvements in care and services.

- Most people disregard learning that does not involve an academic course, but flexible approaches to learning and a willingness to accept new technologies are vital.

- The NHS Knowledge and Skills Framework demands that participation in annual appraisal is undertaken by all staff, leading to the production of a personal development plan.

- Personal development planning identifies the learning and development needs of individuals and also identifies how these needs are taken forward.

- Students undertaking a practice placement within the clinical setting are supported by a range of qualified and unqualified personnel.

- The primary personnel actively involved in supporting pre-registration students include qualified nurses with mentor status and education co-ordinators or clinical facilitators.

- Education co-ordinators plan practice placements, allocate students to appropriate learning situations and provide personal support to students, mentors and all qualified and unqualified staff.

- Training needs analysis is a strategy for training and education that meets the continuing professional needs of health care staff.

- Clinical governance is a framework that unites a range of quality initiatives including clinical effectiveness, evidence-based practice, reflective practice, and quality improvement processes such as clinical audit.
- Clinical effectiveness, which is part of the clinical governance framework, emphasizes the need for practitioners to be clinically effective in their practice.
- Evidence-based practice offers opportunities for addressing clinical problems through rigorous selection of the best available evidence and applying those findings in the clinical situation.
- Clinical audit is the component of clinical governance that offers the greatest potential to assess the quality of care routinely provided for NHS users.
- Self-assessment is the process of identifying your strengths, weaknesses, opportunities and threats.

References

Adams, C. (1999) Clinical effectiveness: a practical guide. *Community Practitioner* 72(5) 125–127

Benner, P. (1984) *From Novice to Expert: Excellence and Power in Clinical Nursing Practice*. London: Addison-Wesley

DH (1997) *The New NHS: Modern, Dependable*. London: The Stationary Office

DH (2003) *Agenda for Change: A Modernised NHS Pay System*. London: The Stationary Office

DH (2004) *The NHS Knowledge and Skills Framework (NHS KSF) and the Development Review Process*. London: The Stationary Office

DH (2008) *Modernising Allied Health Professions (AHP) Careers: A Competence-Based Career Framework*. London: The Stationary Office

Flanagan, J. (1954) The critical incident technique. *Psychological Bulletin* 51, 327–358

Gould, D., Kelly, D. and White, I. (2004) Training-needs analysis: an evaluation framework. *Nursing Standard* 18(20) 33–36

Harding, S. and Salmon, F. (2005) Career development: identify your style. *Nursing Standard* 20(8) 69

Hughes, S.J. (2006) Evaluating operating theatre experience: student nurses in South East Wales. *Journal of Perioperative Practice* 16(6) 290–298

Jenkins, A. (2006) There's no need to stop. *Nursing Standard* 20(18) 72

Koh, L.C. (2002) Practice-based teaching and nurse education. *Nursing Standard* 16(19) 38–42

McClarey, M. (1997) Clinical effectiveness and evidence-based practice. *Nursing Standard* 11(52) 33–37

McCormack, B. and Slater, P. (2006) An evaluation of the role of the clinical education facilitator. *Journal of Clinical Nursing* 15(2) 135–144

NHS Staff Council (2010) *Appraisals and KSF Made Simple: A Practical Guide*. London: NHS Employers

NIHCE (2012) Clinical audit. Available from: http://www.nice.org.uk/usingguidance/implementationtools/clinicalaudit.jsp

NMC (2006) *A–Z Advice Sheet: Clinical Governance*, www.nmc-uk.org

NMC (2008) *The Code: Standards of Conduct, Performance and Ethics for Nurses and Midwives*. London: Nursing Midwifery Council

NMC (2011) *The PREP handbook*. London: Nursing Midwifery Council

Pedder, .L (1998) Training-needs analysis. *Nursing Standard* 13(6) 50–56

Redfern, E. (1998) The power of the professional profile. In F.M. Quinn (ed.) *Continuing Professional Development in Nursing: A Guide for Practitioners and Educators*. Cheltenham: Nelson Thornes

Rees, C. (2011) *Introduction to research for midwives* (3rd Edition). London: Churchill-Livingstone

RCN (2003a) *Nursing education: a statement of principles*. London: Royal College of Nursing

RCN (2003b) *Clinical governance: an RCN resource guide*. London: Royal College of Nursing

RCN (2004) *Quality education for quality care: priorities and actions*. London: Royal College of Nursing

Rich, A. and Parker, D. (1995) Reflection and critical incident analysis: ethical and moral implications of their use within nursing and midwifery education. *Journal of Advanced Nursing* 22 1050–1057

Wood, S. (1998) Ethics and communication: developing reflective practice. *Nursing Standard* 12(18) 44–47

Further Reading

McSherry, R. and Pearce, P. (2007) *Clinical governance: a guide to implementation* (2nd Edition). London: Blackwell

RCN (2009) *Integrated core career and competence framework for registered nurses*. London: Royal College of Nursing

RCN (2006) *Discussing and preparing evidence at your first personal development review*. London: Royal College of Nursing

GLOSSARY

accountability professional or organizational responsibility for the quality of services provided

accreditation the approval and recognition of an organization, qualification or programme of study by an external professional body

acrostic a series of words or phrases in which the initial letters, when read in sequence, form a memorable word

andragogy the teaching and training of adults (rather than children) in which the learner's own needs and motivation are central to the learning process

annotation observations or notes added to a text, such as the comments a tutor writes on a student's essay

appraisal a formal system to consider the qualities an individual brings to an organization and to reflect on how the individual, and organization, could develop in the future

augmented feedback feedback on the performance of a task that is provided by an external source, such as a coach or teacher

autonomy the ability to make one's own decisions and act independently

blended learning learning that makes use of more than one mode of delivery, usually combining online and face-to-face approaches

central-tendency error a type of bias in which an assessor gives all students average marks

clinical academic a health professional who is engaged in both clinical and academic activities

clinical audit the systematic review of clinical care in which specific aspects are evaluated against explicit criteria

clinical competence the capability of practising safely and effectively

clinical credibility a quality usually defined as an awareness of current issues and changes in the practice setting

clinical governance the system through which NHS organizations are accountable for continuously improving the quality of their services and safeguarding high standards of care

cognitive concerned with thinking or conscious mental processes

collaborative practice practice in which different disciplines or professions work together with mutual understanding and respect to achieve shared goals

competency framework a structure that identifies and defines the abilities an individual needs in order to perform a job effectively

computer-mediated tutoring (CMT) a type of computer-based seminar in which a tutor and students come together online to discuss issues, although not in real time

concept mapping a method of generating concepts and organizing them in a graphical format

congruent corresponding or appropriate

continuing professional development (CPD) the means by which professionals maintain, build upon and broaden the knowledge and skills acquired during their initial training

critical incident technique (CIT) a tool for identifying aspects of practice which the student felt were particularly positive or negative and which can be used for reflection and analysis

critical thinking the disciplined, purposeful and reflective examination of evidence in order to make informed judgements on one's own values and actions

curriculum a plan or design for education or training that encompasses learning objectives, subject matter, teaching and learning process and assessment

cybernetic relating to control systems in which goals are set, results are monitored, corrections are made and the original goals are reviewed and modified as necessary

decision theory a theory explaining how individuals take decisions, based on their estimation of the value to them of various possible outcomes

deductively teaching by giving a definition of a concept and following it with examples

developmental framework a structure that sets out the knowledge and skills that professionals must apply when supporting and assessing students who are working towards registration or a qualification that is recordable on the register

deviance a negative term used in relation to individuals who are stigmatized because they differ from social norms

discrimination index a measure of the extent to which responses to an item in a test reflect performance in the test as a whole

distance learning a form of education in which learning happens at a geographical distance and teaching and training are delivered remotely, usually with the use of online technology

domain a sphere of activity or interest

dyadic involving an interaction between two individuals

educational audit the regular assessment of a health care provider by a member of academic staff to ensure that it offers an appropriate learning environment for student nurses

episodic knowledge knowledge stored in the long-term memory that relates to particular autobiographical events

ethology a branch of zoology concerned with the study of animals in their natural settings rather than under artificial laboratory conditions

evaluation the considered judgement about the quality of a product, a process or an experience

evidence-based practice practice in which decisions on treatment and care are based on the best current evidence from research

experiential learning learning that results from personal experience, rather than from instruction by others

experiential taxonomy a system of classifying levels of experience, from initial exposure to the ability to disseminate knowledge and skills, that can be used to plan learning and teaching

expositive a method of teaching in which an existing body of knowledge is transmitted to the student

facilitation the process of helping members of a group to work together more effectively and achieve their objectives

facility index a measure of the easiness of a test item given by the percentage of students who answer the item correctly

feedback a response or reaction to an action that can be used to gauge performance

feeding forward using information about the performance of a past activity to guide and improve performance of a future activity

formative describes assessment that takes place during the learning process in order to modify teaching and learning activities and improve the performance of students

health education an aspect of health promotion concerned with giving information to individuals or groups with the aim of increasing health and well-being; also sometimes used interchangeably with 'health promotion'

health informatics (HI) the science of generating, recording, classifying, storing, retrieving, processing, analyzing, and transmitting health information

health promotion the process of enabling people to increase control over their health, thereby improving their health

humanistic concept a concept related to the development of an individual as a whole human being, focussing on their inner values, beliefs and needs

improvidence shortsightedness, lack of thought about the future

incubation the time that elapses before one returns to a problem, after which one sometimes has an unexpected insight into the solution

inductively teaching by giving examples and then drawing out a general concept

interprofessional bringing together individuals from different disciplines or professions with the aim of increasing mutual understanding and collaboration

kinaesthetic feedback feedback based on a sense of the movement of one's own body

learning outcome a description of the knowledge, skills, attitudes and values that a student should acquire as a result of the educational process

lifelong learning all learning activity undertaken throughout one's life, undertaken with the aim of improving knowledge, skills and competence

mathemagenic behaviours behaviours that give birth to, or bring about, learning

mentor an experienced practitioner who provides educational and personal support

meta-cognitive showing an awareness of one's own thinking and learning processes

microskill a specific skill that forms a component of a wider skill

motor skill a learned sequence of physical actions

multiprofessional involving people from different professions

NMC standards a framework of competencies and skills designed by the Nursing and Midwifery Council that reflects changes in healthcare delivery and ensures that pre-registration nursing education prepares the nurses of the future for effective, safe and compassionate practice

objective test a test requiring short, factual answers that can be marked impartially

obliterative subsumption the process by which new knowledge is assimilated into an existing framework of understanding and can then no longer be retrieved separately

open learning an approach to learning which gives students flexibility over what, when, where, and how they learn

pattern recognition the process of checking the long-term memory to determine whether a stimulus has been encountered before

pedagogy the teaching of children (rather than adults), in which the role of the teacher is to supply subject matter, structure and motivation

peer assessment the assessment of students' written or practical work by their own peer group

peer review a system in which an academic article or paper is reviewed and checked by other members of the author's profession before publication

performance indicator (PI) a quantifiable measure used by organizations to monitor progress towards achieving its mission and goals

phonological relating to the sounds of speech

plagiarism deliberately taking other people's written work and passing it off as one's own

portfolio a collection of evidence of a student's achievements, feedback and reflection that demonstrates learning and the development of professional competence

preceptorship a period of time during which a newly qualified practitioner is supported and guided by an experienced colleague

predicate the part of a proposition or statement that provides information about the subject

premise a proposition, or statement, from which another proposition can be inferred or concluded

PREP Post-Registration Education and Practice

proactive interference the process of forgetting new information because of interference from information that was received earlier

proposition a statement that asserts or denies something about a subject

proprioceptive relating to the body's awareness of its own movement and spatial position

proprioceptive feedback feedback based on an awareness of the movement and spatial position of one's own body

psychomotor relating to physical activity that is the result of mental processes

psychomotor skill a skill that involves both mental and physical ability

quality assurance the process for checking that the standards and quality of an organization's services or products meet agreed expectations

reflective practice the way in which professionals examine their experiences and behaviour within their own practice and so increase their expertise and understanding

retroactive interference the process of forgetting new information because of interference from information that was received subsequently

schema a mental model that gives meaning to, and helps one deal with, aspects of the external world

scheme of work a document that gives an overview of the key components of each teaching session within a module

scrutineer a member of academic staff who inspects, checks and reports on the monitoring procedures for a particular course or programme

self-actualization the achievement of one's full potential as a human being

self-directed learner an individual who is able to take the initiative in their own learning and is capable of study with or without a teacher

self-reinforcement a study method that involves setting onesown goals and rewarding oneself when these goals are achieved

semantic knowledge knowledge stored in the long-term memory that relates to general concepts and not to particular events or episodes

socialization the process by which individuals learn the values, knowledge and patterns of behaviour that make them members of a particular society

stress an adverse reaction to excessive pressure, which can result in reduced performance and ill health

structured impressionistic marking a method of marking in which answers to individual questions are rapidly reviewed and graded on a scale from excellent to unsatisfactory

student-centred learning an approach to learning that gives importance to student empowerment and autonomy

summative describes assessment that takes place at the end of a unit or course to measure the extent to which students have achieved the learning objectives

synectics a creative approach to solving problems that involves looking at a problem from a different perspective, often by the use of analogy

systematic desensitization a technique used to overcome phobias in which the subject is encouraged to relax and then confront the feared situation in a series of small steps

tautological using different words to convey the same sense

taxonomy a system of classification

triadic involving a group of three individuals

validation the process of ensuring that a course or programme is of an appropriate standard and is suitable for adoption

value added the enhancement of a student's ability, learning and experience as a result of pursuing an educational programme

INDEX